The Case for Christ

The Case for Faith

Lee Strobel

ZONDERVAN®

These titles are also available as Zondervan ebook products.
Visit www.zondervan.com/ebooks for more information.

These titles are also available as Zondervan audio products.
Visit www.zondervan.com/audiopages for more information.

Requests for information should be addressed to:

Zondervan, *Grand Rapids, Michigan 49530*

ISBN-10: 0-310-60882-1
ISBN-13: 978-0-310-60882-0

Interior design by Sherri L. Hoffman

Printed in the United States of America

06 07 08 09 10 11 12 • 18 17 16 15 14 13 12 11 10 9 8 7 6 5 4 3 2 1

CONTENTS

THE CASE FOR CHRIST

THE CASE FOR FAITH

The Case for Christ

ACKNOWLEDGMENTS

I am extremely thankful for the insights and contributions that a variety of people have made to this book. In particular, I'm indebted to Bill Hybels, who allowed me to produce a series of presentations on this topic at Willow Creek Community Church; my wife, Leslie, who came up with the idea of translating that concept into a book; and my editor, John Sloan, whose creative input greatly enhanced the project.

Also, I'm grateful to Mark Mittelberg and Garry Poole for their ongoing encouragement and assistance; Chad Meister and Bob and Gretchen Passantino for their research and ideas; Russ Robinson for his legal perspective; my assistant Jodi Walle for her invaluable help; and my daughter, Alison, and son, Kyle, for their behind-the-scenes contributions.

Finally, I'd like to thank the scholars who allowed me to interview them for this book. Again and again I was impressed not only by their knowledge and wisdom but also by their humble and sincere faith—as well as their desire to help spiritual seekers investigate the outrageous claims of Jesus.

INTRODUCTION

Reopening the Investigation of a Lifetime

In the parlance of prosecutors, the attempted murder case against James Dixon was "a dead-bang winner." Open and shut. Even a cursory examination of the evidence was enough to establish that Dixon shot police sergeant Richard Scanlon in the abdomen during a scuffle on Chicago's south side.

Piece by piece, item by item, witness by witness, the evidence tightened a noose around Dixon's neck. There were fingerprints and a weapon, eyewitnesses and a motive, a wounded cop and a defendant with a history of violence. Now the criminal justice system was poised to trip the trap door that would leave Dixon dangling by the weight of his own guilt.

The facts were simple. Sergeant Scanlon had rushed to West 108th Place after a neighbor called police to report a man with a gun. Scanlon arrived to find Dixon noisily arguing with his girlfriend through the front door of her house. Her father emerged when he saw Scanlon, figuring it was safe to come outside.

Suddenly a fight broke out between Dixon and the father. The sergeant quickly intervened in an attempt to break it up. A shot rang out; Scanlon staggered away, wounded in his midsection. Just then two other squad cars arrived, screeching to a halt, and officers ran over to restrain Dixon.

A .22-caliber gun belonging to Dixon—covered with his fingerprints and with one bullet having been fired—was found nearby, where he had apparently flung it after the shooting. The father had been unarmed; Scanlon's revolver remained in his holster. Powder burns on Scanlon's skin showed that he had been shot at extremely close range.

Fortunately, his wound wasn't life-threatening, although it was serious enough to earn him a medal for bravery, proudly pinned on his chest by the police superintendent himself. As for Dixon, when police ran his rap sheet, they found he had previously been convicted of shooting someone else. Apparently, he had a propensity for violence.

And there I sat almost a year later, taking notes in a nearly deserted Chicago courtroom while Dixon publicly admitted that, yes, he was guilty of shooting the fifteen-year police veteran. On top of all the other evidence, the confession clinched it. Criminal court judge Frank Machala ordered Dixon imprisoned, then rapped his gavel to signal that the case was closed. Justice had been served.

I slipped my notebook into the inside pocket of my sports coat and ambled downstairs toward the press room. At the most, I figured my editor would give me three paragraphs to tell the story in the next day's *Chicago Tribune.* Certainly, that's all it deserved. This wasn't much of a tale.

Or so I thought.

THE WHISPER OF AN INFORMANT

I answered the phone in the pressroom and recognized the voice right away—it was an informant I had cultivated during the year I had been covering the criminal courts building. I could tell he had something hot for me, because the bigger the tip, the faster and softer he would talk—and he was whispering a mile a minute.

"Lee, do you know that Dixon case?" he asked.

"Yeah, sure," I replied. "Covered it two days ago. Pretty routine."

"Don't be so sure. The word is that a few weeks before the shooting, Sergeant Scanlon was at a party, showing off his pen gun."

"His what?"

"A pen gun. It's a .22-caliber pistol that's made to look like a fountain pen. They're illegal for anyone to carry, including cops."

When I told him I didn't see the relevance of this, his voice got even more animated. "Here's the thing: Dixon didn't shoot Scanlon. Scanlon was wounded when his own pen gun accidentally went off in his shirt pocket. He framed Dixon so he wouldn't get in trouble for carrying an unauthorized weapon. Don't you see? Dixon is innocent!"

"Impossible!" I exclaimed.

"Check out the evidence yourself," came his reply. "See where it really points."

I hung up the phone and dashed up the stairs to the prosecutor's office, pausing briefly to catch my breath before strolling inside. "You know the Dixon case?" I asked casually, not wanting to tip my hand too early. "If you don't mind, I'd like to go over the details once more."

Color drained from his face. "Uh, I can't talk about it," he stammered. "No comment."

It turned out that my informant had already passed along his suspicions to the prosecutor's office. Behind the scenes, a grand jury was being convened to reconsider the evidence. Amazingly, unexpectedly, the once airtight case against James Dixon was being reopened.

NEW FACTS FOR A NEW THEORY

At the same time, I started my own investigation, studying the crime scene, interviewing witnesses, talking with Dixon, and examining the physical evidence. As I thoroughly checked out the case, the strangest thing happened: all the new facts that I uncovered—and even the old evidence that had once pointed so convincingly toward Dixon's guilt—snugly fit the pen gun theory.

- Witnesses said that before Scanlon arrived on the scene, Dixon had been pounding his gun on the door of his girlfriend's house. The gun discharged in a downward direction; in the cement of the front porch there was a chip that was consistent with a bullet's impact. This would account for the bullet that was missing from Dixon's gun.
- Dixon said he didn't want to be caught with a gun, so he hid it in some grass across the street before police arrived. I found a witness who corroborated that. This explained why the gun had been found some distance from the shooting scene even though nobody had ever seen Dixon throw it.
- There were powder burns concentrated inside—but not above—the left pocket of Scanlon's shirt. The bullet hole was at the bottom of the pocket. Conclusion: a weapon had somehow discharged in the pocket's interior.
- Contrary to statements in the police report, the bullet's trajectory had been at a downward angle. Below Scanlon's shirt pocket was a bloody rip where the bullet had exited after going through some flesh.
- Dixon's rap sheet hadn't told the whole story about him. Although he had spent three years in prison for an earlier shooting, the appellate court had freed him after determining that he had been wrongly convicted. It turns out that police had concealed a key defense witness and that a prosecution

witness had lied. So much for Dixon's record of violent tendencies.

AN INNOCENT MAN IS FREED

Finally I put the crucial question to Dixon: "If you were innocent, why in the world did you plead guilty?"

Dixon sighed. "It was a plea bargain," he said, referring to the practice in which prosecutors recommend a reduced sentence if a defendant pleads guilty and thus saves everybody the time and expense of a trial.

"They said if I pleaded guilty, they would sentence me to one year in prison. I'd already spent 362 days in jail waiting for my trial. All I had to do was admit I did it and I'd go home in a few days. But if I insisted on a trial and the jury found me guilty—well, they'd throw the book at me. They'd give me twenty years for shooting a cop. It wasn't worth the gamble. I wanted to go home. . . ."

"And so," I said, "you admitted doing something that you didn't do."

Dixon nodded. "That's right."

In the end Dixon was exonerated, and he later won a lawsuit against the police department. Scanlon was stripped of his medal, was indicted by a grand jury, pleaded guilty to official misconduct, and was fired from the department.[1] As for me, my stories were splashed across the front page. Much more important, I had learned some big lessons as a young reporter.

One of the most obvious lessons was that evidence can be aligned to point in more than one direction. For example, there had easily been enough proof to convict Dixon of shooting the sergeant. But the key questions were these: *Had the collection of evidence really been thorough? And which explanation best fit the totality of the facts?* Once the pen gun theory was offered, it became clear that this scenario accounted for the full body of evidence in the most optimal way.

And there was another lesson. One reason the evidence originally looked so convincing to me was because it fit my preconceptions at the time. To me, Dixon was an obvious troublemaker, a failure, the unemployed product of a broken family. The cops were the good guys. Prosecutors didn't make mistakes.

Looking through those lenses, all the original evidence seemed to fall neatly into place. Where there had been inconsistencies or gaps,

I naively glossed them over. When police told me the case was airtight, I took them at their word and didn't delve much further.

But when I changed those lenses—trading my biases for an attempt at objectivity—I saw the case in a whole new light. Finally I allowed the evidence to lead me to the truth, regardless of whether it fit my original presuppositions.

That was more than twenty years ago. My biggest lessons were yet to come.

FROM DIXON TO JESUS

The reason I've recounted this unusual case is because in a way my spiritual journey has been a lot like my experience with James Dixon.

For much of my life I was a skeptic. In fact, I considered myself an atheist. To me, there was far too much evidence that God was merely a product of wishful thinking, of ancient mythology, of primitive superstition. How could there be a loving God if he consigned people to hell just for not believing in him? How could miracles contravene the basic laws of nature? Didn't evolution satisfactorily explain how life originated? Doesn't scientific reasoning dispel belief in the supernatural?

As for Jesus, didn't you know that he never claimed to be God? He was a revolutionary, a sage, an iconoclastic Jew—but God? No, that thought never occurred to him! I could point you to plenty of university professors who said so—and certainly they could be trusted, couldn't they? Let's face it: even a cursory examination of the evidence demonstrates convincingly that Jesus had only been a human being just like you and me, although with unusual gifts of kindness and wisdom.

But that's all I had ever really given the evidence: a cursory look. I had read just enough philosophy and history to find support for my skepticism—a fact here, a scientific theory there, a pithy quote, a clever argument. Sure, I could see some gaps and inconsistencies, but I had a strong motivation to ignore them: a self-serving and immoral lifestyle that I would be compelled to abandon if I were ever to change my views and become a follower of Jesus.

As far as I was concerned, the case was closed. There was enough proof for me to rest easy with the conclusion that the divinity of Jesus was nothing more than the fanciful invention of superstitious people.

Or so I thought.

ANSWERS FOR AN ATHEIST

It wasn't a phone call from an informant that prompted me to reexamine the case for Christ. It was my wife.

Leslie stunned me in the autumn of 1979 by announcing that she had become a Christian. I rolled my eyes and braced for the worst, feeling like the victim of a bait-and-switch scam. I had married one Leslie—the fun Leslie, the carefree Leslie, the risk-taking Leslie—and now I feared she was going to turn into some sort of sexually repressed prude who would trade our upwardly mobile lifestyle for all-night prayer vigils and volunteer work in grimy soup kitchens.

Instead I was pleasantly surprised—even fascinated—by the fundamental changes in her character, her integrity, and her personal confidence. Eventually I wanted to get to the bottom of what was prompting these subtle but significant shifts in my wife's attitudes, so I launched an all-out investigation into the facts surrounding the case for Christianity.

Setting aside my self-interest and prejudices as best I could, I read books, interviewed experts, asked questions, analyzed history, explored archaeology, studied ancient literature, and for the first time in my life picked apart the Bible verse by verse.

I plunged into the case with more vigor than with any story I had ever pursued. I applied the training I had received at Yale Law School as well as my experience as legal affairs editor of the *Chicago Tribune*. And over time the evidence of the world—of history, of science, of philosophy, of psychology—began to point toward the unthinkable.

It was like the James Dixon case revisited.

JUDGING FOR YOURSELF

Maybe you too have been basing your spiritual outlook on the evidence you've observed around you or gleaned long ago from books, college professors, family members, or friends. But is your conclusion really the best possible explanation for the evidence? If you were to dig deeper—to confront your preconceptions and systematically seek out proof—what would you find?

That's what this book is about. In effect, I'm going to retrace and expand upon the spiritual journey I took for nearly two years. I'll take you along as I interview thirteen leading scholars and authorities who have impeccable academic credentials.

I have crisscrossed the country—from Minnesota to Georgia, from Virginia to California—to elicit their expert opinions, to challenge them with the objections I had when I was a skeptic, to force them to defend their positions with solid data and cogent arguments, and to test them with the very questions that you might ask if given the opportunity.

In this quest for truth, I've used my experience as a legal affairs journalist to look at numerous categories of proof—eyewitness evidence, documentary evidence, corroborating evidence, rebuttal evidence, scientific evidence, psychological evidence, circumstantial evidence, and, yes, even fingerprint evidence (*that* sounds intriguing, doesn't it?).

These are the same classifications that you'd encounter in a courtroom. And maybe taking a legal perspective is the best way to envision this process—with you in the role of a juror.

If you were selected for a jury in a real trial, you would be asked to affirm up front that you haven't formed any preconceptions about the case. You would be required to vow that you would be open-minded and fair, drawing your conclusions based on the weight of the facts and not on your whims or prejudices. You would be urged to thoughtfully consider the credibility of the witnesses, carefully sift the testimony, and rigorously subject the evidence to your common sense and logic. I'm asking you to do the same thing while reading this book.

Ultimately it's the responsibility of jurors to reach a verdict. That doesn't mean they have one-hundred-percent certainty, because we can't have absolute proof about anything in life. In a trial, jurors are asked to weigh the evidence and come to the best possible conclusion. In other words, harkening back to the James Dixon case, which scenario fits the facts most snugly?

That's your task. I hope you take it seriously, because there may be more than just idle curiosity hanging in the balance. If Jesus is to be believed—and I realize that may be a big *if* for you at this point—then nothing is more important than how you respond to him.

But who was he really? Who did he claim to be? And is there any credible evidence to back up his assertions? That's what we'll seek to determine as we board a flight for Denver to conduct our first interview.

PART 1

Examining the Record

1

THE EYEWITNESS EVIDENCE

Can the Biographies of Jesus Be Trusted?

When I first met shy and soft-spoken Leo Carter, he was a seventeen-year-old veteran of Chicago's grittiest neighborhood. His testimony had put three killers in prison. And he was still carrying a .38-caliber slug in his skull—a grisly reminder of a horrific saga that began when he witnessed Elijah Baptist gun down a local grocer.

Leo and a friend, Leslie Scott, were playing basketball when they saw Elijah, then a sixteen-year-old delinquent with thirty arrests on his rap sheet, slay Sam Blue outside his grocery store.

Leo had known the grocer since childhood. "When we didn't have any food, he'd give us some," Leo explained to me in a quiet voice. "So when I went to the hospital and they said he was dead, I knew I'd have to testify about what I saw."

Eyewitness testimony is powerful. One of the most dramatic moments in a trial is when a witness describes in detail the crime that he or she saw and then points confidently toward the defendant as being the perpetrator. Elijah Baptist knew that the only way to avoid prison would be to somehow prevent Leo Carter and Leslie Scott from doing just that.

So Elijah and two of his pals went hunting. Soon they tracked down Leo and Leslie, who were walking down the street with Leo's brother Henry, and they dragged all three at gunpoint to a darkened loading dock nearby.

"I like you," Elijah's cousin said to Leo, "but I've got to do this." With that he pressed a pistol to the bridge of Leo's nose and yanked the trigger.

The gun roared; the bullet penetrated at a slight angle, blinding Leo in his right eye and embedding in his head. When he crumbled to the ground, another shot was fired, this bullet lodging two inches from his spine.

As Leo watched from his sprawled position, pretending he was dead, he saw his sobbing brother and friend ruthlessly executed at close range. When Elijah and his gang fled, Leo crawled to safety.

Somehow, against all odds, Leo Carter lived. The bullet, too precarious to be removed, remained in his skull. Despite searing headaches that strong medication couldn't dull, he became the sole eyewitness against Elijah Baptist at his trial for killing grocer Sam Blue. The jurors believed Leo, and Elijah was sentenced to eighty years in prison.

Again Leo was the only eyewitness to testify against Elijah and his two companions in the slayings of his brother and his friend. And once more his word was good enough to land the trio in prison for the rest of their lives.

Leo Carter is one of my heroes. He made sure justice was served, even though he paid a monumental price for it. When I think of eyewitness testimony, even to this day—more than twenty years later—his face still appears in my mind.[1]

TESTIMONY FROM DISTANT TIME

Yes, eyewitness testimony can be compelling and convincing. When a witness has had ample opportunity to observe a crime, when there's no bias or ulterior motives, when the witness is truthful and fair, the climactic act of pointing out a defendant in a courtroom can be enough to doom that person to prison or worse.

And eyewitness testimony is just as crucial in investigating historical matters—even the issue of whether Jesus Christ is the unique Son of God.

But what eyewitness accounts do we possess? Do we have the testimony of anyone who personally interacted with Jesus, who listened to his teachings, who saw his miracles, who witnessed his death, and who perhaps even encountered him after his alleged resurrection? Do we have any records from first-century "journalists" who interviewed eyewitnesses, asked tough questions, and faithfully recorded what they scrupulously determined to be true? Equally important, how well would these accounts withstand the scrutiny of skeptics?

I knew that just as Leo Carter's testimony clinched the convictions of three brutal murderers, eyewitness accounts from the mists of distant time could help resolve the most important spiritual issue of all. To get solid answers, I arranged to interview the nationally renowned scholar who literally wrote the book on the topic: Dr. Craig Blomberg, author of *The Historical Reliability of the Gospels.*

I knew Blomberg was smart; in fact, even his appearance fit the stereotype. Tall (six feet two) and lanky, with short, wavy brown hair unceremoniously combed forward, a fuzzy beard, and thick, rimless glasses, he looked like the type who would have been valedictorian of his high school (he was), a National Merit Scholar (he was), and a magna cum laude graduate from a prestigious seminary (he was, from Trinity Evangelical Divinity School).

But I wanted someone who was more than just intelligent and educated. I was searching for an expert who wouldn't gloss over nuances or blithely dismiss challenges to the records of Christianity. I wanted someone with integrity, someone who has grappled with the most potent critiques of the faith and who speaks authoritatively but without the kind of sweeping statements that conceal rather than deal with critical issues.

I was told Blomberg was exactly what I was looking for, and I flew to Denver wondering if he could measure up. Admittedly, I had a few doubts, especially when my research yielded one profoundly disturbing fact that he would probably have preferred had remained hidden: Blomberg still holds out hope that his beloved childhood heroes, the Chicago Cubs, will win the World Series in his lifetime.

Frankly, that was enough to make me a bit suspicious of his discernment.

THE FIRST INTERVIEW: CRAIG L. BLOMBERG, PH.D.

Craig Blomberg is widely considered to be one of the country's foremost authorities on the biographies of Jesus, which are called the four gospels. He received his doctorate in New Testament from Aberdeen University in Scotland, later serving as a senior research fellow at Tyndale House at Cambridge University in England, where he was part of an elite group of international scholars that produced a series of acclaimed works on Jesus. For the last dozen years he has been a professor of New Testament at the highly respected Denver Seminary.

Blomberg's books include *Jesus and the Gospels; Interpreting the Parables; How Wide the Divide?;* and commentaries on the gospel of

Matthew and 1 Corinthians. He also helped edit volume six of *Gospel Perspectives,* which deals at length with the miracles of Jesus, and he coauthored *Introduction to Biblical Interpretation.* He contributed chapters on the historicity of the gospels to the book *Reasonable Faith* and the award-winning *Jesus under Fire*. His memberships include the Society for the Study of the New Testament, Society of Biblical Literature, and the Institute for Biblical Research.

As I expected, his office had more than its share of scholarly volumes stacked on the shelves (he was even wearing a tie emblazoned with drawings of books).

However, I quickly noted that his office walls were dominated not by dusty tomes from ancient historians but by artwork from his young daughters. Their whimsical and colorful depictions of llamas, houses, and flowers weren't haphazardly pinned up as a casual afterthought; they had obviously been treated as prizes—painstakingly matted, carefully framed, and personally autographed by Elizabeth and Rachel themselves. Clearly, I thought to myself, this man has a heart as well as a brain.

Blomberg speaks with the precision of a mathematician (yes, he taught mathematics too, earlier in his career), carefully measuring each word out of an apparent reluctance to tread even one nuance beyond where the evidence warrants. Exactly what I was looking for.

As he settled into a high-back chair, cup of coffee in hand, I too sipped some coffee to ward off the Colorado chill. Since I sensed Blomberg was a get-to-the-point kind of guy, I decided to start my interview by cutting to the core of the issue.

EYEWITNESSES TO HISTORY

"Tell me this," I said with an edge of challenge in my voice, "is it really possible to be an intelligent, critically thinking person and still believe that the four gospels were written by the people whose names have been attached to them?"

Blomberg set his cup of coffee on the edge of his desk and looked intently at me. "The answer is yes," he said with conviction.

He sat back and continued. "It's important to acknowledge that strictly speaking, the gospels are anonymous. But the uniform testimony of the early church was that Matthew, also known as Levi, the tax collector and one of the twelve disciples, was the author of the first gospel in the New Testament; that John Mark, a companion of

Peter, was the author of the gospel we call Mark; and that Luke, known as Paul's 'beloved physician,' wrote both the gospel of Luke and the Acts of the Apostles."

"How uniform was the belief that they were the authors?" I asked.

"There are no known competitors for these three gospels," he said. "Apparently, it was just not in dispute."

Even so, I wanted to test the issue further. "Excuse my skepticism," I said, "but would anyone have had a motivation to lie by claiming these people wrote these gospels, when they really didn't?"

Blomberg shook his head. "Probably not. Remember, these were unlikely characters," he said, a grin breaking on his face. "Mark and Luke weren't even among the twelve disciples. Matthew was, but as a former hated tax collector, he would have been the most infamous character next to Judas Iscariot, who betrayed Jesus!

"Contrast this with what happened when the fanciful apocryphal gospels were written much later. People chose the names of well-known and exemplary figures to be their fictitious authors—Philip, Peter, Mary, James. Those names carried a lot more weight than the names of Matthew, Mark, and Luke. So to answer your question, there would not have been any reason to attribute authorship to these three less respected people if it weren't true."

That sounded logical, but it was obvious that he was conveniently leaving out one of the gospel writers. "What about John?" I asked. "He was extremely prominent; in fact, he wasn't just one of the twelve disciples but one of Jesus' inner three, along with James and Peter."

"Yes, he's the one exception," Blomberg conceded with a nod. "And interestingly, John is the only gospel about which there is some question about authorship."

"What exactly is in dispute?"

"The name of the author isn't in doubt—it's certainly John," Blomberg replied. "The question is whether it was John the apostle or a different John.

"You see, the testimony of a Christian writer named Papias, dated about A.D. 125, refers to John the apostle and John the elder, and it's not clear from the context whether he's talking about one person from two perspectives or two different people. But granted that exception, the rest of the early testimony is unanimous that it was John the apostle—the son of Zebedee—who wrote the gospel."

"And," I said in an effort to pin him down further, "you're convinced that he did?"

"Yes, I believe the substantial majority of the material goes back to the apostle," he replied. "However, if you read the gospel closely, you can see some indication that its concluding verses may have been finalized by an editor. Personally, I have no problem believing that somebody closely associated with John may have functioned in that role, putting the last verses into shape and potentially creating the stylistic uniformity of the entire document.

"But in any event," he stressed, "the gospel is obviously based on eyewitness material, as are the other three gospels."

DELVING INTO SPECIFICS

While I appreciated Blomberg's comments so far, I wasn't ready to move on yet. The issue of who wrote the gospels is tremendously important, and I wanted specific details—names, dates, quotations. I finished off my coffee and put the cup on his desk. Pen poised, I prepared to dig deeper.

"Let's go back to Mark, Matthew, and Luke," I said. "What specific evidence do you have that they are the authors of the gospels?"

Blomberg leaned forward. "Again, the oldest and probably most significant testimony comes from Papias, who in about A.D. 125 specifically affirmed that Mark had carefully and accurately recorded Peter's eyewitness observations. In fact, he said Mark 'made no mistake' and did not include 'any false statement.' And Papias said Matthew had preserved the teachings of Jesus as well.

"Then Irenaeus, writing about A.D. 180, confirmed the traditional authorship. In fact, here—," he said, reaching for a book. He flipped it open and read Irenaeus' words.

> Matthew published his own Gospel among the Hebrews in their own tongue, when Peter and Paul were preaching the Gospel in Rome and founding the church there. After their departure, Mark, the disciple and interpreter of Peter, himself handed down to us in writing the substance of Peter's preaching. Luke, the follower of Paul, set down in a book the Gospel preached by his teacher. Then John, the disciple of the Lord, who also leaned on his breast, himself produced his Gospel while he was living at Ephesus in Asia.[2]

I looked up from the notes I was taking. "OK, let me clarify this," I said. "If we can have confidence that the gospels were written by the disciples Matthew and John, by Mark, the companion of the disciple Peter, and by Luke, the historian, companion of Paul, and sort of a first-century journalist, we can be assured that the events they record are based on either direct or indirect eyewitness testimony."

As I was speaking, Blomberg was mentally sifting my words. When I finished, he nodded.

"Exactly," he said crisply.

ANCIENT VERSUS MODERN BIOGRAPHIES

There were still some troubling aspects of the gospels that I needed to clarify. In particular, I wanted to better understand the kind of literary genre they represented.

"When I go to the bookstore and look in the biography section, I don't see the same kind of writing that I see in the gospels," I said. "When somebody writes a biography these days, they thoroughly delve into the person's life. But look at Mark—he doesn't talk about the birth of Jesus or really anything through Jesus' early adult years. Instead he focuses on a three-year period and spends half his gospel on the events leading up to and culminating in Jesus' last week. How do you explain that?"

Blomberg held up a couple of fingers. "There are two reasons," he replied. "One is literary and the other is theological.

"The literary reason is that basically, this is how people wrote biographies in the ancient world. They did not have the sense, as we do today, that it was important to give equal proportion to all periods of an individual's life or that it was necessary to tell the story in strictly chronological order or even to quote people verbatim, as long as the essence of what they said was preserved. Ancient Greek and Hebrew didn't even have a symbol for quotation marks.

"The only purpose for which they thought history was worth recording was because there were some lessons to be learned from the characters described. Therefore the biographer wanted to dwell at length on those portions of the person's life that were exemplary, that were illustrative, that could help other people, that gave meaning to a period of history."

"And what's the theological reason?" I asked.

"It flows out of the point I just made. Christians believe that as wonderful as Jesus' life and teachings and miracles were, they were meaningless if it were not historically factual that Christ died and was raised from the dead and that this provided atonement, or forgiveness, of the sins of humanity.

"So Mark in particular, as the writer of probably the earliest gospel, devotes roughly half his narrative to the events leading up to and including one week's period of time and culminating in Christ's death and resurrection.

"Given the significance of the Crucifixion," he concluded, "this makes perfect sense in ancient literature."

THE MYSTERY OF Q

In addition to the four gospels, scholars often refer to what they call Q, which stands for the German word *Quelle*, or "source."[3] Because of similarities in language and content, it has traditionally been assumed that Matthew and Luke drew upon Mark's earlier gospel in writing their own. In addition, scholars have said that Matthew and Luke also incorporated some material from this mysterious Q, material that is absent from Mark.

"What exactly is Q?" I asked Blomberg.

"It's nothing more than a hypothesis," he replied, again leaning back comfortably in his chair. "With few exceptions, it's just sayings or teachings of Jesus, which once may have formed an independent, separate document.

"You see, it was a common literary genre to collect the sayings of respected teachers, sort of as we compile the top music of a singer and put it into a 'best of' album. Q may have been something like that. At least that's the theory."

But if Q existed before Matthew and Luke, it would constitute early material about Jesus. Perhaps, I thought, it can shed some fresh light on what Jesus was really like.

"Let me ask this," I said. "If you isolate just the material from Q, what kind of picture of Jesus do you get?"

Blomberg stroked his beard and stared at the ceiling for a moment as he pondered the question. "Well, you have to keep in mind that Q was a collection of sayings, and therefore it didn't have the narrative material that would have given us a more fully orbed picture of Jesus," he replied, speaking slowly as he chose each word with care.

"Even so, you find Jesus making some very strong claims—for instance, that he was wisdom personified and that he was the one by whom God will judge all humanity, whether they confess him or disavow him. A significant scholarly book has argued recently that if you isolate all the Q sayings, one actually gets the same kind of picture of Jesus—of someone who made audacious claims about himself—as you find in the gospels more generally."

I wanted to push him further on this point. "Would he be seen as a miracle worker?" I inquired.

"Again," he replied, "you have to remember that you wouldn't get many miracle stories per se, because they're normally found in the narrative, and Q is primarily a list of sayings."

He stopped to reach over to his desk, pick up a leather-bound Bible, and rustle through its well-worn pages.

"But, for example, Luke 7:18–23 and Matthew 11:2–6 say that John the Baptist sent his messengers to ask Jesus if he really was the Christ, the Messiah they were waiting for. Jesus replied in essence, 'Tell him to consider my miracles. Tell him what you've seen: the blind see, the deaf hear, the lame walk, the poor have good news preached to them.'

"So even in Q," he concluded, "there is clearly an awareness of Jesus' ministry of miracles."

Blomberg's mention of Matthew brought to mind another question concerning how the gospels were put together. "Why," I asked, "would Matthew—purported to be an eyewitness to Jesus—incorporate part of a gospel written by Mark, who everybody agrees was not an eyewitness? If Matthew's gospel was really written by an eyewitness, you would think he would have relied on his own observations."

Blomberg smiled. "It only makes sense if Mark was indeed basing his account on the recollections of the eyewitness Peter," he said. "As you've said yourself, Peter was among the inner circle of Jesus and was privy to seeing and hearing things that other disciples didn't. So it would make sense for Matthew, even though he was an eyewitness, to rely on Peter's version of events as transmitted through Mark."

Yes, I thought to myself, that did make some sense. In fact, an analogy began to form in my mind from my years as a newspaper reporter. I recalled being part of a crowd of journalists that once cornered the famous Chicago political patriarch, the late Mayor Richard J. Daley, to pepper him with questions about a scandal that was brewing in the police department. He made some remarks before escaping to his limousine.

Even though I was an eyewitness to what had taken place, I immediately went to a radio reporter who had been closer to Daley, and asked him to play back his tape of what Daley had just said. This way, I could make sure I had his words correctly written down.

That, I mused, was apparently what Matthew did with Mark—although Matthew had his own recollections as a disciple, his quest for accuracy prompted him to rely on some material that came directly from Peter in Jesus' inner circle.

THE UNIQUE PERSPECTIVE OF JOHN

Feeling satisfied with Blomberg's initial answers concerning the first three gospels—called the synoptics, which means "to view at the same time," because of their similar outline and interrelationship[4]—next I turned my attention to John's gospel. Anyone who reads all four gospels will immediately recognize that there are obvious differences between the synoptics and the gospel of John, and I wanted to know whether this means there are irreconcilable contradictions between them.

"Could you clarify the differences between the synoptic gospels and John's gospel?" I asked Blomberg.

His eyebrows shot up. "*Huge* question!" he exclaimed. "I hope to write a whole book on the topic."

After I assured him I was only after the essentials of the issue, not an exhaustive discussion, he settled back into his chair.

"Well, it's true that John is more different than similar to the synoptics," he began. "Only a handful of the major stories that appear in the other three gospels reappear in John, although that changes noticeably when one comes to Jesus' last week. From that point forward the parallels are much closer.

"There also seems to be a very different linguistic style. In John, Jesus uses different terminology, he speaks in long sermons, and there seems to be a higher Christology—that is, more direct and more blatant claims that Jesus is one with the Father; God himself; the Way, the Truth, and the Life; the Resurrection and the Life."

"What accounts for the differences?" I asked.

"For many years the assumption was that John knew everything Matthew, Mark, and Luke wrote, and he saw no need to repeat it, so he consciously chose to supplement them. More recently it has been assumed that John is largely independent of the other three gospels, which could account for not only the different choices of material but also the different perspectives on Jesus."

JESUS' MOST AUDACIOUS CLAIM

"There are some theological distinctives to John," I observed.

"No question, but do they deserve to be called contradictions? I think the answer is no, and here's why: for almost every major theme or distinctive in John, you can find parallels in Matthew, Mark, and Luke, even if they're not as plentiful."

That was a bold assertion. I promptly decided to put it to the test by raising perhaps the most significant issue of all concerning the differences between the synoptics and John's gospel.

"John makes very explicit claims of Jesus being God, which some attribute to the fact that he wrote later than the others and began embellishing things," I said. "Can you find this theme of deity in the synoptics?"

"Yes, I can," he said. "It's more implicit but you find it there. Think of the story of Jesus walking on the water, found in Matthew 14:22–33 and Mark 6:45–52. Most English translations hide the Greek by quoting Jesus as saying, 'Fear not, it is I.' Actually, the Greek literally says, 'Fear not, I am.' Those last two words are identical to what Jesus said in John 8:58, when he took upon himself the divine name 'I AM,' which is the way God revealed himself to Moses in the burning bush in Exodus 3:14. So Jesus is revealing himself as the one who has the same divine power over nature as Yahweh, the God of the Old Testament."

I nodded. "That's one example," I said. "Do you have any others?"

"Yes, I could go on along these lines," Blomberg said. "For instance, Jesus' most common title for himself in the first three gospels is 'Son of Man,' and—"

I raised my hand to stop him. "Hold on," I said. Reaching into my briefcase, I pulled out a book and leafed through it until I located the quote I was looking for. "Karen Armstrong, the former nun who wrote the best-seller *A History of God,* said it seems that the term 'Son of Man' 'simply stressed the weakness and mortality of the human condition,' so by using it, Jesus was merely emphasizing that 'he was a frail human being who would one day suffer and die.'[5] If that's true," I said, "that doesn't sound like much of a claim to deity."

Blomberg's expression turned sour. "Look," he said firmly, "contrary to popular belief, 'Son of Man' does not primarily refer to Jesus' humanity. Instead it's a direct allusion to Daniel 7:13–14."

With that he opened the Old Testament and read those words of the prophet Daniel.

> In my vision at night I looked, and there before me was one like a son of man, coming with the clouds of heaven. He approached the Ancient of Days and was led into his presence. He was given authority, glory and sovereign power; all peoples, nations and men of every language worshiped him. His dominion is an everlasting dominion that will not pass away, and his kingdom is one that will never be destroyed.

Blomberg shut the Bible. "So look at what Jesus is doing by applying the term 'Son of Man' to himself," he continued. "This is someone who approaches God himself in his heavenly throne room and is given universal authority and dominion. That makes 'Son of Man' a title of great exaltation, not of mere humanity."

Later I came upon a comment by another scholar whom I would soon interview for this book, William Lane Craig, who has made a similar observation.

> "Son of Man" is often thought to indicate the humanity of Jesus, just as the reflex expression "Son of God" indicates his divinity. In fact, just the opposite is true. The Son of Man was a divine figure in the Old Testament book of Daniel who would come at the end of the world to judge mankind and rule forever. Thus, the claim to be the Son of Man would be in effect a claim to divinity.[6]

Continued Blomberg: "In addition, Jesus claims to forgive sins in the synoptics, and that's something only God can do. Jesus accepts prayer and worship. Jesus says, 'Whoever acknowledges me, I will acknowledge before my Father in heaven.' Final judgment is based on one's reaction to—whom? This mere human being? No, that would be a very arrogant claim. Final judgment is based on one's reaction to Jesus *as God*.

"As you can see, there's all sorts of material in the synoptics about the deity of Christ, that then merely becomes more explicit in John's gospel."

THE GOSPELS' THEOLOGICAL AGENDA

In authoring the last gospel, John did have the advantage of being able to mull over theological issues for a longer period of time. So I asked Blomberg, "Doesn't the fact that John was writing with more of a theological bent mean that his historical material may have been tainted and therefore less reliable?"

"I don't believe John is more theological," Blomberg stressed. "He just has a different cluster of theological emphases. Matthew, Mark, and Luke each have very distinctive theological angles that they want to highlight: Luke, the theologian of the poor and of social concern; Matthew, the theologian trying to understand the relationship of Christianity and Judaism; Mark, who shows Jesus as the suffering servant. You can make a long list of the distinctive theologies of Matthew, Mark, and Luke."

I interrupted because I was afraid Blomberg was missing my broader point. "OK, but don't those theological motivations cast doubt on their ability and willingness to accurately report what happened?" I asked. "Isn't it likely that their theological agenda would prompt them to color and twist the history they recorded?"

"It certainly means that as with any ideological document, we have to consider that as a possibility," he admitted. "There are people with axes to grind who distort history to serve their ideological ends, but unfortunately people have concluded that always happens, which is a mistake.

"In the ancient world the idea of writing dispassionate, objective history merely to chronicle events, with no ideological purpose, was unheard of. Nobody wrote history if there wasn't a reason to learn from it."

I smiled. "I suppose you could say that makes everything suspect," I suggested.

"Yes, at one level it does," he replied. "But if we can reconstruct reasonably accurate history from all kinds of other ancient sources, we ought to be able to do that from the gospels, even though they too are ideological."

Blomberg thought for a moment, searching his mind for an appropriate analogy to drive home his point. Finally he said, "Here's a modern parallel, from the experience of the Jewish community, that might clarify what I mean.

"Some people, usually for anti-Semitic purposes, deny or downplay the horrors of the Holocaust. But it has been the Jewish scholars who've created museums, written books, preserved artifacts, and documented eyewitness testimony concerning the Holocaust.

"Now, they have a very ideological purpose—namely, to ensure that such an atrocity never occurs again—but they have also been the most faithful and objective in their reporting of historical truth.

"Christianity was likewise based on certain historical claims that God uniquely entered into space and time in the person of Jesus of Nazareth, so the very ideology that Christians were trying to promote required as careful historical work as possible."

He let his analogy sink in. Turning to face me more directly, he asked, "Do you see my point?"

I nodded to indicate that I did.

HOT NEWS FROM HISTORY

It's one thing to say that the gospels are rooted in direct or indirect eyewitness testimony; it's another to claim that this information was reliably preserved until it was finally written down years later. This, I knew, was a major point of contention, and I wanted to challenge Blomberg with this issue as forthrightly as I could.

Again I picked up Armstrong's popular book *A History of God*. "Listen to something else she wrote," I said.

> We know very little about Jesus. The first full-length account of his life was St. Mark's gospel, which was not written until about the year 70, some forty years after his death. By that time, historical facts had been overlaid with mythical elements which expressed the meaning Jesus had acquired for his followers. It is this meaning that St. Mark primarily conveys rather than a reliable straightforward portrayal.[7]

Tossing the book back into my open briefcase, I turned to Blomberg and continued. "Some scholars say the gospels were written so far after the events that legend developed and distorted what was finally written down, turning Jesus from merely a wise teacher into the mythological Son of God. Is that a reasonable hypothesis, or is there good evidence that the gospels were recorded earlier than that, before legend could totally corrupt what was ultimately recorded?"

Blomberg's eyes narrowed, and his voice took on an adamant tone. "There are two separate issues here, and it's important to keep them separate," he said. "I do think there's good evidence for suggesting early dates for the writing of the gospels. But even if there wasn't, Armstrong's argument doesn't work anyway."

"Why not?" I asked.

"The standard scholarly dating, even in very liberal circles, is Mark in the 70s, Matthew and Luke in the 80s, John in the 90s. But listen: that's still within the lifetimes of various eyewitnesses of the life of Jesus, including hostile eyewitnesses who would have served as a corrective if false teachings about Jesus were going around.

"Consequently, these late dates for the gospels really aren't all that late. In fact, we can make a comparison that's very instructive.

"The two earliest biographies of Alexander the Great were written by Arrian and Plutarch more than four hundred years after Alexander's death in 323 B.C., yet historians consider them to be generally trustworthy. Yes, legendary material about Alexander did develop over time, but it was only in the centuries after these two writers.

"In other words, the first five hundred years kept Alexander's story pretty much intact; legendary material began to emerge over the next five hundred years. So whether the gospels were written sixty years or thirty years after the life of Jesus, the amount of time is negligible by comparison. It's almost a nonissue."

I could see what Blomberg was saying. At the same time, I had some reservations about it. To me, it seemed intuitively obvious that the shorter the gap between an event and when it was recorded in writing, the less likely those writings would fall victim to legend or faulty memories.

"Let me concede your point for the moment, but let's get back to the dating of the gospels," I said. "You indicated that you believe they were written sooner than the dates you mentioned."

"Yes, sooner," he said. "And we can support that by looking at the book of Acts, which was written by Luke. Acts ends apparently unfinished—Paul is a central figure of the book, and he's under house arrest in Rome. With that the book abruptly halts. What happens to Paul? We don't find out from Acts, probably because the book was written before Paul was put to death."

Blomberg was getting more wound up as he went. "That means Acts cannot be dated any later than A.D. 62. Having established that, we can then move backward from there. Since Acts is the second of a two-part work, we know the first part—the gospel of Luke—must have been written earlier than that. And since Luke incorporates parts of the gospel of Mark, that means Mark is even earlier.

"If you allow maybe a year for each of those, you end up with Mark written no later than about A.D. 60, maybe even the late 50s. If Jesus was put to death in A.D. 30 or 33, we're talking about a maximum gap of thirty years or so."

He sat back in his chair with an air of triumph. "Historically speaking, especially compared with Alexander the Great," he said, "that's like a news flash!"

Indeed, that was impressive, closing the gap between the events of Jesus' life and the writing of the gospels to the point where it was negligible by historical standards. However, I still wanted to push the issue. My goal was to turn the clock back as far as I could to get to the very earliest information about Jesus.

GOING BACK TO THE BEGINNING

I stood and strolled over to the bookcase. "Let's see if we can go back even further," I said, turning toward Blomberg. "How early can we date the fundamental beliefs in Jesus' atonement, his resurrection, and his unique association with God?"

"It's important to remember that the books of the New Testament are not in chronological order," he began. "The gospels were written after almost all the letters of Paul, whose writing ministry probably began in the late 40s. Most of his major letters appeared during the 50s. To find the earliest information, one goes to Paul's epistles and then asks, 'Are there signs that even earlier sources were used in writing them?'"

"And," I prompted, "what do we find?"

"We find that Paul incorporated some creeds, confessions of faith, or hymns from the earliest Christian church. These go way back to the dawning of the church soon after the Resurrection.

"The most famous creeds include Philippians 2:6–11, which talks about Jesus being 'in very nature God,' and Colossians 1:15–20, which describes him as being 'the image of the invisible God,' who created all things and through whom all things are reconciled with God 'by making peace through his blood, shed on the cross.'

"Those are certainly significant in explaining what the earliest Christians were convinced about Jesus. But perhaps the most important creed in terms of the historical Jesus is 1 Corinthians 15, where Paul uses technical language to indicate he was passing along this oral tradition in relatively fixed form."

Blomberg located the passage in his Bible and read it to me.

> For what I received I passed on to you as of first importance: that Christ died for our sins according to the Scriptures, that he was buried, that he was raised on the third day according to the Scriptures, and that he appeared to Peter, and then to the Twelve. After that, he appeared to more than five hundred of the brothers at the same time, most of whom are still living, though some have fallen asleep. Then he appeared to James, then to all the apostles. [8]

"And here's the point," Blomberg said. "If the Crucifixion was as early as A.D. 30, Paul's conversion was about 32. Immediately Paul was ushered into Damascus, where he met with a Christian named Ananias and some other disciples. His first meeting with the apostles in Jerusalem would have been about A.D. 35. At some point along there, Paul was given this creed, which had already been formulated and was being used in the early church.

"Now, here you have the key facts about Jesus' death for our sins, plus a detailed list of those to whom he appeared in resurrected form—all dating back to within two to five years of the events themselves!

"That's not later mythology from forty or more years down the road, as Armstrong suggested. A good case can be made for saying that Christian belief in the Resurrection, though not yet written down, can be dated to within two years of that very event.

"This is enormously significant," he said, his voice rising a bit in emphasis. "Now you're not comparing thirty to sixty years with the five hundred years that's generally acceptable for other data—you're talking about two!"

I couldn't deny the importance of that evidence. It certainly seemed to take the wind out of the charge that the Resurrection—which is cited by Christians as the crowning confirmation of Jesus' divinity—was merely a mythological concept that developed over long periods of time as legends corrupted the eyewitness accounts of

Christ's life. For me, this struck especially close to home—as a skeptic, that was one of my biggest objections to Christianity.

I leaned against the bookcase. We had covered a lot of material, and Blomberg's climactic assertion seemed like a good place to pause.

A SHORT RECESS

It was getting late in the afternoon. We had been talking for quite a while without a break. However, I didn't want to end our conversation without putting the eyewitness accounts to the same kind of tests to which a lawyer or journalist would subject them. I needed to know: would they stand up under that scrutiny, or would they be exposed as questionable at best or unreliable at worst?

The necessary groundwork having been laid, I invited Blomberg to stand and stretch his legs before we sat back down to resume our discussion.

Deliberations

Questions for Reflection or Group Study

1. How have your opinions been influenced by someone's eyewitness account of an event? What are some factors you routinely use to evaluate whether someone's story is honest and accurate? How do you think the gospels would stand up to that kind of scrutiny?
2. Do you believe that the gospels can have a theological agenda while at the same time being trustworthy in what they report? Why or why not? Do you find Blomberg's Holocaust analogy helpful in thinking through this issue?
3. How and why does Blomberg's description of the early information about Jesus affect your opinion about the reliability of the gospels?

For Further Evidence

More Resources on This Topic

Barnett, Paul. *Is the New Testament History?* Ann Arbor, Mich.: Vine, 1986.

_______. *Jesus and the Logic of History.* Grand Rapids: Eerdmans, 1997.

Blomberg, Craig. *The Historical Reliability of the Gospels.* Downers Grove, Ill.: InterVarsity Press, 1987.

Bruce, F. F. *The New Testament Documents: Are They Reliable?* Grand Rapids: Eerdmans, 1960.

France, R. T. *The Evidence for Jesus.* Downers Grove, Ill.: InterVarsity Press, 1986.

2

TESTING THE EYEWITNESS EVIDENCE

Do the Biographies of Jesus Stand Up to Scrutiny?

Sixteen-year-old Michael McCullough's words were so faint that jurors couldn't hear them above the soft puffing sound of the mechanical respirator that was keeping him alive. A lip-reader had to hunch over Michael's bed, discern what he was saying, and repeat his testimony to the makeshift courtroom.

Paralyzed from the neck down by a bullet that severed his spinal cord, Michael was too frail to be transported to the courthouse for the trial of the two youths accused of attacking him. Instead the judge, jury, defendants, lawyers, reporters, and spectators crowded into Michael's hospital room, which was declared a temporary branch of Cook County Circuit Court.

Under questioning by prosecutors, Michael recalled how he left his apartment at a Chicago housing project with two dollars in his pocket. He said he was accosted in a stairway by the two defendants, who intentionally shot him in the face as they tried to steal his money. His story was backed up by two other youths who had watched in horror as the assault took place.

The defendants never denied the shooting; instead they claimed that the gun accidentally discharged while they were waving it around. Defense attorneys knew that the only way they could get their clients off with a reduced sentence was if they could succeed in undermining the testimony that the shooting was a vicious and premeditated act of violence.

They did their best to cast doubt on the eyewitness accounts. They questioned the witnesses' ability to view what happened, but they failed to make any inroads. They tried to exploit inconsistencies in the stories, but the accounts harmonized on the central points. They demanded more corroboration, but clearly no more was needed.

They raised hints about character, but the victim and witnesses were law-abiding youths with no criminal record. They hoped to show a bias against the defendants, but they couldn't find one. They questioned whether one witness, a nine-year-old boy named Keith, was old enough to understand what it meant to tell the truth under oath, but it was obvious to everyone that he did.

With defense attorneys unable to shake the credibility of the victim and the prosecution witnesses, the two defendants were convicted of attempted murder and sentenced to fifty years in the penitentiary. Eighteen days later Michael died.[1]

Defense attorneys have a challenging job: to raise questions, to generate doubts, to probe the soft and vulnerable spots of a witness's story. They do this by subjecting the testimony to a variety of tests. The idea is that honest and accurate testimony will withstand scrutiny, while false, exaggerated, or misleading testimony will be exposed.

In Michael's case justice prevailed because the jurors could tell that the witnesses and victim were sincerely and precisely recounting what they had experienced.

Now let's return to our investigation of the historical evidence concerning Jesus. The time had come to subject Dr. Blomberg's testimony to tests that would either reveal its weaknesses or underscore its strength. Many of these would be the same tests that had been used by defense attorneys in Michael's case so many years earlier.

"There are eight different tests I'd like to ask you about," I said to Blomberg as we sat down after our fifteen-minute break.

Blomberg picked up a fresh cup of steaming black coffee and leaned back. I wasn't sure, but it seemed he was looking forward to the challenge.

"Go ahead," he said.

1. THE INTENTION TEST

This test seeks to determine whether it was the stated or implied intention of the writers to accurately preserve history. "Were these first-century writers even interested in recording what actually happened?" I asked.

Blomberg nodded. "Yes, they were," he said. "You can see that at the beginning of the gospel of Luke, which reads very much like prefaces to other generally trusted historical and biographical works of antiquity."

Picking up his Bible, Blomberg read the opening of Luke's gospel.

> Many have undertaken to draw up an account of the things that have been fulfilled among us, just as they were handed down to us by those who from the first were eyewitnesses and servants of the word. Therefore, since I myself have carefully investigated everything from the beginning, it seemed good also to me to write an orderly account for you, most excellent Theophilus, so that you may know the certainty of the things you have been taught.[2]

"As you can see," Blomberg continued, "Luke is clearly saying he intended to write accurately about the things he investigated and found to be well-supported by witnesses."

"What about the other gospels?" I asked. "They don't start with similar declarations; does that mean their writers didn't have the same intentions?"

"It's true that Mark and Matthew don't have this kind of explicit statement," came Blomberg's reply. "However, they are close to Luke in terms of genre, and it seems reasonable that Luke's historical intent would closely mirror theirs."

"And John?" I asked.

"The only other statement of purpose in the gospels comes in John 20:31: 'These are written that you may believe that Jesus is the Christ, the Son of God, and that by believing you may have life in his name.'"

"That," I objected, "sounds more like a theological statement than a historical one."

"I'll grant you that," Blomberg replied. "But if you're going to be convinced enough to believe, the theology has to flow from accurate history. Besides, there's an important piece of implicit evidence that can't be overlooked. Consider the way the gospels are written—in a sober and responsible fashion, with accurate incidental details, with obvious care and exactitude. You don't find the outlandish flourishes and blatant mythologizing that you see in a lot of other ancient writings.

"What does all that add up to?" he asked. Then he answered his own question: "It seems quite apparent that the goal of the gospel writers was to attempt to record what had actually occurred."

Answering Objections

However, is that what really happened? There's a competing and contradictory scenario that has been promoted by some critics.

They have said that early Christians were convinced Jesus was going to be returning during their lifetime to consummate history, so they didn't think it was necessary to preserve any historical records about his life or teachings. After all, why bother if he's going to come and end the world at any moment?

"So," I said, "years later when it became obvious that Jesus wasn't coming back right away, they found they didn't have any accurate historical material to draw on in writing the gospels. Nothing had been captured for historical purposes. Isn't that what really happened?"

"There are certainly sects and groups, including religious ones throughout history, for which that argument works, but not with early Christianity," Blomberg replied.

"Why not?" I challenged him. "What was so different about Christianity?"

"First, I think the premise is a bit overstated. The truth is that the majority of Jesus' teachings presuppose a significant span of time before the end of the world," he said. "But second, even if some of Jesus' followers did think he might come back fairly quickly, remember that Christianity was born out of Judaism.

"For eight centuries the Jews lived with the tension between the repeated pronouncements of prophets that the Day of the Lord was at hand and the continuing history of Israel. And still the followers of these prophets recorded, valued, and preserved the words of the prophets. Given that Jesus' followers looked upon him as being even greater than a prophet, it seems very reasonable that they would have done the same thing."

While that did seem reasonable, some scholars have also raised a second objection that I wanted to pose to Blomberg. "They say that early Christians frequently believed that the physically departed Jesus was speaking through them with messages, or 'prophecies,' for their church," I said. "Since these prophecies were considered as authoritative as Jesus' own words when he was alive on earth, the early Christians didn't distinguish between these newer sayings and the original words of the historical Jesus. As a result, the gospels blend these two types of material, so we don't really know what goes back to the historical Jesus and what doesn't. That's a troubling charge to a lot of people. How do you respond to that?"

"That argument has less historical support than the previous one," he said with a smile. "In fact, within the New Testament itself there is evidence that disproves this hypothesis.

"There are occasions when early Christian prophecy is referred to, but it's always distinguished from what the Lord has said. For example, in 1 Corinthians 7 Paul clearly distinguishes when he has a word from the Lord and when he is quoting the historical Jesus. In the book of Revelation one can clearly distinguish the handful of times in which Jesus directly speaks to this prophet—traditionally assumed to be John the apostle—and when John is recounting his own inspired visions.

"And in 1 Corinthians 14, when Paul is discussing the criteria for true prophecy, he talks about the responsibility of the local church to test the prophets. Drawing on his Jewish background, we know that the criteria for true prophecy would have included whether the prediction comes true and whether these new statements cohere with previously revealed words of the Lord.

"But the strongest argument is what we never find in the gospels. After Jesus' ascension there were a number of controversies that threatened the early church—should believers be circumcised, how should speaking in tongues be regulated, how to keep Jew and Gentile united, what are the appropriate roles for women in ministry, whether believers could divorce non-Christian spouses.

"These issues could have been conveniently resolved if the early Christians had simply read back into the gospels what Jesus had told them from the world beyond. But this never happened. The continuance of these controversies demonstrates that Christians were interested in distinguishing between what happened during Jesus' lifetime and what was debated later in the churches."

2. THE ABILITY TEST

Even if the writers intended to reliably record history, were they able to do so? How can we be sure that the material about Jesus' life and teachings was well preserved for thirty years before it was finally written down in the gospels?

I asked Blomberg, "Won't you concede that faulty memories, wishful thinking, and the development of legend would have irreparably contaminated the Jesus tradition prior to the writing of the gospels?"

He started his answer by establishing the context. "We have to remember that we're in a foreign land in a distant time and place and in a culture that has not yet invented computers or even the printing press," he replied. "Books—or actually, scrolls of papyrus—were relatively rare. Therefore education, learning, worship, teaching in religious communities—all this was done by word of mouth.

"Rabbis became famous for having the entire Old Testament committed to memory. So it would have been well within the capability of Jesus' disciples to have committed much more to memory than appears in all four gospels put together—and to have passed it along accurately."

"Wait a second," I interjected. "Frankly, that kind of memorization seems incredible. How is that possible?"

"Yes, it is difficult for us to imagine today," he conceded, "but this was an oral culture, in which there was great emphasis placed on memorization. And remember that eighty to ninety percent of Jesus' words were originally in poetic form. This doesn't mean stuff that rhymes, but it has a meter, balanced lines, parallelism, and so forth—and this would have created a great memory help.

"The other thing that needs to be said is that the definition of memorization was more flexible back then. In studies of cultures with oral traditions, there was freedom to vary how much of the story was told on any given occasion—what was included, what was left out, what was paraphrased, what was explained, and so forth.

"One study suggested that in the ancient Middle East, anywhere from ten to forty percent of any given retelling of sacred tradition could vary from one occasion to the next. However, there were always fixed points that were unalterable, and the community had the right to intervene and correct the storyteller if he erred on those important aspects of the story.

"It's an interesting"—he paused, searching his mind for the right word—"*coincidence* that ten to forty percent is pretty consistently the amount of variation among the synoptics on any given passage."

Blomberg was hinting at something; I wanted him to be more explicit. "Spell it out for me," I said. "What precisely are you saying?"

"I'm saying that it's likely that a lot of the similarities and differences among the synoptics can be explained by assuming that the disciples and other early Christians had committed to memory a lot of what Jesus said and did, but they felt free to recount this information in various forms, always preserving the significance of Jesus' original teachings and deeds."

Still, I had some question about the ability of these early Christians to accurately preserve this oral tradition. I had too many memories of childhood party games in which words got garbled within a matter of minutes.

Playing Telephone

You've probably played the game of telephone yourself: one child whispers something into another child's ear—for instance, "You're my best friend"—and this gets whispered to others around a big circle until at the end it comes out grossly distorted—perhaps, "You're a brutish fiend."

"Let's be candid," I said to Blomberg. "Isn't this a good analogy for what probably happened to the oral tradition about Jesus?"

Blomberg wasn't buying that explanation. "No, not really," he said. "Here's why: When you're carefully memorizing something and taking care not to pass it along until you're sure you've got it right, you're doing something very different from playing the game of telephone.

"In telephone half the fun is that the person may not have got it right or even heard it right the first time, and they cannot ask the person to repeat it. Then you immediately pass it along, also in whispered tones that make it more likely the next person will goof something up even more. So yes, by the time it has circulated through a room of thirty people, the results can be hilarious."

"Then why," I asked, "isn't that a good analogy for passing along ancient oral tradition?"

Blomberg sipped his coffee before answering. "If you really wanted to develop that analogy in light of the checks and balances of the first-century community, you'd have to say that every third person, out loud in a very clear voice, would have to ask the first person, 'Do I still have it right?' and change it if he didn't.

"The community would constantly be monitoring what was said and intervening to make corrections along the way. That would preserve the integrity of the message," he said. "And the result would be very different from that of a childish game of telephone."

3. THE CHARACTER TEST

This test looks at whether it was in the character of these writers to be truthful. Was there any evidence of dishonesty or immorality that might taint their ability or willingness to transmit history accurately?

Blomberg shook his head. "We simply do not have any reasonable evidence to suggest they were anything but people of great integrity," he said.

"We see them reporting the words and actions of a man who called them to as exacting a level of integrity as any religion has ever known. They were willing to live out their beliefs even to the point of ten of the eleven remaining disciples being put to grisly deaths, which shows great character.

"In terms of honesty, in terms of truthfulness, in terms of virtue and morality, these people had a track record that should be envied."

4. THE CONSISTENCY TEST

Here's a test that skeptics often charge the gospels with failing. After all, aren't they hopelessly contradictory with each other? Aren't there irreconcilable discrepancies among the various gospel accounts? And if there are, how can anyone trust anything they say?

Blomberg acknowledged that there are numerous points at which the gospels appear to disagree. "These range all the way from very minor variations in wording to the most famous apparent contradictions," he said.

"My own conviction is, once you allow for the elements I've talked about earlier—of paraphrase, of abridgment, of explanatory additions, of selection, of omission—the gospels are extremely consistent with each other by ancient standards, which are the only standards by which it's fair to judge them."

"Ironically," I pointed out, "if the gospels had been identical to each other, word for word, this would have raised charges that the authors had conspired among themselves to coordinate their stories in advance, and that would have cast doubt on them."

"That's right," Blomberg agreed. "If the gospels were too consistent, that in itself would invalidate them as independent witnesses. People would then say we really only have one testimony that everybody else is just parroting."

My mind flashed to the words of Simon Greenleaf of Harvard Law School, one of history's most important legal figures and the author of an influential treatise on evidence. After studying the consistency among the four gospel writers, he offered this evaluation: "There is enough of a discrepancy to show that there could have been no previous concert among them; and at the same time such substantial agreement as to show that they all were independent narrators of the same great transaction."[3]

From the perspective of a classical historian, German scholar Hans Stier has concurred that agreement over basic data and divergence of details suggest credibility, because fabricated accounts tend to be fully consistent and harmonized. "Every historian," he wrote, "is especially skeptical at that moment when an extraordinary happening is only reported in accounts which are completely free of contradictions."[4]

While that's true, I didn't want to ignore the difficulties that are raised by the ostensible discrepancies among the gospels. I decided to probe the issue further by pressing Blomberg on some apparent clear-cut contradictions that skeptics frequently seize upon as examples of why the gospels are unreliable.

Coping with Contradictions

I began with a well-known story of a healing. "In Matthew it says a centurion himself came to ask Jesus to heal his servant," I pointed out. "However, Luke says the centurion sent the elders to do this. Now, that's an obvious contradiction, isn't it?"

"No, I don't think so," Blomberg replied. "Think about it this way: in our world today, we may hear a news report that says, 'The president today announced that . . .' when in fact the speech was written by a speechwriter and delivered by the press secretary—and with a little luck, the president might have glanced at it somewhere in between. Yet nobody accuses that broadcast of being in error.

"In a similar way, in the ancient world it was perfectly understood and accepted that actions were often attributed to people when in fact they occurred through their subordinates or emissaries—in this case through the elders of the Jewish people."

"So you're saying that Matthew and Luke can both be right at the same time?"

"That's exactly what I'm saying," he replied.

That seemed plausible, so I posed a second example. "What about Mark and Luke saying that Jesus sent the demons into the swine at Gerasa, while Matthew says it was in Gadara. People look at that and say this is an obvious contradiction that cannot be reconciled—it's two different places. Case closed."

"Well, don't shut the case yet," Blomberg chuckled. "Here's one possible solution: one was a town; the other was a province."

That seemed a little too glib for me. He appeared to be skimming over the real difficulties that are raised by this issue.

"It gets more complicated than that," I said. "Gerasa, the town, wasn't anywhere near the Sea of Galilee, yet that's where the demons, after going into the swine, supposedly took the herd over the cliff to their deaths."

"OK, good point," he said. "But there have been ruins of a town that have been excavated at exactly the right point on the eastern shore of the Sea of Galilee. The English form of the town's name often gets pronounced 'Khersa,' but as a Hebrew word translated or transliterated into Greek, it could have come out sounding something very much like 'Gerasa.' So it may very well have been in Khersa—whose spelling in Greek was rendered as Gerasa—in the province of Gadara."

"Well done," I conceded with a smile. "I'll surrender on that one. But here's a problem that's not so easy: what about the discrepancies between the genealogies of Jesus in Matthew and Luke? Skeptics often point to them as being hopelessly in conflict."

"This is another case of multiple options," he said.

"Such as?"

"The two most common have been that Matthew reflects Joseph's lineage, because most of his opening chapter is told from Joseph's perspective and Joseph, as the adoptive father, would have been the legal ancestor through whom Jesus' royal lineage would have been traced. These are themes that are important for Matthew.

"Luke, then, would have traced the genealogy through Mary's lineage. And since both are from the ancestry of David, once you get that far back the lines converge.

"A second option is that both genealogies reflect Joseph's lineage in order to create the necessary legalities. But one is Joseph's human lineage—the gospel of Luke—and the other is Joseph's legal lineage, with the two diverging at the points where somebody in the line did not have a direct offspring. They had to raise up legal heirs through various Old Testament practices.

"The problem is made greater because some names are omitted, which was perfectly acceptable by standards of the ancient world.

And there are textual variants—names, being translated from one language into another, often took on different spellings and were then easily confused for the name of a different individual."

Blomberg had made his point: there are at least some rational explanations. Even if they might not be airtight, at least they provide a reasonable harmonization of the gospel accounts.

Not wanting our conversation to degenerate into a stump-the-scholar game, I decided to move on. In the meantime Blomberg and I agreed that the best overall approach would be to study each issue individually to see whether there's a rational way to resolve the apparent conflict among the gospels. Certainly there's no shortage of authoritative books that thoroughly examine, sometimes in excruciating detail, how these differences might be reconciled.[5]

"And," said Blomberg, "there are occasions when we may need to hold judgment in abeyance and simply say that since we've made sense out of the vast majority of the texts and determined them to be trustworthy, we can then give them the benefit of the doubt when we're not sure on some of the other details."

5. THE BIAS TEST

This test analyzes whether the gospel writers had any biases that would have colored their work. Did they have any vested interest in skewing the material they were reporting on?

"We can't underestimate the fact that these people loved Jesus," I pointed out. "They were not neutral observers; they were his devoted followers. Wouldn't that make it likely that they would change things to make him look good?"

"Well, I'll concede this much," Blomberg replied, "it creates the potential for this to happen. But on the other hand, people can so honor and respect someone that it prompts them to record his life with great integrity. That's the way they would show their love for him. And I think that's what happened here.

"Besides, these disciples had nothing to gain except criticism, ostracism, and martyrdom. They certainly had nothing to win financially. If anything, this would have provided pressure to keep quiet, to deny Jesus, to downplay him, even to forget they ever met him—yet because of their integrity, they proclaimed what they saw, even when it meant suffering and death."

6. THE COVER-UP TEST

When people testify about events they saw, they will often try to protect themselves or others by conveniently forgetting to mention details that are embarrassing or hard to explain. As a result, this raises uncertainty about the veracity of their entire testimony.

So I asked Blomberg, "Did the gospel writers include any material that might be embarrassing, or did they cover it up to make themselves look good? Did they report anything that would be uncomfortable or difficult for them to explain?"

"There's actually quite a bit along those lines," he said. "There's a large body of Jesus' teaching called the hard sayings of Jesus. Some of it is very ethically demanding. If I were inventing a religion to suit my fancy, I probably wouldn't tell myself to be as perfect as my heavenly Father is perfect, or define adultery to include lust in my heart."

"But," I protested, "there are demanding statements in other religions as well."

"Yes, that's true, which is why the more persuasive kind of hard sayings are those that could be embarrassing for what the church wanted to teach about Jesus."

That response seemed vague. "Give me some examples," I said.

Blomberg thought for a moment, then said, "For instance, Mark 6:5 says that Jesus could do few miracles in Nazareth because the people there had little faith, which seems to limit Jesus' power. Jesus said in Mark 13:32 that he didn't know the day or the hour of his return, which seems to limit his omniscience.

"Now, ultimately theology hasn't had a problem with these statements, because Paul himself, in Philippians 2:5–8, talks about God in Christ voluntarily and consciously limiting the independent exercise of his divine attributes.

"But if I felt free to play fast and loose with gospel history, it would be much more convenient to just leave out that material altogether, and then I wouldn't have to go through the hassle of explaining it.

"Jesus' baptism is another example. You can explain why Jesus, who was without sin, allowed himself to be baptized, but why not make things easier by leaving it out altogether? On the cross Jesus cried out, 'My God, my God, why hast thou forsaken me?' It would have been in the self-interest of the writers to omit that because it raises too many questions."

"Certainly," I added, "there's plenty of embarrassing material about the disciples."

"Absolutely," Blomberg said. "Mark's perspective of Peter is pretty consistently unflattering. And he's the ringleader! The disciples repeatedly misunderstand Jesus. James and John want the places at Jesus' right and left hand, and he has to teach them hard lessons about servant leadership instead. They look like a bunch of self-serving, self-seeking, dull-witted people a lot of the time.

"Now, we already know that the gospel writers were selective; John's gospel ends by saying, somewhat hyperbolically, that the whole world couldn't contain all the information that could have been written about Jesus. So had they left some of this out, that in and of itself wouldn't necessarily have been seen as falsifying the story.

"But here's the point: if they didn't feel free to leave out stuff when it would have been convenient and helpful to do so, is it really plausible to believe that they outright added and fabricated material with no historical basis?"

Blomberg let the question hang for a while before concluding with confidence, "I'd say not."

7. THE CORROBORATION TEST

I introduced this next test by asking Blomberg, "When the gospels mention people, places, and events, do they check out to be correct in cases in which they can be independently verified?" Often such corroboration is invaluable in assessing whether a writer has a commitment to accuracy.

"Yes, they do, and the longer people explore this, the more the details get confirmed," Blomberg replied. "Within the last hundred years archaeology has repeatedly unearthed discoveries that have confirmed specific references in the gospels, particularly the gospel of John—ironically, the one that's supposedly so suspect!

"Now, yes, there are still some unresolved issues, and there have been times when archaeology has created new problems, but those are a tiny minority compared with the number of examples of corroboration.

"In addition, we can learn through non-Christian sources a lot of facts about Jesus that corroborate key teachings and events in his life. And when you stop to think that ancient historians for the most part dealt only with political rulers, emperors, kings, military battles, official religious people, and major philosophical movements, it's remarkable how much we can learn about Jesus and his followers even though they fit none of those categories at the time these historians were writing."

That was a concise and helpful answer. However, while I had no reason to doubt Blomberg's assessment, I decided it would be worthwhile to do some further research along these lines. I picked up my pen and jotted a reminder to myself in the margin of my notes: *Get expert opinions from archaeologist and historian.*

8. THE ADVERSE WITNESS TEST

This test asks the question, Were others present who would have contradicted or corrected the gospels if they had been distorted or false? In other words, do we see examples of contemporaries of Jesus complaining that the gospel accounts were just plain wrong?

"Many people had reasons for wanting to discredit this movement and would have done so if they could have simply told history better," Blomberg said.

"Yet look at what his opponents did say. In later Jewish writings Jesus is called a sorcerer who led Israel astray—which acknowledges that he really did work marvelous wonders, although the writers dispute the source of his power.

"This would have been a perfect opportunity to say something like, 'The Christians will tell you he worked miracles, but we're here to tell you he didn't.' Yet that's the one thing we never see his opponents saying. Instead they implicitly acknowledge that what the gospels wrote—that Jesus performed miracles—is true."

I asked, "Could this Christian movement have taken root right there in Jerusalem—in the very area where Jesus had done much of his ministry, had been crucified, buried, and resurrected—if people who knew him were aware that the disciples were exaggerating or distorting the things that he did?"

"I don't believe so," Blomberg replied. "We have a picture of what was initially a very vulnerable and fragile movement that was being subjected to persecution. If critics could have attacked it on the basis that it was full of falsehoods or distortions, they would have.

"But," he emphasized in conclusion, "that's exactly what we don't see."

A FAITH BUTTRESSED BY FACTS

I'll admit I was impressed by Blomberg. Informed and articulate, scholarly and convincing, he had constructed a strong case for the reliability of the gospels. His evidence for their traditional authorship, his analysis of the extremely early date of fundamental beliefs about Jesus, his well-reasoned defense of the accuracy of the oral tradition, his thoughtful examination of apparent discrepancies—all of his testimony had established a solid foundation for me to build on.

Yet there was still a long way to go in determining whether Jesus is the unique Son of God. In fact, after talking with Blomberg, my next assignment became clear: figure out whether these gospels, shown by Blomberg to be so trustworthy, have been reliably handed down to us over the centuries. How can we be sure that the texts we're reading today bear any resemblance to what was originally written in the first century? What's more, how do we know that the gospels are telling us the full story about Jesus?

I looked at my watch. If traffic was light, I'd make my plane back to Chicago. As I gathered my notes and unplugged my recording equipment, I happened to glance once more at the children's paintings on Blomberg's wall—and suddenly for a moment I thought of him not as a scholar, not as an author, not as a professor, but as a father who sits on the edge of his daughters' beds at night and speaks quietly to them about what's really important in life.

What does he tell them, I wondered, about the Bible, about God, about this Jesus who makes such outrageous claims about himself?

I couldn't resist one last line of questions. "What about your own faith?" I asked. "How has all your research affected your beliefs?"

I barely got the words out of my mouth before he replied. "It has strengthened them, no question. I know from my own research that there's very strong evidence for the trustworthiness of the gospel accounts."

He was quiet for a moment, then continued. "You know, it's ironic: The Bible considers it praiseworthy to have a faith that does not require evidence. Remember how Jesus replied to doubting Thomas: 'You believe because you see; blessed are those who have not seen and yet believe.' And I know evidence can never compel or coerce faith. We cannot supplant the role of the Holy Spirit, which is often a concern of Christians when they hear discussions of this kind.

"But I'll tell you this: there are plenty of stories of scholars in the New Testament field who have not been Christians, yet through their study of these very issues have come to faith in Christ. And there have been countless more scholars, already believers, whose faith has been made stronger, more solid, more grounded, because of the evidence—and that's the category I fall into."

As for me, I had originally been in the first category—no, not a scholar but a skeptic, an iconoclast, a hard-nosed reporter on a quest for the truth about this Jesus who said he was the Way and the Truth and the Life.

I clicked my briefcase closed and stood to thank Blomberg. I would fly back to Chicago satisfied that once again my spiritual quest was off to a good start.

Deliberations

Questions for Reflection or Group Study

1. Overall, how have Blomberg's responses to these eight evidential tests affected your confidence in the reliability of the gospels? Why?
2. Which of these eight tests do you consider the most persuasive and why?
3. When people you trust give slightly different details of the same event, do you automatically doubt their credibility, or do you see if there's a reasonable way to reconcile their accounts? How convincing did you find Blomberg's analysis of the apparent contradictions among the gospels?

For Further Evidence

More Resources on This Topic

Archer, Gleason L. *The Encyclopedia of Bible Difficulties*. Grand Rapids: Zondervan, 1982.

Blomberg, Craig. "The Historical Reliability of the New Testament." In *Reasonable Faith,* by William Lane Craig, 193–231. Westchester, Ill.: Crossway, 1994.

______. "Where Do We Start Studying Jesus?" In *Jesus under Fire*, edited by Michael J. Wilkins and J. P. Moreland, 17–50. Grand Rapids: Zondervan, 1995.

Dunn, James. *The Living Word*. Philadelphia: Fortress, 1988.

Marshall, I. Howard. *I Believe in the Historical Jesus*. Grand Rapids: Eerdmans, 1977.

3

THE DOCUMENTARY EVIDENCE

Were Jesus' Biographies Reliably Preserved for Us?

As a reporter at the *Chicago Tribune,* I was a "document rat"—I spent countless hours rummaging through court files and sniffing for tidbits of news. It was painstaking and time consuming, but the rewards were worth it. I managed to scoop the competition with front-page stories on a regular basis.

For example, I once stumbled upon some top-secret grand jury transcripts that had inadvertently been put in a public file. My subsequent articles exposed massive bid-rigging behind some of Chicago's biggest public works projects, including the construction of major expressways.

But the most eye-popping cache of documents I ever uncovered came in a landmark case in which Ford Motor Company was charged with reckless homicide for the fiery deaths of three teenagers in a subcompact Pinto. It was the first time a U.S. manufacturer had been criminally charged for allegedly marketing a dangerous product.

When I checked the court file in tiny Winamac, Indiana, I found scores of confidential Ford memos revealing that the automaker knew in advance that the Pinto could explode when struck from behind at about twenty miles an hour. The documents indicated that the automaker decided against improving the car's safety to save a few dollars per vehicle and to increase its luggage space.

A Ford lawyer, who happened to be strolling through the courthouse, spotted me making photocopies of the documents. Frantically he rushed into court to get a judicial order sealing the file from the public's view.

But it was too late. My story, headlined "Ford Ignored Pinto Fire Peril, Secret Memos Show," was bannered in the *Tribune* and then flashed throughout the country.[1]

AUTHENTICATING THE DOCUMENTS

Obtaining secret corporate memos is one thing; verifying their authenticity is another. Before a journalist can publish their contents or a prosecutor can admit the documents as evidence in a trial, steps must be taken to make sure they're genuine.

Concerning the so-called Pinto papers, could the Ford letterheads on which they were written be counterfeits? Could the signatures be forgeries? How could I know for sure? And since the memos had obviously been photocopied numerous times, how could I be confident that their contents hadn't been tampered with? In other words, how could I be certain that each copied document was identical to the original memo, which I didn't possess?

What's more, how could I be positive that these memos told the whole story? After all, they represented just a small fraction of the internal correspondence at Ford. What if there were other memos, still hidden from the public's view, that would shed a whole different light on the matter if they were revealed?

These are significant questions, and they're equally relevant in examining the New Testament. When I hold a Bible in my hands, essentially I'm holding copies of ancient historical records. The original manuscripts of the biographies of Jesus—Matthew, Mark, Luke, and John—and all the other books of the Old and New Testaments have long ago crumbled into dust. So how can I be sure that these modern-day versions—the end product of countless copying throughout the ages—bear any resemblance to what the authors originally wrote?

In addition, how can I tell if these four biographies are telling the whole story? What if there were other biographies of Jesus that have been censored because the early church didn't like the image of Jesus they portrayed? How could I have confidence that church politics haven't squelched biographies of Jesus that were every bit as accurate as the four that were finally included in the New Testament, and that would shed important new light on the words and deeds of this controversial carpenter from Nazareth?

These two issues—whether Jesus' biographies were reliably preserved for us and whether equally accurate biographies have been suppressed by the church—merited careful consideration. I knew that there was one scholar universally recognized as a leading authority on these matters. I flew to Newark and drove a rental car to Princeton to visit him on short notice.

THE SECOND INTERVIEW: BRUCE M. METZGER, PH.D.

I found eighty-four-year-old Bruce Metzger on a Saturday afternoon at his usual hangout, the library at Princeton Theological Seminary, where, he says with a smile, "I like to dust off the books."

Actually, he has written some of the best of them, especially when the topic is the text of the New Testament. In all, he has authored or edited fifty books, including *The New Testament: Its Background, Growth, and Content; The Text of the New Testament; The Canon of the New Testament; Manuscripts of the Greek Bible; Textual Commentary on the Greek New Testament; Introduction to the Apocrypha;* and *The Oxford Companion to the Bible*. Several have been translated into German, Chinese, Japanese, Korean, Malagasy, and other languages. He also is coeditor of *The New Oxford Annotated Bible with the Apocrypha* and general editor of more than twenty-five volumes in the series New Testament Tools and Studies.

Metzger's education includes a master's degree from Princeton Theological Seminary and both a master's degree and a doctorate from Princeton University. He has been awarded honorary doctorates by five colleges and universities, including St. Andrews University in Scotland, the University of Munster in Germany, and Potchefstroom University in South Africa.

In 1969 he served as resident scholar at Tyndale House, Cambridge, England. He was a visiting fellow at Clare Hall, University of Cambridge, in 1974 and at Wolfson College, Oxford, in 1979. He is currently professor emeritus at Princeton Theological Seminary after a forty-six-year career teaching the New Testament.

Metzger is chairman of the New Revised Standard Version Bible Committee, a corresponding fellow of the British Academy, and serves on the Kuratorium of the Vetus Latina Institute at the Monastery of Beuron, Germany. He is past president of the Society of Biblical Literature, the International Society for New Testament Studies, and the North American Patristic Society.

If you scan the footnotes of any authoritative book on the text of the New Testament, the odds are you're going to see Metzger cited time after time. His books are mandatory reading in universities and seminaries around the world. He is held in the highest regard by scholars from across a wide range of theological beliefs.

In many ways Metzger, born in 1914, is a throwback to an earlier generation. Alighting from a gray Buick he calls "my gas buggy," he is wearing a dark gray suit and blue paisley tie, which is about as casual as he gets during his visits to the library, even on a weekend. His white hair is neatly combed; his eyes, bright and alert, are framed by rimless glasses. He walks slower than he used to, but he has no difficulty methodically climbing the stairway to the second floor, where he conducts his research in an obscure and austere office.

And he hasn't lost his sense of humor. He showed me a tin canister he inherited as chairman of the Revised Standard Version Bible Committee. He opened the lid to reveal the ashes of an RSV Bible that had been torched in a 1952 bonfire during a protest by a fundamentalist preacher.

"It seems he didn't like it when the committee changed 'fellows' of the King James Version to 'comrades' in Hebrews 1:9," Metzger explained with a chuckle. "He accused them of being communists!"

Though Metzger's speech is hesitant at times and he's prone to replying in quaint phrases like "Quite so," he continues to remain on the cutting edge of New Testament scholarship. When I asked for some statistics, he didn't rely on the numbers in his 1992 book on the New Testament; he had conducted fresh research to get up-to-date figures. His quick mind has no problem recalling details of people and places, and he's fully conversant with all the current debates among New Testament experts. In fact, they continue to look to him for insight and wisdom.

His office, about the size of a jail cell, is windowless and painted institutional gray. It has two wooden chairs; he insisted I take the more comfortable one. That was part of his charm. He was thoroughly kind, surprisingly modest and self-effacing, with a gentle spirit that made me want to someday grow old with the same mellow kind of grace.

We got acquainted with each other for a while, and then I turned to the first issue I wanted to address: how can we be sure the biographies of Jesus were handed down to us in a reliable way?

COPIES OF COPIES OF COPIES

"I'll be honest with you," I said to Metzger. "When I first found out that there are no surviving originals of the New Testament, I was really skeptical. I thought, If all we have are copies of copies of copies, how can I have any confidence that the New Testament we have today bears any resemblance whatsoever to what was originally written? How do you respond to that?"

"This isn't an issue that's unique to the Bible; it's a question we can ask of other documents that have come down to us from antiquity," he replied. "But what the New Testament has in its favor, especially when compared with other ancient writings, is the unprecedented multiplicity of copies that have survived."

"Why is that important?" I asked.

"Well, the more often you have copies that agree with each other, especially if they emerge from different geographical areas, the more you can cross-check them to figure out what the original document was like. The only way they'd agree would be where they went back genealogically in a family tree that represents the descent of the manuscripts."

"OK," I said, "I can see that having a lot of copies from various places can help. But what about the age of the documents? Certainly that's important as well, isn't it?"

"Quite so," he replied. "And this is something else that favors the New Testament. We have copies commencing within a couple of generations from the writing of the originals, whereas in the case of other ancient texts, maybe five, eight, or ten centuries elapsed between the original and the earliest surviving copy.

"In addition to Greek manuscripts, we also have translations of the gospels into other languages at a relatively early time—into Latin, Syriac, and Coptic. And beyond that, we have what may be called secondary translations made a little later, like Armenian and Gothic. And a lot of others—Georgian, Ethiopic, a great variety."

"How does that help?"

"Because even if we had no Greek manuscripts today, by piecing together the information from these translations from a relatively early date, we could actually reproduce the contents of the New Testament. In addition to that, even if we lost all the Greek manuscripts and the early translations, we could still reproduce the contents of the New Testament from the multiplicity of quotations in commentaries, sermons, letters, and so forth of the early church fathers."

While that seemed impressive, it was difficult to judge this evidence in isolation. I needed some context to better appreciate the uniqueness of the New Testament. How, I wondered, did it compare with other well-known works of antiquity?

A MOUNTAIN OF MANUSCRIPTS

"When you talk about a great multiplicity of manuscripts," I said, "how does that contrast with other ancient books that are routinely accepted by scholars as being reliable? For instance, tell me about the writing of authors from about the time of Jesus."

Having anticipated the question, Metzger referred to some handwritten notes he had brought along.

"Consider Tacitus, the Roman historian who wrote his *Annals of Imperial Rome* in about A.D. 116," he began. "His first six books exist today in only one manuscript, and it was copied about A.D. 850. Books eleven through sixteen are in another manuscript dating from the eleventh century. Books seven through ten are lost. So there is a long gap between the time that Tacitus sought his information and wrote it down and the only existing copies.

"With regard to the first-century historian Josephus, we have nine Greek manuscripts of his work *The Jewish War,* and these copies were written in the tenth, eleventh, and twelfth centuries. There is a Latin translation from the fourth century and medieval Russian materials from the eleventh or twelfth century."

Those numbers were surprising. There is but the thinnest thread of manuscripts connecting these ancient works to the modern world. "By comparison," I asked, "how many New Testament Greek manuscripts are in existence today?"

Metzger's eyes got wide. "More than five thousand have been cataloged," he said with enthusiasm, his voice going up an octave.

That was a mountain of manuscripts compared to the anthills of Tacitus and Josephus! "Is that unusual in the ancient world? What would the runner-up be?" I asked.

"The quantity of New Testament material is almost embarrassing in comparison with other works of antiquity," he said. "Next to the New Testament, the greatest amount of manuscript testimony is of Homer's *Iliad,* which was the bible of the ancient Greeks. There are fewer than 650 Greek manuscripts of it today. Some are quite fragmentary. They come down to us from the second and third century A.D. and following. When you consider that Homer composed his epic about 800 B.C., you can see there's a very lengthy gap."

"Very lengthy" was an understatement; it was a thousand years! There was in fact no comparison: the manuscript evidence for the New Testament was overwhelming when juxtaposed against other revered writings of antiquity—works that modern scholars have absolutely no reluctance treating as authentic.

My curiosity about the New Testament manuscripts having been piqued, I asked Metzger to describe some of them for me.

"The earliest are fragments of papyrus, which was a writing material made from the papyrus plant that grew in the marshes of the Nile Delta in Egypt," he said. "There are now ninety-nine fragmentary pieces of papyrus that contain one or more passages or books of the New Testament.

"The most significant to come to light are the Chester Beatty Biblical Papyri, discovered about 1930. Of these, Beatty Biblical Papyrus number one contains portions of the four gospels and the book of Acts, and it dates from the third century. Papyrus number two contains large portions of eight letters of Paul, plus portions of Hebrews, dating to about the year 200. Papyrus number three has a sizable section of the book of Revelation, dating from the third century.

"Another group of important papyrus manuscripts was purchased by a Swiss bibliophile, M. Martin Bodmer. The earliest of these, dating from about 200, contains about two-thirds of the gospel of John. Another papyrus, containing portions of the gospels of Luke and John, dates from the third century."

At this point the gap between the writing of the biographies of Jesus and the earliest manuscripts was extremely small. But what is the oldest manuscript we possess? How close in time, I wondered, can we get to the original writings, which experts call "autographs"?

THE SCRAP THAT CHANGED HISTORY

"Of the entire New Testament," I said, "what is the earliest portion that we possess today?"

Metzger didn't have to ponder the answer. "That would be a fragment of the gospel of John, containing material from chapter eighteen. It has five verses—three on one side, two on the other—and it measures about two and a half by three and a half inches," he said.

"How was it discovered?"

"It was purchased in Egypt as early as 1920, but it sat unnoticed for years among similar fragments of papyri. Then in 1934 C. H.

Roberts of Saint John's College, Oxford, was sorting through the papyri at the John Rylands Library in Manchester, England. He immediately recognized this as preserving a portion of John's gospel. He was able to date it from the style of the script."

"And what was his conclusion?" I asked. "How far back does it go?"

"He concluded it originated between A.D. 100 to 150. Lots of other prominent paleographers, like Sir Frederic Kenyon, Sir Harold Bell, Adolf Deissmann, W. H. P. Hatch, Ulrich Wilcken, and others, have agreed with his assessment. Deissmann was convinced that it goes back at least to the reign of Emperor Hadrian, which was A.D. 117–138, or even Emperor Trajan, which was A.D. 98–117."

That was a stunning discovery. The reason: skeptical German theologians in the last century argued strenuously that the fourth gospel was not even composed until at least the year 160—too distant from the events of Jesus' life to be of much historical use. They were able to influence generations of scholars, who scoffed at this gospel's reliability.

"This certainly blows that opinion out of the water," I commented.

"Yes, it does," he said. "Here we have, at a very early date, a fragment of a copy of John all the way over in a community along the Nile River in Egypt, far from Ephesus in Asia Minor, where the gospel was probably originally composed."

This finding has literally rewritten popular views of history, pushing the composition of John's gospel much closer to the days when Jesus walked the earth. I made a mental note to check with an archaeologist about whether any other findings have bolstered the confidence we can have in the fourth gospel.

A WEALTH OF EVIDENCE

While papyrus manuscripts represent the earliest copies of the New Testament, there are also ancient copies written on parchment, which was made from the skins of cattle, sheep, goats, and antelope.

"We have what are called uncial manuscripts, which are written in all-capital Greek letters," Metzger explained. "Today we have 306 of these, several dating back as early as the third century. The most important are *Codex Sinaiticus,* which is the only complete New Testament in uncial letters, and *Codex Vaticanus,* which is not quite complete. Both date to about A.D. 350.

"A new style of writing, more cursive in nature, emerged in roughly A.D. 800. It's called minuscule, and we have 2,856 of these manuscripts. Then there are also lectionaries, which contain New Testament Scripture in the sequence it was to be read in the early churches at appropriate times during the year. A total of 2,403 of these have been cataloged. That puts the grand total of Greek manuscripts at 5,664."

In addition to the Greek documents, he said, there are thousands of other ancient New Testament manuscripts in other languages. There are 8,000 to 10,000 Latin Vulgate manuscripts, plus a total of 8,000 in Ethiopic, Slavic, and Armenian. In all, there are about 24,000 manuscripts in existence.

"What's your opinion, then?" I asked, wanting to confirm clearly what I thought I was hearing him say. "In terms of the multiplicity of manuscripts and the time gap between the originals and our first copies, how does the New Testament stack up against other well-known works of antiquity?"

"Extremely well," he replied. "We can have great confidence in the fidelity with which this material has come down to us, especially compared with any other ancient literary work."

That conclusion is shared by distinguished scholars throughout the world. Said the late F. F. Bruce, eminent professor at the University of Manchester, England, and author of *The New Testament Documents: Are They Reliable?*: "There is no body of ancient literature in the world which enjoys such a wealth of good textual attestation as the New Testament."[2]

Metzger had already mentioned the name of Sir Frederic Kenyon, former director of the British Museum and author of *The Palaeography of Greek Papyri*. Kenyon has said that "in no other case is the interval of time between the composition of the book and the date of the earliest manuscripts so short as in that of the New Testament."[3]

His conclusion: "The last foundation for any doubt that the scriptures have come down to us substantially as they were written has now been removed."[4]

However, what about discrepancies among the various manuscripts? In the days before lightning-fast photocopying machines, manuscripts were laboriously hand-copied by scribes, letter by letter, word by word, line by line, in a process that was ripe for errors. Now I wanted to zero in on whether these copying mistakes have rendered our modern Bibles hopelessly riddled with inaccuracies.

EXAMINING THE ERRORS

"With the similarities in the way Greek letters are written and with the primitive conditions under which the scribes worked, it would seem inevitable that copying errors would creep into the text," I said.

"Quite so," Metzger conceded.

"And in fact, aren't there literally tens of thousands of variations among the ancient manuscripts that we have?"

"Quite so."

"Doesn't that therefore mean we can't trust them?" I asked, sounding more accusatory than inquisitive.

"No sir, it does not," Metzger replied firmly. "First let me say this: Eyeglasses weren't invented until 1373 in Venice, and I'm sure that astigmatism existed among the ancient scribes. That was compounded by the fact that it was difficult under any circumstances to read faded manuscripts on which some of the ink had flaked away. And there were other hazards—inattentiveness on the part of scribes, for example. So yes, although for the most part scribes were scrupulously careful, errors did creep in.

"But," he was quick to add, "there are factors counteracting that. For example, sometimes the scribe's memory would play tricks on him. Between the time it took for him to look at the text and then to write down the words, the order of words might get shifted. He may write down the right words but in the wrong sequence. This is nothing to be alarmed at, because Greek, unlike English, is an inflected language."

"Meaning . . . ," I prompted him.

"Meaning it makes a whale of a difference in English if you say, 'Dog bites man' or 'Man bites dog'—sequence matters in English. But in Greek it doesn't. One word functions as the subject of the sentence regardless of where it stands in the sequence; consequently, the meaning of the sentence isn't distorted if the words are out of what we consider to be the right order. So yes, some variations among manuscripts exist, but generally they're inconsequential variations like that. Differences in spelling would be another example."

Still, the high number of "variants," or differences among manuscripts, was troubling. I had seen estimates as high as two hundred thousand of them.[5] However, Metzger downplayed the significance of that figure.

"The number sounds big, but it's a bit misleading because of the way variants are counted," he said. He explained that if a single word is misspelled in two thousand manuscripts, that's counted as two thousand variants.

I keyed in on the most important issue. "How many doctrines of the church are in jeopardy because of variants?"

"I don't know of any doctrine that is in jeopardy," he responded confidently.

"None?"

"None," he repeated. "Now, the Jehovah's Witnesses come to our door and say, 'Your Bible is wrong in the King James Version of 1 John 5:7–8, where it talks about 'the Father, the Word, and the Holy Ghost: and these three are one.' They'll say, 'That's not in the earliest manuscripts.'

"And that's true enough. I think that these words are found in only about seven or eight copies, all from the fifteenth or sixteenth century. I acknowledge that is not part of what the author of 1 John was inspired to write.

"But that does not dislodge the firmly witnessed testimony of the Bible to the doctrine of the Trinity. At the baptism of Jesus, the Father speaks, his beloved Son is baptized, and the Holy Spirit descends on him. At the ending of 2 Corinthians Paul says, 'May the grace of the Lord Jesus Christ, and the love of God, and the fellowship of the Holy Spirit be with you all.' There are many places where the Trinity is represented."

"So the variations, when they occur, tend to be minor rather than substantive?"

"Yes, yes, that's correct, and scholars work very carefully to try to resolve them by getting back to the original meaning. The more significant variations do not overthrow any doctrine of the church. Any good Bible will have notes that will alert the reader to variant readings of any consequence. But again, these are rare."

So rare that scholars Norman Geisler and William Nix conclude, "The New Testament, then, has not only survived in more manuscripts than any other book from antiquity, but it has survived in a purer form than any other great book—*a form that is 99.5 percent pure*."[6]

However, even if it's true that the transmission of the New Testament through history has been unprecedented in its reliability, how do we know that we have the whole picture?

What about allegations that church councils squelched equally legitimate documents because they didn't like the picture of Jesus they portrayed? How do we know that the twenty-seven books of the New Testament represent the best and most reliable information? Why is it that our Bibles contain Matthew, Mark, Luke, and John, but many other ancient gospels—the Gospel of Philip, the Gospel of the Egyptians, the Gospel of Truth, the Gospel of Nativity of Mary—were excluded?

It was time to turn to the question of the "canon," a term that comes from a Greek word meaning "rule," "norm," or "standard" and that describes the books that have become accepted as official in the church and included in the New Testament.[7] Metzger is considered a leading authority in that field.

"A HIGH DEGREE OF UNANIMITY"

"How did the early church leaders determine which books would be considered authoritative and which would be discarded?" I asked. "What criteria did they use in determining which documents would be included in the New Testament?"

"Basically, the early church had three criteria," he said. "First, the books must have apostolic authority—that is, they must have been written either by apostles themselves, who were eyewitnesses to what they wrote about, or by followers of apostles. So in the case of Mark and Luke, while they weren't among the twelve disciples, early tradition has it that Mark was a helper of Peter, and Luke was an associate of Paul.

"Second, there was the criterion of conformity to what was called the rule of faith. That is, was the document congruent with the basic Christian tradition that the church recognized as normative? And third, there was the criterion of whether a document had had continuous acceptance and usage by the church at large."

"They merely applied those criteria and let the chips fall where they may?" I asked.

"Well, it wouldn't be accurate to say that these criteria were simply applied in a mechanical fashion," he replied. "There were certainly different opinions about which criterion should be given the most weight.

"But what's remarkable is that even though the fringes of the canon remained unsettled for a while, there was actually a high degree of unanimity concerning the greater part of the New Testament within the first two centuries. And this was true among very diverse congregations scattered over a wide area."

"So," I said, "the four gospels we have in the New Testament today met those criteria, while others didn't?"

"Yes," he said. "It was, if I may put it this way, an example of 'survival of the fittest.' In talking about the canon, Arthur Darby Nock used to tell his students at Harvard, 'The most traveled roads in Europe are the best roads; that's why they're so heavily traveled.' That's a good analogy. British commentator William Barclay said it this way: 'It is the simple truth to say that the New Testament books became canonical because no one could stop them doing so.'

"We can be confident that no other ancient books can compare with the New Testament in terms of importance for Christian history or doctrine. When one studies the early history of the canon, one walks away convinced that the New Testament contains the best sources for the history of Jesus. Those who discerned the limits of the canon had a clear and balanced perspective of the gospel of Christ.

"Just read these other documents for yourself. They're written later than the four gospels, in the second, third, fourth, fifth, even sixth century, long after Jesus, and they're generally quite banal. They carry names—like the Gospel of Peter and the Gospel of Mary—that are unrelated to their real authorship. On the other hand, the four gospels in the New Testament were readily accepted with remarkable unanimity as being authentic in the story they told."

Yet I knew that some liberal scholars, most notably members of the well-publicized Jesus Seminar, believe the Gospel of Thomas ought to be elevated to equal status with the four traditional gospels. Did this mysterious gospel fall victim to political wars within the church, eventually being excluded because of its unpopular doctrines? I decided I'd better probe Metzger on this point.

THE "SECRET WORDS" OF JESUS

"Dr. Metzger, the Gospel of Thomas, which was among the Nag Hammadi documents found in Egypt in 1945, claims it contains 'the secret words which the living Jesus spoke and Didymus Judas Thomas wrote down.' Why was it excluded by the church?"

Metzger was thoroughly acquainted with the work. "The Gospel of Thomas came to light in a fifth-century copy in Coptic, which I've translated into English," he said. "It contains 114 sayings attributed to Jesus but no narrative of what he did, and seems to have been written in

Greek in Syria about A.D. 140. In some cases I think this gospel correctly reports what Jesus said, with slight modifications."

This was certainly an intriguing statement. "Please elaborate," I said.

"For instance, in the Gospel of Thomas Jesus says, 'A city built on a high hill cannot be hidden.' Here the adjective *high* is added, but the rest reads like Matthew's gospel. Or Jesus says, 'Render to Caesar the things that are Caesar's, render to God the things that are God's, render to me the things that are mine.' In this case the later phrase has been added.

"However, there are some things in Thomas that are totally alien to the canonical gospels. Jesus says, 'Split wood; I am there. Lift up a stone, and you will find me there.' That's pantheism, the idea that Jesus is coterminous with the substance of this world. That's contrary to anything in the canonical gospels.

"The Gospel of Thomas ends with a note saying, 'Let Mary go away from us, because women are not worthy of life.' Jesus is quoted as saying, 'Lo, I shall lead her in order to make her a male, so that she too may become a living spirit, resembling you males. For every woman who makes herself male will enter into the kingdom of heaven.'"

Metzger's eyebrows shot up as if he were surprised at what he had just uttered. "Now, this is *not* the Jesus we know from the four canonical gospels!" he said emphatically.

I asked, "What about the charge that Thomas was purposefully excluded by church councils in some sort of conspiracy to silence it?"

"That's just not historically accurate," came Metzger's response. "What the synods and councils did in the fifth century and following was to ratify what already had been accepted by high and low Christians alike. It is not right to say that the Gospel of Thomas was excluded by some fiat on the part of a council; the right way to put it is, the Gospel of Thomas excluded itself! It did not harmonize with other testimony about Jesus that early Christians accepted as trustworthy."

"So you would disagree with anyone who would try to elevate Thomas to the same status as that of the four gospels?" I asked.

"Yes, I would very much disagree. I think the early church exercised a judicious act in discarding it. To take it up now, it seems to me, would be to accept something that's less valid than the other gospels," he replied. "Now, don't get me wrong. I think the Gospel of Thomas is an interesting document, but it's mixed up with pantheistic and antifeminist statements that certainly deserve to be given the left foot of fellowship, if you know what I mean.

"You have to understand that the canon was not the result of a series of contests involving church politics. The canon is rather the separation that came about because of the intuitive insight of Christian believers. They could hear the voice of the Good Shepherd in the gospel of John; they could hear it only in a muffled and distorted way in the Gospel of Thomas, mixed in with a lot of other things.

"When the pronouncement was made about the canon, it merely ratified what the general sensitivity of the church had already determined. You see, the canon is a list of authoritative books more than it is an authoritative list of books. These documents didn't derive their authority from being selected; each one was authoritative before anyone gathered them together. The early church merely listened and sensed that these were authoritative accounts.

"For somebody now to say that the canon emerged only after councils and synods made these pronouncements would be like saying, 'Let's get several academies of musicians to make a pronouncement that the music of Bach and Beethoven is wonderful.' I would say, 'Thank you for nothing! We knew that before the pronouncement was made.' We know it because of sensitivity to what is good music and what is not. The same with the canon."

Even so, I pointed out that some New Testament books, notably James, Hebrews, and Revelation, were more slowly accepted into the canon than others. "Should we therefore be suspicious of them?" I asked.

"To my mind, that just shows how careful the early church was," he replied. "They weren't 'gung ho,' sweeping in every last document that happened to have anything about Jesus in it. This shows deliberation and careful analysis.

"Of course, even today parts of the Syrian church refuse to accept the book of Revelation, yet the people belonging to that church are Christian believers. From my point of view, I accept the book of Revelation as a wonderful part of the Scriptures."

He shook his head. "I think they impoverish themselves by not accepting it."

THE "UNRIVALED" NEW TESTAMENT

Metzger had been persuasive. No serious doubts lingered concerning whether the New Testament's text had been reliably preserved for us through the centuries. One of Metzger's distinguished predecessors at Princeton Theological Seminary, Benjamin Warfield, who held four doctorates and taught systematic theology until his death in 1921, put it this way:

> If we compare the present state of the New Testament text with that of any other ancient writing, we must . . . declare it to be marvelously correct. Such has been the care with which the New Testament has been copied—a care which has doubtless grown out of true reverence for its holy words. . . . The New Testament [is] unrivaled among ancient writings in the purity of its text as actually transmitted and kept in use.[8]

In terms of which documents were accepted into the New Testament, generally there has never been any serious dispute about the authoritative nature of twenty of the New Testament's twenty-seven books—from Matthew through Philemon, plus 1 Peter and 1 John. This of course includes the four gospels that represent Jesus' biographies.[9] The remaining seven books, though questioned for a time by some early church leaders, "were finally and fully recognized by the church generally," according to Geisler and Nix.[10]

As for the "pseudepigraphia," the proliferation of gospels, epistles, and apocalypses in the first few centuries after Jesus—including the Gospels of Nicodemus, Barnabas, Bartholomew, Andrew, the Epistle of Paul to the Laodiceans, the Apocalypse of Stephen, and others—they are "fanciful and heretical . . . neither genuine nor valuable as a whole," and "virtually no orthodox Father, canon or council" considered them to be authoritative or deserving of inclusion in the New Testament.[11]

In fact, I accepted Metzger's challenge by reading many of them myself. Compared with the careful, sober, precise, eyewitness quality of Matthew, Mark, Luke, and John, these works truly deserve the description they received from Eusebius, the early church historian: "Totally absurd and impious."[12] They were too far removed from Jesus' ministry to contribute anything meaningful to my investigation, having been written as late as the fifth and sixth centuries, and their often mythical qualities disqualify them from being historically credible.

With all that established, the time had arrived for my investigation to advance to its next phase. I was curious: how much evidence is there for this miracle-working first-century carpenter *outside* the gospels? Do ancient historians confirm or contradict the New Testament's claims about his life, teachings, and miracles? I knew this required a trip to Ohio to visit one of the country's leading scholars in that field.

As we stood, I thanked Dr. Metzger for his time and expertise. He smiled warmly and offered to walk me downstairs. I didn't want to consume any more of his Saturday afternoon, but my curiosity wouldn't let me leave Princeton without satisfying myself about one remaining issue.

"All these decades of scholarship, of study, of writing textbooks, of delving into the minutiae of the New Testament text—what has all this done to your personal faith?" I asked.

"Oh," he said, sounding happy to discuss the topic, "it has increased the basis of my personal faith to see the firmness with which these materials have come down to us, with a multiplicity of copies, some of which are very, very ancient."

"So," I started to say, "scholarship has not diluted your faith—"

He jumped in before I could finish my sentence. "On the contrary," he stressed, "it has built it. I've asked questions all my life, I've dug into the text, I've studied this thoroughly, and today I know with confidence that my trust in Jesus has been well placed."

He paused while his eyes surveyed my face. Then he added, for emphasis, "*Very* well placed."

Deliberations

Questions for Reflection or Group Study

1. Having read the interview with Dr. Metzger, how would you rate the reliability of the process by which the New Testament was transmitted to us? What are some reasons you find this process trustworthy or not?
2. Scan a copy of the New Testament and examine some of the notes in the margins that talk about variant readings. What are some examples you find? How does the presence of these notations affect your understanding of the passages?
3. Do the criteria for determining whether a document should be included in the New Testament seem reasonable? Why or why not? Are there other criteria you believe should be added? What

disadvantages do modern scholars have in second-guessing the early church's decisions concerning whether a document should be included in the Bible?

For Further Evidence

More Resources on This Topic

Bruce, F. F. *The Canon of Scripture*. Downers Grove, Ill.: InterVarsity Press, 1988.

Geisler, Norman L., and William E. Nix. *A General Introduction to the Bible*. 1968; reprint, Chicago: Moody Press, 1980.

Metzger, Bruce M. *The Canon of the New Testament*. Oxford: Clarendon Press, 1987.

———. *The Text of the New Testament*. New York: Oxford Univ. Press, 1992.

Patzia, Arthur G. *The Making of the New Testament*. Downers Grove, Ill.: InterVarsity Press, 1995.

4

THE CORROBORATING EVIDENCE

Is There Credible Evidence for Jesus outside His Biographies?

Harry Aleman turned and stabbed his finger at me. "*You,*" he sputtered, spitting out the word with disgust. "Why do you keep writing those things about me?" Then he spun around and disappeared down a back stairwell to escape the reporters who were pursuing him through the courthouse.

Actually, it was hard to be a crime reporter in Chicago during the 1970s and *not* write about Harry Aleman. He was, after all, the quintessential crime syndicate hit man. And Chicagoans, in a perverse way, love to read about the mob.

Prosecutors desperately wanted to put Aleman in prison for one of the cold-blooded executions they suspected he had committed on behalf of his syndicate bosses. The problem, of course, was the difficulty of finding anyone willing to testify against a mobster of Aleman's frightening reputation.

Then came their big break. One of Aleman's former cronies, Louis Almeida, was arrested on his way to murder a labor official in Pennsylvania. Convicted of weapons charges and sentenced to a decade in prison, Almeida agreed to testify against Aleman in the unsolved slaying of a Teamsters Union shop steward in Chicago—if prosecutors would agree to show leniency toward Almeida.

This meant Almeida had a motive to cooperate, which would undoubtedly tarnish his credibility to some degree. Prosecutors realized they would need to bolster his testimony to ensure a conviction, so they went searching for someone to corroborate Almeida's account.

Webster's dictionary defines *corroborate* this way: "To make more certain; confirm: He corroborated my account of the accident."[1]

Corroborative evidence supports other testimony; it affirms or backs up the essential elements of an eyewitness account. It can be a public record, a photograph, or additional testimony from a second or third person. It can verify a person's entire testimony or just key parts of it.

In effect, corroborative evidence acts like the support wires that keep a tall antenna straight and unwavering. The more corroborative evidence, the stronger and more secure the case.

But where would prosecutors find corroboration of Almeida's story? It came from a surprising source: a quiet, law-abiding citizen named Bobby Lowe told investigators he had been walking his dog when he saw Aleman murder the union steward. Despite Aleman's bone-chilling notoriety, Lowe agreed to back up Almeida's story by testifying against the mobster.

THE POWER OF CORROBORATION

At Aleman's trial Lowe and Almeida mesmerized jurors with their stories. Almeida's account of driving the getaway car dovetailed with Lowe's straightforward description of seeing Aleman murder his victim on a public sidewalk the evening of September 27, 1972.

Prosecutors thought they had woven an airtight case against the feared hit man, yet throughout the trial they sensed something was amiss. Their skepticism first surfaced when Aleman decided against having a jury trial, opting instead to have a judge hear his case.

At the end of the trial the prosecutors' worst suspicions were realized: despite compelling testimony by Lowe and Almeida, the judge ended up declaring Aleman innocent and letting him go free.

What had happened? Remember, this took place in Cook County, Illinois, where corruption so often lurks. Years later it was revealed that the judge had been slipped ten thousand dollars in return for the acquittal. When an FBI informant disclosed the bribe, the then-retired judge committed suicide—and prosecutors refiled the murder charge against Aleman.

By the time the second trial was held, the law had been changed so that prosecutors could demand that a jury hear the case. That's what they did—and finally, a full twenty-five years after the murder, Aleman was found guilty and sentenced to one hundred to three hundred years in prison.[2]

In spite of the delays, the Aleman saga shows how significant corroborative evidence can be. And the same is true in dealing with historical issues. We've already heard, through Dr. Craig Blomberg's testimony, that in the gospels there is excellent eyewitness evidence for the life, teachings, death, and resurrection of Jesus. But is there any other evidence to corroborate that? Are there writings outside the gospels that affirm or support any of the essentials about Jesus or early Christianity?

In other words, is there any additional documentation that can help seal the case for Christ, as Bobby Lowe's testimony sealed the case against Harry Aleman? The answer, according to our next witness, is yes—and the amount and quality of that evidence may very well surprise you.

THE THIRD INTERVIEW: EDWIN M. YAMAUCHI, PH.D.

As I entered the imposing brick building that houses the office of Edwin Yamauchi at Miami University in picturesque Oxford, Ohio, I walked underneath a stone arch bearing this inscription: "Ye shall know the truth, and the truth will make you free." As one of the country's leading experts in ancient history, Yamauchi has been on a quest for historical truth for much of his life.

Born in Hawaii in 1937, the son of immigrants from Okinawa, Yamauchi started from humble beginnings. His father died just before the Japanese attack on Pearl Harbor, leaving his mother to earn a meager living as a maid for wealthy families. While lacking formal education herself, she encouraged her son to read and study, giving him beautifully illustrated books that instilled in him a lifelong love of learning.

Certainly his academic accomplishments have been impressive. After earning a bachelor's degree in Hebrew and Hellenistics, Yamauchi received master's and doctoral degrees in Mediterranean studies from Brandeis University.

He has been awarded eight fellowships, from the Rutgers Research Council, National Endowment for the Humanities, the American Philosophical Society, and others. He has studied twenty-two languages, including Arabic, Chinese, Egyptian, Russian, Syriac, Ugaritic, and even Comanche.

He has delivered seventy-one papers before learned societies; lectured at more than one hundred seminaries, universities, and colleges, including Yale, Princeton, and Cornell; served as chairman and then president of the Institute for Biblical Research and president of the Conference on Faith and History; and published eighty articles in thirty-seven scholarly journals.

In 1968 he participated in the first excavations of the Herodian temple in Jerusalem, revealing evidence of the temple's destruction in A.D. 70. Archaeology has also been the theme of several of his books, including *The Stones and the Scriptures; The Scriptures and Archaeology;* and *The World of the First Christians*.

Though born into a Buddhist background, Yamauchi has been following Jesus ever since 1952, the year I was born. I was especially curious to see whether his long-term commitment to Christ would color his assessment of the historical evidence. In other words, would he scrupulously stick to the facts or be tempted to draw conclusions that went beyond where the evidence warranted?

I found Yamauchi to have a gentle and unassuming demeanor. Although generally soft-spoken, he's intensely focused. He provides thorough and detailed answers to questions, often pausing to supplement his verbal response by offering photocopies of scholarly articles he has written on the topic. A good scholar knows you can never have too much data.

Inside his book-cluttered office, in the heart of a heavily wooded campus ablaze in autumn colors, we sat down to talk about the topic that still brings a glint to his eyes, even after so many years of research and teaching.

AFFIRMING THE GOSPELS

Because of my interview with Blomberg, I didn't want to suggest that we needed to go beyond the gospels in order to find reliable evidence concerning Jesus. So I started by asking Yamauchi this question: "As a historian, could you give me your assessment of the historical reliability of the gospels themselves?"

"On the whole, the gospels are excellent sources," he replied. "As a matter of fact, they're the most trustworthy, complete, and reliable sources for Jesus. The incidental sources really don't add much detailed information; however, they are valuable as corroborative evidence."

"OK, that's what I want to discuss—the corroborative evidence," I said. "Let's be honest: some people scoff at how much there really is. For example, in 1979 Charles Templeton wrote a novel called *Act of God,* in which a fictional archaeologist made a statement that reflects the beliefs of a lot of people."

I pulled out the book and read the relevant paragraph.

> The [Christian] church bases its claims mostly on the teachings of an obscure young Jew with messianic pretentions who, let's face it, didn't make much of an impression in his lifetime. There isn't a single word about him in secular history. Not a word. No mention of him by the Romans. Not so much as a reference by Josephus.[3]

"Now," I said a little pointedly, "that doesn't sound as if there's much corroboration of the life of Jesus outside the Bible."

Yamauchi smiled and shook his head. "Templeton's archaeologist is simply mistaken," he replied in a dismissive tone, "because we do have very, very important references to Jesus in Josephus and Tacitus.

"The gospels themselves say that many who heard him—even members of his own family—did not believe in Jesus during his lifetime, yet he made such an impression that today Jesus is remembered everywhere, whereas Herod the Great, Pontius Pilate, and other ancient rulers are not as widely known. So he certainly did make an impression on those who believed in him."

He paused, then added, "He did not, of course, among those who did not believe in him."

TESTIMONY BY A TRAITOR

Templeton and Yamauchi had both mentioned Josephus, a first-century historian who's well known among scholars but whose name is unfamiliar to most people today. "Give me some background about him," I said, "and tell me how his testimony provides corroboration concerning Jesus."

"Yes, of course," Yamauchi answered as he crossed his legs and settled deeper into his chair. "Josephus was a very important Jewish historian of the first century. He was born in A.D. 37, and he wrote most of his four works toward the end of the first century.

"In his autobiography he defended his behavior in the Jewish-Roman War, which took place from A.D. 66 to 74. You see, he had surrendered to the Roman general Vespasian during the siege of Jotapata, even though many of his colleagues committed suicide rather than give up."

The professor chuckled and said, "Josephus decided it wasn't God's will for him to commit suicide. He then became a defender of the Romans."

Josephus sounded like a colorful character; I wanted more details about him so I could better understand his motivations and prejudices. "Paint me a portrait of him," I said.

"He was a priest, a Pharisee, and he was somewhat egotistical. His most ambitious work was called *The Antiquities,* which was a history of the Jewish people from Creation until his time. He probably completed it in about A.D. 93.

"As you can imagine from his collaboration with the hated Romans, Josephus was extremely disliked by his fellow Jews. But he became very popular among Christians, because in his writings he refers to James, the brother of Jesus, and to Jesus himself."

Here was our first example of corroboration for Jesus outside the gospels. "Tell me about those references," I said.

Replied Yamauchi, "In *The Antiquities* he describes how a high priest named Ananias took advantage of the death of the Roman governor Festus—who is also mentioned in the New Testament—in order to have James killed."

He leaned over to his bookshelf, pulled out a thick volume, and flipped to a page whose location he seemed to know by heart. "Ah, here it is," he said. "'He convened a meeting of the Sanhedrin and brought before them a man named James, the brother of Jesus, who was called the Christ, and certain others. He accused them of having transgressed the law and delivered them up to be stoned.'[4]

"I know of no scholar," Yamauchi asserted confidently, "who has successfully disputed this passage. L. H. Feldman noted that if this had been a later Christian addition to the text, it would have likely been more laudatory of James. So here you have a reference to the brother of Jesus—who had apparently been converted by the appearance of the risen Christ, if you compare John 7:5 and 1 Corinthians 15:7—and corroboration of the fact that some people considered Jesus to be the Christ, which means 'the Anointed One' or 'Messiah.'"

"THERE LIVED JESUS . . ."

I knew that Josephus had written an even lengthier section about Jesus, which is called the *Testimonium Flavianum.* I knew too that this passage was among the most hotly disputed in ancient literature because on its surface it appears to provide sweeping corroboration of Jesus' life, miracles, death, and resurrection. But is it authentic? Or has it been doctored through the years by people favorable to Jesus?

I asked Yamauchi for his opinion, and it was instantly clear I had tapped into an area of high interest for him. He uncrossed his legs and sat up straight in his chair. "This is a fascinating passage," he said with enthusiasm, leaning forward, book in hand. "But yes, it is controversial." With that he read it to me.

> About this time there lived Jesus, a wise man, if indeed one ought to call him a man. For he was one who wrought surprising feats and was a teacher of such people as accept the truth gladly. He won over many Jews and many of the Greeks. He was the Christ. When Pilate, upon hearing him accused by men of the highest standing among us, had condemned him to be crucified, those who had in the first place come to love him did not give up their affection for him. On the third day he appeared to them restored to life, for the prophets of God had prophesied these and countless other marvelous things about him. And the tribe of Christians, so called after him, has still to this day not disappeared.[5]

The wealth of corroboration for Jesus was readily evident. "You agreed this was controversial—what have scholars concluded about this passage?" I asked.

"Scholarship has gone through three trends about it," he said. "For obvious reasons, the early Christians thought it was a wonderful and thoroughly authentic attestation of Jesus and his resurrection. They loved it. Then the entire passage was questioned by at least some scholars during the Enlightenment.

"But today there's a remarkable consensus among both Jewish and Christian scholars that the passage as a whole is authentic, although there may be some interpolations."

I raised an eyebrow. "Interpolations—would you define what you mean by that?"

"That means early Christian copyists inserted some phrases that a Jewish writer like Josephus would not have written," Yamauchi said.

He pointed to a sentence in the book. "For instance, the first line says, 'About this time there lived Jesus, a wise man.' That phrase is not normally used of Jesus by Christians, so it seems authentic for

Josephus. But the next phrase says, 'if indeed one ought to call him a man.' This implies Jesus was more than human, which appears to be an interpolation."

I nodded to let him know I was following him so far.

"It goes on to say, 'For he was one who wrought surprising feats and was a teacher of such people as accept the truth gladly. He won over many Jews and many of the Greeks.' That seems to be quite in accord with the vocabulary Josephus uses elsewhere, and it's generally considered authentic.

"But then there's this unambiguous statement, 'He was the Christ.' That seems to be an interpolation—"

"Because," I interrupted, "Josephus says in his reference to James that Jesus was '*called* the Christ.'"

"That's right," said Yamauchi. "It's unlikely Josephus would have flatly said Jesus was the Messiah here, when elsewhere he merely said he was *considered* to be the Messiah by his followers.

"The next part of the passage—which talks about Jesus' trial and crucifixion and the fact that his followers still loved him—is unexceptional and considered genuine. Then there's this phrase: 'On the third day he appeared to them restored to life.'

"Again, this is a clear declaration of belief in the Resurrection, and thus it's unlikely that Josephus wrote it. So these three elements seem to have been interpolations."

"What's the bottom line?" I asked.

"That the passage in Josephus probably was originally written about Jesus, although without those three points I mentioned. But even so, Josephus corroborates important information about Jesus: that he was the martyred leader of the church in Jerusalem and that he was a wise teacher who had established a wide and lasting following, despite the fact that he had been crucified under Pilate at the instigation of some of the Jewish leaders."

THE IMPORTANCE OF JOSEPHUS

While these references did offer some important independent verification about Jesus, I wondered why a historian like Josephus wouldn't have said more about such an important figure of the first century. I knew that some skeptics, like Boston University philosopher Michael Martin, have made this same critique.

So I asked for Yamauchi's reaction to this statement by Martin, who doesn't believe Jesus ever lived: "If Jesus did exist, one would have expected Josephus ... to have said more about him.... It is unexpected that Josephus mentioned him ... in passing while mentioning other Messianic figures and John the Baptist in greater detail."[6]

Yamauchi's response seemed uncharacteristically strong. "From time to time some people have tried to deny the existence of Jesus, but this is really a lost cause," he said with a tone of exasperation. "There is overwhelming evidence that Jesus did exist, and these hypothetical questions are really very vacuous and fallacious.

"But I'd answer by saying this: Josephus was interested in political matters and the struggle against Rome, so for him John the Baptist was more important because he seemed to pose a greater political threat than did Jesus."

I jumped in. "Hold on a second. Aren't there some scholars who have portrayed Jesus as a Zealot or at least sympathetic to the Zealots?" I asked, referring to a first-century revolutionary group that opposed Rome politically.

Yamauchi dismissed the objection with a wave of his hand. "That is a position the gospels themselves do not support," he replied, "because remember, Jesus didn't even object to paying taxes to the Romans. Therefore because Jesus and his followers didn't pose an immediate political threat, it's certainly understandable that Josephus isn't more interested in this sect—even though in hindsight it turned out to be very important indeed."

"So in your assessment, how significant are these two references by Josephus?"

"Highly significant," Yamauchi replied, "especially since his accounts of the Jewish War have proved to be very accurate; for example, they've been corroborated through archaeological excavations at Masada as well as by historians like Tacitus. He's considered to be a pretty reliable historian, and his mentioning of Jesus is considered extremely important."

"A MOST MISCHIEVOUS SUPERSTITION"

Yamauchi had just mentioned the most important Roman historian of the first century, and I wanted to discuss what Tacitus had to say about Jesus and Christianity. "Could you spell out what he corroborates?" I asked.

Yamauchi nodded. "Tacitus recorded what is probably the most important reference to Jesus outside the New Testament," he said. "In A.D. 115 he explicitly states that Nero persecuted the Christians as scapegoats to divert suspicion away from himself for the great fire that had devastated Rome in A.D. 64."

Yamauchi stood and walked over to a shelf, scanning it for a certain book. "Ah yes, here it is," he said, withdrawing a thick volume and leafing through it until he found the right passage, which he then read to me.

> Nero fastened the guilt and inflicted the most exquisite tortures on a class hated for their abominations, called Christians by the populace. Christus, from whom the name had its origin, suffered the extreme penalty during the reign of Tiberius at the hands of one of our procurators, Pontius Pilatus, and a most mischievous superstitution, thus checked for the moment, again broke out not only in Judaea, the first source of the evil, but even in Rome.... Accordingly, an arrest was first made of all who pleaded guilty: then, upon their information, an immense multitude was convicted, not so much of the crime of firing the city, as of hatred against mankind.[7]

I was already familiar with that passage, and I was wondering how Yamauchi would respond to an observation by a leading scholar named J. N. D. Anderson. "He speculates that when Tacitus says this 'mischievous superstition' was 'checked for the moment' but later 'again broke out,' he was unconsciously bearing testimony to the belief of early Christians that Jesus had been crucified but then rose from the grave," I said. "Do you agree with him?"

Yamauchi thought for a moment. "This has certainly been the interpretation of some scholars," he replied, seeming to duck my request for his opinion. But then he made a crucial point: "Regardless of whether the passage had this specifically in mind, it does provide us with a very remarkable fact, which is this: crucifixion was the most abhorrent fate that anyone could undergo, and the fact that there was a movement based on a crucified man has to be explained.

"How can you explain the spread of a religion based on the worship of a man who had suffered the most ignominious death possible? Of course, the Christian answer is that he was resurrected. Others have to come up with some alternative theory if they don't believe that. But none of the alternative views, to my mind, are very persuasive."

I asked him to characterize the weight of Tacitus's writings concerning Jesus.

"This is an important testimony by an unsympathetic witness to the success and spread of Christianity, based on a historical figure—Jesus—who was crucified under Pontius Pilate," he said. "And it's significant that Tacitus reported that an 'immense multitude' held so strongly to their beliefs that they were willing to die rather than recant."

CHANTING "AS IF TO A GOD"

I knew that another Roman, called Pliny the Younger, had also referred to Christianity in his writings. "He corroborated some important matters, too, didn't he?" I asked.

"That's right. He was the nephew of Pliny the Elder, the famous encyclopedist who died in the eruption of Vesuvius in A.D. 79. Pliny the Younger became governor of Bithynia in northwestern Turkey. Much of his correspondence with his friend, Emperor Trajan, has been preserved to the present time."

Yamauchi pulled out a photocopy of a book page, saying, "In book 10 of these letters he specifically refers to the Christians he has arrested."

> I have asked them if they are Christians, and if they admit it, I repeat the question a second and third time, with a warning of the punishment awaiting them. If they persist, I order them to be led away for execution; for, whatever the nature of their admission, I am convinced that their stubbornness and unshakable obstinacy ought not to go unpunished....
>
> They also declared that the sum total of their guilt or error amounted to no more than this: they had met regularly before dawn on a fixed day to chant verses alternately amongst themselves in honor of Christ as if to a god, and also to bind themselves by oath, not for any criminal purpose, but to abstain from theft, robbery, and adultery....
>
> This made me decide it was all the more necessary to extract the truth by torture from two slave-women, whom they called

deaconesses. I found nothing but a degenerate sort of cult carried to extravagant lengths.[8]

"How important is this reference?" I asked.

"Very important. It was probably written about A.D. 111, and it attests to the rapid spread of Christianity, both in the city and in the rural area, among every class of persons, slave women as well as Roman citizens, since he also says that he sends Christians who are Roman citizens to Rome for trial.

"And it talks about the worship of Jesus as God, that Christians maintained high ethical standards, and that they were not easily swayed from their beliefs."

THE DAY THE EARTH WENT DARK

To me, one of the most problematic references in the New Testament is where the gospel writers claim that the earth went dark during part of the time that Jesus hung on the cross. Wasn't this merely a literary device to stress the significance of the Crucifixion, and not a reference to an actual historical occurrence? After all, if darkness had fallen over the earth, wouldn't there be at least some mention of this extraordinary event outside the Bible?

However, Dr. Gary Habermas has written about a historian named Thallus who in A.D. 52 wrote a history of the eastern Mediterranean world since the Trojan War. Although Thallus's work has been lost, it was quoted by Julius Africanus in about A.D. 221—and it made reference to the darkness that the gospels had written about![9]

"Could this," I asked, "be independent corroboration of this biblical claim?"

Explained Yamauchi, "In this passage Julius Africanus says, 'Thallus, in the third book of his histories, explains away the darkness as an eclipse of the sun—unreasonably, as it seems to me.'

"So Thallus apparently was saying yes, there had been darkness at the time of the Crucifixion, and he speculated it had been caused by an eclipse. Africanus then argues that it couldn't have been an eclipse, given when the Crucifixion occurred."

Yamauchi reached over to his desk to retrieve a piece of paper. "Let me quote what scholar Paul Maier said about the darkness in a footnote in his 1968 book *Pontius Pilate*," he said, reading these words:

> This phenomenon, evidently, was visible in Rome, Athens, and other Mediterranean cities. According to Tertullian . . . it was a "cosmic" or "world event." Phlegon, a Greek author from Caria writing a chronology soon after 137 A.D., reported that in the fourth year of the 202nd Olympiad (i.e., 33 A.D.) there was "the greatest eclipse of the sun" and that "it became night in the sixth hour of the day [i.e., noon] so that stars even appeared in the heavens. There was a great earthquake in Bithynia, and many things were overturned in Nicaea."[10]

Yamauchi concluded, "So there is, as Paul Maier points out, non-biblical attestation of the darkness that occurred at the time of Jesus' crucifixion. Apparently, some found the need to try to give it a natural explanation by saying it was an eclipse."

A PORTRAIT OF PILATE

Yamauchi's mentioning of Pilate reminded me of how some critics have questioned the accuracy of the gospels because of the way they portray this Roman leader. While the New Testament paints him as being vacillating and willing to yield to the pressures of a Jewish mob by executing Jesus, other historical accounts picture him as being obstinate and inflexible.

"Doesn't this represent a contradiction between the Bible and secular historians?" I asked.

"No, it really doesn't," said Yamauchi. "Maier's study of Pilate shows that his protector or patron was Sejanus and that Sejanus fell from power in A.D. 31 because he was plotting against the emperor."

I was puzzled. "What does that have to do with anything?" I asked.

"Well, this loss would have made Pilate's position very weak in A.D. 33, which is most likely when Jesus was crucified," the professor responded. "So it would certainly be understandable that Pilate would have been reluctant to offend the Jews at that time and to get into further trouble with the emperor. That means the biblical description is most likely correct."[11]

OTHER JEWISH ACCOUNTS

Having talked primarily about Roman corroboration of Jesus, I wanted to turn a corner at this point and discuss whether any other

Jewish accounts besides that of Josephus verify anything about Jesus. I asked Yamauchi about references to Jesus in the Talmud, an important Jewish work finished about A.D. 500 that incorporates the Mishnah, compiled about A.D. 200.

"Jews, as a whole, did not go into great detail about heretics," he replied. "There are a few passages in the Talmud that mention Jesus, calling him a false messiah who practiced magic and who was justly condemned to death. They also repeat the rumor that Jesus was born of a Roman soldier and Mary, suggesting there was something unusual about his birth."

"So," I said, "in a negative way these Jewish references do corroborate some things about Jesus."

"Yes, that's right," he said. "Professor M. Wilcox put it this way in an article that appeared in a scholarly reference work:"

> The Jewish traditional literature, although it mentions Jesus only quite sparingly (and must in any case be used with caution), supports the gospel claim that he was a healer and miracle-worker, even though it ascribes these activities to sorcery. In addition, it preserves the recollection that he was a teacher, and that he had disciples (five of them), and that at least in the earlier Rabbinic period not all of the sages had finally made up their minds that he was a "heretic" or a "deceiver."[12]

EVIDENCE APART FROM THE BIBLE

Although we were finding quite a few references to Jesus outside the gospels, I was wondering why there were not even more of them. While I knew that few historical documents from the first century have survived, I asked, "Overall, shouldn't we have expected to find more about Jesus in ancient writings outside the Bible?"

"When people begin religious movements, it's often not until many generations later that people record things about them," Yamauchi said. "But the fact is that we have better historical documentation for Jesus than for the founder of any other ancient religion."

That caught me off guard. "Really?" I said. "Can you elaborate on that?"

"For example, although the Gathas of Zoroaster, about 1000 B.C., are believed to be authentic, most of the Zoroastrian scriptures were not put into writing until after the third century A.D. The most popular Parsi biography of Zoroaster was written in A.D. 1278.

"The scriptures of Buddha, who lived in the sixth century B.C., were not put into writing until after the Christian era, and the first biography of Buddha was written in the first century A.D. Although we have the sayings of Muhammad, who lived from A.D. 570 to 632, in the Koran, his biography was not written until 767—more than a full century after his death.

"So the situation with Jesus is unique—and quite impressive in terms of how much we can learn about him aside from the New Testament."

I wanted to pick up on that theme and summarize what we had gleaned about Jesus so far from nonbiblical sources. "Let's pretend we didn't have any of the New Testament or other Christian writings," I said. "Even without them, what would we be able to conclude about Jesus from ancient non-Christian sources, such as Josephus, the Talmud, Tacitus, Pliny the Younger, and others?"

Yamauchi smiled. "We would still have a considerable amount of important historical evidence; in fact, it would provide a kind of outline for the life of Jesus," he said.

Then he went on, raising a finger to emphasize each point. "We would know that first, Jesus was a Jewish teacher; second, many people believed that he performed healings and exorcisms; third, some people believed he was the Messiah; fourth, he was rejected by the Jewish leaders; fifth, he was crucified under Pontius Pilate in the reign of Tiberius; sixth, despite this shameful death, his followers, who believed that he was still alive, spread beyond Palestine so that there were multitudes of them in Rome by A.D. 64; and seventh, all kinds of people from the cities and countryside—men and women, slave and free—worshiped him as God."

This was indeed an impressive amount of independent corroboration. And not only can the contours of Jesus' life be reconstructed apart from the Bible, but there's even more that can be gleaned about him from material so old that it actually predates the gospels themselves.

CORROBORATING EARLY DETAILS

The apostle Paul never met Jesus prior to Jesus' death, but he said he did encounter the resurrected Christ and later consulted with some of the eyewitnesses to make sure he was preaching the same message they were. Because he began writing his New Testament letters years before the gospels were written down, they contain extremely early reports concerning Jesus—so early that nobody can make a credible claim that they had been seriously distorted by legendary development.

"Luke Timothy Johnson, the scholar from Emory University, contends that Paul's letters represent 'valuable external verification' of the 'antiquity and ubiquity' of the traditions about Jesus,"[13] I said to Yamauchi. "Do you agree with him?"

We had been talking for quite a while. Yamauchi stood briefly to stretch his legs before settling back down. "There's no question that Paul's writings are the earliest in the New Testament," he said, "and that they do make some very significant references to the life of Jesus."

"Can you spell them out?" I asked.

"Well, he refers to the fact that Jesus was a descendant of David, that he was the Messiah, that he was betrayed, that he was tried, crucified for our sins, and buried, and that he rose again on the third day and was seen by many people—including James, the brother of Jesus who hadn't believed in him prior to his crucifixion.

"It's also interesting that Paul doesn't mention some of the things that are highly significant in the gospels—for instance, Jesus' parables and miracles—but he focuses on Jesus' atoning death and resurrection. Those, for Paul, were the most important things about Jesus—and indeed they transformed Paul from being a persecutor of Christians into becoming history's foremost Christian missionary, who was willing to go through all sorts of hardships and deprivation because of his faith.

"Paul also corroborates some important aspects of the character of Jesus—his humility, his obedience, his love for sinners, and so forth. He calls Christians to have the mind of Christ in the second chapter of Philippians. This is a famous passage in which Paul is probably quoting from an early Christian hymn about the emptying of Christ, who was equal to God yet took the form of a man, of a slave, and suffered the extreme penalty, the Crucifixion. So Paul's letters are an important witness to the deity of Christ—he calls Jesus 'the Son of God' and 'the image of God.'"

I interrupted by saying, "The fact that Paul, who came from a monotheistic Jewish background, worshiped Jesus as God is extremely significant, isn't it?"

"Yes," he said, "and it undermines a popular theory that the deity of Christ was later imported into Christianity by Gentile beliefs. It's just not so. Even Paul at this very early date was worshiping Jesus as God.

"I have to say that all this corroboration by Paul is of the utmost importance. And we have other early letters by the eyewitnesses James and Peter, too. James, for instance, has recollections of Jesus' Sermon on the Mount."

TRULY RAISED FROM THE DEAD

We also have volumes of writings by the "apostolic fathers," who were the earliest Christian writers after the New Testament. They authored the Epistle of Clement of Rome, the Epistles of Ignatius, the Epistle of Polycarp, the Epistle of Barnabas, and others. In many places these writings attest to the basic facts about Jesus, particularly his teachings, his crucifixion, his resurrection, and his divine nature.

"Which of these writings do you consider most significant?" I asked.

Yamauchi pondered the question. While he didn't name the one he thought was most significant, he did cite the seven letters of Ignatius as being among the most important of the writings of the apostolic fathers. Ignatius, the bishop of Antioch in Syria, was martyred during the reign of Trajan before A.D. 117.

"What is significant about Ignatius," said Yamauchi, "is that he emphasized both the deity of Jesus and the humanity of Jesus, as against the docetic heresy, which denied that Jesus was really human. He also stressed the historical underpinnings of Christianity; he wrote in one letter, on his way to being executed, that Jesus was truly persecuted under Pilate, was truly crucified, was truly raised from the dead, and that those who believe in him would be raised, too."[14]

Put all this together—Josephus, the Roman historians and officials, the Jewish writings, the letters of Paul and the apostolic fathers—and you've got persuasive evidence that corroborates all the essentials found in the biographies of Jesus. Even if you were to throw away every last copy of the gospels, you'd still have a picture of Jesus that's extremely compelling—in fact, it's a portrait of the unique Son of God.

I stood and thanked Yamauchi for sharing his time and expertise. "I know there's a lot more we could talk about, since entire books have been written on this topic," I said. "But before we end, I'd like to ask you one last question. A personal one, if that's all right."

The professor rose to his feet. "Yes, that's fine," he said.

I glanced around his modest office, which was filled to the brim with books and manuscripts, records and journals, computer disks and papers, all products of a lifetime of scholarly research into a world of long ago.

"You've spent forty years studying ancient history and archaeology," I said. "What has been the result in your own spiritual life? Have your studies bolstered or weakened your faith in Jesus Christ?"

He looked down at the floor momentarily, then raised his eyes and looked squarely into mine. He said in a firm but sincere voice, "There's no question—my studies have greatly strengthened and enriched my spiritual life. They have given me a better understanding of the culture and historical context of the events.

"This doesn't mean that I don't recognize that there are some issues that still remain; within this lifetime we will not have full knowledge. But these issues don't even begin to undermine my faith in the essential trustworthiness of the gospels and the rest of the New Testament.

"I think the alternative explanations, which try to account for the spread of Christianity through sociological or psychological reasons, are very weak." He shook his head. "Very weak."

Then he added, "For me, the historical evidence has reinforced my commitment to Jesus Christ as the Son of God who loves us and died for us and was raised from the dead. It's that simple."

TRUTH THAT SETS US FREE

As I emerged from Yamauchi's building into a sea of college students scurrying from place to place in order to make their next class, I reflected on how satisfying my drive to tiny Oxford, Ohio, had been. I came seeking corroboration for Jesus, and I walked away with a rich reservoir of material affirming every major aspect of his life, miracles, deity, and victory over death.

I knew that our brief conversation had only scratched the surface. Under my arm I was carrying *The Verdict of History,* which I had reread in preparation for my interview. In it historian Gary Habermas details a total of thirty-nine ancient sources documenting the life of

Jesus, from which he enumerates more than one hundred reported facts concerning Jesus' life, teachings, crucifixion, and resurrection.[15]

What's more, twenty-four of the sources cited by Habermas, including seven secular sources and several of the earliest creeds of the church, specifically concern the divine nature of Jesus. "These creeds reveal that the church did not simply teach Jesus' deity a generation later, as is so often repeated in contemporary theology, because this doctrine is definitely present in the earliest church," Habermas writes. His conclusion: "The best explanation for these creeds is that they properly represent Jesus' own teachings."[16]

That is stunning corroboration for the most important assertion by the most influential individual who has ever lived.

I zipped up my coat as I headed for my car. Glancing back one more time, I saw the October sun illuminating the stone inscription I had first noticed when I walked onto the campus of this thoroughly secular university: "Ye shall know the truth, and the truth will make you free."

Deliberations

Questions for Reflection or Group Study

1. Is there an incident in your life in which you doubted someone's story until he or she offered some corroborating evidence? How was that experience similar to learning about the kind of corroborative evidence that Yamauchi presented?
2. What do you consider to be the most persuasive corroboration that Yamauchi talked about? Why?
3. Ancient sources say that early Christians clung to their beliefs rather than disavow them in the face of torture. Why do you think they had such strongly held convictions?

For Further Evidence

More Resources on This Topic

Bruce, F. F. *Jesus and Christian Origins outside the New Testament.* Grand Rapids: Eerdmans, 1974.

Habermas, Gary. *The Historical Jesus.* Joplin, Mo.: College Press, 1996.

McDowell, Josh, and Bill Wilson. *He Walked among Us.* Nashville: Nelson, 1994.

5

THE SCIENTIFIC EVIDENCE

Does Archaeology Confirm or Contradict Jesus' Biographies?

There was something surreal about my lunch with Dr. Jeffrey MacDonald. There he was, casually munching on a tuna fish sandwich and potato chips in a conference room of a North Carolina courthouse, making upbeat comments and generally enjoying himself. In a nearby room a dozen jurors were taking a break after hearing gruesome evidence that MacDonald had brutally murdered his wife and two young daughters.

As we were finishing our meal, I couldn't restrain myself from asking MacDonald the obvious questions. "How can you act as if nothing is wrong?" I said, my voice mixed with astonishment and indignation. "Aren't you the slightest bit concerned that those jurors are going to find you guilty?"

MacDonald casually waved his half-eaten sandwich in the general direction of the jury room. "Them?" he chortled. "They'll never convict me!"

Then, apparently realizing how cynical those words sounded, he quickly added, "I'm innocent, you know."

That was the last time I ever heard him laugh. Within days the former Green Beret and emergency room physician was found guilty of stabbing to death his wife, Colette, and his daughters, Kimberly, age five, and Kristen, age two. He was promptly sentenced to life in prison and carted off in handcuffs.

MacDonald, whose story was masterfully recounted by Joe McGinniss in the best-seller and TV movie *Fatal Vision,* was cocky enough to think that his alibi would help him get away with murder.

He had told investigators that he was asleep on the couch when drug-crazed hippies awakened him in the middle of the night. He said he fought them off, getting stabbed and knocked unconscious in the process. When he awakened, he found his family slaughtered.

Detectives were skeptical from the start. The living room showed few signs of a life-and-death struggle. MacDonald's wounds were superficial. Though he had poor eyesight, he was somehow able to provide detailed descriptions of his attackers even though he had not been wearing his glasses.

However, skepticism alone doesn't win convictions; that requires hard evidence. In MacDonald's case detectives relied on scientific proof to untangle his web of lies and convict him of the slayings.

There's a wide variety of scientific evidence that's commonly used in trials, ranging from DNA typing to forensic anthropology to toxicology. In MacDonald's case it was serology (blood evidence) and trace evidence that dispatched him to the penitentiary.

In an extraordinary—and for prosecutors, fortuitous—coincidence, each member of MacDonald's family had a different blood type. By analyzing where bloodstains were found, investigators were able to reconstruct the sequence of events that deadly evening—and it directly contradicted MacDonald's version of what happened.

Scientific study of tiny blue pajama threads, which were found scattered in various locations, also refuted his alibi. And microscopic analysis demonstrated that holes in his pajamas could not have been made, as he claimed, by an ice pick wielded by the home invaders. In short, it was FBI technicians in white lab coats who were really behind MacDonald's conviction.[1]

Scientific evidence can also make important contributions to the question of whether the New Testament accounts of Jesus are accurate. While serology and toxicology aren't able to shed any light on the issue, another category of scientific proof—the discipline of archaeology—has great bearing on the reliability of the gospels.

Sometimes called the study of durable rubbish, archaeology involves the uncovering of artifacts, architecture, art, coins, monuments, documents, and other remains of ancient cultures. Experts study these relics to learn what life was like in the days when Jesus walked the dusty roads of ancient Palestine.

Hundreds of archaeological findings from the first century have been unearthed, and I was curious: did they undermine or undergird the eyewitness stories about Jesus? At the same time, my curiosity was tempered by skepticism. I have heard too many Christians make exorbitant claims that archaeology can prove a lot more than it really can. I wasn't interested in more of the same.

So I went on a quest for a recognized authority who has personally dug among the ruins of the Middle East, who has an encyclopedic knowledge of ancient findings, and who possesses enough scientific restraint to acknowledge the limits of archaeology while at the same time explaining how it can illuminate life in the first century.

THE FOURTH INTERVIEW: JOHN MCRAY, PH.D.

When scholars and students study archaeology, many turn to John McRay's thorough and dispassionate 432-page textbook *Archaeology and the New Testament*. When the Arts and Entertainment Television Network wanted to ensure the accuracy of its *Mysteries of the Bible* program, they called McRay as well. And when *National Geographic* needed a scientist who could explain the intricacies of the biblical world, again the phone rang in McRay's office at well-respected Wheaton College in suburban Chicago.

Having studied at Hebrew University, the École Biblique et Archéologique Française in Jerusalem, Vanderbilt University Divinity School, and the University of Chicago (where he earned his doctorate in 1967), McRay has been a professor of New Testament and archaeology at Wheaton for more than fifteen years. His articles have appeared in seventeen encyclopedias and dictionaries, his research has been featured in the *Bulletin of the Near East Archaeology Society* and other academic journals, and he has presented twenty-nine scholarly papers at professional societies.

McRay is also a former research associate and trustee of the W. F. Albright Institute of Archaeological Research in Jerusalem; a former trustee of the American Schools of Oriental Research; a current trustee of the Near East Archaeological Society; and a member of the editorial boards of *Archaeology in the Biblical World* and the *Bulletin for Biblical Research*, which is published by the Institute for Biblical Research.

As much as McRay enjoys writing and teaching about the ancient world, he relishes opportunities to personally explore archaeological digs. He supervised excavating teams at Caesarea, Sepphoris, and

Herodium, all in Israel, over an eight-year period. He has studied Roman archaeological sites in England and Wales, analyzed digs in Greece, and retraced much of the apostle Paul's journeys.

At age sixty-six, McRay's hair is turning silvery and his glasses have become thicker, but he still exudes an air of adventure. Over the desk in his office—and in fact also over his bed at home—is a detailed horizontal photograph of Jerusalem. "I live in the shadow of it," he remarked, a sense of longing in his voice, as he pointed out specific locations of excavations and significant findings.

His office features the kind of cozy couch you'd find on the front porch of a country home. I settled into it while McRay, casually dressed in an open-necked shirt and a sports jacket that looked comfortably worn, leaned back in his desk chair.

Seeking to test whether he would overstate the influence of archaeology, I decided to open our interview by asking him what it *can't* tell us about the reliability of the New Testament. After all, as McRay notes in his textbook, even if archaeology can establish that the cities of Medina and Mecca existed in western Arabia during the sixth and seventh centuries, that doesn't prove that Muhammad lived there or that the Koran is true.

"Archaeology has made some important contributions," he began, speaking in a drawl he picked up as a child in southeastern Oklahoma, "but it certainly can't prove whether the New Testament is the Word of God. If we dig in Israel and find ancient sites that are consistent with where the Bible said we'd find them, that shows that its history and geography are accurate. However, it doesn't confirm that what Jesus Christ said is right. Spiritual truths cannot be proved or disproved by archaeological discoveries."

As an analogy, he offered the story of Heinrich Schliemann, who searched for Troy in an effort to prove the historical accuracy of Homer's *Iliad*. "He did find Troy," McRay observed with a gentle smile, "but that didn't prove the *Iliad* was true. It was merely accurate in a particular geographical reference."

Once we had set some boundaries for what archaeology can't establish, I was anxious to begin exploring what it can tell us about the New Testament. I decided to launch into this topic by making an observation that grew out of my experience as an investigative journalist with a legal background.

DIGGING FOR THE TRUTH

In trying to determine if a witness is being truthful, journalists and lawyers will test all the elements of his or her testimony that can be tested. If this investigation reveals that the person was wrong in those details, this casts considerable doubt on the veracity of his or her entire story. However, if the minutiae check out, this is some indication—not conclusive proof but some evidence—that maybe the witness is being reliable in his or her overall account.

For instance, if a man were telling about a trip he took from St. Louis to Chicago, and he mentioned that he had stopped in Springfield, Illinois, to see the movie *Titanic* at the Odeon Theater and that he had eaten a large Clark bar he bought at the concession counter, investigators could determine whether such a theater exists in Springfield as well as if it was showing this particular film and selling this specific brand and size of candy bar at the time he said he was there. If their findings contradict what the person claimed, this seriously tarnishes his trustworthiness. If the details check out, this doesn't prove that his entire story is true, but it does enhance his reputation for being accurate.

In a sense, this is what archaeology accomplishes. The premise is that if an ancient historian's incidental details check out to be accurate time after time, this increases our confidence in other material that the historian wrote but that cannot be as readily cross-checked.

So I asked McRay for his professional opinion. "Does archaeology affirm or undermine the New Testament when it checks out the details in those accounts?"

McRay was quick to answer. "Oh, there's no question that the credibility of the New Testament is enhanced," he said, "just as the credibility of any ancient document is enhanced when you excavate and find that the author was accurate in talking about a particular place or event."

As an example, he brought up his own digs in Caesarea on the coast of Israel, where he and others excavated the harbor of Herod the Great.

"For a long time people questioned the validity of a statement by Josephus, the first-century historian, that this harbor was as large as the one at Piraeus, which is a major harbor of Athens. People thought Josephus was wrong, because when you see the stones above the surface of the water in the contemporary harbor, it's not very big.

"But when we began to do underwater excavation, we found that the harbor extended far out into the water underground, that it had fallen down, and that its total dimensions were indeed comparable to the harbor at Piraeus. So it turns out Josephus was right after all. This was one more bit of evidence that Josephus knew what he was talking about."

So what about the New Testament writers? Did they really know what they were talking about? I wanted to put that issue to the test in my next line of questioning.

LUKE'S ACCURACY AS A HISTORIAN

The physician and historian Luke authored both the gospel bearing his name and the book of Acts, which together constitute about one-quarter of the entire New Testament. Consequently, a critical issue is whether Luke was a historian who could be trusted to get things right. "When archaeologists check out the details of what he wrote," I said, "do they find that he was careful or sloppy?"

"The general consensus of both liberal and conservative scholars is that Luke is very accurate as a historian," McRay replied. "He's erudite, he's eloquent, his Greek approaches classical quality, he writes as an educated man, and archaeological discoveries are showing over and over again that Luke is accurate in what he has to say."

In fact, he added, there have been several instances, similar to the story about the harbor, in which scholars initially thought Luke was wrong in a particular reference, only to have later discoveries confirm that he was correct in what he wrote.

For instance, in Luke 3:1 he refers to Lysanias being the tetrarch of Abilene in about A.D. 27. For years scholars pointed to this as evidence that Luke didn't know what he was talking about, since everybody knew that Lysanias was not a tetrarch but rather the ruler of Chalcis half a century earlier. If Luke can't get that basic fact right, they suggested, nothing he has written can be trusted.

That's when archaeology stepped in. "An inscription was later found from the time of Tiberius, from A.D. 14 to 37, which names Lysanias as tetrarch in Abila near Damascus—just as Luke had written," McRay explained. "It turned out there had been two government officials named Lysanias! Once more Luke was shown to be exactly right."

Another example is Luke's reference in Acts 17:6 to "politarchs," which is translated as "city officials" by the NIV, in the city of Thessalonica. "For a long time people thought Luke was mistaken, because no evidence of the term 'politarchs' had been found in any ancient Roman documents," McRay said.

"However, an inscription on a first-century arch was later found that begins, 'In the time of the politarchs . . .' You can go to the British Museum and see it for yourself. And then, lo and behold, archaeologists have found more than thirty-five inscriptions that mention politarchs, several of these in Thessalonica from the same period Luke was referring to. Once again the critics were wrong and Luke was shown to be right."

An objection popped into my mind. "Yes, but in his gospel Luke says that Jesus was walking *into* Jericho when he healed the blind man Bartimaeus, while Mark says he was coming *out* of Jericho.[2] Isn't this a clear-cut contradiction that casts doubt on the reliability of the New Testament?"

McRay wasn't stung by the directness of my question. "Not at all," came his response. "It only appears to be a contradiction because you're thinking in contemporary terms, in which cities are built and stay put. But that wasn't necessarily the case long ago.

"Jericho was in at least four different locations as much as a quarter of a mile apart in ancient times. The city was destroyed and resettled near another water supply or a new road or nearer a mountain or whatever. The point is, you can be coming out of one site where Jericho existed and be going into another one, like moving from one part of suburban Chicago to another part of suburban Chicago."

"What you're saying is that both Luke and Mark could be right?" I asked.

"That's correct. Jesus could have been going out of one area of Jericho and into another at the same time."

Again archaeology had answered another challenge to Luke. And given the large portion of the New Testament written by him, it's extremely significant that Luke has been established to be a scrupulously accurate historian, even in the smallest details. One prominent archaeologist carefully examined Luke's references to thirty-two countries, fifty-four cities, and nine islands, finding not a single mistake.[3]

Here's the bottom line: "If Luke was so painstakingly accurate in his historical reporting," said one book on the topic, "on what logical basis may we assume he was credulous or inaccurate in his reporting of matters that were far more important, not only to him but to others as well?"[4]

Matters, for example, like the resurrection of Jesus, the most influential evidence of his deity, which Luke says was firmly established by "many convincing proofs" (Acts 1:3).

THE RELIABILITY OF JOHN AND MARK

Archaeology may support the credibility of Luke, but he isn't the only author of the New Testament. I wondered what scientists would have to say about John, whose gospel was sometimes considered suspect because he talked about locations that couldn't be verified. Some scholars charged that since he failed to get these basic details straight, John must not have been close to the events of Jesus' life.

That conclusion, however, has been turned upside down in recent years. "There have been several discoveries that have shown John to be very accurate," McRay pointed out. "For example, John 5:1–15 records how Jesus healed an invalid by the Pool of Bethesda. John provides the detail that the pool had five porticoes. For a long time people cited this as an example of John being inaccurate, because no such place had been found.

"But more recently the Pool of Bethesda has been excavated—it lies maybe forty feet below ground—and sure enough, there were five porticoes, which means colonnaded porches or walkways, exactly as John had described. And you have other discoveries—the Pool of Siloam from John 9:7, Jacob's Well from John 4:12, the probable location of the Stone Pavement near the Jaffa Gate where Jesus appeared before Pilate in John 19:13, even Pilate's own identity—all of which have lent historical credibility to John's gospel."

"So this challenges the allegation that the gospel of John was written so long after Jesus that it can't possibly be accurate," I said.

"Most definitely," he replied.

In fact, McRay reiterated what Dr. Bruce Metzger had told me about archaeologists finding a fragment of a copy of John 18 that leading papyrologists have dated to about A.D. 125. By demonstrating that copies of John existed this early and as far away as Egypt, archaeology has effectively dismantled speculation that John had been composed well into the second century, too long after Jesus' life to be reliable.

Other scholars have attacked the gospel of Mark, generally considered the first account of Jesus' life to be written. Atheist Michael Martin accuses Mark of being ignorant about Palestinian geography, which he says demonstrates that he could not have lived in the region at the time of Jesus. Specifically he cites Mark 7:31: "Then Jesus left the vicinity of Tyre and went through Sidon, down to the Sea of Galilee and into the region of the Decapolis."

"It has been pointed out," said Martin, "that given these directions Jesus would have been traveling directly *away* from the Sea of Galilee."[5]

When I posed Martin's critique to McRay, he furrowed his brow and then went into a flurry of activity, pulling a Greek version of Mark off his shelf, grabbing reference books, and unfolding large maps of ancient Palestine.

"What these critics seem to be assuming is that Jesus is getting in his car and zipping around on an interstate, but he obviously wasn't," he said.

Reading the text in the original language, taking into account the mountainous terrain and probable roads of the region, and considering the loose way "Decapolis" was used to refer to a confederation of ten cities that varied from time to time, McRay traced a logical route on the map that corresponded precisely with Mark's description.

"When everything is put into the appropriate context," he concluded, "there's no problem with Mark's account."

Again archaeological insights had helped explain what appeared at first to be a sticking point in the New Testament. I asked McRay a broad question about that: had he ever encountered an archaeological finding that blatantly contravened a New Testament reference?

He shook his head. "Archaeology has not produced anything that is unequivocally a contradiction to the Bible," he replied with confidence. "On the contrary, as we've seen, there have been many opinions of skeptical scholars that have become codified into 'fact' over the years but that archaeology has shown to be wrong."

Still, there were some matters I needed to resolve. I pulled out my notes and got ready to challenge McRay with three long-standing riddles that I thought archaeology might have some trouble explaining.

PUZZLE 1: THE CENSUS

The birth narratives of Jesus claim that Mary and Joseph were required by a census to return to Joseph's hometown of Bethlehem. "Let me be blunt: this seems absurd on the face of it," I said. "How could the government possibly force all its citizens to return to their birthplace? Is there any archaeological evidence whatsoever that this kind of census ever took place?"

McRay calmly pulled out a copy of his book. "Actually, the discovery of ancient census forms has shed quite a bit of light on this practice," he said as he leafed through the pages. Finding the reference he was searching for, he quoted from an official governmental order dated A.D. 104.

> Gaius Vibius Maximus, Prefect of Egypt [says]: Seeing that the time has come for the house to house census, it is necessary to compel all those who for any cause whatsoever are residing out of their provinces to *return to their own homes,* that they may both carry out the regular order of the census and may also attend diligently to the cultivation of their allotments.[6]

"As you can see," he said as he closed the book, "that practice is confirmed by this document, even though this particular manner of counting people might seem odd to you. And another papyrus, this one from A.D. 48, indicates that the entire family was involved in the census."

This, however, did not entirely dispose of the issue. Luke said the census that brought Joseph and Mary to Bethlehem was conducted when Quirinius was governing Syria and during the reign of Herod the Great.

"That poses a significant problem," I pointed out, "because Herod died in 4 B.C., and Quirinius didn't begin ruling Syria until A.D. 6, conducting the census soon after that. There's a big gap there; how can you deal with such a major discrepancy in the dates?"

McRay knew I was raising an issue that archaeologists have wrestled with for years. He responded by saying, "An eminent archaeologist named Jerry Vardaman has done a great deal of work in this regard. He has found a coin with the name of Quirinius on it in very small writing, or what we call 'micrographic' letters. This places him as proconsul of Syria and Cilicia from 11 B.C. until after the death of Herod."

I was confused. "What does that mean?" I asked.

"It means that there were apparently two Quiriniuses," he replied. "It's not uncommon to have lots of people with the same Roman names, so there's no reason to doubt that there were two people by the name of Quirinius. The census would have taken place under the reign of the earlier Quirinius. Given the cycle of a census every fourteen years, that would work out quite well."

This sounded a bit speculative to me, but rather than bog down this conversation, I decided to mentally file this issue away for further analysis later.

When I did some additional research, I found that Sir William Ramsay, the late archaeologist and professor at both Oxford and Cambridge Universities in England, had come up with a similar theory. He concluded from various inscriptions that while there was only one Quirinius, he ruled Syria on two separate occasions, which would cover the time period of the earlier census.[7]

Other scholars have pointed out that Luke's text can be translated, "This census took place *before* Quirinius was governing Syria," which would also resolve the problem.[8]

The matter was not as precisely pinned down as I would like. However, I had to admit that McRay and others had offered some plausible explanations. I could conclude with confidence that censuses were held during the time frame of Jesus' birth and that there is evidence people were indeed required to return to their hometowns—which I still thought was odd!

PUZZLE 2: EXISTENCE OF NAZARETH

Many Christians are unaware that skeptics have been asserting for a long time that Nazareth never existed during the time when the New Testament says Jesus spent his childhood there.

In an article called "Where Jesus Never Walked," atheist Frank Zindler noted that Nazareth is not mentioned in the Old Testament, by the apostle Paul, by the Talmud (although sixty-three other Galilean towns are cited), or by Josephus (who listed forty-five other villages and cities of Galilee, including Japha, which was located just over a mile from present-day Nazareth). No ancient historians or geographers mention Nazareth before the beginning of the fourth century.[9] The name first appears in Jewish literature in a poem written about the seventh century A.D.[10]

This absence of evidence paints a suspicious picture. So I put the issue directly to McRay: "Is there any archaeological confirmation that Nazareth was in existence during the first century?"

This issue wasn't new to McRay. "Dr. James Strange of the University of South Florida is an expert on this area, and he describes Nazareth as being a very small place, about sixty acres, with a maximum population of about four hundred and eighty at the beginning of the first century," McRay replied.

However, that was a conclusion; I wanted the evidence. "How does he know that?" I asked.

"Well, Strange notes that when Jerusalem fell in A.D. 70, priests were no longer needed in the temple because it had been destroyed, so they were sent out to various other locations, even up into Galilee. Archaeologists have found a list in Aramaic describing the twenty-four 'courses,' or families, of priests who were relocated, and one of them was registered as having been moved to Nazareth. That shows that this tiny village must have been there at the time."

In addition, he said there have been archaeological digs that have uncovered first-century tombs in the vicinity of Nazareth, which would establish the village's limits because by Jewish law burials had to take place outside the town proper. Two tombs contained objects such as pottery lamps, glass vessels, and vases from the first, third, or fourth centuries.

McRay picked up a copy of a book by renowned archaeologist Jack Finegan, published by Princeton University Press. He leafed through it, then read Finegan's analysis: "From the tombs . . . it can be concluded that Nazareth was a strongly Jewish settlement in the Roman period."[11]

McRay looked up at me. "There has been discussion about the location of some sites from the first century, such as exactly where Jesus' tomb is situated, but among archaeologists there has never really been a big doubt about the location of Nazareth. The burden of proof ought to be on those who dispute its existence."

That seemed reasonable. Even the usually skeptical Ian Wilson, citing pre-Christian remains found in 1955 under the Church of the Annunciation in present-day Nazareth, has managed to concede, "Such findings suggest that Nazareth may have existed in Jesus' time, but there is no doubt that it must have been a very small and insignificant place."[12]

So insignificant that Nathanael's musings in John 1:46 now make more sense: "Nazareth!" he said. "Can anything good come from there?"

PUZZLE 3: SLAUGHTER AT BETHLEHEM

The gospel of Matthew paints a grisly scene: Herod the Great, the king of Judea, feeling threatened by the birth of a baby who he feared would eventually seize his throne, dispatches his troops to murder all the children under the age of two in Bethlehem. Warned by an angel, however, Joseph escapes to Egypt with Mary and Jesus. Only after Herod dies do they return to settle in Nazareth, the entire episode having fulfilled three ancient prophecies about the Messiah. (See Matt. 2:13–23.)

The problem: there is no independent confirmation that this mass murder ever took place. There's nothing in the writings of Josephus or other historians. There's no archaeological support. There are no records or documents.

"Certainly an event of this magnitude would have been noticed by someone other than Matthew," I insisted. "With the complete absence of any historical or archaeological corroboration, isn't it logical to conclude that this slaughter never occurred?"

"I can see why you'd say that," McRay replied, "since today an event like that would probably be splashed all over CNN and the rest of the news media."

I agreed. In fact, in 1997 and 1998 there was a steady stream of news accounts about Muslim extremists repeatedly staging commando raids and slaying virtually entire villages, including women and children, in Algeria. The entire world was taking notice.

"But," added McRay, "you have to put yourself back in the first century and keep a few things in mind. First, Bethlehem was probably no bigger than Nazareth, so how many babies of that age would there be in a village of five hundred or six hundred people? Not thousands, not hundreds, although certainly a few.

"Second, Herod the Great was a bloodthirsty king: he killed members of his own family; he executed lots of people who he thought might challenge him. So the fact that he killed some babies in Bethlehem is not going to captivate the attention of people in the Roman world.

"And third, there was no television, no radio, no newspapers. It would have taken a long time for word of this to get out, especially from such a minor village way in the back hills of nowhere, and historians had much bigger stories to write about."

As a journalist, this was still hard to fathom. "This just wasn't much of a story?" I asked, a bit incredulous.

"I don't think it was, at least not in those days," he said. "A madman killing everybody who seems to be a potential threat to him—that was business as usual for Herod. Later, of course, as Christianity developed, this incident became more important, but I would have been surprised if this had made a big splash back then."

Maybe so, but this was difficult to imagine for a journalist who was trained to sniff out news in a highly technological age of rapid and worldwide communications. At the same time, I had to acknowledge that from what I knew of the bloody landscape of ancient Palestine, McRay's explanation did seem reasonable.

This left one other area I wanted to inquire about. And to me, it was the most fascinating of all.

RIDDLE OF THE DEAD SEA SCROLLS

Admittedly, there is an allure to archaeology. Ancient tombs, cryptic inscriptions etched in stone or scratched onto papyrus, bits of broken pottery, worn coins—they're tantalizing clues for an inveterate investigator. But few vestiges of the past have generated as much intrigue as the Dead Sea Scrolls, hundreds of manuscripts dating from 250 B.C. to A.D. 68 that were found in caves twenty miles east of Jerusalem in 1947. They apparently had been hidden by a strict sect of Jews called the Essenes before the Romans destroyed their settlement.

Some bizarre claims have been made about the scrolls, including John Marco Allegro's absurd book in which he theorized that Christianity emerged from a fertility cult in which adherents tripped out on hallucinogenic mushrooms![13] In a more legitimate but nevertheless much-questioned assertion, papyri expert Jose O'Callaghan said one Dead Sea fragment is part of the earliest manuscript ever found of the gospel of Mark, dating back to a mere seventeen to twenty years after Jesus was crucified. However, many scholars continue to be skeptical of his interpretation.[14]

In any event, no inquiry into the archaeology of the first century would be complete without asking about the scrolls. "Do they tell us anything directly about Jesus?" I asked McRay.

"Well, no, Jesus isn't specifically mentioned in any of the scrolls," he replied. "Primarily these documents give us insights into Jewish life and customs." Then he pulled out some papers and pointed to an article that was published in late 1997. "Although," he added, "there is a very interesting development involving a manuscript called 4Q521 that could tell us something about who Jesus was claiming to be."

That whet my appetite. "Tell me about it," I said with some urgency in my voice.

McRay unfolded the mystery. The gospel of Matthew describes how John the Baptist, imprisoned and wrestling with lingering doubts about Jesus' identity, sent his followers to ask Jesus this monumental question: "Are you the one who was to come, or should we expect someone else?" (Matt. 11:3). He was seeking a straight answer about whether Jesus really was the long-awaited Messiah.

Through the centuries, Christians have wondered about Jesus' rather enigmatic answer. Instead of directly saying yes or no, Jesus replied, "Go back and report to John what you hear and see: The blind receive sight, the lame walk, those who have leprosy are cured, the deaf hear, the dead are raised, and the good news is preached to the poor" (Matt. 11:4–5).

Jesus' response was an allusion to Isaiah 35. But for some reason Jesus included the phrase "the dead are raised," which is conspicuously absent from the Old Testament text.

This is where 4Q521 comes in. This nonbiblical manuscript from the Dead Sea collection, written in Hebrew, dates back to thirty years before Jesus was born. It contains a version of Isaiah 61 that does include this missing phrase, "the dead are raised."

"[Scroll scholar Craig] Evans has pointed out that this phrase in 4Q521 is unquestionably embedded in a messianic context," McRay said. "It refers to the wonders that the Messiah will do when he comes and when heaven and earth will obey him. So when Jesus gave his response to John, he was not being ambiguous at all. John would have instantly recognized his words as a distinct claim that Jesus was the Messiah."

McRay tossed me the article in which Evans was quoted as saying, "4Q521 makes it clear that [Jesus'] appeal to Isaiah 35 is indeed messianic. In essence, Jesus is telling John through his messengers that messianic things are happening. So that answers [John's] question: *Yes, he is the one who is to come.*"[15]

I sat back in my chair. To me, Evans' discovery was a remarkable confirmation of Jesus' self-identity. It was staggering to me how modern archaeology could finally unlock the significance of a statement in which Jesus boldly asserted nearly two thousand years ago that he was indeed the anointed one of God.

"A REMARKABLY ACCURATE SOURCE BOOK"

Archaeology's repeated affirmation of the New Testament's accuracy provides important corroboration for its reliability. This is in stark contrast with how archaeology has proved to be devastating for Mormonism.

Although Joseph Smith, the founder of the Mormon church, claimed that his *Book of Mormon* is "the most correct of any book upon the earth,"[16] archaeology has repeatedly failed to substantiate its claims about events that supposedly occurred long ago in the Americas.

I remember writing to the Smithsonian Institute to inquire about whether there was any evidence supporting the claims of Mormonism, only to be told in unequivocal terms that its archaeologists see "no direct connection between the archaeology of the New World and the subject matter of the book."

As authors John Ankerberg and John Weldon concluded in a book on the topic, "In other words, no *Book of Mormon* cities have ever been located, no *Book of Mormon* person, place, nation, or name has ever been found, no *Book of Mormon* artifacts, no *Book of Mormon* scriptures, no *Book of Mormon* inscriptions . . . nothing which demonstrates the *Book of Mormon* is anything other than myth or invention has *ever* been found."[17]

However, the story is totally different for the New Testament. McRay's conclusions have been echoed by many other scientists, including prominent Australian archaeologist Clifford Wilson, who wrote, "Those who know the facts now recognize that the New Testament must be accepted as a remarkably accurate source book."[18]

With Craig Blomberg having established the essential reliability of the New Testament documents, Bruce Metzger having confirmed their accurate transmittal through history, Edwin Yamauchi having demonstrated extensive corroboration by ancient historians and others, and now John McRay having shown how archaeology underscores their trustworthiness, I had to agree with Wilson. The case for Christ, while far from complete, was being constructed on solid bedrock.

At the same time, I knew there were some high-profile professors who would dissent from that assessment. You've seen them quoted in *Newsweek* and being interviewed on the evening news, talking about their radical reassessment of Jesus. The time had come for me to confront their critiques head-on before I went any further in my investigation. That meant a trip to Minnesota to interview a feisty, Yale-educated scholar named Dr. Gregory Boyd.

Deliberations

Questions for Reflection or Group Study

1. What do you see as some of the shortcomings and benefits of using archaeology to corroborate the New Testament?
2. If Luke and other New Testament writers are shown to be accurate in reporting incidental details, does this increase your confidence that they would be similarly careful in recording more important events? Why or why not?
3. Why do you find Dr. McRay's analysis of the puzzles concerning the census, the existence of Nazareth, and the slaughter at Bethlehem to be generally plausible or implausible?
4. After having considered the eyewitness, documentary, corroborating, and scientific evidence in the case for Christ, stop and assess your conclusions so far. On a scale of zero to ten, with zero being "no confidence" in the essential reliability of the gospels and ten being "full confidence," where would you rate yourself at this point? What are some reasons you chose that number?

For Further Evidence

More Resources on This Topic

Finegan, Jack. *The Archaeology of the New Testament.* Princeton: Princeton Univ. Press, 1992.

McRay, John. *Archaeology and the New Testament.* Grand Rapids: Baker, 1991.

Thompson, J. A. *The Bible and Archaeology.* Grand Rapids: Eerdmans, 1975.

Yamauchi, Edwin. *The Stones and the Scriptures.* New York: J. B. Lippencott, 1972.

6

THE REBUTTAL EVIDENCE

Is the Jesus of History the Same As the Jesus of Faith?

It happens all the time on *Perry Mason* reruns and in paperback novels, but it's extremely rare in real-life legal dramas. So when an eyewitness in a murder trial refused to point out the defendant as the slayer and instead confessed that he was the killer, the entire courtroom was stunned—and I had an amazing story for the *Chicago Tribune*.

Richard Moss was accused of shooting a nineteen-year-old Chicagoan to death outside a northwest-side tavern. Moss's lifelong friend, Ed Passeri, was called to the witness stand to describe the altercation that led to the slaying.

Passeri painted the scene that occurred outside the Rusty Nail Pub, and then the defense attorney asked him what happened to the victim.

Without blinking, Passeri replied that after the victim stabbed him with a pair of scissors, "I shot him."

The court transcriber's jaw dropped open. Prosecutors threw up their hands. The judge immediately halted the proceedings to advise Passeri of his constitutional right against self-incrimination. And then the defendant got on the stand to say yes, that's right—it was Passeri who committed the crime.

"What Passeri did [by confessing] was an act of raw courage," crowed the defense attorney.

But prosecutors were unconvinced. "What courage?" asked one of them. "Passeri knows he's not running the risk of prosecution, because the only evidence the state has points to Richard Moss!"

Still overwhelmingly persuaded of Moss's guilt, prosecutors knew they had to present strong testimony to controvert Passeri's claim. In legal terminology, what they needed was "rebuttal evidence," defined as any proof that's offered to "explain, counteract, or disprove" a witness's account.[1]

The next day, prosecutors questioned three other eyewitnesses who said there was no doubt that it was Moss who had committed the slaying. Sure enough, based on this and other evidence, the jurors found Moss guilty.[2]

Prosecutors did the right thing. When the overpowering strength of the evidence clearly pointed toward the guilt of the defendant, they were wise to be skeptical of an essentially unsupported assertion made by someone with a vested interest in helping his friend.

CAN THE JESUS SEMINAR BE REFUTED?

How does this legal concept of rebuttal evidence fit into my investigation of Jesus?

Now that I had heard powerfully convincing and well-reasoned evidence from the scholars I questioned for this book, I needed to turn my attention to the decidedly contrary opinions of a small group of academics who have been the subject of a whirlwind of news coverage.

I'm sure you've seen the articles. In recent years the news media have been saturated with uncritical reports about the Jesus Seminar, a self-selected group that represents a minuscule percentage of New Testament scholars but that generates coverage vastly out of proportion to the group's influence.

The Seminar's publicity-savvy participants attracted the press by voting with colored beads on whether they thought Jesus said what the gospels quote him as saying. A red bead meant Jesus undoubtedly said this or something like it; a pink bead meant he probably said it; a gray bead meant he didn't say it but the ideas are similar to his own; and a black bead meant he didn't utter these words at all.

In the end they concluded Jesus did not say 82 percent of what the gospels attribute to him. Most of the remaining 18 percent was considered somewhat doubtful, with only 2 percent of Jesus' sayings confidently determined to be authentic.[3] Craving controversy and lacking the expertise to scrutinize the Seminar's methodology, journalists devoted fountains of ink to the story.

Then the Seminar published *The Five Gospels*, containing the four traditional gospels plus the questionable Gospel of Thomas, with Jesus' words color-coded to match the group's findings. Flip through it and you find expanses of black type but precious little in red. For example, the only words in the Lord's Prayer that the Seminar is convinced Jesus said are "Our Father."

But I wanted to go beyond the headlines and to unearth, as commentator Paul Harvey likes to say, "the rest of the story." I needed to know if there was any credible rebuttal evidence to refute these troubling and widely publicized opinions. Were the Jesus Seminar's findings solidly based on unbiased scholarly research, or were they like Passeri's ill-fated testimony: well meaning but ultimately unsupported?

For answers, I made the six-hour drive to St. Paul, Minnesota, to confer with Dr. Gregory Boyd, the Ivy League–educated theology professor whose books and articles have challenged the Jesus Seminar head-on.

THE FIFTH INTERVIEW: GREGORY A. BOYD, PH.D.

Boyd first clashed with the Jesus Seminar in 1996, when he wrote a devastating critique of liberal perspectives of Jesus, called *Cynic Sage or Son of God? Recovering the Real Jesus in an Age of Revisionist Replies*. The heavily footnoted, 416-page tome was honored by readers of *Christianity Today* as one of their favorite books of the year. His popular paperback *Jesus under Siege* continues the same themes on a more introductory level.

Boyd's other books include the award-winning *Letters from a Skeptic*, in which he and his then-doubting father wrestle through tough issues involving Christianity (culminating in his father becoming a committed Christian), and *God at War: The Bible and Spiritual Conflict*. In addition, he was a contributing scholar to *The Quest Study Bible*, which was designed for people who are asking intellectual questions about the Christian faith.

After receiving a bachelor's degree in philosophy from the University of Minnesota, Boyd earned a master of divinity degree (cum laude) from Yale University Divinity School and a doctorate (magna cum laude) from Princeton Theological Seminary.

He is not, however, a stereotypical ivory tower intellectual. With wavy black hair, a wiry frame, and a wry smile, Boyd looks like the academic counterpart of comedian Howie Mandell. And like Mandell, he is pure kinetic energy.

Words gush from him like water from a ruptured pipe. He spins out sophisticated ideas and theological concepts at a dizzying rate. He fidgets, he gestures, he squirms in his chair. There's no time to tuck in his shirt all the way, to file the flurry of papers strewn about his office, or to shelve the books that sit in untidy stacks on his floor. He's too busy thinking, debating, questioning, wondering, dreaming, contemplating, inventing—and tackling one project after another.

In fact, one career can't contain him. In addition to his position as professor of theology at Bethel College, he's also a pastor at Woodland Hills Church, where his passionate preaching has helped attendance grow from forty-two in 1992 to twenty-five hundred today. This real-world environment helps anchor him in the reality of everyday life.

For fun, he debates atheists. He grappled with the late Gordon Stein on the topic "Does God Exist?" He and pastor-turned-skeptic Dan Barker sparred over "Did Jesus Rise from the Dead?" And in a program sponsored by the Islamic Center of Minnesota, he challenged a Muslim on the issue "Is God a Trinity?" Boyd's agile mind, quick wit, empathy with people, and deep reservoir of biblical and philosophical knowledge make him a formidable foe.

What's more, he blends popular culture and serious scholarship as well as anyone I know. He knows football as well as footnotes. He can start a sentence with an offhand observation about a new movie and end it with a stratospheric reference to a profound philosophical conundrum. He's as comfortable reading *Dilbert* or watching *Seinfeld* as he is writing his impressive book *Trinity and Process: A Critical Evaluation and Reconstruction of Hartshorne's Di-Polar Theism towards a Trinitarian Metaphysics.*

His casual and colloquial style (what other biblical scholar gets away with words like "funky" and "wacko"?) quickly made me feel at home as we squeezed into his second-floor office. It was soon clear that Boyd was wound up and ready to go.

WRITINGS FROM THE RADICAL FRINGE

I decided to start from the perspective of the average consumer of news. "People pick up a magazine or newspaper, read the conclusions of the Jesus Seminar, and assume that this represents the mainstream of New Testament scholarship," I said. "But is that really the case?"

"No," he said, looking as if he had just bitten into something sour. "No, no, that's *not* the case. But you're right—people get that impression."

He rocked in his chair until he got comfortable enough to tell a story. "When *Time* came out with its first major article on the Jesus

Seminar," he said, "I happened to be in the process of talking about Christianity with a guy whom I was building a relationship with. He was very skeptical by nature and quite inebriated with New Age ideas.

"We had a mutual friend who was hospitalized, and when I went to visit him, this other guy was already there, reading *Time*. As I walked into the room, he said to me, 'Well, Greg, it looks like the scholars disagree with you,' and he threw the magazine at me!"

Boyd shook his head in both sadness and disbelief. "You see, that article gave him the reason to stop taking me seriously. Even though he knew I was a scholar, he interpreted this article as saying that the majority of scholars—at least, those who aren't wacko fundamentalists—hold these views."

I could empathize with Boyd's story, having heard too many people equate the Jesus Seminar with all scholars. "Do you think that impression is an accident?" I asked.

"Well, the Jesus Seminar certainly portrays itself that way," Boyd replied. "In fact, this is one of its most irritating facets, not just to evangelicals but to other scholars as well.

"If you look at their book *The Five Gospels,* they give 'seven pillars of scholarly wisdom,' as if you must follow their methodology if you're going to be a true scholar. But a lot of scholars, from a wide spectrum of backgrounds, would have serious reservations about one or even most of these pillars. And the Jesus Seminar calls its translation of the Bible 'The Scholars Version'—well, what does that imply? That other versions aren't scholarly?"

He paused for a moment, then cut to the core of the issue. "Here's the truth," he said. "The Jesus Seminar represents an extremely small number of radical-fringe scholars who are on the far, far left wing of New Testament thinking. It does not represent mainstream scholarship.

"And ironically, they have their own brand of fundamentalism. They say they have the right way of doing things, period." He smiled. "In the name of diversity," he added with a chuckle, "they can actually be quite narrow."

DISCOVERING THE "REAL" JESUS

"At least," I said, "the participants in the Jesus Seminar have been very up-front about their goals, haven't they?"

"Yes, that's right. They're explicit in saying they want to rescue the Bible from fundamentalism and to free Americans from the 'naive' belief that the Jesus of the Bible is the 'real' Jesus. They say they want a Jesus who's relevant for today. One of them said that the traditional Jesus did not speak to the needs of the ecological crisis, the nuclear crisis, the feminist crisis, so we need a new picture of Jesus. As another one said, we need 'a new fiction.'

"One of the twists is that they're going directly to the masses instead of to other scholars. They want to take their findings out of the ivory tower and bring them into the marketplace to influence popular opinion. And what they have in mind is a totally new form of Christianity."

The idea of a new Jesus, a new faith, a new Christianity, was intriguing. "So tell me about this Jesus that people from the Jesus Seminar have discovered," I said. "What's he like?"

"Basically, they've discovered what they set out to find. Some think he was a political revolutionary, some a religious fanatic, some a wonder worker, some a feminist, some an egalitarian, some a subversive—there's a lot of diversity," he said.

Then he zeroed in on the key issue. "But there is one picture that they all agree with: Jesus first of all must be a naturalistic Jesus.

"In other words, whatever else is said about him, Jesus was a man like you or me. Maybe he was an extraordinary man, maybe he tapped into our inherent potential as nobody else ever has, but he was not supernatural.

"So they say Jesus and his early followers didn't see him as God or the Messiah, and they didn't see his death as having any special significance. His crucifixion was unfortunate and untimely, and stories about his resurrection came later as a way of trying to deal with that sad reality."

GIVING EVIDENCE A FAIR HEARING

I stood and strolled over to his bookshelf as I formulated my next question. "OK, but you personally have faith that Jesus was resurrected, and maybe your faith taints your viewpoint too much," I said. "The Jesus Seminar paints itself as being on an unbiased quest for truth, as compared with religiously committed people—people like you—who have a theological agenda."

Boyd turned in his seat to face me. "Ah, but that's not what's really going on," he insisted. "The participants of the Jesus Seminar are at least as biased as evangelicals—and I would say more so. They bring a whole set of assumptions to their scholarship, which of course we all do to some degree.

"Their major assumption—which, incidentally, is not the product of unbiased scholarly research—is that the gospels are not even generally reliable. They conclude this at the outset because the gospels include things that seem historically unlikely, like miracles—walking on water, raising the dead. These things, they say, just don't happen. That's naturalism, which says that for every effect in the natural or physical world, there is a natural cause."

"Yeah, but isn't that the way people typically live their lives?" I asked. "Are you saying we should be looking for supernatural explanations behind everything that takes place?"

"Everyone would agree that you don't appeal to supernatural causes if you don't have to," Boyd said. "But these scholars go beyond that and say you don't *ever* have to. They operate under the assumption that everything in history has happened according to their own experiences, and since they've never seen the supernatural, they assume miracles have never occurred in history.

"Here's what they do: they rule out the possibility of the supernatural from the beginning, and then they say, 'Now bring on the evidence about Jesus.' No wonder they get the results they do!"

I wanted to turn the tables a bit. "All right, then how would you proceed?" I asked.

"I would grant that you shouldn't appeal to the supernatural until you have to. Yes, first look for a natural explanation. I do that in my own life. A tree falls—OK, maybe there were termites. Now, could an angel have pushed it over? Well, I wouldn't go to that conclusion until there was definite evidence for it.

"So I grant that. But what I can't grant is the tremendous presumption that we know enough about the universe to say that God—if there is a God—can never break into our world in a supernatural way. That's a very presumptuous assumption. That's not a presumption based on history; now you're doing metaphysics.

"I think there should be a certain amount of humility in the historical investigation to say, 'You know what? It is just possible that Jesus Christ did rise from the dead. It's just possible that his disciples actually saw what the gospels say they saw.' And if there's no other way of accounting adequately for the evidence, let's investigate that possibility.'

"That, I think, is the only way to give the evidence a fair hearing."

CRITIQUING THE CRITERIA

To come up with their conclusion that Jesus never spoke most of the words in the gospels, members of the Jesus Seminar used their own set of assumptions and criteria. But are these standards reasonable and appropriate? Or were they loaded from the outset, like dice that are weighted so they yield the result that was desired all along?

"There are multiple problems with their assumptions and criteria," Boyd began in analyzing the group's approach. "For instance, they assume that the later church put these sayings into the mouth of Jesus, unless they have good evidence to think otherwise. That assumption is rooted in their suspicion of the gospels, and that comes from their assumption that the supernatural can't occur.

"Historians usually operate with the burden of proof on the historian to prove falsity or unreliability, since people are generally not compulsive liars. Without that assumption we'd know very little about ancient history.

"The Jesus Seminar turns this on its head and says you've got to affirmatively prove that a saying came from Jesus. Then they come up with questionable criteria to do that. Now, it's OK for scholars to use appropriate criteria in considering whether Jesus said something. But I'm against the idea that if Jesus doesn't meet these criteria, he must not have said it. That kind of negative conclusion can be a problem."

Dealing in this theoretical realm was starting to bring more murkiness than clarity for me. I needed some concrete examples so I could follow Boyd's point. "Talk about some of the specific criteria they used," I said.

"One is called double dissimilarity," he replied. "This means they can believe Jesus said something if it doesn't look like something a rabbi or the later church would say. Otherwise they assume it got into the gospels from a Jewish or Christian source.

"The obvious problem is that Jesus was Jewish and he founded the Christian church, so it shouldn't be surprising if he sounds Jewish and Christian! Yet they've applied this criterion to reach the negative conclusion that Jesus didn't say a whole lot.

"Then there's the criterion of 'multiple attestation,' which means we can only be sure Jesus said something if it's found in more than one source. Now, this can be a helpful test in confirming a saying. However, why argue in the other direction—if it's only found in one source, it's not valid? In fact, most of ancient history is based on single sources.

Generally, if a source is considered reliable—and I would argue that there are plenty of reasons to believe that the gospels are reliable—it should be considered credible, even if it can't be confirmed by other sources.

"Even when Jesus' sayings are found in two or three gospels, they don't consider this as passing the 'multiple attestation' criterion. If a saying is found in Matthew, Mark, and Luke, they consider that only one source, because they assume that Matthew and Luke used Mark in writing their gospels. They're failing to recognize that an increasing number of scholars are expressing serious reservations about the theory that Matthew and Luke used Mark. With this line of thinking, you can see why it's extremely difficult to prove multiple attestation."

Boyd started to go on, but I told him he had already made his point: loaded criteria, like weighted dice, inevitably bring the results that were desired from the beginning.

JESUS THE WONDER WORKER

One approach taken by naturalistic scholars has been to look for parallels between Jesus and others from ancient history as a way of demonstrating that his claims and deeds were not completely unique. Their goal is to explain away the view that Jesus was one of a kind.

"How do you respond to this?" I asked Boyd. "For example, there were ancient rabbis who did exorcisms or prayed for rain and it came, so some scholars have said Jesus was merely another example of a Jewish wonder worker. Do those parallels hold up?"

I was about to see Boyd the debater in action as he responded point by point to a complex issue without the benefit of notes. I was glad I was taping our conversation; my note taking would never have kept up with his rapid-fire delivery.

"Actually, the parallels break down quickly when you look more closely," he began, picking up speed as he went. "For one thing, the sheer centrality of the supernatural in the life of Jesus has no parallel whatsoever in Jewish history.

"Second, the radical nature of his miracles distinguishes him. It didn't just rain when he prayed for it; we're talking about blindness, deafness, leprosy, and scoliosis being healed, storms being stopped, bread and fish being multiplied, sons and daughters being raised from the dead. This is beyond any parallels.

"Third, Jesus' biggest distinctive is how he did miracles on his own authority. He is the one who says, 'If I, by the finger of God, cast out demons, then the kingdom of God is among you'—he's referring to himself. He says, 'I have been anointed to set the captives free.' He does give God the Father credit for what he does, but you never find him asking God the Father to do it—he does it in the power of God the Father. And for that there is just no parallel.

"This goes right along with the different way Jesus talked about himself—'all authority has been given to me,' 'honor me even as you honor the Father,' 'heaven and earth shall pass away but my word will not pass away.' You don't find rabbis talking like this anywhere."

Having been on the receiving end of that quick burst of arguments, I said with a chuckle, "So what's your point?"

Boyd laughed. "Any parallels with wonder-working rabbis," he said, "are going to be very, very stretched."

JESUS AND THE AMAZING APOLLONIUS

I wasn't going to let Boyd's debating skills intimidate me. I decided to raise a more difficult issue: the seemingly stronger parallels between Jesus and a historical figure named Apollonius of Tyana.

"You know the evidence as well as I do," I said to Boyd. "Here's someone from the first century who was said to have healed people and to have exorcised demons; who may have raised a young girl from the dead; and who appeared to some of his followers after he died. People point to that and say, 'Aha! If you're going to admit that the Apollonius story is legendary, why not say the same thing about the Jesus story?'"

Boyd was nodding to indicate he was tracking with me. "I'll admit that initially this sounds impressive," he said. "When I first heard about Apollonius as a college student, I was really taken aback. But if you do the historical work calmly and objectively, you find that the alleged parallels just don't stand up."

I needed specifics, not generalities. "Go ahead," I said. "Do your best to shoot it down."

"OK. Well, first, his biographer, Philostratus, was writing a century and a half after Apollonius lived, whereas the gospels were written within a generation of Jesus. The closer the proximity to the event, the less chance there is for legendary development, for error, or for memories to get confused.

"Another thing is that we have four gospels, corroborated with Paul, that can be cross-checked to some degree with nonbiblical authors, like Josephus and others. With Apollonius we're dealing with one source. Plus the gospels pass the standard tests used to assess historical reliability, but we can't say that about the stories of Apollonius.

"On top of that, Philostratus was commissioned by an empress to write a biography in order to dedicate a temple to Apollonius. She was a follower of Apollonius, so Philostratus would have had a financial motive to embellish the story and give the empress what she wanted. On the other hand, the writers of the gospel had nothing to gain—and much to lose—by writing Jesus' story, and they didn't have ulterior motives such as financial gain.

"Also, the way Philostratus writes is very different than the gospels. The gospels have a very confident eyewitness perspective, as if they had a camera there. But Philostratus includes a lot of tentative statements, like 'It is reported that . . .' or 'Some say this young girl had died; others say she was just ill.' To his credit, he backs off and treats stories like stories.

"And here's a biggie: Philostratus was writing in the early third century in Cappadocia, where Christianity had already been present for quite a while. So any borrowing would have been done by him, not by Christians. You can imagine the followers of Apollonius seeing Christianity as competition and saying, 'Oh, yeah? Well, Apollonius did the same things Jesus did!' Sort of like, 'My dad can beat up your dad!'

"One final point. I'm willing to admit that Apollonius may have done some amazing things or at least tricked people into thinking he did. But that doesn't in any way compromise the evidence for Jesus. Even if you grant the evidence for Apollonius, you're still left with having to deal with the evidence for Christ."

JESUS AND THE "MYSTERY RELIGIONS"

OK, I thought to myself, let's give this one more try. A lot of college students are taught that many of the themes seen in the life of Jesus are merely echoes of ancient "mystery religions," in which there are stories about gods dying and rising, and rituals of baptism and communion. "What about those parallels?" I asked.

"That was a very popular argument at the beginning of the century, but it generally died off because it was so discredited. For one thing, given the timing involved, if you're going to argue for borrowing, it should be from the direction of Christianity to the mystery religions, not vice versa.

"Also, the mystery religions were do-your-own-thing religions that freely borrowed ideas from various places. However, the Jews carefully guarded their beliefs from outside influences. They saw themselves as a separate people and strongly resisted pagan ideas and rituals."

To me, the most interesting potential parallels were the mythological tales of gods dying and rising. "Aren't those stories similar to Christian beliefs?" I asked.

"While it's true that some mystery religions had stories of gods dying and rising, these stories always revolved around the natural life cycle of death and rebirth," Boyd said. "Crops die in the fall and come to life in the spring. People express the wonder of this ongoing phenomenon through mythological stories about gods dying and rising. These stories were always cast in a legendary form. They depicted events that happened 'once upon a time.'

"Contrast that with the depiction of Jesus Christ in the gospels. They talk about someone who actually lived several decades earlier, and they name names—crucified under Pontius Pilate, when Caiaphas was the high priest, and the father of Alexander and Rufus carried his cross, for example. That's concrete historical stuff. It has nothing in common with stories about what supposedly happened 'once upon a time.'

"And Christianity has nothing to do with life cycles or the harvest. It has to do with a very Jewish belief—which is absent from the mystery religions—about the resurrection of the dead and about life eternal and reconciliation with God.

"As for the suggestion that the New Testament doctrines of baptism or communion come from mystery religions, that's just nonsense. For one thing, the evidence for these supposed parallels comes after the second century, so any borrowing would have come from Christianity, not the other way around.

"And when you look carefully, the similarities vanish. For instance, to get to a higher level in the Mithra cult, followers had to stand under a bull while it was slain, so they could be bathed in its blood and guts. Then they'd join the others in eating the bull.

"Now, to suggest that Jews would find anything attractive about this and want to model baptism and communion after this barbaric practice is extremely implausible, which is why most scholars don't go for it."

SECRET GOSPELS AND TALKING CROSSES

As disorderly and disorganized as his office was, Boyd's mind was sharp and systematized. His analysis of these much touted parallels left little room for doubt. So I decided to advance to another area that the media often write about: the "new discoveries" that are often the subject of books by Jesus Seminar participants.

"There has been a lot written in the popular press about the Gospel of Thomas, Secret Mark, the Cross Gospel, and Q," I said. "Have there really been any new discoveries that change the way we should think about Jesus?"

Boyd sighed in exasperation. "No, there are no new discoveries that tell us anything new about Jesus. The Gospel of Thomas was discovered long ago, but it's only now being used to create an alternative Jesus. Some theories about the Gospel of Thomas may be new, but the gospel itself is not.

"As for Q, it's not a discovery but a theory that has been around for one and a half centuries, which tries to account for the material that Luke and Matthew have in common. What's new is the highly questionable way that left-wing scholars are using their presuppositions to slice this hypothetical Q into various layers of legendary development to back up their preconceived theories."

I knew that John Dominic Crossan, perhaps the most influential scholar in the Jesus Seminar, has made some strong claims about a gospel called Secret Mark. In fact, he asserts that Secret Mark may actually be an uncensored version of the gospel of Mark, containing confidential matters for spiritual insiders.[4] Some have used it to claim that Jesus was actually a magician or that a number of early Christians practiced homosexuality. This conspiratorial scenario has captured the media's imagination.

"What proof is there for this?" I asked Boyd.

His answer came quickly. "None," he said.

Though he apparently didn't see the need to elaborate, I asked him to explain what he meant.

"You see, we don't have Secret Mark," he said. "What we have is one scholar who found a quote from Clement of Alexandria, from late in the second century, that supposedly comes from this gospel. And now, mysteriously, even that is gone, disappeared.

"We don't have it, we don't have a quote from it, and even if we did have a quote from it, we don't have any reason to think that it has given us any valid information about the historical Jesus or what early Christians thought about him. On top of that, we already know that Clement had a track record of being very gullible in accepting spurious writings.

"So Secret Mark is a nonexistent work cited by a now nonexistent text by a late second-century writer who's known for being naive about these things. The vast majority of scholars don't give this any credibility. Unfortunately, those who do get a lot of press, because the media love the sensational."

Crossan also gives credence to what he calls the Cross Gospel. "Does that fare any better?" I asked.

"No, most scholars don't give it credibility, because it includes such outlandishly legendary material. For instance, Jesus comes out of his tomb and he's huge—he goes up beyond the sky—and the cross comes out of the tomb and actually talks! Obviously, the much more sober gospels are more reliable than anything found in this account. It fits better with later apocryphal writings. In fact, it's dependent on biblical material, so it should be dated later."

Unlike the overwhelming majority of biblical experts, the Jesus Seminar has accorded extremely high status to the Gospel of Thomas, elevating it to a place alongside the four traditional gospels. In chapter 3 Dr. Bruce Metzger strongly criticized that position as being unwarranted.

I asked Boyd for his opinion. "Why shouldn't Thomas be given that kind of honor?"

"Everyone concedes that this gospel has been significantly influenced by Gnosticism, which was a religious movement in the second, third, and fourth centuries that supposedly had secret insights, knowledge, or revelations that would allow people to know the key to the universe. Salvation was by what you knew—*gnosis* is Greek for 'know,'" he said.

"So most scholars date the Gospel of Thomas to the mid-second century, in which it fits well into the cultural milieu. Let me give you an example: Jesus is quoted as saying, 'Every woman who will make herself male will enter the kingdom of heaven.' That contradicts the attitude that we know Jesus had toward women, but it fits well with the Gnostic mind-set.

"However, the Jesus Seminar has arbitrarily latched onto certain passages of the Gospel of Thomas and has argued that these passages represent an early strand of tradition about Jesus, even earlier than the canonical gospels.

"Because none of these passages include Jesus making exalted claims for himself or doing supernatural feats, they argue that the earliest view of Jesus was that he was only a great teacher. But the whole line of reasoning is circular. The only reason for thinking these passages in Thomas are early in the first place is because they contain a view of Jesus that these scholars already believed was the original Jesus. In truth there is no good reason for preferring the second-century Gospel of Thomas over the first-century gospels of the New Testament."

HISTORY VERSUS FAITH

The Jesus of history and the Jesus of faith: the Jesus Seminar believes there's a big gulf between the two. In its view the historical Jesus was a bright, witty, countercultural man who never claimed to be the Son of God, while the Jesus of faith is a cluster of feel-good ideas that help people live right but are ultimately based on wishful thinking.

"There's not just a gulf between the Jesus of history and the Jesus of faith," Boyd said as I brought up this subject. "If you discredit everything that says Jesus is divine and reconciles people with God, there's an outright contradiction between the two.

"Generally speaking, they define the Jesus of faith this way: there are religious symbols that are quite meaningful to people—the symbol of Jesus being divine, of the cross, of self-sacrificial love, of the Resurrection. Even though people don't really believe that those things actually happened, they nevertheless can inspire people to live a good life, to overcome existential angst, to realize new potentialities, to resurrect hope in the midst of despair—blah, blah, blah."

He shrugged his shoulders. "Sorry," he said, "I've heard this stuff so much, it comes out my ears!

"So these liberals say historical research can't possibly discover the Jesus of faith, because the Jesus of faith is not rooted in history. He's merely a symbol," Boyd continued. "But listen: Jesus is not a symbol of anything unless he's rooted in history. The Nicene Creed doesn't say, 'We wish these things were true.' It says, 'Jesus Christ was crucified under Pontius Pilate, and the third day he rose again from the dead,' and it goes on from there.

"The theological truth is based on historical truth. That's the way the New Testament talks. Look at the sermon of Peter in the second chapter of Acts. He stands up and says, 'You guys are a witness of these things; they weren't done in secret. David's tomb is still with us, but God has raised Jesus from the dead. Therefore we proclaim him to be the Son of God.'

"Take away miracles and you take away the Resurrection, and then you've got nothing to proclaim. Paul said that if Jesus wasn't raised from the dead, our faith is futile, it's useless, it's empty."

Boyd stopped for a moment. His voice dropped a notch, from preaching mode to an intense expression of personal conviction.

"I don't want to base my life on a symbol," he said resolutely. "I want reality, and the Christian faith has always been rooted in reality. What's not rooted in reality is the faith of liberal scholars. They're the ones who are following a pipe dream, but Christianity is not a pipe dream."

COMBINING HISTORY AND FAITH

We had spent a lot of time talking about the Jesus of the Jesus Seminar—a symbolic Jesus, but one who's impotent to offer the world anything except the illusion of hope. But before we left, I wanted to hear about the Jesus of Gregory Boyd. I needed to know whether the Jesus he researches and writes scholarly books about as a theology professor is the same Jesus he preaches about in his church on Sunday mornings.

"Let me get this straight," I said. "Your Jesus—the Jesus you relate to—is both a Jesus of history *and* a Jesus of faith."

Boyd clenched his fist for emphasis, as if I'd just scored a touchdown. "Yes, that's it exactly, Lee!" he exclaimed. Moving to the very edge of his chair, he spelled out precisely what his scholarship—and his heart—have brought him to believe.

"It's like this: if you love a person, your love goes beyond the facts of that person, but it's rooted in the facts about that person. For example, you love your wife because she's gorgeous, she's nice, she's sweet, she's kind. All these things are facts about your wife, and therefore you love her.

"But your love goes beyond that. You can know all these things about your wife and not be in love with her and put your trust in her, but you do. So the decision goes beyond the evidence, yet it is there also on the basis of the evidence.

"So it is with falling in love with Jesus. To have a relationship with Jesus Christ goes beyond just knowing the historical facts about him, yet it's rooted in the historical facts about him. I believe in Jesus on the basis of the historical evidence, but my relationship with Jesus goes way beyond the evidence. I have to put my trust in him and walk with him on a daily basis."

I interrupted to say, "Yes, but will you acknowledge that Christianity makes some claims about Jesus that are just plain hard to believe?"

"Yes, of course I do," he replied. "That's why I'm glad we have such incredibly strong evidence to show us they're true.

"For me," he added, "it comes down to this: there's no competition. The evidence for Jesus being who the disciples said he was—for having done the miracles that he did, for rising from the dead, for making the claims that he did—is just light-years beyond my reasons for thinking that the left-wing scholarship of the Jesus Seminar is correct.

"What do these scholars have? Well, there's a brief allusion to a lost 'secret' gospel in a late-second-century letter that has unfortunately only been seen by one person and has now itself been lost. There's a third-century account of the Crucifixion and Resurrection that stars a talking cross and that less than a handful of scholars think predates the gospels. There's a second-century Gnostic document, parts of which some scholars now want to date early to back up their own preconceptions. And there is a hypothetical document built on shaky assumptions that is being sliced thinner and thinner by using circular reasoning."

Boyd flopped back in his chair. "No, I'm sorry," he said, shaking his head. "I don't buy it. It's far more reasonable to put my trust in the gospels—which pass the tests of historical scrutiny with flying colors—than to put my hope in what the Jesus Seminar is saying."

A CHORUS OF CRITICISM

Back at my motel, I mentally played back my interview with Boyd. I felt the same way he did: If the Jesus of faith is not also the Jesus of history, he's powerless and he's meaningless. Unless he's rooted in reality, unless he established his divinity by rising from the dead, he's just a feel-good symbol who's as irrelevant as Santa Claus.

But there's good evidence that he's more than that. I had already heard well-supported eyewitness, documentary, corroborating, and scientific evidence supporting the New Testament claim that he is God incarnate, and I was getting ready to hit the road again to dig out even more historical material about his character and resurrection.

Meanwhile Greg Boyd isn't a lone voice crying out against the Jesus Seminar. He's part of a growing crescendo of criticism coming not just from prominent conservative evangelicals but also from other well-respected scholars representing a wide variety of theological backgrounds.

An example was as close as my motel's nightstand, where I reached over to pick up a book called *The Real Jesus,* which I had recently purchased. Its author is Dr. Luke Timothy Johnson, the highly regarded professor of New Testament and Christian origins at the Candler School of Theology of Emory University. Johnson is a Roman Catholic who was a Benedictine monk before becoming a biblical scholar and writing a number of influential books.

Johnson systematically skewers the Jesus Seminar, saying it "by no means represents the cream of New Testament scholarship," it follows a process that is "biased against the authenticity of the gospel traditions," and its results were "already determined ahead of time."[5] He concludes, "This is not responsible, or even critical, scholarship. It is a self-indulgent charade."[6]

He goes on to quote other distinguished scholars with similar opinions, including Dr. Howard Clark Kee, who called the Seminar "an academic disgrace," and Richard Hayes of Duke University, whose review of *The Five Gospels* asserted that "the case argued by this book would not stand up in any court."[7]

I closed the book and turned off the light. Tomorrow I'd resume my hunt for evidence that *would* stand up.

Deliberations

Questions for Reflection or Group Study

1. Have you read news accounts of the Jesus Seminar's opinions? What was your response to what was reported? Did the articles give you the impression that the Seminar's findings represent the opinions of the majority of scholars? What dangers do you see in relying on the news media in reporting on issues of this kind?
2. As you conduct your own investigation of Jesus, should you rule out any possibility of the supernatural at the outset, or should you allow yourself to consider all the evidence of history, even if it points toward the miraculous as having occurred? Why?
3. Boyd said, "I don't want to base my life on a symbol. I want reality. . . ." Why do you agree or disagree? Is it enough that Jesus is a symbol of hope, or is it important for you to be confident that his life, teachings, and resurrection are rooted in history? Why?

For Further Evidence

More Resources on This Topic

Boyd, Gregory A. *Cynic Sage or Son of God? Recovering the Real Jesus in an Age of Revisionist Replies.* Wheaton, Ill.: BridgePoint, 1995.

______. *Jesus under Siege.* Wheaton, Ill.: Victor, 1995.

Johnson, Luke Timothy. *The Real Jesus.* San Francisco: HarperSanFrancisco, 1996.

Wilkins, Michael J., and J. P. Moreland, eds. *Jesus under Fire.* Grand Rapids: Zondervan, 1995.

PART 2

Analyzing Jesus

7

THE IDENTITY EVIDENCE

Was Jesus Really Convinced That He Was the Son of God?

John Douglas has an uncanny ability to look into the minds of people he has never met.

As the original "psychological profiler" for the Federal Bureau of Investigation, Douglas would gather information at a crime scene and then use his insights to peer inside the personality of the still-at-large perpetrator.

Case in point: Douglas predicted that the "Trailside Killer," a serial murderer who stalked wooded areas near San Francisco from 1979 to 1981, would be someone who had a speech impediment as well as tendencies toward animal cruelty, bed-wetting, and arson. Sure enough, the person finally arrested and convicted in the case fit those descriptions perfectly.[1]

With a doctorate in psychology, years of experience as a detective, and a natural talent for understanding human behavior, Douglas has become renowned for his profiling prowess. He has coauthored several best-sellers on the topic, and when Jodie Foster won the Oscar for her performance in *Silence of the Lambs,* she publicly thanked Douglas for being the real-life figure behind her character's FBI mentor.

How is Douglas able to understand the thinking process of individuals he has never even talked to? "Behavior reflects personality," Douglas explained to *Biography* magazine.[2]

In other words, Douglas closely examines the evidence left behind at the crime scene and, where possible, interviews victims to find out exactly what the criminal said and did. From these clues—the left-behind products of the person's behavior—he deduces the individual's psychological makeup.

Now to Jesus: without dialoguing with him, how can we possibly delve into his mind to determine what his motivations, intentions, and self-understanding were? How do we know who he thought he was and what he understood his mission to be?

By looking at his behavior, Douglas would say. If we want to figure out whether Jesus thought he was the Messiah or Son of God—or merely considered himself to be a rabbi or prophet—we need to look at what he did, what he said, and how he related to others.

The question of what Jesus thought about himself is a critical issue. Some professors maintain that the myth of Jesus' deity was superimposed on the Jesus tradition by overzealous supporters years after his death. The real Jesus, these professors believe, would roll over in his grave if he knew people were worshiping him. If you strip away the legends and go back to the earliest material about him, they say you'll find he never aspired to be anything more than an itinerant teacher and occasional rabble-rouser.

But is the evidence of history on their side? To find out, I flew to Lexington, Kentucky, and drove the winding roads past a series of picturesque horse farms to track down the scholar whose acclaimed book *The Christology of Jesus* confronts this very subject.

THE SIXTH INTERVIEW: BEN WITHERINGTON III, PH.D.

There isn't much to tiny Wilmore, Kentucky, except Asbury Theological Seminary, where I found Ben Witherington's office on the fourth floor of a colonial-style building off the rustic community's main drag. With the gracious hospitality of a Southern gentleman, the North Carolina native offered me a comfortable chair and some coffee as we sat down to discuss who Jesus of Nazareth thought he was.

The topic is familiar territory to Witherington, whose books include *Jesus the Sage; The Many Faces of the Christ; The Jesus Quest; Jesus, Paul, and the End of the World;* and *Women in the Ministry of Jesus* and whose articles about Jesus have appeared in specialized dictionaries and academic journals.

Educated at Gordon-Conwell Theological Seminary (master of divinity degree, summa cum laude) and the University of Durham in England (doctorate in theology with a concentration in New Testament), Witherington has taught at Asbury, Ashland Theological Seminary, the Divinity School of Duke University, and Gordon-Conwell. His memberships include the Society for the Study of the New Testament, the Society of Biblical Literature, and the Institute for Biblical Research.

Speaking distinctly and deliberately, weighing his words with care, Witherington definitely sounded like a scholar, yet his voice betrayed an unmistakable undercurrent of fascination—even awe—for his subject. This attitude emerged even further when he took me on a tour of a high-tech studio where he had been mixing images of Jesus with songs whose lyrics illuminate the compassion, the sacrifice, the humanity, and the majesty of his life and ministry.

For a scholar who writes heavily footnoted, cautiously nuanced, and academically precise prose on the technical issues involving Jesus, this artistic wedding of video and music is a poetic outlet for exploring the side of Jesus that only the creative arts can come close to capturing.

Back in Witherington's office, I decided to begin examining the issue of Jesus' self-understanding with a question that often springs to the minds of readers when they're exposed to the gospels for the first time.

"The truth is that Jesus was a bit mysterious about his identity, wasn't he?" I asked as Witherington pulled up a chair across from me. "He tended to shy away from forthrightly proclaiming himself to be the Messiah or Son of God. Was that because he didn't think of himself in those terms or because he had other reasons?"

"No, it's not because he didn't think of himself in those terms," Witherington said as he settled into his chair and crossed his legs. "If he had simply announced, 'Hi, folks; I'm God,' that would have been heard as 'I'm Yahweh,' because the Jews of his day didn't have any concept of the Trinity. They only knew of God the Father—whom they called Yahweh—and not God the Son or God the Holy Spirit.

"So if someone were to say he was God, that wouldn't have made any sense to them and would have been seen as clear-cut blasphemy. And it would have been counterproductive to Jesus in his efforts to get people to listen to his message.

"Besides, there were already a host of expectations about what the Messiah would look like, and Jesus didn't want to be pigeonholed into somebody else's categories. Consequently, he was very careful about what he said publicly. In private with his disciples—that was a different story, but the gospels primarily tell us about what he did in public."

EXPLORING THE EARLIEST TRADITIONS

It was a 1977 book by British theologian John Hick and half a dozen like-minded colleagues that prompted a firestorm of controversy by charging that Jesus never thought of himself as God incarnate or the Messiah. These concepts, they wrote, developed later and were written into the gospels so it appeared that Jesus was making these claims about himself.

To explore that allegation, Witherington has gone back to the very earliest traditions about Jesus—the most primitive material, unquestionably safe from legendary development—and discovered persuasive clues concerning how Jesus really regarded himself.

I wanted to delve into that research, starting with this question: "What clues can we find about Jesus' self-understanding from the way he related to others?"

Witherington thought for a moment, then replied, "Look at his relationship with his disciples. Jesus has twelve disciples, yet notice that he's not one of the Twelve."

While that may sound like a detail without a difference, Witherington said it's quite significant.

"If the Twelve represent a renewed Israel, where does Jesus fit in?" he asked. "He's not just part of Israel, not merely part of the redeemed group, he's forming the group—just as God in the Old Testament formed his people and set up the twelve tribes of Israel. That's a clue about what Jesus thought of himself."

Witherington went on to describe a clue that can be found in Jesus' relationship with John the Baptist. "Jesus says, 'Of all people born of woman, John is the greatest man on earth.' Having said that, he then goes even further in his ministry than the Baptist did—by doing miracles, for example. What does that say about what he thinks of himself?

"And his relationship with the religious leaders is perhaps the most revealing. Jesus makes the truly radical statement that it's not what enters a person that defiles him but what comes out of his heart. Frankly, this sets aside huge portions of the Old Testament book of Leviticus, with its meticulous rules concerning purity.

"Now, the Pharisees didn't like this message. They wanted to keep things as they were, but Jesus said, 'No, God has further plans.

He's doing a new thing.' We have to ask, What kind of person thinks he has the authority to set aside the divinely inspired Jewish Scriptures and supplant them with his own teaching?

"And what about his relationship—if we can call it that—with the Roman authorities? We have to ask why they crucified him. If he had merely been an innocuous sage telling nice little parables, how did he end up on a cross, especially at a Passover season, when no Jew wants any Jew to be executed? There had to be a reason why the sign above his head said, 'This is the King of the Jews.'"

Witherington let that last comment hang in the air, before providing the explanation himself: "Either Jesus had made that verbal claim," he said, "or someone clearly thought he did."

BY THE FINGER OF GOD

While Jesus' relationships provide one window into his self-understanding, Witherington said that Jesus' deeds—especially his miracles—offer additional insights. However, I raised my hand to stop him.

"Certainly you can't say that Jesus' miracles establish that he thought he was God," I said, "since later his own disciples went out and did the same things—and certainly they weren't making claims of deity."

"No, it's not the fact that Jesus did miracles that illuminates his self-understanding," replied Witherington. "What's important is how he interprets his miracles."

"What do you mean?" I asked.

"Jesus says, 'If I, by the finger of God, cast out demons, then you will know that the kingdom of God has come upon you.' He's not like other miracle workers who do amazing things and then life proceeds as it always has. No—to Jesus, his miracles are a sign indicating the coming of the kingdom of God. They are a foretaste of what the kingdom is going to be like. And that sets Jesus apart."

Again I interrupted. "Elaborate on that a bit," I said. "How does it set him apart?"

"Jesus sees his miracles as bringing about something unprecedented—the coming of God's dominion," replied Witherington. "He doesn't merely see himself as a worker of miracles; he sees himself as the one in whom and through whom the promises of God come to pass. And that's a not-too-thinly-veiled claim of transcendence."

I nodded. Now his point made sense to me. With that I turned to the words of Jesus, in search of more clues concerning his self-understanding.

"He was called *Rabbouni,* or 'Rabbi,' by his followers," I said. "Doesn't this imply that he merely taught like the other rabbis of his day?"

Witherington grinned. "Actually," he said, "Jesus taught in a radical new way. He begins his teachings with the phrase 'Amen I say to you,' which is to say, 'I swear in advance to the truthfulness of what I'm about to say.' This was absolutely revolutionary."

"How so?" I asked.

He replied, "In Judaism you needed the testimony of two witnesses, so witness A could witness the truth of witness B and vice versa. But Jesus witnesses to the truth of his own sayings. Instead of basing his teaching on the authority of others, he speaks on his own authority.

"So here is someone who considered himself to have authority above and beyond what the Old Testament prophets had. He believed he possessed not only divine inspiration, as King David did, but also divine authority and the power of direct divine utterance."

In addition to employing the "Amen" phrase in his teaching, Jesus used the term "Abba" when he was relating to God. "What does that tell us about what he thought about himself?" I asked.

"'Abba' connotes intimacy in a relationship between a child and his father," Witherington explained. "Interestingly, it's also the term disciples used for a beloved teacher in early Judaism. But Jesus used it of God—and as far as I can tell, he and his followers were the only ones praying to God that way."

When I asked Witherington to expand on the importance of this, he said, "In the context in which Jesus operated, it was customary for Jews to work around having to say the name of God. His name was the most holy word you could speak, and they even feared mispronouncing it. If they were going to address God, they might say something like, 'The Holy One, blessed be he,' but they were not going to use his personal name."

"And 'Abba' is a personal term," I said.

"Very personal," he replied. "It's the term of endearment in which a child would say to a parent, 'Father Dearest, what would you have me do?'"

However, I spotted an apparent inconsistency. "Wait a second," I interjected. "Praying 'Abba' must not imply that Jesus thinks he's God, because he taught his disciples to use the same term in their own prayers, and they're not God."

"Actually," came Witherington's reply, "the significance of 'Abba' is that Jesus is the initiator of an intimate relationship that was previously unavailable. The question is, What kind of person can change the terms of relating to God? What kind of person can initiate a new covenental relationship with God?"

His distinction made sense to me. "So how significant do you consider Jesus' use of 'Abba' to be?" I asked.

"Quite significant," he answered. "It implies that Jesus had a degree of intimacy with God that is unlike anything in the Judaism of his day. And listen, here's the kicker: Jesus is saying that only through having a relationship with him does this kind of prayer language—this kind of 'Abba' relationship with God—become possible. That says volumes about how he regarded himself."

Witherington started to add another important clue—Jesus' repeated reference to himself as the "Son of Man"—but I let him know that a previous expert, Craig Blomberg, had already explained that this was a reference to Daniel 7. This term, Witherington agreed, is extremely important in revealing Jesus' messianic or transcendent self-understanding.

At this point I paused to take stock of what Witherington had said. When I put together the clues from Jesus' relationships, miracles, and words, his perception of his identity came into sharp focus.

There seemed little question, based upon the earliest evidence, that Jesus considered himself to be more than a doer of great deeds, more than a teacher, more than another prophet in a line of many. There was ample evidence to conclude that he thought of himself in unique and supreme terms—but exactly how sweeping was this self-understanding?

JOHN'S PORTRAIT OF JESUS

In its opening scene the gospel of John uses majestic and unambiguous language to boldly assert the deity of Jesus.

> In the beginning was the Word, and the Word was with God, and the Word was God. He was with God in the beginning.

> Through him all things were made; without him nothing was made that has been made. . . . The Word became flesh and made his dwelling among us. We have seen his glory, the glory of the One and Only, who came from the Father, full of grace and truth.
>
> John 1:1–3, 14

I remember reading that regal introduction when I went through the gospel of John for the first time. I recall asking myself, I wonder how Jesus would respond if he were to read John's words about him? Would he recoil and say, "Whoa, John has got me all wrong! He has embellished and mythologized me to the point where I don't even recognize myself"? Or would he nod approvingly and say, "Yep, I'm all that—and more"?

Later I encountered the words of scholar Raymond Brown, who had come to his own conclusion: "I have no difficulty with the thesis that if Jesus . . . could have read John he would have found that gospel a suitable expression of his identity."[3]

Now here was my chance to hear directly from Witherington, who has spent a lifetime analyzing the scholarly minutiae concerning Jesus' self-perception, about whether he agrees with Brown's assessment.

There was no hesitation and no equivocation. "Yes, I do," he said. "I don't have a problem with that. When you're dealing with the gospel of John, you're dealing with a somewhat interpreted picture of Jesus, but I also believe it's a logical drawing out of what was implicit in the historical Jesus.

"And I'll add this: even if you eliminate the gospel of John, there's still no non-messianic Jesus to be conjured up out of the material in the other three gospels. It's just not there."

Immediately I thought of the famous exchange, recorded in Matthew, in which Jesus asked his disciples in a private meeting, "Who do you say I am?" Peter replied with clarity, "You are the Christ, the Son of the living God." Instead of ducking the issue, Jesus affirmed Peter for his observation. "Blessed are you," he said, "for this was not revealed to you by man, but by my Father in heaven." (See Matt. 16:15–17.)

Even so, some popular depictions of Jesus, such as in the movie *The Last Temptation of Christ,* show him as basically uncertain about his identity and mission. He's saddled with ambiguity and angst.

"Is there any evidence," I asked Witherington, "that Jesus ever had an identity crisis?"

"Not an identity crisis, although I do believe he had points of identity confirmation," the professor replied. "At his baptism, at his temptation, at the Transfiguration, in the Garden of Gethsemane—these are crisis moments in which God confirmed to him who he was and what his mission was.

"For instance, I don't think it's accidental that his ministry does not begin in earnest until after his baptism, when he hears the voice saying, 'You are my Son, with whom I am well pleased.'"

"What did he think his mission was?"

"He saw his job as coming to free the people of God, so his mission was directed to Israel."

"Specifically to Israel," I stressed.

"Yes, that's correct," Witherington said. "There's very little evidence that he sought out Gentiles during his ministry—that was a mission for the later church. You see, the promises of the prophets had come to Israel—and to Israel he must go."

"I AND THE FATHER ARE ONE"

In his book *Reasonable Faith* William Lane Craig points to a substantial amount of evidence that within twenty years of the Crucifixion there was a full-blown Christology proclaiming Jesus as God incarnate.

Church historian Jaroslav Pelikan has pointed out that the oldest Christian sermon, the oldest account of a Christian martyr, the oldest pagan report of the church, and the oldest liturgical prayer (1 Cor. 16:22) all refer to Jesus as Lord and God. Pelikan said, "Clearly, it was the message of what the church believed and taught that 'God' was an appropriate name for Jesus Christ."[4]

In light of this, I asked Witherington, "Do you see any possible way this could have developed—especially so soon—if Jesus had never made transcendent and messianic claims about himself?"

Witherington was adamant. "Not unless you're prepared to argue that the disciples completely forgot what the historical Jesus was like and that they had nothing to do with the traditions that start showing up twenty years after his death," he said. "Frankly, as a historian, this would not make any sense at all."

In dealing with history, he added, all sorts of things are possible, but not all possible things are equally probable.

"Is it probable," he asked, "that all this stuff was conjured up out of thin air within twenty years after Jesus died, when there were still living witnesses to what Jesus the historical figure was really like? I find that just about as unlikely a historical hypothesis as you could possibly come up with.

"The real issue is, what happened after the crucifixion of Jesus that changed the minds of the disciples, who had denied, disobeyed, and deserted Jesus? Very simply, something happened to them that was similar to what Jesus experienced at his baptism—it was confirmed to them that what they had hoped Jesus was, he was."

And what exactly was he? As I was wrapping up my time with Witherington, I wanted him to sum it up for me. Taking all his research into consideration, what was his personal conclusion about who Jesus saw himself to be? I posed the question, sat back, and let him spell it out—which he did, with eloquence and conviction.

"Jesus thought he was the person appointed by God to bring in the climactic saving act of God in human history. He believed he was the agent of God to carry that out—that he had been authorized by God, empowered by God, he spoke for God, and he was directed by God to do this task. So what Jesus said, God said. What Jesus did was the work of God.

"Under the Jewish concept of agency, 'a man's agent is as himself.' Remember how Jesus sent out his apostles and said, 'Whatever they do to you, they've done to me'? There was a strong connection between a man and his agent whom he sends on a mission.

"Well, Jesus believed he was on a divine mission, and the mission was to redeem the people of God. The implication is that the people of God were lost and that God had to do something—as he had always done—to intervene and set them back on the right track. But there was a difference this time. This was the last time. This was the last chance.

"Did Jesus believe he was the Son of God, the anointed one of God? The answer is yes. Did he see himself as the Son of Man? The answer is yes. Did he see himself as the final Messiah? Yes, that's the way he viewed himself. Did he believe that anybody less than God could save the world? No, I don't believe he did.

"And here's where the paradox gets as quizzical as it can possibly get: the way God was going to save the world was by his Son dying. The most human of all human acts—to die.

"Now, God, in his divine nature, doesn't die. So how was God going to get this done? How was God going to be the Savior of the human race? He had to come as a human being to accomplish that task. And Jesus believed he was the one to do it.

"Jesus said in Mark 10:45, 'I did not come to be served but to serve and give my life as a ransom in place of the many.' This is either the highest form of megalomania or it's the example of somebody who really believes, as he said, 'I and the Father are one.' In other words, 'I have the authority to speak for the Father; I have the power to act for the Father; if you reject me, you've rejected the Father.'

"Even if you eliminated the fourth gospel and just read the synoptics, this would still be the conclusion you would come to. And it is the conclusion that Jesus would have led us to if we had a Bible study and asked him this question.

"We have to ask, Why is there no other first-century Jew who has millions of followers today? Why isn't there a John the Baptist movement? Why, of all first-century figures, including the Roman emperors, is Jesus still worshiped today, while the others have crumbled into the dust of history?

"It's because this Jesus—the historical Jesus—is also the living Lord. That's why. It's because he's still around, while the others are long gone."

IN THE VERY PLACE OF GOD

Like Witherington, many other scholars have painstakingly picked apart the earliest evidence for Jesus and reached the same conclusions.

Wrote Craig, "Here is a man who thought of himself as the Son of God in a unique sense, who claimed to act and speak with divine authority, who held himself to be a worker of miracles, and who believed that people's eternal destiny hinged on whether or not they believed in him."[5]

Then he added a remark that's especially startling: "The clues sufficient for a high Christological self-understanding of Jesus are present even in the attenuated twenty percent of Jesus' sayings recognized by the members of the Jesus Seminar as authentic."[6]

The evidence for concluding that Jesus intended to stand in the very place of God is "absolutely convincing," concurred theologian Royce Gordon Gruenler.[7]

So extraordinary is Jesus' assertion, said Craig, that inevitably the issue of his sanity has to come up. He notes that after James Dunn completed his own epic study of this issue, Dunn was compelled to comment, "One last question cannot be ignored: *Was Jesus mad?*"[8]

At the airport in Lexington, waiting for my flight back to Chicago, I dropped coins into a pay phone and called for an appointment to interview one of the country's leading experts on psychology.

It was time to find out.

Deliberations

Questions for Reflection or Group Study

1. What, do you think, are some reasons why Jesus was evasive in disclosing who he was to the public? Can you imagine some ways in which an early proclamation of his deity could have harmed his mission?
2. What are some of the difficulties we face in determining what historical figures thought about themselves? What clues would you find most helpful in trying to determine this? Why did the clues offered by Witherington convince or fail to persuade you that Jesus thought he was God and the Messiah?
3. Jesus taught his disciples to use the term "Abba," or "Dearest Father," in addressing God. What does this tell you about Jesus' relationship with the Father? Is that kind of relationship attractive to you? Why or why not?

For Further Evidence

More Resources on This Topic

Craig, William Lane. "The Self-Understanding of Jesus." In *Reasonable Faith,* by William Lane Craig, 233–54. Westchester, Ill.: Crossway, 1994.

Marshall, I. Howard. *The Origins of New Testament Christology.* Downers Grove, Ill.: InterVarsity Press, 1976.

Moule, C. F. D. *The Origins of Christology.* Cambridge: Cambridge Univ. Press, 1977.

Witherington, Ben, III. *The Christology of Jesus.* Minneapolis: Fortress, 1990.

8

THE PSYCHOLOGICAL EVIDENCE

Was Jesus Crazy When He Claimed to Be the Son of God?

> When a psychologist or psychiatrist testifies, he shall wear a cone-shaped hat that is not less than two feet tall. The surface of the hat shall be imprinted with stars and lightning bolts. Additionally, he shall be required to don a white beard that is not less than eighteen inches in length and shall punctuate crucial elements of his testimony by stabbing the air with a wand. Whenever a psychologist or psychiatrist provides testimony, the bailiff shall contemporaneously dim the courtroom lights and administer two strikes to a Chinese gong.

By suggesting this amendment to the state statutes in 1997, New Mexico state senator Duncan Scott left no doubt about his attitude toward experts who testify that defendants are insane and therefore not legally responsible for their crimes. Apparently, Scott's cynicism was shared by a majority of his colleagues—they voted to approve his tongue-in-cheek proposal! The joke got as far as the House of Representatives, which eventually blocked it from becoming law.[1]

Admittedly, there's an undercurrent of skepticism in courthouses over psychiatrists and psychologists who testify concerning the mental state of defendants, their ability to cooperate with their attorney in preparing their defense, and whether they were legally insane at the time they committed their crime. Even so, most lawyers recognize that mental health professionals offer important insights for the criminal justice system.

I recall a case in which a mild-mannered housewife stood accused of murdering her husband. At first glance she appeared no different from anybody's mother—well dressed, pleasant, kindly, looking as if she had just emerged from baking a fresh batch of chocolate chip cookies for the neighborhood children. I scoffed when a psychologist testified she was mentally unable to stand trial.

Then her lawyer put her on the witness stand. Initially her testimony was clear, rational, and lucid. However, slowly it became more and more bizarre as she described, calmly and with great seriousness, how she had been assaulted by a succession of famous individuals, including Dwight Eisenhower and the ghost of Napoleon. By the time she finished, nobody in the courtroom doubted that she was totally out of touch with reality. The judge committed her to a mental institution until she was well enough to face the charges against her.

Looks can be deceiving. It's the psychologist's job to peer beneath the defendant's veneer and draw conclusions concerning his or her mental condition. It's an inexact science, which means mistakes and even abuses can occur, but overall psychological testimony provides important safeguards for defendants.

How does all this relate to Jesus? In the preceding chapter Dr. Ben Witherington III offered convincing evidence that even the earliest material about Jesus showed he was claiming to be God incarnate. That naturally raises the issue of whether Jesus was crazy when he made those assertions.

In search of an expert's assessment of Jesus' mental state, I drove to a suburban Chicago office building to elicit testimony from one of the country's leading authorities on psychological issues.

THE SEVENTH INTERVIEW: GARY R. COLLINS, PH.D.

With a master's degree in psychology from the University of Toronto and a doctorate in clinical psychology from Purdue University, Collins has been studying, teaching, and writing about human behavior for thirty-five years. He was a professor of psychology at Trinity Evangelical Divinity School for two decades, most of that time as chairman of its psychology division.

A live wire with boundless energy and enthusiasm, Collins is a prolific author. He has written nearly 150 articles for journals and other periodicals and currently is editor of *Christian Counseling Today* and contributing editor of the *Journal of Psychology and Theology*.

He also has produced an astounding forty-five books on psychology-related topics, including *The Magnificent Mind; Family*

Shock; Can You Trust Psychology?; and the classic textbook *Christian Counseling: A Comprehensive Guide*. In addition, he was general editor of the thirty-volume *Resources for Christian Counseling*, a series of books for mental health professionals.

I found Collins in his bright and airy office at the American Association of Christian Counselors, a fifteen-thousand-member society of which he is the president. With salt-and-pepper hair and silver-rimmed glasses, he was looking dapper in a maroon turtleneck sweater, herringbone sports jacket, and gray slacks (but sorry, no pointy hat or flowing white beard).

I started our interview by gesturing out the window, where snow was gently falling on evergreen trees. "A few miles in that direction is a state mental institution," I said. "If we were to go over there, I'm sure we'd find some people who claim that they're God. We'd say they were insane. Jesus said he was God—was he crazy, too?"

"If you want the short answer," Collins said with a chuckle, "it's no."

But, I insisted, this is a legitimate topic that's worthy of further analysis. Experts say that people suffering from delusional psychosis may appear rational much of the time yet can have grandiose beliefs that they are superlative individuals. Some can even attract followers who believe they're geniuses. Maybe that's what happened with Jesus, I suggested.

"Well, it's true that people with psychological difficulties will often claim to be somebody they're not," Collins replied as he clasped his hands behind his head. "They'll sometimes claim to be Jesus himself or the president of the United States or someone else famous—like Lee Strobel," he quipped.

"However," he continued, "psychologists don't just look at what a person says. They'll go much deeper than that. They'll look at a person's emotions, because disturbed individuals frequently show inappropriate depression, or they might be vehemently angry, or perhaps they're plagued with anxiety. But look at Jesus: he never demonstrated inappropriate emotions. For instance, he cried at the death of his friend Lazarus—that's natural for an emotionally healthy individual."

"He certainly got angry at times," I asserted.

"Yes, he did, but it was a healthy kind of anger at people taking advantage of the downtrodden by lining their pockets at the temple. He wasn't just irrationally ticked off because someone was annoying him; this was a righteous reaction against injustice and the blatant mistreatment of people.

"Other deluded people will have misperceptions," he added. "They think people are watching them or are trying to get them when they're not. They're out of contact with reality. They misperceive the actions of other people and accuse them of doing things they have no intention of ever doing. Again, we don't see this in Jesus. He was obviously in contact with reality. He wasn't paranoid, although he rightfully understood that there were some very real dangers around him.

"Or people with psychological difficulties may have thinking disorders—they can't carry on a logical conversation, they'll jump to faulty conclusions, they're irrational. We don't see this in Jesus. He spoke clearly, powerfully, and eloquently. He was brilliant and had absolutely amazing insights into human nature.

"Another sign of mental disturbances is unsuitable behavior, such as dressing oddly or being unable to relate socially to others. Jesus' behavior was quite in line with what would be expected, and he had deep and abiding relationships with a wide variety of people from different walks of life."

He paused, although I sensed he wasn't finished yet. I prompted him to continue by asking, "What else do you observe about him?"

Collins gazed out the window at the beautiful and peaceful snow-blanketed landscape. When he resumed, it was as if he were reminiscing about an old friend.

"He was loving but didn't let his compassion immobilize him; he didn't have a bloated ego, even though he was often surrounded by adoring crowds; he maintained balance despite an often demanding lifestyle; he always knew what he was doing and where he was going; he cared deeply about people, including women and children, who weren't seen as being important back then; he was able to accept people while not merely winking at their sin; he responded to individuals based on where they were at and what they uniquely needed."

"So, Doctor—your diagnosis?" I asked.

"All in all, I just don't see signs that Jesus was suffering from any known mental illness," he concluded, adding with a smile, "He was much healthier than anyone else I know—including me!"

"RAVING MAD"

Granted, as we look back through history, we don't see obvious signs of delusion in Jesus. But what about people who were directly interacting with him? What did they see from their much closer vantage point?

"Some people who were on the scene in the first century would vehemently disagree with you," I pointed out to Collins. "They did conclude that Jesus was crazy. John 10:20 tells us that many Jews thought he was 'demon-possessed and raving mad.' Those are strong words!"

"Yes, but that's hardly a diagnosis by a trained mental health professional," Collins countered. "Look at what prompted those words—Jesus' moving and profound teaching about being the Good Shepherd. They were reacting because his assertions about himself were so far beyond their understanding of the norm, not because Jesus was truly mentally unbalanced.

"And notice that their comments were immediately challenged by others, who said in verse 21, 'These are not the sayings of a man possessed by a demon. Can a demon open the eyes of the blind?'"

"Why is that significant?" I asked.

"Because Jesus wasn't just making outrageous claims about himself. He was backing them up with miraculous acts of compassion, like healing the blind.

"You see, if I claimed to be the president of the United States, that would be crazy. You'd look at me and see none of the trappings of the office of president. I wouldn't look like the president. People wouldn't accept my authority as president. No Secret Service agents would be guarding me. But if the real president claimed to be president, that wouldn't be crazy, because he *is* president and there would be plenty of confirming evidence of that.

"In an analogous way, Jesus didn't just claim to be God—he backed it up with amazing feats of healing, with astounding demonstrations of power over nature, with transcendent and unprecedented teaching, with divine insights into people, and ultimately with his own resurrection from the dead, which absolutely nobody else has been able to duplicate. So when Jesus claimed to be God, it wasn't crazy. It was the truth."

However, Collins' appeal to Jesus' miracles opened the door to other objections. "Some people have tried to shoot down these miracles that supposedly help authenticate Jesus' claim to being the Son of God," I said, pulling out a book from my briefcase. I read him the words of skeptic Charles Templeton.

> Many illnesses, then as now, were psychosomatic, and could be "cured" when the sufferer's perception changed. Just as today a placebo prescribed by a physician in whom the patient

has faith can effect an apparent cure, so, in an early time, faith in the healer could banish adverse symptoms. With each success the healer's reputation would grow and his powers would, as a consequence, become more efficacious.[2]

"Does this," I demanded, "explain away the miracles that supposedly back up Jesus' claim to being the Son of God?"

Collins' reaction surprised me. "I wouldn't have a whole lot of disagreement with what Templeton wrote," Collins replied.

"You wouldn't?"

"Not really. Might Jesus have sometimes healed by suggestion? I have no problem with that. Sometimes people can have a psychologically induced illness, and if they get a new purpose for living, a new direction, they don't need the illness anymore.

"The placebo effect? If you think you're going to get better, you often do get better. That's a well-established medical fact. And when people came to Jesus, they believed he could heal them, so he did. But the fact remains: regardless of how he did it, Jesus did heal them.

"Of course," he quickly added, "that doesn't explain all of Jesus' healings. Often a psychosomatic healing takes time; Jesus' healings were spontaneous. Many times people who are healed psychologically have their symptoms return a few days later, but we don't see any evidence of this. And Jesus healed conditions like lifelong blindness and leprosy, for which a psychosomatic explanation isn't very likely.

"On top of that, he brought people back from the dead—and death is not a psychologically induced state! Plus you have all of his nature miracles—the calming of the sea, turning water into wine. They defy naturalistic answers."

Well . . . maybe. However, Collins' mention of the miracle of turning water into wine brought up another possible explanation of Jesus' amazing feats.

JESUS THE HYPNOTIST

Have you ever seen a stage hypnotist give water to someone they've put in a trance and then suggest to them that they were drinking wine? They smack their lips, they get giddy, they start feeling intoxicated, just as if they were swigging a cheap Bordeaux.

British author Ian Wilson has raised the question of whether this is how Jesus convinced the wedding guests at Cana that he had transformed jugs of water into the finest fermented libation.

In fact, Wilson discusses the possibility that Jesus may have been a master hypnotist, which could explain the supposedly supernatural aspects of his life. For instance, hypnosis could account for his exorcisms; his transfiguration, during which three of his followers saw his face glow and his garments shine as white as light; and even his healings. As evidence, Wilson cites the modern example of a sixteen-year-old boy whose serious skin disorder was inexplicably healed through hypnotic suggestion.

Perhaps Lazarus wasn't really brought back from the dead. Couldn't he have been in a deathlike trance that had been induced by hypnosis? As for the Resurrection, Jesus "could have effectively conditioned [the disciples] to hallucinate his appearances in response to certain pre-arranged cues (the breaking of bread?) for a predetermined period after his death," Wilson speculated.[3]

This would even explain the enigmatic reference in the gospels to Jesus' inability to perform many miracles in his hometown of Nazareth. Said Wilson,

> Jesus failed precisely where *as a hypnotist* we would most expect him to fail, among those who knew him best, those who had seen him grow up as an ordinary child. Largely responsible for any hypnotist's success rate are the awe and mystery with which he surrounds himself, and these essential factors would have been entirely lacking in Jesus' home town.[4]

"You have to admit," I said to Collins, "that this is a rather interesting way of trying to explain away Jesus' miracles."

There was a look of incredulity on his face. "This guy has a whole lot more faith in hypnosis than I do!" he exclaimed. "While it's a clever argument, it just doesn't stand up to analysis. It's full of holes."

One by one, Collins began to enumerate them. "First, there's the problem of a whole bunch of people being hypnotized. Not everybody is equally susceptible.

"Stage hypnotists will talk in a certain soothing tone of voice to the audience and watch for people who seem to be responding, and then they'll pick these people as their volunteers, because they're readily susceptible to hypnosis. In a big group many people are resistant. When Jesus multiplied the bread and fish, there were five thousand witnesses. How could he have hypnotized them all?

"Second, hypnosis doesn't generally work on people who are skeptics and doubters. So how did Jesus hypnotize his brother James, who doubted him but later saw the resurrected Christ? How did he hypnotize Saul of Tarsus, the opponent of Christianity who never even met Jesus until he saw him after his resurrection? How did he hypnotize Thomas, who was so skeptical he wouldn't believe in the Resurrection until he put his fingers in the nail holes in Jesus' hands?

"Third, concerning the Resurrection, hypnosis wouldn't explain the empty tomb.

I jumped in. "I suppose someone could claim that the disciples had been hypnotized to imagine the tomb was empty," I offered.

"Even if that were possible," Collins replied, "Jesus certainly couldn't have hypnotized the Pharisees and Roman authorities, and they would have gladly produced his body if it had remained in the tomb. The fact that they didn't tells us the tomb was really empty.

"Fourth, look at the miracle of turning water into wine. Jesus never addressed the wedding guests. He didn't even suggest to the servants that the water had been turned into wine—he merely told them to take some water to the master of the banquet. He's the one who tasted it and said it was wine, with no prior prompting.

"Fifth, the skin healing that Wilson talks about wasn't spontaneous, was it?"

Actually, I said, the *British Medical Journal* says it took five days after the hypnosis for the reptilian skin, called ichthyosis, to fall off the teenager's left arm, and several more days for the skin to appear normal. The hypnotic success rate for dealing with other parts of his body over a period of several weeks was 50 to 95 percent.[5]

"Compare that," Collins said, "with Jesus healing ten lepers in Luke 17. They were instantaneously healed—and 100 percent. That's not explainable merely by hypnosis. And neither is his healing of a man with a shriveled hand in Mark 3. Even if people were in a trance and merely thought his hand had been healed, eventually they would have found out the truth. Hypnosis doesn't last a real long time.

"And finally, the gospels record all sorts of details about what Jesus said and did, but never once do they portray him as saying or doing anything that would suggest he was hypnotizing people. I could go on and on."

I laughed. "I told you it was an interesting explanation; I didn't say it was convincing!" I said. "Yet books are being written to advance these kinds of ideas."

"It's just amazing to me," Collins replied, "how people will grasp at anything to try to disprove Jesus' miracles."

JESUS THE EXORCIST

Before we finished our interview, I wanted to tap into Collins' psychological expertise in one more area that skeptics find troubling.

"Jesus was an exorcist," I observed. "He talked to demons and cast them out of the people they supposedly possessed. But is it really rational to believe that evil spirits are responsible for some illnesses and bizarre behavior?"

Collins wasn't disturbed by the question. "From my theological beliefs, I accept that demons exist," he replied. "We live in a society in which many people believe in angels. They know there are spiritual forces out there, and it's not too hard to conclude that some might be malevolent. Where you see God working, sometimes those forces are more active, and that's what was probably going on in the time of Jesus."

I noticed Collins had referred to his theological beliefs and not his clinical experience. "Have you, as a psychologist, ever seen clear evidence of the demonic?" I asked.

"I haven't personally, but then I haven't spent my whole career in clinical settings," he said. "My friends in clinical work have said that sometimes they have seen this, and these are not people who are inclined to see a demon behind every problem. They tend to be skeptical. The psychiatrist M. Scott Peck wrote a bit about this kind of thing in his book *People of the Lie*."[6]

I pointed out that Ian Wilson, in suggesting that Jesus may have used hypnosis to cure people who only believed they were possessed, said dismissively that no "realistic individual" would explain a state of possession "as the work of real demons."[7]

"To some degree, you find what you set out to find," Collins said in response. "People who deny the existence of the supernatural will find some way, no matter how far-fetched, to explain a situation apart from the demonic. They'll keep giving medication, keep drugging the person, but he or she doesn't get better. There are cases that don't respond to normal medical or psychiatric treatment."

"Could Jesus' exorcisms really have been psychosomatic healings?" I asked.

"Yes, in some cases, but again you have to look at the whole context. What about the man who was possessed and Jesus sent the demons into the pigs and the pigs ran off the cliff? What's going on if that was a psychosomatic situation? I think Jesus really did drive out demons, and I think some people do that today.

"At the same time, we shouldn't be too quick to jump to a demonic conclusion when faced with a recalcitrant problem. As C. S. Lewis put it, there are two equal and opposite errors we can fall into concerning demons: 'One is to disbelieve in their existence. The other is to believe, and to feel an excessive and unhealthy interest in them. They themselves are equally pleased with both errors.'"[8]

"You know, Gary, that idea might fly with the American Association of Christian Counselors, but would secular psychologists consider it rational to believe in the demonic?" I asked.

I thought Collins might take offense at the question, which came out sounding more condescending than I had intended, but he didn't.

"It's interesting how things are changing," he mused. "Our society today is caught up in 'spirituality.' That's a term that can mean almost anything, but it does recognize the supernatural. It's very interesting what psychologists are believing in these days. Some are into Eastern mystical stuff; some talk about the power of shamans to influence people's lives.

"Whereas twenty-five years ago the suggestion of demonic activity would have been immediately dismissed, many psychologists are beginning to recognize that maybe there are more things in heaven and earth than our philosophies can account for."

"PREPOSTEROUS IMAGINATION!"

Collins and I had drifted a bit from the original point of our interview. As I thought about our talk while I was driving home, I returned to the central issue that had brought me to him: Jesus claimed to be God. Nobody is suggesting he was intentionally deceptive. And now Collins has concluded, based on thirty-five years of psychological experience, that he was not mentally impaired.

However, that left me with a new question: Did Jesus fulfill the attributes of God? After all, it's one thing to claim divinity; it's quite another to embody the characteristics that make God, God.

At a stoplight, I pulled a notebook out of my briefcase and scrawled a note to myself: *Track down D. A. Carson*. I knew that I'd want to talk to one of the country's leading theologians about this next matter.

In the meantime my talk with Gary Collins prompted me to spend time that night carefully rereading the discourses of Jesus. I could detect no sign of dementia, delusions, or paranoia. On the contrary, I was moved once more by his profound wisdom, his uncanny insights, his poetic eloquence, and his deep compassion. Historian Philip Schaff said it better than I can.

> Is such an intellect—clear as the sky, bracing as the mountain air, sharp and penetrating as a sword, thoroughly healthy and vigorous, always ready and always self-possessed—liable to a radical and most serious delusion concerning his own character and mission? *Preposterous imagination!*[9]

Deliberations

Questions for Reflection or Group Study

1. What are some of the differences between a patient in a mental hospital claiming to be God and Jesus making the same assertion about himself?
2. Read Jesus' teaching called the Beatitudes in Matthew 5:1–12. What observations can you make about his intellect, eloquence, compassion, insight into human nature, ability to teach profound truths, and overall psychological health?
3. Having read Collins' response to the theory that hypnosis can account for Jesus' miracles, do you believe this is a viable hypothesis? Why or why not?

For Further Evidence

More Resources on This Topic

Collins, Gary R. *Can You Trust Psychology?* Downers Grove, Ill.: InterVarsity Press, 1988.

______. *Christian Counseling: A Comprehensive Guide.* Waco, Tex.: Word, 1988.

______. *The Soul Search.* Nashville: Nelson, 1998.

Lewis, C. S. *The Screwtape Letters.* London: Collins-Fontana, 1942.

9

THE PROFILE EVIDENCE

Did Jesus Fulfill the Attributes of God?

Shortly after eight student nurses were murdered in a Chicago apartment, the trembling lone survivor huddled with a police sketch artist and described in detail the killer she had seen from her secret vantage point beneath a bed.

Quickly the drawing was flashed around the city—to police officers, to hospitals, to transit stations, to the airport. Soon an emergency room physician called detectives to say he was treating a man who looked suspiciously like the flinty-eyed fugitive depicted in the sketch.

That's how police arrested a drifter named Richard Speck, who was promptly convicted of the heinous slayings and ended up dying in prison thirty years later.[1]

Ever since Scotland Yard first turned a witness's recollections into a sketch of a murder suspect in 1889, forensic artists have played an important role in law enforcement. Today more than three hundred sketch artists work with U.S. police agencies, and an increasing number of departments are relying on a computerized system called EFIT (Electronic Facial Identification Technique).

This recently developed technology was successfully used to solve a 1997 kidnapping that occurred at a shopping mall just a few miles from my suburban Chicago home. The victim provided details about the kidnapper's appearance to a technician, who used a computer to create an electronic likeness of the offender by choosing from different styles of noses, mouths, hairlines, and so forth.

Just moments after the drawing was faxed to police agencies throughout the area, an investigator in another suburb recognized the picture as a dead-ringer for a criminal he had encountered earlier. Fortunately, this led to a quick arrest of the kidnapping suspect.[2]

Oddly enough, the concept of an artist's drawing can provide a rough analogy that can help us in our quest for the truth about Jesus.

Here's how: The Old Testament provides numerous details about God that sketch out in great specificity what he's like. For instance, God is described as omnipresent, or existing everywhere in the universe; as omniscient, or knowing everything that can be known throughout eternity; as omnipotent, or all-powerful; as eternal, or being both beyond time and the source of all time; and as immutable, or unchanging in his attributes. He's loving, he's holy, he's righteous, he's wise, he's just.

Now, Jesus claims to be God. But does he fulfill these characteristics of deity? In other words, if we examine Jesus carefully, does his likeness closely match the sketch of God that we find elsewhere in the Bible? If it doesn't, we can conclude that his claim to being God is false.

This is an extremely complex and mind-stretching issue. For example, when Jesus was delivering the Sermon on the Mount on a hillside outside Capernaum, he wasn't simultaneously standing on Main Street of Jericho, so in what sense could he be called omnipresent? How can he be called omniscient if he readily admits in Mark 13:32 that he doesn't know everything about the future? If he's eternal, why does Colossians 1:15 call him "the firstborn over all creation"?

On the surface these issues seem to suggest that Jesus doesn't resemble the sketch of God. Nevertheless, I've learned over the years that initial impressions can be deceiving. That's why I was glad I would be able to discuss these issues with Dr. D. A. Carson, the theologian who has emerged in recent years as one of the most distinguished thinkers in Christianity.

THE EIGHTH INTERVIEW: DONALD A. CARSON, PH.D.

D. A. Carson, a research professor of New Testament at Trinity Evangelical Divinity School, has written or edited more than forty books, including *The Sermon on the Mount; Exegetical Fallacies; The Gospel According to John;* and his award-winning *The Gagging of God.*

He can read a dozen languages (his mastery of French stems from a childhood spent in Quebec) and is a member of the Tyndale Fellowship for Biblical Research, the Society for Biblical Literature, and the Institute for Biblical Research. His areas of expertise include the historical Jesus, postmodernism, Greek grammar, and the theology of the apostles Paul and John.

After initially studying chemistry (receiving a bachelor of science degree from McGill University), Carson went on to receive a master of divinity degree before going to England, where he earned a doctorate in New Testament at prestigious Cambridge University. He taught at three other colleges and seminaries before joining Trinity in 1978.

I had never met Carson before I drove onto Trinity's Deerfield, Illinois, campus for our interview. Frankly, I was expecting a starched academic. But while I found Carson to be every bit the scholar I had anticipated, I was taken aback by his warm, sincere, and pastoral tone as he responded to what turned out to be, in some cases, rather caustic questions.

Our conversation was held in an otherwise deserted faculty lounge over Christmas break. Carson was wearing a white windbreaker over a button-down shirt, blue jeans, and Adidas. After some preliminary banter about our mutual appreciation of England (Carson has lived there off and on through the years, and his wife, Joy, is British), I pulled out my notebook, started my recorder, and posed a background question to help determine whether Jesus has "the right stuff" to be God.

LIVING AND FORGIVING LIKE GOD

My initial question centered on why Carson thinks Jesus is God in the first place. "What did he say or do," I asked, "that convinces you that he is divine?" I wasn't sure how he would respond, although I anticipated he would focus on Jesus' supernatural feats. I was wrong.

"One could point to such things as his miracles," Carson said as he leaned back in the comfortably upholstered chair, "but other people have done miracles, so while this may be indicative, it's not decisive. Of course, the Resurrection was the ultimate vindication of his identity. But of the many things he did, one of the most striking to me is his forgiving of sin."

"Really?" I said, shifting in my chair, which was perpendicular to his, in order to face him more directly. "How so?"

"The point is, if you do something against me, I have the right to forgive you. However, if you do something against me and somebody else comes along and says, 'I forgive you,' what kind of cheek is that? The only person who can say that sort of thing meaningfully is God himself, because sin, even if it is against other people, is first and foremost a defiance of God and his laws.

"When David sinned by committing adultery and arranging the death of the woman's husband, he ultimately says to God in Psalm 51, 'Against you only have I sinned and done this evil in your sight.' He recognized that although he had wronged people, in the end he had sinned against the God who made him in his image, and God needed to forgive him.

"So along comes Jesus and says to sinners, 'I forgive you.' The Jews immediately recognize the blasphemy of this. They react by saying, 'Who can forgive sins but God alone?' To my mind, that is one of the most striking things Jesus did."

"Not only did Jesus forgive sin," I observed, "but he asserted that he himself was without sin. And certainly sinlessness is an attribute of deity."

"Yes," he replied. "Historically in the West, people considered most holy have also been the most conscious of their own failures and sins. They are people who are aware of their shortcomings and lusts and resentments, and they're fighting them honestly by the grace of God. In fact, they're fighting them so well that others take notice and say, 'There is a holy man or woman.'

"But along comes Jesus, who can say with a straight face, 'Which of you can convict me of sin?' If I said that, my wife and children and all who know me would be glad to stand up and testify, whereas no one could with respect to Christ."

Although moral perfection and the forgiveness of sin are undoubtedly characteristics of deity, there are several additional attributes that Jesus must fulfill if he is to match the sketch of God. It was time to progress to those. After having started by lobbing softballs at Carson, I got ready to throw some curves.

MYSTERY OF THE INCARNATION

Using some notes I had brought along, I hit Carson in rapid-fire succession with some of the biggest obstacles to Jesus' claim of deity.

"Dr. Carson, how in the world could Jesus be omnipresent if he couldn't be in two places at once?" I asked. "How could he be omniscient when he says, 'Not even the Son of Man knows the hour of his return'? How could he be omnipotent when the gospels plainly tell us that he was unable to do many miracles in his hometown?"

Pointing my pen at him for emphasis, I concluded by saying, "Let's admit it: the Bible itself seems to argue against Jesus being God."

While Carson didn't flinch, he did concede that these questions have no simple answers. After all, they strike at the very heart of the Incarnation—God becoming man, spirit taking on flesh, the infinite becoming finite, the eternal becoming time-bound. It's a doctrine that has kept theologians busy for centuries. And that's where Carson chose to start his answer: by going back to the way scholars have tried to respond to these matters through the years.

"Historically, there have been two or three approaches to this," he began, sounding a bit as if he were beginning a classroom lecture. "For example, at the end of the last century, the great theologian Benjamin Warfield worked through the gospels and ascribed various bits either to Christ's humanity or to his deity. When Jesus does something that's a reflection of him being God, that's ascribed to Christ's deity. When there's something reflecting his limitations or finiteness or his humanness—for example, his tears; does God cry?—that's ascribed to his humanity."

That explanation was fraught with problems, it seemed to me. "If you do that, wouldn't you end up with a schizophrenic Jesus?" I asked.

"It's easy to slip into that unwittingly," he replied. "All the confessional statements have insisted that both Jesus' humanity and his deity remained distinct, yet they combined in one person. So you want to avoid a solution in which there are essentially two minds—sort of a Jesus human mind and a Christ heavenly mind. However, this is one kind of solution, and there may be something to it.

"The other kind of solution is some form of *kenosis,* which means 'emptying.' This spins out of Philippians 2, where Paul tells us that Jesus, 'being in the form of God, did not think equality with God was something to be exploited'—that's the way it should be translated—'but emptied himself.' He became a nobody."

That seemed a little ambiguous to me. "Can you be more explicit?" I asked. "What exactly did he empty himself of?"

Apparently, I had put my finger on the issue. "Ah, that's the question," Carson replied with a nod. "Through the centuries, people have given various answers to that. For instance, did he empty himself of his deity? Well, then he would no longer be God.

"Did he empty himself of the attributes of his deity? I have a problem with that too, because it's difficult to separate attributes from reality. If you have an animal that looks like a horse, smells like a horse, walks like a horse, and has all the attributes of a horse, you've got a horse. So I don't know what it means for God to empty himself of his attributes and still be God.

"Some have said, 'He didn't empty himself of his attributes, but he emptied himself of the use of his attributes'—a self-limiting type of thing. That's getting closer, although there are times when that was not what he was doing—he was forgiving sins the way only God can, which is an attribute of deity.

"Others go further by saying, 'He emptied himself of the independent use of his attributes.' That is, he functioned like God when his heavenly Father gave him explicit sanction to do so. Now, that's much closer. The difficulty is that there is a sense in which the eternal Son has always acted in line with his Father's commandments. You don't want to lose that, even in eternity past. But it's getting closer."

I sensed we were somewhere in the vicinity of the bull's-eye, but I wasn't sure we were going to get much closer. That seemed to be Carson's sentiment, too.

"Strictly speaking," he said, "Philippians 2 does not tell us precisely what the eternal Son emptied himself of. He emptied himself; he became a nobody. Some kind of emptying is at issue, but let's be frank—you're talking about the Incarnation, one of the central mysteries of the Christian faith.

"You're dealing with formless, bodiless, omniscient, omnipresent, omnipotent Spirit and finite, touchable, physical, time-bound creatures. For one to become the other inevitably binds you up in mysteries.

"So part of Christian theology has been concerned not with 'explaining it all away' but with trying to take the biblical evidence and, retaining all of it fairly, find ways of synthesis that are rationally coherent, even if they're not exhaustively explanatory."

That was a sophisticated way of saying that theologians can come up with explanations that seem to make sense, even though they might not be able to explain every nuance about the Incarnation. In a way, that seemed logical. If the Incarnation is true, it's not surprising that finite minds couldn't totally comprehend it.

It seemed to me that some sort of voluntary "emptying" of Jesus' independent use of his attributes was reasonable in explaining why he generally didn't exhibit the "omnis"—omniscience, omnipotence, and omnipresence—in his earthly existence, even though the New Testament clearly states that all these qualities are ultimately true of him.

That, however, was only part of the problem. I flipped to the next page of my notes and began another line of questioning about some specific biblical passages that seemed to directly contradict Jesus' claim to being God.

CREATOR OR CREATED?

Part of the sketch that Jesus must match is that God is an uncreated being who has existed from eternity past. Isaiah 57:15 describes God as "he who lives forever." But, I said to Carson, there are some verses that seem to strongly suggest that Jesus was a created being.

"For instance," I said, "John 3:16 calls Jesus the 'begotten' Son of God, and Colossians 1:15 says he was the 'firstborn over all creation.' Don't they clearly imply that Jesus was created, as opposed to being the Creator?"

One of Carson's areas of expertise is Greek grammar, which he called upon in responding to both of those verses.

"Let's take John 3:16," he said. "It's the King James Version that translates the Greek with the words 'his only begotten Son.' Those who consider this the correct rendering usually bind that up with the Incarnation itself—that is, his begetting in the Virgin Mary. But in fact, that's not what the word in Greek means.

"It really means 'unique one.' The way it was usually used in the first century is 'unique and beloved.' So John 3:16 is simply saying that Jesus is the unique and beloved Son—or as the New International Version translates it, 'the one and only Son'—rather than saying that he's ontologically begotten in time."

"That only explains that one passage," I pointed out.

"OK, let's look at the Colossians verse, which uses the term 'firstborn.' The vast majority of commentators, whether conservative or liberal, recognize that in the Old Testament the firstborn, because of the laws of succession, normally received the lion's share of the estate, or the firstborn would become king in the case of a royal family. The firstborn therefore was the one ultimately with all the rights of the father.

"By the second century before Christ, there are places where the word no longer has any notion of actual begetting or of being born first but carries the idea of the authority that comes with the position of being the rightful heir. That's the way it applies to Jesus, as virtually all scholars admit. In light of that, the very expression 'firstborn' is slightly misleading."

"What would be a better translation?" I asked.

"I think 'supreme heir' would be more appropriate," he responded.

While that would explain the Colossians passage, Carson went even further, with one last point.

"If you're going to quote Colossians 1:15, you have to keep it in context by going on to Colossians 2:9, where the very same author stresses, 'For in Christ all the fullness of the Deity lives in bodily form.' The author wouldn't contradict himself. So the term 'firstborn' cannot exclude Jesus' eternality, since that is part of what it means to possess the fullness of the divine."

For me, that nailed the issue. But there were other troubling passages as well. For example, in Mark 10 someone addresses Jesus as "good teacher," promoting him to reply, "Why do you call me good? No one is good—except God alone."

"Wasn't he denying his divinity by saying this?" I asked.

"No, I think he was trying to get the fellow to stop and think about what he was saying," Carson explained. "The parallel passage in Matthew is a little more expansive and does not find Jesus downplaying his deity at all.

"I think all he's saying is, 'Wait a minute; why are you calling me good? Is this just a polite thing, like you say, "Good day"? What do you mean by good? You call me good master—is this because you're trying to honey up to me?'

"In a fundamental sense there's only one who is good, and that's God. But Jesus is not implicitly saying, 'So don't call me that.' He's saying, 'Do you really understand what you're saying when you say that? Are you really ascribing to me what should only be ascribed to God?'

"That could be teased out to mean, 'I really am what you say; you speak better than you know' or 'Don't you dare call me that; next time call me "sinner Jesus" like everybody else does.' In terms of all that Jesus says and does elsewhere, which way does it make sense to take it?"

With so many verses that call Jesus "sinless," "holy," "righteous," "innocent," "undefiled," and "separate from sinners," the answer was pretty obvious.

WAS JESUS A LESSER GOD?

If Jesus was God, what kind of God was he? Was he equal to the Father, or some sort of junior God, possessing the attributes of deity and yet somehow failing to match the total sketch that the Old Testament provides of the divine?

That question comes out of another passage that I pointed out to Carson. "Jesus said in John 14:28, 'The Father is greater than I.' Some people look at this and conclude that Jesus must have been a lesser God. Are they right?" I asked.

Carson sighed. "My father was a preacher," he replied, "and a dictum in our home when I was growing up was, 'A text without a context becomes a pretext for a prooftext.' It's very important to see this passage in its context.

"The disciples are moaning because Jesus has said he's going away. Jesus says, 'If you loved me, you'd be glad for my sake when I say I'm going away, because the Father is greater than I.' That is to say, Jesus is returning to the glory that is properly his, so if they really know who he is and really love him properly, they'll be glad that he's going back to the realm where he really is greater. Jesus says in John 17:5, 'Glorify me with the glory that I had with the Father before the world began'—that is, 'the Father is greater than I.'

"When you use a category like 'greater,' it doesn't have to mean ontologically greater. If I say, for example, that the president of the United States is greater than I, I'm not saying he's an ontologically superior being. He's greater in military capability, political prowess, and public acclaim, but he's not more of a man than I am. He's a human being and I'm a human being.

"So when Jesus says, 'The Father is greater than I,' one must look at the context and ask if Jesus is saying, 'The Father is greater than I because he's God and I'm not.' Frankly, that would be a pretty ridiculous thing to say. Suppose I got up on some podium to preach and said, 'I solemnly declare to you that God is greater than I am.' That would be a rather useless observation.

"The comparison is only meaningful if they're already on the same plane and there's some delimitation going on. Jesus is in the limitations of the Incarnation—he's going to the cross; he's going to die—but he's about to return to the Father and to the glory he had with the Father before the world began.

"He's saying, 'You guys are moaning for my sake; you ought to be glad because I'm going home.' It's in that sense that 'the Father is greater than I.'"

"So," I said, "this isn't an implicit denial of his deity."

"No," he concluded, "it's really not. The context makes that clear."

While I was ready to accept the fact that Jesus was not a lesser God, I had a different and more sensitive issue to raise: how could Jesus be a compassionate God yet endorse the idea of eternal suffering for those who reject him?

THE DISQUIETING QUESTION OF HELL

The Bible says that the Father is loving. The New Testament affirms the same about Jesus. But can they really be loving while at the same time sending people to hell? After all, Jesus teaches more about hell than anyone in the entire Bible. Doesn't that contradict his supposed gentle and compassionate character?

In posing this question to Carson, I quoted the hard-edged words of agnostic Charles Templeton: "How could a loving Heavenly Father create an endless hell and, over the centuries, consign millions of people to it because they do not or cannot or will not accept certain religious beliefs?"[3]

That question, though tweaked for maximum impact, didn't raise Carson's ire. He began with a clarification. "First of all," he said, "I'm not sure that God simply casts people into hell because they don't accept certain beliefs."

He thought for a moment, then backed up to take a run at a more thorough answer by discussing a subject that many modern people consider a quaint anachronism: sin.

"Picture God in the beginning of creation with a man and woman made in his image," Carson said. "They wake up in the morning and think about God. They love him truly. They delight to do what he wants; it's their whole pleasure. They're rightly related to him and they're rightly related to each other.

"Then, with the entrance of sin and rebellion into the world, these image bearers begin to think that they are at the center of the universe. Not literally, but that's the way they think. And that's the way we think. All the things we call 'social pathologies'—war, rape, bitterness, nurtured envies, secret jealousies, pride, inferiority complexes—are bound up in the first instance with the fact that we're not rightly related with God. The consequence is that people get hurt.

"From God's perspective, that is shockingly disgusting. So what should God do about it? If he says, 'Well, I don't give a rip,' he's saying that evil doesn't matter to him. It's a bit like saying, "Oh yeah, the Holocaust—I don't care." Wouldn't we be shocked if we thought God didn't have moral judgments on such matters?

"But in principle, if he's the sort of God who has moral judgments on those matters, he's got to have moral judgments on this huge matter of all these divine image bearers shaking their puny fists at his face and singing with Frank Sinatra, 'I did it my way.' That's the real nature of sin.

"Having said that, hell is not a place where people are consigned because they were pretty good blokes but just didn't believe the right stuff. They're consigned there, first and foremost, because they defy their Maker and want to be at the center of the universe. Hell is not filled with people who have already repented, only God isn't gentle enough or good enough to let them out. It's filled with people who, for all eternity, still want to be at the center of the universe and who persist in their God-defying rebellion.

"What is God to do? If he says it doesn't matter to him, God is no longer a God to be admired. He's either amoral or positively creepy. For him to act in any other way in the face of such blatant defiance would be to reduce God himself."

I interjected, "Yes, but what seems to bother people the most is the idea that God will torment people for eternity. That seems vicious, doesn't it?"

Replied Carson, "In the first place, the Bible says that there are different degrees of punishment, so I'm not sure that it's the same level of intensity for all people.

"In the second place, if God took his hands off this fallen world so that there were no restraint on human wickedness, we would make hell. Thus if you allow a whole lot of sinners to live somewhere in a confined place where they're not doing damage to anyone but themselves, what do you get but hell? There's a sense in which they're doing it to themselves, and it's what they want because they still don't repent."

I thought Carson was finished with his answer, because he hesitated for a moment. However, he had one more crucial point. "One of the things that the Bible does insist is that in the end not only will justice be done, but justice will be seen to be done, so that every mouth will be stopped."

I grabbed ahold of that last statement. "In other words," I said, "at the time of judgment there is nobody in the world who will walk away from that experience saying that they have been treated unfairly by God. Everyone will recognize the fundamental justice in the way God judges them and the world."

"That's right," Carson said firmly. "Justice is not always done in this world; we see that every day. But on the Last Day it will be done for all to see. And no one will be able to complain by saying, 'This isn't fair.'"

JESUS AND SLAVERY

There was one other issue I wanted to raise with Carson. I glanced at my watch. "Do you have a few more minutes?" I asked. When he indicated he did, I began to address one more controversial topic.

To be God, Jesus must be ethically perfect. But some critics of Christianity have charged that he fell short because, they say, he tacitly approved of the morally abhorrent practice of slavery. As Morton Smith wrote,

> There were innumerable slaves of the emperor and of the Roman state; the Jerusalem Temple owned slaves; the High Priest owned slaves (one of them lost an ear in Jesus' arrest); all of the rich and almost all of the middle class owned slaves. So far as we are told, Jesus never attacked this practice.... There seem to have been slave revolts in Palestine and Jordan in Jesus' youth; a miracle-working leader of such a revolt would have attracted a large following. If Jesus had denounced slavery or promised liberation, we should almost certainly have heard of his doing it. We hear nothing, so the most likely supposition is that he said nothing.[4]

How can Jesus' failure to push for the abolition of slavery be squared with God's love for all people? "Why didn't Jesus stand up and shout, 'Slavery is wrong'?" I asked. "Was he morally deficient for not working to dismantle an institution that demeaned people who were made in the image of God?"

Carson straightened up in his chair. "I really think that people who raise that objection are missing the point," he said. "If you'll permit me, I'll set the stage by talking about slavery, ancient and modern, because in our culture the issue is understandably charged with overtones that it didn't have in the ancient world."

I gestured for him to continue. "Please go ahead," I said.

OVERTHROWING OPPRESSION

"In his book *Race and Culture,*[5] African-American scholar Thomas Sowell points out that every major world culture until the modern period, without exception, has had slavery," Carson explained. "While it could be tied to military conquests, usually slavery served an economic function. They didn't have bankruptcy laws, so if you got yourself into terrible hock, you sold yourself and/or your family into slavery. As it was discharging a debt, slavery was also providing work. It wasn't necessarily all bad; at least it was an option for survival.

"Please understand me: I'm not trying to romanticize slavery in any way. However, in Roman times there were menial laborers who were slaves, and there were also others who were the equivalent of distinguished Ph.D.'s, who were teaching families. And there was no association of a particular race with slavery.

"In American slavery, though, all blacks and only blacks were slaves. That was one of the peculiar horrors of it, and it generated an unfair sense of black inferiority that many of us continue to fight to this day.

"Now let's look at the Bible. In Jewish society, under the Law everyone was to be freed every Jubilee. In other words, there was a slavery liberation every seventh year. Whether or not things actually worked out that way, this was nevertheless what God said, and this was the framework in which Jesus was brought up.

"But you have to keep your eye on Jesus' mission. Essentially, he did not come to overturn the Roman economic system, which included slavery. He came to free men and women from their sins. And here's my point: what his message does is transform people so they begin to love God with all their heart, soul, mind, and strength and to love their neighbor as themselves. Naturally, that has an impact on the idea of slavery.

"Look at what the apostle Paul says in his letter to Philemon concerning a runaway slave named Onesimus. Paul doesn't say to overthrow slavery, because all that would do would be to get him executed. Instead he tells Philemon he'd better treat Onesimus as a brother in Christ, just as he would treat Paul himself. And then, to make matters perfectly clear, Paul emphasizes, 'Remember, you owe your whole life to me because of the gospel.'

"The overthrowing of slavery, then, is through the transformation of men and women by the gospel rather than through merely changing an economic system. We've all seen what can happen when you merely overthrow an economic system and impose a new order. The whole communist dream was to have a 'revolutionary man' followed by the 'new man.' Trouble is, they never found the 'new man.' They got rid of the oppressors of the peasants, but that didn't mean the peasants were suddenly free—they were just under a new regime of darkness. In the final analysis, if you want lasting change, you've got to transform the hearts of human beings. And that was Jesus' mission.

"It's also worth asking the question that Sowell poses: how did slavery stop? He points out that the driving impetus for the abolition of slavery was the evangelical awakening in England. Christians rammed abolition through Parliament in the beginning of the nineteenth century and then eventually used British gunboats to stop the slave trade across the Atlantic.

"While there were about eleven million Africans who were shipped to America—and many didn't make it—there were about thirteen million Africans shipped to become slaves in the Arab world. Again it was the British, prompted by people whose hearts had been changed by Christ, who sent their gunboats to the Persian Gulf to oppose this."

Carson's response made sense not only historically but also in my own experience. For example, years ago I knew a businessman who was a rabid racist with a superior and condescending attitude toward anyone of another color. He hardly made any effort to conceal his contempt for African-Americans, letting his bigoted bile frequently spill out in crude jokes and caustic remarks. No amount of arguments could dissuade him from his disgusting opinions.

Then he became a follower of Jesus. As I watched in amazement, his attitudes, his perspective, and his values changed over time as his heart was renewed by God. He came to realize that he could no longer harbor ill-will toward any person, since the Bible teaches that all people are made in the image of God. Today I can honestly say that he's genuinely caring and accepting toward others, including those who are different from him.

Legislation didn't change him. Reasoning didn't change him. Emotional appeals didn't change him. He'll tell you that God changed him from the inside out—decisively, completely, permanently. That's one of many examples I've seen of the power of the gospel that Carson was talking about—the power to transform vengeful haters into humanitarians, hardhearted hoarders into softhearted givers, power-mongers into selfless servants, and people who exploit others—through slavery or some other form of oppression—into people who embrace all.

This squares with what the apostle Paul said in Galatians 3:28: "There is neither Jew nor Greek, slave nor free, male nor female, for you are all one in Christ Jesus."

MATCHING THE SKETCH OF GOD

Carson and I talked, sometimes in animated tones, for two hours, filling more tapes than would fit in this chapter. I found his answers to be well reasoned and theologically sound. In the end, however, how the Incarnation works—how Spirit takes on flesh—remained a mind-boggling concept.

Even so, according to the Bible, the fact that it did occur is not in any doubt. Every attribute of God, says the New Testament, is found in Jesus Christ:

- Omniscience? In John 16:30 the apostle John affirms of Jesus, "Now we can see that you know all things."
- Omnipresence? Jesus said in Matthew 28:20, "Surely I am with you always, to the very end of the age" and in Matthew 18:20, "Where two or three come together in my name, there am I with them."
- Omnipotence? "All authority in heaven and on earth has been given to me," Jesus said in Matthew 28:18.
- Eternality? John 1:1 declares of Jesus, "In the beginning was the Word, and the Word was with God, and the Word was God."
- Immutability? Hebrews 13:8 says, "Jesus Christ is the same yesterday and today and forever."

Also, the Old Testament paints a portrait of God by using such titles and descriptions as Alpha and Omega, Lord, Savior, King, Judge, Light, Rock, Redeemer, Shepherd, Creator, giver of life, forgiver of sin, and speaker with divine authority. It's fascinating to note that in the New Testament each and every one is applied to Jesus.[6]

Jesus said it all in John 14:7: "If you really knew me, you would know my Father as well." Loose translation: "When you look at the sketch of God from the Old Testament, you will see a likeness of me."

Deliberations

Questions for Reflection or Group Study

1. Read Philippians 2:5–8, which talks about Jesus emptying himself and being born into humble circumstances, with the cross as his destination. What are some possible motivations for Jesus to do this? Then read verses 9–11. What happens as a result of Jesus' mission? What could prompt everyone to someday conclude that Jesus is Lord?
2. Has the idea of hell been an impediment in your spiritual journey? How do you respond to Carson's explanation of this issue?
3. Carson addressed some verses that on the surface seemed to suggest that Jesus was a created being or a lesser God. Did you find his reasoning persuasive? Why or why not? What did his analysis of these issues teach you in terms of the need for appropriate background information in interpreting Scripture?

For Further Evidence

More Resources on This Topic

Harris, Murray J. *Jesus As God.* Grand Rapids: Baker, 1993.
Martin, W. J. *The Deity of Christ.* Chicago: Moody Press, 1964.
McDowell, Josh, and Bart Larson. *Jesus: A Biblical Defense of His Deity.* San Bernardino, Calif.: Here's Life, 1983.
Stott, John. *Basic Christianity.* Grand Rapids: Eerdmans, 1986.
Zodhiates, Spiros. *Was Christ God?* Grand Rapids: Eerdmans, 1966.

10

THE FINGERPRINT EVIDENCE

Did Jesus—and Jesus Alone—Match the Identity of the Messiah?

It was an uneventful Saturday at the Hiller home in Chicago. Clarence Hiller spent the afternoon painting the trim on the outside of his two-story house on West 104th Street. By early evening he and his family had retired to bed. However, what happened next would change criminal law in America forever.

The Hillers woke in the early morning hours of September 19, 1910, and became suspicious that a gaslight near their daughter's bedroom had gone out. Clarence went to investigate. His wife heard a quick succession of sounds: a scuffle, two men tumbling down the stairs, two gunshots, and the slamming of the front door. She emerged to find Clarence dead at the foot of the stairs.

Police arrested Thomas Jennings, a convicted burglar, less than a mile away. There was blood on his clothes and his left arm had been injured—both, he said, from falling on a streetcar. In his pocket they found the same kind of gun that had been used to shoot Clarence Hiller, but they couldn't determine if it was the murder weapon.

Knowing they needed more to convict Jennings, detectives scoured the inside of Hiller's home in a search for additional clues. One fact soon became obvious: the killer had entered through a rear kitchen window. Detectives went outside—and there, next to that window, forever imprinted in the white paint that the murder victim himself had so carefully applied to a railing only hours before his death, they found four clear fingerprints from someone's left hand.

Fingerprint evidence was a new concept at the time, having been recently introduced at an international police exhibition in St. Louis. So far, fingerprints had never been used to convict anyone of murder in the United States.

Despite strong objections by defense attorneys that such evidence was unscientific and inadmissible, four officers testified that the fingerprints in the paint perfectly matched those of Thomas Jennings—and him alone. The jury found Jennings guilty, the Illinois Supreme Court upheld his conviction in a historic ruling, and he was later hanged.[1]

The premise behind fingerprint evidence is simple: each individual has unique ridges on his or her fingers. When a print found on an object matches the pattern of ridges on a person's finger, investigators can conclude with scientific certainty that this specific individual has touched that object.

In many criminal cases, fingerprint identification is the pivotal evidence. I remember covering a trial in which a single thumbprint found on the cellophane wrapper of a cigarette package was the determining factor in convicting a twenty-year-old burglar of murdering a college coed.[2] That's how conclusive fingerprint evidence can be.

OK, but what has this got to do with Jesus Christ? Simply this: There is another kind of evidence that's analogous to fingerprints and establishes to an astounding degree of certainty that Jesus is indeed the Messiah of Israel and the world.

In the Jewish Scriptures, which Christians call the Old Testament, there are several dozen major prophecies about the coming of the Messiah, who would be sent by God to redeem his people. In effect, these predictions formed a figurative fingerprint that only the Anointed One would be able to match. This way, the Israelites could rule out any impostors and validate the credentials of the authentic Messiah.

The Greek word for "Messiah" is *Christ*. But was Jesus really the Christ? Did he miraculously fulfill these predictions that were written hundreds of years before he was born? And how do we know he was the only individual throughout history who fit the prophetic fingerprint?

There are plenty of scholars with long strings of initials after their names whom I could have asked about this topic. However, I wanted to interview someone for whom this was more than just an abstract academic exercise, and that took me to a very unlikely setting in southern California.

THE NINTH INTERVIEW: LOUIS S. LAPIDES, M.DIV., TH.M.

Usually a church would be a natural location in which to question someone about a biblical issue. But there was something different about sitting down with Pastor Louis Lapides in the sanctuary of his congregation on the morning after Sunday worship services. This setting of pews and stained glass was not where you would expect to find a nice Jewish boy from Newark, New Jersey.

Yet that's Lapides' background. For someone with his heritage, the question of whether Jesus is the long-anticipated Messiah goes beyond theory. It's intensely personal, and I had sought out Lapides so I could hear the story of his own investigation of this critical issue.

Lapides earned a bachelor's degree in theology from Dallas Baptist University as well as a master of divinity and a master of theology degree in Old Testament and Semitics from Talbot Theological Seminary. He served for a decade with Chosen People Ministries, talking about Jesus to Jewish college students. He has taught in the Bible department of Biola University and worked for seven years as an instructor for Walk Through the Bible seminars. He is also the former president of a national network of fifteen messianic congregations.

Slender and bespectacled, Lapides is soft-spoken but has a quick smile and ready laugh. He was upbeat and polite as he ushered me to a chair near the front of Beth Ariel Fellowship in Sherman Oaks, California. I didn't want to begin by debating biblical nuances; instead I started by inviting Lapides to tell me the story of his spiritual journey.

He folded his hands in his lap, looked at the dark wood walls for a moment as he decided where to start, and then began unfolding an extraordinary tale that took us from Newark to Greenwich Village to Vietnam to Los Angeles, from skepticism to faith, from Judaism to Christianity, from Jesus as irrelevant to Jesus as Messiah.

"As you know, I came from a Jewish family," he began. "I attended a conservative Jewish synagogue for seven years in preparation for bar mitzvah. Although we considered those studies to be very important, our family's faith didn't affect our everyday life very much. We didn't stop work on the Sabbath; we didn't have a kosher home."

He smiled. "However, on the High Holy Days we attended the stricter Orthodox synagogue, because somehow my dad felt that's where you went if you really wanted to get serious with God!"

When I interjected to ask what his parents had taught him about the Messiah, Lapides' answer was crisp. "It never came up," he said matter-of-factly.

I was incredulous. In fact, I thought I had misunderstood him. "You're saying it wasn't even discussed?" I asked.

"Never," he reiterated. "I don't even remember it being an issue in Hebrew school."

This was amazing to me. "How about Jesus?" I asked. "Was he ever talked about? Was his name used?"

"Only derogatorily!" Lapides quipped. "Basically, he was never discussed. My impressions of Jesus came from seeing Catholic churches: there was the cross, the crown of thorns, the pierced side, the blood coming from his head. It didn't make any sense to me. Why would you worship a man on a cross with nails in his hands and his feet? I never once thought Jesus had any connection to the Jewish people. I just thought he was a god of the Gentiles."

I suspected that Lapides' attitudes toward Christians had gone beyond mere confusion over their beliefs. "Did you believe Christians were at the root of anti-Semitism?" I asked.

"Gentiles were looked upon as synonymous with Christians, and we were taught to be cautious because there could be anti-Semitism among the Gentiles," he said, sounding a bit diplomatic.

I pursued the issue further. "Would you say you developed some negative attitudes toward Christians?"

This time he didn't mince words. "Yes, actually I did," he said. "In fact, later when the New Testament was first presented to me, I sincerely thought it was going to basically be a handbook on anti-Semitism: how to hate Jews, how to kill Jews, how to massacre them. I thought the American Nazi Party would have been very comfortable using it as a guidebook."

I shook my head, saddened at the thought of how many other Jewish children have grown up thinking of Christians as their enemies.

A SPIRITUAL QUEST BEGINS

Lapides said several incidents dimmed his allegiance to Judaism as he was growing up. Curious about the details, I asked him to elaborate, and he immediately turned to what was clearly the most heartrending episode of his life.

"My parents got divorced when I was seventeen," he said—and surprisingly, even after all these years I could still detect hurt in his voice. "That really put a stake in any religious heart I may have had. I wondered, Where does God come in? Why didn't they go to a rabbi for counseling? What good is religion if it can't help people in a practical way? It sure couldn't keep my parents together. When they split up, part of me split as well.

"On top of that, in Judaism I didn't feel as if I had a personal relationship with God. I had a lot of beautiful ceremonies and traditions, but he was the distant and detached God of Mount Sinai who said, 'Here are the rules—you live by them, you'll be OK; I'll see you later.' And there I was, an adolescent with raging hormones, wondering, Does God relate to my struggles? Does he care about me as an individual? Well, not in any way I could see."

The divorce prompted an era of rebellion. Consumed with music and influenced by the writings of Jack Kerouac and Timothy Leary, he spent too much time in Greenwich Village coffeehouses to go to college—making him vulnerable to the draft. By 1967 he found himself on the other side of the world in a cargo boat whose volatile freight—ammunition, bombs, rockets, and other high explosives—made it a tempting target for the Vietcong.

"I remember being told at our orientation in Vietnam, 'Twenty percent of you will probably get killed, and the other eighty percent will probably get a venereal disease or become alcoholics or get hooked on drugs.' I thought, I don't even have a one percent chance of coming out normal!

"It was a very dark period. I witnessed suffering. I saw body bags; I saw the devastation from war. And I encountered anti-Semitism among some of the GIs. A few of them from the South even burned a cross one night. I probably wanted to distance myself from my Jewish identity—maybe that's why I began delving into Eastern religions."

Lapides read books on Eastern philosophies and visited Buddhist temples while in Japan. "I was extremely bothered by the evil I had seen, and I was trying to figure out how faith can deal with it," he told me. "I used to say, 'If there's a God, I don't care if I find him on Mount Sinai or Mount Fuji. I'll take him either way.'"

He survived Vietnam, returning home with a newfound taste for marijuana and plans to become a Buddhist priest. He tried to live an ascetic lifestyle of self-denial in an effort to work off the bad karma for the misdeeds of his past, but soon he realized he'd never be able to make up for all his wrongs.

Lapides was quiet for a moment. "I got depressed," he said. "I remember getting on the subway and thinking, Maybe jumping onto the tracks is the answer. I could free myself from this body and just merge with God. I was very confused. To make matters worse, I started experimenting with LSD."

Looking for a new start, he decided to move to California, where his spiritual quest continued. "I went to Buddhist meetings, but that was empty," he said. "Chinese Buddhism was atheistic, Japanese Buddhism worshiped statues of Buddha, Zen Buddhism was too elusive. I went to Scientology meetings, but they were too manipulative and controlling. Hinduism believed in all these crazy orgies that the gods would have and in gods who were blue elephants. None of it made sense; none of it was satisfying."

He even accompanied friends to meetings that had Satanic undercurrents. "I would watch and think, Something is going on here, but it's not good," he said. "In the midst of my drug-crazed world, I told my friends I believed there's a power of evil that's beyond me, that can work in me, that exists as an entity. I had seen enough evil in my life to believe that."

He looked at me with an ironic smile. "I guess I accepted Satan's existence," he said, "before I accepted God's."

"I CAN'T BELIEVE IN JESUS"

It was 1969. Lapides' curiosity prompted him to visit Sunset Strip to gawk at an evangelist who had chained himself to an eight-foot cross to protest the way local tavern owners had managed to get him evicted from his storefront ministry. There on the sidewalk Lapides encountered some Christians who engaged him in an impromptu spiritual debate.

A bit cocky, he started throwing Eastern philosophy at them. "There is no God out there," he said, gesturing toward the heavens. "We're God. I'm God. You're God. You just have to realize it."

"Well, if you're God, why don't you create a rock?" one person replied. "Just make something appear. That's what God does."

In his drug-addled mind Lapides imagined he was holding a rock. "Yeah, well, here's a rock," he said, extending his empty hand.

The Christian scoffed. "That's the difference between you and the true God," he said. "When God creates something, everyone can see it. It's objective, not subjective."

That registered with Lapides. After thinking about it for a while, he said to himself, If I find God, he's got to be objective. I'm through with this Eastern philosophy that says it's all in my mind and that I can create my own reality. God has to be an objective reality if he's going to have any meaning beyond my own imagination.

When one of the Christians brought up the name of Jesus, Lapides tried to fend him off with his stock answer. "I'm Jewish," he said. "I can't believe in Jesus."

A pastor spoke up. "Do you know of the prophecies about the Messiah?" he asked.

Lapides was taken off guard. "Prophecies?" he said. "I've never heard of them."

The minister startled Lapides by referring to some of the Old Testament predictions. Wait a minute! Lapides thought. Those are my Jewish Scriptures he's quoting! How could Jesus be in there?

When the pastor offered him a Bible, Lapides was skeptical. "Is the New Testament in there?" he asked. The pastor nodded. "OK, I'll read the Old Testament, but I'm not going to open up the other one," Lapides told him.

He was taken aback by the minister's response. "Fine," said the pastor. "Just read the Old Testament and ask the God of Abraham, Isaac, and Jacob—the God of Israel—to show you if Jesus is the Messiah. Because he *is* your Messiah. He came to the Jewish people initially, and then he was also the Savior of the world."

To Lapides, this was new information. Intriguing information. Astonishing information. So he went back to his apartment, opened the Old Testament to its first book, Genesis, and went hunting for Jesus among words that had been written hundreds of years before the carpenter of Nazareth had ever been born.

"PIERCED FOR OUR TRANSGRESSIONS"

"Pretty soon," Lapides told me, "I was reading the Old Testament every day and seeing one prophecy after another. For instance, Deuteronomy talked about a prophet greater than Moses who will come and whom we should listen to. I thought, Who can be greater than Moses? It sounded like the Messiah—someone as great and as respected as Moses but a greater teacher and a greater authority. I grabbed ahold of that and went searching for him."

As Lapides progressed through the Scriptures, he was stopped cold by Isaiah 53. With clarity and specificity, in a haunting prediction wrapped in exquisite poetry, here was the picture of a Messiah who would suffer and die for the sins of Israel and the world—all written more than seven hundred years before Jesus walked the earth.

> He was despised and rejected by men,
>   a man of sorrows, and familiar with suffering.
> Like one from whom men hide their faces
>   he was despised, and we esteemed him not.
>
> Surely he took up our infirmities
>   and carried our sorrows,
> yet we considered him stricken by God,
>   smitten by him, and afflicted.
> But he was pierced for our transgressions,
>   he was crushed for our iniquities;
> the punishment that brought us peace was upon him,
>   and by his wounds we are healed.
> We all, like sheep, have gone astray,
>   each of us has turned to his own way;
> and the LORD has laid on him
>   the iniquity of us all.
>
> He was oppressed and afflicted,
>   yet he did not open his mouth;
> he was led like a lamb to the slaughter,
>   and as a sheep before her shearers is silent,
>   so he did not open his mouth.
> By oppression and judgment he was taken away.
>   And who can speak of his descendants?
> For he was cut off from the land of the living;
>   for the transgression of my people he was stricken.
> He was assigned a grave with the wicked,
>   and with the rich in his death,
> though he had done no violence,
>   nor was any deceit in his mouth....
>
> For he bore the sin of many,
>   and made intercession for the transgressors.
>
> Isaiah 53:3–9, 12

Instantly Lapides recognized the portrait: this was Jesus of Nazareth! Now he was beginning to understand the paintings he had seen in the Catholic churches he had passed as a child: the suffering Jesus, the crucified Jesus, the Jesus who he now realized had been "pierced for our transgressions" as he "bore the sin of many."

As Jews in the Old Testament sought to atone for their sins through a system of animal sacrifices, here was Jesus, the ultimate sacrificial lamb of God, who paid for sin once and for all. Here was the personification of God's plan of redemption.

So breathtaking was this discovery that Lapides could only come to one conclusion: it was a fraud! He believed that Christians had rewritten the Old Testament and twisted Isaiah's words to make it sound as if the prophet had been foreshadowing Jesus.

Lapides set out to expose the deception. "I asked my stepmother to send me a Jewish Bible so I could check it out myself," he told me. "She did, and guess what? I found that it said the same thing! Now I really had to deal with it."

THE JEWISHNESS OF JESUS

Over and over Lapides would come upon prophecies in the Old Testament—more than four dozen major predictions in all. Isaiah revealed the manner of the Messiah's birth (of a virgin); Micah pinpointed the place of his birth (Bethlehem); Genesis and Jeremiah specified his ancestry (a descendent of Abraham, Isaac, and Jacob, from the tribe of Judah, the house of David); the Psalms foretold his betrayal, his accusation by false witnesses, his manner of death (pierced in the hands and feet, although crucifixion hadn't been invented yet), and his resurrection (he would not decay but would ascend on high); and on and on.[3] Each one chipped away at Lapides' skepticism until he was finally willing to take a drastic step.

"I decided to open the New Testament and just read the first page," he said. "With trepidation I slowly turned to Matthew as I looked up to heaven, waiting for the lightning bolt to strike!"

Matthew's initial words leaped off the page: "A record of the genealogy of Jesus Christ the son of David, the son of Abraham . . ."

Lapides' eyes widened as he recalled the moment he first read that sentence. "I thought, Wow! Son of Abraham, son of David—it was all fitting together! I went to the birth narratives and thought, Look at this! Matthew is quoting from Isaiah 7:14: 'The virgin will be with child and will give birth to a son.' And then I saw him quoting from the prophet Jeremiah. I sat there thinking, You know, this is about Jewish people. Where do the Gentiles come in? What's going on here?

"I couldn't put it down. I read through the rest of the gospels, and I realized this wasn't a handbook for the American Nazi Party; it was an interaction between Jesus and the Jewish community. I got to the book of Acts and—this was incredible!—they were trying to figure out how the Jews could bring the story of Jesus to the Gentiles. Talk about role reversal!"

So convincing were the fulfilled prophecies that Lapides started telling people that he thought Jesus was the Messiah. At the time, this was merely an intellectual possibility to him, yet its implications were deeply troubling.

"I realized that if I were to accept Jesus into my life, there would have to be some significant changes in the way I was living," he explained. "I'd have to deal with the drugs, the sex, and so forth. I didn't understand that God would help me make those changes; I thought I had to clean up my life on my own."

EPIPHANY IN THE DESERT

Lapides and some friends headed into the Mojave Desert for a getaway. Spiritually he was feeling conflicted. He had been unsettled by nightmares of being torn apart by dogs pulling at him from opposite directions. Sitting among the desert scrub, he recalled the words someone had spoken to him on Sunset Strip: "You're either on God's side or on Satan's side."

He believed in the embodiment of evil—and that's not whose side he wanted to be on. So Lapides prayed, "God, I've got to come to the end of this struggle. I have to know beyond a shadow of a doubt that Jesus is the Messiah. I need to know that you, as the God of Israel, want me to believe this."

As he related the story to me, Lapides hesitated, unsure how to put into words what happened next. A few moments passed. Then he told me, "The best I can put together out of that experience is that God objectively spoke to my heart. He convinced me, experientially, that he exists. And at that point, out in the desert, in my heart I said, 'God, I accept Jesus into my life. I don't understand what I'm supposed to do with him, but I want him. I've pretty much made a mess of my life; I need you to change me.'"

And God began to do that in a process that continues to this day. "My friends knew my life had changed, and they couldn't understand it," he said. "They'd say, 'Something happened to you in the desert. You don't want to do drugs anymore. There's something different about you.'

"I would say, 'Well, I can't explain what happened. All I know is that there's someone in my life, and it's someone who's holy, who's righteous, who's a source of positive thoughts about life—and I just feel whole.'"

That last word, it seemed, said everything. "*Whole,*" he emphasized to me, "in a way I had never felt before."

Despite the positive changes, he was concerned about breaking the news to his parents. When he finally did, reaction was mixed. "At first they were joyful because they could tell I was no longer dependent on drugs and I sounded much better emotionally," he recalled. "But that began to unravel when they understood the source of all the changes. They winced, as if to say, 'Why does it have to be Jesus? Why can't it be something else?' They didn't know what to do with it."

With a trace of sadness in his voice, he added, "I'm still not sure they really do."

Through a remarkable string of circumstances, Lapides' prayer for a wife was answered when he met Deborah, who was also Jewish and a follower of Jesus. She took him to her church—the same one, it turned out, that was pastored by the minister who many months earlier on Sunset Strip had challenged Lapides to read the Old Testament.

Lapides laughed. "I'll tell you what—his jaw dropped open when he saw me walk into the church!"

That congregation was filled with ex-bikers, ex-hippies, and ex-addicts from the Strip, along with a spattering of transplanted Southerners. For a young Jewish man from Newark who was relationally gun-shy with people who were different from him, because of the anti-Semitism he feared he would encounter, it was healing to learn to call such a diverse crowd "brothers and sisters."

Lapides married Deborah a year after they met. Since then she has given birth to two sons. And together they've given birth to Beth Ariel Fellowship, a home for Jews and Gentiles who also are finding wholeness in Christ.

RESPONDING TO OBJECTIONS

Lapides finished his story and relaxed in his chair. I let the moment linger. The sanctuary was peaceful; the stained glass was glowing red and yellow and blue from the California sun. I sat musing over the power of one person's story of a faith found. I marveled at this saga of war and drugs, of Greenwich Village and Sunset Strip and a barren desert, none of which I ever would have associated with the pleasant, well-adjusted minister sitting in front of me.

But I didn't want to ignore the obvious questions that his story raised. With Lapides' permission I started by asking the one that was foremost on my mind: "If the prophecies were so obvious to you and pointed so unquestionably toward Jesus, why don't more Jews accept him as their Messiah?"

It was a question Lapides has asked himself a lot during the three decades since he was challenged by a Christian to investigate the Jewish Scriptures. "In my case, I took the time to read them," he replied. "Oddly enough, even though the Jewish people are known for having high intellects, in this area there's a lot of ignorance.

"Plus you have countermissionary organizations that hold seminars in synagogues to try to disprove the messianic prophecies. Jewish people hear them and use them as an excuse for not exploring the prophecies personally. They'll say, 'The rabbi told me there's nothing to this.'

"I'll ask them, 'Do you think the rabbi just brought up an objection that Christianity has never heard before? I mean, scholars have been working on this for hundreds of years! There's great literature out there and powerful Christian answers to those challenges.' If they're interested, I help them go further."

I wondered about the ostracism a Jewish person faces if he or she becomes a Christian. "That's definitely a factor," he said. "Some people won't let the messianic prophecies grab them, because they're afraid of the repercussions—potential rejection by their family and the Jewish community. That's not easy to face. Believe me, I know."

Even so, some of the challenges to the prophecies sound pretty convincing when a person first hears them. So one by one I posed the most common objections to Lapides to see how he would respond.

1. The Coincidence Argument

First, I asked Lapides whether it's possible that Jesus merely fulfilled the prophecies by accident. Maybe he's just one of many throughout history who have coincidentally fit the prophetic fingerprint.

"Not a chance," came his response. "The odds are so astronomical that they rule that out. Someone did the math and figured out that the probability of just eight prophecies being fulfilled is one chance in one hundred million billion. That number is millions of times greater than the total number of people who've ever walked the planet!

"He calculated that if you took this number of silver dollars, they would cover the state of Texas to a depth of two feet. If you marked one silver dollar among them and then had a blindfolded person wander the whole state and bend down to pick up one coin, what would be the odds he'd choose the one that had been marked?"

With that he answered his own question: "The same odds that anybody in history could have fulfilled just eight of the prophecies."

I had studied this same statistical analysis by mathematician Peter W. Stoner when I was investigating the messianic prophecies for myself. Stoner also computed that the probability of fulfilling forty-eight prophecies was one chance in a trillion, trillion, trillion, trillion, trillion, trillion, trillion, trillion, trillion, trillion, trillion, trillion, trillion![4]

Our minds can't comprehend a number that big. This is a staggering statistic that's equal to the number of minuscule atoms in a trillion, trillion, trillion, trillion, billion universes the size of our universe!

"The odds alone say it would be impossible for anyone to fulfill the Old Testament prophecies," Lapides concluded. "Yet Jesus—and only Jesus throughout all of history—managed to do it."

The words of the apostle Peter popped into my head: "But the things which God announced beforehand by the mouth of all the prophets, that His Christ should suffer, He has thus fulfilled" (Acts 3:18 NASB).

2. The Altered Gospel Argument

I painted another scenario for Lapides, asking, "Isn't it possible that the gospel writers fabricated details to make it appear that Jesus fulfilled the prophecies?

"For example," I said, "the prophecies say the Messiah's bones would remain unbroken, so maybe John invented the story about the Romans breaking the legs of the two thieves being crucified with Jesus, and not breaking his legs. And the prophecies talk about betrayal for thirty pieces of silver, so maybe Matthew played fast and loose with the facts and said, yeah, Judas sold out Jesus for that same amount."

But that objection didn't fly any further than the previous one. "In God's wisdom, he created checks and balances both inside and outside the Christian community," Lapides explained. "When the gospels were being circulated, there were people living who had been around when all these things happened. Someone would have said to Matthew, 'You know it didn't happen that way. We're trying to communicate a life of righteousness and truth, so don't taint it with a lie.'"

Besides, he added, why would Matthew have fabricated fulfilled prophecies and then willingly allowed himself to be put to death for following someone who he secretly knew was really not the Messiah? That wouldn't make any sense.

What's more, the Jewish community would have jumped on any opportunity to discredit the gospels by pointing out falsehoods. "They would have said, 'I was there, and Jesus' bones *were* broken by the Romans during the Crucifixion,'" Lapides said. "But even though the Jewish Talmud refers to Jesus in derogatory ways, it never once makes the claim that the fulfillment of prophecies was falsified. Not one time."

3. The Intentional Fulfillment Argument

Some skeptics have asserted that Jesus merely maneuvered his life in a way to fulfill the prophecies. "Couldn't he have read in Zechariah that the Messiah would ride a donkey into Jerusalem, and then arrange to do exactly that?" I asked.

Lapides made a small concession. "For a few of the prophecies, yes, that's certainly conceivable," he said. "But there are many others for which this just wouldn't have been possible.

"For instance, how would he control the fact that the Sanhedrin offered Judas thirty pieces of silver to betray him? How could he arrange for his ancestry, or the place of his birth, or his method of execution, or that soldiers gambled for his clothing, or that his legs remained unbroken on the cross? How would he arrange to perform miracles in front of skeptics? How would he arrange for his resurrection? And how would he arrange to be born when he was?"

That last comment piqued my curiosity. "What do you mean by when he was born?" I asked.

"When you interpret Daniel 9:24–26, it foretells that the Messiah would appear a certain length of time after King Artaxerxes I issued a decree for the Jewish people to go from Persia to rebuild the walls in Jerusalem," Lapides replied.

He leaned forward to deliver the clincher: "That puts the anticipated appearance of the Messiah at the exact moment in history when

Jesus showed up," he said. "Certainly that's nothing he could have prearranged."[5]

4. The Context Argument

One other objection needed to be addressed: were the passages that Christians identify as messianic prophecies really intended to point to the coming of the Anointed One, or do Christians rip them out of context and misinterpret them?

Lapides sighed. "You know, I go through the books that people write to try to tear down what we believe. That's not fun to do, but I spend the time to look at each objection individually and then to research the context and the wording in the original language," he said. "And every single time, the prophecies have stood up and shown themselves to be true.

"So here's my challenge to skeptics: don't accept my word for it, but don't accept your rabbi's either. Spend the time to research it yourself. Today nobody can say, 'There's no information.' There are plenty of books out there to help you.

"And one more thing: sincerely ask God to show you whether or not Jesus is the Messiah. That's what I did—and without any coaching it became clear to me who fit the fingerprint of the Messiah."

"EVERYTHING MUST BE FULFILLED . . ."

I appreciated the way Lapides had responded to the objections, but ultimately it was the story of his spiritual journey that kept replaying in my mind as I flew back to Chicago late that night. I reflected on how many times I had encountered similar stories, especially among successful and thoughtful Jewish people who had specifically set out to refute Jesus' messianic claims.

I thought about Stan Telchin, the East Coast businessman who had embarked on a quest to expose the "cult" of Christianity after his daughter went away to college and received *Y'shua* (Jesus) as her Messiah. He was astonished to find that his investigation led him—and his wife and second daughter—to the same Messiah. He later became a Christian minister, and his book that recounts his story, *Betrayed!*, has been translated into more than twenty languages.[6]

There was Jack Sternberg, a prominent cancer physician in Little Rock, Arkansas, who was so alarmed at what he found in the Old Testament that he challenged three rabbis to disprove that Jesus was the Messiah. They couldn't, and he too has claimed to have found wholeness in Christ.[7]

And there was Peter Greenspan, an obstetrician-gynecologist who practices in the Kansas City area and is a clinical assistant professor at the University of Missouri–Kansas City School of Medicine. Like Lapides, he had been challenged to look for Jesus in Judaism. What he found troubled him, so he went to the Torah and Talmud, seeking to discredit Jesus' messianic credentials. Instead he concluded that Jesus did miraculously fulfill the prophecies.

For him, the more he read books by those trying to undermine the evidence for Jesus as the Messiah, the more he saw the flaws in their arguments. Ironically, concluded Greenspan, "I think I actually came to faith in *Y'shua* by reading what detractors wrote."[8]

He found, as have Lapides and others, that Jesus' words in the gospel of Luke have proved true: "Everything must be fulfilled that is written about me in the Law of Moses, the Prophets and the Psalms" (Luke 24:44). It was fulfilled, and only in Jesus—the sole individual in history who has matched the prophetic fingerprint of God's anointed one.

Deliberations

Questions for Reflection or Group Study

1. Even if you're not Jewish, is there an aspect of Lapides' spiritual journey that is similar to your own? Were there any lessons you learned from Lapides about how you should proceed?
2. Lapides considered his Jewish heritage and unbiblical lifestyle impediments to becoming a follower of Jesus. Is there anything in your life that would make it difficult to become a Christian? Do you see any costs that you might incur if you became a Christian? How might they compare with the benefits?
3. Lapides thought Christians were anti-Semitic. In a recent word-association exercise at an East Coast university, the word most often associated with *Christian* was *intolerant*. Do you have negative perceptions of Christians? What do they stem from? How might this influence your receptivity to the evidence about Jesus?

For Further Evidence

More Resources on This Topic

Fruchtenbaum, Arnold. *Jesus Was a Jew.* Tustin, Calif.: Ariel Ministries, 1981.

Frydland, Rachmiel. *What the Rabbis Know about the Messiah.* Cincinnati: Messianic, 1993.

Kaiser, Walter C., Jr. *The Messiah in the Old Testament.* Grand Rapids: Zondervan, 1995.

Rosen, Moishe. *Y'shua, the Jewish Way to Say Jesus.* Chicago: Moody Press, 1982.

Rosen, Ruth, ed. *Jewish Doctors Meet the Great Physician.* San Francisco: Purple Pomegranate, 1997.

Telchin, Stan. *Betrayed!* Grand Rapids: Chosen, 1982.

PART 3

Researching the Resurrection

11

THE MEDICAL EVIDENCE

Was Jesus' Death a Sham and His Resurrection a Hoax?

I paused to read the plaque hanging in the waiting room of a doctor's office: "Let conversation cease. Let laughter flee. This is the place where death delights to help the living."

Obviously, this was no ordinary physician. I was paying another visit to Dr. Robert J. Stein, one of the world's foremost forensic pathologists, a flamboyant, husky-voiced medical detective who used to regale me with stories about the unexpected clues he had uncovered while examining corpses. For him, dead men *did* tell tales—in fact, tales that would often bring justice to the living.

During his lengthy tenure as medical examiner of Cook County, Illinois, Stein performed more than twenty thousand autopsies, each time meticulously searching for insights into the circumstances surrounding the victim's death. Repeatedly his sharp eye for detail, his encyclopedic knowledge of the human anatomy, and his uncanny investigative intuition helped this medical sleuth reconstruct the victim's violent demise.

Sometimes innocent people were vindicated as a result of his findings. But more often Stein's work was the final nail in a defendant's coffin. Such was the case with John Wayne Gacy, who faced the executioner after Stein helped convict him of thirty-three grisly murders.

That's how crucial medical evidence can be. It can determine whether a child died of abuse or an accidental fall. It can establish whether a person succumbed to natural causes or was murdered by someone who spiked the person's coffee with arsenic. It can uphold or dismantle a defendant's alibi by pinpointing the victim's time of death, using an ingenious procedure that measures the amount of potassium in the eyes of the deceased.

And yes, even in the case of someone brutally executed on a Roman cross two millennia ago, medical evidence can still make a crucial contribution: it can destroy one of the most persistent arguments used by those who claim that the resurrection of Jesus—the supreme vindication of his claim to deity—was nothing more than an elaborate hoax.

RESURRECTION OR RESUSCITATION?

The idea that Jesus never really died on the cross can be found in the Koran,[1] which was written in the seventh century—in fact, Ahmadiya Muslims contend that Jesus actually fled to India. To this day there's a shrine that supposedly marks his real burial place in Srinagar, Kashmir.[2]

As the nineteenth century dawned, Karl Bahrdt, Karl Venturini, and others tried to explain away the Resurrection by suggesting that Jesus only fainted from exhaustion on the cross, or he had been given a drug that made him appear to die, and that he had later been revived by the cool, damp air of the tomb.[3]

Conspiracy theorists bolstered this hypothesis by pointing out that Jesus had been given some liquid on a sponge while on the cross (Mark 15:36) and that Pilate seemed surprised at how quickly Jesus had succumbed (Mark 15:44). Consequently, they said, Jesus' reappearance wasn't a miraculous resurrection but merely a fortuitous resuscitation, and his tomb was empty because he continued to live.

While reputable scholars have repudiated this so-called swoon theory, it keeps recurring in popular literature. In 1929 D. H. Lawrence wove this theme into a short story in which he suggested that Jesus had fled to Egypt, where he fell in love with the priestess Isis.[4]

In 1965 Hugh Schonfield's best-seller *The Passover Plot* alleged that it was only the unanticipated stabbing of Jesus by the Roman soldier that foiled his complicated scheme to escape the cross alive, even though Schonfield conceded, "We are nowhere claiming . . . that [the book] represents what actually happened."[5]

The swoon hypothesis popped up again in Donovan Joyce's 1972 book *The Jesus Scroll,* which "contains an even more incredible string of improbabilities than Schonfield's," according to Resurrection expert Gary Habermas.[6] In 1982 *Holy Blood, Holy Grail* added the twist that Pontius Pilate had been bribed to allow Jesus to be taken down from the cross before he was dead. Even so, the authors confessed, "We could not—and still cannot—prove the accuracy of our conclusion."[7]

As recently as 1992 a little-known academic from Australia, Barbara Thiering, caused a stir by reviving the swoon theory in her book *Jesus and the Riddle of the Dead Sea Scrolls,* which was introduced with much fanfare by a well-respected U.S. publisher and then derisively dismissed by Emory University scholar Luke Timothy Johnson as being "the purest poppycock, the product of fevered imagination rather than careful analysis."[8]

Like an urban myth, the swoon theory continues to flourish. I hear it all the time in discussing the Resurrection with spiritual seekers. But what does the evidence really establish? What actually happened at the Crucifixion? What was Jesus' cause of death? Is there any possible way he could have survived this ordeal? Those are the kinds of questions that I hoped medical evidence could help resolve.

So I flew to southern California and knocked on the door of a prominent physician who has extensively studied the historical, archaeological, and medical data concerning the death of Jesus of Nazareth—although it seems that, due to the mysteriously missing body, no autopsy has ever been performed.

THE TENTH INTERVIEW: ALEXANDER METHERELL, M.D., PH.D.

The plush setting was starkly incongruous with the subject we were discussing. There we were, sitting in the living room of Metherell's comfortable California home on a balmy spring evening, warm ocean breezes whispering through the windows, while we were talking about a topic of unimaginable brutality: a beating so barbarous that it shocks the conscience, and a form of capital punishment so depraved that it stands as wretched testimony to man's inhumanity to man.

I had sought out Metherell because I heard he possessed the medical and scientific credentials to explain the Crucifixion. But I also had another motivation: I had been told he could discuss the topic dispassionately as well as accurately. That was important to me, because I wanted the facts to speak for themselves, without the hyperbole or charged language that might otherwise manipulate emotions.

As you would expect from someone with a medical degree (University of Miami in Florida) and a doctorate in engineering (University of Bristol in England), Metherell speaks with scientific precision. He is board certified in diagnosis by the American Board of Radiology and has been a consultant to the National Heart, Lung, and Blood Institute of the National Institutes of Health of Bethesda, Maryland.

A former research scientist who has taught at the University of California, Metherell is editor of five scientific books and has written for publications ranging from *Aerospace Medicine* to *Scientific American*. His ingenious analysis of muscular contraction has been published in *The Physiologist* and *Biophysics Journal*. He even looks the role of a distinguished medical authority: he's an imposing figure with silver hair and a courteous yet formal demeanor.

I'll be honest: at times I wondered what was going on inside Metherell. With scientific reserve, speaking slowly and methodically, he gave no hint of any inner turmoil as he calmly described the chilling details of Jesus' demise. Whatever was going on underneath, whatever distress it caused him as a Christian to talk about the cruel fate that befell Jesus, he was able to mask with a professionalism born out of decades of laboratory research.

He just gave me the facts—and after all, that was what I had traveled halfway across the country to get.

THE TORTURE BEFORE THE CROSS

Initially I wanted to elicit from Metherell a basic description of the events leading up to Jesus' death. So after a time of social chat, I put down my iced tea and shifted in my chair to face him squarely. "Could you paint a picture of what happened to Jesus?" I asked.

He cleared his throat. "It began after the Last Supper," he said. "Jesus went with his disciples to the Mount of Olives—specifically, to the Garden of Gethsemane. And there, if you remember, he prayed all night. Now, during that process he was anticipating the coming events of the next day. Since he knew the amount of suffering he was going to have to endure, he was quite naturally experiencing a great deal of psychological stress."

I raised my hand to stop him. "Whoa—here's where skeptics have a field day," I told him. "The gospels tell us he began to sweat blood at this point. Now, c'mon, isn't that just a product of some overactive imaginations? Doesn't that call into question the accuracy of the gospel writers?"

Unfazed, Metherell shook his head. "Not at all," he replied. "This is a known medical condition called hematidrosis. It's not very common, but it is associated with a high degree of psychological stress.

"What happens is that severe anxiety causes the release of chemicals that break down the capillaries in the sweat glands. As a result, there's a small amount of bleeding into these glands, and the sweat comes out tinged with blood. We're not talking about a lot of blood; it's just a very, very small amount."

Though a bit chastened, I pressed on. "Did this have any other effect on the body?"

"What this did was set up the skin to be extremely fragile so that when Jesus was flogged by the Roman soldier the next day, his skin would be very, very sensitive."

Well, I thought, here we go. I braced myself for the grim images I knew were about to flood my mind. I had seen plenty of dead bodies as a journalist—casualties of car accidents, fires, and crime syndicate retribution—but there was something especially unnerving in hearing about someone being intentionally brutalized by executioners determined to extract maximum suffering.

"Tell me," I said, "what was the flogging like?"

Metherell's eyes never left me. "Roman floggings were known to be terribly brutal. They usually consisted of thirty-nine lashes but frequently were a lot more than that, depending on the mood of the soldier applying the blows.

"The soldier would use a whip of braided leather thongs with metal balls woven into them. When the whip would strike the flesh, these balls would cause deep bruises or contusions, which would break open with further blows. And the whip had pieces of sharp bone as well, which would cut the flesh severely.

"The back would be so shredded that part of the spine was sometimes exposed by the deep, deep cuts. The whipping would have gone all the way from the shoulders down to the back, the buttocks, and the back of the legs. It was just terrible."

Metherell paused. "Go on," I said.

"One physician who has studied Roman beatings said, 'As the flogging continued, the lacerations would tear into the underlying skeletal muscles and produce quivering ribbons of bleeding flesh.' A third-century historian by the name of Eusebius described a flogging by saying, 'The sufferer's veins were laid bare, and the very muscles, sinews, and bowels of the victim were open to exposure.'

"We know that many people would die from this kind of beating even before they could be crucified. At the least, the victim would experience tremendous pain and go into hypovolemic shock."

Metherell had thrown in a medical term I didn't know. "What does hypovolemic shock mean?" I asked.

"*Hypo* means 'low,' *vol* refers to volume, and *emic* means 'blood,' so hypovolemic shock means the person is suffering the effects of losing a large amount of blood," the doctor explained. "This does four things. First, the heart races to try to pump blood that isn't there; second, the blood pressure drops, causing fainting or collapse; third, the kidneys stop producing urine to maintain what volume is left; and fourth, the person becomes very thirsty as the body craves fluids to replace the lost blood volume."

"Do you see evidence of this in the gospel accounts?"

"Yes, most definitely," he replied. "Jesus was in hypovolemic shock as he staggered up the road to the execution site at Calvary, carrying the horizontal beam of the cross. Finally Jesus collapsed, and the Roman soldier ordered Simon to carry the cross for him. Later we read that Jesus said, 'I thirst,' at which point a sip of vinegar was offered to him.

"Because of the terrible effects of this beating, there's no question that Jesus was already in serious to critical condition even before the nails were driven through his hands and feet."

THE AGONY OF THE CROSS

As distasteful as the description of the flogging was, I knew that even more repugnant testimony was yet to come. That's because historians are unanimous that Jesus survived the beating that day and went on to the cross—which is where the real issue lies.

These days when condemned criminals are strapped down and injected with poisons, or secured to a wooden chair and subjected to a surge of electricity, the circumstances are highly controlled. Death comes quickly and predictably. Medical examiners carefully certify the victim's passing. From close proximity witnesses scrutinize everything from beginning to end.

But how certain was death by this crude, slow, and rather inexact form of execution called crucifixion? In fact, most people aren't sure how the cross kills its victims. And without a trained medical examiner to officially attest that Jesus had died, might he have escaped the experience brutalized and bleeding but nevertheless alive?

I began to unpack these issues. "What happened when he arrived at the site of the Crucifixion?" I asked.

"He would have been laid down, and his hands would have been nailed in the outstretched position to the horizontal beam. This crossbar was called the patibulum, and at this stage it was separate from the vertical beam, which was permanently set in the ground."

I was having difficulty visualizing this; I needed more details. "Nailed with what?" I asked. "Nailed where?"

"The Romans used spikes that were five to seven inches long and tapered to a sharp point. They were driven through the wrists," Metherell said, pointing about an inch or so below his left palm.

"Hold it," I interrupted. "I thought the nails pierced his palms. That's what all the paintings show. In fact, it's become a standard symbol representing the Crucifixion."

"Through the wrists," Metherell repeated. "This was a solid position that would lock the hand; if the nails had been driven through the palms, his weight would have caused the skin to tear and he would have fallen off the cross. So the nails went through the wrists, although this was considered part of the hand in the language of the day.

"And it's important to understand that the nail would go through the place where the median nerve runs. This is the largest nerve going out to the hand, and it would be crushed by the nail that was being pounded in."

Since I have only a rudimentary knowledge of the human anatomy, I wasn't sure what this meant. "What sort of pain would that have produced?" I asked.

"Let me put it this way," he replied. "Do you know the kind of pain you feel when you bang your elbow and hit your funny bone? That's actually another nerve, called the ulna nerve. It's extremely painful when you accidentally hit it.

"Well, picture taking a pair of pliers and squeezing and crushing that nerve," he said, emphasizing the word *squeezing* as he twisted an imaginary pair of pliers. "That effect would be similar to what Jesus experienced."

I winced at the image and squirmed in my chair.

"The pain was absolutely unbearable," he continued. "In fact, it was literally beyond words to describe; they had to invent a new word:

excruciating. Literally, *excruciating* means 'out of the cross.' Think of that: they needed to create a new word, because there was nothing in the language that could describe the intense anguish caused during the crucifixion.

"At this point Jesus was hoisted as the crossbar was attached to the vertical stake, and then nails were driven through Jesus' feet. Again, the nerves in his feet would have been crushed, and there would have been a similar type of pain."

Crushed and severed nerves were certainly bad enough, but I needed to know about the effect that hanging from the cross would have had on Jesus. "What stresses would this have put on his body?"

Metherell answered, "First of all, his arms would have immediately been stretched, probably about six inches in length, and both shoulders would have become dislocated—you can determine this with simple mathematical equations.

"This fulfilled the Old Testament prophecy in Psalm 22, which foretold the Crucifixion hundreds of years before it took place and says, 'My bones are out of joint.'"

THE CAUSE OF DEATH

Metherell had made his point—graphically—about the pain endured as the crucifixion process began. But I needed to get to what finally claims the life of a crucifixion victim, because that's the pivotal issue in determining whether death can be faked or eluded. So I put the cause-of-death question directly to Metherell.

"Once a person is hanging in the vertical position," he replied, "crucifixion is essentially an agonizingly slow death by asphyxiation.

"The reason is that the stresses on the muscles and diaphragm put the chest into the inhaled position; basically, in order to exhale, the individual must push up on his feet so the tension on the muscles would be eased for a moment. In doing so, the nail would tear through the foot, eventually locking up against the tarsal bones.

"After managing to exhale, the person would then be able to relax down and take another breath in. Again he'd have to push himself up to exhale, scraping his bloodied back against the coarse wood of the cross. This would go on and on until complete exhaustion would take over, and the person wouldn't be able to push up and breathe anymore.

"As the person slows down his breathing, he goes into what is called respiratory acidosis—the carbon dioxide in the blood is dissolved as carbonic acid, causing the acidity of the blood to increase. This eventually leads to an irregular heartbeat. In fact, with his heart beating erratically, Jesus would have known that he was at the moment of death, which is when he was able to say, 'Lord, into your hands I commit my spirit.' And then he died of cardiac arrest."

It was the clearest explanation I had ever heard of death by crucifixion—but Metherell wasn't done.

"Even before he died—and this is important, too—the hypovolemic shock would have caused a sustained rapid heart rate that would have contributed to heart failure, resulting in the collection of fluid in the membrane around the heart, called a pericardial effusion, as well as around the lungs, which is called a pleural effusion."

"Why is that significant?"

"Because of what happened when the Roman soldier came around and, being fairly certain that Jesus was dead, confirmed it by thrusting a spear into his right side. It was probably his right side; that's not certain, but from the description it was probably the right side, between the ribs.

"The spear apparently went through the right lung and into the heart, so when the spear was pulled out, some fluid—the pericardial effusion and the pleural effusion—came out. This would have the appearance of a clear fluid, like water, followed by a large volume of blood, as the eyewitness John described in his gospel."

John probably had no idea why he saw both blood and a clear fluid come out—certainly that's not what an untrained person like him would have anticipated. Yet John's description is consistent with what modern medicine would expect to have happened. At first this would seem to give credibility to John being an eyewitness; however, there seemed to be one big flaw in all this.

I pulled out my Bible and flipped to John 19:34. "Wait a minute, Doc," I protested. "When you carefully read what John said, he saw 'blood and water' come out; he intentionally put the words in that order. But according to you, the clear fluid would have come out first. So there's a significant discrepancy here."

Metherell smiled slightly. "I'm not a Greek scholar," he replied, "but according to people who are, the order of words in ancient Greek was determined not necessarily by sequence but by prominence. This means that since there was a lot more blood than water, it would have made sense for John to mention the blood first."

I conceded the point but made a mental note to confirm it myself later. "At this juncture," I said, "what would Jesus' condition have been?"

Metherell's gaze locked with mine. He replied with authority, "There was absolutely no doubt that Jesus was dead."

ANSWERING THE SKEPTICS

Dr. Metherell's assertion seemed well supported by the evidence. But there were still some details I wanted to address—as well as at least one soft spot in his account that could very well undermine the credibility of the biblical account.

"The gospels say the soldiers broke the legs of the two criminals being crucified with Jesus," I said. "Why would they have done that?"

"If they wanted to speed up death—and with the Sabbath and Passover coming, the Jewish leaders certainly wanted to get this over before sundown—the Romans would use the steel shaft of a short Roman spear to shatter the victim's lower leg bones. This would prevent him from pushing up with his legs so he could breathe, and death by asphyxiation would result in a matter of minutes.

"Of course, we're told in the New Testament that Jesus' legs were not broken, because the soldiers had already determined that he was dead, and they just used the spear to confirm it. This fulfilled another Old Testament prophecy about the Messiah, which is that his bones would remain unbroken."

Again I jumped in. "Some people have tried to cast doubt on the gospel accounts by attacking the Crucifixion story," I said. "For instance, an article in the *Harvard Theological Review* concluded many years ago that there was 'astonishing little evidence that the feet of a crucified person were ever pierced by nails.' Instead, the article said, the victim's hands and feet were tied to the cross by ropes.[9] Won't you concede that this raises credibility problems with the New Testament account?"

Dr. Metherell moved forward until he was sitting on the edge of his chair. "No," he said, "because archaeology has now established that the use of nails was historical—although I'll certainly concede that ropes were indeed sometimes used."

"What's the evidence?"

"In 1968 archaeologists in Jerusalem found the remains of about three dozen Jews who had died during the uprising against Rome around A.D. 70. One victim, whose name was apparently Yohanan, had been crucified. And sure enough, they found a seven-inch nail still driven into his feet, with small pieces of olive wood from the cross still attached. This was excellent archaeological confirmation of a key detail in the gospel's description of the Crucifixion."

Touché, I thought. "But one other point of dispute concerns the expertise of the Romans to determine whether Jesus was dead," I pointed out. "These people were very primitive in terms of their understanding of medicine and anatomy and so forth—how do we know they weren't just mistaken when they declared that Jesus was no longer living?"

"I'll grant you that these soldiers didn't go to medical school. But remember that they were experts in killing people—that was their job, and they did it very well. They knew without a doubt when a person was dead, and really it's not so terribly difficult to figure out.

"Besides, if a prisoner somehow escaped, the responsible soldiers would be put to death themselves, so they had a huge incentive to make absolutely sure that each and every victim was dead when he was removed from the cross."

THE FINAL ARGUMENT

Appealing to history and medicine, to archaeology and even Roman military rules, Metherell had closed every loophole: Jesus could not have come down from the cross alive. But still, I pushed him further. "Is there any possible way—*any possible way*—that Jesus could have survived this?"

Metherell shook his head and pointed his finger at me for emphasis. "Absolutely not," he said. "Remember that he was already in hypovolemic shock from the massive blood loss even before the crucifixion started. He couldn't possibly have faked his death, because you can't fake the inability to breathe for long. Besides, the spear thrust into his heart would have settled the issue once and for all. And the Romans weren't about to risk their own death by allowing him to walk away alive."

"So," I said, "when someone suggests to you that Jesus merely swooned on the cross . . ."

"I tell them it's impossible. It's a fanciful theory without any possible basis in fact."

Yet I wasn't quite ready to let go of the issue. At the risk of frustrating the doctor, I said, "Let's speculate that the impossible happened and that Jesus somehow managed to survive the crucifixion. Let's say he was able to escape from his linen wrappings, roll the huge rock away from the mouth of his tomb, and get past the Roman soldiers who were standing guard. Medically speaking, what condition would he have been in after he tracked down his disciples?"

Metherell was reluctant to play that game. "Again," he stressed, becoming a bit more animated, "there's just no way he could have survived the cross.

"But if he had, how could he walk around after nails had been driven through his feet? How could he have appeared on the road to Emmaus just a short time later, strolling for long distances? How could he have used his arms after they were stretched and pulled from their joints? Remember, he also had massive wounds on his back and a spear wound to his chest."

Then he paused. Something clicked in his mind, and now he was ready to make a closing point that would drive a final stake through the heart of the swoon theory once and for all. It was an argument that nobody has been able to refute ever since it was first advanced by German theologian David Strauss in 1835.

"Listen," Metherell said, "a person in that kind of pathetic condition would never have inspired his disciples to go out and proclaim that he's the Lord of life who had triumphed over the grave.

"Do you see what I'm saying? After suffering that horrible abuse, with all the catastrophic blood loss and trauma, he would have looked so pitiful that the disciples would never have hailed him as a victorious conqueror of death; they would have felt sorry for him and tried to nurse him back to health.

"So it's preposterous to think that if he had appeared to them in that awful state, his followers would have been prompted to start a worldwide movement based on the hope that someday they too would have a resurrection body like his. There's just no way."

A QUESTION FOR THE HEART

Convincingly, masterfully, Metherell had established his case beyond a reasonable doubt. He had done it by focusing exclusively on the "how" question: How was Jesus executed in a way that absolutely ensured his death? But as we ended, I sensed that something was missing. I had tapped into his knowledge, but I hadn't touched his heart. So as we stood to shake hands, I felt compelled to ask the "why" question that begged to be posed.

"Alex, before I go, let me ask your opinion about something—not your medical opinion, not your scientific evaluation, just something from your heart."

I felt him let down his guard a bit. "Yes," he said, "I'll try."

"Jesus intentionally walked into the arms of his betrayer, he didn't resist arrest, he didn't defend himself at his trial—it was clear that he was willingly subjecting himself to what you've described as a humiliating and agonizing form of torture. And I'd like to know why. What could possibly have motivated a person to agree to endure this sort of punishment?"

Alexander Metherell—the man this time, not the doctor—searched for the right words.

"Frankly, I don't think a typical person could have done it," he finally replied. "But Jesus knew what was coming, and he was willing to go through it, because this was the only way he could redeem us—by serving as our substitute and paying the death penalty that we deserve because of our rebellion against God. That was his whole mission in coming to earth."

Having said that, I could still sense that Metherell's relentlessly rational and logical and organized mind was continuing to crunch down my question to its most basic, nonreducible answer.

"So when you ask what motivated him," he concluded, "well ... I suppose the answer can be summed up in one word—and that would be *love*."

Driving away that night, it was this answer that played over and over in my mind.

All in all, my trip to California had been thoroughly helpful. Metherell had persuasively established that Jesus could not have survived the ordeal of the cross, a form of cruelty so vile that the Romans exempted their own citizens from it, except for cases of high treason.

Metherell's conclusions were consistent with the findings of other physicians who have carefully studied the issue. Among them is Dr. William D. Edwards, whose 1986 article in the *Journal of the American Medical Association* concluded, "Clearly, the weight of the historical and medical evidence indicates that Jesus was dead before the wound to his side was inflicted.... Accordingly, interpretations based on the assumption that Jesus did not die on the cross appear to be at odds with modern medical knowledge."[10]

Those who seek to explain away the resurrection of Jesus by claiming that he somehow escaped the clutches of death at Galgotha need to offer a more plausible theory that fits the facts.

And then they too must end up pondering the haunting question that all of us need to consider: What could possibly have motivated Jesus to willingly allow himself to be degraded and brutalized the way that he did?

Deliberations

Questions for Reflection or Group Study

1. After considering Metherell's account, do you see any validity to the swoon theory? Why or why not?
2. For two millennia the cross has been a symbol for Christians. Now that you've read Metherell's testimony, how might your own view of that symbol be different in the future?
3. Would you be willing to suffer for the sake of another person? For whom and why? What would it take to motivate you to endure torture in the place of someone else?
4. How would you react to the soldiers if they were abusing, humiliating, and torturing you, as they did Jesus? What could possibly account for Jesus' reaction, which was to utter in the midst of his agony, "Father, forgive them"?

For Further Evidence

More Resources on This Topic

Edwards, William D., et al. "On the Physical Death of Jesus Christ." *Journal of the American Medical Association* (March 21, 1986), 1455–63.

Foreman, Dale. *Crucify Him.* Grand Rapids: Zondervan, 1990.

Hengel, M. *Crucifixion in the Ancient World.* Philadelphia: Fortress, 1977.

McDowell, Josh. *The Resurrection Factor.* San Bernardino, Calif.: Here's Life, 1981.

12

THE EVIDENCE OF THE MISSING BODY

Was Jesus' Body Really Absent from His Tomb?

Candy heiress Helen Vorhees Brach flew into the world's busiest airport on a crisp autumn afternoon, stepped into a crowd, and promptly disappeared without a trace. For more than twenty years the mystery of what happened to this red-haired, animal-loving philanthropist has baffled police and journalists alike.

While investigators are convinced she was murdered, they haven't been able to determine the specific circumstances, largely because they've never found her body. Police have floated some speculation, leaked tantalizing possibilities to the press, and even got a judge to declare that a con man was responsible for her disappearance. But absent a corpse, her murder officially remains unsolved. Nobody has ever been charged with her slaying.

The Brach case is one of those frustrating enigmas that keep me awake from time to time as I mentally sift through the sparse evidence and try to piece together what happened. Ultimately it's an unsatisfying exercise; I want to *know* what happened, and there just aren't enough facts to chase away the conjecture.

Occasionally bodies turn up missing in pulp fiction and real life, but rarely do you encounter an empty tomb. Unlike the case of Helen Brach, the issue with Jesus isn't that he was nowhere to be seen. It's that he *was* seen, alive; he *was* seen, dead; and he *was* seen, alive once more. If we believe the gospel accounts, this isn't a matter of a missing body. No, it's a matter of Jesus still being alive, even to this day, even after publicly succumbing to the horrors of crucifixion so graphically depicted in the preceding chapter.

The empty tomb, as an enduring symbol of the Resurrection, is the ultimate representation of Jesus' claim to being God. The apostle

Paul said in 1 Corinthians 15:17 that the Resurrection is the very linchpin of the Christian faith: "If Christ has not been raised, your faith is futile; you are still in your sins."

Theologian Gerald O'Collins put it this way: "In a profound sense, Christianity without the resurrection is not simply Christianity without its final chapter. It is not Christianity at all."[1]

The Resurrection is the supreme vindication of Jesus' divine identity and his inspired teaching. It's the proof of his triumph over sin and death. It's the foreshadowing of the resurrection of his followers. It's the basis of Christian hope. It's the miracle of all miracles.

If it's true. Skeptics claim that what happened to Jesus' body is still a mystery akin to Helen Brach's disappearance—there's not enough evidence, they say, to reach a firm conclusion.

But others assert that the case is effectively closed, because there is conclusive proof that the tomb was vacant on that first Easter Morning. And if you want someone to compellingly present that case, your best bet is to visit with William Lane Craig, widely considered to be among the world's foremost experts on the Resurrection.

THE ELEVENTH INTERVIEW: WILLIAM LANE CRAIG, PH.D., D.TH.

I had an unusual perspective the first time I saw Bill Craig in action: I was seated behind him as he defended Christianity before a crowd of nearly eight thousand people, with countless others listening on more than one hundred radio stations across the country.

As moderator of a debate between Craig and an atheist selected by the national spokesman for American Atheists, Inc., I marveled as Craig politely but powerfully built the case for Christianity while simultaneously dismantling the arguments for atheism. From where I was sitting, I could watch the faces of people as they discovered—many for the first time—that Christianity can stand up to rational analysis and rugged scrutiny.

In the end it was no contest. Among those who had entered the auditorium that evening as avowed atheists, agnostics, or skeptics, an overwhelming 82 percent walked out concluding that the case for Christianity had been the most compelling. Forty-seven people entered as nonbelievers and exited as Christians—Craig's arguments for the faith were that persuasive, especially compared with the paucity of evidence for atheism. Incidentally, nobody became an atheist.[2]

So when I flew down to Atlanta to interview him for this book, I was anxious to see how he'd respond to the challenges concerning the empty tomb of Jesus.

He hadn't changed since I had seen him a few years earlier. With his close-cropped black beard, angular features, and riveting gaze, Craig still looks the role of a serious scholar. He speaks in cogent sentences, never losing his train of thought, always working through an answer methodically, point by point, fact by fact.

Yet he isn't a dry theologian. Craig has a refreshing enthusiasm for his work. His pale blue eyes dance as he weaves elaborate propositions and theories; he punctuates his sentences with hand gestures that beckon for understanding and agreement; his voice modulates from near giddiness over some arcane theological point that he finds fascinating to hushed sincerity as he ponders why some scholars resist the evidence that he finds so compelling.

In short, his mind is fully engaged, but so is his heart. When he talks about skeptics he has debated, it isn't with a smug or adversarial tone. He goes out of his way to mention their endearing qualities when he can—this one was a wonderful speaker, that one was charming over dinner.

In the subtleties of our conversation, I sensed that he isn't out to pummel opponents with his arguments; he's sincerely seeking to win over people who he believes matter to God. He seems genuinely perplexed why some people cannot, or will not, recognize the reality of the empty tomb.

DEFENDING THE EMPTY TOMB

Wearing blue jeans, white socks, and a dark-blue sweater with red turtleneck collar, Craig lounged on a floral couch in his living room. On the wall behind him was a large framed scene of Munich.

It was there, fresh with a master of arts degree from Trinity Evangelical Divinity School and a doctorate in philosophy from the University of Birmingham, England, that Craig studied the Resurrection for the first time, while earning another doctorate, this one in theology from the University of Munich. Later he taught at Trinity Evangelical Divinity School and then served as a visiting scholar at the Higher Institute of Philosophy at the University of Louvain near Brussels.

His books include *Reasonable Faith; No Easy Answers; Knowing the Truth about the Resurrection; The Only Wise God; The Existence of*

God and the Beginning of the Universe; and (with Quentin Smith) *Theism, Atheism, and Big Bang Cosmology*, published by Oxford University Press.

He also contributed to *The Intellectuals Speak Out about God; Jesus under Fire; In Defense of Miracles;* and *Does God Exist?* In addition, his scholarly articles have appeared in such journals as *New Testament Studies; Journal for the Study of the New Testament; Gospel Perspectives; Journal of the American Scientific Affiliation;* and *Philosophy*. He is a member of nine professional societies, including the American Academy of Religion and the American Philosophical Association.

While he is internationally known for his writings about the intersection of science, philosophy, and theology, he needed no prompting to discuss the subject that still makes his heart beat fast: the resurrection of Jesus.

WAS JESUS REALLY BURIED IN THE TOMB?

Before looking at whether the tomb of Jesus was empty, I needed to establish whether his body had been there in the first place. History tells us that as a rule, crucified criminals were left on the cross to be devoured by birds or were thrown into a common grave. This has prompted John Dominic Crossan of the Jesus Seminar to conclude that Jesus' body probably was dug up and consumed by wild dogs.

"Based on these customary practices," I said to Craig, "wouldn't you admit that this is most likely what happened?"

"If all you looked at was customary practice, yes, I'd agree," came his reply. "But that would ignore the specific evidence in this case."

"OK, then let's look at the specific evidence," I said. With that I pointed out an immediate problem: the gospels say Jesus' corpse was turned over to Joseph of Arimathea, a member of the very council—the Sanhedrin—that voted to condemn Jesus. "That's rather implausible, isn't it?" I demanded in a tone that sounded more pointed than I had intended.

Craig shifted on the couch as if he were getting ready to pounce on my question. "No, not when you look at all the evidence for the burial," he said. "So let me go through it. For one thing, the burial is mentioned by the apostle Paul in 1 Corinthians 15:3–7, where he passes on a very early creed of the church."

I acknowledged this with a nod, since Dr. Craig Blomberg had already described this creed in some detail during our earlier interview. Craig agreed with Blomberg that the creed undoubtedly goes back to within a few years of Jesus' crucifixion, having been given to Paul, after his conversion, in Damascus or in his subsequent visit to Jerusalem when he met with the apostles James and Peter.

Since Craig was going to be referring to the creed, I opened the Bible in my lap and quickly reviewed the passage: "For what I received I passed on to you as of first importance: that Christ died for our sins according to the Scriptures, that he was buried, that he was raised on the third day according to the Scriptures . . ." The creed then goes on to list several appearances of the resurrected Jesus.

"This creed is incredibly early and therefore trustworthy material," Craig said. "Essentially, it's a four-line formula. The first line refers to the Crucifixion, the second to the burial, the third to the Resurrection, and the fourth to Jesus' appearances. As you can see, the second line affirms that Jesus was buried."

That was too vague for me. "Wait a minute," I interjected. "He may have been buried, but was it in a tomb? And was it through Joseph of Arimathea, this mysterious character who comes out of nowhere to claim the body?"

Craig remained patient. "This creed is actually a summary that corresponds line by line with what the gospels teach," he explained. "When we turn to the gospels, we find multiple, independent attestation of this burial story, and Joseph of Arimathea is specifically named in all four accounts. On top of that, the burial story in Mark is so extremely early that it's simply not possible for it to have been subject to legendary corruption."

"How can you tell it's early?" I asked.

"Two reasons," he said. "First, Mark is generally considered to be the earliest gospel. Second, his gospel basically consists of short anecdotes about Jesus, more like pearls on a string than a smooth, continuous narrative.

"But when you get to the last week of Jesus' life—the so-called passion story—then you do have a continuous narrative of events in sequence. This passion story was apparently taken by Mark from an even earlier source—and this source included the story of Jesus being buried in the tomb."

IS JOSEPH OF ARIMATHEA HISTORICAL?

While those were good arguments, I spotted a problem with Mark's account of what happened. "Mark says that the entire Sanhedrin voted to condemn Jesus," I said. "If that's true, this means Joseph of Arimathea cast his ballot to kill Jesus. Isn't it highly unlikely that he would have then come to give Jesus an honorable burial?"

Apparently, my observation put me in good company. "Luke may have felt this same discomfort," Craig said, "which would explain why he added one important detail—Joseph of Arimathea wasn't present when the official vote was taken. So that would explain things. But the significant point about Joseph of Arimathea is that he would not be the sort of person who would have been invented by Christian legend or Christian authors."

I needed more than merely a conclusion on that matter; I wanted some solid reasoning. "Why not?" I asked.

"Given the early Christian anger and bitterness toward the Jewish leaders who had instigated the crucifixion of Jesus," he said, "it's highly improbable that they would have invented one who did the right thing by giving Jesus an honorable burial—especially while all of Jesus' disciples deserted him! Besides, they wouldn't make up a specific member of a specific group, whom people could check out for themselves and ask about this. So Joseph is undoubtedly a historical figure."

Before I could ask a follow-up question, Craig continued. "I'll add that if this burial by Joseph were a legend that developed later, you'd expect to find other competing burial traditions about what happened to Jesus' body. However, you don't find these at all.

"As a result, the majority of New Testament scholars today agree that the burial account of Jesus is fundamentally reliable. John A. T. Robinson, the late Cambridge University New Testament scholar, said the honorable burial of Jesus is one of the earliest and best-attested facts that we have about the historical Jesus."

Craig's explanations satisfied me that Jesus' body was indeed placed in Joseph's tomb. But the creed left an ambiguity: perhaps, even after the Resurrection, his body remained entombed.

"While the creed says Jesus was crucified, buried, and then resurrected, it doesn't specifically say the tomb was empty," I pointed out. "Doesn't this leave room for the possibility that the Resurrection was only spiritual in nature and that Jesus' body was still in the tomb?"

"The creed definitely implies the empty tomb," Craig countered. "You see, the Jews had a physical concept of resurrection. For them, the primary object of the resurrection was the bones of the deceased—not even the flesh, which was thought to be perishable. After the flesh rotted away, the Jews would gather the bones of their deceased and put them in boxes to be preserved until the resurrection at the end of the world, when God would raise the righteous dead of Israel and they would come together in the final kingdom of God.

"In light of this, it would have been simply a contradiction of terms for an early Jew to say that someone was raised from the dead but his body still was left in the tomb. So when this early Christian creed says Jesus was buried and then raised on the third day, it's saying implicitly but quite clearly: an empty tomb was left behind."

HOW SECURE WAS THE TOMB?

Having heard convincing evidence that Jesus had been in the tomb, it seemed important to know how secure his grave was from outside influences. The tighter the security, the less likely the body could have been tampered with. "How protected was Jesus' tomb?" I asked.

Craig proceeded to describe how this kind of tomb looked, as best as archaeologists have been able to determine from excavations of first-century sites.

"There was a slanted groove that led down to a low entrance, and a large disk-shaped stone was rolled down this groove and lodged into place across the door," he said, using his hands to illustrate what he was saying. "A smaller stone was then used to secure the disk. Although it would be easy to roll this big disk down the groove, it would take several men to roll the stone back up in order to reopen the tomb. In that sense it was quite secure."

However, was Jesus' tomb also guarded? I knew that some skeptics have attempted to cast doubt on the popular belief that Jesus' tomb was carefully watched around the clock by highly disciplined Roman soldiers, who faced death themselves if they failed in their duty.

"Are you convinced there were Roman guards?" I asked.

"Only Matthew reports that guards were placed around the tomb," he replied. "But in any event, I don't think the guard story is an important facet of the evidence for the Resurrection. For one thing, it's too disputed by contemporary scholarship. I find it's prudent to base my arguments on evidence that's most widely accepted by the majority of scholars, so the guard story is better left aside."

I was surprised by his approach. "Doesn't that weaken your case?" I asked.

Craig shook his head. "Frankly, the guard story may have been important in the eighteenth century, when critics were suggesting that the disciples stole Jesus' body, but nobody espouses that theory today," he responded.

"When you read the New Testament," he continued, "there's no doubt that the disciples sincerely believed the truth of the Resurrection, which they proclaimed to their deaths. The idea that the empty tomb is the result of some hoax, conspiracy, or theft is simply dismissed today. So the guard story has become sort of incidental."

WERE ANY GUARDS PRESENT?

Even so, I was interested in whether there was any evidence to back up Matthew's assertion about the guards. Although I understood Craig's reasons for setting aside the issue, I pressed ahead by asking whether there was any good evidence that the guard story is historical.

"Yes, there is," he said. "Think about the claims and counterclaims about the Resurrection that went back and forth between the Jews and Christians in the first century.

"The initial Christian proclamation was, 'Jesus is risen.' The Jews responded, 'The disciples stole his body.' To this Christians said, 'Ah, but the guards at the tomb would have prevented such a theft.' The Jews responded, 'Oh, but the guards at the tomb fell asleep.' To that the Christians replied, 'No, the Jews bribed the guards to say they fell asleep.'

"Now, if there had not been any guards, the exchange would have gone like this: In response to the claim Jesus is risen, the Jews would say, 'No, the disciples stole his body.' Christians would reply, 'But the guards would have prevented the theft.' Then the Jewish response would have been, 'What guards? You're crazy! There were no guards!' Yet history tells us that's not what the Jews said.

"This suggests the guards really were historical and that the Jews knew it, which is why they had to invent the absurd story about the guards having been asleep while the disciples took the body."

Again a nagging question prompted me to jump in. "There seems to be another problem here," I said, pausing as I tried to formulate my objection as succinctly as I could.

"Why would the Jewish authorities have placed guards at the tomb in the first place? If they were anticipating a resurrection or the disciples faking one, this would mean they had a better understanding of Jesus' predictions about his resurrection than the disciples did! After all, the disciples were surprised by the whole thing."

"You've hit on something there," Craig conceded. "However, maybe they placed the guards there to prevent any sort of tomb robbery or other disturbances from happening during Passover. We don't know. That's a good argument; I grant its full force. But I don't think it's insuperable."

Yes, but it does raise some question concerning the guard story. Plus another objection came to mind. "Matthew says the Roman guards reported to the Jewish authorities," I said. "But doesn't that seem unlikely, since they were responsible to Pilate?"

A slight smile came to Craig's face. "If you look carefully," he said, "Matthew doesn't say the guards are Romans. When the Jews go to Pilate and ask for a guard, Pilate says, 'You have a guard.' Now, does he mean, 'All right, here's a detachment of Roman soldiers'? Or does he mean, 'You've got your own temple guards; use them'?

"Scholars have debated whether or not it was a Jewish guard. I was initially inclined, for the reason you mentioned, to think that the guard was Jewish. I've rethought that, however, because the word Matthew uses to refer to the guards is often used with respect to Roman soldiers rather than just temple officers.

"And remember, John tells us it was a Roman centurion who led Roman soldiers to arrest Jesus under the direction of Jewish leadership. So there is precedent for Roman guards reporting to Jewish religious leaders. It seems plausible that they could also be involved in the guarding of the tomb."

Weighing the evidence, I felt persuaded that guards had been present, but I decided to drop this line of questioning, since Craig doesn't rely on the guard story anyway. Meanwhile I was anxious to confront Craig with what seems to be the most persuasive argument against the idea that Jesus' tomb was vacant on Easter Morning.

WHAT ABOUT THE CONTRADICTIONS?

Through the years, critics of Christianity have attacked the empty tomb story by pointing out apparent discrepancies among the gospel accounts. For example, skeptic Charles Templeton said recently, "The four descriptions of events . . . differ so markedly at so many points that, with all the good will in the world, they cannot be reconciled."[3]

Taken at face value, this objection seems to penetrate to the heart of the reliability of the empty tomb narratives. Consider this summary by Dr. Michael Martin of Boston University, which I read to Craig that morning:

> In Matthew, when Mary Magdalene and the other Mary arrived toward dawn at the tomb there is a rock in front of it, there is a violent earthquake, and an angel descends and rolls back the stone. In Mark, the women arrive at the tomb at sunrise and the stone had been rolled back. In Luke, when the women arrive at early dawn they find the stone had already been rolled back.
>
> In Matthew, an angel is sitting on the rock outside the tomb and in Mark a youth is inside the tomb. In Luke, two men are inside.
>
> In Matthew, the women present at the tomb are Mary Magdalene and the other Mary. In Mark, the women present at the tomb are the two Marys and Salome. In Luke, Mary Magdalene, Mary the mother of James, Joanna, and the other women are present at the tomb.
>
> In Matthew, the two Marys rush from the tomb in great fear and joy, run to tell the disciples, and meet Jesus on the way. In Mark, they run out of the tomb in fear and say nothing to anyone. In Luke, the women report the story to the disciples who do not believe them and there is no suggestion that they meet Jesus.[4]

"And," I said to Craig, "Martin points out that John conflicts with much of the other three gospels. He concludes, 'In sum, the accounts of what happened at the tomb are either inconsistent or can only be made consistent with the aid of implausible interpretations.'"[5]

I stopped reading and looked up from my notes. My eyes locking with Craig's, I asked him point-blank, "In light of all this, how in the world can you possibly consider the empty tomb story to be credible?"

Immediately I noticed something about Craig's demeanor. In casual conversation or when discussing tepid objections to the empty tomb, he's rather mellow. But the tougher the question and the more piercing the challenge, the more animated and focused he gets. And at this point his body language told me he couldn't wait to dive into these seemingly dangerous waters.

Clearing his throat, Craig began. "With all due respect," he said, "Michael Martin is a philosopher, not a historian, and I don't think he understands the historian's craft. For a philosopher, if something is inconsistent, the law of contradiction says, 'This cannot be true, throw it out!' However, the historian looks at these narratives and says, 'I see some inconsistencies, but I notice something about them: they're all in the secondary details.'

"The core of the story is the same: Joseph of Arimathea takes the body of Jesus, puts it in a tomb, the tomb is visited by a small group of women followers of Jesus early on the Sunday morning following his crucifixion, and they find that the tomb is empty. They see a vision of angels saying that Jesus is risen.

"The careful historian, unlike the philosopher, doesn't throw out the baby with the bathwater. He says, 'This suggests that there is a historical core to this story that is reliable and can be depended upon, however conflicting the secondary details might be.'

"So we can have great confidence in the core that's common to the narratives and that would be agreed upon by the majority of New Testament scholars today, even if there are some differences concerning the names of the women, the exact time of the morning, the number of the angels, and so forth. Those kinds of secondary discrepancies wouldn't bother a historian."

Even the usually skeptical historian Michael Grant, a fellow of Trinity College, Cambridge, and professor at Edinburgh University, concedes in his book *Jesus: An Historian's Review of the Gospels,* "True, the discovery of the empty tomb is differently described by the various gospels, but if we apply the same sort of criteria that we would apply to any other ancient literary sources, then the evidence is firm and plausible enough to necessitate the conclusion that the tomb was, indeed, found empty."[6]

CAN DISCREPANCIES BE HARMONIZED?

Sometimes while covering criminal trials, I've seen two witnesses give the exact same testimony, down to the nitty-gritty details, only to find themselves ripped apart by the defense attorney for having colluded before the trial. So I remarked to Craig, "I suppose if all four gospels were identical in all their minutiae, that would have raised the suspicion of plagiarism."

"Yes, that's a very good point," he said. "The differences between the empty tomb narratives suggest that we have multiple, independent attestation of the empty tomb story. Sometimes people say, 'Matthew and Luke just plagiarized from Mark,' but when you look at the narratives closely, you see divergences that suggest that even if Matthew and Luke did know Mark's account, nevertheless they also had separate, independent sources for the empty tomb story.

"So with these multiple and independent accounts, no historian would disregard this evidence just because of secondary discrepancies. Let me give you a secular example.

"We have two narratives of Hannibal crossing the Alps to attack Rome, and they're incompatible and irreconcilable. Yet no classical historian doubts the fact that Hannibal did mount such a campaign. That's a nonbiblical illustration of discrepancies in secondary details failing to undermine the historical core of a historical story."

I conceded the power of that argument. And as I reflected on Martin's critique, it seemed to me that some of his alleged contradictions could be rather easily reconciled. I mentioned this to Craig by saying, "Aren't there ways to harmonize some of the differences among these accounts?"

"Yes, that's right, there are," Craig replied. "For example, the time of the visit to the tomb. One writer might describe it as still being dark, the other might be saying it was getting light, but that's sort of like the optimist and the pessimist arguing over whether the glass was half empty or half full. It was around dawn, and they were describing the same thing with different words.

"As for the number and names of the women, none of the gospels pretend to give a complete list. They all include Mary Magdalene and other women, so there was probably a gaggle of these early disciples that included those who were named and probably a couple of others. I think it would be pedantic to say that's a contradiction."

"What about the different accounts of what happened afterward?" I asked. "Mark said the women didn't tell anybody, and the other gospels say they did."

Craig explained, "When you look at Mark's theology, he loves to emphasize awe and fright and terror and worship in the presence of the divine. So this reaction of the women—of fleeing with fear and trembling, and saying nothing to anyone because they were afraid—is all part of Mark's literary and theological style.

"It could well be that this was a temporary silence, and then the women went back and told the others what had happened. In fact," he concluded with a grin, "it *had* to be a temporary silence; otherwise Mark couldn't be telling the story about it!"

I wanted to ask about one other commonly cited discrepancy. "Jesus said in Matthew 12:40, 'For as Jonah was three days and three nights in the belly of a huge fish, so the Son of Man will be three days and three nights in the heart of the earth.' However, the gospels report that Jesus was really in the tomb one full day, two full nights, and part of two days. Isn't this an example of Jesus being wrong in not fulfilling his own prophecy?"

"Some well-meaning Christians have used this verse to suggest Jesus was crucified on Wednesday rather than on Friday, in order to get the full time in there!" Craig said. "But most scholars recognize that according to early Jewish time-reckoning, any part of a day counted as a full day. Jesus was in the tomb Friday afternoon, all day Saturday, and on Sunday morning—under the way the Jews conceptualized time back then, this would have counted as three days.

"Again," he concluded, "that's just another example of how many of these discrepancies can be explained or minimized with some background knowledge or by just thinking them through with an open mind."

CAN THE WITNESSES BE TRUSTED?

The gospels agree that the empty tomb was discovered by women who were friends and followers of Jesus. But that, in Martin's estimation, makes their testimony suspect, since they were "probably not objective observers."

So I put the question to Craig: "Does the women's relationship with Jesus call the reliability of their testimony into question?"

Unwittingly I had played right into Craig's hand. "Actually, this argument backfires on people who use it," Craig said in response. "Certainly these women were friends of Jesus. But when you understand the role of women in first-century Jewish society, what's really extraordinary is that this empty tomb story should feature women as the discoverers of the empty tomb in the first place.

"Women were on a very low rung of the social ladder in first-century Palestine. There are old rabbinical sayings that said, 'Let the words of the Law be burned rather than delivered to women' and 'Blessed is he whose children are male, but woe to him whose children are female.'

Women's testimony was regarded as so worthless that they weren't even allowed to serve as legal witnesses in a Jewish court of law.

"In light of this, it's absolutely remarkable that the chief witnesses to the empty tomb are these women who were friends of Jesus. Any later legendary account would have certainly portrayed male disciples as discovering the tomb—Peter or John, for example. The fact that women are the first witnesses to the empty tomb is most plausibly explained by the reality that—like it or not—they *were* the discoverers of the empty tomb! This shows that the gospel writers faithfully recorded what happened, even if it was embarrassing. This bespeaks the historicity of this tradition rather than its legendary status."

WHY DID THE WOMEN VISIT THE TOMB?

Craig's explanation, however, left yet another question lingering: why were the women going to anoint the body of Jesus if they already knew that his tomb was securely sealed? "Do their actions really make sense?" I asked.

Craig thought for a moment before he answered—this time not in his debater's voice but in a more tender tone. "Lee, I strongly feel that scholars who have not known the love and devotion that these women felt for Jesus have no right to pronounce cool judgments upon the feasibility of what they wanted to do.

"For people who are grieving, who have lost someone they desperately loved and followed, to want to go to the tomb in a forlorn hope of anointing the body—I just don't think some later critic can treat them like robots and say, 'They shouldn't have gone.'"

He shrugged his shoulders. "Maybe they thought there would be men around who could move the stone. If there were guards, maybe they thought they would. I don't know.

"Certainly the notion of visiting a tomb to pour oils over a body is a historical Jewish practice; the only question is the feasibility of who would move the stone for them. And I don't think we're in the right position to pronounce judgment on whether or not they should have simply stayed at home."

WHY DIDN'T CHRISTIANS CITE THE EMPTY TOMB?

In preparing for my interview with Craig, I had gone to the Internet sites of several atheist organizations to see the kind of arguments they were raising against the Resurrection. For some reason few atheists deal with this topic. However, one critic raised an objection that I wanted to present to Craig.

Essentially, he said a major argument against the empty tomb is that none of the disciples or later Christian preachers bothered to point to it. He wrote, "We would expect the early Christian preachers to have said: 'You don't believe us? Go look in the tomb yourselves! It's at the corner of Fifth and Main, third sepulcher on the right.'"

Yet, he said, Peter doesn't mention the empty tomb in his preaching in Acts 2. Concluded this critic, "If even the disciples didn't think the empty tomb tradition was any good, why should we?"

Craig's eyes widened as I posed the question. "I just don't think that's true," he replied, a bit of astonishment in his voice, as he picked up his Bible and turned to the second chapter of Acts, which records Peter's sermon at Pentecost.

"The empty tomb *is* found in Peter's speech," Craig insisted. "He proclaims in verse 24 that 'God raised him from the dead, freeing him from the agony of death.'

"Then he quotes from a psalm about how God would not allow his Holy One to undergo decay. This had been written by David, and Peter says, 'I can tell you confidently that the patriarch David died and was buried, and his tomb is here to this day.' But, he says, Christ 'was not abandoned to the grave, nor did his body see decay. God has raised this Jesus to life, and we are all witnesses of the fact.'"

Craig looked up from the Bible. "This speech contrasts David's tomb, which remained to that day, with the prophecy in which David says Christ would be raised up—his flesh wouldn't suffer decay. It's clearly implicit that the tomb was left empty."

Then he turned to a later chapter in the book of Acts. "In Acts 13:29–31, Paul says, 'When they had carried out all that was written about him, they took him down from the tree and laid him in a tomb. But God raised him from the dead, and for many days he was seen by those who had traveled with him from Galilee to Jerusalem.' Certainly the empty tomb is implicit there."

He shut his Bible, then added, "I think it's rather wooden and unreasonable to contend that these early preachers didn't refer to the empty tomb, just because they didn't use the two specific words *empty tomb*. There's no question that they knew—and their audiences understood from their preaching—that Jesus' tomb was vacant."

WHAT'S THE AFFIRMATIVE EVIDENCE?

I had spent the first part of our interview peppering Craig with objections and arguments challenging the empty tomb. But I suddenly realized that I hadn't given him the opportunity to spell out his affirmative case. While he had already alluded to several reasons why he believes Jesus' tomb was unoccupied, I said, "Why don't you give me your best shot? Convince me with your top four or five reasons that the empty tomb is a historical fact."

Craig rose to the challenge. One by one he spelled out his arguments concisely and powerfully.

"First," he said, "the empty tomb is definitely implicit in the early tradition that is passed along by Paul in 1 Corinthians 15, which is a very old and reliable source of historical information about Jesus.

"Second, the site of Jesus' tomb was known to Christian and Jew alike. So if it weren't empty, it would be impossible for a movement founded on belief in the Resurrection to have come into existence in the same city where this man had been publicly executed and buried.

"Third, we can tell from the language, grammar, and style that Mark got his empty tomb story—actually, his whole passion narrative—from an earlier source. In fact, there's evidence it was written before A.D. 37, which is much too early for legend to have seriously corrupted it.

"A. N. Sherwin-White, the respected Greco-Roman classical historian from Oxford University, said it would have been without precedent anywhere in history for legend to have grown up that fast and significantly distorted the gospels.

"Fourth, there's the simplicity of the empty tomb story in Mark. Fictional apocryphal accounts from the second century contain all kinds of flowery narratives, in which Jesus comes out of the tomb in glory and power, with everybody seeing him, including the priests, Jewish authorities, and Roman guards. Those are the way legends read, but these don't come until generations after the events, which is after eyewitnesses have died off. By contrast, Mark's account of the story of the empty tomb is stark in its simplicity and unadorned by theological reflection.

"Fifth, the unanimous testimony that the empty tomb was discovered by women argues for the authenticity of the story, because this would have been embarrassing for the disciples to admit and most certainly would have been covered up if this were a legend.

"Sixth, the earliest Jewish polemic presupposes the historicity of the empty tomb. In other words, there was nobody who was claiming that the tomb still contained Jesus' body. The question always was, 'What happened to the body?'

"The Jews proposed the ridiculous story that the guards had fallen asleep. Obviously, they were grasping at straws. But the point is this: they started with the assumption that the tomb was vacant! Why? Because they knew it was!"

WHAT ABOUT ALTERNATIVE THEORIES?

I listened intently as Craig articulated each point, and to me the six arguments added up to an impressive case. However, I still wanted to see if there were any loopholes before concluding it was airtight.

"Kirsopp Lake suggested in 1907 that the women merely went to the wrong tomb," I said. "He says they got lost and a caretaker at an unoccupied tomb told them, 'You're looking for Jesus of Nazareth. He is not here,' and they ran away, afraid. Isn't that a plausible explanation?"[7]

Craig sighed. "Lake didn't generate any following with this," he said. "The reason is that the site of Jesus' tomb was known to the Jewish authorities. Even if the women had made this mistake, the authorities would have been only too happy to point out the tomb and correct the disciples' error when they began to proclaim that Jesus had risen from the dead. I don't know anybody who holds to Lake's theory today."

Frankly, other options didn't sound very likely, either. Obviously, the disciples had no motive to steal the body and then die for a lie, and certainly the Jewish authorities wouldn't have removed the body. I said, "We're left with the theory that the empty tomb was a later legend and that by the time it developed, people were unable to disprove it, because the location of the tomb had been forgotten."

"That has been the issue ever since 1835, when David Strauss claimed these stories are legendary," Craig replied. "And that's why in our conversation today we've focused so much on this legendary hypothesis by showing that the empty tomb story goes back to within a few years of the events themselves. This renders the legend theory worthless. Even if there are some legendary elements in the secondary details of the story, the historical core of the story remains securely established."

Yes, there were answers for these alternative explanations. Upon analysis, every theory seemed to crumble under the weight of evidence and logic. But the only remaining option was to believe that the crucified Jesus returned to life—a conclusion some people find too extraordinary to swallow.

I thought for a moment about how I could phrase this in a question to Craig. Finally I said, "Even though these alternative theories admittedly have holes in them, aren't they more plausible than the absolutely incredible idea that Jesus was God incarnate who was raised from the dead?"

"This, I think, is the issue," he said, leaning forward. "I think people who push these alternative theories would admit, 'Yes, our theories are implausible, but they're not as improbable as the idea that this spectacular miracle occurred.' However, at this point the matter is no longer a historical issue; instead it's a philosophical question about whether miracles are possible."

"And what," I asked, "would you say to that?"

"I would argue that the hypothesis that God raised Jesus from the dead is not at all improbable. In fact, based on the evidence, it's the best explanation for what happened. What is improbable is the hypothesis that Jesus rose naturally from the dead. That, I would agree, is outlandish. Any hypothesis would be more probable than saying the corpse of Jesus spontaneously came back to life.

"But the hypothesis that God raised Jesus from the dead doesn't contradict science or any known facts of experience. All it requires is the hypothesis that God exists, and I think there are good independent reasons for believing that he does."

With that Craig added this clincher: "As long as the existence of God is even possible, it's possible that he acted in history by raising Jesus from the dead."

CONCLUSION: THE TOMB WAS VACANT

Craig was convincing: the empty tomb—admittedly, a miracle of staggering proportions—did make sense in light of the evidence. And it was only part of the case for the Resurrection. From Craig's Atlanta home I was getting ready to go to Virginia to interview a renowned expert on the evidence for the appearances of the resurrected Jesus, and then to California to speak with another scholar about the considerable circumstantial evidence.

As I thanked Craig and his wife, Jan, for their hospitality, I reflected to myself that up close, in his blue jeans and white socks,

Craig didn't look like the kind of formidable adversary who would devastate the best Resurrection critics in the world. But I had heard the tapes of the debates for myself.

In the face of the facts, they have been impotent to put Jesus' body back into the tomb. They flounder, they struggle, they snatch at straws, they contradict themselves, they pursue desperate and extraordinary theories to try to account for the evidence. Yet each time, in the end, the tomb remains vacant.

I was reminded of the assessment by one of the towering legal intellects of all time, the Cambridge-educated Sir Norman Anderson, who lectured at Princeton University, was offered a professorship for life at Harvard University, and served as dean of the Faculty of Laws at the University of London.

His conclusion, after a lifetime of analyzing this issue from a legal perspective, was summed up in one sentence: "The empty tomb, then, forms a veritable rock on which all rationalistic theories of the resurrection dash themselves in vain."[8]

Deliberations

Questions for Reflection or Group Study

1. What's your own conclusion concerning whether Jesus' tomb was empty on Easter Morning? What evidence did you find most convincing in coming to that judgment?
2. As Craig pointed out, everyone in the ancient world admitted the tomb was empty; the issue was how it got that way. Can you think of any logical explanation for the vacant tomb other than the resurrection of Jesus? If so, how do you imagine someone like Bill Craig might respond to your theory?
3. Read Mark 15:42–16:8, the earliest account of Jesus' burial and empty tomb. Do you agree with Craig that it is "stark in its simplicity and unadorned by theological reflection"? Why or why not?

For Further Evidence

More Resources on This Topic

Craig, William Lane. "Did Jesus Rise from the Dead?" In *Jesus under Fire,* edited by Michael J. Wilkins and J. P. Moreland, 147–82. Grand Rapids: Zondervan, 1995.

______. "The Empty Tomb of Jesus." In *In Defense of Miracles,* edited by R. Douglas Geivett and Gary R. Habermas, 247–61. Downers Grove, Ill.: InterVarsity Press, 1997.

______. *Knowing the Truth about the Resurrection.* Ann Arbor, Mich.: Servant, 1988.

______. *Reasonable Faith.* Westchester, Ill.: Crossway, 1994.

Craig, William Lane, and Frank Zindler. *Atheism vs. Christianity: Where Does the Evidence Point?* Grand Rapids: Zondervan, 1993. Videocassette.

Harris, Murray J. *Three Crucial Questions about Jesus.* Grand Rapids: Baker, 1994.

13

THE EVIDENCE OF APPEARANCES

Was Jesus Seen Alive After His Death on the Cross?

In 1963 the body of fourteen-year-old Addie Mae Collins, one of four African-American girls tragically murdered in an infamous church bombing by white racists, was buried in Birmingham, Alabama. For years family members kept returning to the grave to pray and leave flowers. In 1998 they made the decision to disinter the deceased for reburial at another cemetery.

When workers were sent to dig up the body, however, they returned with a shocking discovery: The grave was empty.

Understandably, family members were terribly distraught. Hampered by poorly kept records, cemetery officials scrambled to figure out what had happened. Several possibilities were raised, the primary one being that her tombstone had been erected in the wrong place.[1]

Yet in the midst of determining what happened, one explanation was never proposed: Nobody suggested that young Addie Mae had been resurrected to walk the earth again. Why? Because by itself an empty grave does not a resurrection make.

My conversation with Dr. William Lane Craig has already elicited powerful evidence that the tomb of Jesus was empty the Sunday after his crucifixion. While I knew that this was important and necessary evidence for his resurrection, I was also aware that a missing body is not conclusive proof by itself. More facts would be needed to establish that Jesus really did return from the dead.

That's what prompted my plane trip to Virginia. As my flight gently banked over the wooded hills below, I was doing some last-minute reading of a book by Michael Martin, the Boston University professor who has sought to discredit Christianity. I smiled at his words:

"Perhaps the most sophisticated defense of the resurrection to date has been produced by Gary Habermas."[2]

I glanced at my watch. I would land with just enough time to rent a car, drive to Lynchburg, and make my two o'clock appointment with Habermas himself.

THE TWELFTH INTERVIEW: GARY HABERMAS, PH.D, D.D.

Two autographed photos of hockey players, shown in flat-out combat on ice, hang on the walls of Habermas's austere office. One features the immortal Bobby Hull of the Chicago Blackhawks; the other depicts Dave "The Hammer" Schultz, the brawling, tough-as-nails forward for the Philadelphia Flyers.

"Hull is my favorite hockey player," explains Habermas. "Schultz is my favorite fighter." He grinned, then added, "There's a difference."

Habermas—bearded, straight-talking, rough-hewn—is also a fighter, an academic pit bull who looks more like a nightclub bouncer than an ivory tower intellectual. Armed with razor-sharp arguments and historical evidence to back them up, he's not afraid to come out swinging.

Antony Flew, one of the leading philosophical atheists in the world, found that out when he tangled with Habermas in a major debate on the topic "Did Jesus Rise from the Dead?" The results were decidedly one-sided. Of the five independent philosophers from various colleges and universities who served as judges of the debate's content, four concluded that Habermas had won. One called the contest a draw. None cast a ballot for Flew. Commented one judge, "I was surprised (shocked might be a more accurate word) to see how weak Flew's own approach was.... I was left with this conclusion: Since the case against the resurrection was no stronger than that presented by Antony Flew, I would think it was time I began to take the resurrection seriously."[3]

One of five other professional debate judges who evaluated the contestants' argumentation techniques (again Habermas was the victor) felt compelled to write, "I conclude that the historical evidence, though flawed, is strong enough to lead reasonable minds to conclude that Christ did indeed rise from the dead.... Habermas does end up providing 'highly probable evidence' for the historicity of the resurrection 'with no plausible naturalistic evidence against it.' Habermas, therefore, in my opinion, wins the debate."[4]

After earning a doctorate from Michigan State University, where he wrote his dissertation on the Resurrection, Habermas received a doctor of divinity degree from Emmanuel College in Oxford, England. He has authored seven books dealing with Jesus rising from the dead, including *The Resurrection of Jesus: A Rational Inquiry; The Resurrection of Jesus: An Apologetic; The Historical Jesus;* and *Did Jesus Rise from the Dead? The Resurrection Debate,* which was based on his debate with Flew. Among his other books are *Dealing with Doubt* and (with J. P. Moreland) *Beyond Death: Exploring the Evidence for Immortality.*

In addition, he coedited *In Defense of Miracles* and contributed to *Jesus under Fire* and *Living Your Faith: Closing the Gap between Mind and Heart.* His one hundred articles have appeared in popular publications (such as the *Saturday Evening Post*), scholarly journals (including *Faith and Philosophy* and *Religious Studies*), and reference books (for example, *The Baker Dictionary of Theology*). He's also the former president of the Evangelical Philosophical Society.

I don't mean to suggest by my earlier description that Habermas is unnecessarily combative; he's friendly and self-effacing in casual conversations. I just wouldn't want to be on the other side of a hockey puck—or an argument—from him. He has an innate radar that helps him zero in on his opponent's vulnerable points. He also has a tender side, which I would discover—quite unexpectedly—before our interview was over.

I found Habermas in his no-nonsense office at Liberty University, where he is currently distinguished professor and chairman of the Department of Philosophy and Theology and director of the master's program in apologetics. The room, with its black file cabinets, metal desk with simulated wood top, threadbare carpet, and folding guest chairs, is certainly no showplace. Like its occupant, it's free from pretension.

"DEAD PEOPLE DON'T DO THAT"

Habermas, sitting behind his desk, rolled up the sleeves of his blue button-down shirt as I turned on my tape recorder and started our interview.

"Isn't it true," I began with prosecutorial bluntness, "that there are absolutely no eyewitnesses to Jesus' resurrection?"

"That's exactly right—there's no descriptive account of the Resurrection," Habermas replied in an admission that might surprise people who only have a casual knowledge of the subject.

"When I was young, I was reading a book by C. S. Lewis, who wrote that the New Testament says nothing about the Resurrection. I wrote a real big 'No!' in the margin. Then I realized what he was saying: nobody was sitting inside the tomb and saw the body start to vibrate, stand up, take the linen wrappings off, fold them, roll back the stone, wow the guards, and leave."

That, it seemed to me, might pose some problems. "Doesn't this hurt your efforts to establish that the Resurrection is a historical event?" I asked.

Habermas pushed back his chair to get more comfortable. "No, this doesn't hurt our case one iota, because science is all about causes and effects. We don't see dinosaurs; we study the fossils. We may not know how a disease originates, but we study its symptoms. Maybe nobody witnesses a crime, but police piece together the evidence after the fact.

"So," he continued, "here's how I look at the evidence for the Resurrection: First, did Jesus die on the cross? And second, did he appear later to people? If you can establish those two things, you've made your case, because dead people don't normally do that."

Historians agree there's plenty of evidence that Jesus was crucified, and Dr. Alexander Metherell demonstrated in an earlier chapter that Jesus could not have survived the rigors of that execution. That leaves the second part of the issue: did Jesus really appear later?

"What evidence is there that people saw him?" I asked.

"I'll start with evidence that virtually all critical scholars will admit," he said, opening the Bible in front of him. "Nobody questions that Paul wrote 1 Corinthians, and we have him affirming in two places that he personally encountered the resurrected Christ. He says in 1 Corinthians 9:1, 'Am I not an apostle? Have I not seen Jesus our Lord?' And he says in 1 Corinthians 15:8, 'Last of all he appeared to me also.'"

I recognized that last quote as being attached to the early church creed that Craig Blomberg and I have already discussed. As William Lane Craig indicated, the first part of the creed (verses 3–4) refers to Jesus' execution, burial, and resurrection.

The final part of the creed (verses 5–8) deals with his post-Resurrection appearances: "[Christ] appeared to Peter, and then to the

Twelve. After that, he appeared to more than five hundred of the brothers at the same time, most of whom are still living, though some have fallen asleep. Then he appeared to James, then to all the apostles." In the next verse, Paul adds, "And last of all he appeared to me also, as to one abnormally born."

On the face of it, this is incredibly influential testimony that Jesus did appear alive after his death. Here were names of specific individuals and groups of people who saw him, written at a time when people could still check them out if they wanted confirmation. Since I knew that the creed would be pivotal in establishing the Resurrection, I decided to subject it to greater scrutiny: Why are historians convinced it's a creed? How trustworthy is it? How far back does it go?

"Do you mind if I cross-examine you on this creed?" I asked Habermas.

He extended his hand as if to invite the inquiry. "Please," he said politely, "go ahead."

"CONVINCE ME IT'S A CREED"

Initially I wanted to determine why Habermas, Craig, Blomberg, and others are convinced that this passage is a creed of the early church and not just the words of Paul, who wrote the letter to the Corinthian church in which it's contained.

My challenge to Habermas was simple and direct: "Convince me it's a creed."

"Well, I can give you several solid reasons. First, Paul introduces it with the words *received* and *delivered* [or *passed on* in the NIV], which are technical rabbinic terms indicating he's passing along holy tradition.

"Second," Habermas said, looking down at his hands as he grabbed a finger at a time to emphasize each point he was making, "the text's parallelism and stylized content indicate it's a creed. Third, the original text uses *Cephas* for Peter, which is his Aramaic name. In fact, the Aramaic itself could indicate a very early origin. Fourth, the creed uses several other primitive phrases that Paul would not customarily use, like 'the Twelve,' 'the third day,' 'he was raised,' and others. Fifth, the use of certain words is similar to Aramaic and Mishnaic Hebrew means of narration."

Having run out of fingers, he looked up at me. "Should I go on?" he asked.

"OK, OK," I said. "You're saying that these facts convince you, as a conservative evangelical Christian, that this is an early creed."

Habermas seemed a bit offended by that admittedly barbed remark. "It's not just conservative Christians who are convinced," he insisted indignantly. "This is an assessment that's shared by a wide range of scholars from across a broad theological spectrum. The eminent scholar Joachim Jeremias refers to this creed as 'the earliest tradition of all,' and Ulrich Wilckens says it 'indubitably goes back to the oldest phase of all in the history of primitive Christianity.'"

That raised the question of how primitive the creed is. "How far back can you date it?" I asked.

"We know that Paul wrote 1 Corinthians between A.D. 55 and 57. He indicates in 1 Corinthians 15:1–4 that he has already passed on this creed to the church at Corinth, which would mean it must predate his visit there in A.D. 51. Therefore the creed was being used within twenty years of the Resurrection, which is quite early.

"However, I'd agree with the various scholars who trace it back even further, to within two to eight years of the Resurrection, or from about A.D. 32 to 38, when Paul received it in either Damascus or Jerusalem. So this is incredibly early material—primitive, unadorned testimony to the fact that Jesus appeared alive to skeptics like Paul and James, as well as to Peter and the rest of the disciples."

"But," I protested, "it's not really a firsthand account. Paul is providing the list second- or thirdhand. Doesn't that diminish its value as evidence?"

Not to Habermas. "Keep in mind that Paul personally affirms that Jesus appeared to him as well, so this provides firsthand testimony. And Paul didn't just pick up this list from strangers on the street. The leading view is that he got it directly from the eyewitnesses Peter and James themselves, and he took great pains to confirm its accuracy."

That was a strong claim. "How do you know that?" I asked.

"I would concur with the scholars who believe Paul received this material three years after his conversion, when he took a trip to Jerusalem and met with Peter and James. Paul describes that trip in Galatians 1:18–19, where he uses a very interesting Greek word—*historeo*."

I wasn't familiar with the meaning of the word. "Why is that significant?"

"Because this word indicates that he didn't just casually shoot the breeze when he met with them. It shows this was an investigative inquiry. Paul was playing the role of an examiner, someone who was carefully checking this out. So the fact that Paul personally confirmed matters with two eyewitnesses who are specifically mentioned in the creed—Peter and James—gives this extra weight. One of the very few Jewish New Testament scholars, Pinchas Lapide, says the evidence in support of the creed is so strong that it 'may be considered as a statement of eyewitnesses.'"

Before I could jump in, Habermas added, "And later, in 1 Corinthians 15:11, Paul emphasizes that the other apostles agreed in preaching the same gospel, this same message about the Resurrection. This means that what the eyewitness Paul is saying is the exact same thing as what the eyewitnesses Peter and James are saying."

I'll admit it: all this sounded pretty convincing. Still, I had some reservations about the creed, and I didn't want Habermas's confident assertions to deter me from probing further.

THE MYSTERY OF THE FIVE HUNDRED

The creed in 1 Corinthians 15 is the only place in ancient literature where it is claimed that Jesus appeared to five hundred people at once. The gospels don't corroborate it. No secular historian mentions it. And to me, that raises a yellow flag.

"If this really happened, why doesn't anyone else talk about it?" I asked Habermas. "You'd think the apostles would cite this as evidence wherever they went. As the atheist Michael Martin says, 'One must conclude that it is extremely unlikely that this incident really occurred' and that this therefore 'indirectly casts doubt on Paul as a reliable source.'"[5]

That remark bothered Habermas. "Well, it's just plain silliness to say this casts doubt on Paul," he replied, sounding both astonished and annoyed that someone would make that claim.

"I mean, give me a break! First, even though it's only reported in one source, it just so happens to be the earliest and best-authenticated passage of all! That counts for *something*.

"Second, Paul apparently had some proximity to these people. He says, 'most of whom are still living, though some have fallen asleep.' Paul either knew some of these people or was told by someone who knew them that they were still walking around and willing to be interviewed.

"Now, stop and think about it: you would never include this phrase unless you were absolutely confident that these folks would confirm that they really did see Jesus alive. I mean, Paul was virtually inviting people to check it out for themselves! He wouldn't have said this if he didn't know they'd back him up.

"Third, when you have only one source, you can ask, 'Why aren't there more?' But you can't say, 'This one source is crummy on the grounds that someone else didn't pick up on it.' You can't downgrade this one source that way. So this doesn't cast any doubt on Paul at all—believe me, Martin would love to be able to do that, but he can't do it legitimately.

"This is an example of how some critics want it both ways. Generally, they denigrate the gospel Resurrection accounts in favor of Paul, since he is taken to be the chief authority. But on this issue, they're questioning Paul for the sake of texts that they don't trust as much in the first place! What does this say about their methodology?"

I was still having trouble envisioning this appearance by Jesus to such a large crowd. "Where would this encounter with five hundred people have taken place?" I asked.

"Well, the Galilean countryside," Habermas speculated. "If Jesus could feed five thousand, he could preach to five hundred. And Matthew does say Jesus appeared on a hillside; maybe more than just the eleven disciples were there."

Picturing that scene in my mind, I still couldn't help but wonder why someone else didn't report on this event. "Wouldn't it be likely that the historian Josephus would have mentioned something of that magnitude?"

"No, I don't think that's necessarily true. Josephus was writing sixty years afterward. How long do local stories circulate before they start to die out?" Habermas asked. "So either Josephus didn't know about it, which is possible, or he chose not to mention it, which would make sense because we know Josephus was not a follower of Jesus. You can't expect Josephus to start building the case for him."

When I didn't respond for a moment, Habermas continued. "Look, I'd love to have five sources for this. I don't. But I do have one excellent source—a creed that's so good that German historian Hans von Campenhausen says, 'This account meets all the demands of historical reliability that could possibly be made of such a text.' Besides, you don't need to rely on the reference to the five hundred to make the case for the Resurrection. Usually I don't even use it."

Habermas's answer carried some logic. Still, there was another aspect of the creed that weighed on me: it says Jesus appeared first to Peter, whereas John said he appeared first to Mary Magdalene. In fact, the creed doesn't mention any women, even though they're prominently featured in the gospel accounts.

"Don't these contradictions hurt its credibility?" I asked.

"Ah, no," came the reply. "First of all, look at the creed carefully: it doesn't say Jesus appeared *first* to Peter. All it does is put Peter's name first on the list. And since women were not considered competent as witnesses in first-century Jewish culture, it's not surprising that they're not mentioned here. In the first-century scheme of things, their testimony wouldn't carry any weight. So placing Peter first could indicate logical priority rather than temporal priority.

"Again," he concluded, "the creed's credibility remains intact. You've raised some questions, but wouldn't you concede that they don't undermine the persuasive evidence that the creed is early, that it's free from legendary contamination, that it's unambiguous and specific, and that it's ultimately rooted in eyewitness accounts?"

All in all, I was forced to agree that he was right. The weight of the evidence clearly and convincingly supports the creed as being powerful evidence for Jesus' post-Resurrection appearances.

So powerful that William Lane Craig, the Resurrection expert I interviewed in the previous chapter, said that Wolfhart Pannenberg, perhaps the greatest living systematic theologian in the world, "has rocked modern, skeptical German theology by building his entire theology precisely on the historical evidence for the resurrection of Jesus as supplied in Paul's list of appearances."[6]

Having satisfied myself about the essential reliability of the 1 Corinthians 15 creed, it was time to begin looking at the four gospels, which recount the various appearances by the resurrected Jesus in more detail.

THE TESTIMONY OF THE GOSPELS

I started this line of inquiry by asking Habermas to describe the post-Resurrection appearances in Matthew, Mark, Luke, and John.

"There are several different appearances to a lot of different people in the gospels and Acts—some individually, some in groups, sometimes indoors, sometimes outdoors, to softhearted people like John and skeptical people like Thomas," he began.

"At times they touched Jesus or ate with him, with the texts teaching that he was physically present. The appearances occurred over several weeks. And there are good reasons to trust these accounts—for example, they're lacking in many typical mythical tendencies."

"Can you enumerate these appearances for me?"

From memory, Habermas described them one at a time. Jesus appeared

- to Mary Magdalene, in John 20:10–18;
- to the other women, in Matthew 28:8–10;
- to Cleopas and another disciple on the road to Emmaus, in Luke 24:13–32;
- to eleven disciples and others, in Luke 24:33–49;
- to ten apostles and others, with Thomas absent, in John 20:19–23;
- to Thomas and the other apostles, in John 20:26–30;
- to seven apostles, in John 21:1–14;
- to the disciples, in Matthew 28:16–20.
- And he was with the apostles at the Mount of Olives before his ascension, in Luke 24:50–52 and Acts 1:4–9.

"It's particularly interesting," Habermas added, "that C. H. Dodd, the Cambridge University scholar, has carefully analyzed these appearances and concluded that several of them are based on especially early material, including Jesus' encounter with the women, in Matthew 28:8–10; his meeting with the eleven apostles, in which he gave them the Great Commission, in Matthew 28:16–20; and his meeting with the disciples, in John 20:19–23, in which he showed them his hands and side."

Again, here was a wealth of sightings of Jesus. This was not merely a fleeting observance of a shadowy figure by one or two people. There were multiple appearances to numerous people, several of the appearances being confirmed in more than one gospel or by the 1 Corinthians 15 creed.

"Is there any further corroboration?" I asked.

"Just look at Acts," replied Habermas, referring to the New Testament book that records the launch of the church. Not only are Jesus' appearances mentioned regularly, but details are provided, and the theme of the disciples being a witness of these things is found in almost every context.

"The key," Habermas said, "is that a number of the accounts in Acts 1–5, 10, and 13 also include some creeds that, like the one in 1 Corinthians 15, report some very early data concerning the death and resurrection of Jesus."

With that Habermas picked up a book and read the conclusion of scholar John Drane.

> The earliest evidence we have for the resurrection almost certainly goes back to the time immediately after the resurrection event is alleged to have taken place. This is the evidence contained in the early sermons in the Acts of the Apostles . . . there can be no doubt that in the first few chapters of Acts its author has preserved material from very early sources.[7]

Indeed, Acts is littered with references to Jesus' appearances. The apostle Peter was especially adamant about it. He says in Acts 2:32, "God has raised this Jesus to life, and we are all witnesses of the fact." In Acts 3:15 he repeats, "You killed the author of life, but God raised him from the dead. We are witnesses of this." He confirms to Cornelius in Acts 10:41 that he and others "ate and drank with him after he rose from the dead."

Not to be outdone, Paul said in a speech recorded in Acts 13:31, "For many days he was seen by those who had traveled with him from Galilee to Jerusalem. They are now his witnesses to our people."

Asserted Habermas, "The Resurrection was undoubtedly the central proclamation of the early church from the very beginning. The earliest Christians didn't just endorse Jesus' teachings; they were convinced they had seen him alive after his crucifixion. *That's* what changed their lives and started the church. Certainly, since this was their centermost conviction, they would have made absolutely sure that it was true."

All of the gospel and Acts evidence—incident after incident, witness after witness, detail after detail, corroboration on top of corroboration—was extremely impressive. Although I tried, I couldn't think of any more thoroughly attested event in ancient history.

However, there was another question that needed to be raised, this one concerning the gospel that most scholars believe was the first account of Jesus to be written.

MARK'S MISSING CONCLUSION

When I first began investigating the Resurrection, I encountered a troubling comment in the margin of my Bible: "The most reliable early manuscripts and other ancient witnesses do not have Mark 16:9–20." In other words, most scholars believe that the gospel of Mark ends at 16:8, with the women discovering the tomb empty but without Jesus having appeared alive to anyone at all. That seemed perplexing.

"Doesn't it bother you that the earliest gospel doesn't even report any post-Resurrection appearances?" I asked Habermas.

On the contrary, he didn't seemed disturbed at all. "I don't have a problem with that whatsoever," he said. "Sure, it would be nice if he had included a list of appearances, but here are some things for you to think about:

"Even if Mark does end there, which not everyone believes, you still have him reporting that the tomb is empty, and a young man proclaiming, 'He is risen!' and telling the women that there will be appearances. So you have, first, a proclamation that the Resurrection has occurred, and second, a prediction that appearances will follow.

"You can close your favorite novel and say, 'I can't believe the author's not telling me the next episode,' but you can't close the book and say, 'The writer doesn't believe in the next episode.' Mark definitely does. He obviously believed the Resurrection had taken place. He ends with the women being told that Jesus will appear in Galilee, and then others later confirm that he did."

According to church tradition, Mark was a companion of the eyewitness Peter. "Isn't it odd," I asked, "that Mark wouldn't mention that Jesus appeared to Peter, if he really had?"

"Mark doesn't mention any appearances, so it wouldn't be peculiar that Peter's isn't listed," he said. "However, note that Mark does single out Peter. Mark 16:7 says, 'But go, tell his disciples and Peter, "He is going ahead of you into Galilee. There you will see him, just as he told you."'

"This agrees with 1 Corinthians 15:5, which confirms that Jesus did appear to Peter, and Luke 24:34, another early creed, which says, 'It is true! The Lord has risen and has appeared to Simon,' or Peter.

"So what Mark predicts about Peter is reported to have been fulfilled, in two early and very reliable creeds of the church—as well as by Peter himself in Acts."

ARE THERE ANY ALTERNATIVES?

Without question, the amount of testimony and corroboration of Jesus' post-Resurrection appearances is staggering. To put it into perspective, if you were to call each one of the witnesses to a court of law to be cross-examined for just fifteen minutes each, and you went around the clock without a break, it would take you from breakfast on Monday until dinner on Friday to hear them all. After listening to 129 straight hours of eyewitness testimony, who could possibly walk away unconvinced?

Having been a legal affairs journalist who has covered scores of trials, both criminal and civil, I had to agree with the assessment of Sir Edward Clarke, a British High Court judge who conducted a thorough legal analysis of the first Easter Day: "To me the evidence is conclusive, and over and over again in the High Court I have secured the verdict on evidence not nearly so compelling. As a lawyer I accept the gospel evidence unreservedly as the testimony of truthful men to facts that they were able to substantiate."[8]

However, could there be any plausible alternatives that could explain away these encounters with the risen Jesus? Could these accounts be legendary in nature? Or might the witnesses have experienced hallucinations? I decided to raise those issues with Habermas to get his response.

Possibility 1: The Appearances Are Legendary

If it's true that the gospel of Mark originally ended before any appearances were reported, it could be argued that there's evolutionary development in the gospels: Mark records no appearances, Matthew has some, Luke has more, and John has the most.

"Doesn't that demonstrate that the appearances are merely legends that grew up over time?" I asked.

"For a lot of reasons, no, it doesn't," Habermas assured me. "First, not everybody believes Mark is the earliest gospel. There are scholars, admittedly in the minority, who believe Matthew was written first.

"Second, even if I accept your thesis as true, it only proves that legends grew up over time—it can't explain away the original belief that Jesus was risen from the dead. *Something* happened that prompted the apostles to make the Resurrection the central proclamation of the earliest church. Legend can't explain those initial eyewitness accounts. In other words, legend can tell you how a story got bigger; it can't tell you how it originated when the participants are both eyewitnesses and reported the events early.

"Third, you're forgetting that the 1 Corinthians 15 creed predates any of the gospels, and it makes huge claims about the appearances. In fact, the claim involving the biggest number—that he was seen alive by five hundred people at once—goes back to this earliest source! That creates problems for the legendary-development theory. The best reasons for rejecting the legend theory come from the early creedal accounts in 1 Corinthians 15 and Acts, both of which predate the gospel material."

"And fourth, what about the empty tomb? If the Resurrection were merely a legend, the tomb would be filled. However, it was empty on Easter Morning. That demands an additional hypothesis."

Possibility 2: The Appearances Were Hallucinations

Maybe the witnesses were sincere in believing they saw Jesus. Perhaps they accurately recorded what took place. But could they have been seeing a hallucination that convinced them they were encountering Jesus when they really weren't?

Habermas smiled at the question. "Do you know Gary Collins?" he asked.

That question took me off guard. Sure, I replied, I know him. "I was in his office just recently to interview him for this same book," I said.

"Do you believe he's qualified as a psychologist?" Habermas asked.

"Yes," I answered warily, since I could tell he was setting me up for something. "A doctorate, a professor for twenty years, the author of dozens of books on psychological issues, president of a national association of psychologists—yeah, sure, I'd consider him qualified."

Habermas handed me a piece of paper. "I asked Gary about the possibility that these were hallucinations, and this is his professional opinion," he told me. I looked at the document.

> Hallucinations are individual occurrences. By their very nature only one person can see a given hallucination at a time. They certainly aren't something which can be seen by a group of people. Neither is it possible that one person could somehow

> induce an hallucination in somebody else. Since an hallucination exists only in this subjective, personal sense, it is obvious that others cannot witness it.[9]

"That," said Habermas, "is a big problem for the hallucination theory, since there are repeated accounts of Jesus appearing to multiple people who reported the same thing.

"And there are several other arguments why hallucinations can't explain away his appearances," he continued. "The disciples were fearful, doubtful, and in despair after the Crucifixion, whereas people who hallucinate need a fertile mind of expectancy or anticipation. Peter was hardheaded, for goodness' sake; James was a skeptic—certainly not good candidates for hallucinations.

"Also, hallucinations are comparably rare. They're usually caused by drugs or bodily deprivation. Chances are, you don't know anybody who's ever had a hallucination not caused by one of those two things. Yet we're supposed to believe that over a course of many weeks, people from all sorts of backgrounds, all kinds of temperaments, in various places, all experienced hallucinations? That strains the hypothesis quite a bit, doesn't it?

"Besides, if we establish the gospel accounts as being reliable, how do you account for the disciples eating with Jesus and touching him? How does he walk along with two of them on the road to Emmaus? And what about the empty tomb? If people only thought they saw Jesus, his body would still be in his grave."

OK, I thought, if it wasn't a hallucination, maybe it was something more subtle.

"Could this have been an example of groupthink, in which people talk each other into seeing something that doesn't exist?" I asked. "As Michael Martin observed, 'A person full of religious zeal may see what he or she wants to see, not what is really there.'"[10]

Habermas laughed. "You know, one of the atheists I debated, Antony Flew, told me he doesn't like it when other atheists use that last argument, because it cuts both ways. As Flew said, 'Christians believe because they want to, but atheists don't believe because they don't want to!'

"Actually, there are several reasons why the disciples couldn't have talked each other into this. As the center of their faith, there was too much at stake; they went to their deaths defending it. Wouldn't some of them rethink the groupthink at a later date and recant or just quietly fall away? And what about James, who didn't believe in Jesus, and Paul, who was a persecutor of Christians—how did they get talked into seeing something? Further, what about the empty tomb?

"And on top of that, this view doesn't account for the forthright language of sight in the 1 Corinthians 15 creed and other passages. The eyewitnesses were at least convinced that they had *seen* Jesus alive, and groupthink doesn't explain this aspect very well."

Habermas paused long enough to pull out a book and cap his argument with a quote from prominent theologian and historian Carl Braaten: "Even the more skeptical historians agree that for primitive Christianity . . . the resurrection of Jesus from the dead was a real event in history, the very foundation of faith, and not a mythical idea arising out of the creative imagination of believers."[11]

"Sometimes," concluded Habermas, "people just grasp at straws trying to account for the appearances. But nothing fits all the evidence better than the explanation that Jesus was alive."

"NO RATIONAL DOUBT"

Jesus was killed on the cross—Alexander Metherell has made that graphically clear. His tomb was empty on Easter Morning—William Lane Craig left no doubt about that. His disciples and others saw him, touched him, and ate with him after the Resurrection—Gary Habermas has built that case with abundant evidence. As prominent British theologian Michael Green said, "The appearances of Jesus are as well authenticated as anything in antiquity.... There can be no rational doubt that they occurred, and that the main reason why Christians became sure of the resurrection in the earliest days was just this. They could say with assurance, 'We have seen the Lord.' They *knew* it was he."[12]

And all this doesn't even exhaust the evidence. I had already made plane reservations for a trip to the other side of the country to interview one more expert on the final category of proof that the Resurrection is a real event of history.

Before I left Habermas's office, however, I had one more question. Frankly, I hesitated to ask it, because it was a bit too predictable and I thought I'd get an answer that was a little too pat.

The question concerned the importance of the Resurrection. I figured if I asked Habermas about that, he'd give the standard reply about it being at the center of Christian doctrine, the axis around which the Christian faith turned. And I was right—he did give a stock answer like that.

But what surprised me was that this wasn't all he said. This nuts-and-bolts scholar, this burly and straight-shooting debater, this combat-ready defender of the faith, allowed me to peer into his soul as he gave an answer that grew out of the deepest valley of despair he had ever walked through.

THE RESURRECTION OF DEBBIE

Habermas rubbed his graying beard. The quick-fire cadence and debater's edge to his voice were gone. No more quoting of scholars, no more citing of Scripture, no more building a case. I had asked about the importance of the Resurrection, and Habermas decided to take a risk by harkening back to 1995, when his wife, Debbie, slowly died of stomach cancer. Caught off guard by the tenderness of the moment, all I could do was listen.

"I sat on our porch," he began, looking off to the side at nothing in particular. He sighed deeply, then went on. "My wife was upstairs dying. Except for a few weeks, she was home through it all. It was an awful time. This was the worst thing that could possibly happen."

He turned and looked straight at me. "But do you know what was amazing? My students would call me—not just one but several of them—and say, 'At a time like this, aren't you glad about the Resurrection?' As sober as those circumstances were, I had to smile for two reasons. First, my students were trying to cheer me up with my own teaching. And second, it worked.

"As I would sit there, I'd picture Job, who went through all that terrible stuff and asked questions of God, but then God turned the tables and asked *him* a few questions.

"I knew if God were to come to me, I'd ask only one question: 'Lord, why is Debbie up there in bed?' And I think God would respond by asking gently, 'Gary, did I raise my Son from the dead?'

"I'd say, 'Come on, Lord, I've written seven books on that topic! Of course he was raised from the dead. But I want to know about Debbie!'

"I think he'd keep coming back to the same question—'Did I raise my Son from the dead?' 'Did I raise my Son from the dead?'—until I got his point: the Resurrection says that if Jesus was raised two thousand years ago, there's an answer to Debbie's death in 1995.

And do you know what? It worked for me while I was sitting on the porch, and it still works today.

"It was a horribly emotional time for me, but I couldn't get around the fact that the Resurrection *is* the answer for her suffering. I still worried; I still wondered what I'd do raising four kids alone. But there wasn't a time when that truth didn't comfort me.

"Losing my wife was the most painful experience I've ever had to face, but if the Resurrection could get me through that, it can get me through anything. It was good for 30 A.D., it's good for 1995, it's good for 1998, and it's good beyond that."

Habermas locked eyes with mine. "That's not some sermon," he said quietly. "I believe that with all my heart. If there's a resurrection, there's a heaven. If Jesus was raised, Debbie was raised. And I will be someday, too.

"Then I'll see them both."

Deliberations

Questions for Reflection or Group Study

1. Habermas reduced the issue of the Resurrection down to two questions: Did Jesus die? And was he later seen alive? Based on the evidence so far, how would you answer those questions and why?
2. How influential is the 1 Corinthians 15 creed in your assessment of whether Jesus was seen alive? What are your reasons for concluding that it's significant or insignificant in your investigation?
3. Spend a few minutes to look up some of the gospel appearances cited by Habermas. Do they have the ring of truth to you? How would you evaluate them as evidence for the Resurrection?
4. Habermas spoke about how the Resurrection had a personal meaning for him. Have you faced a loss in your life? How would belief in the Resurrection affect the way you view it?

For Further Evidence

More Resources on This Topic

Ankerberg, John, and John Weldon. *Ready with an Answer.* Eugene, Ore.: Harvest House, 1997.

Geivett, R. Douglas, and Gary R. Habermas, eds. *In Defense of Miracles.* Downers Grove, Ill.: InterVarsity Press, 1997.

Habermas, Gary, and Antony Flew. *Did Jesus Rise from the Dead? The Resurrection Debate.* San Francisco: Harper & Row, 1987.

Habermas, Gary, and J. P. Moreland. *Beyond Death: Exploring the Evidence for Immortality.* Westchester, Ill.: Crossway, 1998.

Morison, Frank. *Who Moved the Stone?* Grand Rapids: Zondervan, 1987.

Proctor, William. *The Resurrection Report.* Nashville: Broadman & Holman, 1998.

14

THE CIRCUMSTANTIAL EVIDENCE

Are There Any Supporting Facts That Point to the Resurrection?

No witnesses watched Timothy McVeigh load two tons of fertilizer-based explosives into a Ryder rental truck. Nobody saw him drive the vehicle to the front of the federal building in Oklahoma City and detonate the bomb, killing 168 people. No video camera captured an image of him fleeing the scene.

Yet a jury was able to conclude beyond a reasonable doubt that McVeigh was guilty of the worst act of domestic terrorism in U.S. history. Why? Because fact by fact, exhibit by exhibit, witness by witness, prosecutors used circumstantial evidence to build an airtight case against him.

While none of the 137 people called to the witness stand had seen McVeigh commit the crime, their testimony did provide indirect evidence of his guilt: a businessman said McVeigh rented a Ryder truck, a friend said McVeigh talked about bombing the building out of anger against the government, and a scientist said McVeigh's clothes contained a residue of explosives when he was arrested.

Prosecutors buttressed this with more than seven hundred exhibits, ranging from motel and taxi receipts to telephone records to a truck key to a bill from a Chinese restaurant. Over eighteen days they skillfully wove a convincing web of evidence from which McVeigh was woefully unable to extricate himself.

Eyewitness testimony is called direct evidence because people describe under oath how they personally saw the defendant commit the crime. While this is often compelling, it can sometimes be subject to faded memories, prejudices, and even outright fabrication. In contrast, circumstantial evidence is made up of indirect facts from which inferences can be rationally drawn.[1] Its cumulative effect can be every bit as strong—and in many instances even more potent—than eyewitness accounts.

Ask Timothy McVeigh. He may have thought he committed the perfect crime by avoiding eyewitnesses, but he nevertheless landed on death row due to the circumstantial facts that pointed toward him as devastatingly as any firsthand witness could have.

Having already considered the persuasive evidence for the empty tomb, and eyewitness accounts of the risen Jesus, now it was time for me to seek out any circumstantial evidence that might bolster the case for the Resurrection. I knew that if an event as extraordinary as the resurrection of Jesus had really occurred, history would be littered with indirect evidence backing it up.

That quest took me once more to southern California, this time to the office of a professor who masterfully blends expertise in history, philosophy, and science.

THE THIRTEENTH INTERVIEW: J. P. MORELAND, PH.D.

J. P. Moreland's dark-gray hair, silvery mustache, and gold-rimmed glasses make him appear a little older than his fifty years. Yet he is brimming with energy. He spoke in animated and enthusiastic tones, frequently leaning forward in his swivel chair to emphasize his points, actually bouncing a bit at times, almost as if he were going to leap out and throttle me with his arguments.

"I love this stuff," he exclaimed during one brief break—the only time during our conversation when he stated the obvious.

Moreland's highly organized mind works so systematically, so logically, that he seems to effortlessly construct his case in complete sentences and whole paragraphs, without wasted words or extraneous thoughts, ready for proofreading and printing. When my tape recorder would stop, he would pause, give me time to slip in a new cassette, and then pick up exactly where he had left off, without missing a beat.

While Moreland is a well-known philosopher (with a doctorate from the University of Southern California) and is comfortable navigating the conceptual worlds of Kant and Kierkegaard, he doesn't dwell exclusively in the abstract. His background in science (he has a chemistry degree from the University of Missouri) and mastery of history (as demonstrated by his excellent book *Scaling the Secular City*) anchor him in the everyday world and prevent him from floating into purely ethereal thinking.

Moreland, who also has a master's degree in theology from Dallas Theological Seminary, currently is a professor at the Talbot School of Theology, where he teaches in the master's program in philosophy and ethics.

His articles have been published in more than thirty professional journals, such as *American Philosophical Quarterly; Metaphilosophy;* and *Philosophy and Phenomeological Research.* He has written, coauthored, or edited a dozen books, including *Christianity and the Nature of Science*; *Does God Exist?* (a debate with Kai Nielsen); *The Life and Death Debate; The Creation Hypothesis*; *Beyond Death: Exploring the Evidence for Immortality; Jesus under Fire*; and *Love Your God with All Your Mind.*

Sitting down with Moreland in his small but homey office, I already knew that circumstantial evidence is plural rather than singular. In other words, it's built brick by brick by brick until there's a sturdy foundation on which conclusions can be confidently based.

So I began our interview with a point-blank challenge: "Can you give me five pieces of circumstantial evidence that convince you Jesus rose from the dead?"

Moreland listened intently to my question. "Five examples?" he asked. "Five things that are not in dispute by anybody?"

I nodded. With that Moreland pushed his chair back from his desk and launched into his first piece of evidence: the changed lives of the disciples and their willingness to die for their conviction that Jesus had risen from the dead.

EXHIBIT 1: THE DISCIPLES DIED FOR THEIR BELIEFS

"When Jesus was crucified," Moreland began, "his followers were discouraged and depressed. They no longer had confidence that Jesus had been sent by God, because they believed anyone crucified was accursed by God. They also had been taught that God would not let his Messiah suffer death. So they dispersed. The Jesus movement was all but stopped in its tracks.

"Then, after a short period of time, we see them abandoning their occupations, regathering, and committing themselves to spreading a very specific message—that Jesus Christ was the Messiah of God who died on a cross, returned to life, and was seen alive by them.

"And they were willing to spend the rest of their lives proclaiming this, without any payoff from a human point of view. It's not as though there were a mansion awaiting them on the Mediterranean. They faced a life of hardship. They often went without food, slept exposed to the elements, were ridiculed, beaten, imprisoned. And finally, most of them were executed in torturous ways.

"For what? For good intentions? No, because they were convinced beyond a shadow of a doubt that they had seen Jesus Christ alive from the dead. What you can't explain is how this particular group of men came up with this particular belief without having had an experience of the resurrected Christ. There's no other adequate explanation."

I interrupted with a "Yes, but . . ." objection. "Yes," I agreed, "they were willing to die for their beliefs. But," I added, "so have Muslims and Mormons and followers of Jim Jones and David Koresh. This may show that they were fanatical, but let's face it: it doesn't prove that what they believed is true."

"Wait a minute—think carefully about the difference," Moreland insisted as he swiveled to face me head-on, planting both of his feet firmly on the floor.

"Muslims might be willing to die for their belief that Allah revealed himself to Muhammad, but this revelation was not done in a publicly observable way. So they could be wrong about it. They may sincerely think it's true, but they can't know for a fact, because they didn't witness it themselves.

"However, the apostles were willing to die for something they had seen with their own eyes and touched with their own hands. They were in a unique position not to just believe Jesus rose from the dead but to know for sure. And when you've got eleven credible people with no ulterior motives, with nothing to gain and a lot to lose, who all agree they observed something with their own eyes—now you've got some difficulty explaining that away."

I smiled because I had been playing devil's advocate by raising my objection. Actually, I knew he was right. In fact, this critical distinction was pivotal in my own spiritual journey.

It had been put to me this way: People will die for their religious beliefs if they sincerely believe they're true, but people won't die for their religious beliefs if they know their beliefs are false.

While most people can only have faith that their beliefs are true, the disciples were in a position to know without a doubt whether or not Jesus had risen from the dead. They claimed that they saw him, talked with him, and ate with him. If they weren't absolutely certain, they wouldn't have allowed themselves to be tortured to death for proclaiming that the Resurrection had happened.[2]

"OK, I'm convinced on that one," I said. "But what else do you have?"

EXHIBIT 2: THE CONVERSION OF SKEPTICS

"Another piece of circumstantial evidence," Moreland went on, "is that there were hardened skeptics who didn't believe in Jesus before his crucifixion—and were to some degree dead-set against Christianity—who turned around and adopted the Christian faith after Jesus' death. There's no good reason for this apart from them having experienced the resurrected Christ."

"You're obviously talking about James, the brother of Jesus, and Saul of Tarsus, who became the apostle Paul," I said. "But do you really have any credible evidence that James had been a skeptic of Jesus?"

"Yes, I do," he said. "The gospels tell us Jesus' family, including James, were embarrassed by what he was claiming to be. They didn't believe in him; they confronted him. In ancient Judaism it was highly embarrassing for a rabbi's family not to accept him. Therefore the gospel writers would have no motive for fabricating this skepticism if it weren't true.

"Later the historian Josephus tells us that James, the brother of Jesus, who was the leader of the Jerusalem church, was stoned to death because of his belief in his brother. Why did James's life change? Paul tells us: the resurrected Jesus appeared to him. There's no other explanation."

Indeed, none jumped to mind. "And Saul?" I asked.

"As a Pharisee, he hated anything that disrupted the traditions of the Jewish people. To him, this new countermovement called Christianity would have been the height of disloyalty. In fact, he worked out his frustration by executing Christians when he had a chance," Moreland replied.

"Suddenly he doesn't just ease off Christians but joins their movement! How did this happen? Well, everyone agrees Paul wrote Galatians, and he tells us himself in that letter what caused him to take a 180-degree turn and become the chief proponent of the Christian faith. By his own pen he says he saw the risen Christ and heard Christ appoint him to be one of his followers."

I was waiting for Moreland to make this point, so I could challenge him with an objection by Christianity critic Michael Martin. He said that if you count Paul's conversion as being evidence for the truth of the Resurrection, you should count Muhammad's conversion to Islam as being evidence for the truth that Jesus was not resurrected, since Muslims deny the Resurrection!

"Basically, he says the evidential values of Paul's conversion and Muhammad's conversion cancel each other out," I told Moreland. "Frankly, that seems like a good point. Won't you admit that he's right?"

Moreland didn't bite. "Let's take a look at Muhammad's conversion," he said with confidence in his voice. "No one knows anything about it. Muhammad claims he went into a cave and had a religious experience in which Allah revealed the Koran to him. There's no other eyewitness to verify this. Muhammad offered no publicly miraculous signs to certify anything.

"And someone easily could have had ulterior motives in following Muhammad, because in the early years Islam was spread largely by warfare. Followers of Muhammad gained political influence and power over the villages that were conquered and 'converted' to Islam by the sword.

"Contrast that with the claims of the early followers of Jesus, including Paul. They claimed to have seen public events that other people saw as well. These were things that happened outside their minds, not just in their minds.

"Furthermore, when Paul wrote 2 Corinthians—which nobody disputes he did—he reminded the people in Corinth that he performed miracles when he was with them earlier. He'd certainly be foolish to make this statement if they knew he hadn't."

"And your point?" I asked.

"Remember," he said, "it's not the simple fact that Paul changed his views. You have to explain how he had this particular change of belief that completely went against his upbringing; how he saw the risen Christ in a public event that was witnessed by others, even though they didn't understand it; and how he performed miracles to back up his claim to being an apostle."

"All right, all right," I said. "I see your point. And I'll admit, it's a good one." With that I gestured for him to go on to his next piece of evidence.

EXHIBIT 3: CHANGES TO KEY SOCIAL STRUCTURES

In order to explain his next category of circumstantial proof, Moreland had to provide some important background information about Jewish culture.

"At the time of Jesus, the Jews had been persecuted for seven hundred years by the Babylonians, Assyrians, Persians, and now by the Greeks and the Romans," Moreland explained. "Many Jews had been scattered and lived as captives in these other nations.

"However, we still see Jews today, while we don't see Hittites, Perizzites, Ammonites, Assyrians, Persians, Babylonians, and other people who had been living in that time. Why? Because these people got captured by other nations, intermarried, and lost their national identity.

"Why didn't that happen to the Jews? Because the things that made the Jews, Jews—the social structures that gave them their national identity—were unbelievably important to them. The Jews would pass these structures down to their children, celebrate them in synagogue meetings every Sabbath, and reinforce them with their rituals, because they knew if they didn't, there soon would be no Jews left. They would be assimilated into the cultures that captured them.

"And there's another reason why these social institutions were so important: they believed these institutions were entrusted to them by God. They believed that to abandon these institutions would be to risk their souls being damned to hell after death.

"Now a rabbi named Jesus appears from a lower-class region. He teaches for three years, gathers a following of lower- and middle-class people, gets in trouble with the authorities, and gets crucified along with thirty thousand other Jewish men who are executed during this time period.

"But five weeks after he's crucified, over ten thousand Jews are following him and claiming that he is the initiator of a new religion. And get this: they're willing to give up or alter all five of the social institutions that they have been taught since childhood have such importance both sociologically and theologically."

"So the implication is that something big was going on," I said.

Moreland exclaimed, "Something *very* big was going on!"

Revolutionizing Jewish Life

I invited Moreland to go through these five social structures and explain how the followers of Jesus had changed or abandoned them.

"First," he said, "they had been taught ever since the time of Abraham and Moses that they needed to offer an animal sacrifice on a yearly basis to atone for their sins. God would transfer their sins to that animal, and their sins would be forgiven so they could be in right standing with him. But all of a sudden, after the death of this Nazarene carpenter, these Jewish people no longer offer sacrifices.

"Second, Jews emphasized obeying the laws that God had entrusted to them through Moses. In their view, this is what separated them from pagan nations. Yet within a short time after Jesus' death, Jews were beginning to say that you don't become an upstanding member of their community merely by keeping Moses' laws.

"Third, Jews scrupulously kept the Sabbath by not doing anything except religious devotion every Saturday. This is how they would earn right standing with God, guarantee the salvation of their family, and be in right standing with the nation. However, after the death of this Nazarene carpenter, this fifteen-hundred-year tradition is abruptly changed. These Christians worship on Sunday—why? Because that's when Jesus rose from the dead.

"Fourth, they believed in monotheism—only one God. While Christians teach a form of monotheism, they say that the Father, Son, and Holy Spirit are one God. This is radically different from what the Jews believed. They would have considered it the height of heresy to say someone could be God and man at the same time. Yet Jews begin to worship Jesus as God within the first decade of the Christian religion.

"And fifth, these Christians pictured the Messiah as someone who suffered and died for the sins of the world, whereas Jews had been trained to believe that the Messiah was going to be a political leader who would destroy the Roman armies."

With that context established, Moreland went in for the rhetorical kill, drilling me with his intense and unwavering gaze. "Lee," he said, "how can you possibly explain why in a short period of time not just one Jew but an entire community of at least ten thousand Jews were willing to give up these five key practices that had served them sociologically and theologically for so many centuries? My explanation is simple: they had seen Jesus risen from the dead."

While Moreland's point was extremely impressive, I saw a problem in people understanding it today. I told him that it's very difficult for twentieth-century Americans to appreciate the radical nature of this transformation.

"These days people are fluid in their faith," I said. "They bounce back and forth between Christianity and New Age beliefs. They dabble in Buddhism, they mix and match and create their own spirituality. For them, making the kind of changes you mentioned wouldn't seem like a big deal."

Moreland nodded. He had apparently heard this objection before. "I'd ask a person like that, 'What's your most cherished belief? That your parents were good people? That murder is immoral? Think about how radical something must be to get you to change or give up that belief you treasure so much. Now we're starting to get close.'

"Keep in mind that this is an entire community of people who are abandoning treasured beliefs that have been passed on for centuries and that they believed were from God himself. They were doing it even though they were jeopardizing their own well-being, and they also believed they were risking the damnation of their souls to hell if they were wrong.

"What's more, they were not doing this because they had come upon better ideas. They were very content with the old traditions. They gave them up because they had seen miracles that they could not explain and that forced them to see the world another way."

"We're Western individualists who like technological and sociological change," I observed. "Traditions don't mean as much to us."

"I'll grant that," Moreland replied. "But these people did value tradition. They lived in a period in which the older something was, the better. In fact, for them the farther back they could trace an idea, the more likely it was to be true. So to come up with new ideas was opposite of the way we are today.

"Believe me," he concluded, "these changes to the Jewish social structures were not just minor adjustments that were casually made—they were absolutely monumental. This was nothing short of a social earthquake! And earthquakes don't happen without a cause."

EXHIBIT 4: COMMUNION AND BAPTISM

Moreland pointed to the emergence of the sacraments of Communion and baptism in the early church as more circumstantial evidence that the Resurrection is true. But I had some doubts.

"Isn't it only natural that religions would create their own rituals and practices?" I asked. "All religions have them. So how does that prove anything about the Resurrection?"

"Ah, but let's consider Communion for a moment," he replied. "What's odd is that these early followers of Jesus didn't get together to celebrate his teachings or how wonderful he was. They came together regularly to have a celebration meal for one reason: to remember that Jesus had been publicly slaughtered in a grotesque and humiliating way.

"Think about this in modern terms. If a group of people loved John F. Kennedy, they might meet regularly to remember his confrontation with Russia, his promotion of civil rights, and his charismatic personality. But they're not going to celebrate the fact that Lee Harvey Oswald murdered him!

"However, that's analogous to what these early Christians did. How do you explain that? I explain it this way: they realized that Jesus' slaying was a necessary step to a much greater victory. His murder wasn't the last word—the last word was that he had conquered death for all of us by rising from the dead. They celebrated his execution because they were convinced that they had seen him alive from the tomb."

"What about baptism?" I asked.

"The early church adopted a form of baptism from their Jewish upbringing, called proselyte baptism. When Gentiles wanted to take upon themselves the laws of Moses, the Jews would baptize those Gentiles in the authority of the God of Israel. But in the New Testament, people were baptized in the name of God the Father, God the Son, and God the Holy Spirit—which meant they had elevated Jesus to the full status of God.

"Not only that, but baptism was a celebration of the death of Jesus, just as Communion was. By going under the water, you're celebrating his death, and by being brought out of the water, you're celebrating the fact that Jesus was raised to newness of life."

I interrupted by saying, "You're assuming that these sacraments weren't merely adapted from the so-called mystery religions."

"And for good reasons," Moreland replied. "First, there's no hard evidence that any mystery religion believed in gods dying and rising, until after the New Testament period. So if there was any borrowing, they borrowed from Christianity.

"Second, the practice of baptism came from Jewish customs, and the Jews were very much against allowing Gentile or Greek ideas to affect their worship. And third, these two sacraments can be dated back to the very earliest Christian community—too early for the influence of any other religions to creep into their understanding of what Jesus' death meant."

EXHIBIT 5: THE EMERGENCE OF THE CHURCH

Moreland prefaced this final point by saying, "When a major cultural shift takes place, historians always look for events that can explain it."

"Yes, that makes sense," I said.

"OK, then let's think about the start of the Christian church. There's no question it began shortly after the death of Jesus and spread so rapidly that within a period of maybe twenty years it had even reached Caesar's palace in Rome. Not only that, but this movement triumphed over a number of competing ideologies and eventually overwhelmed the entire Roman empire.

"Now, if you were a Martian looking down on the first century, would you think Christianity or the Roman Empire would survive? You probably wouldn't put money on a ragtag group of people whose primary message was that a crucified carpenter from an obscure village had triumphed over the grave. Yet it was so successful that today we name our children Peter and Paul and our dogs Caesar and Nero!

"I like the way C. F. D. Moule, the Cambridge New Testament scholar, put it: 'If the coming into existence of the Nazarenes, a phenomenon undeniably attested by the New Testament, rips a great hole in history, a hole the size and shape of Resurrection, what does the secular historian propose to stop it up with?'"[3]

While this wasn't Moreland's strongest point, since other religious movements have popped up and spread too, circumstantial evidence doesn't rely solely on the strength of one fact. Rather it's the cumulative weight of several facts that together tip the scales toward a conclusion. And to Moreland, the conclusion is clear.

"Look," he said, "if someone wants to consider this circumstantial evidence and reach the verdict that Jesus did not rise from the dead—fair enough. But they've got to offer an alternative explanation that is plausible for all five of these facts.

"Remember, there's no doubt these facts are true; what's in question is how to explain them. And I've never seen a better explanation than the Resurrection."

I mentally played back the tape of the circumstantial evidence: the willingness of the disciples to die for what they experienced; the revolutionized lives of skeptics like James and Saul; the radical changes in social structures cherished by Jews for centuries; the sudden appearance of Communion and baptism; and the amazing emergence and growth of the church.

Given all five uncontested facts, I had to agree with Moreland that the Resurrection, and only the Resurrection, makes sense of them all. No other explanation comes close. And that's just the indirect evidence. When I added the potent proof for the empty tomb of Jesus, and the convincing testimony about his post-Resurrection appearances, the case seemed conclusive.

That was also the assessment of Sir Lionel Luckhoo, the brilliant and savvy attorney whose astounding 245 consecutive murder acquittals earned him a place in *The Guinness Book of World Records* as the world's most successful lawyer.[4] Knighted twice by Queen Elizabeth, this former justice and diplomat subjected the historical facts about the Resurrection to his own rigorous analysis for several years before declaring, "I say unequivocally that the evidence for the resurrection of Jesus Christ is so overwhelming that it compels acceptance by proof which leaves absolutely no room for doubt."[5]

But wait. There is more.

TAKING THE FINAL STEP

Our interview over, Moreland and I were bantering about football as I unplugged my tape recorder and began packing away my notes. Though I was in a bit of a hurry to catch my flight back to Chicago, he said something that prompted me to pause.

"There's one other category of evidence you haven't asked about," he remarked.

My mind reviewed our interview. "I give up," I said. "What is it?"

"It's the ongoing encounter with the resurrected Christ that happens all over the world, in every culture, to people from all kinds of backgrounds and personalities—well educated and not, rich and poor, thinkers and feelers, men and women," he said. "They all will testify that more than any single thing in their lives, Jesus Christ has changed them."

Moreland leaned forward for emphasis. "To me, this provides the final evidence—not the only evidence but the final confirming proof—that the message of Jesus can open the door to a direct encounter with the risen Christ."

"I assume you've had an encounter like that," I said. "Tell me about it."

"In 1968 I was a cynical chemistry major at the University of Missouri, when I was confronted with the fact that if I examined the claims of Jesus Christ critically but with an open mind, there was more than enough evidence for me to believe it.

"So I took a step of faith in the same direction the evidence was pointing, by receiving Jesus as my forgiver and leader, and I began to relate to him—to the resurrected Christ—in a very real and ongoing way.

"In three decades I've had hundreds of specific answers to prayers, I've had things happen that simply cannot be explained by natural explanations, and I have experienced a changed life beyond anything I could have imagined."

But, I protested, people experience life change in other religions whose tenets contradict Christianity. "Isn't it dangerous to base a decision on subjective experiences?" I asked.

"Let me make two things clear," he said. "First, I'm not saying, 'Just trust your experience.' I'm saying, 'Use your mind calmly and weigh the evidence, and then let experience be a confirming piece of evidence.' Second, if what this evidence points to is true—that is, if all these lines of evidence really do point to the resurrection of Jesus—the evidence itself begs for an experiential test."

"Define that," I said.

"The experiential test is, 'He's still alive, and I can find out by relating to him.' If you were on a jury and heard enough evidence to convince you of someone's guilt, it wouldn't make sense to stop short of the final step of convicting him. And for people to accept the evidence for the resurrection of Jesus and not take the final step of testing it experientially would be to miss where the evidence is ultimately pointing."

"So," I said, "if the evidence points strongly in this direction, it's only rational and logical to follow it into the experiential realm."

He nodded in approval. "That's precisely right," he said. "It's the final confirmation of the evidence. In fact, I'll say this: the evidence screams out for the experiential test."

Deliberations

Questions for Reflection or Group Study

1. The disciples were in the unique position of knowing for certain whether Jesus had returned from the dead, and they were willing to die for their conviction that he did. Can you think of anyone in history who has knowingly and willingly died for a lie? What degree of certainty would you need before you would be willing to lay down your life for a belief? How thoroughly would you investigate a matter if you were going to base your life on it?
2. What are your most cherished beliefs? What would it take for you to abandon or radically rethink those treasured opinions—especially if you truly believed you were risking the damnation of your soul if you were wrong? How does your answer relate to the historical fact that thousands of Jews suddenly abandoned five key social and religious structures shortly after the crucifixion of Jesus?
3. Other than the resurrection of Jesus, can you think of any explanation that would simultaneously account for all five categories of evidence that J. P. Moreland discussed? How do you think someone like him would respond to your hypothesis?
4. Moreland ended his interview by talking about the experiential test. What would have to happen before you would be willing to take that step yourself?

For Further Evidence

More Resources on This Topic

Green, Michael. *Christ Is Risen: So What?* Kent, England: Sovereign World, 1995.

McDowell, Josh. *The Resurrection Factor*, 105–20. San Bernardino, Calif.: Here's Life, 1981.

Moreland, J. P. *Scaling the Secular City*. Grand Rapids: Baker, 1987.

Moule, C. F. D. *The Phenomenon of the New Testament*. London: SCM Press, 1967.

CONCLUSION: THE VERDICT OF HISTORY

What Does the Evidence Establish—And What Does It Mean Today?

The date was November 8, 1981. It was a Sunday. I locked myself in my home office and spent the afternoon replaying the spiritual journey I had been traveling for twenty-one months.

My investigation into Jesus was similar to what you've just read, except that I primarily studied books and other historical research instead of personally interacting with scholars. I had asked questions and analyzed answers with as much of an open mind as I could muster. Now I had reached critical mass. The evidence was clear. The one remaining issue was what I would do with it.

Pulling out a legal pad, I began listing the questions I had posed as I embarked on my investigation, and some of the key facts I had uncovered. In a similar way, I could sum up the substance of what we've learned in our own examination of the evidence.

• CAN THE BIOGRAPHIES OF JESUS BE TRUSTED?

I once thought the gospels were merely religious propaganda, hopelessly tainted by overactive imaginations and evangelistic zeal. However, Craig Blomberg, one of the country's foremost authorities on the topic, built a convincing case that they reflect eyewitness testimony and bear the unmistakable earmarks of accuracy. So early are these biographies that they cannot be explained away as legendary invention. In fact, the fundamental beliefs in Jesus' miracles, resurrection, and deity go way back to the very dawning of the Christian movement.

• DO THE BIOGRAPHIES OF JESUS STAND UP TO SCRUTINY?

Blomberg argued persuasively that the gospel writers intended to preserve reliable history, were able to do so, were honest and willing to include difficult-to-explain material, and didn't allow bias to unduly color their reporting. The harmony among the gospels on essential facts, coupled with divergence on some details, lends historical credibility to the accounts. What's more, the early church couldn't have taken root and flourished right there in Jerusalem if it had been teaching facts about Jesus that his own contemporaries could have exposed as exaggerated or false. In short, the gospels were able to pass all eight evidential tests.

- **WERE JESUS' BIOGRAPHIES RELIABLY PRESERVED FOR US?**

World-class scholar Bruce Metzger said that compared with other ancient documents, there is an unprecedented number of New Testament manuscripts and that they can be dated extremely close to the original writings. The modern New Testament is 99.5 percent free of textual discrepancies, with no major Christian doctrines in doubt. The criteria used by the early church to determine which books should be considered authoritative have ensured that we possess the best records about Jesus.

- **IS THERE CREDIBLE EVIDENCE FOR JESUS OUTSIDE HIS BIOGRAPHIES?**

"We have better historical documentation for Jesus than for the founder of any other ancient religion," said Edwin Yamauchi. Sources from outside the Bible corroborate that many people believed Jesus performed healings and was the Messiah, that he was crucified, and that despite this shameful death, his followers, who believed he was still alive, worshiped him as God. One expert documented thirty-nine ancient sources that corroborate more than one hundred facts concerning Jesus' life, teachings, crucifixion, and resurrection. Seven secular sources and several early creeds concern the deity of Jesus, a doctrine "definitely present in the earliest church," according to scholar Gary Habermas.

- **DOES ARCHAEOLOGY CONFIRM OR CONTRADICT JESUS' BIOGRAPHIES?**

Archaeologist John McRay said there's no question that archaeological findings have enhanced the New Testament's credibility. No discovery has ever disproved a biblical reference. Further, archaeology has established that Luke, who wrote about one-quarter of the New Testament, was an especially careful historian. Concluded one expert, "If Luke was so painstakingly accurate in his historical reporting [of minor details], on what logical basis may we assume he was credulous or inaccurate in his reporting of matters that were far more important, not only to him but to others as well?" Like, for instance, the resurrection of Jesus.

• IS THE JESUS OF HISTORY THE SAME AS THE JESUS OF FAITH?

Gregory Boyd said the much-publicized Jesus Seminar, which doubts Jesus said most of what's attributed to him, represents "an extremely small number of radical-fringe scholars who are on the far, far left wing of New Testament thinking." The Seminar ruled out the possibility of miracles at the outset, it employed questionable criteria, and some participants have touted myth-riddled documents of extremely dubious quality. Further, the idea that stories about Jesus emerged from mythology about gods dying and rising fails to withstand scrutiny. Said Boyd, "The evidence for Jesus being who the disciples said he was . . . is just light-years beyond my reasons for thinking that the left-wing scholarship of the Jesus Seminar is correct." In sum, the Jesus of faith is the same as the Jesus of history.

• WAS JESUS REALLY CONVINCED THAT HE WAS THE SON OF GOD?

By going back to the very earliest traditions, which are unquestionably safe from legendary development, Ben Witherington III was able to show that Jesus had a supreme and transcendent self-understanding. Based on the evidence, Witherington said, "Did Jesus believe he was the Son of God, the anointed one of God? The answer is yes. Did he see himself as the Son of Man? The answer is yes. Did he see himself as the final Messiah? Yes, that's the way he viewed himself. Did he believe that anybody less than God could save the world? No, I don't believe he did."

• WAS JESUS CRAZY WHEN HE CLAIMED TO BE THE SON OF GOD?

Well-known psychologist Gary Collins said Jesus exhibited no inappropriate emotions, was in contact with reality, was brilliant and had amazing insights into human nature, and enjoyed deep and abiding relationships. "I just don't see signs that Jesus was suffering from any known mental illness," he concluded. In addition, Jesus backed up his claim to being God through miraculous feats of healing, astounding demonstrations of power over nature, unrivaled teaching, divine understanding of people, and with his own resurrection, which was the final authentication of his identity.

I

• DID JESUS FULFILL THE ATTRIBUTES OF GOD?

While the Incarnation—God becoming man, the infinite becoming finite—stretches our imagination, prominent theologian D. A. Carson pointed out that there's lots of evidence that Jesus exhibited the characteristics of deity. Based on Philippians 2, many theologians believe Jesus voluntarily emptied himself of the independent use of these divine attributes as he pursued his mission of human redemption. Even so, the New Testament specifically confirms that Jesus ultimately possessed every qualification of deity, including omniscience, omnipresence, omnipotence, eternality, and immutability.

J

• DID JESUS—AND JESUS ALONE—MATCH THE IDENTITY OF THE MESSIAH?

Hundreds of years before Jesus was born, prophets foretold the coming of the Messiah, or the Anointed One, who would redeem God's people. In effect, dozens of these Old Testament prophecies created a fingerprint that only the true Messiah could fit. This gave Israel a way to rule out impostors and validate the credentials of the authentic Messiah. Against astronomical odds—one chance in a trillion, trillion, trillion, trillion, trillion, trillion, trillion, trillion, trillion, trillion, trillion, trillion, trillion—Jesus, and only Jesus throughout history, matched this prophetic fingerprint. This confirms Jesus' identity to an incredible degree of certainty.

K

• WAS JESUS' DEATH A SHAM AND HIS RESURRECTION A HOAX?

By analyzing the medical and historical data, Dr. Alexander Metherell concluded Jesus could not have survived the gruesome rigors of crucifixion, much less the gaping wound that pierced his lung and heart. The idea that he somehow swooned on the cross and pretended to be dead lacks any evidential basis. Roman executioners were grimly efficient, knowing that they themselves would face death if any of their victims were to come down from the cross alive. Even if Jesus had somehow lived through the torture, his ghastly condition could never have inspired a worldwide movement based on the premise that he had gloriously triumphed over the grave.

• WAS JESUS' BODY REALLY ABSENT FROM HIS TOMB?

William Lane Craig presented striking evidence that the enduring symbol of Easter—the vacant tomb of Jesus—was a historical reality. The empty grave is reported or implied in extremely early sources—Mark's gospel and the 1 Corinthians 15 creed—which date so close to the event that they could not possibly have been products of legend. The fact that the gospels report that women discovered the empty tomb bolsters the story's authenticity. The site of Jesus' tomb was known to both Christian and Jew alike, so it could have been checked by skeptics. In fact, nobody, not even the Roman authorities or Jewish leaders, ever claimed that the tomb still contained Jesus' body. Instead they were forced to invent the absurd story that the disciples, despite having no motive or opportunity, had stolen the body—a theory that not even the most skeptical critic believes today.

• WAS JESUS SEEN ALIVE AFTER HIS DEATH ON THE CROSS?

The evidence for the post-Resurrection appearances of Jesus didn't develop gradually over the years as mythology distorted memories of his life. Rather, said Resurrection expert Gary Habermas, the Resurrection was "the central proclamation of the early church from the very beginning." The ancient creed from 1 Corinthians 15 mentions specific individuals who encountered the risen Christ, and Paul even challenged first-century doubters to talk with these individuals personally to determine the truth of the matter for themselves. The book of Acts is littered with extremely early affirmations of Jesus' resurrection, while the gospels describe numerous encounters in detail. Concluded British theologian Michael Green, "The appearances of Jesus are as well authenticated as anything in antiquity.... There can be no rational doubt that they occurred."

• ARE THERE ANY SUPPORTING FACTS THAT POINT TO THE RESURRECTION?

J. P. Moreland's circumstantial evidence added final documentation for the Resurrection. First, the disciples were in a unique position to know whether the Resurrection happened, and they went to their deaths proclaiming it was true. Nobody knowingly and willingly dies for a lie. Second, apart from the Resurrection, there's no good reason why skeptics like Paul and James would have been converted and would have died for their faith. Third, within weeks of the Crucifixion, thousands of Jews began abandoning key social practices that had critical sociological and religious importance for centuries. They believed they risked damnation if they were wrong. Fourth, the early sacraments of Communion and baptism affirmed Jesus' resurrection and deity. And fifth, the miraculous emergence of the church in the face of brutal Roman persecution "rips a great hole in history, a hole the size and shape of Resurrection," as C. F. D. Moule put it.

FAILING MÜLLER'S CHALLENGE

I'll admit it: I was ambushed by the amount and quality of the evidence that Jesus is the unique Son of God. As I sat at my desk that Sunday afternoon, I shook my head in amazement. I had seen defendants carted off to the death chamber on much less convincing proof! The cumulative facts and data pointed unmistakably toward a conclusion that I wasn't entirely comfortable in reaching.

Frankly, I had wanted to believe that the deification of Jesus was the result of legendary development in which well-meaning but misguided people slowly turned a wise sage into the mythological Son of God. That seemed safe and reassuring; after all, a roving apocalyptic preacher from the first century could make no demands on me. But while I went into my investigation thinking that this legendary explanation was intuitively obvious, I emerged convinced it was totally without basis.

What clinched it for me was the famous study by A. N. Sherwin-White, the great classical historian from Oxford University, which William Lane Craig alluded to in our interview. Sherwin-White meticulously examined the rate at which legend accrued in the ancient world. His conclusion: not even two full generations was enough time for legend to develop and to wipe out a solid core of historical truth.[1]

Now consider the case of Jesus. Historically speaking, the news of his empty tomb, the eyewitness accounts of his post-Resurrection appearances, and the conviction that he was indeed God's unique Son emerged virtually instantaneously.

The 1 Corinthians 15 creed, affirming Jesus' death for our sins and listing his post-Resurrection appearances to named eyewitnesses, was already being recited by Christians as soon as twenty-four months after the Crucifixion. Mark's account of the empty tomb was drawn from material that dates back to within a few years of the event itself.

The gospels, attesting to Jesus' teachings, miracles, and resurrection, were circulating within the lifetimes of Jesus' contemporaries, who would have been only too glad to set the record straight if there had been embellishment or falsehood. The most primitive Christian hymns affirm Jesus' divine nature.

Blomberg summed it up this way: "*Within the first two years after his death,* then, significant numbers of Jesus' followers seem to have formulated a doctrine of the atonement, were convinced that he had been raised from the dead in bodily form, associated Jesus with God, and believed they found support for all these convictions in the Old Testament."[2]

Concluded William Lane Craig, "The time span necessary for significant accrual of legend concerning the events of the gospels would place us in the second century A.D., *just the time in fact when the legendary apocryphal gospels were born.* These are the legendary accounts sought by the critics."[3]

There was simply nowhere near enough time for mythology to thoroughly corrupt the historical record of Jesus, especially in the midst of eyewitnesses who still had personal knowledge of him. When German theologian Julius Müller in 1844 challenged anyone to find a single example of legend developing that fast anywhere in history, the response from the scholars of his day—and to the present time—was resounding silence.[4]

On November 8, 1981, I realized that my biggest objection to Jesus also had been quieted by the evidence of history. I found myself chuckling at how the tables had been turned.

In light of the convincing facts I had learned during my investigation, in the face of this overwhelming avalanche of evidence in the case for Christ, the great irony was this: it would require much more faith for me to maintain my atheism than to trust in Jesus of Nazareth!

IMPLICATIONS OF THE EVIDENCE

Remember the story of James Dixon in the introduction of this book? The evidence pointed powerfully toward his guilt for shooting a Chicago police sergeant. He even admitted he did it!

Yet when a more thorough investigation was conducted, suddenly a shift occurred: the scenario that fit the facts most perfectly was that the sergeant had framed Dixon, who was innocent of the shooting. Dixon was set free, and it was the officer who found himself convicted.

As we conclude our investigation in the case for Christ, it's worth revisiting the two big lessons from that story.

- **First, Has the Collection of Evidence Really Been Thorough?**

Yes, it has been. I selected experts who could state their position and defend it with historical evidence that I could then test through cross-examination. I wasn't merely interested in their opinions; I wanted facts. I challenged them with the current theories of atheists and liberal professors. Given their background, credentials, experience, and character, these scholars were more than qualified to present reliable historical data concerning Jesus.

- **Second, Which Explanation Best Fits the Totality of the Evidence?**

By November 8, 1981, my legend thesis, to which I had doggedly clung for so many years, had been thoroughly dismantled. What's more, my journalistic skepticism toward the supernatural had melted in light of the breathtaking historical evidence that the resurrection of Jesus was a real, historical event. In fact, my mind could not conjure up a single explanation that fit the evidence of history nearly as well as the conclusion that Jesus was who he claimed to be: the one and only Son of God.

The atheism I had embraced for so long buckled under the weight of historical truth. It was a stunning and radical outcome, certainly not what I had anticipated when I embarked on this investigative process. But it was, in my opinion, a decision compelled by the facts.

All of which led me to the "So what?" question. If this is true, what difference does it make? There were several obvious implications.

- If Jesus is the Son of God, his teachings are more than just good ideas from a wise teacher; they are divine insights on which I can confidently build my life.
- If Jesus sets the standard for morality, I can now have an unwavering foundation for my choices and decisions, rather than basing them on the ever-shifting sands of expediency and self-centeredness.

- If Jesus did rise from the dead, he's still alive today and available for me to encounter on a personal basis.
- If Jesus conquered death, he can open the door of eternal life for me, too.
- If Jesus has divine power, he has the supernatural ability to guide me and help me and transform me as I follow him.
- If Jesus personally knows the pain of loss and suffering, he can comfort and encourage me in the midst of the turbulence that he himself warned is inevitable in a world corrupted by sin.
- If Jesus loves me as he says, he has my best interests at heart. That means I have nothing to lose and everything to gain by committing myself to him and his purposes.
- If Jesus is who he claims to be (and remember, no leader of any other major religion has even pretended to be God), as my Creator he rightfully deserves my allegiance, obedience, and worship.

I remember writing out these implications on my legal pad and then leaning back in my chair. I had reached the culmination of my nearly two-year journey. It was finally time to deal with the most pressing question of all: "Now what?"

THE FORMULA OF FAITH

After a personal investigation that spanned more than six hundred days and countless hours, my own verdict in the case for Christ was clear. However, as I sat at my desk, I realized that I needed more than an intellectual decision. I wanted to take the experiential step that J. P. Moreland had described in the last interview.

Looking for a way to bring that about, I reached over to a Bible and opened it to John 1:12, a verse I had encountered during my investigation: "Yet to all who received him, to those who believed in his name, he gave the right to become children of God."

The key verbs in that verse spell out with mathematical precision what it takes to go beyond mere mental assent to Jesus' deity and enter into an ongoing relationship with him by becoming adopted into God's family: believe + receive = become.

1. Believe

As someone educated in journalism and law, I was trained to respond to the facts, wherever they lead. For me, the data demonstrated convincingly that Jesus is the Son of God who died as my substitute to pay the penalty I deserved for the wrongdoing I had committed.

And there was plenty of wrongdoing. I'll spare myself the embarrassment of going into details, but the truth is that I had been living a profane, drunken, self-absorbed, and immoral lifestyle. In my career, I had backstabbed my colleagues to gain a personal advantage and had routinely violated legal and ethical standards in pursuit of stories. In my personal life, I was sacrificing my wife and children on the altar of success. I was a liar, a cheater, and a deceiver.

My heart had shrunk to the point where it was rock hard toward anyone else. My main motivator was personal pleasure—and ironically, the more I hungrily sought after it, the more elusive and self-destructive it became.

When I read in the Bible that these sins separated me from God, who is holy and morally pure, this resonated as being true. Certainly God, whose existence I had denied for years, seemed extremely distant, and it became obvious to me that I needed the cross of Jesus to bridge that gulf. Said the apostle Peter, "For Christ died for sins once for all, the righteous for the unrighteous, to bring you to God" (1 Peter 3:18).

All this I now believed. The evidence of history and of my own experience was too strong to ignore.

2. Receive

Every other faith system I studied during my investigation was based on the "do" plan. In other words, it was necessary for people to do something—for example, use a Tibetan prayer wheel, pay alms, go on pilgrimages, undergo reincarnations, work off karma from past misdeeds, reform their character—to try to somehow earn their way back to God. Despite their best efforts, lots of sincere people just wouldn't make it.

Christianity is unique. It's based on the "done" plan—Jesus has done for us on the cross what we cannot do for ourselves: he has paid the death penalty that we deserve for our rebellion and wrongdoing, so we can become reconciled with God.

I didn't have to struggle and strive to try to do the impossible of making myself worthy. Over and over the Bible says that Jesus offers forgiveness and eternal life as a free gift that cannot be earned (see Rom. 6:23; Eph. 2:8–9; Titus 3:5). It's called grace—*amazing* grace, unmerited favor. It's available to anyone who receives it in a sincere prayer of repentance. Even someone like me.

Yes, I had to take a step of faith, as we do in every decision we make in life. But here's the crucial distinction: I was no longer trying to swim upstream against the strong current of evidence; instead I was choosing to go in the same direction that the torrent of facts was flowing. That was reasonable, that was rational, that was logical. What's more, in an inner and inexplicable way, it was also what I sensed God's Spirit was nudging me to do.

So on November 8, 1981, I talked with God in a heartfelt and unedited prayer, admitting and turning from my wrongdoing, and receiving the gift of forgiveness and eternal life through Jesus. I told him that with his help I wanted to follow him and his ways from here on out.

There were no lightning bolts, no audible replies, no tingly sensations. I know that some people feel a rush of emotion at such a moment; as for me, however, there was something else that was equally exhilarating: there was the rush of reason.

3. Become

After taking that step, I knew from John 1:12 that I had crossed the threshold into a new experience. I had become something different: a child of God, forever adopted into his family through the historical, risen Jesus. Said the apostle Paul, "Therefore, if anyone is in Christ, he is a new creation; the old has gone, the new has come" (2 Cor. 5:17).

Sure enough, over time as I endeavored to follow Jesus' teachings and open myself to his transforming power, my priorities, my values, and my character were (and continue to be) gradually changed. Increasingly I want Jesus' motives and perspective to be my own. To paraphrase Martin Luther King Jr., I may not yet be the man I should be or the man, with Christ's help, I someday will be—but thank God I'm not the man I used to be!

Maybe that sounds mystical to you; I don't know. Not so long ago it would have to me. But it's very real to me now and to those around me. In fact, so radical was the difference in my life that a few months after I became a follower of Jesus, our five-year-old daughter Alison went up to my wife and said, "Mommy, I want God to do for me what he's done for Daddy."

Here was a little girl who had only known a father who was profane, angry, verbally harsh, and all too often absent. And even though she had never interviewed a scholar, never analyzed the data, never investigated historical evidence, she had seen up close the influence that Jesus can have on one person's life. In effect, she was saying, "If this is what God does to a human being, that's what I want for me."

Looking back nearly two decades, I can see with clarity that the day I personally made a decision in the case for Christ was nothing less than the pivotal event of my entire life.

REACHING YOUR OWN VERDICT

Now to you. At the outset I encouraged you to approach the evidence in this book as a fair and impartial juror as much as possible, drawing your conclusions based on the weight of the evidence. In the end the verdict is yours and yours alone. Nobody else can cast the ballot for you.

Perhaps after reading expert after expert, listening to argument after argument, seeing the answers to question after question, and testing the evidence with your logic and common sense, you've found, as I have, that the case for Christ is conclusive.

The believe part of John 1:12 is firmly in place; all that's left is to receive Jesus' grace, and then you'll become his son or daughter, engaged in a spiritual adventure that can flourish for the rest of your life and into eternity. For you, the time for the experiential step has arrived, and I can't encourage you more strongly to take that step with enthusiasm.

On the other hand, maybe questions still linger for you. Perhaps I didn't address the objection that's uppermost in your mind. Fair enough. No single book can deal with every nuance. However, I trust that the amount of information reported in these pages will at least have convinced you that it's reasonable—in fact, imperative—to continue your investigation.

Pinpoint where you think the evidence needs to be bolstered and then seek out additional answers from well-respected experts. If you believe you've come up with a scenario that better accounts for the facts, be willing to subject it to tough-minded scrutiny. Use the suggested resources in this book to delve deeper. Study the Bible yourself (one suggestion: *The Journey*, a special edition of the Bible that's designed for people who don't yet believe it's the word of God).[5]

Resolve that you'll reach a verdict when you've gathered a sufficient amount of information, knowing that you'll never have full resolution of every single issue. You may even want to whisper a prayer to the God who you're not sure exists, asking him to guide you to the truth about him. And through it all, you'll have my sincere encouragement as you continue in your spiritual quest.

At the same time, I do feel a strong obligation to urge you to make this a front-burner issue in your life. Don't approach it casually or flippantly, because there's a lot riding on your conclusion. As Michael Murphy aptly put it, "We ourselves—and not merely the truth claims—are at stake in the investigation."[6] In other words, if my conclusion in the case for Christ is correct, your future and eternity hinge on how you respond to Christ. As Jesus declared, "If you do not believe that I am the one I claim to be, you will indeed die in your sins" (John 8:24).

Those are sober words, offered out of authentic and loving concern. I cite them to underline the magnitude of this matter and in the hope that they will spur you to actively and thoroughly examine the case for Christ.

In the end, however, remember that some options just aren't viable. The accumulated evidence has already closed them off. Observed C. S. Lewis, the brilliant and once skeptical Cambridge University professor who was eventually won over by evidence for Jesus,

> I am trying here to prevent anyone saying the really foolish thing that people often say about Him: "I'm ready to accept Jesus as a great moral teacher, but I don't accept His claim to be God." That is the one thing we must not say. A man who was merely a man and said the sort of things Jesus said would not be a great moral teacher. He would either be a lunatic ... or else he would be the Devil of Hell. You must make your choice. Either this man was, and is, the Son of God: or else a madman or something worse. You can shut Him up for a fool, you can spit at Him and kill Him as a demon; or you can fall at His feet and call Him Lord and God. But let us not come with any patronizing nonsense about His being a great human teacher. He has not left that open to us. He did not intend to.[7]

LIST OF CITATIONS

Archer—Gleason L. Archer, *The Encyclopedia of Bible Difficulties* (Grand Rapids: Zondervan, 1982).

Anderson—J. N. D. Anderson, *The Evidence for the Resurrection* (Downers Grove, Ill.: InterVarsity Press, 1966).

Ankerberg—John Ankerberg and John Weldon, *The Facts on the Mormon Church* (Eugene, Ore.: Harvest House, 1991).

Ankerberg—John Ankerberg and John Weldon, *Knowing the Truth about the Resurrection* (Eugene, Ore.: Harvest House, 1996).

Ankerberg—John Ankerberg and John Weldon, *Ready with an Answer* (Eugene, Ore.: Harvest House, 1997).

Armstrong—Karen Armstrong, *A History of God* (New York: Ballantine/Epiphany, 1993).

Baigent—Michael Baigent, Richard Leigh, and Henry Lincoln, *Holy Blood, Holy Grail* (New York: Delacorte, 1982).

Barnett—Paul Barnett, *Is the New Testament History?* (Ann Arbor, Mich.: Vine, 1986).

Barnett—Paul Barnett, *Jesus and the Logic of History* (Grand Rapids: Eerdmans, 1997).

Black—Henry Campbell Black, *Black's Law Dictionary*, 5th ed. (St. Paul, Minn.: West, 1979).

Blomberg—Craig Blomberg, *The Historical Reliability of the Gospels* (Downers Grove, Ill.: InterVarsity Press, 1987).

Boyd, Gregory A. *Cynic Sage or Son of God? Recovering the Real Jesus in an Age of Revisionist Replies.* Wheaton, Ill.: BridgePoint, 1995.

Boyd—Gregory A. Boyd, *Jesus under Siege* (Wheaton, Ill.: Victor, 1995).

Boyd—Robert Boyd, *Tells, Tombs, and Treasure* (Grand Rapids: Baker, 1969).

Braaten—Carl Braaten, *History and Hermeneutics*, vol. 2 of *New Directions in Theology Today*, ed. William Hordern (Philadelphia: Westminster Press, 1966).

British Medical Journal—"A Case of Congenital Ichthyosiform Erythrodermia of Brocq Treated by Hypnosis," *British Medical Journal* 2 (1952).

Brown—R. E. Brown, "Did Jesus Know He Was God?" *Biblical Theology Bulletin* 15 (1985).

Bruce—F. F. Bruce, *The New Testament Documents: Are They Reliable?* (Grand Rapids: Eerdmans, 1960).

Bruce—F. F. Bruce, *The Books and the Parchments* (Old Tappan, N.J.: Revell, 1963).

Bruce—F. F. Bruce, *Jesus and Christian Origins outside the New Testament* (Grand Rapids: Eerdmans, 1974).

Bruce—F. F. Bruce, *The Canon of Scripture* (Downers Grove, Ill.: Inter-Varsity Press, 1988).

Chicago Tribune—"Bomb Victim's Body Not in Grave," *Chicago Tribune* (January 14, 1998).

Clifford—Ross Clifford, *The Case for the Empty Tomb* (Claremont, Calif.: Albatross, 1991).

Collins, Gary R. *Can You Trust Psychology?* Downers Grove, Ill.: Inter-Varsity Press, 1988.

Collins, Gary R. *Christian Counseling: A Comprehensive Guide.* Dallas: Word, 1988.

Collins, Gary R. *The Soul Search.* Nashville: Nelson, 1998.

Craig—William Lane Craig, *Knowing the Truth about the Resurrection* (Ann Arbor, Mich.: Servant, 1988).

Craig—William Lane Craig, *Reasonable Faith* (Westchester, Ill.: Crossway, 1994).

Craig—William Lane Craig, *The Son Rises: Historical Evidence for the Resurrection of Jesus* (Chicago: Moody Press, 1981).

Craig, William Lane, and Frank Zindler. *Atheism vs. Christianity: Where Does the Evidence Point?* Grand Rapids: Zondervan, 1993. Videocassette.

Crossan—John Dominic Crossan, *The Historical Jesus* (San Francisco: HarperSanFrancisco, 1991).

Donato—Marla Donato, "That Guilty Look," *Chicago Tribune* (April 1, 1994).

Drane—John Drane, *Introducing the New Testament* (San Francisco: Harper & Row, 1986).

Dunn—James D. G. Dunn, *Jesus and the Spirit* (London: SCM Press, 1975).

Dunn—James Dunn, *The Living Word* (Philadelphia: Fortress, 1988).

Edwards—William D. Edwards et al., "On the Physical Death of Jesus Christ," *Journal of the American Medical Association* (March 21, 1986), 1455–63.

Evans—Colin Evans, *The Casebook of Forensic Detection* (New York: John Wiley & Sons, 1996).

Finegan—Jack Finegan, *The Archaeology of the New Testament* (Princeton: Princeton Univ. Press, 1992).

Foreman, Dale. *Crucify Him.* Grand Rapids: Zondervan, 1990.

France—R. T. France, *The Evidence for Jesus* (Downers Grove, Ill.: InterVarsity Press, 1986).

Fruchtenbaum, Arnold. *Jesus Was a Jew.* Tustin, Calif.: Ariel Ministries, 1981.

Frydland, Rachmiel. *What the Rabbis Know about the Messiah.* Cincinnati: Messianic, 1993.

Geisler—Norman Geisler and Thomas Howe, *When Critics Ask* (Wheaton, Ill.: Victor, 1992).

Geisler—Norman L. Geisler and William E. Nix, *A General Introduction to the Bible* (1968; reprint, Chicago: Moody Press, 1980).

Geivett—R. Douglas Geivett and Gary R. Habermas, eds., *In Defense of Miracles* (Downers Grove, Ill.: InterVarsity Press, 1997).

Grant—Michael Grant, *Jesus: An Historian's Review of the Gospels* (New York: Charles Schribner's Sons, 1977).

Green—Michael Green, *Christ Is Risen: So What?* (Kent, England: Sovereign World, 1995).

Green—Michael Green, *The Empty Cross of Jesus* (Downers Grove, Ill.: InterVarsity Press, 1984).

Greenleaf—Simon Greenleaf, *The Testimony of the Evangelists* (Grand Rapids: Baker, 1984).

Gregory—Leland H. Gregory III, "Top Ten Government Bloopers," *George* (November 1997).

Gruenler—Royce Gordon Gruenler, *New Approaches to Jesus and the Gospels* (Grand Rapids: Baker, 1982).

Habermas—Gary Habermas, *The Historical Jesus* (Joplin, Mo.: College Press, 1996).

Habermas—Gary Habermas, *The Verdict of History* (Nashville: Nelson, 1988).

Habermas—Gary Habermas and Antony Flew, *Did Jesus Rise from the Dead? The Resurrection Debate* (San Francisco: Harper & Row, 1987), xiv.

Habermas, Gary, and J. P. Moreland. *Beyond Death: Exploring the Evidence for Immortality.* Westchester, Ill.: Crossway, 1998.

Habermas—Gary Habermas and J. P. Moreland, *Immortality: The Other Side of Death* (Nashville: Nelson, 1992).

Harris, Murray J. *Jesus As God.* Grand Rapids: Baker, 1993.

Harris, Murray J. *Three Crucial Questions about Jesus.* Grand Rapids: Baker, 1994.

Hengel, M. *Crucifixion in the Ancient World.* Philadelphia: Fortress, 1977.

Ignatius—Ignatius, *Trallians* 9.

Irenaeus—Irenaeus, *Adversus haereses* 3.3.4.
Johnson—Denny Johnson, "Police Add Electronic 'Sketch Artist' to Their Bag of Tricks," *Chicago Tribune* (June 22, 1997).
Johnson—Luke Timothy Johnson, *The Real Jesus* (San Francisco: HarperSanFrancisco, 1996).
Josephus—Josephus, *The Antiquities* 20.200.
Kaiser, Walter C., Jr. *The Messiah in the Old Testament.* Grand Rapids: Zondervan, 1995.
Kenyon—Frederic Kenyon, *Handbook to the Textual Criticism of the New Testament* (New York: Macmillan, 1912).
Kenyon—Frederic Kenyon, *The Bible and Archaeology* (New York: Harper, 1940).
Lake—Kirsopp Lake, *The Historical Evidence for the Resurrection of Jesus Christ* (London: Williams & Norgate, 1907).
Lawrence—D. H. Lawrence, *Love among the Haystacks and Other Stories* (New York: Penguin, 1960).
Lewis—C. S. Lewis, *Mere Christianity* (New York: Macmillan-Collier, 1960).
Lewis—C. S. Lewis, *The Screwtape Letters* (London: Collins-Fontana, 1942).
Maier—Paul L. Maier, *Pontius Pilate* (Wheaton, Ill.: Tyndale House, 1968).
Maier—P. Maier, "Sejanus, Pilate, and the Date of the Crucifixion," *Church History* 37 (1968).
Marshall—I. Howard Marshall, *I Believe in the Historical Jesus* (Grand Rapids: Eerdmans, 1977).
Martin—Michael Martin, *The Case against Christianity* (Philadelphia: Temple Univ. Press, 1991).
Martin, W. J. *The Deity of Christ.* Chicago: Moody Press, 1964.
McDowell—Josh McDowell, *Evidence That Demands a Verdict* (1972; reprint, San Bernardino, Calif.: Here's Life, 1986).
McDowell—Josh McDowell, *More Than a Carpenter* (Wheaton, Ill.: Living Books, 1977).
McDowell—Josh McDowell, *The Resurrection Factor* (San Bernardino, Calif.: Here's Life, 1981).
McDowell—Josh McDowell and Bart Larson, *Jesus: A Biblical Defense of His Deity* (San Bernardino, Calif.: Here's Life, 1983).
McDowell—Josh McDowell and Bill Wilson, *He Walked among Us* (Nashville: Nelson, 1994).
McFarlan—Donald McFarlan, ed., *The Guinness Book of World Records* (New York: Bantam, 1991).
McGinniss—Joe McGinniss, *Fatal Vision* (New York: New American Library, 1989).

McRay—John McRay, *Archaeology and the New Testament* (Grand Rapids: Baker, 1991).
Metzger—Bruce M. Metzger, *The Canon of the New Testament* (Oxford: Clarendon Press, 1988).
Metzger—Bruce M. Metzger, *The Text of the New Testament* (Oxford: Oxford Univ. Press, 1992).
Miller—Kevin D. Miller, "The War of the Scrolls," *Christianity Today* (October 6, 1997).
Montgomery—John Warwick Montgomery, ed., *Christianity for the Tough-Minded* (Minneapolis: Bethany House, 1973).
Moreland, J. P. *Scaling the Secular City.* Grand Rapids: Baker, 1987.
Morison, Frank. *Who Moved the Stone?* Grand Rapids: Zondervan, 1987.
Moule—C. F. D. Moule, *The Phenomenon of the New Testament* (London: SCM Press, 1967).
Müller—Julius Müller, *The Theory of Myths, in Its Application to the Gospel History, Examined and Confuted* (London: John Chapman, 1844).
Neill—Stephen Neill, *The Interpretation of the New Testament 1861–1961* (London: O.U.P., 1964).
O'Collins—Gerald O'Collins, *The Easter Jesus* (London: Darton, Longman & Todd, 1973).
Patzia—Arthur G. Patzia, *The Making of the New Testament* (Downers Grove, Ill.: InterVarsity Press, 1995).
Peck—M. Scott Peck, *People of the Lie* (New York: Touchstone, 1997).
Pelikan—Jaroslav Pelikan, *The Christian Tradition: A History of the Development of Doctrine,* vol. 1, *The Emergence of the Catholic Tradition (100–600)* (Chicago: Univ. of Chicago Press, 1971).
Phlegon—Phlegon, *Olympiades he Chronika* 13, ed. Otto Keller, *Rerum Naturalium Scriptores Graeci Minores,* I (Leipzig: Teurber, 1877).
Possley—Maurice Possley, "Mob Hit Man Aleman Gets One Hundred to Three Hundred Years," *Chicago Tribune* (November 26, 1997).
Proctor, William. *The Resurrection Report.* Nashville: Broadman & Holman, 1998.
Rosen—Marjorie Rosen, "Getting Inside the Mind of a Serial Killer," *Biography* (October 1997).
Rosen, Moishe. *Y'shua, the Jewish Way to Say Jesus.* Chicago: Moody Press, 1982.
Rosen—Ruth Rosen, ed., *Jewish Doctors Meet the Great Physician* (San Francisco: Purple Pomegranate, 1997).
Schaff—Philip Schaff, *The Person of Christ* (New York: American Tract Society, 1918).

Schonfield—Hugh Schonfield, *The Passover Plot* (New York: Bantam, 1965).
Sherwin-White—A. N. Sherwin-White, *Roman Society and Roman Law in the New Testament* (Oxford: Clarendon Press, 1963).
Smith—Morton Smith, "Biblical Arguments for Slavery," *Free Inquiry* (Spring 1987), 30.
Sowell—Thomas Sowell, *Race and Culture* (New York: Basic, 1995).
Stoner—Peter W. Stoner, *Science Speaks* (Chicago: Moody Press, 1969).
Stott, John. *Basic Christianity.* Grand Rapids: Eerdmans, 1986.
Strobel—Lee Strobel, "His 'I Shot Him' Stuns Courtroom," *Chicago Tribune* (June 20, 1975).
Strobel—Lee Strobel, "Pal's Confession Fails; Defendant Ruled Guilty," *Chicago Tribune* (June 21, 1975).
Strobel—Lee Strobel, "Jury in Makeshift Courtroom Hears Dying Boy Tell of Attack," *Chicago Tribune* (February 24, 1976).
Strobel—Lee Strobel, "'Textbook' Thumbprint Aids Conviction in Coed's Killing," *Chicago Tribune* (June 29, 1976).
Strobel—Lee Strobel, "Four Years in Jail—and Innocent," *Chicago Tribune* (August 22, 1976).
Strobel—Lee Strobel, "Youth's Testimony Convicts Killers, but Death Stays Near," *Chicago Tribune* (October 25, 1976).
Strobel—Lee Strobel, "Did Justice Close Her Eyes?" *Chicago Tribune* (August 21, 1977).
Strobel—Lee Patrick Strobel, *Reckless Homicide: Ford's Pinto Trial* (South Bend, Ind.: And Books, 1980).
Strobel—Lee Strobel, *God's Outrageous Claims* (Grand Rapids: Zondervan, 1997).
Telchin—Stan Telchin, *Betrayed!* (Grand Rapids: Chosen, 1982).
Templeton—Charles Templeton, *Act of God* (New York: Bantam, 1979).
Templeton—Charles Templeton, *Farewell to God* (Toronto: McClelland & Stewart, 1996).
Thompson, J. A. *The Bible and Archaeology.* Grand Rapids: Eerdmans, 1975.
Warfield—Benjamin B. Warfield, *Introduction to Textual Criticism of the New Testament* (London: Hodder & Stoughton, 1907).
Webster's—*Webster's Encyclopedic Unabridged Dictionary of the English Language* (New York: Gramercy, 1989).
Wilcox—M. Wilcox, "Jesus in the Light of His Jewish Environment," *Aufstieg und Niedergang der römischen Welt* 2, no. 25.1 (1982).
Wilkins—Michael J. Wilkins and J. P. Moreland, eds., *Jesus under Fire* (Grand Rapids: Zondervan, 1995).
Wilson—Ian Wilson, *Jesus: The Evidence* (1984; reprint, San Francisco: HarperSanFrancisco, 1988).

Witherington—Ben Witherington III, *The Christology of Jesus* (Minneapolis: Fortress, 1990).

Yamauchi—Edwin Yamauchi, "Josephus and the Scriptures," *Fides et Historia* 13 (1980).

Yamauchi, Edwin. *The Stones and the Scriptures.* New York: J. B. Lippencott, 1972.

Zindler—Frank Zindler, "Where Jesus Never Walked," *American Atheist* (Winter 1996-1997).

Zodhiates, Spiros. *Was Christ God?* Grand Rapids: Eerdmans, 1966.

Zondervan—*The Journey* (Grand Rapids: Zondervan, 1996).

NOTES

INTRODUCTION: REOPENING THE INVESTIGATION OF A LIFETIME

1. Lee Strobel, "Four Years in Jail—and Innocent," *Chicago Tribune* (August 22, 1976) and "Did Justice Close Her Eyes?" *Chicago Tribune* (August 21, 1977).

CHAPTER 1: THE EYEWITNESS EVIDENCE

1. Lee Strobel, "Youth's Testimony Convicts Killers, but Death Stays Near," *Chicago Tribune* (October 25, 1976).
2. Irenaeus, *Adversus haereses* 3.3.4.
3. Arthur G. Patzia, *The Making of the New Testament* (Downers Grove, Ill.: InterVarsity Press, 1995), 164.
4. Ibid., 49.
5. Karen Armstrong, *A History of God* (New York: Ballantine/Epiphany, 1993), 82.
6. William Lane Craig, *The Son Rises: Historical Evidence for the Resurrection of Jesus* (Chicago: Moody Press, 1981), 140.
7. Armstrong, *A History of God,* 79.
8. 1 Corinthians 15:3–7.

CHAPTER 2: TESTING THE EYEWITNESS EVIDENCE

1. Lee Strobel, "Jury in Makeshift Courtroom Hears Dying Boy Tell of Attack," *Chicago Tribune* (February 24, 1976).
2. Luke 1:1–4.
3. Simon Greenleaf, *The Testimony of the Evangelists* (Grand Rapids: Baker, 1984), vii.
4. Cited in Craig Blomberg, "Where Do We Start Studying Jesus?" in Michael J. Wilkins and J. P. Moreland, eds., *Jesus under Fire* (Grand Rapids: Zondervan, 1995), 34.
5. See Gleason L. Archer, *The Encyclopedia of Bible Difficulties* (Grand Rapids: Zondervan, 1982) and Norman Geisler and Thomas Howe, *When Critics Ask* (Wheaton, Ill.: Victor, 1992).

CHAPTER 3: THE DOCUMENTARY EVIDENCE

1. See Lee Patrick Strobel, *Reckless Homicide: Ford's Pinto Trial* (South Bend, Ind.: And Books, 1980), 75–92 and Lee Strobel, *God's Outrageous Claims* (Grand Rapids: Zondervan, 1997), 43–58. Ford was ultimately acquitted of criminal charges after the judge withheld key documents from the jury, though the automaker was successfully sued in civil cases. Allegations about the Pinto were first reported in *Mother Jones* magazine.

2. F. F. Bruce, *The Books and the Parchments* (Old Tappan, N.J.: Revell, 1963), 178, cited in Josh McDowell, *Evidence That Demands a Verdict* (1972; reprint, San Bernardino, Calif.: Here's Life, 1986), 42.

3. Frederic Kenyon, *Handbook to the Textual Criticism of the New Testament* (New York: Macmillan, 1912), 5, cited in Ross Clifford, *The Case for the Empty Tomb* (Claremont, Calif.: Albatross, 1991), 33.

4. Frederic Kenyon, *The Bible and Archaeology* (New York: Harper, 1940), 288.

5. Norman L. Geisler and William E. Nix, *A General Introduction to the Bible* (1968; reprint, Chicago: Moody Press, 1980), 361.

6. Ibid., 367, emphasis added.

7. Patzia, *The Making of the New Testament,* 158.

8. Benjamin B. Warfield, *Introduction to Textual Criticism of the New Testament* (London: Hodder & Stoughton, 1907), 12–13.

9. Geisler and Nix, *A General Introduction to the Bible,* 195. They note that some include Philemon, 1 Peter, and 1 John among the disputed books, but "it is probably better to refer to these as omitted rather than disputed books."

10. Ibid., 207.

11. Ibid., 199. This does not include the Apocrypha, which were accepted by particular churches for a particular period of time and today are considered valuable though not canonical. Examples: Shepherd of Hermas, Epistle to the Corinthians, Epistle of Pseudo-Barnabas, Didache, Apocalypse of Peter, The Acts of Paul and Thecla, and Ancient Homily or the Second Epistle of Clement.

12. Ibid.

CHAPTER 4: THE CORROBORATING EVIDENCE

1. *Webster's Encyclopedic Unabridged Dictionary of the English Language* (New York: Gramercy, 1989), 328.

2. Maurice Possley, "Mob Hit Man Aleman Gets One Hundred to Three Hundred Years," *Chicago Tribune* (November 26, 1997).

3. Charles Templeton, *Act of God* (New York: Bantam, 1979), 152.

4. Josephus, *The Antiquities* 20.200. See also Edwin Yamauchi, "Josephus and the Scriptures," *Fides et Historia* 13 (1980), 42–63.

5. Josephus, *The Antiquities* 18.63–64.

6. Michael Martin, *The Case against Christianity* (Philadelphia: Temple Univ. Press, 1991), 49.

7. Tacitus, *Annals* 15.44.

8. Pliny the Younger, *Letters* 10.96.

9. Gary Habermas, *The Historical Jesus* (Joplin, Mo.: College Press, 1996), 196–97.

10. Paul L. Maier, *Pontius Pilate* (Wheaton, Ill.: Tyndale House, 1968), 366, citing a fragment from Phlegon, *Olympiades he Chronika* 13, ed. Otto Keller, *Rerum Naturalium Scriptores Graeci Minores,* 1 (Leipzig: Teurber, 1877), 101. Translation by Maier.

11. See P. Maier, "Sejanus, Pilate, and the Date of the Crucifixion," *Church History* 37 (1968), 1–11.

12. M. Wilcox, "Jesus in the Light of His Jewish Environment," *Aufstieg und Niedergang der römischen Welt* 2, no. 25.1 (1982), 133.

13. Luke Timothy Johnson, *The Real Jesus* (San Francisco: HarperSanFrancisco, 1996), 120.

14. Ignatius, *Trallians* 9.

15. See Gary Habermas, *The Verdict of History* (Nashville: Nelson, 1988).

16. Ibid, 169.

CHAPTER 5: THE SCIENTIFIC EVIDENCE

1. For the full story, see Joe McGinniss, *Fatal Vision* (New York: New American Library, 1989). For a description of the scientific evidence, see Colin Evans, *The Casebook of Forensic Detection* (New York: John Wiley & Sons, 1996), 277–80.

2. Luke 18:35, Mark 10:46.

3. Norman Geisler and Thomas Howe, *When Critics Ask* (Wheaton, Ill.: Victor, 1992), 385.

4. John Ankerberg and John Weldon, *Ready with an Answer* (Eugene, Ore.: Harvest House, 1997), 272.

5. Michael Martin, *The Case Against Christianity* (Philadelphia: Temple Univ. Press, 1991), 69, emphasis added.

6. John McRay, *Archaeology and the New Testament* (Grand Rapids: Baker, 1991), 155, emphasis added.

7. Robert Boyd, *Tells, Tombs, and Treasure* (Grand Rapids: Baker, 1969), 175, cited in Habermas, *The Historical Jesus,* 172.

8. Geisler and Howe, *When Critics Ask,* 185.

9. Frank Zindler, "Where Jesus Never Walked," *American Atheist* (Winter 1996-1997), 34.

10. Ian Wilson, *Jesus: The Evidence* (1984; reprint, San Francisco: HarperSanFrancisco, 1988), 67.

11. Jack Finegan, *The Archaeology of the New Testament* (Princeton: Princeton Univ. Press, 1992), 46.

12. Wilson, *Jesus: The Evidence*, 67.

13. Wilkins and Moreland, *Jesus under Fire*, 209.

14. Ibid., 211.

15. Kevin D. Miller, "The War of the Scrolls," *Christianity Today* (October 6, 1997), 44, emphasis added.

16. Joseph Smith, *History of the Church*, 8 vols. (Salt Lake City: Deseret, 1978), 4:461, cited in Donald S. Tingle, *Mormonism* (Downers Grove, Ill.: InterVarsity Press, 1981), 17.

17. John Ankerberg and John Weldon, *The Facts on the Mormon Church* (Eugene, Ore.: Harvest House, 1991), 30, emphasis in original.

18. Clifford Wilson, *Rocks, Relics and Biblical Reliability* (Grand Rapids: Zondervan; Richardson, Tex.: Probe, 1977), 120, cited in Ankerberg and Weldon, *Ready with an Answer*, 272.

CHAPTER 6: THE REBUTTAL EVIDENCE

1. Henry Campbell Black, *Black's Law Dictionary*, 5th ed. (St. Paul, Minn.: West, 1979), 1139.

2. Lee Strobel, "His 'I Shot Him' Stuns Courtroom," *Chicago Tribune* (June 20, 1975) and "Pal's Confession Fails; Defendant Ruled Guilty," *Chicago Tribune* (June 21, 1975).

3. Gregory A. Boyd, *Jesus under Siege* (Wheaton, Ill.: Victor, 1995), 88.

4. John Dominic Crossan, *The Historical Jesus* (San Francisco: HarperSanFrancisco, 1991), 329.

5. Johnson, *The Real Jesus*, 3, 5, 8.

6. Ibid, 26.

7. Ibid.

CHAPTER 7: THE IDENTITY EVIDENCE

1. Marjorie Rosen, "Getting Inside the Mind of a Serial Killer," *Biography* (October 1997), 62–65.

2. Ibid., 64.

3. R. E. Brown, "Did Jesus Know He Was God?" *Biblical Theology Bulletin* 15 (1985), 78, cited in Ben Witherington III, *The Christology of Jesus* (Minneapolis: Fortress, 1990), 277.

4. Jaroslav Pelikan, *The Christian Tradition: A History of the Development of Doctrine*, vol. 1, *The Emergence of the Catholic Tradition (100–600)* (Chicago: Univ. of Chicago Press, 1971), 173, cited in William Lane Craig, *Reasonable Faith* (Westchester, Ill.: Crossway, 1994), 243.

5. Craig, *Reasonable Faith*, 252.

6. Ibid., 244.

7. Royce Gordon Gruenler, *New Approaches to Jesus and the Gospels* (Grand Rapids: Baker, 1982), 74.

8. James D. G. Dunn, *Jesus and the Spirit* (London: SCM Press, 1975), 60, cited in Craig, *Reasonable Faith,* 252, emphasis added.

CHAPTER 8: THE PSYCHOLOGICAL EVIDENCE

1. Leland H. Gregory III, "Top Ten Government Bloopers," *George* (November 1997), 78.

2. Charles Templeton, *Farewell to God* (Toronto: McClelland & Stewart, 1996), 112.

3. Wilson, *Jesus: The Evidence,* 141.

4. Ibid., 109, emphasis in original.

5. "A Case of Congenital Ichthyosiform Erythrodermia of Brocq Treated by Hypnosis," *British Medical Journal* 2 (1952), 996, cited in Wilson, *Jesus: The Evidence,* 103.

6. M. Scott Peck, *People of the Lie* (New York: Touchstone, 1997).

7. Wilson, *Jesus: The Evidence,* 107.

8. C. S. Lewis, *The Screwtape Letters* (London: Collins-Fontana, 1942), 9.

9. Philip Schaff, *The Person of Christ* (New York: American Tract Society, 1918), 97, cited in McDowell, *Evidence That Demands a Verdict,* 107, emphasis added.

CHAPTER 9: THE PROFILE EVIDENCE

1. Marla Donato, "That Guilty Look," *Chicago Tribune* (April 1, 1994).

2. Denny Johnson, "Police Add Electronic 'Sketch Artist' to Their Bag of Tricks," *Chicago Tribune* (June 22, 1997).

3. Templeton, *Farewell to God,* 230.

4. Morton Smith, "Biblical Arguments for Slavery," *Free Inquiry* (Spring 1987), 30.

5. Thomas Sowell, *Race and Culture* (New York: Basic, 1995).

6. Josh McDowell and Bart Larson, *Jesus: A Biblical Defense of His Deity* (San Bernardino, Calif.: Here's Life, 1983), 62–64.

CHAPTER 10: THE FINGERPRINT EVIDENCE

1. Evans, *The Casebook of Forensic Detection,* 98–100.

2. Lee Strobel, "'Textbook' Thumbprint Aids Conviction in Coed's Killing," *Chicago Tribune* (June 29, 1976).

3. For basic details on fulfilled prophecies, see McDowell, *Evidence That Demands a Verdict,* 141–77.

4. Peter W. Stoner, *Science Speaks* (Chicago: Moody Press, 1969), 109.
5. For a discussion of the Daniel prophecy, see Robert C. Newman, "Fulfilled Prophecy As Miracle," in R. Douglas Geivett and Gary R. Habermas, eds., *In Defense of Miracles* (Downers Grove, Ill.: InterVarsity Press, 1997), 214–25.
6. Stan Telchin, *Betrayed!* (Grand Rapids: Chosen, 1982).
7. Ruth Rosen, ed., *Jewish Doctors Meet the Great Physician* (San Francisco: Purple Pomegranate, 1997), 9–23.
8. Ibid., 34–35.

CHAPTER 11: THE MEDICAL EVIDENCE

1. Surah IV: 156–57.
2. Wilson, *Jesus: The Evidence,* 140.
3. Craig, *Reasonable Faith,* 234.
4. D. H. Lawrence, *Love among the Haystacks and Other Stories* (New York: Penguin, 1960), 125.
5. Hugh Schonfield, *The Passover Plot* (New York: Bantam, 1965), 165.
6. Habermas, *The Verdict of History,* 56.
7. Michael Baigent, Richard Leigh, and Henry Lincoln, *Holy Blood, Holy Grail* (New York: Delacorte, 1982), 372.
8. Johnson, *The Real Jesus,* 30.
9. J. W. Hewitt, "The Use of Nails in the Crucifixion," *Harvard Theological Review* 25 (1932), 29–45, cited in Josh McDowell, *The Resurrection Factor* (San Bernardino, Calif.: Here's Life, 1981), 45.
10. William D. Edwards et al., "On the Physical Death of Jesus Christ," *Journal of the American Medical Association* (March 21, 1986), 1455–63.

CHAPTER 12: THE EVIDENCE OF THE MISSING BODY

1. Gerald O'Collins, *The Easter Jesus* (London: Darton, Longman & Todd, 1973), 134, cited in Craig, *The Son Rises,* 136.
2. For a tape of the debate, see William Lane Craig and Frank Zindler, *Atheism vs. Christianity: Where Does the Evidence Point?* (Grand Rapids: Zondervan, 1993), videocassette.
3. Templeton, *Farewell to God,* 120.
4. Martin, *The Case against Christianity,* 78–79.
5. Ibid., 81.
6. Michael Grant, *Jesus: An Historian's Review of the Gospels* (New York: Charles Schribner's Sons, 1977), 176.
7. Kirsopp Lake, *The Historical Evidence for the Resurrection of Jesus Christ* (London: Williams & Norgate, 1907), 247–79, cited in William Lane Craig, *Knowing the Truth about the Resurrection* (Ann Arbor, Mich.: Servant, 1988), 35–36.

8. J. N. D. Anderson, *The Evidence for the Resurrection* (Downers Grove, Ill.: InterVarsity Press, 1966), 20.

CHAPTER 13: THE EVIDENCE OF APPEARANCES

1. "Bomb Victim's Body Not in Grave," *Chicago Tribune* (January 14, 1998).

2. Martin, *The Case against Christianity,* 87.

3. Gary Habermas and Antony Flew, *Did Jesus Rise from the Dead? The Resurrection Debate* (San Francisco: Harper & Row, 1987), xiv.

4. Ibid., xv.

5. Martin, *The Case against Christianity,* 90.

6. Craig, *The Son Rises,* 125.

7. John Drane, *Introducing the New Testament* (San Francisco: Harper & Row, 1986), 99.

8. Michael Green, *Christ Is Risen: So What?* (Kent, England: Sovereign World, 1995), 34.

9. Also cited in Gary Habermas and J. P. Moreland, *Immortality: The Other Side of Death* (Nashville: Nelson, 1992), 60.

10. Martin, *The Case against Christianity,* 75.

11. Carl Braaten, *History and Hermeneutics,* vol. 2 of *New Directions in Theology Today,* ed. William Hordern (Philadelphia: Westminster Press, 1966), 78, cited in Habermas and Flew, *Did Jesus Rise from the Dead?* 24.

12. Michael Green, *The Empty Cross of Jesus* (Downers Grove, Ill.: InterVarsity Press, 1984), 97, cited in Ankerberg and Weldon, *Knowing the Truth about the Resurrection,* 22, emphasis in original.

CHAPTER 14: THE CIRCUMSTANTIAL EVIDENCE

1. Black, *Black's Law Dictionary,* 221.

2. See Josh McDowell, *More Than a Carpenter* (Wheaton, Ill.: Living Books, 1977), 60–71.

3. C. F. D. Moule, *The Phenomenon of the New Testament* (London: SCM Press, 1967), 3.

4. Donald McFarlan, ed., *The Guinness Book of World Records* (New York: Bantam, 1991), 547.

5. Clifford, *The Case for the Empty Tomb,* 112.

CONCLUSION: THE VERDICT OF HISTORY

1. A. N. Sherwin-White, *Roman Society and Roman Law in the New Testament* (Oxford: Clarendon Press, 1963), 188–91.

2. Blomberg, "Where Do We Start Studying Jesus?" in Wilkins and Moreland, *Jesus under Fire,* 43, emphasis added.

3. Craig, *The Son Rises,* 102, emphasis added.

4. Julius Müller, *The Theory of Myths, in Its Application to the Gospel History, Examined and Confuted* (London: John Chapman, 1844), 26, cited in Craig, *The Son Rises,* 101.

5. *The Journey* (Grand Rapids: Zondervan, 1996).

6. Michael Murphy, "The Two-Sided Game of Christian Faith," in John Warwick Montgomery, ed., *Christianity for the Tough-Minded* (Minneapolis: Bethany House, 1973), 125, cited in Ankerberg and Weldon, *Knowing the Truth about the Resurrection,* 44.

7. C. S. Lewis, *Mere Christianity* (New York: Macmillan-Collier, 1960), 55–56.

The Case for Faith

INTRODUCTION: THE CHALLENGE OF FAITH

Christian theism must be rejected by any person with even a shred of respect for reason.

George H. Smith, atheist[1]

Christian faith is not an irrational leap. Examined objectively, the claims of the Bible are rational propositions well supported by reason and evidence.

Charles Colson, Christian[2]

William Franklin Graham steadied himself by gripping both sides of the podium. He was eighty years old, fighting Parkinson's disease, but he stared intently at the throngs inside the RCA Dome in Indianapolis and spoke in a steady, forceful voice. There was no hint of hesitation, no uncertainty or ambiguity. His sermon was essentially the same simple and direct message he had been preaching for fifty years.

He referenced the chaos and violence around the world, and he zeroed in on the anguish, pain, and confusion in the hearts of individuals. He talked about sin, about forgiveness, about redemption, and about the loneliness, despair, and depression that weigh so many people down.

"All of us want to be loved," he said in his familiar North Carolina cadence as he approached the conclusion of his talk. "All of us want somebody to love us. Well, I want to tell you that God loves you. He loves you so much that he gave us his Son to die on the cross for our sins. And he loves you so much that he will come into your life and change the direction of your life and make you a new person, whoever you are.

"Are you sure that you know Christ? There comes a moment in which the Spirit of God convicts you, calls you, speaks to you about opening your heart and making certain of your relationship to God.

And hundreds of you here tonight are not sure. You'd like to be sure. You'd like to leave here tonight knowing that if you died on the way home, you would be ready to meet God."

So he urged them to come. And they did—at first, there was a trickle of people, and then the floodgates opened, with individuals, couples, and entire families pouring into the empty space in front of the platform. Soon they were shoulder-to-shoulder, the crowd wrapping around the sides of the stage, nearly three thousand in all. Some were weeping, gripped by somber conviction; others stared downward, still stewing in shame over their past; many were smiling from ear to ear—liberated, joyous . . . home, finally.

One married woman was typical. "My mom died of cancer when I was young, and at the time I thought I was being punished by God," she told a counselor. "Tonight I realized that God loves me—it is something I've known but couldn't really grasp. Tonight a peacefulness came into my heart."[3]

What is faith? There would have been no need to define it for these people on that sultry June night. Faith was almost palpable to them. They reached out to God almost as if they were expecting to physically embrace him. Faith drained them of the guilt that had oppressed them. Faith replaced despondency with hope. Faith infused them with new direction and purpose. Faith unlocked heaven. Faith was like cool water soaking their parched soul.

But faith isn't always that easy, even for people who desperately want it. Some people hunger for spiritual certainty, yet something hinders them from experiencing it. They wish they could taste that kind of freedom, but obstacles block their paths. Objections pester them. Doubts mock them. Their hearts want to soar to God; their intellects keep them securely tied down.

They see the television coverage of the crowds who have come forward to pray with Billy Graham and they shake their heads. If it were only that simple, they sigh to themselves. If only there weren't so many questions.

For Charles Templeton—ironically, once Billy Graham's pulpit partner and close friend—questions about God have hardened into bitter opposition toward Christianity. Like Graham, Templeton once spoke powerfully to crowds in vast arenas and called for people to commit themselves to Jesus Christ. Some even predicted Templeton would eventually eclipse Graham as an evangelist.

But that was a long time ago. That was before the crippling questions. Today Templeton's faith—repeatedly punctured by persistent and obstinate doubts—has leaked away. Maybe forever.

Maybe.

FROM FAITH TO DOUBT

The year was 1949. Thirty-year-old Billy Graham was unaware that he was on the brink of being catapulted into worldwide fame and influence. Ironically, as he readied himself for his breakthrough crusade in Los Angeles, he found himself grappling with uncertainty—not over the existence of God or the divinity of Jesus but over the fundamental issue of whether he could totally trust what his Bible was telling him.

In his autobiography, Graham said he felt as if he were being stretched on a rack. Pulling him toward God was Henrietta Mears, the bright and compassionate Christian educator who had a thorough understanding of modern scholarship and an abounding confidence in the reliability of the Scriptures. Yanking him the other way was Graham's close companion and preaching colleague, thirty-three-year-old Charles Templeton.[4]

According to Templeton, he became a Christian fifteen years earlier when he found himself increasingly disgusted with his lifestyle on the sports staff of the Toronto *Globe*. Fresh from a night out at a sleazy strip joint, feeling shoddy and unclean, he went to his room and knelt by his bed in the darkness.

"Suddenly," he would recall later, "it was as though a black blanket had been draped over me. A sense of guilt pervaded my entire mind and body. The only words that would come were, 'Lord, come down. Come down....'" And then:

> Slowly, a weight began to lift, a weight as heavy as I. It passed through my thighs, my torso, my arms and shoulders, and lifted off. An ineffable warmth began to suffuse my body. It seemed that a light had turned on in my chest and that it had cleansed me.... I hardly dared breathe, fearing that I might alter or end the moment. And I heard myself whispering softly over and over again, "Thank you, Lord. Thank you. Thank you. Thank you." Later, in bed, I lay quietly at the center of a radiant, overwhelming, all-pervasive happiness.[5]

After abandoning journalism for the ministry, Templeton met Graham in 1945 at a Youth for Christ rally. They were roommates and constant companions during an adventurous tour of Europe, alternating in the pulpit as they preached at rallies. Templeton founded a church that soon overflowed its 1,200-seat sanctuary. *American Magazine* said he "set a new standard for mass evangelism."[6] His friendship with Graham grew. "He's one of the few men I have ever loved in my life," Graham once told a biographer.[7]

But soon doubts began gnawing at Templeton. "I had gone through a conversion experience as an incredibly green youth," he recalled later. "I lacked the intellectual skills and the theological training needed to buttress my beliefs when—as was inevitable—questions and doubts began to plague me.... My reason had begun to challenge and sometimes to rebut the central beliefs of the Christian faith."[8]

A TRIUMPH OF FAITH

Now, there was the skeptical Templeton, a counterpoint to the faith-filled Henrietta Mears, tugging his friend Billy Graham away from her repeated assurances that the Scriptures are trustworthy. "Billy, you're fifty years out of date," he argued. "People no longer accept the Bible as being inspired the way you do. Your faith is too simple."

Templeton seemed to be winning the tug-of-war. "If I was not exactly doubtful," Graham would recall, "I was certainly disturbed." He knew that if he could not trust the Bible, he could not go on. The Los Angeles crusade—the event that would open the door to Graham's worldwide ministry—was hanging in the balance.

Graham searched the Scriptures for answers, he prayed, he pondered. Finally, in a heavy-hearted walk in the moonlit San Bernardino Mountains, everything came to a climax. Gripping a Bible, Graham dropped to his knees and confessed he couldn't answer some of the philosophical and psychological questions that Templeton and others were raising.

"I was trying to be on the level with God, but something remained unspoken," he wrote. "At last the Holy Spirit freed me to say it. 'Father, I am going to accept this as Thy Word—by *faith!* I'm going to allow faith to go beyond my intellectual questions and doubts, and I will believe this to be Your inspired Word.'"

Rising from his knees, tears in his eyes, Graham said he sensed the power of God as he hadn't felt it for months. "Not all my questions were answered, but a major bridge had been crossed," he said. "In my heart and mind, I knew a spiritual battle in my soul had been fought and won."[9]

For Graham, it was a pivotal moment. For Templeton, though, it was a bitterly disappointing turn of events. "He committed intellectual suicide by closing his mind," Templeton declared. The emotion he felt most toward his friend was pity. Now on different paths, their lives began to diverge.

History knows what would happen to Graham in the succeeding years. He would become the most persuasive and effective evangelist of modern times and one of the most admired men in the world. But what would happen to Templeton? Decimated by doubts, he resigned from the ministry and moved back to Canada, where he became a commentator and novelist.

Templeton's reasoning had chased away his faith. But are faith and intellect really incompatible? Is it possible to be a thinker and a Bible-believing Christian at the same time? Some don't believe so.

"Reason and faith are opposites, two mutually exclusive terms: there is no reconciliation or common ground," asserts atheist George H. Smith. "Faith is belief without, or in spite of, reason."[10]

Christian educator W. Bingham Hunter takes the opposite view. "Faith," he said, "is a rational response to the evidence of God's self-revelation in nature, human history, the Scriptures and his resurrected Son."[11]

For me, having lived much of my life as an atheist, the last thing I want is a naive faith built on a paper-thin foundation of wishful thinking or make-believe. I need a faith that's consistent with reason, not contradictory to it; I want beliefs that are grounded in reality, not detached from it. I need to find out once and for all whether the Christian faith can stand up to scrutiny.

It was time for me to talk face to face with Charles Templeton.

FROM MINISTER TO AGNOSTIC

Some five hundred miles north of where Billy Graham was staging his Indianapolis campaign, I tracked Templeton to a modern high-rise building in a middle-class neighborhood of Toronto. Taking the elevator to the twenty-fifth floor, I went to a door marked "Penthouse" and used the brass knocker.

Under my arm I carried a copy of Templeton's latest book, whose title leaves no ambiguity concerning his spiritual perspective. It's called *Farewell to God: My Reasons for Rejecting the Christian Faith.* The often-acerbic tome seeks to eviscerate Christian beliefs, attacking them with passion for being "outdated, demonstrably untrue, and often, in their various manifestations, deleterious to individuals and to society."[12]

Templeton draws upon a variety of illustrations as he strives to undermine faith in the God of the Bible. But I was especially struck by one moving passage in which he pointed to the horrors of Alzheimer's disease, describing in gripping detail the way it hideously strips people of their personal identity by rotting their mind and memory. How, he demanded, could a compassionate God allow such a ghastly illness to torture its victims and their loved ones?

The answer, he concluded, is simple: Alzheimer's would not exist if there were a loving God. And because it does exist, that's one more bit of persuasive evidence that God does not.[13] For someone like me, whose wife's family has endured the ugly ravages of Alzheimer's, it was an argument that carried considerable emotional punch.

I wasn't sure what to expect as I waited at Templeton's doorstep. Would he be as combative as he was in his book? Would he be bitter toward Billy Graham? Would he even go through with our interview? When he had consented in a brief telephone conversation two days earlier, he had said vaguely that his health was not good.

Madeleine Templeton, fresh from tending flowers in her rooftop garden, opened the door and greeted me warmly. "I know you've come all the way from Chicago," she said, "but Charles is very sick, I'm sorry to say."

"I could come back another time," I offered.

"Well, let's see how he's feeling," she said. She led me up a red-carpeted staircase into their luxury apartment, two large and frisky poodles at her heels. "He's been sleeping. . . ."

At that moment, her eighty-three-year-old husband emerged from his bedroom. He was wearing a dark brown, lightweight robe over similarly colored pajamas. Black slippers were on his feet. His thinning gray hair was a bit disheveled. He was gaunt and pale, although his blue-gray eyes appeared alert and expressive. He politely extended his hand to be shaken.

"Please excuse me," he said, clearing his throat, "but I'm not well." Then he added matter-of-factly: "Actually, I'm dying."

"What's wrong?" I asked.

His answer almost knocked me on my heels. "Alzheimer's disease," he replied.

My mind raced to what he'd written about Alzheimer's being evidence for the nonexistence of God; suddenly, I had an insight into at least some of the motivation for his book.

"I've had it . . . let's see, has it been three years?" he said, furrowing his brow and turning to his wife for help. "That's right, isn't it, Madeleine?"

She nodded. "Yes, dear, three years."

"My memory isn't what it was," he said. "And, as you may know, Alzheimer's is always fatal. Always. It sounds melodramatic, but the truth is I'm doomed. Sooner or later, it will kill me. But first, it will take my mind." He smiled faintly. "It's already started, I'm afraid. Madeleine can attest to that."

"Look, I'm sorry to intrude," I said. "If you're not feeling up to this . . ."

But Templeton insisted. He ushered me into the living room, brightly decorated in a contemporary style and awash in afternoon sunshine, which poured through glass doors that offered a breath-taking panoramic view of the city. We sat on adjacent cushioned chairs, and in a matter of minutes Templeton seemed to have mustered fresh energy.

"I suppose you want me to explain how I went from the ministry to agnosticism," he said. With that, he proceeded to describe the events that led to the shedding of his faith in God.

That was what I had expected. But I could never have anticipated how our conversation would end.

THE POWER OF A PICTURE

Templeton was fully engaged now. Occasionally, I could see evidence of his Alzheimer's, such as when he was unable to recall a precise sequence of events or when he'd repeat himself. But for the most part he spoke with eloquence and enthusiasm, using an impressive vocabulary, his rich and robust voice rising and lowering for emphasis. He had an aristocratic tone that sounded nearly theatrical at times.

"Was there one thing in particular that caused you to lose your faith in God?" I asked at the outset.

He thought for a moment. "It was a photograph in *Life* magazine," he said finally.

"Really?" I said. "A photograph? How so?"

He narrowed his eyes a bit and looked off to the side, as if he were viewing the photo afresh and reliving the moment. "It was a picture of a black woman in Northern Africa," he explained. "They were experiencing a devastating drought. And she was holding her dead baby in her arms and looking up to heaven with the most forlorn expression. I looked at it and I thought, 'Is it possible to believe that there is a loving or caring Creator when all this woman needed was *rain?*'"

As he emphasized the word *rain*, his bushy gray eyebrows shot up and his arms gestured toward heaven as if beckoning for a response.

"How could a loving God *do this* to that woman?" he implored as he got more animated, moving to the edge of his chair. "Who runs the rain? I don't; you don't. *He* does—or that's what I thought. But when I saw that photograph, I immediately knew it is not possible for this to happen and for there to be a loving God. There was no way. Who else but a fiend could destroy a baby and virtually kill its mother with agony—when all that was needed was *rain*?"

He paused, letting the question hang heavily in the air. Then he settled back into his chair. "That was the climactic moment," he said. "And then I began to think further about the world being the creation of God. I started considering the plagues that sweep across parts of the planet and indiscriminately kill—more often than not, painfully—all kinds of people, the ordinary, the decent, and the rotten. And it just became crystal clear to me that it is not possible for an intelligent person to believe that there is a deity who loves."

Templeton was tapping into an issue that had vexed me for years. In my career as a newspaper reporter, I hadn't merely seen photos of intense suffering; I was a frequent first-hand observer of the underbelly of life where tragedy and suffering festered—the rotting inner cities of the United States; the filthy slums of India; Cook County Jail and the major penitentiaries; the hospice wards for the hopeless; all sorts of disaster scenes. More than once, my mind reeled at trying to reconcile the idea of a loving God with the depravity and heartache and anguish before my eyes.

But Templeton wasn't done. "My mind then went to the whole concept of hell. My goodness," he said, his voice infused with astonishment, "I couldn't hold someone's hand to a fire for a moment. Not an instant! How could a loving God, just because you don't obey him and do what he wants, torture you forever—not allowing you to die, but to continue in that pain for eternity? There is no criminal who would do this!"

"So these were the first doubts you had?" I asked.

"Prior to that, I had been having more and more questions. I had preached to hundreds of thousands of people the antithetical message, and then I found to my dismay that I could no longer believe it. To believe it would be to deny the brain I had been given. It became quite clear that I had been wrong. So I made up my mind that I would leave the ministry. That's essentially how I came to be agnostic."

"Define what you mean by that," I said, since various people have offered different interpretations of that term.

"The atheist says there is no God," he replied. "The Christian and Jew say there is a God. The agnostic says, 'I cannot know.' Not *do not* know but *cannot* know. I never would presume to say flatly that there is no God. I don't know everything; I'm not the embodiment of wisdom. But it is not possible for me to believe in God."

I hesitated to ask the next question. "As you get older," I began in a tentative tone, "and you're facing a disease that's always fatal, do you—"

"Worry about being wrong?" he interjected. He smiled. "No, I don't."

"Why not?"

"Because I have spent a lifetime thinking about it. If this were a simplistic conclusion reached on a whim, that would be different. But it's impossible for me—*impossible*—to believe that there is any thing or person or being that could be described as a loving God who could allow what happens in our world daily."

"Would you *like* to believe?" I asked.

"Of course!" he exclaimed. "If I could, I would. I'm eighty-three years old. I've got Alzheimer's. I'm dying, for goodness sake! But I've spent my life thinking about it and I'm not going to change now. Hypothetically, if someone came up to me and said, 'Look, old boy, the reason you're ill is God's punishment for your refusal to continue on the path your feet were set in'—would that make any difference to me?"

He answered himself emphatically: "No," he declared. "*No.* There cannot be, in our world, a loving God."

His eyes locked with mine. "*Cannot* be."

THE ILLUSION OF FAITH

Templeton ran his fingers through his hair. He had been talking in adamant tones, and I could tell he was beginning to tire. I wanted to be sensitive to his condition, but I had a few other questions I wanted to pursue. With his permission, I continued.

"As we're talking, Billy Graham is in the midst of a series of rallies in Indiana," I told Templeton. "What would you say to the people who've stepped forward to put their faith in Christ?"

Templeton's eyes got wide. "Why, I wouldn't interfere in their lives at all," he replied. "If a person has faith and it makes them a better individual, then I'm all for that—even if I think they're nuts. Having been a Christian, I know how important it is to people's lives—how it alters their decisions, how it helps them deal with difficult problems. For most people, it's a boon beyond description. But is it because there is a God? No, it's not."

Templeton's voice carried no condescension, and yet the implications of what he was saying were thoroughly patronizing. Is that what faith is all about—fooling yourself into becoming a better person? Convincing yourself there's a God so that you'll become motivated to ratchet up your morality a notch or two? Embracing a fairy tale so you'll sleep better at night? *No, thank you*, I thought to myself. If that's faith, I wasn't interested.

"What about Billy Graham himself?" I asked. "You said in your book that you feel sorry for him."

"Oh, no, no," he insisted, contrary to his writings. "Who am I to feel sorry for what another man believes? I may regret it on his behalf, if I may put it that way, because he has closed his mind to reality. But would I wish him ill? Not for anything at all!"

Templeton glanced over to an adjacent glass coffee table where Billy Graham's autobiography was sitting.

"Billy is pure gold," he remarked fondly. "There's no feigning or fakery in him. He's a first-rate human being. Billy is profoundly Christian—he's the genuine goods, as they say. He sincerely believes—unquestionably. He is as wholesome and faithful as anyone can be."

And what about Jesus? I wanted to know what Templeton thought of the cornerstone of Christianity. "Do you believe Jesus ever lived?" I asked.

"No question," came the quick reply.

"Did he think he was God?"

He shook his head. "That would have been the last thought that would have entered his mind."

"And his teaching—did you admire what he taught?"

"Well, he wasn't a very good preacher. What he said was too simple. He hadn't thought about it. He hadn't agonized over the biggest question there is to ask."

"Which is . . ."

"Is there a God? How could anyone believe in a God who does, or allows, what goes on in the world?"

"And so how do you assess this Jesus?" It seemed like the next logical question—but I wasn't ready for the response it would evoke.

THE ALLURE OF JESUS

Templeton's body language softened. It was as if he suddenly felt relaxed and comfortable in talking about an old and dear friend. His voice, which at times had displayed such a sharp and insistent edge, now took on a melancholy and reflective tone. His guard seemingly down, he spoke in an unhurried pace, almost nostalgically, carefully choosing his words as he talked about Jesus.

"He was," Templeton began, "the greatest human being who has ever lived. He was a moral genius. His ethical sense was unique. He was the intrinsically wisest person that I've ever encountered in my life or in my readings. His commitment was total and led to his own death, much to the detriment of the world. What could one say about him except that this was a form of greatness?"

I was taken aback. "You sound like you really care about him," I said.

"Well, yes, he's the most important thing in my life," came his reply. "I . . . I . . . I," he stuttered, searching for the right word, "I know it may sound strange, but I have to say . . . I *adore* him!"

I wasn't sure how to respond. "You say that with some emotion," I said.

"Well, yes. Everything good I know, everything decent I know, everything pure I know, I learned from Jesus. Yes . . . yes. And tough!

Just look at Jesus. He castigated people. He was angry. People don't think of him that way, but they don't read the Bible. He had a righteous anger. He cared for the oppressed and exploited. There's no question that he had the highest moral standard, the least duplicity, the greatest compassion, of any human being in history. There have been many other wonderful people, but Jesus is Jesus."

"And so the world would do well to emulate him?"

"Oh, my goodness, yes! I have tried—and try is as far as I can go—to act as I have believed he would act. That doesn't mean I could read his mind, because one of the most fascinating things about him was that he often did the opposite thing you'd expect—"

Abruptly, Templeton cut short his thoughts. There was a brief pause, almost as if he was uncertain whether he should continue.

"Uh . . . but . . . no," he said slowly, "he's the most . . ." He stopped, then started again. "In my view," he declared, "he is the most important human being who has ever existed."

That's when Templeton uttered the words I never expected to hear from him. "And if I may put it this way," he said as his voice began to crack, *"I . . . miss . . . him!"*

With that, tears flooded his eyes. He turned his head and looked downward, raising his left hand to shield his face from me. His shoulders bobbed as he wept.

What was going on? Was this an unguarded glimpse into his soul? I felt drawn to him and wanted to comfort him; at the same time, the journalist in me wanted to dig to the core of what was prompting this reaction. Missed him *why?* Missed him *how?*

In a gentle voice, I asked, "In what way?"

Templeton fought to compose himself. I could tell it wasn't like him to lose control in front of a stranger. He sighed deeply and wiped away a tear. After a few more awkward moments, he waved his hand dismissively. Finally, quietly but adamantly, he insisted: "Enough of that."

He leaned forward to pick up his coffee. He took a sip, holding the cup tightly in both hands as if drawing warmth from it. It was obvious that he wanted to pretend this unvarnished look into his soul had never happened.

But I couldn't let it go. Nor could I gloss over Templeton's pointed but heartfelt objections about God. Clearly, they demanded a response.

For him, as well as for me.

ON THE ROAD TO ANSWERS

1.6 billion [Christians] can be wrong.... My claim is simply that ... rational people should give up these beliefs.

Michael Martin, atheist[1]

Today, it seems to me, there is no good reason for an intelligent person to embrace the illusion of atheism or agnosticism, to make the same intellectual mistakes I made. I wish ... I had known then what I know now.

Patrick Glynn, atheist-turned-Christian[2]

A short time after the interview with Charles Templeton, my wife, Leslie, and I began driving back to Chicago, spending much of the way in an animated discussion about my enigmatic encounter with the former evangelist.

Frankly, I needed some time to process the experience. It had been an unusual interview, ranging all the way from the resolute rejection of God to an emotional desire to reconnect with the Jesus he used to worship.

"It sounds like you really like Templeton," Leslie remarked at one point.

"I do," I said.

The truth is that my heart went out to him. He hungers for faith; he conceded as much. As someone facing death, he has every incentive to want to believe in God. There's an undeniable pull toward Jesus that clearly comes from deep inside him. But then there are those formidable intellectual barriers that stand squarely in his path.

Like Templeton, I've always been someone who has grappled with questions. In my former role as legal affairs editor of the *Chicago Tribune,* I had been notorious for raising what I called *"Yes, but"* objections. *Yes,* I could see that the evidence in a trial was pointing toward a certain verdict, *but* what about that inconsistency, or this flaw, or that weak link? *Yes,* the prosecutor may have presented a convincing case for the defendant's guilt, *but* what about his alibi or the lack of fingerprints?

And the same was true of my personal investigation of Jesus. I started out as an atheist, utterly convinced that God didn't create people but that people created God in a pathetic effort to explain the unknown and temper their overpowering fear of death. My previous book, *The Case for Christ,* described my nearly two-year examination of the historical evidence that pointed me toward the verdict that God really exists and that Jesus actually is his unique Son. (For a summary of those findings, please see the Appendix.)

But that hadn't been enough by itself to completely settle the matter for me. There were still those nagging objections. *Yes,* I could see how the historical evidence for Jesus' resurrection can support a verdict that he's divine, *but* what about the flurry of problems that raises? I called these conundrums "The Big Eight":

- If there's a loving God, why does this pain-wracked world groan under so much suffering and evil?
- If the miracles of God contradict science, then how can any rational person believe that they're true?
- If God really created the universe, why does the persuasive evidence of science compel so many to conclude that the unguided process of evolution accounts for life?
- If God is morally pure, how can he sanction the slaughter of innocent children as the Old Testament says he did?
- If Jesus is the only way to heaven, then what about the millions of people who have never heard of him?
- If God cares about the people he created, how could he consign so many of them to an eternity of torture in hell just because they didn't believe the right things about him?
- If God is the ultimate overseer of the church, why has it been rife with hypocrisy and brutality throughout the ages?
- If I'm still plagued by doubts, then is it still possible to be a Christian?

These are among the most commonly posed questions about God. In fact, they were some of the very issues discussed by Charles Templeton in my interview with him and in his book. And just like with Templeton, these obstacles also once stood solidly between me and faith.

OVERCOMING OBJECTIONS

While I could relate to many of the objections that Templeton had raised, at the same time I wasn't naïve enough to accept each of them at face value. It was clear that some of his obstacles to faith shouldn't be impediments at all.

For example, Templeton was plain wrong about Jesus considering himself to be a mere human being. Even if you go back to the earliest and most primitive information about him—data that could not have been tainted by legendary development—you find that Jesus undoubtedly saw himself in transcendent, divine, and messianic terms.[3]

In fact, here's an irony: the very historical documents that Templeton relied upon for his information about the inspiring moral life of Jesus are actually the exact same records that repeatedly affirm his deity. So if Templeton is willing to accept their accuracy concerning Jesus' character, then he also ought to consider them trustworthy when they assert that Jesus claimed to be divine and then backed up that assertion by rising from the dead.

In addition, the resurrection of Jesus could not have been a legend as Templeton claimed. The apostle Paul preserved a creed of the early church that was based on eyewitness accounts of Jesus' return from the dead—and which various scholars have dated to as early as twenty-four to thirty-six months after Jesus' death.[4] That's far too quick for mythology to have tainted the record. The truth is that nobody has ever been able to show one example in history of a legend developing that quickly and wiping out a solid core of historical truth.[5]

As I systematically documented in *The Case for Christ,* the eyewitness evidence, the corroborating evidence, the documentary evidence, the scientific evidence, the psychological evidence, the "fingerprint" or prophetic evidence, and other historical data point powerfully toward the conclusion that Jesus really is God's one and only Son.

Yes, but . . .

What about those nettlesome issues that hinder Templeton from embracing the faith that he admittedly desires so much to have? They haunted me. They were the same issues that had once perplexed me—and as Leslie and I drove along the interstate toward home, some of them began to nag at me anew.

TRAVELING THE SAME PATH

Leslie and I were quiet for a while. I gazed out the window at the undulating meadows of the Canadian countryside. Finally, Leslie said, "It sounds like your interview ended a little abruptly. What did Templeton say before you left?"

"Actually, he was very warm. He even gave me a tour of his apartment," I told her. "It was like he didn't want me to leave. But no matter how much I tried, I couldn't get him to reengage in discussing his feelings about Jesus."

I thought for a moment before continuing. "He did say one other thing that struck me. Just as I was getting ready to leave, he looked me in the eyes—very intensely—and shook my hand and said with great sincerity, 'We've been on the same path.'"

Leslie nodded. "You *have* been," she said. "You're both writers, you've both been skeptics." Then she added with a smile, "And you're both too hardheaded to buy into faith until you're sure it's not riddled with holes."

She was right. "But, you know, his mind seemed so closed," I said. "He insisted there *cannot* be a loving God. And yet at the same time, his heart seemed so open. In a way, I think he wants Jesus just as much as the people who came forward in Indianapolis. Only he can't have him. At least, he doesn't think so. Not with his objections."

Leslie and I spent the night in a Michigan hotel and finally arrived home before noon the following day. I lugged our suitcase up the stairs and tossed it onto the bed. Leslie unzipped it and began taking out clothes.

"At least we're home for a while," she remarked.

"Well, not quite," I said.

I couldn't let Templeton's questions go. They resonated too deeply with my own. So I decided to retrace and expand upon my spiritual journey in a different direction than I had pursued when I wrote *The Case for Christ,* which was an investigation of the historical evidence for the life, death, and resurrection of Jesus Christ. I wanted to determine once again whether there are soul-satisfying responses when Christianity is confronted with life's harshest and most perplexing questions that send nagging doubts into our hearts and minds. Can faith really stand up to reason? Or will rigorous intellectual scrutiny chase God away?

I resolved to track down the most knowledgeable and ardent defenders of Christianity. My intent was not to take a cynical or confrontational approach by badgering them with nitpicking questions or seeing whether I could trick them into painting themselves into a rhetorical corner. This wasn't a game to me.

I was sincerely interested in determining whether they had rational answers to "The Big Eight." I wanted to give them ample opportunity to spell out their reasoning and evidence in detail so that, in the end, I could evaluate whether their positions made sense. Most of all, I wanted to find out whether God was telling the truth when he said, "You will seek me and find me when you seek me with all your heart."[6]

I picked up the telephone. It was time to make plans to hit the road in search of answers.

Charles Templeton would have expected nothing less.

1

OBJECTION #1: SINCE EVIL AND SUFFERING EXIST, A LOVING GOD CANNOT

Either God wants to abolish evil, and cannot; or he can, but does not want to; or he cannot and does not want to. If he wants to, but cannot, he is impotent. If he can, and does not want to, he is wicked. But, if God both can and wants to abolish evil, then how comes evil in the world?

Epicurus, philosopher

The fact of suffering undoubtedly constitutes the single greatest challenge to the Christian faith, and has been in every generation. Its distribution and degree appear to be entirely random and therefore unfair. Sensitive spirits ask if it can possibly be reconciled with God's justice and love.

John Stott, theologian[1]

As an idealistic young reporter fresh out of journalism school, one of my first assignments at the *Chicago Tribune* was to write a thirty-part series in which I would profile destitute families living in the city. Having been raised in the homogenized suburbs, where being "needy" meant having only one Cadillac, I quickly found myself immersed in Chicago's underbelly of deprivation and desperation. In a way, my experience was akin to Charles Templeton's reaction to the photo of the African woman with her deceased baby.

Just a short drive from Chicago's Magnificent Mile, where stately Tribune Tower rubs shoulders with elegant fashion boutiques and luxury hotels, I walked into the tiny, dim, and barren hovel being shared by sixty-year-old Perfecta de Jesus and her two granddaughters. They had lived there about a month, ever since their previous cockroach-infested tenement erupted in flames.

Perfecta, frail and sickly, had run out of money weeks earlier and had received a small amount of emergency food stamps. She stretched the food by serving only rice and beans with bits of meat for meal after meal. The meat ran out quickly. Then the beans. Now all that was left was a handful of rice. When the overdue public-aid check would finally come, it would be quickly consumed by the rent and utility bills, and the family would be right back where it started.

The apartment was almost completely empty, without furniture, appliances, or carpets. Words echoed off the bare walls and cold wooden floor. When her eleven-year-old granddaughter, Lydia, would set off for her half-mile walk to school on the biting cold winter mornings, she would wear only a thin gray sweater over her short-sleeved, print dress. Halfway to school, she would give the sweater to her shivering thirteen-year-old sister, Jenny, clad in just a sleeveless dress, who would wrap the sweater around herself for the rest of the way. Those were the only clothes they owned.

"I try to take care of the girls as best I can," Perfecta explained to me in Spanish. "They are good. They don't complain."[2]

Hours later, safely back in my plush lakefront high-rise with an inspiring view of Chicago's wealthiest neighborhoods, I felt staggered by the contrast. If there is a God, why would kind and decent people like Perfecta and her grandchildren be cold and hungry in the midst of one of the greatest cities in the world? Day after day as I conducted research for my series, I encountered people in circumstances that were similar or even worse. My response was to settle deeper into my atheism.

Hardships, suffering, heartbreak, man's inhumanity to man—those were my daily diet as a journalist. This wasn't looking at magazine photos from faraway places; this was the grit and pain of life, up close and personal.

I've looked into the eyes of a young mother who had just been told that her only daughter had been molested, mutilated, and murdered. I've listened to courtroom testimony describing gruesome horrors that had been perpetrated against innocent victims. I've visited noisy and chaotic prisons, the trash heaps of society; low-budget nursing homes where the elderly languish after being abandoned by their loved ones; pediatric hospital wards where emaciated children fight vainly against the inexorable advance of cancer; and crime-addled inner cities where drug trafficking and drive-by shootings are all too common.

But nothing shocked me as much as my visit to the slums of Bombay, India. Lining both sides of the noisy, filthy, congested streets, as far as the eye could see, were small cardboard and burlap shanties, situated right next to the road where buses and cars would spew their exhaust and soot. Naked children played in the open sewage ditches that coursed through the area. People with missing limbs or bodies contorted by deformities sat passively in the dirt. Insects buzzed everywhere. It was a horrific scene, a place where, one taxi driver told me, people are born on the sidewalk, live their entire lives on the sidewalk, and die a premature death on the sidewalk.

Then I came face-to-face with a ten-year-old boy, about the same age as my son Kyle at the time. The Indian child was scrawny and malnourished, his hair filthy and matted. One eye was diseased and half closed; the other stared vacantly. Blood oozed from scabs on his face. He extended his hand and mumbled something in Hindi, apparently begging for coins. But his voice was a dull, lifeless monotone, as if he didn't expect any response. As if he had been drained of all hope.

Where was God in that festering hellhole? If he had the power to instantly heal that youngster, why did he turn his back? If he loved these people, why didn't he show it by rescuing them? Is this, I wondered, the real reason: because the very presence of such awful, heart-wrenching suffering actually disproves the existence of a good and loving Father?

MAKING SENSE OF SUFFERING

Everyone has encountered pain and sorrow. Heart disease claimed my father when he should have had many years left to see his grandchildren grow up. I kept a vigil at a neonatal intensive care unit as my newborn daughter battled a mysterious illness that both threatened her life and baffled her doctors. I've rushed to the hospital after the anguished call of a friend whose daughter had been hit by a drunk driver, and I was holding their hands at the moment life slipped away from her. I've had to break the news to a friend's two small children that their mother had committed suicide. I've seen childhood buddies succumb to cancer, to Lou Gehrig's disease, to heart ailments, to car accidents. I've seen Alzheimer's ravage the mind of a loved one. I'm sure you could tell similar stories of personal pain.

We recently emerged from a century unprecedented in its cruelty and inhumanity, where victims of tyrants like Hitler, Stalin, Pol Pot, and Mao Tse-tung are numbered in the tens of millions. The vastness of the cruelty numbs our minds, but then occasionally we come across a story that personalizes the horror and makes us shudder anew.

Like the account I was reading recently of an Italian journalist during World War II who was visiting a smiling Ante Pavelic, the pro-Nazi leader of Croatia. Pavelic proudly showed him a basket of what looked like oysters. It was, he said, a gift from his troops—forty pounds of human eyes. A small memento from their slaughter of Serbs, Jews, and Gypsies.[3]

We read stories like that—horrible evils like the Holocaust, the Killing Fields of Cambodia, the genocide of Rwanda, and the torture chambers of South America—and we can't help but wonder: *Where is God?* We watch television coverage of earthquakes and hurricanes in which thousands perish, and we wonder: *Why didn't God stop it?* We read the statistic that one thousand million people in the world lack the basic necessities of life, and we wonder: *Why doesn't God care?* We may suffer ourselves with persistent pain or aching loss or seemingly hopeless circumstances, and we wonder: *Why doesn't God help?* If he is loving and if he is all-powerful and if he is good, then surely all of this suffering should not exist. And yet it does.

What's worse, it's often the innocent who are victimized. "If only villains got broken backs or cancers, if only cheaters and crooks got Parkinson's disease, we should see a sort of celestial justice in the universe," wrote agnostic-turned-Christian Sheldon Vanauken.

> But, as it is, a sweet-tempered child lies dying of a brain tumor, a happy young wife sees her husband and child killed before her eyes by a drunken driver; and . . . we soundlessly scream at the stars, "Why? Why?" A mention of God—of God's will—doesn't help a bit. How could a good God, a loving God, do that? How could he even let it happen? And no answer comes from the indifferent stars.[4]

Christian author Philip Yancey begins his celebrated book on suffering with a chapter appropriately titled, "A Problem That Won't Go Away."[5] This is not just an intellectual issue to be debated in sterile academic arenas; it's an intensely personal matter that can tie our emotions into knots and leave us with spiritual vertigo—disoriented, frightened, and angry. One writer referred to the problem of pain as "the question mark turned like a fishhook in the human heart."[6]

In fact, this is the single biggest obstacle for spiritual seekers. I commissioned George Barna, the public-opinion pollster, to conduct a national survey in which he asked a scientifically selected cross-section of adults: "If you could ask God only one question and you knew he would give you an answer, what would you ask?" The top response, offered by 17 percent of those who said they had a question, was: "Why is there pain and suffering in the world?"[7]

Charles Templeton also demanded an answer to that question. His retreat from faith began with that *Life* magazine photo of the African mother holding her child who had died because of a simple lack of rain. In his book denouncing Christianity, Templeton recounts a litany of tragedies from ancient and modern history, and then declares:

> "A loving God" could not possibly be the author of the horrors we have been describing—horrors that continue every day, have continued since time began, and will continue as long as life exists. It is an inconceivable tale of suffering and death, and because the tale is fact—is, in truth, the history of the world—it is obvious that there cannot be a loving God.[8]

Cannot? Does the presence of suffering necessarily mean the absence of God? Is this obstacle to faith insurmountable? To believe wholeheartedly in a loving and omnipotent Father, do I have to paper over the reality of evil and pain around me? As a journalist, that was simply not an option. I had to account for all the facts, for all the evidence, minimizing nothing.

I was discussing these issues with Leslie at a sensitive time in her life. Her uncle had just died, and her aunt had been diagnosed with Alzheimer's disease and terminal cancer. Rocked by that turbulence, Leslie was wary of anyone who might try to give easy answers.

"If someone thinks he can wrap everything up in a neat little package and put a fancy theological bow on it," she cautioned, "go somewhere else."

I knew she was right. That's why I placed a call to Boston College and asked to make an appointment with the author of *Making Sense Out of Suffering*—a book whose title summed up exactly what I was seeking to do.

THE FIRST INTERVIEW: PETER JOHN KREEFT, PH.D.

I like to refer to Peter Kreeft as "the un-philosopher." Not that he isn't a philosopher; in fact, he's a first-rate philosophical thinker, with a doctorate from Fordham University, postgraduate study at Yale University, and thirty-eight years of experience as a philosophy professor at Villanova University and (since 1965) Boston College. He has taught such courses as metaphysics, ethics, mysticism, sexuality, and Oriental, Greek, medieval, and contemporary philosophy, earning such honors as the Woodrow Wilson and Yale-Sterling fellowships.

Still, if you were to conjure up a mental image of a stereotypical philosopher, Kreeft would probably not come to mind. Unfairly or not, philosophers are generally imagined to be a bit boring, speaking in vague and convoluted sentences, residing in the cloistered ivory towers of academia, and being serious to the point of dour.

In contrast, Kreeft gives real-world answers in an engaging and even entertaining way; communicates crisply, often with a memorable twist of a phrase; wears a bemused grin and can't restrain himself from cracking jokes about even the most sacrosanct subject; and, although he's sixty-two years old, can frequently be found at any given beach pursuing his hobby of surfing. (In a forthcoming book, one of his chapter titles is "I Surf, Therefore I Am.")

Kreeft, a Catholic also widely read by Protestants, has written more than forty books, including *Love is Stronger than Death, Heaven: the Heart's Deepest Longing, Prayer: the Great Conversation*, *A Refutation of Moral Relativism,* and *Handbook of Christian Apologetics* (with Ronald K. Tacelli). His whimsical imagination is especially evident in *Between Heaven and Hell,* which envisions C. S. Lewis, John F. Kennedy, and Aldous Huxley, after death, arguing about Christ, and *Socrates Meets Jesus,* in which the ancient thinker becomes a Christian at Harvard Divinity School.

I encountered Kreeft's offbeat sense of humor even before I walked into his office. While the other sixteen office doors on his drab and dimly lit corridor were undefaced, Kreeft's was festooned with Doonesbury and Dilbert cartoons and other tongue-in-cheek mementos—a drawing of a bull with a slash through it, a photo of Albert Einstein playfully sticking out his tongue, and a cartoon in which Satan greets people in hell by saying: "You'll find that there's no right or wrong here—just what works for you."

What drew me to Kreeft was his insightful book about suffering, in which he skillfully weaves a journey of discovery through Socrates, Plato, and Aristotle; through Augustine, Kierkegaard, and Dostoyevski; through *Star Trek, The Velveteen Rabbit,* and *Hamlet;* and through Moses, Job, and Jeremiah. All along the way, there are clues that eventually, ultimately, finally, converge on Jesus and the tears of God.

I arrived early and waited for Kreeft in the hallway. He soon arrived fresh from a philosophical conclave that was being held elsewhere in Boston. His brown tweed jacket, thick glasses, and neatly combed dark gray hair gave him a fatherly appearance. He sat behind his desk (under a sign that said, "No Dumping"), and we started by casually chatting about his beloved Boston Red Sox—an appropriate subject given our topic of suffering.

But then I turned a corner. There was no other approach than to hit Kreeft head-on with Templeton's blunt objections to Christianity, embodied by that *Life* magazine photo of an anguished mother clutching her dead infant in drought-ravaged Africa.

A BEAR, A TRAP, A HUNTER, AND GOD

Confronting Kreeft with the same emotional intensity that Templeton had displayed to me, I described the photo and then quoted the former evangelist word for word:

> I thought, "Is it possible to believe that there is a loving or caring Creator when all this woman needed was *rain*?" How could a loving God *do this* to that woman? Who runs the rain? I don't; you don't. *He* does—or that's what I thought. But when I saw that photograph, I immediately knew it is not possible for this to happen and for there to be a loving God. There was no way. Who else but a fiend could destroy a baby and virtually kill its mother with agony—when all that was needed was *rain*?... And then I began ... considering the plagues that sweep across parts of the planet and indiscriminately kill ... and it just became crystal clear to me that it is not possible for an intelligent person to believe that there is a deity who loves.

I looked up from my notes. The professor's eyes were riveted on me. Facing him squarely, leaning forward in my chair for emphasis, I said in a rather accusatory tone: "Dr. Kreeft, you're an intelligent person and you believe in a deity who loves. How in the world would you respond to Templeton?"

Kreeft cleared his throat. "First of all," he began, "I'd focus on his words, 'it is not possible.' Even David Hume, one of history's most famous skeptics, said it's just *barely* possible that God exists. That's at least a somewhat reasonable position—to say that there's at least a small possibility. But to say there's *no* possibility that a loving God who knows far more than we do, including about our future, could possibly tolerate such evil as Templeton sees in Africa—well, that strikes me as intellectually arrogant."

That took me aback. "Really?" I asked. "How so?"

"How can a mere finite human be sure that infinite wisdom would not tolerate certain short-range evils in order for more long-range goods that we couldn't foresee?" he asked.

I could see his point but needed an example. "Elaborate a bit," I prodded.

Kreeft thought for a moment. "Look at it this way," he said. "Would you agree that the difference between us and God is greater than the difference between us and, say, a bear?"

I nodded.

"Okay, then, imagine a bear in a trap and a hunter who, out of sympathy, wants to liberate him. He tries to win the bear's confidence, but he can't do it, so he has to shoot the bear full of drugs. The bear, however, thinks this is an attack and that the hunter is trying to kill him. He doesn't realize that this is being done out of compassion.

"Then, in order to get the bear out of the trap, the hunter has to push him further into the trap to release the tension on the spring. If the bear were semiconscious at that point, he would be even more convinced that the hunter was his enemy who was out to cause him suffering and pain. But the bear would be wrong. He reaches this incorrect conclusion because he's not a human being."

Kreeft let the illustration soak in for a moment. "Now," he concluded, "how can anyone be certain that's not an analogy between us and God? I believe God does the same to us sometimes, and we can't comprehend why he does it any more than the bear can understand the motivations of the hunter. As the bear could have trusted the hunter, so we can trust God."

FAITH AND PREJUDICE

I paused to think about Kreeft's point, but he continued before I could reply.

"However," he said, "I certainly don't want to demean Templeton. He's responding in a very honest and heartfelt way to the fact that something counts against God. Only in a world where faith is difficult can faith exist. I don't have faith in two plus two equals four or in the noonday sun. Those are beyond question. But Scripture describes God as a hidden God. You have to make an effort of faith to find him. There are clues you can follow.

"And if that weren't so, if there were something more or less than clues, it's difficult for me to understand how we could really be free to make a choice about him. If we had absolute proof instead of clues, then you could no more deny God than you could deny the sun. If we had no evidence at all, you could never get there. God gives us just enough evidence so that those who want him can have him. Those who want to follow the clues will.

"The Bible says, 'Seek and you shall find.'[9] It doesn't say everybody will find him; it doesn't say nobody will find him. *Some* will find. Who? Those who seek. Those whose hearts are set on finding him and who follow the clues."

I jumped in. "Wait a minute—a moment ago you admitted that 'something counts against God'—that evil and suffering *are* evidence against him," I pointed out. "Aren't you conceding, therefore, that evil disproves God's existence?" I thumped my hand on his desk. "Case closed!" I declared with a mock air of triumph.

Kreeft recoiled a bit at my outburst. "No, no," he insisted, shaking his head. "First of all, evidence is not necessarily certain or conclusive. I'm saying in this world there is evidence against and evidence for God. Augustine put it very simply: 'If there is no God, why is there so much good? If there is a God, why is there so much evil?'

"There's no question that the existence of evil is one argument against God—but in one of my books I summarize twenty arguments that point persuasively in the other direction, in favor of the existence of God.[10] Atheists must answer all twenty arguments; theists must only answer one. However, each of us gets to cast a vote. Faith is active; it demands a response. Unlike reason, which bows down faithfully to the evidence, faith is prejudiced."

That last word jumped out at me. "What do you mean, 'prejudiced'?"

"Suppose a policeman came into this room and said they just captured my wife in the act of murdering thirteen neighbors by chopping off their heads, and they have witnesses. I would laugh at him. I would say, 'No, this cannot be. You do not know her as I do.' He would say, 'Where's your evidence?' I'd say, 'It's of a different kind than yours. But there is evidence that this could not be.' So I'm prejudiced.

"However, my prejudice is a *reasonable* prejudice because it's based on the evidence I've gathered in my very real experience. So someone who knows God has evidence—and therefore prejudices based on that evidence—which someone who does not know God does not have."

EVIL AS EVIDENCE *FOR* GOD

Kreeft stopped for a few seconds before adding this unexpected and counter-intuitive remark: "Besides, the evidence of evil and suffering can go both ways—it can actually be used in *favor* of God."

I sat up straight in my chair. "How," I demanded, "is *that* possible?"

"Consider this," Kreeft said. "If Templeton is right in responding to these events with outrage, that presupposes there really is a difference between good and evil. The fact that he's using the standard of good to judge evil—the fact that he's saying quite rightly that this horrible suffering isn't what ought to be—means that he has a notion of what ought to be; that this notion corresponds to something real; and that there is, therefore, a reality called the Supreme Good. Well, that's another name for God."

That sounded suspiciously like philosophical sleight of hand. Warily, I summarized Kreeft's point to see if I understood it. "You mean that unintentionally Templeton may be testifying to the reality of God because by recognizing evil he's assuming there's an objective standard on which it's based?"

"Right. If I give one student a ninety and another an eighty, that presupposes that one hundred is a real standard. And my point is this: if there is no God, where did we get the standard of goodness by which we judge evil as evil?

"What's more, as C. S. Lewis said, 'If the universe is so bad ... how on earth did human beings ever come to attribute it to the activity of a wise and good Creator?' In other words, the very presence of these ideas in our minds—that is, the idea of evil, thus of goodness and of God as the origin and standard of goodness—needs to be accounted for."

An interesting counter-punch, I mused. "Are there any other ways in which you believe evil works against atheism?" I asked.

"Yes, there are," he replied. "If there is no Creator and therefore no moment of creation, then everything is the result of evolution. If there was no beginning or first cause, then the universe must have always existed. That means the universe has been evolving for an infinite period of time—and, by now, everything should already be perfect. There would have been plenty of time for evolution to have finished and evil to have been vanquished. But there still is evil and suffering and imperfection—and that proves the atheist wrong about the universe."

"Then atheism," I said, "is an inadequate answer to the problem of evil?"

"It's an easy answer—maybe, if I may use the word, a cheap answer," he said. "Atheism is cheap on people, because it snobbishly says nine out of ten people through history have been wrong about God and have had a lie at the core of their hearts.

"Think about that. How is it possible that over ninety percent of all the human beings who have ever lived—usually in far more painful circumstances than we—could believe in God? The objective evidence, just looking at the balance of pleasure and suffering in the world, would not seem to justify believing in an absolutely good God. Yet this has been almost universally believed.

"Are they all crazy? Well, I suppose you can believe that if you're a bit of an elitist. But maybe, like Leo Tolstoy, we have to learn from the peasants. In his autobiography, he wrestles with the problem of evil. He saw life had more suffering than pleasure and more evil than good and was therefore apparently meaningless. He was so despairing that he was tempted to kill himself. He said he didn't know how he could endure.

"Then he said, in effect, 'Wait a minute—most people *do* endure. Most people have a life that's harder than mine and yet they find it wonderful. How can they do that? Not with explanations, but with faith.' He learned from the peasants and found faith and hope.[11]

"So atheism treats people cheaply. Also, it robs death of meaning, and if death has no meaning, how can life ultimately have meaning?

Atheism cheapens everything it touches—look at the results of communism, the most powerful form of atheism on earth.

"And in the end, when the atheist dies and encounters God instead of the nothingness he had predicted, he'll recognize that atheism was a cheap answer because it refused the only thing that's not cheap—the God of infinite value."

A PROBLEM OF LOGIC

Kreeft had made some interesting initial points, but we had been dancing around the subject a bit. It was time to cut to the core of the issue. Pulling out some notes that I had scrawled on the airplane, I challenged Kreeft with a question that crystallized the controversy.

"Christians believe in five things," I said. "First, God exists. Second, God is all-good. Third, God is all-powerful. Fourth, God is all-wise. And, fifth, evil exists. Now, how can all of those statements be true at the same time?"

An enigmatic smile crept onto Kreeft's face. "It looks like they can't be," he conceded. "I remember a liberal preacher who once tried to dissuade me from taking up with the fundamentalists. He said, 'There's a logical problem here—you can be intelligent, or you can be honest, or you can be a fundamentalist, or any two of the three, but not all three.' And my fundamentalist friend said, 'I'd say, you can be honest, or you can be intelligent, or you can be liberal, or any of the two, but not all three.'"

I laughed at the story. "We have the same kind of logical problem here," I said.

"That's right. It seems you have to drop one of those beliefs. If God is all-powerful, he can do anything. If God is all-good, he wants only good. If God is all-wise, he knows what is good. So if all of those beliefs are true—and Christians believe they are—then it would seem that the consequence is that no evil can exist."

"But evil *does* exist," I said. "Therefore, isn't it logical to assume that such a God doesn't exist?"

"No, I'd say one of those beliefs about him must be false, or we must not be understanding it in the right way."

It was time to find out. With a sweep of my hand, I invited Kreeft to examine these three divine attributes—God being all-powerful, all-good, and all-knowing—one at a time in light of the existence of evil.

Attribute #1: God Is All-Powerful

"What does it mean when we say that God is all-powerful?" Kreeft asked, and then he answered his own question: "That means he can do everything that is meaningful, everything that is possible, everything that makes any sense at all. God cannot make himself to cease to exist. He cannot make good evil."

"So," I said, "there are some things he can't do even though he's all-powerful."

"Precisely *because* he is all powerful, he can't do some things. He can't make mistakes. Only weak and stupid beings make mistakes. One such mistake would be to try to create a self-contradiction, like two plus two equals five or a round square.

"Now, the classic defense of God against the problem of evil is that it's not logically possible to have free will and no possibility of moral evil. In other words, once God chose to create human beings with free will, then it was up to them, rather than to God, as to whether there was sin or not. That's what free will means. Built into the situation of God deciding to create human beings is the chance of evil and, consequently, the suffering that results."

"Then God is the creator of evil."

"No, he created the *possibility* of evil; people actualized that potentiality. The source of evil is not God's power but mankind's freedom. Even an all-powerful God could not have created a world in which people had genuine freedom and yet there was no potentiality for sin, because our freedom includes the possibility of sin within its own meaning. It's a self-contradiction—a meaningless nothing—to have a world where there's real choice while at the same time no possibility of choosing evil. To ask why God didn't create such a world is like asking why God didn't create colorless color or round squares."

"Then why didn't God create a world without human freedom?"

"Because that would have been a world without humans. Would it have been a place without hate? Yes. A place without suffering? Yes. But it also would have been a world without love, which is the highest value in the universe. That highest good never could have been experienced. Real love—our love of God and our love of each other—must involve a choice. But with the granting of that choice comes the possibility that people would choose instead to hate."

"But look at Genesis," I said. "God did create a world where people were free and yet there was no sin."

"That's precisely what he did," Kreeft said. "After creation, he declared that the world was 'good.' People were free to choose to love God or turn away from him. However, such a world is necessarily a place where sin is freely possible—and, indeed, that potentiality for sin was actualized not by God, but by people. The blame, ultimately, lies with us. He did his part perfectly; we're the ones who messed up."

"Rabbi Harold Kushner reaches a different conclusion in his bestseller *When Bad Things Happen to Good People*," I pointed out. "He says God isn't all-powerful after all—that he would *like* to help, but he just isn't capable of solving all the problems in the world. He said, 'Even God has a hard time keeping chaos in check.'"[12]

Kreeft raised an eyebrow. "For a rabbi, that's hard to understand, because the distinctively Jewish notion of God is the opposite of that," he said. "Surprisingly—against the evidence, it seems—the Jews insisted that there is a God who is all-powerful and nevertheless all good.

"Now, that doesn't seem as reasonable as paganism, which says if there is evil in the world, then there must be many gods, each of them less than all-powerful, some of them good, some of them evil, or if there's one God, then he's facing forces he can't quite control. Until Judaism's revelation of the true God, that was a very popular philosophy."

"You don't think much of Kushner's God," I said, more as a statement than a question.

"Frankly, that God is hardly worth believing in. Do I have a big brother who's doing what he can but it's not very much? Well, who cares?" he said, shrugging his shoulders. "Practically speaking, that's the same as atheism. Rely on yourself first and then maybe God, maybe not.

"No, the evidence is that God *is* all-powerful. The point to remember is that creating a world where there's free will and no possibility of sin is a self-contradiction—and that opens the door to people choosing evil over God, with suffering being the result. The overwhelming majority of the pain in the world is caused by our choices to kill, to slander, to be selfish, to stray sexually, to break our promises, to be reckless."

Attribute #2: God Is All-Knowing

I asked Kreeft to move on to the next divine quality—God's omniscience. He pushed back his chair to get more comfortable, then looked off to the side as he collected his thoughts once more.

"Let's begin this way," he said. "God, if he is all-wise, knows not only the present but the future. And he knows not only present good and evil but future good and evil. If his wisdom vastly exceeds ours, as the hunter's exceeds the bear's, it is at least possible—contrary to Templeton's analysis—that a loving God could deliberately tolerate horrible things like starvation because he foresees that in the long run that more people will be better and happier than if he miraculously intervened. That's at least intellectually possible."

I shook my head. "That's still hard to accept," I said. "It sounds like a cop-out to me."

"Okay, then, let's put it to the test," Kreeft replied. "You see, God has specifically shown us very clearly how this can work. He has demonstrated how the very worst thing that has ever happened in the history of the world ended up resulting in the very best thing that has ever happened in the history of the world."

"What do you mean?

"I'm referring to dei-cide," he replied. "The death of God himself on the cross. At the time, nobody saw how anything good could ever result from this tragedy. And yet God foresaw that the result would be the opening of heaven to human beings. So the worst tragedy in history brought about the most glorious event in history. And if it happened there—if the ultimate evil can result in the ultimate good—it can happen elsewhere, even in our own individual lives. Here, God lifts the curtain and lets us see it. Elsewhere he simply says, 'Trust me.'

"All of which would mean that human life is incredibly dramatic, like a story for which you don't know the ending rather than a scientific formula. In fact, let's follow this dramatic story line for a minute.

"Suppose you're the devil. You're the enemy of God and you want to kill him, but you can't. However, he has this ridiculous weakness of creating and loving human beings, whom you *can* get at. Aha! Now you've got hostages! So you simply come down into the world, corrupt humankind, and drag some of them to hell. When God sends prophets to enlighten them, you kill the prophets.

"Then God does the most foolish thing of all—he sends his own Son and he plays by the rules of the world. You say to yourself, 'I can't believe he's that stupid! Love has addled his brains! All I have to do is inspire some of my agents—Herod, Pilate, Caiaphas, the Roman soldiers—and get him crucified.' And that's what you do.

"So there he hangs on the cross—forsaken by man and seemingly by God, bleeding to death and crying, 'My God, my God, why hast thou forsaken me?' What do you feel now as the devil? You feel triumph and vindication! But of course you couldn't be more wrong. This is *his* supreme triumph and your supreme defeat. He stuck his heel into your mouth and you bit it and that blood destroyed you.

"Now, if that is not a freak occurrence, but it's a paradigm of the human situation, then when we bleed and when we suffer, as Christ did, maybe the same thing is happening. Maybe this is God's way of defeating the devil.

"At the time of the crucifixion, the disciples couldn't see how anything good could result; similarly, as we face struggles and trials and suffering, we sometimes can't imagine good emerging. But we've seen how it did in the case of Jesus, and we can trust it will in our case too. For instance, the greatest Christians in history seem to say that their sufferings ended up bringing them the closest to God—so this is the best thing that could happen, not the worst."

Attribute #3: God Is All-Good

That left us with God's attribute of goodness.

"*Good* is a notoriously tricky word," Kreeft began, "because even in human affairs there's such a wide range of meaning. But the difference, once again, between us and God is certainly greater than the difference between us and animals, and since good varies enormously between us and animals, it must vary even more enormously between us and God."

"Granted," I said. "But if I sat there and did nothing while my child got run over by a truck, I wouldn't be good in any sense of the word. I'd be an evil father if I did that. And God does the equivalent of that. He sits by and refuses to perform miracles to take us out of dangers even greater than being hit by a truck. So why isn't he bad?"

Kreeft nodded. "It looks like he is," he said. "But the fact that God deliberately allows certain things, which if we allowed them would turn us into monsters, doesn't necessarily count against God."

I couldn't see his reasoning. "You'll have to explain why that is," I said.

"Okay, let me give you an analogy in human relationships," he replied. "If I said to my brother, who's about my age, 'I could bail you out of a problem but I won't,' I would probably be irresponsible and perhaps wicked. But we do that with our children all the time. We don't do their homework for them. We don't put a bubble around them and protect them from every hurt.

"I remember when one of my daughters was about four or five years old and she was trying to thread a needle in Brownies. It was very difficult for her. Every time she tried, she hit herself in the finger and a couple of times she bled. I was watching her, but she didn't see me. She just kept trying and trying.

"My first instinct was to go and do it for her, since I saw a drop of blood. But wisely I held back, because I said to myself, 'She can do it.' After about five minutes, she finally did it. I came out of hiding and she said, "Daddy, daddy—look what I did! Look at what I did!' She was so proud she had threaded the needle that she had forgotten all about the pain.

"That time the pain was a good thing for her. I was wise enough to have foreseen it was good for her. Now, certainly God is much wiser than I was with my daughter. So it's at least possible that God is wise enough to foresee that we need some pain for reasons which we may not understand but which he foresees as being necessary to some eventual good. Therefore, he's not being evil by allowing that pain to exist.

"Dentists, athletic trainers, teachers, parents—they all know that sometimes to be good is *not* to be kind. Certainly there are times when God allows suffering and deprives us of the lesser good of pleasure in order to help us toward the greater good of moral and spiritual education. Even the ancient Greeks believed the gods taught wisdom through suffering. Aeschylus wrote: 'Day by day, hour by hour / Pain drips upon the heart / As, against our will, and even in our own despite / Comes Wisdom from the awful grace of God.'

"We know that moral character gets formed through hardship, through overcoming obstacles, through enduring despite difficulties. Courage, for example, would be impossible in a world without pain. The apostle Paul testified to this refining quality of suffering when he wrote that 'suffering produces perseverance; perseverance, character; and character, hope.'[13]

"Let's face it: we learn from the mistakes we make and the suffering they bring. The universe is a soul-making machine, and part of that process is learning, maturing, and growing through difficult and challenging and painful experiences. The point of our lives in this world isn't comfort, but training and preparation for eternity. Scripture tells us that even Jesus 'learned obedience through suffering'[14]—and if that was true for him, why wouldn't it be even more true for us?"

Kreeft let the question hang in the air for a moment while his mental gears whirred. Then he continued. "Suppose we didn't have any suffering at all," he added. "Suppose we had drugs for every pain, free entertainment, free love—everything but pain. No Shakespeare, no Beethoven, no Boston Red Sox, no death—no meaning. Impossibly spoiled little brats—that's what we'd become.

"It's like that old Twilight Zone television show where a gang of bank robbers gets shot and one of them wakes up walking on fluffy clouds at the golden gate of a celestial city. A kindly white-robed man offers him everything he wants. But soon he's bored with the gold, since everything's free, and with the beautiful girls, who only laugh when he tries to hurt them, since he has a sadistic streak.

"So he summons the St. Peter figure. 'There must be some mistake.' 'No, we make no mistakes here.' 'Can't you send me back to earth?' 'Of course not, you're dead.' 'Well, then, I must belong with my friends in the Other Place. Send me there.' 'Oh, no, we can't do that. Rules, you know.' 'What is this place, anyway?' 'This is the place where you get everything you want.' 'But I thought I was supposed to *like* heaven.' 'Heaven? Who said anything about heaven? Heaven is the Other Place.' The point is that a world without suffering appears more like hell than heaven."

That seemed hyperbolic. "Do you really believe that?" I asked.

"Yes, I do. In fact, if you don't, then pretend you're God and try to create a better world in your imagination. Try to create utopia. But you have to think through the consequences of everything you try to improve. Every time you use force to prevent evil, you take away freedom. To prevent all evil, you must remove all freedom and reduce people to puppets, which means they would then lack the ability to freely choose love.

"You may end up creating a world of precision that an engineer might like—*maybe*. But one thing's for sure: you'll lose the kind of world that a Father would want."

THE MEGAPHONE OF PAIN

Clue by clue, Kreeft was shedding more and more light on the mystery of suffering. But each new insight seemed to spawn new questions.

"Evil people get away with hurting others all the time. Certainly God can't consider that fair," I said. "How can he stand there and watch that happen? Why doesn't he intervene and deal with all the evil in the world?"

"People *aren't* getting away with it," Kreeft insisted. "Justice delayed is not necessarily justice denied. There will come a day when God will settle accounts and people will be held responsible for the evil they've perpetrated and the suffering they've caused. Criticizing God for not doing it right now is like reading half a novel and criticizing the author for not resolving the plot. God will bring accountability at the right time—in fact, the Bible says one reason he's delaying is because some people are still following the clues and have yet to find him.[15] He's actually delaying the consummation of history out of his great love for them."

"But in the meantime, doesn't the sheer amount of suffering in the world bother you?" I asked. "Couldn't God curtail at least some of the more horrific evil? One philosopher formulated an argument against God this way: First, there is no reason that would justify God in permitting so much evil rather than a lot less; second, if God exists, then there must be such a reason; so, three, God does not exist."

Kreeft was sympathetic to the problem, but wasn't buying that solution. "That's like saying it's reasonable to believe in God if six Jews die in a Holocaust, but not seven. Or sixty thousand but not sixty thousand and one, or 5,999,999, but not six million," he said. "When you translate the general statement 'so much' into particular examples like that, it shows how absurd it is. There can't be a dividing line.

"It's true that there are some instances where quantity does becomes quality. For example, boiling water: once a temperature of 212 degrees is reached, you get a new state—gas—and gas laws rather than liquid laws apply. But suffering isn't like that. At what point does suffering disprove the existence of God? No such point can be shown. Besides, because we're not God, we can't say how much suffering is needed. Maybe every single element of pain in the universe is necessary. How can we know?"

I chuckled. "I suppose a person could say, 'If *I'm* having the pain, then that's too much suffering in the world!'"

Kreeft laughed. "Aha, of course!" he exclaimed. "That's the subjective 'too much.' That's a classic case of anthropomorphism. If I were God, I wouldn't allow this much pain; God couldn't possibly disagree with me; God did allow this pain; and therefore there is no God."

"You said a moment ago that some pain might be necessary. That indicates there is a meaning to suffering," I said. "If so, what is it?"

"One purpose of suffering in history has been that it leads to repentance," he said. "Only after suffering, only after disaster, did Old Testament Israel, do nations, do individual people turn back to God. Again, let's face it: we learn the hard way. To quote C. S. Lewis: 'God whispers to us in our pleasures, speaks in our conscience, but shouts in our pains. It is his megaphone to rouse a deaf world.'[16] And, of course, repentance leads to something wonderful—to blessedness, since God is the source of all joy and all life. The outcome is good—in fact, better than good.

"Simply put, I believe that suffering is compatible with God's love if it is medicinal, remedial, and necessary; that is, if we are very sick and desperately need a cure. And that's our situation. Jesus said, 'It is not the healthy who need a doctor, but the sick. . . . I have not come to call the righteous, but sinners.'"[17]

"But good people suffer just as much—or sometimes more—than the bad," I pointed out. "That's what's so striking about the title of Kushner's book: *When Bad Things Happen to Good People*. How is that fair?"

"Well, the answer to that is that there are no good people," Kreeft replied.

"What about that old saying, 'God don't make no junk?'"

"Yes, we're ontologically good—we still bear God's image—but morally we're not. His image in us has been tarnished. The prophet Jeremiah said that 'from the least to the greatest, all are greedy for gain,'[18] and the prophet Isaiah said, 'all of us have become like one who is unclean, and all our righteous acts are like filthy rags.'[19] Our good deeds are stained with self-interest and our demands for justice are mixed with lust for vengeance. Ironically, it's the best people who most readily recognize and admit their own shortcomings and sin.

"We are good stuff gone bad, a defaced masterpiece, a rebellious child. Lewis pointed out that we're not just imperfect people who need growth, but we're rebels who need to lay down our arms. Pain and suffering are frequently the means by which we become motivated to finally surrender to God and to seek the cure of Christ.

"That's what we need most desperately. That's what will bring us the supreme joy of knowing Jesus. Any suffering, the great Christians from history will tell you, is worth that result."

BEARING THE PAIN

I sat back in my chair and reflected on what Kreeft had said so far. Some of his arguments were stronger than others, but at least he wasn't merely offering canned explanations. The clues seemed to be leading somewhere.

I decided to ask him about a quote from Augustine, who said: "Since God is the highest good, he would not allow any evil to exist in his works unless his omnipotence and goodness were such as to bring good even out of evil." After reading him those words, I said, "Does that mean suffering and evil contain the potential for good?"

"Yes, I believe all suffering contains at least the opportunity for good," came his response, "but not everyone actualizes that potential. Not all of us learn and benefit from suffering; that's where free will comes in. One prisoner in a concentration camp will react quite differently from another, because of the choice each one makes to respond to the environment.

"But just about every human being can reflect on his or her past and say, 'I learned from that hardship. I didn't think I would at the time, but I'm a bigger and better person for having endured it and persevered.' Even people without religious faith are aware of that dimension of suffering. And if we can bring good out of evil even without bringing God into the picture, you can imagine how much more, with God's help, evil can work out for the greater good."

Bringing God into the picture, however, raised another issue: if he loves people, how could he emotionally tolerate the ongoing onslaught of pain and suffering? Wouldn't it overwhelm him? I pulled out Templeton's book and read Kreeft this quote:

> Jesus said, "Are not five sparrows sold for a penny, and not one of them is forgotten before God; and are you not of more value than many sparrows?" But if God grieves over the death of one sparrow, how could even his eternal spirit bear the sickness, suffering, and death of the multiplied millions of men, women, children, animals, birds, and other sensate creatures, in every part of the world, in every century since time began?[20]

"I think Mr. Templeton is anthropomorphizing God by saying, 'I couldn't imagine how any intelligent being could bear this,'" Kreeft said. "And, yes, he's right—we *can't* imagine it. But we can believe it. God does, in fact, weep over every sparrow and grieve over every evil and every suffering. So the suffering that Christ endured on the cross is literally unimaginable. It's not just what you and I would have experienced in our own finite human agony, physical and mental, but all the sufferings of the world were there.

"Let's go back to Templeton's photo of the starving woman in Africa—all she needed was rain. *Where is God?* He was entering into her agony. Not just her physical agony, but her moral agony. *Where is God? Why doesn't he send the rain?* God's answer is the Incarnation. He himself entered into all that agony, he himself bore all of the pain of this world, and that's unimaginable and shattering and even more impressive than the divine power of creating the world in the first place.

"Just imagine every single pain in the history of the world, all rolled together into a ball, eaten by God, digested, fully tasted, eternally. In the act of creating the world, God not only said, let there be pretty little bunny rabbits and flowers and sunsets, but also let there be blood and guts and the buzzing flies around the cross. In a sense, Templeton is right. God is intimately involved in the act of creating a world of suffering. He didn't do it—we did it—yet he did say, 'Let this world be.'

"And if he did that and then just sat back and said, 'Well, it's your fault after all'—although he'd be perfectly justified in doing that—I don't see how we could love him. The fact that he went beyond justice and quite incredibly took all the suffering upon himself, makes him so winsome that the answer to suffering is—" Kreeft's eyes darted around the room as he searched for the right words. "The answer," he said, "is . . . how could you not love this being who went the extra mile, who practiced more than he preached, who entered into our world, who suffered our pains, who offers himself to us in the midst of our sorrows? What more could he do?"

I said, "In effect, then, the answer to Templeton's question about how could God bear all that suffering is—he did."

"He did!" Kreeft declared. "God's answer to the problem of suffering is that he came right down into it. Many Christians try to get God off the hook for suffering; God put himself on the hook, so to speak—on the cross. And therefore the practical conclusion is that if we want to be with God, we have to be with suffering, we have to not avoid the cross, either in thought or in fact. We must go where he is and the cross is one of the places where he is. And when he sends us

the sunrises, we thank him for the sunrises; when he sends us sunsets and deaths and sufferings and crosses, we thank him for that."

I bristled. "Is it possible, really, to thank God for the pain that befalls us?"

"Yes. In heaven, we will do exactly that. We will say to God, 'Thank you so much for this little pain I didn't understand at the time, and that little pain that I didn't understand at the time; these I now see were the most precious things in my life.'

"Even if I don't find myself emotionally capable of doing that right now, even if I cannot honestly say to God in the middle of pain, 'God, thank you for this pain,' but have to say instead, 'Deliver me from evil,' that's perfectly right and perfectly honest—yet I believe that's not the last word. The last words of the Lord's prayer aren't 'deliver us from evil;' the last words are, 'Thine is the glory and the honor.'

"I do think that any fairly mature Christian can look back on his or her life and identify some moment of suffering that made them much closer to God than they had ever thought possible. Before this happened, they would have said, 'I don't really see how this can accomplish any good at all,' but after they emerge from the suffering, they say, 'That's amazing. I learned something I never thought I could have learned. I didn't think that my weak and rebellious will was capable of such strength, but God, with his grace, gave me the strength for a moment.' If it weren't for suffering, it wouldn't have been possible.

"The closeness to God, the similarity to God, the conformity to God, not just the feeling of being close to God but the ontological real closeness to God, the God-likeness of the soul, emerges from suffering with remarkable efficiency."

"You mentioned heaven," I said. "And the Bible does talk about our sufferings in this world being light and momentary compared to what God's followers will experience in heaven. How does the heaven part play into all this story?"

Kreeft's eyes widened. "If it weren't for that, there would hardly be a story," he said. "Excise all the references to heaven from the New Testament and you have very little left. Saint Teresa said, 'In light of heaven, the worst suffering on earth, a life full of the most atrocious tortures on earth, will be seen to be no more serious than one night in an inconvenient hotel.' That's a challenging or even an outrageous statement! But she didn't speak from the kind of insulated bubble that so many of us live in; she spoke from a life full of suffering.

"The apostle Paul uses another outrageous word in a similar context when he's comparing earthly pleasures with the pleasure of knowing Christ. He said the privileges of Roman citizenship, of being a Pharisee of the Pharisees, of being highly educated, as to the law blameless—all of this, as compared to knowing Christ, is 'dung.'[21] That's a very bold word!

"Similarly, compared with knowing God eternally, compared to the intimacy with God that Scripture calls a spiritual marriage, nothing else counts. If the way to that is through torture, well, torture is nothing compared with that. Yes, it's enormous in itself, but compared to that, it's nothing.

"So the answer to Templeton is, yes, you're perfectly right in saying that this photograph of the African woman is outrageous. This lack of rain, this starvation, is indeed outrageous in itself. And in one sense, the answer is not to figure it out; one answer is to look in the face of God and compare those two things.

"On the one side of the scale, this torture or all the tortures of the world; on the other side of the scale, the face of God—the God available to all who seek him in the midst of their pain. The good of God, the joy of God, is going to infinitely outweigh all of the sufferings—and even the joys—of this world."

THE POWER OF GOD'S PRESENCE

I was glad that Kreeft had brought the conversation back around to the woman from Templeton's photograph. I didn't want the interview to get too far afield from her. She personalized the issue of suffering, standing as a powerful representative of the world's one billion destitute people.

"If she were here right now," I said to Kreeft, "what would you say to her?"

Kreeft didn't hesitate. "Nothing," he said simply.

I blinked in disbelief. "*Nothing*?"

"Not at first, anyway," he said. "I'd let her talk to me. The founder of an organization for the multiply handicapped says that he works with the handicapped for a very selfish reason: they teach him something much more valuable than he could ever teach them. Namely, who he is. That sounds sentimental, but it's true.

"One of my four children is moderately handicapped, and I've learned more from her than from the other three. I've learned that I'm handicapped and that we're all handicapped, and listening to her helps me to understand myself.

"So the first thing we'd need to do with this woman is to listen to her. To be aware of her. To see her pain. To feel her pain. We live in a relative bubble of comfort, and we look at pain as an observer, as a philosophical puzzle or theological problem. That's the wrong way to look at pain. The thing to do with pain is to enter it, be one with her, and then you learn something from it.

"In fact, it's significant that most objections to the existence of God from the problem of suffering come from outside observers who are quite comfortable, whereas those who actually suffer are, as often as not, made into stronger believers by their suffering."

That's a phenomenon many writers have noted. After wide-ranging research into the topic of suffering, Philip Yancey wrote, "As I visited people whose pain far exceeded my own . . . I was surprised by its effects. Suffering seemed as likely to reinforce faith as to sow agnosticism."[22] Scottish theologian James S. Stewart said: "It is the spectators, the people who are outside, looking at the tragedy, from whose ranks the skeptics come; it is not those who are actually in the arena and who know suffering from the inside. Indeed, the fact is that it is the world's greatest sufferers who have produced the most shining examples of unconquerable faith."[23]

"Why is that?" I asked Kreeft.

His response was crisp. "Free will," he said. "There's a story of the two rabbis in a concentration camp. One had lost his faith and said there is no God; the other had kept his faith and said, 'God will rescue us.' Both were in a line to enter the death showers. The believer looked around and said, 'God will rescue us,' but when it became his turn to go in, his last words were: 'There is no God.'

"Then the unbelieving rabbi, who had constantly heckled the other rabbi's faith, entered the gas chamber with the prayer 'Shema Israel' on his lips. He became a believer. Free will, both ways. Why do some people in starving Africa or concentration camps become believers and some lose their faith? That's a mystery of human unpredictability."

"Let's go back to the woman," I replied. "You said we should listen and react to her, which sounds like a good thing. But there must be more."

"Yes," he said. "We would want to be Jesus to her, to minister to her, to love her, to comfort her, to embrace her, to weep with her. Our love—a reflection of God's love—should spur us to help her and others who are hurting."

Kreeft gestured toward the hallway. "On my door there's a cartoon of two turtles. One says, 'Sometimes I'd like to ask why he allows poverty, famine, and injustice when he could do something about it.' The other turtle says, 'I'm afraid God might ask me the same question.' Those who have Jesus' heart toward hurting people need to live out their faith by alleviating suffering where they can, by making a difference, by embodying his love in practical ways."

"That cartoon reminds me of the way God likes to turn questions around," I commented.

"Yes, he's constantly doing that. This happened to Job. Job was wondering who God was, because it looked as if God was a cosmic sadist. At the end of the book of Job, the all-time classic on the problem of suffering, God finally shows up with the answer—and the answer is a question.

"He says to Job, 'Who are you? Are you God? Did you write this script? Were you there when I laid the foundations of the earth?' And Job realizes the answer is no. Then he's satisfied. Why? *Because he sees God!* God doesn't write him a book. He could have written the best book on the problem of evil ever written. Instead, he shows himself to Job."

"And that satisfied him—"

"Yes! It *has* to—that's what's going to satisfy us forever in heaven. I think Job gets a foretaste of heaven at the end of the book of Job, because he meets God. If it were only words that God gave him, that would mean that Job could dialogue and ask God another question and God would give a good answer and Job would ask another question the next day and the next day, because Job was a very demanding philosopher. This would go on and on and never end. What could make it end? God's presence!

"God didn't let Job suffer because he lacked love, but because he *did* love, in order to bring Job to the point of encountering God face to face, which is humanity's supreme happiness. Job's suffering hollowed out a big space in him so that God and joy could fill it.

"As we look at human relationships, what we see is that lovers don't want explanations, but presence. And what God is, essentially, is presence—the doctrine of the Trinity says God is three persons who are present to each other in perfect knowledge and perfect love. That's why God is infinite joy. And insofar as we can participate in that presence, we too have infinite joy. So that's what Job has—even on his dung heap, even before he gets any of his worldly goods back—once he sees God face to face.

"As I said, this makes sense even among human beings. Let's say Romeo and Juliet have a much deeper and more mature love than in Shakespeare's play. Let's say that what Romeo wants most in all the world is Juliet. And let's say that he has lost all his friends and possessions, and he's bleeding and he thinks Juliet is dead.

"Then he sees Juliet rise up and say, 'Romeo, where are you? I'm not dead; are you?' Is Romeo completely happy? Yes. *Completely* happy? Yes. Does he mind at all that he's bleeding and tattered and poor? Not at all! He would much rather be in love in the South Bronx than divorced in Honolulu."

EVERY TEAR, HIS TEAR

We were clearly moving toward the climax of our discussion. The clues Kreeft had mentioned at the outset of our interview were converging, and I could sense an increasing passion and conviction in his voice. I wanted to see more of his heart—and I wouldn't be disappointed.

"The answer, then, to suffering," I said in trying to sum up where we've come, "is not an answer at all."

"Correct," he emphasized, leaning forward as he pleaded his case. "It's the Answerer. It's Jesus himself. It's not a bunch of words, it's *the* Word. It's not a tightly woven philosophical argument; it's a person. *The* person. The answer to suffering cannot just be an abstract idea, because this isn't an abstract issue; it's a personal issue. It requires a personal response. The answer must be someone, not just something, because the issue involves someone—*God, where are you?*"

That question almost echoed in his small office. It demanded a response. To Kreeft, there is one—a very real one. A living One.

"Jesus is there, sitting beside us in the lowest places of our lives," he said. "Are we broken? He was broken, like bread, for us. Are we despised? He was despised and rejected of men. Do we cry out that we can't take any more? He was a man of sorrows and acquainted with grief. Do people betray us? He was sold out himself. Are our tenderest relationships broken? He too loved and was rejected. Do people turn from us? They hid their faces from him as from a leper.

"Does he descend into all of our hells? *Yes*, he does. From the depths of a Nazi death camp, Corrie ten Boom wrote: 'No matter how deep our darkness, he is deeper still.' He not only rose from the dead, he changed the meaning of death and therefore of all the little deaths—the sufferings that anticipate death and make up parts of it.

"He is gassed in Auschwitz. He is sneered at in Soweto. He is mocked in Northern Ireland. He is enslaved in the Sudan. He's the one we love to hate, yet to us he has chosen to return love. Every tear we shed becomes his tear. He may not wipe them away yet, but he will."

He paused, his confident tone downshifting to tentative. "In the end, God has only given us partial explanations," he said slowly, a shrug in his voice. "Maybe that's because he saw that a better explanation wouldn't have been good for us. I don't know why. As a philosopher, I'm obviously curious. Humanly, I wish he had given us more information."

With that, he looked fully into my face.

"But he knew Jesus was more than an explanation," he said firmly. "He's what we really need. If your friend is sick and dying, the most important thing he wants is not an explanation; he wants you to sit with him. He's terrified of being alone more than anything else. So God has not left us alone."

Kreeft leaned back in his chair and let himself relax. There was only one more thing he wanted me to know.

"And for that," he said, *"I love him."*

DRAWING GOOD FROM EVIL

Less than an hour later, everything was quiet in the car as it snaked through Boston's rain-slickened streets on the way back to the airport. My friend Marc Harrienger, a long-time Boston resident, had graciously volunteered to drive me to and from Kreeft's office. Looking out the window at nothing in particular, I was reviewing the interview in my mind. Most of all, I was wondering how that African woman would have responded to the philosopher's earnest words.

Marc had sat through the interview, listening intently from a wooden chair propped up against the wall. This was not a topic of idle speculation to him.

He broke the silence in the car. “It’s true,” he said.

“What’s true?” I asked.

“What Kreeft said—it’s true. I know it. I’ve lived it.”

Several years earlier, Marc had been shoveling snow on his driveway when his wife said she was going to move the car and asked him to watch their young daughter. As the car backed out, they were suddenly thrust into the worst nightmare that parents can imagine: their toddler was crushed beneath a wheel.

Like the African woman, Marc has known what it’s like to hold a dying child in his arms. While I wasn’t able to talk with that grieving mother, I could converse with him.

So deep was Marc’s initial despair that he had to ask God to help him breathe, to help him eat, to help him function at the most fundamental level. Otherwise, he was paralyzed by the emotional pain. But he increasingly felt God’s presence, his grace, his warmth, his comfort, and very slowly, over time, his wounds began to heal.

Having experienced God at his point of greatest need, Marc would emerge from this crucible a changed person, abandoning his career in business to attend seminary. Through his suffering—though he never would have chosen it, though it was horribly painful, though it was life-shattering at the time—Marc has been transformed into someone who would devote the rest of life to bringing God’s compassion to others who are alone in their desperation.

In the pulpit for the first time, Marc was able to draw on his own experiences with God in the depths of sorrow. People were captivated because his own loss had given him special insights, empathy, and credibility. In the end, dozens of them responded by saying they too wanted to know this Jesus, this God of tears. Now other hearts were being healed because of Marc’s having been broken. From one couple’s despair emerges new hope for many.

“Sometimes skeptics scoff at the Bible saying that God can cause good to emerge from our pain if we run toward him instead of away from him,” Marc said. “But I’ve watched it happen in my own life. I’ve experienced God’s goodness through deep pain, and no skeptic can dispute that. The God who the skeptic denies is the same God who held our hands in the deep, dark places, who strengthened our marriage, who deepened our faith, who increased our reliance on him, who gave us two more children, and who infused our lives with new purpose and meaning so that we can make a difference to others.”

I asked gently, "Do you wish you had more answers about why suffering happens in the first place?"

"We live in a broken world; Jesus was honest enough to tell us we'd have trials and tribulations.[24] Sure, I'd like to understand more about why. But Kreeft's conclusion was right—the ultimate answer is Jesus' presence. That sounds sappy, I know. But just wait—when your world is rocked, you don't want philosophy or theology as much as you want the reality of Christ. He *was* the answer for me. He was the very answer we needed."

The existence of pain and suffering are powerful accusations against God. The question, however, is whether the evidence succeeds in convicting him. I thought Kreeft's deft analysis and analogies went a long way toward undermining this formidable obstacle to faith, but many other kinds of objections remained. This was just the beginning of a long journey of discovery, and I decided to withhold my final verdict until all the obstacles to faith were confronted and all the facts were in.

In the meantime, prominent British pastor John R. W. Stott, who acknowledged that suffering is "the single greatest challenge to the Christian faith," has reached his own conclusion:

> I could never myself believe in God, if it were not for the cross.... In the real world of pain, how could one worship a God who was immune to it? I have entered many Buddhist temples in different Asian countries and stood respectfully before the statue of Buddha, his legs crossed, arms folded, eyes closed, the ghost of a smile playing round his mouth, a remote look on his face, detached from the agonies of the world. But each time after a while I have had to turn away. And in imagination I have turned instead to that lonely, twisted, tortured figure on the cross, nails through hands and feet, back lacerated, limbs wrenched, brow bleeding from thorn-pricks, mouth dry and intolerably thirsty, plunged in God-forsaken darkness. That is the God for me! He laid aside his immunity to pain. He entered our world of flesh and blood, tears and death. He suffered for us. Our sufferings become more manageable in light of his. There is still a question mark against human suffering, but over it we boldly stamp another mark, the cross which symbolizes divine suffering. 'The cross of Christ ... is God's only self-justification in such a world' as ours.[25]

DELIBERATIONS

Questions for Reflection or Group Study

- How have difficulties, challenges, and even pain shaped your character and values? How are you different today as a result of the problems you've had to face in life? Can you ever imagine thanking God someday for how suffering has molded you? Kreeft said, "I believe all suffering contains at least the opportunity for good." Was that true in your case?
- What were Kreeft's strongest points? What were his weakest? If you had an opportunity to question him, what would you ask? Based on his other observations, how do you think he might respond to your question?
- If you were God, how would you have designed the world differently? As you remove suffering or evil and tinker with people's free will, think through the consequences that would result. How would people form character in your utopia? Would they be motivated to seek God in the midst of their pleasures? If you supernaturally intervened to eliminate evil, where would you draw the line—to prevent murder? Child abuse? Theft? Slander? Evil thoughts that may prompt evil actions? At what point are people turned into puppets who lack free will and therefore cannot truly express love?
- If Marc were to sit down with the woman in the *Life* magazine photo, what three things do you think he would say to her? How do you believe she might respond?

FOR FURTHER EVIDENCE

More Resources on This Topic

- Peter Kreeft. *Making Sense Out of Suffering*. Ann Arbor, Mich.: Servant, 1986.
- Philip Yancey. *Where Is God When It Hurts*. Grand Rapids, Mich.: Zondervan, 1990.
- Joni Eareckson Tada and Steven Estes. *When God Weeps*. Grand Rapids, Mich.: Zondervan, 1997.
- Luis Palau. *Where Is God When Bad Things Happen?* New York: Doubleday, 1999.

2

OBJECTION #2: SINCE MIRACLES CONTRADICT SCIENCE, THEY CANNOT BE TRUE

The virgin birth, the Resurrection, the raising of Lazarus, even the Old Testament miracles, all are freely used for religious propaganda, and they are very effective with an audience of unsophisticates and children.

Richard Dawkins, atheist[1]

It is not just a provocative rumor that God has acted in history, but a fact worthy of our intellectual conviction. The miracles of Christianity are not an embarrassment to the Christian worldview. Rather, they are testimony to the compassion of God for human beings benighted by sin and circumstance.

Gary Habermas, Christian[2]

I've seen guilty defendants squirm and sweat on the witness stand as they feel the noose of justice slowly tightening around their neck. They try to lie their way out of their predicament. They concoct improbable stories in a futile effort to explain away incriminating evidence. They manufacture transparently false alibis; they cast blame on innocent people; they attempt to discredit police and prosecutors; they rewrite history; they deny and obfuscate and try to hoodwink the judge and jurors.

But there's one tactic I've never seen: a defendant claiming that the reason his fingerprints ended up on the murder weapon is—somehow, for some inexplicable reason, an act of God occurred, a mysterious, unrepeatable, supernatural event that made his fingerprints suddenly appear somewhere he had never touched.

Once a defendant tried a "Twinkie defense" by making the dubious assertion that his elevated sugar levels were somehow responsible for his criminal behavior, but not even the most audacious defendant would try a "miracle defense."

Why? Because nobody would believe him! After all, we're modern and scientific people living in the Third Millennium. We don't subscribe to superstition, sorcery, or direct intervention from some unseen divine source. Claiming a miracle would be so blatantly silly that even the most desperate defendant wouldn't resort to that strategy.

One time I saw Penn and Teller, the comedian-magicians, select a ten-year-old boy named Isaiah from the audience and show him a long strip of polyester, which they proceeded to knot and cut in the middle. Then, with a big flourish, they shook out the cloth and—voilà!—it was in one piece again.

"What do you think?" Penn asked little Isaiah. "Was that a miracle or a magic trick?"

Isaiah didn't hesitate. "A magic trick," he replied with confidence.

A mere child, it seems, is smart enough to know that when we can't quite understand what might have caused a mysterious event, there's still undoubtedly a reasonable explanation apart from the miraculous.

I knew from my conversation with agnostic Charles Templeton that he had shed his belief in miracles many years ago. "Our early forefathers sought within the limits of their experience to interpret life's imponderables, usually attributing the inexplicable to the intervention of one or more of their gods, demi-deities, and evil spirits," he wrote. "But surely . . . it is time to have done with primitive speculation and superstition and look at life in rational terms."[3]

There are scientists who agree, predicting that the march of knowledge will ultimately trample belief in supernatural events. In 1937, German physicist Max Planck said: "Faith in miracles must yield ground, step by step, before the steady and firm advance of the forces of science, and its total defeat is indubitably a mere matter of time."[4]

Atheist Richard Dawkins, professor of public understanding of science at Oxford University and author of *The Selfish Gene*, believes that time is rapidly coming. "We're working on . . . a complete understanding of the universe and everything that is in it," he said in a television interview.[5]

That means, *violà!* as with Penn and Teller's magically restored sash, there would be no need to appeal to the miraculous in order to explain away what previously had been shrouded in mystery.

But can a person be scientifically sophisticated and still believe in the possibility of miracles? "My faith can be summed up in this one paradox: I believe in science, and I believe in God," said nuclear physicist Hugh Siefken. "I plan to continue testifying to both."[6]

He and many other scientists see no inherent conflict between their profession and their conclusion that a miracle-working God is responsible for creating and sustaining the universe.

Is that a form of professional denial? Can a person write off elves and fairies as being fanciful and yet at the same time embrace manna from heaven, the virgin birth, and the Resurrection as being credible events of history? If miracles are direct violations of natural laws, then how can a reasonable person believe they could ever occur?

I knew that William Lane Craig was a rational man. And I was aware that he has used his considerable intellectual skills to defend the idea that God has—and does—intervene in the world through miraculous acts. I called him and asked whether he'd be willing to let me question him on the topic.

"Sure," he said. "Come on down."

I jotted down a long list of challenges and booked a flight to Atlanta. On the plane, I mused that primitive people probably would have considered jet travel to be a miracle. How else could fifty tons of metal be kept aloft in apparent defiance of the law of gravity? Surely God's invisible hand must be beneath it.

People today know better. They understand aerodynamics and jet propulsion. But has our knowledge of science and technology really rendered all belief in miracles obsolete? Or would Craig be able to provide convincing evidence that a person can be sober-minded and discerning while at the same time maintaining the validity of the miraculous?

THE SECOND INTERVIEW: WILLIAM LANE CRAIG, PH.D.

My initial reaction to seeing Bill Craig was disbelief. His beard, which for twenty-three years had given him a serious and scholarly demeanor, was gone. My face must have registered my shock.

"I turned fifty," he explained, "so I celebrated by shaving it off."

Craig ushered me down a flight of stairs to his office, a well-organized room dominated by a dark wood desk and floor-to-ceiling bookshelves with neatly arranged rows of books and scholarly journals. I settled into a comfortable chair while Craig sat behind the desk, leaning back in a leather-clad office chair that protested with a loud squeak.

Craig has written extensively about miracles, especially the resurrection of Jesus. His books include *Reasonable Faith, Knowing the Truth about the Resurrection, The Historical Argument for the Resurrection of Jesus,* and *Assessing the New Testament Evidence for the Historicity of the Resurrection of Jesus,* and he contributed to *In Defense of Miracles, Does God Exist? Jesus Under Fire,* and *The Intellectuals Speak Out about God.*

He holds doctorates in philosophy from the University of Birmingham, England, and in theology from the University of Munich, and is currently a Research Professor of Philosophy at the Talbot School of Theology. He is the member of nine professional societies, including the American Academy of Religion, Society of Biblical Literature, and the American Philosophical Association, and he has written for *New Testament Studies, Journal for the Study of the New Testament, Journal of the American Scientific Affiliation, Gospel Perspectives, Philosophy,* and other scholarly publications.

Sans beard and wearing blue jeans, Craig looked a decade younger than his age, with piercing blue eyes, brown hair combed casually to the side, and a quick and enthusiastic laugh. He stroked his chin—subconsciously missing his beard, perhaps—as he listened intently to my first question, which admittedly came with an edge of challenge.

"Okay, Dr. Craig, you're an intelligent and educated individual," I began. "Tell me: how can a modern and rational person still believe in babies being born from virgins, people walking on water, and cadavers emerging alive from tombs?"

Craig smiled. "It's funny you should ask specifically about the virgin birth," he replied, "because that was a major stumbling block to my becoming a Christian. I thought it was totally absurd."

"Really?" I said. "What happened?"

"When the Christian message was first shared with me as a teenager, I had already studied biology. I knew that for the virgin birth to be true, a Y chromosome had to be created out of nothing in Mary's ovum, because Mary didn't possess the genetic material to produce a male child. To me, this was utterly fantastic. It just didn't make sense."

"You're not alone," I observed. "Other skeptics have problems with it too. How did you proceed?"

Craig thought back for a moment. "Well, I sort of put that issue aside and became a Christian anyway, even though I didn't really believe in the virgin birth. But then, after becoming a Christian, it occurred to me that if I really do believe in a God who created the universe, then for him to create a Y chromosome would be child's play!"

I told Craig that I found it interesting he could have become a Christian despite misgivings about a doctrine as significant as the virgin birth.

"I guess the authenticity of the person of Jesus and the truth of his message were so powerful that they simply overwhelmed any residual doubts that I had," he replied.

I pressed him by asking, "Weren't you rushing headlong into something you didn't totally accept?"

"No, I think this can be a good procedure," he said. "You don't need to have all your questions answered to come to faith. You just have to say, 'The weight of the evidence seems to show this is true, so even though I don't have answers to all my questions, I'm going to believe and hope for answers in the long run.' That's what happened with me."

"Does a person have to suspend their critical judgment in order to believe in something as improbable as miracles?"

Craig sat upright in his chair and raised his index finger as if to punctuate his point. "Only if you believe that God does not exist!" he stressed. "Then I would agree—the miraculous would be absurd. But if there is a Creator who designed and brought the universe into being, who sustains its existence moment by moment, who is responsible for the very natural laws that govern the physical world, then certainly it's rational to believe that the miraculous is possible."

MIRACLES VERSUS SCIENCE

We were already getting into the interview but we had not yet paused to define our terms. Before going any further, I knew it was important that we settled on what 'miracle' means.

"We throw around the word pretty haphazardly," I said. Harking back to my day thus far, I added, "For example, I might say, 'It was a miracle I made my flight to Atlanta,' or, 'It's a miracle I found your house.' Is that being too loose with the word?"

"Yes, I think it's a misuse to talk about these things as miracles," he said. "They're clearly natural events with natural consequences."

"Then how do you define the term?"

Craig spelled out his definition with precision. "In the proper sense," he said, "a miracle is an event which is not producible by the natural causes that are operative at the time and place that the event occurs."

As he said it, I silently repeated the definition in order to cement it in my mind. I mulled it for a few moments before continuing with what I considered to be the next logical question.

"But then isn't there a contradiction between science and miracles?" I asked. "Atheistic philosopher Michael Ruse said, 'Creationists believe the world started miraculously. But miracles lie outside of science, which by definition deals with the natural, the repeatable, that which is governed by law.'"[7]

"Notice that Ruse does not say miracles are *contradictory* to science," Craig pointed out. "He says miracles lie *outside* of science, and that's quite different. I think a Christian who believes in miracles could agree with him on that. He could say that miracles, properly speaking, lie outside the province of natural science—but that's not to say they contradict science."

I tried to digest the distinction. "Can you think of another example of something like that?" I asked.

Craig thought for a moment before answering. "Well, ethics, for instance, lie outside the province of science," he replied. "Science doesn't make ethical judgments. So I wouldn't necessarily object to Ruse's statement. He's saying that the goal of science is to seek natural explanations, and therefore miracles lie outside of the scientific realm."

Before I could ask another question, Craig spoke up again. "I should add, though, that you can do a theistic form of science. For example, there's a whole movement of people like mathematician William Dembski and biochemist Michael Behe who infer by principled means that there is an Intelligent Designer of the universe and the biological world.[8] They aren't being arbitrary—from a rational and scientific perspective, they're concluding from the evidence that there must be an intelligent Creator."

"So," I said, "you're disagreeing with the great skeptic David Hume, who defined miracles as being violations of the laws of nature."

"Yes, absolutely. That's an improper understanding of miracles," he said. "You see, natural laws have implicit *ceteris paribus* conditions—that's Latin meaning, 'all other things being equal.' In other words, natural laws assume that no other natural or supernatural factors are interfering with the operation that the law describes."

"Can you give me an example of that?"

Craig's eyes swept the room in search of an illustration. He finally landed on one as near as his own body.

"Well, it's a law of nature that oxygen and potassium combust when they're combined," he explained. "But I have oxygen and potassium in my body, and yet I'm not bursting into flames. Does that mean it's a miracle and I'm violating the laws of nature? No, because the law merely states what happens under idealized conditions, assuming no other factors are interfering. In this case, however, there *are* other factors interfering with the combustion, and so it doesn't take place. That's not a violation of the law.

"Similarly, if there's a supernatural agent that is working in the natural world, then the idealized conditions described by the law are no longer in effect. The law isn't violated because the law has this implicit provision that nothing is messing around with the conditions."

I told Craig that his explanation reminded me of a conversation I had several years earlier with J. P. Moreland, the noted philosopher who wrote *Christianity and the Nature of Science*. He used an illustration of the law of gravity, which says that if you drop an object, it will fall to the earth. But, he said, if an apple falls from a tree and you reach out to catch it before it hits the ground, you're not violating or negating the law of gravity; you're merely intervening.

"Yes, that's my point with the *ceteris paribus* conditions," Craig said. "The law of gravity states what will happen under idealized conditions with no natural or supernatural factors intervening. Catching the apple doesn't overturn the law of gravity or require the formulation of a new law. It's merely the intervention of a person with free will who overrides the natural causes operative in that particular circumstance. And that, essentially, is what God does when he causes a miracle to occur."

That made sense to me. I knew, however, that some scientists would nevertheless dismiss the miraculous as mere superstition. I decided to pursue this line of questioning further.

REAL ACTS OF GOD

I asked Craig what he thought about physicist Max Plank's prediction that faith in miracles would inevitably yield ground to the advance of science and biologist Richard Dawkin's remark that scientists would someday understand the workings of the universe and thus vanquish the need for miraculous explanations. Craig's reaction surprised me.

"I think they're right," he declared.

I looked up from my notes, thinking perhaps he had misunderstood my question. "Excuse me?" I said.

"Really," he insisted, "I think they're correct—insofar as some superstitious people use miracles as an excuse for ignorance and sort of punt to God every time they can't explain something. I think it's a good thing that science will squeeze out that kind of simplistic thinking.

"But those aren't the miracles I've been talking about. I'm referring to events by which, in a principled way, you could legitimately infer that there was a supernatural agent intervening in the process. Those miracles—*real acts of God*—won't be squeezed out by the advance of science, because they're not based on an appeal to ignorance. They're substantiated by the weight of the scientific and historical evidence.

"Michael Behe does this in his book *Darwin's Black Box.* Behe explores 'irreducible complexity' in nature—organisms that could not have evolved step-by-step by a gradual Darwinian process of natural selection and genetic mutation. Now, he's not saying that this is merely scientifically inexplicable. He's giving a principled inference to an Intelligent Designer based on what the evidence shows. This is rational. His conclusions are based on solid scientific analysis."

Craig's discussion of evidence for miracles prompted me to ask about another point that was made by Hume, the eighteenth-century Scottish skeptic and history's most famous doubter of the miraculous. "Hume said the evidence for the uniformity of nature is so conclusive that any evidence for miracles would never be able to overcome it," I pointed out. "For instance, look at the Resurrection. We have thousands of years of uniform evidence that dead people simply do not return from the dead. So Hume says no amount of evidence would be able to overcome that tremendous presumption."

Craig shook his head. "There's no contradiction between believing that men generally stay in their graves and that Jesus of Nazareth rose from the dead. In fact, Christians believe both of these. The opposite of the statement that Jesus rose from the dead is not that all other men remained in their graves; it's that Jesus of Nazareth remained in *his* grave.

"In order to argue against the evidence for the Resurrection, you have to present evidence against the Resurrection itself, not evidence that everybody else has always remained in their grave. So I think his argument is simply fallacious.

"Now, I would agree with Hume that a *natural* resurrection of Jesus from the dead, without any sort of divine intervention, is enormously improbable. But that's *not* the hypothesis. The hypothesis is God raised Jesus from the dead. That doesn't say anything against the laws of nature, which say dead men don't come back to life *naturally*."

EXTRAORDINARY EVIDENCE

While I could see Craig's point, I wanted to pursue this avenue further. "Some critics say that the Resurrection is an extraordinary event and therefore it requires extraordinary evidence," I said. "Doesn't that assertion have a certain amount of appeal?"

"Yes, that sounds like common sense," he replied. "But it's demonstrably false."

"How so?"

"Because this standard would prevent you from believing in all sorts of events that we do rationally embrace. For example, you would not believe the report on the evening news that the numbers chosen in last night's lottery were 4, 2, 9, 7, 8, and 3, because that would be an event of extraordinary improbability. The odds against that are millions and millions to one, and therefore you should not believe it when the news reports it. Yet we obviously believe we're rational in concluding it's true. How is that possible?

"Well, probability theorists say that you must weigh the improbability of the event's occurring against the probability that the evidence would be just as it is if the event had not taken place."

Craig rattled off that statement so fast that my mind was having trouble assimilating it. "Whoa," I said, holding up my hand. "You're going to have to slow down and give me an example."

"Okay, look at it this way: if the evening news has a very high probability of being accurate, then it's highly improbable that they would inaccurately report the numbers chosen in the lottery. That counterbalances any improbability in the choosing of those numbers, so you're quite rational to believe in this highly improbable event.

"In the same way, any improbability that you might think resides in the resurrection of Jesus is counterbalanced by the improbability of the empty tomb, Jesus' resurrection appearances, the sudden change in the first disciples taking place if there were no such event as the resurrection of Jesus. Do you see what I mean?"

Yes, I said, that illustration made his point clear. As improbable as the Resurrection might seem to skeptics, this has to be weighed against how improbable it would be to have all of the various historical evidence for its occurrence if it never actually took place.

"So," Craig concluded, "it becomes quite rational to believe in an event like the miraculous resurrection of Jesus. Besides, I look at it this way: if God really exists, then in what sense *is* it improbable that he would raise Jesus from the dead? I can't think of any."

"Have you seen skeptics who have become believers in Christianity because of the quality and quantity of the evidence for the Resurrection?" I asked.

Craig's eyes got wide. "Oh, yes, certainly!" he said. "I recently met a fellow who became a Christian out of the so-called 'free thought' movement. He looked into the Resurrection and concluded from the evidence that God raised Jesus from the dead. Of course, his free-thought colleagues bitterly railed against him. He said, 'Why are they so hostile? I merely followed the principles of free thought, and this is where the evidence and reason led me!'"

I chuckled. "Are you saying some 'free thought' folks aren't as free thinking as they would have people believe?"

"Frankly," he replied, "I think many skeptics act in a close-minded way."

As a former skeptic myself, I have noticed the same phenomenon. "Are you referring to the fact that some of them rule out even the possibility of miracles from the outset?" I asked.

"Precisely," Craig said. "Logicians have a term: 'inference to the best explanation.' This means you have a body of data to be explained, and then you have a pool of live options or various explanations for that data. You need to choose which explanation from that pool would, if true, best explain the observed data.

"Some skeptics, however, will not allow supernatural explanations even to be in the pool of live options. Consequently, if there is no natural explanation for an event, they're simply left with ignorance.

"That's prejudice. Apart from some proof of atheism, there's no warrant for excluding supernatural explanations from being a member of the pool of live options. If you do put them in that pool, then you've got to be an open, honest investigator to see which is the best explanation of any given event."

THE MIRACLES OF JESUS

"Let's say you're an honest investigator," I said, picking up on his last thought. "What would you look for to convince you that something miraculous has occurred?"

"You would have a number of criteria. You would have to investigate to see if something cannot be accounted for in terms of the natural forces that were operable at that time and place. And you'd look for a religio-historical context."

I wanted to pursue this idea of context. Hume said that if historians uniformly agreed that the Queen of England died and then reappeared alive a month later, he would be inclined to accept any explanation other than God having performed a miracle. I asked Craig for his response to that.

"I would agree that a miracle without context is inherently ambiguous," Craig replied. "The context of a miracle can help us determine if it's from God or not. For instance, the Queen's revivification would lack any religious context and would basically be a bald and unexplained anomaly.

"But that's not the case with Jesus. His supernatural feats took place in a context charged with religious significance because he performed his miracles and exorcisms as signs of the in-breaking of the kingdom of God into human history, and they served as an authentication of his message. And his resurrection comes as the climax to his own unparalleled life and ministry and his radical claims to divine authority which got him crucified. This is why the Resurrection gives us pause, while the Queen's return would only perplex us. Therefore, the religio-historical context is crucial in understanding miraculous events."

But I pressed further: "*Did* Jesus perform miracles? What convinces you that he did?"

"The fact is that most New Testament critics today admit he performed what we would call miracles. Granted, they may not all believe these were *genuine* miracles, but the idea of Jesus of Nazareth as a miracle-worker and exorcist is part of the historical Jesus that's generally accepted by critics today."

With that, Craig swiveled his chair and withdrew a file from the shelf behind his desk. He flipped through some pages until he landed the one he was after. "Let me read you a quote from Rudolf Bultmann, who's recognized as one of the most skeptical New Testament critics of this century":

> The Christian fellowship was convinced that Jesus had done miracles and they told many stories of miracles about him. Most of these stories contained in the gospels are legendary or are at least dressed up with legend. But, there can be no doubt that Jesus did such deeds, which were, in his and his contemporaries' understanding, miracles; that is to say, events that were the result of supernatural divine causality. Doubtless he healed the sick and cast out demons.[9]

Craig closed the file. "Even Bultmann says miracles and exorcisms belong to the historical Jesus. Now, in Bultmann's day these stories were considered legendary because of the supposed influence of Greco-Roman mythology on the gospels, but scholars today realize this influence was virtually nil. They now believe the role of Jesus as a miracle-worker must be understood against the backdrop of first century Palestinian Judaism, where it fits right in.

"In fact," he concluded, "the only reason to be skeptical that these were genuine miracles rather than psychosomatic healings would be philosophical—do you believe that such events can occur or not? The historicity of the events is not in doubt."

MIRACLES AND LEGENDS

The conclusions of these scholars was helpful, but I wanted more than that. "What is the specific evidence that Jesus performed miracles?" I asked.

"Part of it is that these events are found in all of the strata of the gospel sources. For example, the miracle of the feeding of the five thousand is found in all of the gospels, so you have independent, multiple attestation to these events. There is no vestige of a non-miraculous

Jesus of Nazareth in any of the sources; therefore, it's very likely that this belongs to the historical Jesus. Moreover, it fits right into the Jewish milieu. There were other Jewish exorcists and miracle workers who preceded Jesus."

That wasn't enough for me. "Just because several people said something extraordinary happened—like the feeding of the five thousand—doesn't necessarily mean it's true," I said.

"In one sense, it's a very individual question of what you will find convincing for yourself," he replied. "I think we can confidently say there isn't any reason to be doubtful about these narratives apart from philosophical reasons. In other words, if you believe God exists, then there's no good reason to be skeptical about these events.

"However, let me add this: regarding the central miracle of the New Testament—the Resurrection—there is a very good case for concluding with confidence that, yes, this is really an event of history. You see, the evidence for the Resurrection is much, much stronger than the evidence, say, that Jesus did a miracle by healing the blind man in John 9. You have a wealth of data concerning the empty tomb, the Resurrection appearances, and the origin of the disciples' belief in the Resurrection."

"Isn't it more likely that the accounts of Jesus' miracles actually were legends that developed years after his life?" I asked. "Atheist George Smith says, 'As one moves from the earlier to the later gospels, some of the miracles become more exaggerated.'[10]

"He illustrates this legendary development by comparing Mark 1, which says *all* were brought to Jesus and *many* were healed; Matthew 8, which says *many* were brought to Jesus and *all* were healed; and Luke 4, which says *all* were brought and *all* were healed. As historian Archibald Robertson said, 'We are witnessing the progressive growth of a legend.'"[11]

Craig got a sour look on his face. "That argument is really quite fanciful," he said, "because the gospel writers don't use the word 'all' or 'many' in the way a police report would."

He pushed aside the Bultmann folder on his desk and reached for his Bible, opening it to the New Testament and running his finger down a page. Finding Mark 1:5, he read the verse aloud: "The whole Judean countryside and all the people of Jerusalem went out to him. Confessing their sins, they were baptized by him in the Jordan River."

"Okay, think about that," he said. "It says John the Baptist was baptizing all of Judea and Jerusalem. *Really? All* of Judea? *All* of

Jerusalem?" Craig said, his voice rising in mock astonishment. "The *whole* province was emptied of people who went to the Jordan River and they were *all* baptized—all the infants, every elderly individual? Well, obviously not. This was not an expression that was meant to be read woodenly like a police report.

"Now, back to the accounts you mentioned earlier—what is the central point they're making? Clearly, that multitudes were going to Jesus for healings and exorcisms, and this is well attested. The fact is that all these accounts are in absolute agreement that there were miracles performed by Jesus and that this involved lots of people."

He added one more point: "And it's important to remember that for the greatest miracle, the Resurrection, we know from historical research that there was nowhere near enough time for legend to have developed and wiped out a solid core of historical truth."

THE "MIRACLES" OF MUHAMMAD

Assuming that there's historical evidence that Jesus did perform feats that eyewitnesses considered to be miraculous, what about miracles in other religions? To the critic Hume, miracles from different religions cancel each other out as being evidence for truth.

For instance, Islamic tradition says Muhammad ascended to heaven on a mule, that he healed the broken leg of a companion, that he fed large groups with little food, that he turned a tree branch into a steel sword, and that he was responsible for other supernatural accomplishments.

"If he and Jesus both performed similar miracles," I said to Craig, "then doesn't that water down the uniqueness of Jesus and negate miracles as being evidence of his truth?"

Craig furrowed his brow. "I think this is based on a misimpression of Islam," he said a bit tentatively. "Correct me if I'm wrong, but as I read the Koran, essentially there aren't any miracles, apart from the supposed miracle of the Koran itself."

"Granted," I replied. "Except for a few disputed passages, I think scholars generally interpret the Koran that way. But I said these miracles are reported in Islamic *tradition*, which is where they really proliferate."[12]

Craig searched his mind and then locked in on the issue. "Ah, yes, exactly—the miracles are mentioned in the so-called Hadith," he said. "And here's what's important: this Islamic tradition comes hundreds of years after Muhammad's life and therefore isn't comparable to the gospels, which were written down within the first generation when the eyewitnesses were still alive.

"For example, in First Corinthians 15, the reports of Jesus' resurrection appearances go back to within the first five years after the event. Consequently, this is fresh data that could have not been the result of legendary development. It's simply not comparable to these legendary stories about Muhammad that accumulated many, many years later in Islamic tradition."

"Do you think it's significant that the Koran itself doesn't emphasize miracles by Muhammad in the way the Bible does about Jesus?"

"Perhaps in the sense that later the Hadith seemed to find it necessary to invent miracles for Muhammad. He never claimed any such things for himself. Basically, these stories illustrate how non-historical reports arise by legendary influences over centuries of time, in contrast to the gospels, where miracle reports are part of the earliest strata of sources."

Still, I sensed a contradiction. If the immediacy of the reporting of miracles is important, then certainly the Book of Mormon passes that test. "There you have claims of the miraculous that are reported soon after they supposedly occurred, yet you wouldn't accept them as being true," I pointed out.

"In this case, what you have is just plain charlatanry by Joseph Smith, who created Mormonism," Craig replied. "It's interesting that Smith and his father, when they lived in New York, were obsessed with finding Captain Kidd's buried gold. Then what does Smith later claim he finds? Golden plates from the Angel Moroni, and then they disappear and are supposedly taken to heaven and never seen again.

"What you have here is an elaborate hoax, compared to the gospels, with the evident sincerity of the people in what they were reporting. The problem with Mormonism is basically one of credibility because of the unreliability of Joseph Smith and a blatant lack of corroboration. Unlike the gospels, whose credibility has been greatly enhanced by archaeology, archaeological discoveries have repeatedly failed to substantiate the Book of Mormon."

THE PERSONAL SIDE OF MIRACLES

My discussion with Craig had been stimulating so far, but it had remained exclusively on an intellectual plane. I wanted to get more personal, to probe beneath Craig's scholarly persona and relate the issue of miracles to his individual life. But I hesitated.

Through my years of acquaintance with Bill Craig, I had noticed some physical challenges he was facing. For instance, I could tell when we shook hands that his right hand was a bit gnarled. Out of politeness, I had never broached the subject with him. Now, as we explored this topic, his apparent ailment raised a troubling question that I could no longer ignore: if God can perform miracles, why hasn't he healed someone who is as devoted to him as Bill Craig has been?

I began slowly. "Look, Bill," I said, "you believe God still does miracles, don't you?"

"I wouldn't deny that miracles can happen today," Craig said. "I would add, though, that there's no reason to expect them to be as frequent or evident as they were with Jesus. Miracles tend to cluster around great moments in salvation history, like the Exodus or the ministry of Jesus, who saw his miracles as signs to the people of the inbreaking of the kingdom of God and his exorcisms as signs of his ability to destroy the powers of darkness."

"Then tell me this," I said gently. "If God loves you and he has the power to heal you, why doesn't he make your physical afflictions disappear?"

Craig didn't seem to be offended by the question. He shifted in his chair and then leaned forward, his voice changing from a professorial tone to one that was more personal and tender.

"Paul the apostle had what he called 'a thorn in his flesh' that he asked God three times to remove," Craig began, "and God's answer was that his grace was sufficient and that his strength is made perfect in weakness. That passage has been a comfort to me in my own life."

He glanced off to the side, perhaps deciding how much to say. When he looked back at me, the sharp, steely intensity of his blue eyes had softened to a vulnerable sincerity.

"I guess I don't discuss this very much publicly," he said, "but I have a congenital neuromuscular disease that causes progressive atrophy in the extremities. In my case it's fairly light. A lot of people with this syndrome have to wear metal braces on their legs. They're completely crippled. I've really been fortunate that mine hasn't been very bad."

"You've asked for a miracle?" I said.

He nodded. "As a young Christian I prayed that God would heal me. But he didn't."

Even though I could tell from his matter-of-fact tone that he wasn't seeking pity, my heart went out to him. "You're disappointed," I said, my words coming out more like an observation than a question.

A slight smile came to his face. "Lee, do you know what has amazed me?" he asked with an unmistakable sense of wonder. "As I look at my life, God has used this disease in so many remarkable ways to shape me and my personality. Because I couldn't do athletics, in order to succeed at something I was driven into academics. I really owe my existence as a scholar to my having this disease. It's what compelled me to the life of the mind.

"And it also affected me psychologically by giving me a tremendous drive to succeed. It caused me to have an achievement and goal orientation, which has helped me to do a lot in life. So I've really seen played out in a very personal way what Paul said—his strength is made perfect in weakness."

"If you could have been healed, would you have wanted to be?"

He let out a laugh. "Well, *now* perhaps it would be nice, having learned the lessons!" he said.

Then he gave a more serious answer that echoed Peter Kreeft's earlier comments about suffering. "On the other hand, I've become quite accustomed to it. As I look back, I can honestly say that I am glad this was the way God directed my life. He can even use the bad things of life to bring about his ultimate purposes and ends.

"That doesn't mean those things aren't bad—they really *are* bad. But they're all within the sovereignty of God. Even good can come out of evil."

FAITH IN A GOD OF MIRACLES

Bill Craig is not an ivory-tower pontificator; he's a man whose everyday life embodies his Christian philosophy. Even when wrestling with the very real issue of his own affliction, he emerges with confirmation that his beliefs are well placed. Everything is undergirded by a supreme confidence in the rationality of Christianity, a religion whose linchpin is a miracle of unprecedented proportions.

"You titled one of your most popular books *Reasonable Faith,*" I said, "but there are skeptics who would call that an oxymoron."

I reached into my briefcase and withdrew a book called *Critiques of God,* turning to a chapter titled, "Religion and Reason." It was written by atheist Richard Robinson, a philosopher educated at Oxford and Cornell universities. I read Craig a quote that I had previously highlighted:

> Christian faith is not merely believing that there is a god. It is believing that there is a god no matter what the evidence on the question may be. 'Have faith,' in the Christian sense, means, 'make yourself believe that there is a god without regard to evidence.'[13]

Closing the book, I looked up at Craig and asked: "How do you see this interplay between faith and reason? Are the two really contradictory as critics contend?"

Craig began with a definition. "Faith is trust or commitment to what you think is true," he replied. "Why a person thinks Christianity is true may differ from individual to individual. For one person, it might be because God speaks to his heart and produces in him a conviction this is true. I certainly believe that's valid.

"To another person, though, it may be a more hardheaded intellectual exploration of the evidence that leads him to the same conclusion. But neither comes to faith until he makes that act of trust or commitment to what he thinks is true. When you understand faith in these categories, you can see it's entirely compatible with reason."

When I asked Craig to elaborate, he thought for a minute and then offered an illustration from his own experience. He began, "I had corneal transplant surgery a while back," but as soon as the words left his mouth, he let out a laugh. One more medical problem did sound like "piling-on" in light of our previous discussion about his health. Craig shrugged. "My wife says I'm a walking medical disaster area," he said with a chuckle, "but the healthiest person she knows!

"Anyway, before I was willing to let anyone operate on my eyes, Jan and I did a thorough search to find the best corneal surgeon in the country. We did research, we looked at the evidence, we contacted him, talked with him, and finally, after becoming convinced on the basis of the evidence he was the best, then I placed my trust in him and let him operate on my eyes. My faith or trust in him was based upon the good evidence that I had in his qualifications and credibility.

"In the same way, with respect to belief in God or miracles, many people make that act of trust or commitment after they have become convinced by the evidence that Christianity is true. Not everybody takes that route, but there are certainly people who do. And that's a logical and rational approach that uses reason rather than negates it."

The subject of evidence opened the door to a fundamental issue that was begging to be explored. Time after time, Craig had referred to the fact that if God exists, then it's reasonable to believe that the miraculous is possible. And while that makes sense, to many people it hinges on a very big "if."

"What affirmative evidence convinces you that such a miracle-working being exists?" I asked. "Can you give me some solid reasons for believing in a divine Creator and the validity of Christianity?"

Craig was nodding all through my question. "In 1986, I heard a lecture in which Alvin Plantinga presented two dozen reasons for believing in God. He's the premiere Christian philosopher today, and it was a dazzling display of theistic arguments," Craig replied.[14]

I glanced at my watch. "How about zeroing in on five main arguments?" I suggested.

"Okay," he said, "I'll go through a conspiracy of arguments for God that reinforce and underline each other."[15]

Pushing up the sleeves of his shirt, Craig settled into his chair. As the author of *The Existence of God and the Beginning of the Universe* and co-author of *Theism, Atheism, and Big Bang Cosmology*, published by Oxford University Press, Craig began his arguments exactly where one would expect.

Reason #1: God Makes Sense of the Universe's Origin

"Both philosophically and scientifically," Craig said, "I would argue that the universe and time itself had a beginning at some point in the finite past. But since something cannot just come out of nothing, there has to be a transcendent cause beyond space and time which brought the universe into being."

"And the universe came into being in what has been called the Big Bang?" I asked.

"Exactly. As Stephen Hawking said, 'Almost everyone now believes that the universe, and time itself, had a beginning at the Big Bang.'[16] That's where the overwhelming scientific evidence points—to an event approximately fourteen billion years ago. Now, this poses a major problem for skeptics. As Anthony Kenny of Oxford University says, 'A proponent of the Big Bang theory, at least if he is an atheist, must believe that the ... universe came from nothing and by nothing.'"[17]

Craig chuckled. "Of course, something coming from nothing doesn't make sense! Lee, you've been quoting the famous skeptic David Hume quite a bit in our interview. Well, even he said: 'But allow me to tell you that I never asserted so absurd a proposition as that anything might arise without a cause.'[18]

"Atheists recognize this. For example, one of contemporary philosophy's most prominent atheists, Kai Nielsen, once said: 'Suppose you suddenly hear a loud bang . . . and you ask me, 'What made that bang?' and I reply, 'Nothing, it just happened.' You would not accept that.'[19]

"And he's absolutely correct. Yet think about it: if there must be a cause for a little bang, then doesn't it also make sense that there would be a cause for a big bang?"

It was a question that didn't seem to need a response. "So how would you summarize this initial argument?" I asked.

As he made each point, Craig grabbed a finger to count them off. "First, whatever begins to exist has a cause. Second, the universe began to exist. And, third, therefore, the universe has a cause. As the eminent scientist Sir Arthur Eddington wrote: 'The beginning seems to present insuperable difficulties unless we agree to look on it as frankly supernatural.'"[20]

I interrupted. "Okay, that points toward a Creator, but does it tell us much about him?"

"Actually, yes, it does," Craig replied. "We know this supernatural cause must be an uncaused, changeless, timeless, and immaterial being."

"What's the basis of your conclusions?"

"It must be uncaused because we know that there cannot be an infinite regress of causes. It must be timeless and therefore changeless, at least without the universe, because it was the creator of time. In addition, because it also created space, it must transcend space and therefore be immaterial rather than physical in nature."

There was an obvious question that had to be asked. "If everything must have a cause, then who or what caused God?" I said.

"Wait a second—I never said *everything* must have a cause," Craig replied. "The premise is that whatever *begins to exist* must have a cause. In other words, 'being' can't come from 'nonbeing.' Since God never began to exist, he doesn't require a cause. He never came into being."

I told him that sounded suspiciously like he was making a special exception for God.

"Atheists themselves used to be very comfortable in maintaining that the universe is eternal and uncaused," he replied. "The problem is that they can no longer hold that position because of modern evidence that the universe started with the Big Bang. So they can't legitimately object when I make the same claim about God—he is eternal and he is uncaused."

Reason #2: God Makes Sense of the Universe's Complexity

"In the last thirty-five years," Craig said, "scientists have been stunned to discover that the Big Bang was not some chaotic, primordial event, but rather a highly ordered event that required an enormous amount of information. In fact, from the very moment of its inception, the universe had to be fine-tuned to an incomprehensible precision for the existence of life like ourselves. And that points in a very compelling way toward the existence of an Intelligent Designer."

"'Fine-tuned' is a subjective term," I pointed out. "It could mean a lot of things. What do you mean by it?"

"Let me put it this way," he said. "Scientifically speaking, it's far more probable for a life-*prohibiting* universe to exist than a life-*sustaining* one. Life is balanced on a razor's edge."

As an example, he cited Hawking's writings. "He has calculated," Craig said, "that if the rate of the universe's expansion one second after the Big Bang had been smaller by even one part in a hundred thousand million million, the universe would have collapsed into a fireball."[21]

In short order, Craig proceeded to go down a list of several other mind-boggling statistics to support his conclusion.[22] Among them:

- British physicist P. C. W. Davies has concluded the odds against the initial conditions being suitable for the formation of stars—a necessity for planets and thus life—is a one followed by at least a thousand billion billion zeroes.[23]
- Davies also estimated that if the strength of gravity or of the weak force were changed by only one part in a ten followed by a hundred zeroes, life could never have developed.[24]
- There are about fifty constants and quantities—for example, the amount of usable energy in the universe, the difference in mass between protons and neutrons, the ratios of the fundamental

forces of nature, and the proportion of matter to antimatter—that must be balanced to a mathematically infinitesimal degree for any life to be possible.[25]

"All of this," said Craig, "amply supports the conclusion that there's an intelligence behind creation. In fact, the alternate explanations just don't add up.

"For instance, one theory is called 'natural necessity,' which means there is some unknown Theory of Everything that would explain the way the universe is. In other words, something in nature made it necessary that things would turn out this way.

"That concept falls apart, however, when you study it deeply. First, anyone who claims the universe must be life-permitting is making a radical claim that requires strong proof, but this alternative is merely an assertion. Second, there are other models of the universe that are different from ours, so it must be possible for the universe to have been different. And, third, even if the laws of nature are necessary, you still have to have initial conditions put in at the beginning on which these laws can operate."

Yet this wasn't the only possible alternative. I interrupted to raise a different scenario that sounded plausible on the surface. "What about the possibility that the fine-tuning of the universe is the result of pure chance?" I asked. "Maybe the whole thing is merely a big cosmic accident—a colossal roll of the dice, so to speak."

Craig sighed. "Lee, I'll tell you this: the precision is so utterly fantastic, so mathematically breathtaking, that it's just plain silly to think it could have been an accident. Especially since we're not just talking about simple odds but what theorists call 'specified probability,' which rules out chance beyond a reasonable doubt."

I wasn't ready to abandon the option of chance. "What if there were an infinite number of other universes existing apart from ours?" I asked. "Then the odds would be that one of them would have the right conditions for sustaining life—and that's the one in which we happen to find ourselves."

Craig had heard that theory before. "It's called the Many Worlds Hypothesis," he said. "Hawking has talked about this concept. Here's the problem: these other theoretical universes are inaccessible to us and therefore there's no possible way to provide any evidence that this might be true. It's purely a concept, an idea, without scientific proof. The prominent British scientist and theologian John Polkinghorne has called it 'pseudo-science' and 'a metaphysical guess.'[26]

"And think about it: if this were true, it would make rational conduct of life impossible, because you could explain away anything—no matter how improbable—by postulating an infinite number of other universes."

I wasn't quite following that line of reasoning. "What do you mean by that?" I asked.

"For example, if you were dealing cards in a poker game and each time you dealt yourself four aces, you couldn't be accused of cheating, no matter how improbable the situation. You could merely point out that in an infinite ensemble of universes, there will occur a universe in which every time a person deals, he deals four aces to himself and therefore—*lucky me!*—I just happen to be in that universe!

"Look—this is pure metaphysics. There's no real reason to believe such parallel worlds exist. The very fact that skeptics have to come up with such an outlandish theory is because the fine-tuning of the universe points powerfully toward an Intelligent Designer—and some people will hypothesize anything to avoid reaching that conclusion."

I knew that this astonishingly precise balance of the universe was one of the main factors in leading Harvard-educated Patrick Glynn, the Associate Director and Scholar-in-Residence at the George Washington University Institute for Communitarian Policy Studies, to abandon atheism and become a Christian. In his book *God: The Evidence,* he shoots holes in such other alternate theories as quantum mechanics and "baby universes," coming to this conclusion:

> Today, the concrete data point strongly in the direction of the God hypothesis.... Those who wish to oppose it have no testable theory to marshal, only speculations about unseen universes spun from fertile scientific imagination.... Ironically, the picture of the universe bequeathed to us by the most advanced twentieth-century science is closer in spirit to the vision presented in the Book of Genesis than anything offered by science since Copernicus.[27]

Reason #3: God Makes Sense of Objective Moral Values

Craig summarized his next point succinctly at the outset: "A third factor pointing toward God is the existence of objective moral values in the universe. If God does not exist, then objective moral values do not exist."

That, of course, raised the question of what he meant by "objective" values. Craig was quick to add both a definition and an illustration.

"Objective moral values are valid and binding independently of whether anyone believes in them or not," he explained. "For example, to label the Holocaust objectively wrong is to say it was wrong even though the Nazis thought that it was right. And it would still be wrong even if the Nazis had won World War II and succeeded in brainwashing or exterminating everybody who disagreed with them. Now, if God does not exist, then moral values are not objective in this way."

I was shaking my head. "Wait a second," I interjected. "If you're saying that an atheist can't have moral values or live a basically ethical life, then I have a problem with that. I have a friend who doesn't believe in God, and he's as kind and caring an individual as many of the Christians I know."

"No, I'm not saying a person must believe in God in order to live a moral life. The question is, 'If God does not exist, do objective moral values exist?' And the answer is, 'No.'"

"Why not?"

"Because if there is no God, then moral values are merely the products of socio-biological evolution. In fact, that's what many atheists think. According to philosopher Michael Ruse: 'Morality is a biological adaptation no less than are hands and feet and teeth,' and morality is 'just an aid to survival and reproduction . . . any deeper meaning is illusory.'[28]

"Or if there is no God, then morality is just a matter of personal taste, akin to statements like, 'Broccoli tastes good.' Well, it tastes good to some people but bad to others. There isn't any objective truth about that; it's a subjective matter of taste. And to say that killing innocent children is wrong would just be an expression of taste, saying, 'I don't like the killing of innocent children.'

"Like Ruse and atheist Bertrand Russell, I don't see any reason to think that in the absence of God, the morality evolved by *homo sapiens* is objective. After all, if there is no God, then what's so special about human beings? They're just accidental byproducts of nature that have only recently evolved on a tiny speck of dust lost somewhere in a mindless universe and are doomed to perish forever in a relatively short time.

"On the atheistic view, some action, like rape, may not be socially advantageous, and therefore it has become taboo in the course of human development. But that doesn't prove that rape is really wrong. In fact, it's conceivable that rape could have evolved as something that's advantageous for the survival of the species. Thus, without God there is no absolute right and wrong which imposes itself on our conscience.

"However, we all know deep down that, in fact, objective moral values *do* exist. All we have to do to see that is to simply ask ourselves: 'Is torturing a child for fun really a morally neutral act?' I'm persuaded you'd say, 'No, that's not morally neutral; it's really wrong to do that.' And you'll say that in full cognizance of the Darwinian theory of evolution and all the rest.

"A good illustration of this is a fund-raising letter sent out in 1991 by John Healey, the executive director of Amnesty International, in which he said: 'I am writing you today because I think you share my profound belief that there are indeed some moral absolutes. When it comes to torture, to government-sanctioned murder, to 'disappearances' ... these are outrages against all of us."[29]

"Actions like rape and child abuse aren't just behaviors that happen to be socially unacceptable—they are clearly moral abominations. They are objectively wrong. And such things as love, equality, and self-sacrifice really are good in an objective sense. We all know these things deep down.

"And since these objective moral values cannot exist without God and they unquestionably do exist, then it follows logically and inescapably that God exists."

Reason #4: God Makes Sense of the Resurrection

With this point, Craig said he was going to switch gears a bit. "We've been saying that if we have good reasons to believe in God, then we can believe in miracles," he said. "I've been giving reasons that point toward God's existence. But miracles themselves also can be part of the cumulative case for God. That's true, for instance, of the Resurrection. If Jesus of Nazareth really did come back from the dead, then we have a divine miracle on our hands and, thus, evidence for the existence of God."

I asked Craig to recap why he believes the historical evidence points toward that conclusion—"But," I stressed, "don't assume that the New Testament is the inspired word of God." He agreed for the sake of his answer to consider the New Testament to be merely a collection of first century Greek documents that can be subjected to analysis like any other ancient records.

"There are at least four facts about the fate of Jesus that are widely accepted by New Testament historians from a broad spectrum," Craig began. "The first is that after Jesus was crucified, he was buried by Joseph of Arimathea in a tomb. This is important because it means the location of the tomb was known to Jew, Christian, and Roman alike."

"What evidence do you have for this?" I asked.

"Jesus' burial is reported in extremely old information that Paul included in his first letter to the church in Corinth.[30] This information can be dated to within five years after Jesus' death, so it wasn't legendary. Further, the burial story is part of very old material that Mark used in writing his gospel, and his story lacks signs of legendary development. There are no traces of any competing burial story. What's more, it would be inexplicable for anyone to make up Joseph's involvement, since he was a member of the Sanhedrin that condemned Jesus.

"The second fact is that on the Sunday after the crucifixion, Jesus' tomb was found empty by a group of his women followers. This is substantiated by Paul's early report to the Corinthians, which implies the empty tomb, and by Mark's very old source material. So again we have early, independent attestation.

"And we have a lot more. For instance, the empty-tomb story lacks signs of legendary embellishment, and the earliest known Jewish response to the proclamation of Jesus' resurrection presupposes that his tomb was empty. In addition, it's reported that women discovered the tomb empty. Now, the testimony of women was considered so unreliable that they couldn't testify in Jewish courts. The only reason to include the highly embarrassing detail that women discovered the empty tomb is that the gospel writers were faithfully recording what really happened.

"The third fact is that on multiple occasions and under various circumstances, different individuals and groups of people experienced appearances of Jesus alive from the dead. This is almost universally acknowledged by New Testament scholars for several reasons.

"For example, the list of eyewitnesses to Jesus' resurrection, provided by Paul to the Corinthians, guarantees that such appearances occurred. Given the early date of the information and Paul's own acquaintance with the people involved, this cannot be dismissed as legendary.

"Also, the appearance narratives in the gospels provide multiple, independent attestation of the appearances. Even the skeptical New Testament critic Gerd Lüdemann has concluded: 'It may be taken as historically certain that Peter and the disciples had experiences after Jesus' death in which Jesus appeared to them as the risen Christ.'[31]

"The fourth fact is that the original disciples suddenly and sincerely came to believe that Jesus was risen from the dead despite their predisposition to the contrary. Jewish beliefs precluded anyone's rising from the dead before the general resurrection at the end of the world. Even so, the original disciples suddenly came to believe so strongly that God had raised Jesus that they were willing to die for that belief. New Testament scholar Luke Johnson said: 'Some sort of powerful, transformative experience is required to generate the sort of movement earliest Christianity was.'"[32]

"Okay, then," I said, "what do you think is the best explanation for these four facts?"

"Frankly, there is absolutely no naturalistic explanation that fits," he replied. "All of the old theories like 'the disciples stole the body' or 'Jesus wasn't really dead' have been universally rejected by modern scholarship.

"Personally, I think the very best explanation is the same one provided by the eyewitnesses: that God raised Jesus from the dead. In fact, this hypothesis easily passes all six tests that historians use in determining what is the best explanation for a given body of historical facts."[33]

Reason #5: God Can Immediately Be Experienced

Craig said that this last point was not so much an argument for God's existence, "but rather it's the claim that you can know that God exists wholly apart from arguments by having an immediate experience of him. Philosophers call this a 'properly basic belief.'"

Craig looked straight at me. "Lee, let me illustrate this concept with a question," he said. "Can you prove that the external world exists?"

The question caught me off guard. I thought about it for a moment and could come up with no logical sequence of arguments that would incontrovertibly establish such a thing. "I'm not sure how I would go about doing that," I conceded.

"That's right," he replied. "Your belief in the reality of the external world is 'properly basic.' You can't prove that the external world exists. After all, you could be a brain in a vat being stimulated with electrodes by a mad scientist so that you just think you're seeing an external world. But you'd have to be crazy to think that. So this 'properly basic belief' in the external world is entirely rational. In other words, it's appropriately grounded in our experience.

"In the same way, in the context of an immediate experience of God, it's rational to believe in God in a properly basic way. And I've had such an experience. God invaded my life as a sixteen-year-old, and for more than thirty years I've walked with him day by day, year by year, as a living reality in my experience.

"In the absence of overwhelming arguments for atheism, it seems to me perfectly rational to go on believing in the reality of that experience. This is the way people in biblical days knew God. As John Hick wrote: 'To them God was not a proposition completing a syllogism, or an idea adopted by the mind, but the experiential reality which gave significance to their lives.'"[34]

"But," I interjected, "what if an atheist says the same thing—that he has a 'properly basic belief' in the absence of God? Then you're deadlocked."

Replied Craig: "Philosopher William Alston says that in that case, the Christian should do whatever is feasible to find common ground, like logic or empirical facts, to show in a noncircular way whose view is correct.[35]

"That's what I've tried to do in these other four arguments. I know God exists in a properly basic way, and I've tried to show he exists by appealing to the common facts of science, ethics, history, and philosophy. Taken together, they form a powerful case for God and Christianity."

A KNOCK ON THE DOOR

As I had been observing Craig while he rattled off his reasons for believing in God, I noticed that he displayed a serene confidence in what he was saying. Before we finished, I wanted to get to the heart of what was producing that conviction.

"As you sit here right now, deep in your soul, do you know for a fact that Christianity is true?" I asked.

Without hesitating, he replied, "Yes, I do."

"Ultimately, how do you know for sure?"

"Ultimately, the way a Christian really knows that Christianity is true is through the self-authenticating witness of God's Spirit," he said. "The Holy Spirit whispers to our spirit that we belong to God.[36] That's one of his roles. Other evidence, though still valid, is basically confirmatory."

Craig thought for a moment, then asked, "You know Peter Grant, don't you?" I replied that, yes, I was a friend of the Atlanta pastor. "Well," Craig said, "he came up with a great illustration of how this works.

"Let's say you're going to the office to see if your boss is in. You see his car in the parking lot. You ask the secretary if he's in, and she says, 'Yes, I just spoke with him.' You see light from under his office door. You listen and hear his voice on the telephone. On the basis of all this evidence, you have good grounds for concluding that your boss is in his office.

"But you could do something quite different. You could go to the door and knock on it and meet the boss face-to-face. At that point, the evidence of the car in the parking lot, the secretary's testimony, the light under the door, the voice on the telephone—all of that would still be valid, but it would take a secondary role, because now you've met the boss face-to-face.

"And in the same way, when we've met God, so to speak, face-to-face, all of the arguments and evidence for his existence—though still perfectly valid—take a secondary role. They now become confirmatory of what God himself has shown us in a supernatural way through the witness of the Holy Spirit in our hearts."

"And this immediate experience of God is available to anyone who seeks it?"

"Absolutely. The Bible says God is knocking on the door of our life, and if we open it we will encounter him and experience him personally. He says in Revelation 3:20: 'Here I am! I stand at the door and knock. If anyone hears my voice and opens the door, I will go in and eat with him, and he with me.'"

Craig gestured toward the tape recorder that had been capturing our conversation. "We've been talking a lot about miracles today," he said in conclusion. "It's no exaggeration to say that knowing God personally and seeing him change lives are the greatest miracles of all."

I reached over and clicked off the recorder. Because of my own experience with God after years of living in the mire of immorality as an atheist, I knew he was right.

Based on how God has transformed my life, my attitudes, my relationships, my motivations, my marriage, and my priorities through his very real ongoing presence in my life, I realized at that moment that miracles like manna from heaven, the virgin birth, and the Resurrection—well, in the end, they're child's play for a God like that.

Deliberations

Questions for Reflection or Group Study

- After reading this interview, do you believe that miracles are possible? What would convince you that something miraculous had occurred? Do you believe the evidence of history establishes that the miraculous resurrection of Jesus actually took place? Why or why not?
- Which one of Craig's arguments for the existence of God was most persuasive to you? Why? Taken together, do these five points convince you that it's rational to believe in the existence of a miracle-working God? If not, how else would you account for these five categories of evidence?
- Craig prayed for God to miraculously cure his medical condition, but he hasn't. What do you think of his reaction to that? Have you prayed for God to intervene with a miracle in your life? What happened? How has this affected your attitude toward God? In what way was Craig's response to his situation helpful or not helpful to you?

For Further Evidence

More Resources on This Topic

- William Lane Craig. "The Problem of Miracles." In *Reasonable Faith*, 127–155. Wheaton, Ill.: Crossway, 1994.
- R. Douglas Geivett and Gary R. Habermas, eds. *In Defense of Miracles*. Downers Grove, Ill.: InterVarsity Press, 1997.
- C. S. Lewis. *Miracles: A Preliminary Study.* New York: Macmillan, 1947.
- J. A. Cover. "Miracles and Christian Theism." In *Reason for the Hope Within*, ed. Michael J. Murray, 345–374. Grand Rapids, Mich.: Eerdmans, 1999.
- Norman L. Geisler. *Miracles and the Modern Mind.* Grand Rapids, Mich.: Baker, 1992.

3

OBJECTION #3: EVOLUTION EXPLAINS LIFE, SO GOD ISN'T NEEDED

Charles Darwin didn't want to murder God, as he once put it. But he did.

Time magazine[1]

[Evolutionary theory] is still, as it was in Darwin's time, a highly speculative hypothesis entirely without direct factual support and very far from that self-evident axiom some of its more aggressive advocates would have us believe.

Michael Denton, molecular biologist[2]

Investigators were desperately searching for some piece of physical evidence to link suspect Ronald Keith Williamson to a brutal slaying that had shocked the tranquil community of Ada, Oklahoma, three years earlier.

They were having a difficult time building a solid case against Williamson, who vigorously denied strangling twenty-one-year-old Debra Sue Carter. So far their only evidence consisted of a witness who had seen Williamson talking with Carter earlier on the evening she was slain; an admission by Williamson that he once dreamed he had killed her; and the testimony of a jailhouse informant who claimed she had overheard him talking about the crime. Obviously, police needed more proof if they wanted to convict him.

Finally, detectives came up with the clincher. An expert took four hairs that had been found on the victim's body and elsewhere at the crime scene, examined them under a microscope, and concluded they were "a match" with samples taken from Williamson, according to a newspaper report. Their case bolstered by scientific evidence, investigators arrested Williamson and put him on trial.

It didn't take long for a jury to find the former minor-league baseball player guilty of the slaying and to dispatch him to Death Row. With the ghastly crime finally solved, the people of Ada breathed a collective sigh of relief. Justice had been done. The killer was going to pay with his life.

There was, however, one big problem: Williamson was telling the truth about his innocence. After he languished in prison for twelve years—nine of them awaiting execution—an analysis of DNA at the crime scene established that someone else had committed the murder. On April 15, 1999, Williamson was finally set free.[3]

But wait a second—what about the hair-comparison evidence that pointed toward Williamson's guilt? If his hair was found at the scene of the crime, didn't that implicate him in the slaying? The answer is disconcerting: hair evidence often purports to prove more than it actually does.

The newspaper report had glossed over some important nuances. The hair from the scene didn't really "match" Williamson's. A criminologist had merely concluded they were "consistent" with each other. In other words, their color, shape, and texture looked similar. Thus, the hairs from the crime scene could have come from Williamson—or perhaps they could have come from someone else.

Far from being as incriminating as fingerprints, hair analysis has been called "pseudo-science" by some legal analysts. Often jurors hear impressive-sounding testimony about what appears to be scientifically valid proof, and they conclude—incorrectly—that it establishes the defendant's guilt. Some prosecutors, in the heat of courtroom battle, have even been known to mischaracterize or subtly overstate the value of hair analysis during their closing arguments.[4]

In the case of Williamson, a federal judge called the hair evidence "scientifically unreliable" and said it never should have been used against the defendant. Even more troubling, hair evidence had been used against eighteen Death Row prisoners who subsequently were declared innocent in the last quarter century.[5]

The case of Ronald Keith Williamson is an eye-opening example of justice gone awry. His unwarranted conviction demonstrates how easy it is for jurors to draw sweeping conclusions that aren't really justified by the actual scientific facts. And in a sense, Williamson's story paralleled my own investigation into one of the most potent bits of scientific evidence that's commonly used against the existence of God.

DARWIN'S ACCOMPLISHMENT

Although there was much that led up to it, I guess you could say I lost the last remnants of my faith in God during biology class in high school. So profound was the experience that I could take you back to the very seat where I was sitting when I first was taught that evolution explained the origin and development of life. The implications were clear: Charles Darwin's theory eliminated the need for a supernatural Creator by demonstrating how naturalistic processes could account for the increasing complexity and diversity of living things.

My experience was not uncommon. Scholar Patrick Glynn has described how he took a similar path that ended up in atheism:

> I embraced skepticism at an early age, when I first learned of Darwin's theory of evolution in, of all places, Catholic grade school. It immediately occurred to me that either Darwin's theory was true or the creation story in the Book of Genesis was true. They could not both be true, and I stood up in class and told the poor nun as much. Thus began a long odyssey away from the devout religious belief and practice that had marked my childhood toward an increasingly secular and rationalistic outlook.[6]

In the popular culture, the case for evolution is generally considered shut. "Darwinism remains one of the most successful scientific theories ever promulgated," *Time* magazine said in its recap of the second millennium.[7] To Charles Templeton, it's simply beyond dispute that "all life is the result of timeless evolutionary forces."[8]

Biologist Francisco Ayala said Darwin's "greatest accomplishment" was to show how the development of life is "the result of a natural process, natural selection, without any need to resort to a Creator."[9] Michael Denton, the Australian molecular biologist and physician, agreed that Darwinism "broke man's link with God" and consequently "set him adrift in the cosmos without purpose."[10] He added:

> As far as Christianity was concerned, the advent of the theory of evolution ... was catastrophic.... The decline in religious belief can probably be attributed more to the propagation and advocacy by the intellectual and scientific community of the Darwinian version of evolution than to any other single factor.[11]

As the textbook *Evolutionary Biology* declares: "By coupling undirected, purposeless variation to the blind, uncaring process of natural selection, Darwin made theological or spiritual explanations of the life processes superfluous."[12] British biologist Richard Dawkins was speaking for many when he said that Darwin "made it possible to be an intellectually fulfilled atheist."[13]

In fact, prominent evolutionist William Provine of Cornell University candidly conceded that if Darwinism is true, then there are five inescapable implications: there's no evidence for God; there's no life after death; there's no absolute foundation for right and wrong; there's no ultimate meaning for life; and people don't really have free will.[14]

But is Darwinism true? I walked away from my formal education convinced it was. As my spiritual journey began taking me into the realm of science, however, I started to have an increasingly uneasy feeling. Like the hair-comparison evidence in the Williamson case, did the evidence for evolution purport to prove more than it actually does?

The more I investigated the issue, the more I saw how I had glossed over significant nuances in a rush to judgment, reminiscent of the Oklahoma murder trial. When I examined the matter thoroughly, I began to question whether the sweeping conclusions of Darwinists are really justified by the hard scientific facts. (A similar journey, incidentally, helped lead Glynn back to faith in God.)

This is not, I soon discovered, a case of religion versus science; rather, this is an issue of science versus science. More and more biologists, biochemists, and other researchers—not just Christians—have raised serious objections to evolutionary theory in recent years, claiming that its broad inferences are sometimes based on flimsy, incomplete, or flawed data.

In other words, what looks at first blush like an airtight scientific case for evolution begins to unravel upon closer examination. New discoveries during the past thirty years have prompted an increasing number of scientists to contradict Darwin by concluding that there was an Intelligent Designer behind the creation and development of life.

"The result of these cumulative efforts to investigate the cell—to investigate life at the molecular level—is a loud, clear, piercing cry of 'design!'" biochemist Michael Behe of Lehigh University said in his ground-breaking critique of Darwinism.[15] He went on to say:

> The conclusion of intelligent design flows naturally from the data itself—not from sacred books or sectarian beliefs.... The reluctance of science to embrace the conclusion of intelligent

> design . . . has no justifiable foundation. . . . Many people, including many important and well-respected scientists, just don't *want* there to be anything beyond nature.[16]

That last sentence described me. I was more than happy to latch onto Darwinism as an excuse to jettison the idea of God so I could unabashedly pursue my own agenda in life without moral constraints.

Yet someone who knows me well once described me as being "a sucker for the truth."[17] My training in journalism and law compels me to dig beneath opinion, speculation, and theories, all the way down until I hit the bedrock of solid facts. And try as I might, I couldn't turn my back on nagging inconsistencies that were undermining the foundation of Darwin's theory.

A PRIMORDIAL DETECTIVE STORY

Everyone concedes that evolution is true to some extent. Undeniably, there are variations within species of animals and plants, which explains why there are more than two hundred different varieties of dogs, cows can be bred for improved milk production, and bacteria can adapt and develop immunity to antibiotics. This is called "micro-evolution."

But Darwin's theory goes much further than that, claiming that life began millions of years ago with simple single-cell creatures and then developed through mutation and natural selection into the vast array of plant and animal life that populate the planet. Human beings came on the scene from the same common ancestor as the ape. Scientists call this more controversial theory "macro-evolution."

Initially troubling to me was the paucity of fossil evidence for the transitions between various species of animals. Even Darwin conceded that the lack of these fossils "is perhaps the most obvious and serious objection" to his theory, although he confidently predicted that future discoveries would vindicate him.

Fast forward to 1979. David M. Raup, the curator of the Field Museum of Natural History in Chicago, said:

> We are now about one hundred and twenty years after Darwin and the knowledge of the fossil record has been greatly expanded. We now have a quarter of a million fossil species, but the situation hasn't changed much. . . . We have even fewer examples of evolutionary transition than we had in Darwin's time.[18]

What the fossil record *does* show is that in rocks dated back some five hundred and seventy million years, there is the sudden appearance of nearly all the animal phyla, and they appear fully formed, "without a trace of the evolutionary ancestors that Darwinists require."[19] It's a phemonenon that points more readily toward a Creator than Darwinism.

That isn't the only argument against evolution. In his book *Origin of Species,* Darwin also admitted: "If it could be demonstrated that any complex organ existed which could not possibly have been formed by numerous, successive, slight modifications, then my theory would absolutely break down."[20] Taking up that challenge, Behe's award-winning book *Darwin's Black Box* showed how recent biochemical discoveries have found numerous examples of this very kind of "irreducible complexity."

I was particularly interested in a more fundamental issue, however. Biological evolution can only take place after there was some sort of living matter that could replicate itself and then grow in complexity through mutation and survival of the fittest. I wanted to go back even further and ask the cornerstone question of human existence: Where did life begin in the first place?

The origin of life has intrigued both theologians and scientists for centuries. "The most amazing thing to me is existence itself," said cosmologist Allan Sandage. "How is it that inanimate matter can organize itself to contemplate itself?"[21]

How, indeed? Darwin's theory presupposes that nonliving chemicals, if given the right amount of time and circumstances, could develop by themselves into living matter. Undeniably, that view has gained widespread popular acceptance through the years. But are there any scientific data to back up that belief? Or, like the hair-comparison evidence in the Oklahoma murder trial, is that analysis long on speculation but short on hard facts?

I knew that if scientists could convincingly demonstrate how life could emerge purely through natural chemical processes, then there's no need for God. On the other hand, if the evidence points in the other direction towards an Intelligent Designer, then Darwin's entire evolutionary house of cards would collapse.

This primordial detective story took me on a journey to Houston, Texas, where I rented a car and drove through the countryside and cattle ranches to the community of College Station, home of Texas A&M University. Down the block from the school, in a modest two-story frame house, I knocked on the door of one of the most influential experts on how life arose on primitive planet Earth.

THE THIRD INTERVIEW: WALTER L. BRADLEY, PH.D.

Walter L. Bradley caused a stir in 1984 when he co-authored the seminal book, *The Mystery of Life's Origin*, which was a devastating analysis of theories about how living matter was created. Eyebrows were raised because its foreword was written by biologist Dean Kenyon of San Francisco State University, whose book *Biological Predestination* had previously argued that chemicals had an inherent ability to evolve into living cells under the right conditions. Calling Bradley's book "cogent, original, and compelling," Kenyon concluded: "The authors believe, and I now concur, that there is a fundamental flaw in all current theories of the chemical origins of life."[22]

Since then, Bradley has written and spoken widely on the topic of how life began. He has contributed to the books *Mere Creation* and *Three Views of Creation and Evolution*, while he and chemist Charles B. Thaxton wrote "Information and the Origin of Life" for the book *The Creation Hypothesis*. His more technical articles include co-authoring, "A Statistical Examination of Self-Ordering of Amino Acids in Proteins," published in *Origins of Life and Evolution of the Biosphere*, which reflects his personal research in the origin-of-life field.

Bradley received his doctorate in materials science from the University of Texas at Austin and was a professor of mechanical engineering at Texas A&M University for twenty-four years, serving as head of the department for four years. An expert on polymers and thermodynamics, both of which are critically important in the life-origin debate, Bradley has been director of the Polymer Technology Center at Texas A&M and has received research grants totaling four million dollars.

He has consulted with such corporations as Dow Chemical, 3M, B. F. Goodrich, General Dynamics, Boeing, and Shell Oil, and has been an expert witness in about seventy-five legal cases. In addition, he is a fellow of the Discovery Institute's Center for the Renewal of Science and Culture and has been elected a fellow of the American Society for Materials and the American Scientific Affiliation.

The soft-spoken, self-effacing Bradley, who talks with an unhurried Texas drawl, is a strong family man. His two children and five grandchildren all live near each other in College Station, and they get together frequently. In fact, his wife, Ann; daughter, Sharon; and grandchildren Rachel, Daniel, and Elizabeth joined us for lunch at a local delicatessen after our interview.

As a scientist concerned with accuracy, Bradley answers questions in careful and complete sentences, making sure to acknowledge nuances and not to overstate his conclusions. He talks respectfully of the evolutionists he has debated through the years, including renowned chemistry professor Robert Shapiro of New York University, who called *The Mystery of Life's Origin* "an important contribution" that "brings together the major scientific arguments that demonstrate the inadequacy of current theories."[23]

Just three months after his retirement from Texas A&M, the fifty-six-year-old Bradley was relaxed and genial as we sat down at his dining room table. He was comfortably attired in a light blue sports shirt, blue jeans, and white socks with no shoes. It was clear from the outset that he had come prepared for our discussion: a pile of research papers was neatly stacked next to him. Ever the scientist, he wanted to be able to back up everything he said.

To lay some groundwork, I started our conversation by going back to Darwin himself. "His theory of evolution sought to explain how simple life forms could develop over long periods of time into increasingly complex creatures," I said. "But that ignores the important issue of how life arose in the first place. What was Darwin's theory about that?"

Bradley picked up a book as he began to answer. "Well, he didn't really have a good idea of how life arose," Bradley said, slipping on his gold-rimmed reading glasses. "In 1871 he wrote a letter in which he did some speculation—it wasn't even a hypothesis, just some brainstorming." With that, Bradley read Darwin's words:

> It is often said that all the conditions for the first production of a living organism are now present which could ever have been present. But if (and oh! what a big if!) we could conceive in some warm little pond, with all sorts of ammonia and phosphoric salts, light, heat, electricity, etc. present, that a protein compound was chemically formed ready to undergo still more complex changes, at the present day such matter would be instantly devoured or absorbed, which would not have been the case before living creatures were formed.[24]

Closing the book, Bradley said, "So Darwin was the first one to theorize that life emerged from chemicals reacting in some 'warm little pond.'"

"He makes it sound pretty easy," I remarked.

"Darwin may have underestimated the problem because it was widely thought back then that life sort of naturally develops every place," he replied. "People thought maggots would spontaneously develop from decaying meat. But two hundred years before the publication of Darwin's *Origin of Species,* Francesco Redi demonstrated that meat that was kept away from flies never developed maggots. Later, Louis Pasteur showed that air contains microorganisms that can multiply in water, giving the illusion of the spontaneous generation of life. He announced at the Sorbonne in Paris that 'never will the doctrine of spontaneous generation recover from the mortal blow of this simple experiment.'"[25]

Bradley let that thoroughly register with me before continuing. "But then in the 1920s, some scientists said they agreed with Pasteur that spontaneous genesis doesn't happen in a short time frame. But they theorized that if you had *billions* and *billions* of years—as the late astronomer Carl Sagan liked to say—then it might really happen after all."

"And that," I concluded, "is the basis for the idea that nonliving chemicals can combine into living cells if given enough time."

"That's exactly right," he said.

BUILDING BLOCKS OF LIFE

I told Bradley that in high school and college I was taught that the primitive earth was covered with pools of chemicals and had an atmosphere that was conducive to the formation of life. With energy supplied by lightning, chemicals in this "prebiotic soup"—over a period of billions of years—linked together and a simple life form emerged. From there, evolution took over.

"Who conceptualized that scenario?" I asked.

"Russian biochemist Alexander Oparin proposed in 1924 that complex molecular arrangements and the functions of living matter evolved from simpler molecules that preexisted on the early earth," he said. "Then in 1928, British biologist J. B. S. Haldane theorized that ultraviolet light acting on the earth's primitive atmosphere caused sugars and amino acids to concentrate in the oceans, and then life eventually emerged from this primordial broth.

"Later Nobel Prize winner Harold Urey suggested that earth's primitive atmosphere would have made it favorable for organic compounds to have emerged. Urey was the Ph.D. advisor to Stanley Miller at the University of Chicago, and it was Miller who decided to test this experimentally."

Miller's name rang a bell. I remember being taught in school about his landmark experiment in which he recreated the atmosphere of the primitive earth in a laboratory and shot electricity through it to simulate the effects of lightning. Before long, he found that amino acids—the building blocks of life—had been created. I can remember my biology teacher recounting the experiment with an infectious enthusiasm, suggesting it proved conclusively that life could have emerged from nonliving chemicals.

"This experiment was hailed as a major breakthrough at the time, wasn't it?" I asked.

"Oh, absolutely!" Bradley declared. "Sagan called it the single most significant step in convincing many scientists that life is likely to be abundant in the cosmos.[26] Chemist William Day said the experiment showed that this first step in the creation of life was not a chance event, but it was inevitable.[27] Astronomer Harlow Shapley said Miller had proven that 'the appearance of life is essentially an automatic biochemical development that comes along naturally when physical conditions are right.'"[28]

That was certainly impressive. "Did that close the issue?" I asked.

"Hardly," replied Bradley. "For a while, evolutionists were euphoric. But there was a major problem with the experiment that has invalidated its results."

I had never been taught anything in school about the Miller experiment being fatally flawed. "What was the problem?" I asked.

"Miller and Oparin didn't have any real proof that the earth's early atmosphere was composed of ammonia, methane, and hydrogen, which Miller used in his experiment. They based their theory on physical chemistry. They wanted to get a chemical reaction that would be favorable, and so they proposed that the atmosphere was rich in those gases. Oparin was smart enough to know that if you start with inert gases like nitrogen and carbon dioxide, they won't react."

My eyes got wide. This was a devastating critique of Miller's experiment. "Are you saying that the deck was stacked in advance to get the results they wanted?" I asked, incredulity in my voice.

"Essentially, yes," he replied.

"What was the real environment of the early earth like?" I asked.

"From 1980 on, NASA scientists have shown that the primitive earth never had any methane, ammonia, or hydrogen to amount to anything," he said. "Instead, it was composed of water, carbon dioxide, and nitrogen—and you absolutely cannot get the same experimental results with that mixture. It just won't work. More recent experiments have confirmed this to be the case."

I slumped back in my chair, amazed at the implications of what Bradley had disclosed. My mind flashed back to my biology teacher, who seemed so utterly confident that Miller's experiment validated the chemical evolution of life. Certainly that was the thinking of his day. Now new discoveries have changed everything—and yet there are generations of former students still living under the impression that the origin of life issue has been resolved.

"So the scientific significance of Miller's experiment today . . . ," I began, prompting Bradley to finish my sentence.

" . . . is zilch," he said. "When textbooks present the Miller experiment, they should be honest enough to say it was interesting historically but not terribly relevant to how life actually developed."[29]

I let out a low whistle. The analogy of the Oklahoma murder trial was proving to be even more accurate than I had thought.

ASSEMBLING A CELL

Before we went any further, I thought it would be important to understand some fundamentals about living matter to determine whether it's reasonable to believe it could have been the product of unguided chemical reactions.

"Let's start by defining the difference between a living system and one that's not living," I said to Bradley.

"A living system must do at least three things: process energy, store information, and replicate," he said. "All living systems do that. Human beings do these three functions, although bacteria do them much more quickly and efficiently. Nonliving things don't do them."

Again thinking back to Darwin's day, I asked, "Did Darwin consider basic living matter—say, for instance, a one-cell organism—to be rather simple?"

"Yes, he undoubtedly would have," came his response. "Darwin probably didn't think it would be very difficult to create life from nonlife because the gap between the two didn't appear very great to him. In 1905, Ernst Haeckel described living cells as being merely 'homogeneous globules of plasm.'[30] In those days they didn't have any way of seeing the complexity that exists within the membrane of the cell. But the truth is that a one-cell organism is more complicated than anything we've been able to recreate through supercomputers.

"One person very creatively—but quite accurately—described a single-cell organism as a high-tech factory, complete with artificial languages and decoding systems; central memory banks that store and retrieve impressive amounts of information; precision control systems that regulate the automatic assembly of components; proofreading and quality control mechanisms that safeguard against errors; assembly systems that use principles of prefabrication and modular construction; and a complete replication system that allows the organism to duplicate itself at bewildering speeds."

"That's extremely impressive," I said. "But maybe one-cell organisms are more complicated today due to the fact that they have developed and evolved through the eons. Maybe the first cells produced on the primitive earth were much more basic and therefore easier to create."

"Let's accept that theory," came Bradley's reply. "But even when you try to imagine what the minimal living cell would have been like, it's still not simple at all."

"What would go into building a living organism?" I asked—and then, before Bradley could open his mouth to reply, I quickly added: "And keep it basic."

"Okay," he said, clearing his throat. "Essentially, you start with amino acids. They come in eighty different types, but only twenty of them are found in living organisms. The trick, then, is to isolate only the correct amino acids. Then the right amino acids have to be linked together in the right sequence in order to produce protein molecules. Picture those plastic stick-together chains that kids play with—you have to put together the right amino acids in the right way to ultimately get biological function."

Imagining kids playing with plastic toys made the process seem—well, like child's play. "That doesn't sound very difficult," I said.

"It wouldn't be if you were applying your intelligence to the problem and purposefully selecting and assembling the amino acids one at a time. But, remember, this is chemical evolution. It would be unguided by any outside help. And there are a lot of other complicating factors to consider."

"Such as what?"

"For instance, other molecules tend to react more readily with amino acids than amino acids react with each other. Now you have the problem of how to eliminate these extraneous molecules. Even in the Miller experiment, only two percent of the material he produced was composed of amino acids, so you'd have a lot of other chemical material that would gum up the process.

"Then there's another complication: there are an equal number of amino acids that are right- and left-handed, and only left-handed ones work in living matter. Now you've got to get only these select ones to link together in the right sequence. And you also need the correct kind of chemical bonds—namely, peptide bonds—in the correct places in order for the protein to be able to fold in a specific three-dimensional way. Otherwise, it won't function.

"It's sort of like a printer taking letters out of a basket and setting type the way they used to do it by hand. If you guide it with your intelligence, it's no problem. But if you just choose letters at random and put them together haphazardly—including upside down and backwards—then what are the chances you'd get words, sentences, and paragraphs that would make sense? It's extremely unlikely.

"In the same way, perhaps one hundred amino acids have to be put together in just the right manner to make a protein molecule. And, remember, that's just the first step. Creating one protein molecule doesn't mean you've created life. Now you have to bring together a collection of protein molecules—maybe two hundred of them—with just the right functions to get a typical living cell."

Whew! Now I was beginning to see the enormity of the challenge. Even if Miller had been right about the ease with which amino acids could be produced in the primitive earth's atmosphere, nevertheless the process of putting them together into protein molecules and then assembling those into a functioning cell would be mindboggling.

"In living systems," continued Bradley, "the guidance that's needed to assemble everything comes from DNA. Every cell of every plant and animal has to have a DNA molecule. Think of it as a little microprocessor that regulates everything. DNA works hand-in-glove with RNA to direct the correct sequencing of amino acids. It's able to do this through biochemical instructions—that is, information—that is encoded on the DNA."

That raised an obvious issue. "Where did the DNA come from?" I asked.

"The making of DNA and RNA would be an even greater problem than creating protein," he replied. "These are much more complex, and there are a host of practical problems. For instance, the synthesis of key building blocks for DNA and RNA has never been successfully done except under highly implausible conditions without any resemblance to those of the early earth. Klaus Dose of the Institute for Biochemistry in Mainz, Germany, admitted that the difficulties in synthesizing DNA and RNA 'are at present beyond our imagination.'[31]

"Frankly, the origin of such a sophisticated system that is both rich in information and capable of reproducing itself has absolutely stymied origin-of-life scientists. As the Nobel Prize-winner Sir Francis Crick said, 'The origin of life appears to be almost a miracle, so many are the conditions which would have had to be satisfied to get it going.'"[32]

Even so, scientists have tried to come up with creative theories to try to explain how biopolymers (such as proteins) became assembled with only the right building blocks (amino acids) and only the correct isomers (left-handed amino acids) joined with only the correct peptide bonds in only the correct sequence. I decided to ask Bradley for his analysis of the most common hypotheses that scientists have proposed in recent years.

Theory #1: Random Chance

I had been taught in school that if chemicals had an ample amount of time to interact in the "warm little ponds" of early earth, eventually the improbable would become probable and life would emerge. Given Bradley's description of what would have to happen, however, I could see why this theory has lost support in recent years.

"Scientists once believed in the idea of random chance plus time yielding life, because they also believed in the steady-state theory of the universe," Bradley said. "This meant the universe was infinitely old, and who knows what could happen if you had an infinite amount of time? But with the discovery of background radiation in 1965, the Big Bang theory came to dominate in cosmology. The bad news for evolution was that this meant the universe was only about fourteen billion years old. More recent work has verified that the earth is probably less than five billion years old."

"Still," I interjected, "that's a long time. A lot can happen in five billion years."

"Actually, it's not as long as you think. The earth spent a long time cooling down to a temperature where it could support life. Based on the discovery of microfossils, scientists have now estimated that the time gap between the earth reaching the right temperature and the first emergence of life was only about four hundred million years. That's not much time for chemical evolution to take place. In fact, Cyril Ponnamperuma of the University of Maryland and Carl Woese of the University of Illinois have suggested that life may be as old as the earth and that its origin may have virtually coincided with the birth of the planet.[33]

"And not only was the time too short, but the mathematical odds of assembling a living organism are so astronomical that nobody still believes that random chance accounts for the origin of life. Even if you optimized the conditions, it wouldn't work. If you took all the carbon in the universe and put it on the face of the earth, allowed it to chemically react at the most rapid rate possible, and left it for a billion years, the odds of creating just one functional protein molecule would be one chance in a 10 with 60 zeroes after it."

Those odds are so infinitesimal that the human mind can't comprehend them. "That makes winning the lottery look like a sure thing," I quipped.

"Absolutely. Behe has said the probability of linking together just one hundred amino acids to create one protein molecule by chance would be the same as a blindfolded man finding one marked grain of sand somewhere in the vastness of the Sahara Desert—and doing it not just once, but three different times.[34] Sir Frederick Hoyle put it colorfully when he said that this scenario is about as likely as a tornado whirling through a junkyard and accidentally assembling a fully functional Boeing 747.

"In other words, the odds for all practical purposes are zero. That's why even though some people who aren't educated in this field still believe life emerged by chance, scientists simply don't believe it anymore."

Theory #2: Chemical Affinity

With random chance being soundly rejected as an explanation for the origin of life, scientists turned to another theory: that there must be some inherent attraction that would cause amino acids to spontaneously link up in the right sequence to create the protein molecules out of which living cells are made. This idea was popularized in a 1969 book, co-authored by Kenyon, which argued that the emergence of life actually might have been "biochemically predestined" because of these chemical bonding preferences.[35]

In fact, researchers studied the *Atlas of Protein Sequence and Structure* to determine whether certain amino acids preferentially positioned themselves next to a particular neighbor. They looked at ten proteins and performed a supporting experiment that seemed to suggest there was merit to this hypothesis.

"That sounds like a plausible explanation," I said to Bradley. "What's wrong with it?"

Although I didn't know it at the time, I was asking the scientist who was part of a team that refuted that hypothesis in 1986.

"We wrote a computer program to analyze not just ten proteins, but every one of the two hundred and fifty proteins in the *Atlas*," Bradley replied. "The results demonstrated conclusively that the sequencing had nothing to do with chemical preferences. Consequently, that theory bit the dust.[36] Even Kenyon, one of its biggest proponents, has repudiated the idea."

Theory #3: Self-Ordering Tendencies

This theory comes with an intimidating title: "non-equilibrium thermodynamics." Basically, the concept says that under certain circumstances, if energy is passed through a system at a fairly high rate, the system becomes unstable and will actually rearrange itself into an alternate and somewhat more complicated form.

An example is water draining out of a bathtub. Initially, the water molecules merely drop at random down the drain. But toward the end, the exit becomes much more orderly as the molecules spontaneously form a vortex.

"Some scientists have suggested that this tendency for molecules to become more orderly could be an analogy for how nature spontaneously organizes itself under certain circumstances," I said to Bradley.

He was thoroughly familiar with this hypothesis. "The problem is that the level of organization you're talking about is quite low. Even Ilya Prigogine, the thermodynamacist who has speculated about this theory, admitted recently that 'there is still a gap between the most complex structures we can produce in nonequilibrium situations in chemistry, and the complexity we find in biology.'[37]

"He's right. Compare the vortex in a bathtub to the mind-boggling complexity I described in creating living matter and you'll see it's an incredibly big gap."

Other scientists have brought up "equilibrium thermodynamics" as another possible solution. As an example, if water is cooled, it turns into ice. The molecules in ice are more orderly than the random molecules of water. Some have pointed to this as another way in which nature orders itself.

But Bradley discounted this theory for a similar reason. "Again," he said, "you have a very low level of information needed to create ice crystals compared to the high level of information required to order the amino acids to create protein molecules. That's why this theory hasn't caught on, either."

Bradley said there's a significant difference between the "order" found in some nonliving things and the "specified complexity" of living cells.

"Ice crystals have a certain amount of order, but it's simple, repetitive, and has a low amount of information, sort of like filling a book with the words "I love you, I love you, I love you" over and over again. In contrast, the kind of complexity we see in living matter has a high information content that specifies how to assemble amino acids in the right sequence, like a book being filled with meaningful sentences that communicate a story.

"Unquestionably, energy can create patterns of simple order. For instance, you could see ripples on the sand at a beach and know they were created by the action of waves. But if you saw the words, "John loves Mary" and a heart with an arrow drawn in the sand, you know that energy alone didn't create that. That's why the prominent information theorist H. P. Yockey has said, 'Attempts to relate the idea of order . . . with biological organization . . . must be regarded as a play on words which cannot stand careful scrutiny.'"[38]

Theory #4: Seeding from Space

Frustrated by the seemingly insurmountable obstacles to chemical evolution on earth, some scientists—including Crick, the co-discoverer of DNA—have proposed that the building blocks for life came from somewhere else in space. Hoyle and N. C. Wickramasinghe have speculated that particles the size of living cells could reach earth without being incinerated by the atmosphere. While in space, a thin layer of graphite dust could protect them from the destructive rays of ultraviolet light.

This theory was bolstered by the discovery of amino acids in the famous Murchison meteorite that fell in Australia in 1969, as well as in another meteorite that plummeted into Antarctica some 3.8 billion years ago.[39]

Crick and Leslie Orgel have gone even further by suggesting that life spores may have been intentionally sent to earth by an advanced civilization, perhaps, some have speculated, with the intention of making earth a wilderness area, zoo, or cosmic dump.[40]

"All of that sounds pretty bizarre," I said to Bradley. "But, then, maybe it's not as bizarre as the idea that God created everything."

Bradley's face betrayed his distaste for this approach. "The fact that scientists come up with these kind of outlandish proposals shows that they just can't imagine any way that life could have naturally developed on earth, and they're right about that," he said. "I like the way Phillip Johnson put it: 'When a scientist of Crick's caliber feels he has to invoke undetectable spacemen, it is time to consider whether the field of prebiological evolution has come to a dead end.'[41]

"The biggest flaw in this theory is that it doesn't solve the origin-of-life problem," Bradley explained. "Think about this: if you say life emerged somewhere else, that just moves the problem to another location! The same obstacles exist."

While that was certainly true, I saw another possibility. "Maybe another planet would have an atmosphere of ammonia, methane, and hydrogen, which would be more conducive to producing the building blocks of life," I suggested.

"Even if that were the case," he responded, "how did these amino acids and proteins get assembled into living matter? That's a problem of information—how to sequence the atoms in the right way—and that problem is independent of what the atmosphere is. Even if meteorites did deliver amino acids to earth, you still have the assembly problem.

"As A. Dauvillier said in *The Photochemical Origin of Life*, this theory 'is a facile hypothesis, a subterfuge which seeks to avoid the fundamental problem of the origin of life.'[42] Even Stanley Miller has no use for the theory. He told *Discover* magazine: 'Organics from outer space—that's garbage, it really is.'"[43]

Bradley picked up a report on a July 1999, international conference of origin-of-life scientists and read an excerpt to me: "Before the end of the conference's second day, researchers had to agree that extraterrestrial delivery could *not* have supplied all the needed prebiotic molecules."[44] The report went on to say that evolutionist Shapiro had studied the Murchison meteorite and "showed that side reactions would effectively prevent any prebiotic molecules in the meteorite from *ever* spontaneously forming life molecules."[45]

"Meanwhile," added Bradley, "Christopher Chyba, a planetary scientist from NASA, said that even though spacecraft have confirmed some organic compounds in comets out in space, 'at these velocities, at least ten to fifteen miles per second, the temperatures you reach on impact are so high that you end up frying just about anything.'[46] Besides, even if they made it to earth, you still have the problem of how they would have become assembled into living matter."

Theory #5: Vents in the Ocean

In 1977, scientists aboard the research submarine *Alvin,* half a mile below the surface of the Pacific west of Ecuador, discovered exotic hydrothermal vents on the sea floor. Tubeworms, clams, and bacteria, whose primary source of energy is sulfur compounds from the vents, were flourishing nearby. Since then, dozens of other vents have been found at various undersea locations.

This has led Jack Corliss, a marine biologist now working at NASA's Goddard Space Flight Center, to suggest that these vents might have provided an environment where the beginning of life might have been nurtured.

"The thing about hot springs is that they provide a nice, safe, continuous process by which you can go from very simple molecules all the way to living cells and primitive bacteria," he told *Discover* magazine.[47]

Some popular periodicals, long on speculation but short on specifics, have promoted this concept. However, when science writer Peter Radetcky asked origin-of-life researcher Miller about it, he got undisguised hostility. "The vent hypothesis is a real loser. I don't understand why we even have to discuss it," an exasperated Miller told him.[48]

Bradley also was skeptical when I brought up this theory. "Granted, the vents might provide an unusual energy source that could prompt some chemicals to become reactive," he said. "But it never even addresses the assembly problem. This theory does nothing to solve the problem of how to put together the building blocks of life in the right sequence and with the right connections."

What's more, he said, experiments by Miller and Jeffrey Bada at the University of California at San Diego have suggested that the high temperatures of these superheated vents would destroy rather than create complex organic compounds.

Explained Bradley: "It's now thought that all of the water in the ocean is periodically recirculated through these vents. If you were finally getting some molecules that were beginning to get bigger and more complex, they would be so fragile that they would get destroyed by the heat when they were recirculated. That means the time scale for chemical evolution would be shrunk dramatically. The vents would make you go back and start over at pretty short intervals—and that would work against the development of life."

Theory #6: Life from Clay

Another hypothesis popularized by the media in recent years was Scottish chemist A. G. Cairns-Smith's suggestion that life somehow arose on clays whose crystalline structure had enough complexity to somehow encourage prebiotic chemicals to assemble together.[49]

"What about that approach?" I asked Bradley.

"In one sense, the clays might help, because molecules don't like to react in water, and the surface of the clay might give them a less-wet environment," Bradley replied.

"But how would the clay be able to impart the information needed to sequence the chemicals together in the right way? The best that crystalline clay can do is provide very, very low-grade sequencing information, and it's going to be very repetitive. It's like the book I talked about a minute ago that's filled with 'I love you, I love you, I love you' over and over again. Is it orderly? Yes. Does it have much information? No. That's what a crystal is—nothing more than redundant information. It's far, far short of the specified complexity that living matter needs.

"Even Cairns-Smith has recognized the problems with his idea. He admitted in 1991, 'No one has been able to coax clay into something resembling evolution in a laboratory; nor has anyone found anything resembling a clay-based organism in nature.'"[50]

THE MOST REASONABLE INFERENCE

Time after time, origin-of-life scientists have come up empty when they've tried to theorize how chemicals could evolve into living matter. Recently, some have used computer models to try to show how chemical reactions might have occurred on the primitive earth, but these scenarios only work if the computer is programmed to eliminate some of the insurmountable obstacles that chemicals would have actually faced in the real world.

When a scientist at the Santa Fe Institute, where some computer simulations have been conducted, commented, "If Darwin had a computer on his desk, who knows what he could have discovered," origin-of-life expert John Horgan wryly remarked, "What indeed: Charles Darwin might have discovered a great deal about computers and very little about nature."[51]

With so many theories evaporating under scrutiny, I asked Bradley for his personal assessment of the state of research into how life emerged.

"There isn't any doubt that science, for the moment at least, is at a dead end," he replied. "The optimism of the 1950s is gone. The mood at the 1999 international conference on origin of life was described as grim—full of frustration, pessimism, and desperation.[52] Nobody pretends that any alternative provides a reasonable path of how life went unguided from simple chemicals to proteins to basic life forms."

Bradley reached over to a book and quickly located the quote he was after. "Klaus Dose, the biochemist who's considered one of the foremost experts in this area, summed up the situation pretty well," Bradley said, reading his words:

> More than thirty years of experimentation on the origin of life in the fields of chemical and molecular evolution have led to a better perception of the immensity of the problem of the origin of life on Earth rather than to its solution. At present all discussions on principle theories and experiments in the field either end in stalemate or in a confession of ignorance.[53]

Continued Bradley: "Shapiro argues strongly that all current theories are bankrupt.[54] Crick said out of frustration, 'Every time I write a paper on the origin of life, I swear I will never write another one, because there is too much speculation running after too few facts.'[55] Even Miller, some forty years after his famous experiment, said in a great understatement to *Scientific American:* 'The problem of the origin of life has turned out to be much more difficult than I, and most other people, envisioned.'"[56]

By coincidence, at about the same time as my interview with Bradley, Harvard University's outspoken evolutionist Stephen Jay Gould was asked to write an essay for *Time* magazine on whether scientists will ever figure out how life began. The result was a vague and equivocating piece that hemmed and hawed but never even came close to suggesting a single hypothesis for how life managed to emerge from nonlife.[57]

"What does one do with this scientific stalemate?" I asked Bradley.

"That depends a lot on one's metaphysics," he said. "Shapiro, whom I highly respect, says there must be some physical laws we haven't discovered yet which will eventually show us how life arose naturally. But there's nothing in science that guarantees a natural explanation for how life began. Science is neutral in regard to the outcome. It's hard to imagine new natural laws, because they're going to have characteristics that are consistent with the existing ones."

"Then what," I said, "is your own best hypothesis?"

Bradley didn't answer immediately. He glanced over at the stack of research papers, lingering for a moment before he looked back at me. When our eyes met, he continued.

"If there isn't a natural explanation and there doesn't seem to be the potential of finding one, then I believe it's appropriate to look at a supernatural explanation. I think that's the most reasonable inference based on the evidence."

That seemed to be a big concession for someone trained in science. "You don't see a problem in saying that the best explanation seems to be an Intelligent Designer?"

"Absolutely not. I think people who believe that life emerged naturalistically need to have a great deal more faith than people who reasonably infer that there's an Intelligent Designer."

"What prevents more scientists from drawing that conclusion?"

"Many *have* reached that conclusion. But for some, their philosophy gets in the way. If they're persuaded ahead of time that there isn't a God, then no matter how compelling the evidence, they'll always say, 'Wait and we'll find something better in the future.' But that's a metaphysical argument. Scientists aren't more objective than anybody else. They all come to questions like this with their preconceived ideas."

I quickly interjected, "Yes, but you came in with a preconceived idea that there *is* a God."

Bradley nodded. "Sure," he conceded. "And I've been pleasantly surprised, because a lower level of evidence probably would have satisfied me. But what I've found is absolutely overwhelming evidence that points toward an Intelligent Designer."

"So you think the facts point convincingly toward a Creator?"

"*Convincingly* is too mild a term," he replied. "The evidence is compelling. 'Convincing' suggests it's a little more likely than not; 'compelling' says you have to really work hard not to get to that conclusion."

"But it sounds so . . . ," I said, stumbling a bit while searching for the right word, "*unscientific*," I finally said.

"On the contrary," Bradley replied, "it's very scientific. For the past one hundred and fifty years, scientists have used arguments based on analogies to things we do understand to formulate new hypotheses in emerging areas of scientific work. And that's what this is about."

REASONING BY ANALOGY

The analogical method was described in the nineteenth century by astronomer John F. W. Herschel, who wrote: "If the analogy of two phenomena be very close and striking, while, at the same time, the cause of one is very obvious, it becomes scarcely possible to refuse to admit the action of an analogous cause in the other, though not so obvious in itself."[58]

"How does this apply to the origin-of-life issue?" I asked Bradley.

"If the only time we see written information—whether it's a painting on a cave wall or a novel from Amazon.com—is when there's an intelligence behind it, then wouldn't that also be true of nature itself?" Bradley said in responding.

"In other words, what is encoded on the DNA inside every cell of every living creature is purely and simply written information. We use a twenty-six-letter alphabet in English; in DNA, there is a four-letter chemical alphabet, whose letters combine in various sequences to form words, sentences, and paragraphs. These comprise all the instructions needed to guide the functioning of the cell. They spell out in coded form the instructions for how a cell makes proteins. It works just the way alphabetical letter sequences do in our language.

"Now, when we see written language, we can infer, based on our experience, that it has an intelligent cause. And we can legitimately use analogical reasoning to conclude that the remarkable information sequences in DNA also had an intelligent cause. Therefore, this means life on earth came from a 'who' instead of a 'what'."

Undeniably, it was a powerful and persuasive argument. Bradley seemed to reflect on it for a few moments before offering an illustration that would clinch his point.

"Did you see the movie *Contact?*"

"Sure," I said. "It was based on Carl Sagan's book."

"That's right," he replied. "In the movie, scientists are scanning the skies for signs of intelligent life in space. Their radiotelescopes just receive static—random sounds from space. It's reasonable to assume there's no intelligence behind that. Then one day they begin receiving a transmission of prime numbers, which are numbers divisible only by themselves and one.

"The scientists reason that it's too improbable that there would be a natural cause behind a string of numbers like that. This wasn't merely unorganized static; it was information, a message with content. From that, they concluded there was an intelligent cause behind it. As Sagan himself once said, 'The receipt of a single message from space' would be enough to know there's an intelligence out there.[59] That's reasoning by analogy—we know that where there's intelligent communication, there's an intelligent cause."

Bradley's eyes bored in on me as he delivered his conclusion. "And if a single message from space is enough for us to conclude there's an intelligence behind it, then what about the vast amounts of information contained in the DNA of every living plant and animal?" he said, his voice rising in emphasis.

"Each cell in the human body contains more information than in all thirty volumes of the *Encyclopaedia Britannica.* It's certainly reasonable to make the inference that this isn't the random product of unguided nature, but it's the unmistakable sign of an Intelligent Designer."

It was an argument without an answer. "Then," I said, "the origin of life is the Achilles heel of evolution."

"That's right. As Phillip Johnson said, 'If Darwinists are to keep the Creator out of the picture, they have to provide a naturalistic explanation for the origin of life.'"[60]

"Lee, they haven't been able to do it. Despite all their efforts, they haven't even come up with a single possibility that even remotely makes sense. And there's no prospect they will. In fact, everything is pointing the other way—in the unmistakable direction of God. Today it takes a great deal of faith to be an honest scientist who is an atheist."

"I BUILD MOLECULES"

By happenstance, over in nearby Houston, nanoscientist James Tour, a professor at Rice University's Department of Chemistry and Center for Nanoscale Science and Technology, had recently finished giving a speech.

With a doctorate in organic chemistry from Purdue University and post-doctoral work at Stanford University and the University of Wisconsin, Tour is on the cutting-edge of research into the molecular world. He has written more than one hundred and forty technical research articles and holds seventeen United States patents.

"I build molecules for a living," he said in introducing himself. "I can't begin to tell you how difficult that job is."

The purpose of his talk was not to dazzle the audience with descriptions of his latest high-tech efforts to store enormous amounts of information on a microscopic scale, replacing silicon chips that are large and unwieldy by comparison. Instead, it was to describe something else he has found the deeper and deeper he has probed into the awe-inspiring wonders of the molecular level: the fingerprints of an Intelligent Designer.

"I stand in awe of God because of what he has done through his creation," he said. "Only a rookie who knows nothing about science would say science takes away from faith. If you really study science, it will bring you closer to God."[61]

How ironic, I thought. Once, a rudimentary understanding of evolutionary science had propelled me toward atheism; now, an increasing grasp of molecular science was cementing my confidence in God. Like the Oklahoma murder case, my initial verdict had been based on flawed evidence that yielded a flawed conclusion.

The idea that undirected processes could somehow be responsible for turning dead chemicals into all the complexity of living things is surely, as microbiologist Denton observed, "no more nor less than the great cosmogenic myth" of our times.[62]

Time magazine was wrong: Darwin didn't murder God. There are simply too many powerful clues—especially in the astounding intricacy of unseen atoms and the uncanny chemical language encoded on the double helix of DNA—to establish that the Creator is alive and well.

DELIBERATIONS

Questions for Reflection or Group Study

- Describe the education you received in evolution. In what ways did it affect your outlook toward God?
- Before reading this interview with Bradley, how specifically did you believe life arose on earth? Did the interview change your viewpoint? How and why?
- Based on the evidence, do you believe it's reasonable to infer the existence of an Intelligent Designer? Why or why not? In light of the facts, do you believe it would take more faith to believe life arose naturalistically or through an intelligent cause?

FOR FURTHER EVIDENCE

More Resources on This Topic

- Charles B. Thaxton, Walter L. Bradley, and Roger L. Olsen. *The Mystery of Life's Origin.* Dallas: Lewis and Stanley, 1984.
- Phillip E. Johnson, *Darwin on Trial,* 2d ed. Downer's Grove, Ill.: InterVarsity Press, 1993.
- William A. Dembski, ed. *Mere Creation*. Downers Grove, Ill: InterVarsity Press, 1998.
- J. P. Moreland, ed. *The Creation Hypothesis*. Downers Grove, Ill.: InterVarsity Press, 1994.
- Michael J. Behe. *Darwin's Black Box.* New York: The Free Press, 1996.
- Michael Denton. *Evolution: A Theory in Crisis.* Chevy Chase, Md.: Adler & Adler, 1986.
- Hank Hanegraaff. *The Face that Demonstrates the Farce of Evolution.* Nashville: Word, 1998.

4

OBJECTION #4: GOD ISN'T WORTHY OF WORSHIP IF HE KILLS INNOCENT CHILDREN

The Bible tells us to be like God, and then on page after page it describes God as a mass murderer.

Robert A. Wilson[1]

But you, O Lord, are a compassionate and gracious God, slow to anger, abounding in love and faithfulness.

King David[2]

As I walked through the metal detectors and past the uniformed guards, I could sense an undercurrent of expectation at the White House. Despite efforts to project a business-as-usual facade, it was clear that something big was going on behind the scenes. The Monica Lewinsky scandal had been escalating, and pressure was building for President Clinton to come clean before Special Prosecutor Kenneth Starr released his long-awaited report.

Clinton arrived half an hour late for breakfast, sitting down directly across from me. His face was drawn, his eyes tired and puffy. Concerned for his health, I asked him how he was feeling.

"I was up until 3:00 A.M.," he replied in a husky whisper.

The press corps noisily jockeyed for position at the rear of the room, cameras whirring, pencils and notebooks poised. Clinton stood and took a few steps to a lectern. A hush fell over the room. His usual glibness was gone.

"I may not be quite as easy with my words today as I have been in years past," he told the small gathering of religious leaders. "I was up rather late last night thinking and praying about what I ought to say today."

He pulled out his glasses so he could read what he had written on a piece of paper. What followed was his most emotional and dramatic statement since news of his affair had broken in the media.

"I don't think there is a fancy way to say that I have sinned," he said, his eyes moist and his face pained. "It is important to me that everybody who has been hurt know that the sorrow I feel is genuine—first and most important, my family, also my friends, my staff, my Cabinet, Monica Lewinsky and her family, and the American people. I have asked all for their forgiveness. I have repented. . . . I must have God's help to be the person that I want to be."

There he was, the most powerful individual in the world, saying he had "a broken spirit" over his grossly immoral conduct with the former intern. All of his economic initiatives, all of his foreign policy efforts and social programs had faded into the background. Taking center stage was the stark and convicting issue of character.

Politicians are expected to fashion a positive public image, burnishing it to a lustrous shine through self-serving press releases and adroit spin-doctoring, but their real character often gets revealed through their private choices far from the spotlight. Certainly a person's behind-the-scenes moral decisions—their marital fidelity and fundamental honesty in their relationships—are relevant to how they will conduct the business of the people. After all, they unmask the true individual.

When I was an atheist I thought Christians could teach politicians a few tricks about creating a positive public image. Christians would focus relentlessly on certain appealing aspects of God's character—his love, his grace, his forgiveness, his compassion, his mercy—but underplay or ignore the biblical passages that seem to reveal more troubling aspects of his character.

When attention is focused on the little-mentioned Old Testament stories of massacres and other broad-scale bloodshed, suddenly God is seen in a different light. Like Clinton, whose carefully crafted public persona fell apart once credible stories of extramarital dalliances were documented, God's image as a loving and benevolent deity gets called into question by stories of seemingly cruel and vengeful behavior. Do these brutal accounts disclose the true character of God? And if they do, does he deserve to be worshiped?

Charles Templeton has his own opinion. "The God of the Old Testament is utterly unlike the God believed in by most practicing

Christians," he said. "His justice is, by modern standards, outrageous. . . . He is biased, querulous, vindictive, and jealous of his prerogatives."[3]

Atheist George H. Smith agrees. "The Old Testament God garnered an impressive list of atrocities," he said. "Jehovah himself was fond of directly exterminating large numbers of people, usually through pestilence or famine, and often for rather unusual offenses."[4] Smith likes to quote former president Thomas Jefferson as saying that the Old Testament accounts reveal God to be "cruel, vindictive, capricious and unjust."[5]

This issue is disturbing enough, but in addition there's an ancillary matter that demands to be explored. In evaluating the character of God, both critics and Christians cite the Bible as their source of information. But is it really a trustworthy book? Isn't the Bible chock full of contradictions and inconsistencies that undermine its reliability? Haven't its references to history been called into question by modern archaeology? Isn't it more likely a collection of imaginative legends than an accurate description of the Creator of the universe?

These two issues—the character of God and the reliability of the book that purports to tell us about him—were major hurdles when I was a spiritual seeker. At the time, I immersed myself in books and articles to try to come to some well-reasoned conclusions. I wish I could have done then what I was about to do now: sit down to interview a scholar who is one of the most well-known and effective defenders of Christianity in the world.

THE FOURTH INTERVIEW: NORMAN L. GEISLER, PH.D.

Norman Geisler can be a tenacious and intimidating debater when he's marshalling biblical references, archaeological findings, scientific discoveries, and historical events to refute someone bent on discrediting Christianity. His encyclopedic memory and rapid-fire delivery have overwhelmed many critics through the years.

But it was a soft-spoken and grandfatherly Geisler who invited me into his modest yet comfortable office at Southern Evangelical Seminary in Charlotte, North Carolina, where he is president of the school. Casually dressed in a multicolored sweater over a blue button-down shirt, he had an easy smile and a down-to-earth sense of humor. Even so, I soon found him focused with laser-beam intensity on the challenges I had come half way across the country to raise with him.

Geisler, a prodigious and award-winning author, has written, co-authored, or edited more than fifty books, including such standards as *General Introduction to the Bible, Inerrancy, Introduction to Philosophy, Philosophy of Religion, When Skeptics Ask, When Critics Ask,* and *When Cultists Ask.* One of his most recent volumes is the ambitious, 841-page *Baker Encyclopedia of Christian Apologetics,* which systematically discusses issues ranging from "absolute truth" to "Zen Buddhism."

Having studied at Wheaton College, the University of Detroit, Wayne State University, William Tyndale College, and Northwestern University, Geisler received his doctorate in philosophy from Loyola University in Chicago. He is the former chairman of philosophy of religion at Trinity Evangelical Divinity School in Deerfield, Illinois, and professor of systematic theology at Dallas Theological Seminary. His memberships include the American Philosophical Society, the American Scientific Association, and the American Academy of Religion.

Geisler has traveled widely—through all fifty states and twenty-five countries on six continents—giving lectures on the evidence for Christianity and debating such well-known skeptics as humanist Paul Kurtz. Consequently, I knew there was little chance that I would take him completely off guard by a question. However, I came armed with some of the most difficult issues of all.

As we sat across from each other in maroon leather chairs, I pulled out a piece of paper on which I had jotted the biting words of an esteemed American patriot whose criticism of Christianity is legendary.

"In 1794," I began, "Thomas Paine wrote in *The Age of Reason:* 'Whenever we read the obscene stories, the voluptuous debaucheries, the cruel and torturous executions, the unrelenting vindictiveness, with which more than half the Bible is filled, it would be more consistent that we called it the work of a demon, than the word of God.'"[6]

I looked up at Geisler to see if he was wincing at the sting of Paine's words. "That's a tough challenge," I said. "How would you respond to him if he were sitting here today?"

Geisler adjusted his gold-rimmed glasses, then remarked with a chuckle, "First of all, I'd say too bad he didn't have a Bible. When he wrote the first part of *The Age of Reason,* he didn't have one. But apart from that, I think he's confusing two things: what the Bible records and what the Bible approves."

"Give me some examples of the difference," I said.

"For instance, the Bible records Satan's lies and David's adultery, but it doesn't approve of them," he explained. "It's true that there are a lot of gross stories in the Bible. The book of Judges reports the raping of a woman, then cutting her in twelve pieces and sending one piece to each of the tribes of Israel.[7] But the Bible certainly doesn't approve of that. Secondly, I think that Paine is just factually wrong. The Bible doesn't have any cruel and torturous executions that God commanded."

I raised my hand to protest. "David was called a man after God's own heart, and yet the Bible says he tortured his enemies," I pointed out. "It says he 'put them under saws, and under axes or iron, and made them pass through the brick-kiln.'[8] That sounds cruel and torturous to me!"

"Not so fast," Geisler cautioned. "You're quoting from the King James Version, and it's open to misinterpretation there. The New International Version clarifies the original Hebrew language and says David 'brought out the people who were there, consigning them to labor with saws and with iron picks and axes, and he made them work at brick-making.' That's labor—not torture—and it's quite humane compared to the cruelties his enemies had unleashed. Besides, this is another case where the Bible records something but doesn't necessarily condone it."

Touché, I thought to myself. Quickly regrouping, I pressed on. "That passage aside, there's still a lot of carnage in the Old Testament," I said. "Isn't there a big difference between the often-cruel God of the Old Testament and the loving God of the New Testament?"

Geisler smiled. "It's interesting you ask that," he replied, "because I just did a study of every time the Bible uses the word that the King James Version translates as 'mercy.' I found it occurs 261 times in the Bible—and seventy-two percent of them are in the Old Testament. That's a three-to-one ratio. Then I studied the word 'love' and found it occurs 322 times in the Bible, about half in each testament. So you have the same emphasis on love in both.

"Ironically," he added, "you could make a case that God is more judgmental in the New Testament than the Old. For example, the Old Testament talks very little about eternal punishment, but the New Testament does."

"There's no evolution in God's character, then?"

"That's right. In fact, the Bible says, 'I the Lord do not change.'[9] In both testaments you've got the identical, unchangeable God—the one who is so holy he cannot look upon sin, and yet the one whose loving, merciful, gracious, and compassionate heart wants to pour forgiveness on all people who repent."

Compassionate? I thought to myself. *Merciful?* The time had come to get to the crux of the character issue.

GOD'S ORDERS TO KILL

I looked intently into Geisler's eyes. My voice leaked sarcasm as I posed the most pointed objection to God's character. "You talk about compassion and mercy," I said, "but those qualities are hard to understand when we see God ordering genocide by telling the Israelites in Deuteronomy 7 to 'totally destroy' the Canaanites and six other nations and to 'show them no mercy.'"

That got me started on a roll. "And that wasn't an isolated incident," I continued, picking up speed as I went. "God ordered the execution of every Egyptian firstborn; he flooded the world and killed untold thousands of people; he told the Israelites: 'Now go, attack the Amalekites and totally destroy everything that belongs to them. Do not spare them; put to death men and women, children and infants, cattle and sheep, camels and donkeys.'[10] That sounds more like a violent and brutal God than a loving one. How can people be expected to worship him if he orders innocent children to be slaughtered?"

Despite the force of the question, Geisler retained a calm and reasoned tone. "This shows," he said, "that God's character is absolutely holy, and that he has got to punish sin and rebellion. He's a righteous judge; that's undeniably part of who he is. But, second, his character is also merciful. Listen: if anyone wants to escape, he will let them."

Geisler paused. My questions clearly required a more extended explanation. "Lee, you've raised a whole bunch of good issues, and they deserve a thoughtful response," he said. "Do you mind if we go through those passages a little more carefully? Because if we do, I think we'll see the same pattern over and over."

I gestured for him to proceed. "Please," I said, "go through them. I really do want to understand."

"Let's start with the Amalekites," he began. "Listen, Lee, they were far from innocent. *Far* from it. These were not nice people. In fact, they were utterly and totally depraved. Their mission was to destroy Israel. In other words, to commit genocide. As if that weren't evil enough, think what was hanging in the balance. The Israelites were the chosen people through whom God would bring salvation to the entire world through Jesus Christ."

"So you're saying they deserved to be destroyed?" I asked.

"The destruction of their nation was necessitated by the gravity of their sin," Geisler said. "Had some hardcore remnant survived, they might have resumed their aggression against the Israelites and God's plan. These were a persistent and vicious and warring people. To show you how reprehensible they were, they had been following the Israelites and had been cowardly slaughtering the most vulnerable among them—the weak, elderly, and disabled who were lagging behind.

"They wanted to wipe every last one of the Israelites off the face of the earth. God could have dealt with them through a natural disaster like a flood, but instead he used Israel as his instrument of judgment. He took action not only for the sake of the Israelites, but ultimately for the sake of everyone through history whose salvation would be provided by the Messiah who was to be born among them."

"But the children," I protested. "Why did innocent children need to be killed?"

"Let's keep in mind," he said, "that technically nobody is truly innocent. The Bible says in Psalm 51 that we're all born in sin; that is, with the propensity to rebel and commit wrongdoing. Also, we need to keep in mind God's sovereignty over life. An atheist once brought up this issue in a debate, and I responded by saying, 'God created life and he has the right to take it. If you can create life, then you can have the right to take it. But if you can't create it, you don't have that right.' And the audience applauded.

"People assume that what's wrong for us is wrong for God. However, it's wrong for me to take your life, because I didn't make it and I don't own it. For example, it's wrong for me to go into your yard and pull up your bushes, cut them down, kill them, transplant them, move them around. I can do that in my yard, because I own the bushes in my yard.

"Well, God is sovereign over all of life and he has the right to take it if he wishes. In fact, we tend to forget that God takes the life of every human being. It's called death. The only question is when and how, which we have to leave up to him."

WHAT ABOUT THE CHILDREN?

Intellectually, I could understand Geisler's answer up to this point. However, emotionally it didn't go far enough. I was still unsettled. "But the children..." I persisted.

Geisler, himself the father of six children and grandfather of nine, was sympathetic. "Socially and physically, the fate of children throughout history has always been with their parents, whether that's for good or for ill," he pointed out.

"But, Lee, you need to understand the situation among the Amalekites. In that thoroughly evil and violent and depraved culture, there was no hope for those children. This nation was so polluted that it was like gangrene that was taking over a person's leg, and God had to amputate the leg or the gangrene would spread and there wouldn't be anything left. In a sense, God's action was an act of mercy."

"Mercy?" I asked. "How so?"

"According to the Bible, every child who dies before the age of accountability goes to heaven to spend eternity in the presence of God," he replied. "Now, if they had continued to live in that horrible society, past the age of accountability, they undoubtedly would have become corrupted and thereby lost forever."

"What makes you think children go to heaven when they die?" I asked.

"Isaiah 7:16 talks about an age before a child is morally accountable, before the child 'knows enough to reject the wrong and choose the right.' King David spoke of going to be with his son who died at birth. Jesus said, 'Let the little children come to me, and do not hinder them, for the kingdom of God belongs to such as these,' which indicates they will go to heaven.[11] There's a considerable amount of other scriptural support for this position as well."

I jumped on an apparent inconsistency. "If ultimately it was best for those children to die before the age of accountability because they would go to heaven, why can't the same be said about unborn children who are aborted today?" I asked. "If they're aborted, they're definitely going to heaven, but if they are born and grow up they might rebel against God and end up in hell. Isn't that a forceful argument in favor of abortion?"

Geisler's response came quickly. "No, that's a false analogy," he insisted. "First, God doesn't command anyone today to have an abortion; in fact, it's contrary to the teachings of the Bible. Remember, he's the only one who can decide to take a life, because he's the ultimate author of life. Second, today we don't have a culture that's as thoroughly corrupt as the Amalekite society. In that culture, there was no hope; today, there's hope."

"So," I said, "you don't think God was being unreasonable by ordering the destruction of the Amalekites?"

"You have to remember that these people were given plenty of opportunity to change their ways and to avoid all of this," he said. "In fact, if you take all of the Canaanites along with the Amalekites, they had four hundred years to repent. That's a very long time. Finally, after waiting centuries to give them an opportunity to abandon their path toward self-destruction, God's nature demanded that he deal with their willful evil. He certainly didn't act precipitously.

"Now, we have to keep in mind that those who had wanted to get out of this situation had already done so; they had ample opportunity through the years. Surely the ones who wanted to be saved from destruction fled and were spared.

"In Joshua 6, where the Bible talks about the destruction of Jericho and the Canaanites, you've got the same pattern. This was a thoroughly evil culture, so much so that the Bible says it nauseated God. They were into brutality, cruelty, incest, bestiality, cultic prostitution, even child sacrifice by fire. They were an aggressive culture that wanted to annihilate the Israelites.

"Again, you've got evil people who were destroyed but the righteous among them who were saved. For instance, Rahab, who protected the Israelite spies, was not judged with the other people. And look at what happened to the corrupt residents of the city of Nineveh. God was going to judge them because they deserved it, but they repented and God saved the whole bunch. So here's the point: *whoever has repented, God has been willing to save.* That's important to remember.

"You see, God's purpose in these instances was to destroy the corrupt nation because the national structure was inherently evil, not to destroy people if they were willing to repent. Many verses indicate that God's primary desire was to drive these evil people out of the land that they already knew had been promised for a long time to Israel. That way, Israel could come in and be relatively free from the outside corruption that could have destroyed it like a cancer. He wanted to create an environment where the Messiah could come for the benefit of millions of people through history."

"The pattern, then, was that people had plenty of warning?" I asked.

"Certainly," he said. "And consider this: most of the women and children would have fled in advance before the actual fighting began, leaving behind the warriors to face the Israelites. The fighters who remained would have been the most hardened, the ones who stubbornly refused to leave, the carriers of the corrupt culture. So it's really questionable how many women and children might actually have been involved anyway.

"Besides, under the rules of conduct God had given to the Israelites, whenever they went into an enemy city they were to first make the people an offer of peace. The people had a choice: they could accept that offer, in which case they wouldn't be killed, or they could reject the offer at their own peril. That's appropriate and fair."

I had to admit that these insights shed new light on the situation, especially his comments about the ample warning that had been given and the likelihood that women and children had probably evacuated the area prior to any battle. And as troubling as these passages are, it helped to know that Israel would offer peace before engaging in a fight and that the biblical pattern was that repentant people are given opportunities to avoid the judgment.

"God, then, was not being capricious?"

"He's not capricious, he's not arbitrary, he's not cruel. But, Lee, I have to tell you something: he is undeniably just. His nature demands that he deal with corrupt people who stubbornly and willfully persist in their evil. And isn't that what he should do? Isn't that what we want—for justice to be done? One of the key things to remember is that throughout history, for those who repent and turn to him, he's compassionate, merciful, gracious, and kind. In the end, we'll all see his fairness."

Still, there was another troubling episode—again, involving children—that seemed to challenge Geisler's opinion that God does not act capriciously. It involves one of the strangest episodes in the entire Bible.

COSMIC OVERKILL?

The prophet Elisha was walking down the road toward Bethel when he was confronted by some little children who teased him by making fun of his baldness. "Go on up, you baldhead!" they taunted. "Go on up, you baldhead!" He reacted by cursing them in the name of God. Then, in a stunning act of retribution, two bears suddenly emerged from the woods and mauled forty-two of them.[12]

"Now, Dr. Geisler, you insisted that God is not capricious," I said. "But that sounds like an outrageous response to a minor and silly offense. Mauling forty-two innocent little children just because they poked fun of some bald guy is awfully severe."

Geisler was well-acquainted with the issue. "The presupposition of your question is wrong," Geisler replied. "These were not small innocent children."

Having anticipated his response, I pulled out a photocopy of the passage and thrust it in his direction. "Yes, they were," I retorted. "Look right there," I said, pointing to the words. "It says 'little children.'"

Geisler glanced briefly at the page, immediately recognizing its source. "Unfortunately, the King James Version has a misleading translation there," he said. "Scholars have established that the original Hebrew is best translated 'young men.' The New International Version renders the word 'youths.' As best we can tell, this was a violent mob of dangerous teenagers, comparable to a modern street gang. The life of the prophet was in danger by the sheer number of them—if forty-two were mauled, who knows how many were threatening him in total?"

"Threatening him?" I asked. "Give me a break! They were just making fun of his baldness."

"When you understand the context, you'll see that this was much more serious than that," Geisler replied. "Commentators have noted that their taunts were intended to challenge Elisha's claim to be a prophet. Essentially, they were saying, 'If you're a man of God, why don't you go up to heaven like the prophet Elijah did?' Apparently, they were mocking the earlier work of God in taking Elijah to heaven. They were contemptuous in their disbelief over what God had done through both of these prophets.

"And their remarks about Elisha being bald were most likely a reference to the fact that lepers in those days shaved their heads. So they were assailing Elisha—a man of dignity and authority as a prophet of God—as a detestable and despicable outcast. They were casting a slur on not only his character, but on God's, since he was God's representative."

"Still," I said, "isn't that a rather minor offense?"

"Not in the context of those days," he said. "Elisha justifiably felt threatened by the gang. His life was in danger. They were, in effect, attacking him and God. This was a kind of preemptory strike to put fear in the hearts of anyone else who would do this, because this could be a dangerous precedent. If a menacing mob of teenagers got away with this and God didn't come to the defense of his prophet, just think of the negative effect that would have on society. It could open the door to further attacks on prophets and consequently a disregard for the urgent message they were trying to bring from God.

"In fact, as one commentator said, 'Instead of demonstrating unleashed cruelty, the bear attack shows God trying repeatedly to bring his people back to himself through smaller judgments until the people's sin is too great and judgment must come full force.... The disastrous fall of Samaria would have been avoided had the people repented after the bear attack.'"[13]

"Last of all," Geisler added, "I'd say once again that we have to consider the sovereignty of God. It wasn't Elisha who took their lives; it was the God who created them who let the bears loose. And if he created life, he has every right to take it away. The attack of this gang on the prophet revealed their true attitudes toward God, and it's always a perilous path that leads to destruction when you defiantly curse and stubbornly oppose God."

I folded the photocopy of the passage. "Then it's a misreading of the original text to see these as mere children," I said.

"That's right," he said. "The Hebrew that was used to describe them indicates they were most likely between the ages of twelve and thirty. In fact, one of the same Hebrew words is used elsewhere to describe men in the army.[14] As you can see, when everything is put into perspective, you get a much different picture than was originally supposed."

By now, Geisler's answers had deflated much of the case against God's character by bringing some balance and context to understanding his apparent intent in these controversial episodes. While these passages were still sticking points, seeing the other side did make it easier to give God the benefit of the doubt, especially in light of the preponderance of other evidence for his compassion and love.

There was also, however, a related matter about God's character that concerns many people these days: how he has dealt with animals.

Why did he create a world where predators constantly stalk prey and where violent death is an integral part of life? And more fundamentally, doesn't that reveal something disturbing about his attitude?

THE PAIN OF ANIMALS

Charles Templeton raised the issue of suffering in the animal kingdom when he wrote in his book *Farewell to God:*

> The grim and inescapable reality is that all life is predicated on death. Every carnivorous creature must kill and devour other creatures.... How could a loving and omnipotent God create such horrors?... Surely it would not be beyond the competence of an omniscient deity to create an animal world that could be sustained and perpetuated without suffering and death.[15]

"What about that?" I asked Geisler after reading Templeton's quote to him.

"He's got a lot of truth in there," Geisler replied.

That wasn't the response I was expecting. "You think so?" I asked.

"Yes," he said. "But, unfortunately, it's like a glass of good water with a drop of arsenic in it. There's good water there, but it's poisoned."

"How so?"

"The good water is, yes, God can create those kind of animals. And the fact is, he did. The original paradise had those kind of animals and the paradise to come—the paradise restored—is going to have those kind of animals. In fact, we're told that God originally created animals and human beings to be herbivorous."

With that, Geisler reached under his chair and removed a Bible. He opened it toward its beginning; his eyes scanned the page until he stopped near the end of the first chapter, reading:

> Then God said, "I give you every seed-bearing plant on the face of the whole earth and every tree that has fruit with seed in it. They will be yours for food. And to all the beasts of the earth and all the birds of the air and all the creatures that move on the ground—everything that has the breath of life in it—I give every green plant for food." And it was so.[16]

Shutting the book, Geisler continued. "God did not appoint animals to be eaten in paradise, and animals weren't eating each other. The prophet Isaiah said someday God will 'create new heavens and a new earth' where 'the wolf and the lamb will feed together, and the lion will eat straw like the ox.'[17] In other words, there's not going to be the kind of killing that goes on now.

"In sum, everything that God created was good. What changed things was the Fall. When God was told, in effect, to shove off, he partially did. Romans 8 says all creation was affected—that includes plant life, human beings, animals, everything. There were fundamental genetic changes; we see, for instance, how life spans rapidly decreased after the Fall. God's plan was not designed to be this way; it's only this way because of sin. Ultimately, it will be remedied."

"But in instituting the animal sacrifice system in the Old Testament, wasn't God being cruel to animals?" I asked.

"The manner in which these animals were killed was quite humane. It was the most painless way to die. And there was no waste. They ate the meat, they used the skin for clothing, so essentially they were growing and harvesting animals. This was not an attempt to eliminate a species. And of course, there was an important reason for the animal sacrifices—they pointed ahead toward the ultimate sacrifice of Jesus Christ, the lamb of God, on the cross as payment for our sin."

"What about all the pain in the world as a result of animals hunting and killing other animals?" I asked. "The sum total of suffering that God allows in the world is absolutely enormous."

"I think that entire presupposition is wrong," he replied. "As C. S. Lewis said, there is no sum total of pain. It's a misnomer. No one person or animal experiences the sum total of pain. In fact, no one person experiences at one time the sum total of pain of their lifetime. If you had thirty ounces of pain spread over thirty years, you only get an ounce a year and therefore only a fraction of an ounce a day.

"As far as animals are concerned, we have to remember that the Bible clearly forbids their abuse. Christians should oppose any mistreatment of animals. However, I would challenge the premise of the animal-rights movement that animals have moral rights. They are not moral creatures. Now, moral people can do immoral things to animals, but the Bible says, 'A righteous man cares for the needs of his animal.'[18] They are to serve us and help us, and it's morally wrong to be cruel to them."

CAN THE BIBLE BE TRUSTED?

In assessing the character of God, Geisler was relying on the Bible. Having authored a book on the inerrancy of Scripture, Geisler's opinion of it is well known: he believes the Bible to be uniquely inspired by God and factual in all it teaches and touches upon. Still, is there any rational reason to believe that the Bible really does accurately reveal the truth about God?

George H. Smith, the atheistic philosopher, thinks not. "The Bible shows no traces whatsoever of supernatural influence," he said. "Quite the contrary, it is obviously the product of superstitious men who, at times, were willing to deceive if it would further their doctrines."[19]

Templeton cavalierly dismisses most of the Bible as being "embellished folk tales," adding that it is "no longer possible for an informed man or woman to believe that ... the Bible is either a reliable document ... or, as the Christian church insists, the infallible Word of God."[20]

During my years as an atheist, I mocked the fantastical tales and blatant mythology that I believed disqualified the Bible from being a divinely inspired book—an opinion, incidentally, that quite conveniently relieved me from any need to follow its moral dictates. Although I had never thoroughly studied its contents, I was quick to reject the Bible in order to free myself to live the kind of corrupt lifestyle that was blatantly at odds with its tenets.

My time with Geisler was a rare opportunity to hear first-hand why he draws the opposite conclusion and so zealously defends the Bible as being trustworthy. I stood to stretch my legs, walking over to a bookshelf and casually scanning the titles. Then I turned and said, "Everything hinges on whether the Bible is true. What's your basis for believing it is?"

With characteristic confidence, Geisler replied, "There's more evidence that the Bible is a reliable source than there is for any other book from the ancient world."

To me, however, that seemed more of a conclusion than evidence. "You're going to have to give me some facts to back that up," I said, sitting back down on the edge of my seat in anticipation of Geisler's response.

"There's lots of evidence I could talk about," he began. "I could talk about the Bible's unity—sixty-six books written in different literary styles by perhaps forty different authors with diverse backgrounds over fifteen hundred years, and yet the Bible amazingly unfolds one continuous drama with one central message. That points to the existence of the divine Mind that the writers claimed inspired them.

"And there's the Bible's transforming power—from the beginning, it has renewed people; given them hope, courage, purpose, wisdom, guidance, and power; and formed an anchor for their lives. While early Islam was spread by the sword, early Christianity spread by the Spirit, even while Christians were being killed by Roman swords.

"I believe the most convincing evidence falls into two categories, however. First, there's archaeological confirmation of its reliability, and, second, there's miraculous confirmation of its divine authority."

Reason #1: Confirmation by Archaeology

Geisler started his discussion of the archaeological evidence by quoting the words of Jesus, who said: "I have spoken to you of earthly things and you do not believe; how then will you believe if I speak of heavenly things?"[21]

"Conversely," said Geisler, "if we can trust the Bible when it's telling us about straightforward earthly things that can be verified, then we can trust it in areas where we can't directly verify it in an empirical way."

"How, then, has the Bible been corroborated?" I asked. Having investigated some of the archaeological confirmation of the New Testament in my previous book, *The Case for Christ,* I was especially interested in archaeology and the Old Testament, and that's where I asked Geisler to begin.

"There have been thousands—not hundreds—of archaeological finds in the Middle East that support the picture presented in the biblical record. There was a discovery not long ago confirming King David. The patriarchs—the narratives about Abraham, Isaac, and Jacob—were once considered legendary, but as more has become known these stories are increasingly corroborated. The destruction of Sodom and Gomorrah was thought to be mythological until evidence was uncovered that all five of the cities mentioned in Genesis were, in fact, situated just as the Old Testament said. As far as their destruction goes, archaeologist Clifford Wilson said there is 'permanent evidence of the great conflagration that took place in the long distant past.'[22]

"Furthermore," Geisler added, "various aspects of the Jewish captivity have been confirmed. Also, every reference in the Old Testament to an Assyrian king has been proven correct; an excavation during the 1960s confirmed that the Israelites could, indeed, have entered Jerusalem by way of a tunnel during David's reign; there is evidence the world did have a single language at one time, as the Bible says; the site of Solomon's temple is now being excavated; and on and on. Many times, archaeologists have been skeptical of the Old Testament, only to have new discoveries corroborate the biblical account."

"For example . . . ," I said.

"For instance, Samuel says that after Saul's death his armor was put in the temple of Ashtoroth, who was a Canaanite fertility goddess, at Bethshan, while Chronicles reports that his head was put in the temple of a Philistine corn god named Dagon. Now, archaeologists thought that must have been an error and therefore the Bible was unreliable. They didn't think enemies would have had temples in the same place at the same time."

"What did the archaeologists find?" I asked.

"They confirmed through excavations that there were two temples at that site, one each for Dagon and Ashtoroth. They were separated by a hallway. As it turned out, the Philistines had apparently adopted Ashtaroth as one of their own goddesses. The Bible was right after all.

"That kind of phenomenon has happened again and again. The Bible makes about three dozen references to the Hittites, but critics used to charge that there was no evidence that such people ever existed. Now archaeologists digging in modern Turkey have discovered the records of the Hittites. As the great archaeologist William F. Albright declared, 'There can be no doubt that archaeology has confirmed the substantial historicity of the Old Testament tradition.'"[23]

I asked Geisler to continue by briefly summarizing why he believes that archaeology corroborates the New Testament.

"The noted Roman historian Colin J. Hemer, in *The Book of Acts in the Setting of Hellenistic History*, shows how archaeology has confirmed not dozens, but hundreds and hundreds of details from the biblical account of the early church," Geisler said. "Even small details have been corroborated, like which way the wind blows, how deep the water is a certain distance from shore, what kind of disease a particular island had, the names of local officials, and so forth.

"Now, Acts was authored by the historian Luke. Hemer gives more than a dozen reasons for why Acts had to have been written before A.D. 62, or about thirty years after Jesus' crucifixion. Even earlier, Luke wrote the gospel of Luke, which is substantially the same as the other biblical accounts of Jesus' life.

"So here you have an impeccable historian, who has been proven right in hundreds of details and never proven wrong, writing the whole history of Jesus and the early church. And it's written within one generation while eyewitnesses were still alive and could have disputed it if it were exaggerated or false. You don't have anything like that from any other religious book from the ancient world."[24]

"Is Hemer a lone voice on that?" I asked.

"Hardly," came the reply. "Prominent historian Sir William Ramsay started out as a skeptic, but after studying Acts he concluded that 'in various details the narrative showed marvelous truth.'[25] The great Oxford University classical historian A. N. Sherwin-White said, 'For Acts the confirmation of historicity is overwhelming,' and that 'any attempt to reject its basic historicity must now appear absurd.'[26]

"Earlier, I mentioned archaeologist William F. Albright, who was a leader in the American School of Oriental Research for forty years. He started out as a liberal but became more and more conservative as he studied the archaeological record. He concluded that the radical New Testament critics are 'pre-archaeological' and their views are 'quite antiquated.'"[27]

I sat back in my leather chair as I reflected on Geisler's barrage of facts and quotes. The argument was strong: if archaeology shows the Bible was accurate in what can be checked out, why would it be any less accurate in its other points? That only proves so much, however.

"Even if archaeology does confirm that the Bible is historically accurate, that doesn't mean it's divinely authoritative," I said.

"Correct," Geisler said crisply. "The only reason why anyone should accept the Bible as divinely authoritative is because it has miraculous confirmation."

Reason #2: Evidence of Divine Origin

Geisler thumbed through his well-worn Bible, turning all the way to its opening sentence and then balancing the open book on his lap.

"It all goes back to whether the first verse of the Bible is true when it says, 'In the beginning God created the heavens and the earth,'" Geisler said. "I believe there's overwhelming scientific evidence that it is true—everything that has a beginning has a beginner, the universe had a beginning, therefore it had a beginner; the universe was tweaked and fine tuned from the very moment of creation for the emergence of human life; and so on."

I interrupted to inform him that I had already interviewed William Lane Craig about the evidence pointing to a divine origin of the universe.

"Ah, good," he said. "What people often forget is that if this first verse is true, not only are miracles possible, but miracles are actual, because the biggest miracle has already happened—making something out of nothing. What's harder: for Jesus to take water and turn it into wine or to take a handful of nothing and make water? It's a lot harder to make water out of nothing than to make wine out of water.

"A skeptic once said to me, 'I don't believe the Bible because it has miracles.' I said, 'Name one.' He said, 'Turning water into wine. Do you believe that?' I said, 'Yeah, it happens all the time.' He said, 'What do you mean?' I said, 'Well, rain goes through the grapevine, up into the grape, and the grape turns into wine. All Jesus did was speed it up a little bit.'

"My point is if you've got a God who can make something out of nothing, then he can make miracles. And then the only thing we have to look at is what book in the world has been miraculously confirmed. There's only one, and that's the Bible."

"Okay," I said. "Tell me how."

Geisler raised two fingers. "Two ways," he said. "First, the Bible is miraculously confirmed by the fulfillment of predictive prophecies, and, second, it's confirmed by the miracles performed by those who purported to be speaking for God."

CONFIRMATION BY PROPHECIES

Geisler began with a sweeping sentence: "The Bible is the only book in the world that has precise, specific predictions that were made hundreds of years in advance and that were literally fulfilled."

Gesturing toward one of the books packed into his shelves, he continued by saying, "According to *Barton Payne's Encyclopedia of Biblical Prophecy*, there are 191 predictions in the Old Testament about the coming of Christ, including his ancestry, the city in which he would be born, that he would be born of a virgin, precisely the time in history when he would die, and so on.

"In fact, Psalm 22:16 says his hands and feet would be pierced; verse 14 says his bones would be out of joint; verse 18 talks about the casting of lots for his garments; and Zechariah 12:10 says he would be pierced, as Jesus was with a lance. That's obviously a picture of his crucifixion—however, it was written before crucifixion was even implemented as a method of execution by the Romans. The Jews stoned people to death back then.

"And, of course, Isaiah 53:2–12 has perhaps the most amazing predictions about Christ in the entire Old Testament. It foretells twelve aspects of his passion that were all fulfilled—he would be rejected, be a man of sorrow, live a life of suffering, be despised by others, carry our sorrow, be smitten and afflicted by God, be pierced for our transgressions, be wounded for our sins, would suffer like a lamb, would die with the wicked, would be sinless, and would pray for others."

I spoke up. "Wait a second," I said. "If you talk to a rabbi, he'll tell you that passage refers symbolically to Israel, not to the Messiah."

Geisler shook his head. "In Old Testament times, the Jewish rabbis *did* consider this to be a prophecy concerning the Messiah. That's the opinion that's really relevant," he said.

"Only later, after Christians pointed out this was obviously referring to Jesus, did they begin saying it was really about the suffering Jewish nation. But clearly that's wrong. Isaiah customarily refers to the Jewish people in the first-person plural, like 'our' or 'we,' but he always refers to the Messiah in the third-person singular, like 'he' and 'him'—and that's what he did in Isaiah 53. Plus, anyone who reads it for themselves will readily see it's referring to Jesus. Maybe that's why it's usually skipped over in synagogues these days.

"So here you have incredible predictions that were literally fulfilled in the life of one man, even though he had no control over most of them. For instance, he couldn't have arranged his ancestry, the timing of his birth, and so on. These prophecies were written two hundred to four hundred years in advance. No other book in the world has this. The Bible is the only book that's supernaturally confirmed this way."

I pondered this. "But Old Testament prophets weren't the only ones in history who have made predictions that have amazingly come true. For instance, Nostradamus, the physician and astrologer who lived in the 1500s, is famous for having made forecasts about the future. Didn't he predict the rise of Hitler and Nazi Germany?" I said, more as a statement than a question. "If he can do that, what's so special about the predictive prophecies of the Bible?"

"The problem with Nostradamus and so many other so-called psychics is that their predictions are often very enigmatic, ambiguous, and inaccurate," Geisler retorted.

"But what about the Hitler prediction?" I demanded. "That's pretty specific."

"Actually, it wasn't specific at all," he replied.

Geisler stood up and strolled over to his bookshelf, pulling down one of his books and rummaging through it until he located what he was after. Then he read the words of Nostradamus' prediction:

> Followers of sects, great troubles are in store for the Messenger. A beast upon the theater prepares the scenical play. The inventor of that wicked feat will be famous. By sects the world will be confused and divided.... Beasts mad with hunger will swim across rivers. Most of the army will be against the Lower Danube *[Hister sera]*. The great one shall be dragged in an iron cage when the child brother *[de Germain]* will observe nothing.[28]

Continued Geisler, "Obviously, this is not a reference to Adolf Hitler. The word isn't 'Hitler' but 'Hister,' and it's clearly not a person but a place. The Latin phrase *de Germain* should be interpreted as 'brother' or 'near relative,' not Germany. He doesn't cite any dates or even a general time frame. Besides, what does he mean by 'beasts' and 'iron cage?' It's so confusing that the entire prophecy is meaningless.

"The pattern is that Nostradamus' predictions are very ambiguous and could fit a great variety of events. His followers are inconsistent in how they interpret what he said. And some of his prophecies have been shown to be false. In fact, not a single prediction of Nostradamus has ever been proven genuine."

"I'll concede that many psychics, like Nostradamus, are vague in their predictions," I said. "But you have to admit that the same is true of some of the biblical prophecies."

"Granted, not all biblical prophecy is sharp," Geisler replied. "However, many prophecies are very specific. How much more detailed can you get than accurately predicting when Jesus would die, as Daniel 9:24–26 did? When you do the math, you find that this passage pinpoints when Jesus would enter human history. And what about predictions of his birth place or how he would suffer and die? The specificity is astounding—and they have invariably proven to be true."

I countered with a contemporary example of a psychic whose predictions often were quite detailed. "In 1956, Jeane Dixon predicted a Democrat would win the 1960 presidential election and be assassinated in office. That was fulfilled in John F. Kennedy—and that's a pretty specific prophecy."

Geisler wasn't impressed. "She also predicted the 1960 election would be dominated by labor, which it wasn't. She later hedged her bets by saying Richard Nixon would win, so there was a one hundred percent chance one of those predictions coming true. As far as the assassination, three of the ten presidents in the twentieth century had died in office and two others were critically ill at the end of their terms. The odds against her weren't too bad.

"Besides, unlike the biblical prophets, she made numerous predictions that turned out to be false—that Red China would plunge the world into war over Quemoy and Matsu in 1958; that World War III would begin in 1954; that Castro would be banished from Cuba in 1970. My favorite is that she predicted Jacqueline Kennedy would not remarry—and the very next day, she wed Aristotle Onassis!" he said with a chuckle.

"A study of the prophecies made by psychics in 1975, including Dixon's, showed they were only accurate six percent of the time. That's pitiful! You probably could just guess and get a better record than that. Besides, you'll find that Dixon, Nostradamus, and other psychics commonly deal with occult practices—she used a crystal ball, for example—and that could account for some of what they predicted."

As someone skeptical of psychics, I didn't want to get pushed further into a position of trying to defend them. And Geisler's point had been made: they are completely different from biblical prophets. I decided to advance to a more potent criticism of biblical prophecy, which is the allegation that Christians wrench them out of context and claim they predicted the coming of Jesus when actually they were dealing with another issue. One example popped into my mind.

"Do you mind?" I asked as I reached over and took Geisler's Bible. I turned to Matthew 2:15, which says: "So [Joseph] got up, took the child and his mother during the night and left for Egypt, where he stayed until the death of Herod. And so was fulfilled what the Lord had said through the prophet: 'Out of Egypt I called my son.'"

That's a reference to Hosea 11:1. I turned to that verse and read it to Geisler: "When Israel was a child, I loved him, and out of Egypt I called my son." Closing the book and handing it back to Geisler, I said: "Now, obviously that passage is about the children of Israel coming out of Egypt in the Exodus. It's not about the Messiah. Isn't that yanking a prophecy out of context?"

"That's a good question," Geisler remarked. "You have to understand, however, that not all prophecies are predictive."

"Meaning what?" I asked.

"It's true that the New Testament did apply certain Old Testament passages to Jesus that were not directly predictive of him. Many scholars see these references as being 'typologically' fulfilled in Christ, without being directly predictive."

"Meaning?"

"In other words, some truth in the passage can appropriately be applied to Christ even though it was not specifically predictive of him. Others scholars say there's a generic meaning in certain Old Testament passages that apply to both Israel and Christ, both of whom were called God's 'son.' This is sometimes called a 'double-reference view' of prophecy.

"I can see the merit of both views. But, again, these passages were not directly predictive, and I don't use them that way. There are certainly, however, a sufficient number of examples of prophecies that are clearly predictive to establish the divine authority of the Bible. Mathematics has shown that there's absolutely no way they could have been fulfilled by mere chance."

CONFIRMATION BY MIRACLES

Advancing to the other reason for the Bible's divine authority, Geisler said there's one sure way to determine whether a prophet is truly a spokesman for God or a charlatan trying to deceive the masses: can he produce clear-cut miracles? All three great monotheistic religions—Christianity, Judaism, and Islam—recognize the validity of miracles as a means of confirming a message from God. Even famed skeptic Bertrand Russell conceded that miracles would authenticate a truth claim.[29]

"In the Bible—which, remember, we've seen is historically reliable—we have prophets who were challenged but who then performed miracles to establish their credentials," Geisler said.

"For example, Moses said in Exodus 4:1, 'What if they do not believe me or listen to me and say, 'The Lord did not appear to you?' How does God respond? By telling Moses to throw his staff to the ground; instantly, it turned into a snake. He told Moses to pick it up by its tail; it turned back into a staff. Then God said in verse 5, 'This is so that they may believe that the Lord, the God of their fathers—the God of Abraham, the God of Isaac and the God of Jacob—has appeared to you.'

"The same thing for Elijah on Mount Carmel—he was challenged and God sent down fire from heaven to confirm he was a true prophet. As for Jesus, he actually came out and said, 'Don't believe me unless I do miracles of God.'[30] And then he did them. Even Nicodemus conceded this when he said to Jesus, 'Rabbi, we know you are a teacher who has come from God. For no one could perform the miraculous signs you are doing if God were not with him.'[31]

"This never happened to Muhammad. In fact, Muhammad actually believed Jesus was a prophet who performed miracles, including raising the dead. Muslims also believe Moses and Elijah performed miracles. That's very interesting, because in the Koran when unbelievers challenged Muhammad to perform a miracle, he refused. He merely said they should read a chapter in the Koran."[32]

"He did?" I interjected.

"Absolutely. And yet Muhammad himself said, 'God hath certainly power to send down a sign.'[33] He even said, 'They [will] say: 'Why is not a sign sent down to him from his Lord?'[34] Unlike Jesus, miracles were not a sign of Muhammad's ministry. It wasn't until a hundred and fifty or two hundred years after his life that his followers invented miracles and ascribed them to him.

"But when John the Baptist raised the question of whether Jesus was the Messiah, Jesus was able to respond confidently to John's disciples: 'Go back and report to John what you have seen and heard: the blind receive sight, the lame walk, those who have leprosy are cured, the deaf hear, the dead are raised, and the good news is preached to the poor.'"[35]

Geisler stopped for a moment while I considered what he was saying. Then he summed up his arguments: "When you add this up—the historical reliability of the Bible as authenticated by archaeology, the miraculous fulfillment of clear predictive prophecies, and the performance of documented miracles—you get a supernaturally confirmed book unlike any other in history."

I wanted to clarify something. "What you're not saying is, 'I believe the Bible is divinely inspired because it says it is.'"

"That's right. That's a circular argument. No, the argument goes like this: the Bible *claims* to be the Word of God and the Bible *proves* to be the Word of God."

That would seem to be a pretty good case—*if* the Bible didn't have so many apparent contradictions within it. But how can the Bible really be trustworthy if it can't keep its own story straight? How can it be considered divinely inspired if it makes statements that simply cannot be reconciled with each other?

COPING WITH CONTRADICTIONS

When I asked about alleged contradictions in the Bible, Geisler leaned back in his chair and smiled. It was an issue he had spent a lifetime studying.

"I've made a hobby of collecting alleged discrepancies, inaccuracies, and conflicting statements in the Bible," he said. "I have a list of about eight hundred of them. A few years ago I coauthored a book called *When Critics Ask,* which devotes nearly six hundred pages to setting the record straight.[36] All I can tell you is that in my experience when critics raise these objections, they invariably violate one of seventeen principles for interpreting Scripture."

"What are those?" I asked.

"For example, assuming the unexplained is unexplainable. I'm sure some sharp critic could say to me, 'What about this issue?' and even though I've done a forty-year study of these things, I wouldn't be able to answer him. What does that prove—that the Bible has an error or Geisler is ignorant? I'd give the benefit of the doubt to the Bible, because of the eight hundred allegations I've studied, I haven't found one single error in the Bible, but I've found a lot of errors by the critics."

I cocked my head. "Is that really reasonable, though, to give the Bible the benefit of the doubt?"

"Yes, it is," he insisted. "When a scientist comes upon an anomaly in nature, does he give up science? When our space probe found braided rings around Jupiter, this was contrary to all scientific explanations. So do you remember when all the NASA scientists resigned because they couldn't explain it?"

I laughed. "Of course not," I said.

"Exactly. They didn't give up. They said, 'Ah, there must be an explanation,' and they continued to study. I approach the Bible the same way. It has proven over and over to be accurate, even when I initially thought it wasn't. Why shouldn't I give it the benefit of the doubt now? We need to approach the Bible the way an American is treated in court: presumed innocent until proven guilty.

"Critics do the opposite. They denied the Hittites of the Old Testament ever existed. Now archaeologists have found the Hittite library. Critics say, 'Well, I guess the Bible was right in that verse, but I don't accept the rest.' Wait a minute—when it has been proven to be accurate over and over again in hundreds of details, the burden of proof is on the critic, not on the Bible."

I asked Geisler to briefly describe some of the other principles for resolving apparent conflicts in Scripture.

"For example," he said, "failing to understand the context of the passage. This is the most common mistake critics make. Taking words out of context, you can even cause the Bible to prove there's no God. After all, Psalm 14:1 comes right out and says it: 'There is no God.' But, of course, in context it says, The fool says in his heart, 'There is no God.' Therefore, context is critically important, and most often critics are guilty of wrenching verses out of context to create an alleged discrepancy when there isn't one.

"Another mistake is assuming a partial report is a false report. Matthew reports that Peter said to Jesus, 'You are the Christ, the Son of the living God.' Mark said, 'You are the Christ.' Luke said, 'The Christ of God.'[37] Critics say, 'See? Error!' I say, 'Where's the error?' Matthew didn't say, 'You *aren't* the Christ' and Mark said, 'You are.' Matthew gave more. That's not an error; those are complementary.

"Other mistakes include neglecting to interpret difficult passages in light of clear ones; basing a teaching on an obscure passage; forgetting that the Bible uses nontechnical, everyday language; failing to remember the Bible uses different literary devices; and forgetting that the Bible is a human book with human characteristics."

"Humans make mistakes," I said. "If it's a human book, aren't errors inevitable?"

"Except for, say, the Ten Commandments, the Bible wasn't dictated," Geisler replied. "The writers weren't secretaries to the Holy Spirit. Sometimes they used human sources or used different literary styles or wrote from different perspectives or emphasized different interests or revealed human thought patterns and emotions. There's no problem with that. But like Christ, the Bible is totally human, yet without error."

"However," I interjected, "people bring up alleged contradictions all the time."

"Like what, for example?" he responded. "What are the most common you hear?"

I thought for a moment. "Matthew says there was one angel at Jesus' tomb; John says there were two. The gospels say Judas hung himself; Acts says his bowels gushed out."

"You're right; those are frequently cited," he replied. "But they're easily reconciled. Concerning the angels, have you ever noticed that whenever you have two of anything, you also have one? It never fails. Matthew didn't say there was *only* one. John was providing more detail by saying there were two.

"As for Judas' suicide, you hang yourself in a tree or over the edge of a cliff. It was against the law to touch a dead body in those days. So somebody came along later, found his body, cut the rope, and the bloated body fell onto the rocks. What happens? The bowels gush out, just as the Bible says. They're not contradictory, they're complementary."

All in all, I had to admit that Geisler was on track. I remember as an atheist peppering ill-prepared Christians with a flurry of apparent biblical contradictions and discrepancies. They would get flustered and embarrassed because they couldn't answer them, and I'd walk away feeling smug and self-satisfied.

But because they weren't able to answer them didn't mean there weren't answers. As with the troubling passages about the Canaanites and Elisha, the more I delved into the historical evidence and subjected the issues to scrutiny, the more they tended to fade away as objections.

WHY IS IT HARD TO BELIEVE?

It was almost time for lunch and I was getting hungry. "Do you want to get a bite to eat?" I asked Geisler.

"Sure," he said. "There's a little sandwich place down the road."

I glanced through my notes. I thought I had covered everything I wanted to discuss—but then I noticed a quotation I had brought along with me. It was a sentiment that reflected the frustration of a lot of people: why does God make it so difficult to believe in him? I didn't want to end the interview without asking Geisler about it.

"One more thing before we go," I said as I read him the colorful words of a frustrated spiritual seeker:

> So if I want to avoid hell, I presumably have to believe that a snake talked to Eve, that a virgin got pregnant from God, that a whale swallowed a prophet, that the Red Sea was parted, and all sorts of other crazy things. Well, if God wants me so bad . . . why does He make believing in Him so . . . impossible? . . . It seems to me that an all-powerful God could do a much better job of convincing people of His existence than any evangelist ever does. . . . Just write it in the sky, nice and big: "Here's your proof, Ed. Believe in Me or go to hell! Sincerely, the Almighty."[38]

Looking up at Geisler, I said, "What would you say to him?"

Geisler was a bit bemused. "My answer would be that God *did* do something like that," he replied. "Psalm 19:1 says, 'The heavens are telling the glory of God; and the firmament proclaims his handiwork.'[39] In fact, it's written across the heavens so vividly that more and more scientists who search the stars are becoming Christians.

"The great cosmologist Allan Sandage, who won astronomy's version of the Nobel Prize, concluded that God is 'the explanation for the miracle of existence.'[40] Sir Fred Hoyle, who devised the steady state theory of the universe to avoid the existence of God, eventually became a believer in an Intelligent Designer of the universe.

"The astrophysicist Hugh Ross, who got his doctorate in astronomy from the University of Toronto and did research on quasars and galaxies, said scientific and historical evidence 'deeply rooted my confidence in the veracity of the Bible.'[41] Robert Jastrow, a confessed agnostic and director of the Mount Wilson Observatory and founder of the Goddard Space Institute, concluded the Big Bang points toward God. And I like what mathematical physicist Robert Griffiths said: 'If we need an atheist for a debate, I go to the philosophy department. The physics department isn't much use.'[42] The evidence, Lee, is so clear."

Not to a skeptic like Bertrand Russell, I noted. "He said if he someday stands before God and is asked why he never put his faith in him, he'll say he hadn't been given enough evidence," I reminded him.

Geisler, one of whose hobbies is collecting quotes from atheists and agnostics, pointed out something else Russell said. "He was asked in a *Look* magazine interview, 'Under what condition would you believe in God,' and he essentially said, "Well, if I heard a voice from heaven and it predicted a series of things and they came to pass, then I guess I'd have to believe there's some kind of supernatural being.'"[43]

In light of our discussion about the miraculous fulfillment of predictive prophecies in the Bible, the irony in Russell's statement was obvious.

"I'd say, 'Mr. Russell, there *has* been a voice from heaven; it has predicted many things; and we've seen them undeniably come to pass,'" Geisler declared.

"Then you don't think God is making it hard for people to believe?"

"On the contrary, the evidence is there if people will be willing to see it. It's not for a lack of evidence that people turn from God; it's from their pride or their will. God is not going to force anyone into the fold. Love never works coercively. It only works persuasively. And there's plenty of persuasive evidence there."

I felt an obligation to disclose the identity of the person I quoted as asking why God makes it so difficult to believe. I told Geisler his name is Edward Boyd, and he made that remark to his son, Christian philosopher Gregory Boyd, as they exchanged a series of letters in which they debated the evidence for Christianity. In 1992, after personally weighing the evidence, the formerly skeptical Edward Boyd decided to become a follower of Jesus.[44]

Geisler smiled at the story, and then he turned personal, even poetic, as he closed by discussing his personal faith.

"For me, I say the same thing that the apostle Peter said: 'Lord, to whom shall we go? You have the words of eternal life.'[45] He's the only one who not only claimed to be God but proved to be God. When I compare this to all other claimants of all other religions, it's like the poet who said the night has a thousand eyes and the day has but one; the light of the whole world dies with the setting of the sun.'"

Geisler's voice softened but kept its intensity. "At the midnight of human ignorance, there are a lot of lights in the sky. Noontime, there's only one. And that's Jesus Christ, the light of the world. Based on the evidence for who he was, there really aren't any competitors.

"So I cast my lot with him—not the one who claimed wisdom, Confucius; or the one who claimed enlightenment, Buddha; or the one who claimed to be a prophet, Muhammad, but with the one who claimed to be God in human flesh. The one who declared, 'Before Abraham was born, I am'[46]—and proved it."

DELIBERATIONS

Questions for Reflection or Group Study

- Evaluate how well you believe Geisler succeeded in dealing with the troublesome issues of how God dealt with the Amalekites, the Canaanites, and the mob that threatened the prophet Elisha. What was the strongest part of his explanation? Is the issue of God's character a "sticking point" in your spiritual journey? Why or why not?
- Do Geisler's guidelines for interpreting Scripture make sense to you? Which ones have you seen violated by critics? Do you agree that it's reasonable to give the Bible the benefit of the doubt on grounds that it has already proven reliable in numerous instances? Why or why not?
- What's your reaction to the quotation by former skeptic Edward Boyd? Do you believe God has made it difficult for us to believe in him? What's your biggest impediment to faith? What specific steps could you take to overcome that obstacle?
- Have you been stumped by an apparent discrepancy or contradiction in the Bible? If so, how would you go about researching an answer? Try posing your question as succinctly as you can, and then take advantage of internet and library resources, including the books listed below, and see if there's an explanation that will satisfy you.

FOR FURTHER EVIDENCE

More Resources on This Topic

• Norman Geisler. *Baker Encyclopedia of Christian Apologetics*. Grand Rapids, Mich.: Baker, 1999.

- Norman Geisler and Thomas Howe. *When Critics Ask.* Grand Rapids, Mich.: Baker, 1992.
- Norman Geisler and Ronald Brooks. *When Skeptics Ask.* Wheaton, Ill.: Victor, 1990.
- Gleason L. Archer. *Encyclopedia of Bible Difficulties.* Grand Rapids, Mich.: Zondervan, 1992.
- Walter C. Kaiser Jr., Peter H. Davids, F. F. Bruce, and Manfred T. Brauch. *Hard Sayings of the Bible.* Downers Grove, Ill.: InterVarsity Press, 1996.

5

OBJECTION #5: IT'S OFFENSIVE TO CLAIM JESUS IS THE ONLY WAY TO GOD

I am absolutely against any religion that says that one faith is superior to another. I don't see how that is anything different than spiritual racism. It's a way of saying that we are closer to God than you, and that's what leads to hatred.

Rabbi Schmuley Boteach[1]

Moses could mediate on the law; Muhammad could brandish a sword; Buddha could give personal counsel; Confucius could offer wise sayings; but none of these men was qualified to offer an atonement for the sins of the world. . . . Christ alone is worthy of unlimited devotion and service.

Theologian R. C. Sproul[2]

Walter Chaplinsky had strong opinions about religion and wasn't shy about expressing them. In 1940 he caused a ruckus in Rochester, New Hampshire, by loudly denouncing organized religion as being "a racket" and condemning several Christian denominations by name. The result: he found himself arrested and convicted under a state law making it a crime to speak "any offensive, derisive or annoying word to any person who is lawfully in any street or other public place."

Believing that his free-speech rights were being violated, Chaplinsky appealed his case all the way to the United States Supreme Court. However, in 1942 the justices unanimously affirmed his conviction, saying that "fighting words" like the ones he shouted fall outside the protection of the First Amendment.[3] Thirty years later, the high court clarified its definition of "fighting words" by calling them "personally abusive epithets" that are "inherently likely to provoke violent action."[4]

"Fighting words" arouse a visceral response in people, making their guts churn and their hands ball into fists. This offensive language strikes deep inside by attacking their most cherished beliefs, virtually taunting them to lash out in retaliation. To some people, such are the outrageous words of Jesus Christ: "I am the way and the truth and the life. No one comes to the Father except through me."[5]

Many people consider it arrogant, narrow-minded, and bigoted for Christians to contend that the only path to God must go through Jesus of Nazareth. In a day of religious pluralism and tolerance, this exclusivity claim is politically incorrect, a verbal slap in the face of other belief systems. Pluralist Rosemary Radford Ruether labeled it "absurd religious chauvinism,"[6] while one Jewish rabbi called it a "spiritual dictatorship" that fosters the kind of smug and superior attitude that can lead to hatred and violence toward people who believe differently.[7]

Certainly an approach like the one expressed by Indian philosopher Swami Vivekenanda is much more acceptable today: "We [Hindus] accept all religions to be true," he told the World Parliament of Religions in 1893. The real sin, he said, is to call someone else a sinner.[8]

That kind of open-mindedness and liberality fits well with our current culture of relativism, where no "fact" is considered universally true at all times, at all places, for all people, and in all cultures. Indeed, fully two-thirds of Americans now deny there's any such thing as truth.[9]

When I was an atheist, I bristled at assertions by Christians that they held a monopoly on the only correct approach to religion. "Who do they think they are?" I'd grouse. "Who are they to judge everyone else? Where's the love of Jesus in that?"

Charles Templeton called it "insufferable presumption"[10] for the Bible to claim that besides Jesus there is "no other name under heaven ... by which we must be saved."[11] Templeton added:

> Christians are a small minority in the world. Approximately four out of every five people on the face of the earth believe in gods other than the Christian God. The more than five billion people who live on earth revere or worship more than three hundred gods. If one includes the animist or tribal religions,

the number rises to more than three thousand. *Are we to believe that only Christians are right?*[12]

Despite Templeton's woeful undercounting of the number of gods worshiped in the world, his point remains. The exclusivity claim of Jesus is among the biggest obstacles to spiritual seekers today. With a subject this volatile, I knew I needed to talk with an expert who has a crisp, analytical mind, a sound philosophical background, and extensive experience with a wide range of different world religions. Those criteria led me to a suburb of Atlanta, Georgia, and the office of Ravi Zacharias, who was born and raised in India.

THE FIFTH INTERVIEW: RAVI ZACHARIAS, D.D., LL.D.

"There's an old Indian saying that says there are two ways to get to your nose," Ravi Zacharias told me as he removed his black suit coat and sat down at a round wooden table in his office.

"There's this way," he said, pointing directly to his nose. Then he reached around the back of his head and touched his nose from the far side. "And there's *this* way," he said with a smile.

In other words, Indians sometimes prefer to take a long and circuitous route to an answer rather than getting to the point too quickly. And sometimes that's true of Zacharias, who has earned a reputation as being among the world's most astute and articulate defenders of Christianity.

Gentle-spirited but with a razor-sharp intellect, Zacharias has been called "a man of great spiritual perception and intellectual integrity" by Billy Graham.[13] He has spoken about Christianity, philosophy, world religions, and cults in fifty countries and numerous universities. His books include the award-winning *Can Man Live Without God,* partly based on a series of penetrating lectures he delivered at Harvard University; *A Shattered Visage: The Real Face of Atheism; Deliver Us From Evil; Cries of the Heart;* and *Jesus Among Other Gods.* His first children's book, *The Merchant and the Thief,* was released in 1999.

Zacharias was educated at Trinity Evangelical Divinity School, where he earned a master's of divinity degree, and he has been a visiting scholar at Cambridge University. He has been honored by the conferring of Doctor of Divinity degrees from Houghton College and Tyndale College and Seminary, as well as a Doctor of Laws degree from Asbury College. He is the former chair of evangelism and contemporary thought at Alliance Theological Seminary.

Currently, Zacharias heads Ravi Zacharias International Ministries, with offices in the United States, Canada, India, and England. He and his wife, Margaret, have three children.

Zacharias is an imposing figure with a boyish smile. His medium bronze skin contrasts with hair that's so white it's almost luminous. He speaks in a soft, husky voice with a distinctive Indian accent and cadence. Unfailingly polite and hospitable, he was generous with his time and completely focused on our interview, even though behind the scenes his staff was feverishly making preparations for another international trip on which he was about to embark.

I had come to question him about Jesus' claim that he is the sole path to God, an assertion he had made to his disciple Thomas. According to tradition, the once-doubting Thomas, his faith bolstered by his encounter with the resurrected Christ, later ventured deep into India to communicate the Christian message, finally being murdered near Madras. Zacharias was born a scant six miles from the memorial erected to his martyrdom.

In a sense, Zacharias' spiritual journey is reminiscent of Thomas's. After spending his early years as a Christian in name only, Zacharias found a tentative kind of faith at age seventeen after hearing an American evangelist speak at a rally. Later he ended up in the hospital after attempting to kill himself over the meaninglessness of life, an experience through which he became a radically devoted follower of Jesus and a missionary from India to places around the world.

I knew his experience in that multicultural, multireligious environment, where he grew up among Muslims, Hindus, and Sikhs, would enrich his perspective on this troubling question of Christ's exclusivity. As he sipped hot tea, I pulled my notes out of my briefcase and immediately zeroed in on the topic at hand.

THE ARROGANCE OF CHRISTIANITY

"Forgive me for being blunt," I said in prefacing my question, "but isn't it grossly arrogant for Christians to claim Jesus is the one and only way to God? Why do Christians think they're justified in asserting that they're right and that everybody else in the world is wrong?"

While Zacharias' accent and conservative business attire—a starched white shirt and muted tie—gave him an air of formality, he was invariably enthusiastic, warm, and engaging in his answers.

"Lee, I hear that question so much, especially in the East," he said, his voice animated and his eyes looking sincere and concerned. "The first thing I do is try to deal with the misinformation that is inherent in it."

"Misinformation?" I asked. "Like what?"

"First," he said, "it's important to understand that Christianity is not the only religion that claims exclusivity. For instance, Muslims radically claim exclusivity—not just theologically, but also linguistically. Muslims believe that the sole, sufficient, and consummate miracle of Islam is the Koran. They say, however, it's only recognizable in Arabic, and that any translation desacralizes it. And it's not just a basic understanding of Arabic that's required, but a sophisticated knowledge of the language.

"As for Buddhism, it was born when Gautama Buddha rejected two fundamental assertions of Hinduism—the ultimate authority of the Vedas, which are their scriptures, and the caste system. Hinduism itself is absolutely uncompromising on two or three issues: the law of karma, which is the law of moral cause and effect, so that every birth is a rebirth that makes recompense for the previous life; the authority of the Vedas; and reincarnation."

I interrupted. "But I've heard Hindus say quite nobly that Hinduism is a very tolerant faith," I said, thinking of statements like the one made by Swami Vivekenanda near the beginning of this chapter.

He smiled. "Whenever you hear that statement, don't take it at face value," he said. "What it really means is that Hinduism allows you to practice your religion so long as it buys into their notion of truth, which is syncretistic," he said. Syncretism is the attempt to blend together different or even opposing beliefs.

"As for Sikhism," he continued, "it came as a challenge to both Hinduism and Buddhism. Then there are the atheists—they reject the viewpoints of those who believe in God. And even Baha'ism, which claims to be a cosmic embrace of all religions, ends up excluding the exclusivists! Therefore, the statement that Christians are arrogant by claiming exclusivity ignores the reality that every other major religion does as well. So when people talk of arrogance, this cannot be a logical attack they are making."

I started to formulate my next question, but Zacharias anticipated where it was headed and jumped in to complete my sentence.

"You believe that all truth—" I began.

"Is, by definition, exclusive," he said. "Yes, yes, I do. If truth does not exclude, then no assertion of a truth claim is being made;

it's just an opinion that is being stated. Any time you make a truth claim, you mean something contrary to it is false. Truth excludes its opposite."

"There are those who deny that," I observed.

"Yes, but think about this: to deny the exclusive nature of truth is to make a truth claim, and is that person then not arrogant too? That's the boomerang effect that the condemner often doesn't pause to consider. The clear implications of Jesus saying he's the way, the truth, and the life are that, first, truth is absolute, and second, truth is knowable. His claim of exclusivity means categorically that anything that contradicts what he says is by definition false."

"It's one thing for Christians to believe that," I said. "It's another thing to communicate it without sounding smug or superior. But Christians often come off that way."

Zacharias sighed. It was a charge he had heard all too often. "Yes, if truth is not undergirded by love, it makes the possessor of that truth obnoxious and the truth repulsive," he said. "Having been raised in India and having all Hindu, Muslim, Buddhist, and Sikh friends growing up, I can appreciate some of their criticisms of Christians. Christianity's history has some explaining to do with its methodology. Violence, antagonism, and hostility are contrary to the love of Christ. One cannot communicate the love of Christ in non-loving terms.

"In India we have a proverb that says once you cut off a person's nose, there's no point in giving him a rose to smell," he continued. "And if a Christian's arrogance turns off somebody, that person won't be receptive to the Christian message. Mahatma Gandhi said, 'I like their Christ, I don't like their Christians.' Friedrich Nietzshe said, 'I will believe in the Redeemer when the Christian looks a little more redeemed.' Their points need to be taken.

"However," he added, "it *is* possible to lovingly claim exclusive truth, just as a scientist can very gently say, 'This is the second law of thermodynamics' without adding, 'Now, can we vote on how many of us can cooperate with it or not?'"

"So the criticism of Christians is often valid?"

"Yes, sometimes we have run afoul of cultural sensitivities. At the same time, however, Eastern religions have a lot of soul-searching to do in this regard today. Clannish and political conflicts aside, I know of no Christianized country where your life is in danger because you are from another faith. But today there are many countries in the world—such as Pakistan, Saudia Arabia, and Iran—where to become a follower of Christ is to put your life and your family at risk."

I had read enough newspaper accounts in recent years to know that was accurate, including in Zacharias' native land, where several Christians have been killed by militant Hindus in recent years. But sometimes it's not the manner in which the Christians try to spread their faith that's offensive. Sometimes people are simply reacting to the message itself.

"Even the one whose life was most perfectly lived ended up on a cross," Zacharias noted. "Resistance to truth can be so strong that it can still engender violence and hate even when the person has done absolutely nothing wrong."

ORIGIN, MEANING, MORALITY, DESTINY

Anyone can claim to be the only path to God. In fact, quite a few crackpots have made that assertion throughout history. The real issue is why anybody should believe Jesus was telling the truth when he said it.

"On what basis do you believe this claim by Jesus is true?" I asked Zacharias.

"Ah, yes, that is the heart of the question," he replied, his head nodding. "On one hand, you can say that the resurrection of Jesus established him as being the son of God. If that's true, then all other faith systems cannot be true, because they each assert something contrary to his divinity. And of course, the historical record concerning the Resurrection is extremely compelling.

"On the other hand, you can approach this issue by looking at the four fundamental questions that every religion seeks to answer: Origin, meaning, morality, and destiny. I believe that only the answers of Jesus Christ correspond to reality. There is a coherence among his answers unlike those of any other religion."

That was a bold statement. "Can you back that up with examples of how other faiths fail those tests?"

"Consider Buddhism," he replied. "Buddha's answer on the question of morality does not cohere with his answer concerning origins. You see, Buddhism is technically nontheistic, if not atheistic. But if there was no Creator, from where does one arrive at a moral law? Or consider the Hindu version of reincarnation. If every birth is a rebirth, and if every life pays for the previous life, then what were you paying for in your first birth? You see—incoherence dominates."

He was quick to add that he was not trying to denigrate those religions. "Great scholars will tell you there is incoherence," he said. "Even Gandhi said that if he had his way he would expunge some of the scriptures from Hinduism, because they are so contradictory with each other. By contrast, Jesus provides answers to these four fundamental questions of life in a way that corresponds with reality and has internal consistency, unlike any other faith system."

That statement invited challenge. "Go through each one," I said, "and tell me how."

"Fair enough," he replied. "Concerning origins, the Bible says we are not identical with God—contrary to the Hindu claim—but we are distinct from him. In other words, we didn't bring ourselves into being, but we are a creation of God. Since we were created in his image, this accounts for human beings having a moral point of reference. No system is able to explain this except the monotheistic ones. Even naturalists have no explanation for humanity's moral framework. However, this moral framework corresponds to the reality of human experience.

"Also, Christianity says we rejected the divine will. The tempter in the garden said if you eat this fruit, you will become as gods, knowing good and evil. The implication is that you become the definer of good and evil. Humanism was born right there; man became the measure of all things. This willful rebellion and rejection of God corresponds to reality. As Malcolm Muggeridge said, human depravity is at once the most empirically verifiable reality but also the most philosophically resistant.

"Next, the issue of meaning. Here again, the Christian faith stands without parallel. The simplest way to describe it is that God does not call us to meaning by asking us to be good people. He does not call us to meaning just by telling us to love one another. It is only in the experience of worship that meaning comes to be. Only something greater than pleasure can provide meaning, and that is the perpetual novelty of God himself in worship. The Bible tells us to love the Lord our God with all our heart, soul, and mind, and only when we've done that can we begin to love our neighbors as ourselves. This also corresponds to experience.

"Next, Christianity says morality is not culturally based, but instead it grows out of the very character of God. Otherwise, you end up with the dilemma from philosophy of old: is the moral law over and above you, or is a moral law subject to you? If it is over and above you, where do you find its root, then? The only way to explain that is to find it in an eternal, moral, omnipotent, infinite God who is inseparable from his character. Thus, Christianity explains morality in a coherent manner.

"Finally, destiny is based on the resurrection of Jesus Christ, the historical event that proved his divinity and that opened the door to heaven for everyone who will follow him. Where else do you have anything that comes close to claiming this?

"Billy Graham once told of meeting Konrad Adenauer, the mayor of Cologne who was imprisoned by Hitler for opposing the Nazi regime and who later became the highly regarded chancellor of West Germany from 1949 to 1963. Adenauer looked Graham in the eyes and asked, 'Do you believe in the resurrection of Jesus Christ from the dead?' Graham said, 'Of course I do.' To which Adenauer replied: 'Mr. Graham, outside of the resurrection of Jesus, I do not know of any other hope for this world.'

"He was right. Because the Resurrection is an actual historical event, we can be forgiven, we can be reconciled with God, we can spend eternity with him, and we can trust Jesus' teachings as being from God.

"One of my friends was a Muslim convert who was later martyred. I remember visiting him in the hospital after his legs had been blown off, and he said: 'The more I understand of what others have claimed and taught, the more beautiful Jesus Christ looks to me.' I've never forgotten that, and I believe that to be absolutely true.

"No man spoke like Jesus. No one ever answered the questions the way he answered them, not only propositionally but also in his person. Existentially, we can test it out. Empirically, we can test it out. The Bible is not just a book of mysticism or spirituality; it is a book that also gives geographical truths and historical truths. If you're an honest skeptic, it's not just calling you to a feeling; it's calling you to a real Person. That's why the apostle Peter said, 'We did not follow cleverly invented stories when we told you about the power and coming of our Lord Jesus Christ, but we were eyewitnesses of his majesty.'[14]

"He's saying, 'This is true. This is reality. This can be trusted.' And, yes, this truth excludes that which is contrary."

OF ELEPHANTS AND FAITH

Even if Zacharias was right about Christianity, however, does this necessarily mean that all other religions are false? Perhaps they're all teaching the same fundamental truths at their core, using different language, diverse images, and various traditions to communicate basically identical beliefs.

"Some people say that when you strip away everything, all the world religions are essentially teaching the universal fatherhood of God and the universal brotherhood of humankind," I said. "That would mean that all the world's faith systems are equally valid."

Zacharias shook his head, his face registering dismay. "Only someone who doesn't understand the world religions would claim they basically teach the same thing," he said.

"What do they mean by the universal fatherhood of God when Buddhism doesn't even claim that there is a God? What do we mean by the fatherhood of God when Shankara, one of the most respected Hindu philosophers, said theism is only a child's way to ultimately get to the top, where you find out God is not distinct from you? What then does the fatherhood of God mean? It's an illusion. This fatherhood of God is not a trans-religious doctrine.

"Secondly, the brotherhood of humanity—yes, we are brothers and sisters as fellow human beings, but the only reason we are is because we have been fashioned by God. Once you take that foundation away," he said with a chuckle, "then brotherhood ends up with more hoods than brothers! In sum, Islam, Buddhism, Hinduism, and Christianity are not saying the same thing. They are distinct and mutually exclusive religious doctrines. They all cannot be true at the same time."

Still, I wasn't through attempting to harmonize them. "Maybe the various religions each have a slice of the truth," I suggested. "Theologian John Hick said the world religions are different culturally conditioned responses to the ultimately 'Real,' or God.[15] Isn't this like the old story of the three blind men feeling the elephant—each religion is a sincere but inadequate attempt to explain the mystery of God, and so each one is valid in its own way?"

Zacharias started with a bit of philosophical judo. "Either Hick is the product of his own culture or he has transcended his culture in making that statement," he countered. "And if he has transcended his culture, why hasn't anyone else transcended culture? It sounds very academically sophisticated, but it has too many problems at its heart."

"Like what?" I asked.

"For instance, does the atheist have a piece of the truth, or is the atheist marginalized here? If the atheist does have a piece of the truth, which piece is it, since the fundamental tenet of atheism is the denial of God's very existence?"

He paused, letting the question answer itself. Then he added: "I will say this: there are aspects of truth in virtually all of the major religions. They contain some great thoughts and ideas. Reading the notable Eastern philosophers is very, very stimulating. But it's not like we are blind people exploring the elephant, with one person feeling the leg and thinking it's a tree; the other person feeling the trunk and thinking it's a rope; and the third feeling the ear and thinking it's a fan.

"The point is," he said, his voice rising for emphasis, "the parable has already given away the fact that this, indeed, is an elephant! The blind man may tell you it's a tree, but he's wrong. It is not a tree or a rope or a fan. The seeing man knows this is an elephant. He knows the truth; his sight has revealed it to him. And Jesus Christ has made it clear that the eternal truths of God may be known. Jesus Christ is the centerpiece of the gospel—in him, all of truth came together. So while there may be aspects of truth elsewhere, the sum total of truth is in Christ.

"Hick's explanation ignores the possibility that God would reveal himself, and that therefore we can have knowledge of who he is. Instead, Hick has made culture and intuition supreme. But the Bible says God *did* reveal himself: 'In the beginning was the Word, and the Word was with God, and the Word was God.... The Word became flesh and made his dwelling among us. We have seen his glory, the glory of the One and Only, who came from the Father, full of grace and truth.'"[16]

REDEMPTION, RIGHTEOUSNESS, WORSHIP

Comedian Quentin Crisp once said: "When I told the people of Northern Ireland that I was an atheist, a woman in the audience stood up and said, 'Yes, but is it the God of the Catholics or the God of the Protestants in whom you don't believe?'"

His humor was actually a sad commentary on the depth of sectarian strife in that land. Through the centuries, the world has seen plenty of acrimony and violence over differences in the way people view God. Disgusted by religious bickering, some people have thrown up their hands and said the world would be a much better place if people simply stopped arguing over doctrinal disputes and instead focused on living in peace with each other.

"There are moral-living Muslims, Jews, Christians, Mormons, and Hindus," I pointed out to Zacharias. "Isn't how a person lives and treats his neighbor more important than what he believes theologically?"

"How a person lives and how he treats his neighbor *is* very important," came his reply. "But it is not more important than what he believes, because the way he lives is reflective of what he believes. Regardless of whether he has ever signed a doctrinal statement, what he really and truly believes is what he will ultimately live out. But this question makes the assumption that morality is what life is all about."

"If life isn't about being moral," I said, "then what is it about?"

"Jesus Christ didn't come into this world to make bad people good," he said. "He came into this world to make dead people live. He came so that those who are dead to God can come alive to God. If this life were only about morality, then how you live would be the most important thing, although it would still be connected to what you believe. But that misunderstands the Christian concept, which is no matter how well we live, we cannot live up to the standard and character of God.

"The word 'sin' means missing the mark. And if that is a correct definition, then the grace of God becomes the most important truth. Apart from him, we cannot even believe what is right, let alone live the right way.

"So, yes, living kindly and morally good lives is important, if purely for survival. But philosophers from Socrates, Plato, and Aristotle, all the way to the Enlightenment thinkers like Immanuel Kant were unable to even define what morality is. Ultimately, they could only give us what morality did for society.

"When I did a study of options by which people can live good lives, I came down to six or seven of them, such as Joseph Fletcher's situation ethics, Ayn Rand's egocentric humanism, Kant's idea of duty, and so forth. But they contradicted one another pretty heavily, and the reason is that there was no transcendent, compelling moral reason. It was all reduced to mere survival. So I believe goodness or badness is the wrong starting point; life and death, spiritually, is where you begin."

"But as you conceded, it *is* important how people live," I said. "People say Gandhi lived a more virtuous life than most Christians. Why should he be sent to hell just because he wasn't a follower of Jesus?"

"That's a tough issue. When I get that question before big audiences, that's the time I want to take a break!" he said with a smile. "But the Bible does give us some guidance in answering this.

"First and foremost, it's important to know that no human being consigns anybody to heaven or hell. In fact, God himself does not send anybody to heaven or to hell; the person chooses to respond to the grace of God or to reject the grace of God, although even that decision is enabled by his grace.

"Second, Abraham asked God in the case of Sodom and Gomorrah whether he was going to let the righteous die with the unrighteous, and it was wonderful how Abraham answered his own question. He said, 'Will not the Judge of all the earth do right?'[17] This means we can be absolutely confident that whatever God does in the case of Gandhi or any other person, he will do what is right.

"Now, think about this: the Bible says anyone spending eternity with God in heaven is there because of the grace and provision of Jesus Christ, which the person has trusted and received. If the person has rejected that grace, then was he a good man or a bad man? That's an interesting question, because Scripture tells us nobody is really good until he or she is first redeemed."

"Elaborate on that," I said.

"The pattern in Exodus is threefold: God brought the people out of Egypt, he gave them the moral law, and then he gave them the tabernacle. In other words, redemption, righteousness, worship. You can never violate that sequence. Unless you are redeemed, you cannot be righteous. Unless you are redeemed and righteous, you cannot worship, 'for who shall ascend unto the hill of the Lord,' says the Bible, 'but he who has clean hands and a pure heart?'[18]

"So redemption is the most important step toward righteousness. If I try to work myself toward goodness, I am essentially saying I don't need to be redeemed by God. I am my own redeemer. Any person, good or bad in our eyes, who says that is in violation of a fundamental principle of God's revelation, which is that redemption is the first step."

SO WHAT ABOUT GANDHI?

Still, my mind was on Gandhi. "He didn't follow Jesus," I said, "so I suppose you would say he was not redeemed."

"That is something that will be determined by God," Zacharias replied. "However, what is it Gandhi believed? He summarized it in one statement: 'God is truth and truth is God.' My question to him would be, 'What does that mean?' We are sitting in a room; that is a true statement. What has this got to do with whether this room is god or not? It doesn't. It only conforms to a statement I have just made. God exists—is that a true statement? If that is a true statement, who is this God?"

I interrupted. "Yet here you have a person like Gandhi, who in the eyes of most people lived a good life, whereas a serial killer like David Berkowitz, the Son of Sam, murdered several innocent people and now says he's prayed a prayer to become a Christian. Christians would say Berkowitz is going to heaven but Gandhi isn't. Where's the equity in that?"

"Because we are moral human beings, we want to see equity. But when we reduce equity to issues of who behaved in what way during a given span of time, we miss the whole concept of equity. We are judging this from the point of view of our system. If God were to truly give what every one of us deserved, none of us would get to heaven.

"There's the joke about two brothers who lived scandalous lives, and when one of them suddenly died, the surviving brother went to a minister and asked if he would preach at his brother's funeral. He said, 'I just have one request: that you refer to my brother as a saint.' The pastor said he would do his best to accommodate him.

"The funeral came and the minister was eulogizing the deceased. 'I want you to know this man was a swindler, a liar, a cheater, and a thief,' he said. 'But compared to his brother, he was a saint!'

"Now, there is a sharp edge to that story. We try desperately to claim goodness by comparing ourselves to others. David Berkowitz can say, 'Wait a minute; I'm not Hitler! I didn't kill millions, I just killed a few.' Or 'I wasn't Jeffrey Dahmer; I didn't eat my victims.' We tend to do the kind of comparisons by which we always emerge better than someone else, and so we think we're good. But by the perfect moral standard of God, we all fail. We all need God's forgiveness and grace.

"Admittedly, what David Berkowitz did was violent and evil. There's no question about that. However, we have to look at this in the whole scheme of God's plan. You see, there are worse things than death or murder."

"Like what?" I asked.

"Though it's hard to comprehend," he said, "the worst thing is to say to God that you don't need him. Why? Because a dead person can be restored to life by God; a bereaved person can find peace from God; a person who has been violated can find God's sustenance and strength and even see God conquer through the dark mystery of evil. In other words, there is recourse through these atrocities and tragedies. But to a person who says he or she doesn't need God, what is the recourse? There is none.

"So the question is not whether I'm a David Berkowitz, a Mahatma Gandhi, an Adolph Hitler, or a Mother Teresa. The question is, 'Have I come to the realization that I've fallen short of God's perfect standard and, therefore, apart from the grace of God, I have no possibility of being with him in heaven?'

"Frankly, if I have lived a life that I think is so good that I don't need God, then ironically Berkowitz will have found the ultimate truth to which my own arrogance and confidence have blinded me. What is hell but the absence of God? And for me to live my life with the absence of God is to already be on the road to hell."

"But," I protested, "is it fair for a killer like Berkowitz to get off scot-free?"

"I'm not sure he has," Zacharias said. "Yes, God has forgiven him if he has confessed and repented and sought God's mercy. But the more he is in tune with who Christ is, the deeper will be his pain for what he has done.

"Let me give you an example. Suppose you're driving and your mind wanders for a moment. Suddenly, a child runs in front of you and you hit that child. The closer you are in touch with the tragedy, the greater will be your burden for the rest of your life. You will never be able to look into the face of another child without thinking, 'What did I do? What did I do?'

"We may think Berkowitz got away in the sense that he didn't go to the gallows, but there is such a thing as the gallows of the heart. Your heart can be very attuned to the hell that you unleashed. I do not believe that a truly converted person would sit in his prison cell and think, 'Well, I've come to know Christ and so I'm off the hook on that.' No. Sometimes the hell of an inner heart may be very deep and painful.

"I believe there is a hell to a delayed salvation because the tears that flow are tears of what was lost before you came to know God. Does he forgive your past? Yes, but sometimes you cannot forget it."

Having said that, Zacharias paused and leaned back in his chair. When he resumed, he said: "Any time grace is misunderstood, it will always lead to comparison and jealousy or discontent and the charge of inequity. Interestingly enough, Jesus addresses this very issue.

"In one of his parables, the workers who labored all day were distressed that those who had come in at the last moment had also received the grace of the landlord.[19] One of the most staggering truths of the Scriptures is to understand that we do not earn our way to heaven. Also, we read in the Bible the story of the woman of ill repute who Jesus received. The Pharisee looked down his merit-formed nose and sneered at the mercy of God.[20] Works have a place—but as a demonstration of having received God's forgiveness, not as a badge of merit of having earned it."

WHAT OF THOSE WHO HAVEN'T HEARD?

Serial killer David Berkowitz was fortunate. He lives in a country where people freely talk about Christianity. Someone told him about Christ's offer of forgiveness, and he says he has confessed his offenses and put his faith in Jesus. But what about people who live in places where the gospel isn't routinely discussed or where its dissemination is actually outlawed?

"Isn't it unfair to condemn them when they never heard about Jesus and merely followed the religious traditions of their parents?" I asked.

Zacharias reached over to pick up his Bible. As he opened it and flipped to Acts, I caught a glimpse of the many places where he had highlighted key verses in yellow.

"The Bible says first of all that nobody will be in the presence of God apart from the fact that the person and work of Christ made it possible. That's the price it took: Christ's death on the cross as our substitute, paying the penalty we deserved to pay. Now, some people are born into one culture or another, but the apostle Paul said something very interesting about that when he was speaking to the Athenians."

Zacharias lifted his reading glasses out of his pocket and slipped them on so that they perched on his nose. Then he read part of a passage where Paul was debating some Greek philosophers:

> From one man he made every nation of men, that they should inhabit the whole earth; and he determined the times set for them and the exact places where they should live. God did this so that men would seek him and perhaps reach out for him and find him, though he is not far from each one of us.[21]

Removing his glasses, Zacharias looked up at me. "This is important," he said, "because he's pointing out that there's a sovereign plan in creation, where each person is assigned a place of birth. God knows where we will be born and raised, and he puts us in a position where we might seek him. We are clearly told that wherever we live—in whatever culture, in whatever nation—he is within reach of every one of us. There is always the possibility of a person crying out on their knees, 'God, help me,' and if that happens there are ways in which God can minister to them that are beyond our understanding."

"For example?"

"For example, he might send someone to share the gospel with them. Or let me tell you what happened in the case of a Muslim woman who worked for a very well-known institution in her country. She told me how she was leaving her office at the end of her day's work and was very unhappy in her heart. As she was walking, she muttered, 'I don't know why I am so empty,' and after that, out of the blue, she said, 'Jesus, can you help me?' She stopped on the sidewalk and said to herself, 'Why did I name him?' Well, that woman ended up becoming a Christian.

"In her case, I think God saw a heart that hungered for him but did not know how to reach him in the cloister of her existence. I think this was God breaking past the barriers of her environment because she was already breaking through the barriers of her inner life, seeking after him. Thus, God can reach into any cultural situation in response to anyone who wants to know him.

"Another way of looking at this issue comes from Romans, where Paul says God's infinite power and deity are revealed to everyone through creation.[22] Then Paul says God put the law in our hearts and our consciences that we might seek after him.[23] And he talks about the word of Christ that is necessary for a person to come to know him.[24] I think more and more that this word of Christ comes within the framework of different cultures.

"What do I mean by that?

"I have spoken in many Islamic countries, where it's tough to talk about Jesus. Virtually every Muslim who has come to follow Christ has done so, first, because of the love of Christ expressed through a Christian, or second, because of a vision, a dream, or some other supernatural intervention. Now, no religion has a more intricate doctrine of angels and visions than Islam, and I think it's extraordinary that God uses that sensitivity to the supernatural world in which he speaks in visions and dreams and reveals himself.

"One of India's greatest converts was a Sikh, Sundar Singh, who came to know Christ through an appearance of Christ in his room in a dream one night. It had a tremendous impact on his life and he became a Christian. So there are ways that God can reveal himself that go far beyond our own understanding.

"Now, if God is able to give the word of Christ in various settings in ways we can't even understand—if he's not far from us wherever we are, if he is able to speak through the general revelation of creation and through our conscience—then we have to accept the fact that we are without excuse. Every human being will know enough truth so that if they respond to that known truth, God will reveal more to them. Does that mean they have to have as much of a volume of truth as someone in another setting does? I don't believe so."

I tried to summarize his point. "You're saying that regardless of where a person lives in the world, regardless of the culture in which they live, anyone who responds to the understanding that they do have and sincerely seeks God will in some way be given an opportunity to respond to him?"

As I spoke, Zacharias was weighing my words with care. "I believe so," he replied. "We have to be very careful here, but I believe that if a person genuinely and sincerely seeks after him, there will be some way God makes available for that person to hear of him. If that person would not have responded to God under any circumstance, then perhaps he will not hear of him. But all people know enough to condemn them; they do not need to hear John 3:16 in order to be lost. They are lost because they've already rejected what God has spoken to them through creation, their conscience, and other ways. Because of that, we will all stand accountable before him."

"So sincerity is important?

"Sincerity is not salvation," came his response. "But I think sincerity brings about the possibility of God revealing himself to you.

Some may seem sincere and when Christ is presented to them, they reject him. They fail the test of truth."

I said, "You believe, then, that the amount of information a person needs to have concerning Christ can vary widely?"

"Yes, I believe so. The danger of a Western perspective is thinking that if something isn't neatly packaged, it's no good. And unfortunately, some Western Christians think that unless a person says the creed just like they do, they don't know God.

"Yet what does an infant know of his mother? He knows she nourishes him, she changes him, she embraces him, she kisses him—she must be a friend. That child doesn't know his mother as well as he will when he's eighteen. But he knows her enough to love her. I believe that as God reveals himself there are levels of understanding that are bound to vary."

WHY NOT JESUS?

If Jesus is the truth, why do so many people reject him? If Christianity is true, shouldn't it ultimately triumph? That's not what the statistics show, however. Christianity is making relatively little progress in winning converts from other major world religions. Basically, people around the globe tend to adopt the religion of their parents.

I asked Zacharias about this, and he said these issues trouble him as a defender of Christianity. There are, though, some explanations, he said.

"To look at this from a different perspective, why is Buddhism so popular in America today?" he asked. "My answer is simple: because you can be good without having God. If you can have a nice little dose of spirituality from three to five in the afternoon and then dichotomize your life once again and go live it any way you please—well, why not? A religion like that would have a lot of attraction.

"Why is Islam attractive to some? Because of geopolitical considerations. What is it about the Hindu faith that's attractive? It is rich in philosophy, and its tenet of treating the earth with reverence has some appeal today."

"Why not Christ?" I asked.

"Because he calls you to die to yourself," he replied. "Any time truth involves a total commitment in which you bring yourself to complete humility, to the surrender of the will, you will always have resistance. Christ violates our power and autonomy. He challenges us in areas of purity. John the Baptist came giving the law. People did not like it. Jesus came giving the message of grace and they said, 'Why don't you give us the firmness of the law?' Whatever Jesus brings into culture, culture will want to change it. At the heart of the rejection is resistance to the claim of who he is.

"Buddhism and other religious systems basically tell people how to pull themselves up by their ethical bootstraps. I have never had a problem knowing what is right and wrong in most situations; what I have lacked is the will to do what is right. That's where Christ comes in. He says if you'll bring all of yourself to him, he will not only give you eternal life, but he will change what you want to do in this life."

Given the level of commitment required by Christianity, I was curious about what prompted Zacharias to respond positively to the message of Jesus. "Tell me a bit of your story," I said.

He looked down for a moment, brushing a crumb off his shirt sleeve. Then he reached over to his cup of tea and took a sip before answering.

"In India, you are what you are born into," he began. "My father and mother were nominal Christians; in fact, the reason they were Christians was simply because they were not Buddhists, Muslims, or Hindus. I don't recall ever hearing the gospel preached at my church, which was very liberal-minded.

"Just prior to my coming to Christ, my sisters were exposed to the gospel and made their commitment. I came to believe in Jesus in two stages. The first stage was when I heard the gospel publicly proclaimed in an auditorium when I was seventeen. I said to myself, 'Something about this is true and I want it.' I went forward and was counseled, but I did not really understand. The baggage was too much.

"At the time, I was under a lot of pressure in a culture where academic performance was of supreme importance. If you're not at the top of the class, then you're not going to succeed. I couldn't cope with it. I also had a very strict father, and I struggled with that. I took a lot of punishment physically.

"So a few months later, I decided to end my own life. I was not depressed; my friends would have been shocked to hear suicide was on my mind. But for me, life had no meaning or purpose. I went to school one day and used the keys to the science lab to check out some poisons. I put them into a glass of water, gobbled it up, and collapsed on my knees."

I stared in disbelief. With Zacharias being as sophisticated, as erudite, as articulate, and as influential as he is today, it was impossible for me to visualize him as a confused and hope-starved teenager crumbling to his knees and gasping for breath as self-administered toxins coursed through his veins.

"My servant in the house rushed me to the hospital; if he were not there, I would be dead," he continued. "They emptied all of the poisons out of me. As I lay in bed, a friend walked in with a New Testament and showed me John chapter 14. I couldn't hold the book; my body was too dehydrated. My mother had to read it to me.

"There she was, reading where Jesus was talking to Thomas and saying, 'I am the way, the truth, and the life. No one comes to the Father except through me.' Then she came to verse 18, where Jesus tells his disciples, 'Because I live, you also will live.'

"That verse touched my soul. I said in a prayer, 'Jesus, I don't know much about who you are, but you are telling me you're the author of true life.' I didn't understand the concept of sin. In that culture, I couldn't have. But what I did understand was that he was offering himself to me to give me life.

"So I said, 'If you take me out of this hospital room, I will leave no stone unturned in my pursuit of truth.' And I walked out of that room five days later an absolutely brand new man. I began to study the Bible, and it dramatically changed my life. My brothers then came to follow Jesus, as did my parents before they died.

"But it was in that hospital room where Christ told me—through nobody explaining it to me—that he could give me what life was really meant to be. And I've never looked back. Years of study have only confirmed my decision to follow him. I took some philosophy courses at Cambridge under a renowned atheist, and I remember thinking in astonishment, 'These are the best arguments atheists have?' It merely confirmed the truth of Scripture."

"You deal with a lot of spiritual seekers now," I said. "What do you tell them?"

"The Bible says, 'You will seek me and find me when you seek me with all your heart.'[25] Think about that—that's an amazing promise. I encourage them to bring their heart and mind into a receptive mode and to not spare their intellect in testing the truth of the Bible. For any genuine person who brings an unprejudiced view, I don't see how he or she can walk away except saying there is nothing like this on the face of the earth.

"I have traveled the world. I have searched high and low. I have found nothing that satisfies my mind, my heart, and the deepest longings of my soul like Jesus does. He is not only the way, the truth, and the life; he is personal to me. He is *my* way, and *my* truth, and *my* life—just as he can be for anyone who reaches out to him.

"Because remember what Paul told the Athenians: 'He is not far,' he said, 'from each one of us.'"

DELIBERATIONS

Questions for Reflection or Group Study

- What was your emotional reaction the first time you heard the claim that Jesus is the only path to God? Has your viewpoint changed since reading Ravi Zacharias' interview? If so, how?
- Zacharias said: "The clear implications of Jesus saying he's the way, the truth, and the life are that, first, truth is absolute, and, second, truth is knowable." Do you believe those two assertions about truth? Why or why not?
- How well do you believe Christianity deals with the four fundamental issues of life: Origin, meaning, morality, and destiny? Does the Bible's teaching on those topics correspond to your experience?
- Have you personally considered any other world religion? If so, what did you find attractive about it? What aspects of Christianity attract you and which ones repel you?
- The Bible says about God, "You will seek me and find me when you seek me with all your heart." What three practical suggestions would you give to a friend who wants to know how he or she can seek God that way? Have you taken those steps yourself? What has been the result so far?

FOR FURTHER EVIDENCE

More Resources on This Topic

- Ravi Zacharias. *Jesus Among Other Gods.* Nashville: Word, 2000.
- Paul Copan. *True for You, But Not for Me.* Minneapolis: Bethany House, 1998.

- Frank Beckwith and Gregory Koukl. *Relativism: Feet Firmly Planted in Mid-Air.* Grand Rapids, Mich.: Baker, 1998.
- Millard J. Erickson. *How Shall They Be Saved?* Grand Rapids, Mich.: Baker, 1996.

6

OBJECTION #6: A LOVING GOD WOULD NEVER TORTURE PEOPLE IN HELL

There is one very serious defect to my mind in Christ's moral character, and that is that he believed in hell. I do not myself feel that any person who is really profoundly humane can believe in everlasting punishment.

Bertrand Russell, atheist[1]

Hell is God's great compliment to the reality of human freedom and the dignity of human choice.

G. K. Chesterton, Christian[2]

Judge Cortland A. Mathers was in a quandary. Standing before him was a defendant who was guilty of playing a minor role in a drug case. She was a thirty-one-year-old impoverished mother with a young family. She was remorseful over her crime. In the judge's opinion, she deserved a second chance. Justice would be served by giving her probation.

But there was a problem: if Mathers found her guilty of the charge against her, he would have no choice under Massachusetts law but to sentence her to six years in the penitentiary. He knew that prison would scar her forever. More than likely, it would destroy her fragile family and leave her embittered, angry, unemployed, and destined for more trouble.

This is a system called "mandatory sentencing," which removes the discretion of judges in disposing of certain kinds of cases. The positive side is that judges are prevented from being too lenient. But the negative consequence is that in some instances the automatic sentence can be too harsh—like in this case, where the defendant stood to serve more time behind bars than most armed robbers.

Mathers was never known to shrink back from sentencing criminals to long prison terms if the circumstances warranted it. But in this case, he considered the mandatory sentence—with no possibility of early release—to be an "absolute miscarriage of justice."

And so Mathers made his choice: "Disobey the law in order to be just." He declared her guilty of a lesser offense that did not carry a pre-set prison term and sentenced her to five years of probation with required counseling.

"If a judge is not capable of doing that, then he shouldn't be on the bench," Mathers told the *Boston Globe* in its investigation of mandatory sentencing. "A judge either is an automaton, rubber-stamping these sentences, or is driven by a sense of justice."[3]

I was thinking about that case as my plane was descending toward Los Angeles International Airport on a sultry September morning. How ironic, I mused, that a law designed to enforce justice threatened to thwart it instead. I could understand the sense of fairness that prompted Mathers to sidestep one-size-fits-all sentencing and instead to impose a punishment that would more appropriately fit the crime.

For a long time as a spiritual seeker, I found my sense of justice outraged by the Christian teaching about hell, which I considered far more unjust than a mandatory prison term would have been in the case before Mathers. The doctrine seemed like cosmic overkill to me, an automatic and unappealable sentence to an eternity of torture and torment. It's mandatory sentencing taken to the extreme: everyone gets the same consequences, regardless of their circumstances. Step out of line with God—even a little bit, even inadvertently—and you're slapped with an endless prison sentence in a place that makes Leavenworth look like Disneyland.

Where's the justice in that? Where's the proportionality between crime and punishment? What kind of a God enjoys seeing his creatures writhe forever—without hope, beyond redemption—in a torture chamber every bit as ghastly and barbaric as a Nazi concentration camp? Wasn't atheist B. C. Johnson right when he charged that "the idea of hell is morally absurd?"[4]

Those are tough and emotionally charged questions. I needed answers from a tough-minded authority, someone who wouldn't flinch from honest challenges. I glanced out the plane's window as suburban Los Angeles passed beneath, shimmering in the bright sunlight. I was anxious for my one-on-one encounter with a well-respected philosopher who has wrestled extensively with this troubling doctrine of eternal damnation.

THE SIXTH INTERVIEW: J. P. MORELAND, PH.D.

It didn't take long to get my rental car and drive to J. P. Moreland's house, which is located not far from the Talbot School of Theology, where he is a professor in the master's program in philosophy and ethics.

Moreland's book, *Beyond Death: Exploring the Evidence for Immortality,* showed that he had done a lot of thorough thinking and personal soul-searching about the doctrine of hell. He and coauthor Gary Habermas also delved into the nature of the soul, near-death experiences, reincarnation, and the theology of heaven.

I also selected Moreland because of his broad background. He is educated in science (with a chemistry degree from the University of Missouri), possesses a thorough knowledge of theology (he has a master's degree from Dallas Theological Seminary), and he's a highly regarded philosopher (having earned his doctorate at the University of Southern California).

He has produced more than a dozen books, including *Scaling the Secular City; Christianity and the Nature of Science; Does God Exist?* (a debate with Kai Nielsen); *The Creation Hypothesis; Body and Soul; Love Your God with All Your Mind;* and the award-winning *Jesus Under Fire.* All of that and he's just fifty-one.

Moreland, dressed casually in a short-sleeve shirt, shorts, and deck shoes without socks, greeted me in the driveway of his ranch-style house. I shook his hand and offered my condolences. I knew he had traveled to San Diego the previous night and watched as his beloved Kansas City Chiefs were humiliated by the lowly Chargers. He was still wearing a baseball-style hat with his team's name emblazoned on the front.

Inside, after exchanging a few pleasantries, I slumped down on his living room couch and sighed. The subject of hell was big, heavy, controversial, a flashpoint for spiritual skeptics. I searched my mind for a starting point.

I finally decided just to be honest. "I'm not sure where to begin," I confessed. "How should we even approach the topic of hell?"

Moreland thought for a moment, then leaned back in his green padded chair. "Maybe," he offered, "we should distinguish between liking or disliking something and judging whether it's right to do."

"What do you mean?"

"Many times something we like isn't the right thing to do," he explained. "Some people say adultery is pleasurable, but most people would agree it's wrong. And often doing the right thing isn't pleasurable. Telling someone a hard truth that they need to hear, or firing someone who isn't doing a good job, can be very unpleasant."

"And," I interjected, "hell evokes a visceral response. People react strongly against the mere idea of it."

"That's right. They tend to evaluate whether it's appropriate based on their feelings or emotional offense to it."

"How do we get beyond that?"

"I think people should try to set aside their feelings," he said. "The basis of their evaluation should be whether hell is a morally just or morally right state of affairs, not whether they like or dislike the concept."

Moreland paused before continuing. "And it's important to understand that if the God of Christianity is real, he hates hell and he hates people going there," he added. "The Bible is very clear: God says he takes no pleasure in the death of the wicked."[5]

Maybe so, but they still end up spending their eternity in a place of absolute horror and abject despair. I thought back to my interview with Charles Templeton, the evangelist-turned-skeptic. Admittedly, he has strong emotions concerning hell, but they seemed to be legitimately fueled by righteous indignation and moral outrage.

Frankly, I was a bit wary of completely divorcing the discussion of hell from our emotional response to it—after all, they seemed hopelessly intertwined.

TACKLING TEMPLETON'S CHALLENGE

Although I understood Moreland's point that the morality or immorality of hell is independent of our feelings toward the issue, I decided my best tactic would be to confront Moreland head-on with Templeton's objections—emotion and all.

I cleared my throat and sat upright, turning to face Moreland more squarely. "Look, Dr. Moreland," I began, my voice notching up in intensity, "I interviewed Charles Templeton about this matter and he was very adamant. He told me: 'I couldn't hold someone's hand to a fire for a moment. Not an instant! How could a loving God, just because you don't obey him and do what he wants, torture you forever—not allowing you to die, but to continue in that pain for eternity?'"

Then I spit out Templeton's last words with the same tone of disgust he had used in talking to me: "'There is no *criminal* who would do this!'"

The challenge almost seemed to reverberate in his living room. Tension quickly mounted. Then, sounding more accusatory than inquisitive, I capped the question by demanding, "Dr. Moreland, what in the world do you say to that?"

So much for his idea of getting beyond feelings.

Now, you have to understand something about J. P. Moreland: he's a philosopher. He's a thinker. He's coolly rational. Nothing seems to rattle his cage. And despite my charged tone, which almost seemed to imply he was personally responsible for the creation of hell, Moreland took no offense. Instead, his mind quickly cut to the core of the issue.

"The key to answering Templeton is in his wording," Moreland began. "He has loaded his question to the point where it's like asking, 'When did you stop beating your wife?' No matter how you reply, you're doomed from the outset if you accept his wording."

"So his premise is wrong," I said. "How so?"

"Well, for one thing, hell is not a torture chamber."

My eyebrows shot up. Certainly that would be news to many generations of Sunday School children who have been frightened into nightmares by gruesome descriptions of the everlasting infliction of fiery agony in Hades.

"It's not?" I asked.

Moreland shook his head. "God doesn't torture people in hell, so he's flat wrong about that," he continued. "Templeton also makes it sound like God is a spoiled child who says to people, 'Look, if you're not willing to obey my arbitrary rules, then I'm going to sentence you for it. You need to know that *my* rules are *my* rules, and if I don't get my way, then I'm going to make you pay.' Well, of course, if God is just a child with arbitrary rules, then it would be capricious for him to sentence people. But that's not at all what is going on here.

"God is the most generous, loving, wonderful, attractive being in the cosmos. He has made us with free will and he has made us for a purpose: to relate lovingly to him and to others. We are not accidents, we're not modified monkeys, we're not random mistakes. And if we fail over and over again to live for the purpose for which we were made—a purpose, by the way, which would allow us to flourish more than living any other way—then God will have absolutely no choice but to give us what we've asked for all along in our lives, which is separation from him."

"And that is hell. . . ."

"Yes, that's hell. One more point: it's wrong to think God is simply a loving being, especially if you mean 'loving' in the sense that most Americans use that word today. Yes, God is a compassionate being, but he's also a just, moral, and pure being. So God's decisions are not based on modern American sentimentalism. This is one of the reasons why people have never had a difficult time with the idea of hell until modern times. People today tend to care only for the softer virtues like love and tenderness, while they've forgotten the hard virtues of holiness, righteousness, and justice.

"So in the wording of his question, Templeton has given us a spiteful being who has imposed these unfair, arbitrary rules and who ultimately stomps his foot and says, 'If I don't get my way, I'm going to torture you forever.'"

Moreland's intense blue-gray eyes locked with mine. "Nothing," he stressed, "could be further from the truth."

GOD'S FALL-BACK POSITION

"Okay, then," I said as I settled deeper into the couch, "here's your chance to set the record straight. Let's lay some groundwork by getting our definitions in order. You said hell is not a torture chamber. Then what is it?"

"The essence of hell is relational," he replied. "Christianity says people are the most valuable things in the entire creation. If people matter, then personal relationships matter, and hell is largely relational.

"In the Bible, hell is separation or banishment from the most beautiful being in the world—God himself. It is exclusion from anything that matters, from all value, not only from God but also from those who have come to know and love him."

I was confused about something. "Is hell a punishment for having broken God's standards?" I asked. "Or is it the natural consequence of people living a life where they say, 'I don't care if I'm separate from God, I want to do things my way,' and then they are given their desire for all eternity by being separated from God forever?"

"It's both," he said. "Make no mistake: hell *is* punishment—but it's not a punish*ing*. It's not torture. The punishment of hell is separation from God, bringing shame, anguish, and regret. And because we will have both body and soul in the resurrected state, the misery experienced can be both mental and physical. But the pain that's suffered will be due to the sorrow from the final, ultimate, unending banishment from God, his kingdom, and the good life for which we were created in the first place. People in hell will deeply grieve all they've lost.

"Hell is the final sentence that says you refused regularly to live for the purpose for which you were made, and the only alternative is to sentence you away for all eternity. So it *is* punishment. But it's also the natural consequence of a life that has been lived in a certain direction."

"According to Genesis, when God created everything, he declared it was 'good,'" I pointed out. "Obviously, God created hell. But how could he possibly think that hell is good? Doesn't that call his character into question?"

"Actually," replied Moreland, "hell was not part of the original creation. Hell is God's fall-back position. Hell is something God was forced to make because people chose to rebel against him and turn against what was best for them and the purpose for which they were created.

"You know, when people founded the United States, they didn't start out by creating jails. They would have much rather had a society without jails. But they were forced to create them because people would not cooperate. The same is true for hell."

"Is hell a physical place?"

"Yes and no. When people die, their soul leaves their body and they're no longer physical. The Bible says when people who are ultimately headed for hell die before Christ's return, they're separated from the presence of God but they're not in a physical place because they're not physical. In that sense, hell is probably not a location, but it's a real part of the universe. It's like you go through a door into another kind of existence."

"Sounds like a near-death experience," I chuckled.

"Well, I think near-death experiences have demonstrated beyond a reasonable doubt that when people die they're still able to be conscious," Moreland replied.

Then he continued: "At the final judgment, our body will be raised and our soul will be reunited with it. At that point, I do think there will be a part of the universe where people will be cut off from the primary place where the activity of God and his people will be manifested. So at that point it does make sense to talk about hell being a place—but it will not be a torture chamber or anything like that."

FLAMES, WORMS, AND GNASHING TEETH

There was that "torture chamber" imagery again. "No wonder that's a popular vision of hell," I said. "When I was about ten years old, I was taken to Sunday school, where the teacher lit a candle and said, 'Do you know how much it hurts to burn your finger? Well, imagine your whole body being in fire forever and ever. That's what hell is.'"

Moreland nodded as if he had heard that kind of story before.

"Now, some kids got scared," I added. "I just got resentful that this guy was trying to manipulate me. I think lots of people have had this sort of experience. You have to admit that when it comes to talking about hell, the Bible certainly does have a tendency to refer to flames."

"That's true," Moreland replied, "but the flames are a figure of speech."

I put up my hand. "Okay, wait a minute," I protested. "I thought you were a conservative scholar. Are you going to try to soften the idea of hell to make it more palatable?"

"Absolutely not," came his reply. "I just want to be biblically accurate. We know that the reference to flames is figurative because if you try to take it literally, it makes no sense. For example, hell is described as a place of utter darkness and yet there are flames, too. How can that be? Flames would light things up.

"In addition, we're told Christ is going to return surrounded by flames and that he's going to have a big sword coming out of his mouth. But nobody thinks Christ won't be able to say anything because he'll be choking on a sword. The figure of the sword stands for the word of God in judgment. The flames stand for Christ coming in judgment. In Hebrews 12:29, God is called a consuming fire. Yet nobody thinks God is a cosmic Bunsen burner. Using the flame imagery is a way of saying he's a God of judgment."

"What about hell being a place where worms constantly eat people's flesh," I asked.

"In Jesus' day thousands of animals were sacrificed every week in the Temple, and there was a sewage system for the blood and fat to flow outside, where it gathered in a pool. There were worms constantly ingesting that. It was a very ugly place," Moreland said. "When Jesus was teaching, he used this metaphor as a way of saying hell is worse than that disgusting place outside the city."

"There's also the phrase 'gnashing of teeth' to describe those in hell," I said. "Doesn't that refer to people reacting to the pain of torture?"

"More precisely, this is meant to describe a state of anger or realization of great loss," Moreland said. "It's an expression of rage at realizing that one has made a huge mistake. If you've ever been around people who are self-absorbed, self-centered, and highly narcissistic, they get angry when they don't get their way. I believe the gnashing of teeth is an expression of the type of personality of people who will belong in hell."

"No flames, no worms, no gnashing of teeth from torture—maybe hell isn't as bad as we thought," I said in an effort to inject a little levity.

Moreland responded quickly. "It would be a mistake to think that way," he said firmly. "Any figure of speech has a literal point. What is figurative is the burning flame; what is literal is that this is a place of utter heartbreak. It is a loss of everything, and it's meant to stand for the fact that hell is the worst possible situation that could ever happen to a person."

"You mentioned people in hell who are self-absorbed and narcissistic, who've rejected God all their life," I said. "Is it possible that, for these kind of people, heaven would be hell?"

"Let me put it this way," he said. "Have you ever been around somebody who was unbelievably good looking, extremely attractive, and a lot smarter than you are? When you're in a social situation, people want to listen to him, not you. Suppose you don't care for that person, but you're kept in a room with him twenty-four hours a day for thirty years. That would be an unbelievably difficult experience.

"Now, multiply those qualities ten thousand times, and that's a little bit of what God is like. He is real, real smart. He's very attractive. He's a lot more morally pure than we are. And if people do not fall passionately in love with him, then to force them to have to be around him forever—doing the kinds of things that people who love him would want to do—would be utterly uncomfortable.

"You have to understand that people's character is not formed by decisions all at once, but by thousands of little choices they make every day without even knowing about it. Each day we're preparing ourselves for either being with God and his people and valuing the things he values, or choosing not to engage with those things. So, yes, hell is primarily a place for people who would not want to go to heaven."

"You're saying people consciously choose hell?"

"No, I don't mean they consciously reject heaven and choose to go to hell instead. But they *do* choose not to care about the kinds of values that will be present in heaven every day."

I said, "So, in effect, by the way we live our lives we're either preparing ourselves for being in God's presence and enjoying him for eternity, or we're preparing ourselves for an existence where we try to make ourselves the center of the universe and we have no interest in being with God or the people who love him."

Moreland nodded. "That's absolutely right. So hell is not simply a sentence. It *is* that, but it's also the end of a path that is chosen, to some degree, in this life right here and now, day by day."

Even so, there are aspects of hell that seem to violate our sense of justice. At least, I've felt that in the past. I took advantage of a pause in our conversation to reach into my briefcase and retrieve a list of them that I had written on the airplane.

"How about if I ask for your reply to each of these issues," I said to Moreland. "My goal isn't to get into an argument with you. I just want you to spell out your perspective, and then at the end I'll weigh whether I think you're giving adequate responses and if, in total, the doctrine of hell stands up to scrutiny."

"Sounds fair," he replied.

I glanced at the list and decided to begin with one of the most emotion-charged objections of all.

Objection 1: How Can God Send Children to Hell?

People recoil at the thought of children languishing in hell. In fact, some atheists like to taunt Christians by dredging up writings by nineteenth-century evangelists who used horrific language to describe the ghastly experiences of children in hell. For example, a British priest nicknamed "the children's apostle" wrote these gruesome words:

> A little child is in this red-hot oven. Hear how it screams to come out! See how it turns and twists itself about in the fire! It beats its head against the roof of the oven. It stamps its little feet on the floor. You can see on the face of this little child what you see on the faces of all in hell—despair, desperate and horrible.[6]

"The idea of children in hell—well, it's too much," I said to Moreland. "How can there be a loving God if children are subjected to hell?" I was interested in seeing whether Moreland's response would be consistent with scholar Norman Geisler's earlier assessment of this issue.

"Remember," Moreland cautioned in light of the quote about the child in the oven, "the biblical language about fire and flames is figurative."

"Yes, okay, but still—will there be children in hell?"

Moreland, who is the father of two daughters, leaned forward as he spoke. "You must understand that in the afterlife, our personalities reflect an adult situation anyway, so we can say for sure that there will be no children in hell," he began.

"And certainly there will be no one in hell who, if they had a chance to grow up to be adults, would have chosen to go to heaven. No one will go to hell simply because all they needed was a little more time and they died prematurely."

Moreland reached over to a table and retrieved his leather-clad Bible. "Besides, in the Bible children are universally viewed as figures of speech for salvation. In all of the texts where children are used in regard to the afterlife, they're used as pictures of being saved. There's no case where children are ever used as figures of damnation."

He flipped through the Old Testament until he settled on Second Samuel. "Here's a good example," he said. "The child that King David conceived in an adulterous relationship with Bathsheba died, and David says in Second Samuel 12:23: 'I will go to him, but he will not return to me.'

"David was expressing the truth that his child will be in heaven and that he would join him someday. So that is another piece of evidence that children will not be in hell."

Objection 2: Why Does Everyone Suffer the Same in Hell?

As I was formulating my next question, I rose from the couch and wandered toward the front window, pausing in a pool of sunlight that was dancing on the carpet. The Massachusetts case involving Judge Mathers was lurking in the back of my mind.

"Our sense of justice demands that evil people be held accountable for the way they've harmed others," I said. "And in that sense, hell might be an appropriate sanction for some. However, it violates our sense of fairness that Adolf Hitler would bear the same eternal punishment as someone who lived a pretty good life by our standards, but who made the decision not to follow God."

Moreland was listening intently. "It seems unjust that everyone is subjected to the same consequences," he said. "Is that what you're saying?"

"Yes, that's right. Doesn't that bother you?"

Moreland turned in his Bible to the New Testament. "Actually," he said, "everyone doesn't experience hell in the same way. The Bible teaches that there are different degrees of suffering and punishment."

He came to Matthew 11 and his index finger searched until it settled on verses 20–24, which he read aloud:

> Then Jesus began to denounce the cities in which most of his miracles had been performed, because they did not repent. "Woe to you, Korazin! Woe to you, Bethsaida! If the miracles that were performed in you had been performed in Tyre and Sidon, they would have repented long ago in sackcloth and ashes. But I tell you, it will be more bearable for Tyre and Sidon on the day of judgment than for you. And you, Capernaum, will you be lifted up to the skies? No, you will go down to the depths. If the miracles that were performed in you had been performed in Sodom, it would have remained to this day. But I tell you that it will be more bearable for Sodom on the day of judgment than for you."

Moreland closed the book. "Jesus is saying that people will be sentenced in accordance with their deeds," he said.

"No one-size-fits-all?" I asked. "Justice will be adjusted according to each individual?"

"Exactly. There will be degrees of separation, isolation, and emptiness in hell. I think this is significant because it emphasizes that God's justice is proportional. There is not exactly the same justice for everyone who refuses the mercy of God.

"Remember, if God really does let people shape their own character by the thousands of choices they make, he is also going to allow them to suffer the natural consequences of the character that they've chosen to have. And those who are in worse shape personally will experience a greater degree of isolation and emptiness."

Objection 3: Why Are People Punished Infinitely for Finite Crimes?

How can any wrongs we've committed in this life merit *eternal* punishment? Isn't it unfair to say that a *finite* life of sin warrants *infinite* punishment? Where's the justice in that?

"Wouldn't a loving God make the punishment fit the crime by not making hell last forever?" I asked as I sat back down on the edge of the couch. "How can we do anything in this life that would warrant eternal torture?"

"Remember, it's not torture," Moreland pointed out. "The wording is critical. It's not eternal conscious torture; it's eternal conscious suffering due to being sentenced away from God."

"Okay," I said, "but that doesn't answer the question."

"No, it doesn't. But let me try. First, we all know that the degree to which a person warrants punishment is not a function of the length of time it took to commit a crime. For example, a murder can take ten seconds to commit; stealing somebody's *Encyclopaedia Britannica* could take half a day if it took a long time to break into the house. My point is that the degree of someone's just punishment is not a function of how long it took to commit the deed; rather, it's a function of how severe the deed itself was.

"And that leads to the second point. What is the most heinous thing a person can do in this life? Most people, because they don't think much about God, will say it's harming animals or destroying the environment or hurting another person. And, no question, all of those are horrible. But they pale in light of the worst thing a person can do, which is to mock and dishonor and refuse to love the person that we owe absolutely everything to, which is our Creator, God himself.

"You have to understand that God is infinitely greater in his goodness, holiness, kindness, and justice than anyone else. To think that a person could go through their whole life constantly ignoring him, constantly mocking him by the way they choose to live without him, saying, 'I couldn't care less about what you put me here to do. I couldn't care less about your values or your Son's death for me. I'm going to ignore all of that'—*that's* the ultimate sin. And the only punishment worthy of that is the ultimate punishment, which is everlasting separation from God.

"As Alan Gomes has pointed out, the nature of the *object* against which the sin is committed, as well as the nature of the sin itself, must be taken into account when determining the degree of heinousness."[7]

Moreland's answer made me think of the incident where a lawyer asked Jesus what the greatest law is. Jesus told him: "Love the Lord your God with all your heart and with all your soul and with all your strength and with all your mind, and, love your neighbor as yourself."[8]

In the United States, the most serious crime—murder—is punishable by its most severe sanction, which is being separated from society for life in prison. And there did seem to be a certain logic in saying that defiantly violating God's ultimate law should bring the ultimate sanction, which is being separated from God and his people for eternity.

Objection 4: Couldn't God Force Everyone to Go to Heaven?

"Let me go back to a point you made at the outset," I said to Moreland. "You said God is grieved by the necessity of hell."

"Yes, that's right."

"Then why can't he simply force everyone to go to heaven? That would seem to be a simple solution."

"Because that," replied Moreland, "would be immoral."

"Immoral?" I said in surprise. "More immoral than hell?"

"Yes, immoral. Follow me on this: there's a difference between *intrinsic* value and *instrumental* value. Something has intrinsic value if it's valuable and good in and of itself; something has instrumental value if it's valuable as a means to an end. For example, saving lives is intrinsically good. Driving on the right side of the street is an instrumental value; it's just good because it helps keep order. If society decided that everyone should drive on the left side, that would be okay. The goal is to preserve order and save lives.

"Now, when you treat people as instrumentally valuable, or only as a means to an end, you're dehumanizing them, and that's wrong. You're treating people as things when you treat them merely as a means to an end. You only respect people when you treat them as having intrinsic value."

"And how does this relate to forcing people to go to heaven?" I asked.

"If you were to force people to do something against their free choice, you would be dehumanizing them. You would be saying that the good of what you want to do is more valuable than respecting their choices, and so you're treating people as a means to an end by requiring them to do something they don't want. That's what it would be like if God forced everyone to go to heaven.

"If God has given people free will, Lee, then there's no guarantee that everybody's going to choose to cooperate with him. The option of forcing everyone to go to heaven is immoral, because it's dehumanizing; it strips them of the dignity of making their own decision; it denies them their freedom of choice; and it treats them as a means to an end.

"God can't make people's character for them, and people who do evil or cultivate false beliefs start a slide away from God that ultimately ends in hell. God respects human freedom. In fact, it would be unloving—a sort of divine rape—to force people to accept heaven and God if they didn't really want them. When God allows people to say 'no' to him, he actually respects and dignifies them."

Objection 5: Why Doesn't God Just Snuff People Out?

Another aspect of hell that's especially troubling to people is that its duration is eternal. But what if hell didn't last forever? Instead, what if God annihilated people—that is, snuffed them out of existence—instead of forcing them to be consciously separated from him forever and ever?

"Surely," I said to Moreland, "that would be more humane than an eternity of regret and remorse."

"Believe it or not, everlasting separation from God is morally superior to annihilation," he replied. "Why would God be morally justified in annihilating somebody? The only way that's a good thing would be the end result, which would be to keep people from experiencing the conscious separation from God forever. Well, then you're treating people as a means to an end.

"It's like forcing people to go to heaven. What you're saying is, 'The thing that really matters is that people no longer suffer consciously, so I'm going to snuff this person out of existence in order to achieve that end.' Do you see? That's treating the person as a means to an end.

"What hell does is recognize that people have intrinsic value. If God loves intrinsic value, then he has got to be a sustainer of persons, because that means he is a sustainer of intrinsic value. He refuses to snuff out a creature that was made in his own image. So in the final analysis, hell is the only morally legitimate option.

"God doesn't like it, but he quarantines them. This honors their freedom of choice. He just will not override that. In fact, God considers people so intrinsically valuable that he sent his Son, Jesus Christ, to suffer and die so that they can, if they choose, spend eternity in heaven with him."

But some theologians claim that annihilation is what's taught by the Scriptures. They say the Bible teaches that while the punish*ment* of hell is eternal, the punish*ing* isn't eternal.

Annihilationists like to cite Psalm 37, which says the wicked "will be no more," "like smoke they [will] vanish away," and "transgressors shall be altogether destroyed." And they point to Psalm 145:20, where David said, "The Lord preserves all who love him; but all the wicked he will destroy." And Isaiah 1:28: "Rebels and sinners shall be destroyed together and those who forsake the Lord shall be consumed." They also contend that the metaphors used by Jesus are evidence of annihilationism: the wicked are "bound in bundles to be burned," the bad fish are thrown away, and the harmful plants are rooted up.[9]

I asked Moreland: "Doesn't this mean that annihilationism is consistent with Scripture and therefore a reasonable way to harmonize God's fairness with the doctrine of hell?"

Moreland stood firm. "No, it's not the biblical teaching," he insisted. "Whenever you're trying to understand what an author is teaching, you begin with clear passages that were intended by the author to speak on the question, and then move to unclear passages that may not be intended to teach on the subject.

"Let me illustrate this. There are passages in the Bible that say Jesus Christ died for everyone. There's also Galatians 2:20, where the apostle Paul says, 'Christ died for me.' Now, am I to assume from that passage that Christ only died for Paul? No, but why not? Because there are clear passages that teach that Christ died for everybody, so when we come to Paul's statement we say that it's obvious he didn't mean Jesus died only for Paul, because we interpret the unclear in light of the clear.

"Now, how about these passages concerning hell? The Old Testament has clear passages on hell being everlasting. Daniel 12:2 says at the end of the age, the just are raised to everlasting life, the unjust to everlasting punishment.[10] The identical Hebrew word for *everlasting* is used in both instances. If we're going to say that people are annihilated in hell, we should say they're annihilated in heaven. You can't have your cake and eat it too. And that passage is clearly meant to be teaching on this question.

"In the New Testament, in Matthew 25, Jesus offers a clear teaching where he's intending to address the question of the eternal state of heaven and hell, and he uses the same word *everlasting* to refer to both.

"So we go from these clear passages to the ambiguous teaching about being 'cut off.' All that talk about being destroyed and being cut off in the Old Testament is usually meant to mean people being cut off from Israel and the land. Most of those passages have little or nothing to do with everlasting life; they have to do with being cut off in this life to the promises Abraham gave to the people in the land."

But, I pointed out, the annihilationists also cite the biblical language of fire as evidence that people are destroyed rather than languish forever in hell. As well-respected British pastor John R. W. Stott put it: "The fire itself is termed 'eternal' and 'unquenchable,' but it would be very odd if what is thrown into it proves indestructible. Our expectation would be the opposite: it would be consumed for ever, not tormented for ever."[11]

Moreland, however, was adamant. "The flame language is figurative," he said. "In Revelation, we are told that hell and death are cast into the lake of fire. Now, hell is not something that can burn. It's a realm. That's like saying heaven could be burned. Heaven's not the kind of thing that burns. And how can you burn death? Death isn't something you can set a torch to and ignite it.

"So it's obvious that the lake of fire is meant to stand for judgment. When it says an end is placed to hell, the word 'hell' is meant to refer to the temporary state of those between their death and the final resurrection. At that point, they're given their bodies again and they will be located away from God. Death is put to an end because there's not going to be any more death. So the flame language of the lake of fire is clearly meant to be a figure of speech for judgment, not a literal burning."

Objection 6: How Can Hell Exist Alongside of Heaven?

"If heaven is supposed to be a place without tears, then how can there be an eternal hell existing at the same time?" I asked. "Wouldn't those in heaven mourn for those who are suffering forever in hell?"

"First of all, I think people in heaven will realize that hell is a way of honoring people as being intrinsically valuable creatures made in God's image," Moreland said.

"Second, many times a person's ability to enjoy something comes from growing older and gaining a more mature perspective. When my children were young, one child was not able to enjoy a gift if the other child got a present that she thought was a little bit better. When they got older, they were able to enjoy their present, irrespective of the other person's. In fact, if they were worrying about what the other person got, they would be allowing the other person to control them.

"C. S. Lewis said hell doesn't have veto power over heaven. He meant that people in heaven will not be denied the privilege of enjoying their life just because they're consciously aware of hell. If they couldn't, then hell would have veto power over heaven.

"You have to remember that the soul is big enough to have an unperturbed sense of joy, well-being, love, and happiness, while at the same time having a sense of grief and sadness for others. Those are not inconsistent states in a person's life, and it is a mark of a person's character and maturity that they're able to have those states at the same time."

Objection 7: Why Didn't God Create Only Those He Knew Would Follow Him?

"If God knows the future, why did he create people whom he knew would never turn to him and who would therefore end up in hell?" I asked. "Couldn't he have created only those whom he knew would follow him and simply not created those whom he knew would reject him? That option would seem to be much more humane than hell."

"It depends on God's goal," said Moreland. "If God had chosen to create just a handful of four, six, or seven people, maybe he could have only created those people who would go to heaven. The problem is that once God starts to create more people, it becomes more difficult to just create the people who would choose him and not create the people who wouldn't."

"Why is that?"

"Because one of the reasons God put us here is to give us a chance to affect other people."

Moreland thought for a moment before coming up with an analogy. "Do you recall the *Back to the Future* movies?" he asked.

"Remember how they went back in time, changed one small detail, and then when they returned to the future the entire town was completely changed? I think there's an element of truth to that.

"The simple fact of the matter is that we are impacted by observing other people. Suppose, for example, that when I was a little boy God gave my parents the choice to move to Illinois as opposed to staying in Missouri. Let's say there was a Christian neighbor who was a hypocrite, and I observed this man and chose because of his life to say 'no' to the gospel the rest of my life. Now suppose that people at work looked at how obnoxious I was and five people become followers of Christ because of my bad example of what a non-Christian life looks like. Well, if we go to Illinois, we get one person lost—me—but five people are redeemed.

"On the other hand, suppose God chooses not to give the offer of a new job to my dad and we stay in Missouri. I might have a track coach who was a Christian and who pours his life into me and I end up choosing to follow God because of that. But because my Christian life is not really what it ought to be, five people are influenced away from Christ.

"Do you see? It's a *Back to the Future* scenario. When God chooses to create somebody, he or she has an impact on other people's choices and it might be that they have an impact on their decisions to trust Christ or not.

"There is another part of this, which has to do with how the soul is created. There's a view that the soul comes into existence at conception and is in some way passed on by the parents. In other words, soulish potentialities are contained in the parents' egg and sperm. It's called *traducianism.* This means my parents created my soul in the act of reproduction. Consequently, I could not have had different parents. That means, then, that the only way God could make me is if my entire ancestral lineage had preceded me, because different grandparents mean different parents and thus different materials for the soul.

"And here's the implication of traducianism for our question: God has to weigh completely different ancestral chains in their entirety. He can't just weigh individual people. So it may be that God allows some chains to come about, with some individuals in them who reject Christ—say, my great, great-grandfather—but which allow for others to be born who do trust Christ. In other words, God would be balancing alternative chains and not just alternative people.

"When God is making these judgments, his purpose is not to keep as many people out of hell as possible. His goal is to get as many people into heaven as possible.

"And it may be, sadly enough, that he's going to have to allow some more people who will choose to go to hell to be created in order to get a larger number of people who choose to go to heaven."

Objection 8: Why Doesn't God Give People a Second Chance?

The Bible says explicitly that people are destined to die once and to then face judgment.[12] Yet if God is really loving, why wouldn't he give people a second chance after death to make the decision to follow him and go to heaven?

"If people tasted hell, wouldn't that give them a strong motivation to change their minds?" I asked.

"This question assumes God didn't do everything he could do before people died, and I reject that," Moreland said. "God does everything he can to give people a chance, and there will be not a single person who will be able to say to God, 'If you had just not allowed me to die prematurely, if you'd have given me another twelve months, I know I would have made that decision.'

"The Bible tells us God is delaying the return of Christ to the earth to give everybody all the time he possibly can so they will come to him.[13] If all a person needed was a little bit more time to come to Christ, then God would extend their time on this earth to give them that chance. So there will be nobody who just needed a little more time or who died prematurely who would have responded to another chance to receive Christ.

"God is fair. He isn't trying to make it difficult for people. I believe it's certainly possible that those who respond to the light from nature that they have received will either have the message of the gospel sent to them, or else it may be that God will judge them based on his knowledge of what they would have done had they had a chance to hear the gospel. The simple fact is God rewards those who seek him."[14]

That only dealt with part of the question, however. "Wait a minute," I said. "Wouldn't death and the awareness of the presence or absence of God after you die be a very motivating thing for people?"

"Yes, it would, but in a negative way. First, you've got to realize that the longer people live separated from God, the less likely they are able to exercise their free choice and trust him. This is why most people who come to Christ do so when they're young. The longer you live with a bad habit, the harder it is to turn that habit around. It's not impossible, but it's harder. So what would make people think that, say, a ten-year incubation period of being separated from God would get their attention?

"Besides, that would make life before death utterly irrelevant. Then the question would be, why didn't God create people from the beginning with the incubation period? Why did he create them on earth for seventy-five years and let them die and then put them in the incubation period if it was the incubation period that they really needed in the first place? Here's the truth, Lee: this life *is* the incubation period!

"The next thing you have to keep in mind is if people saw the judgment seat of God after death, it would be so coercive that they would no longer have the power of free choice. Any 'decision' they made would not be a real genuine free choice; it would be totally coerced.

"It would be like me holding a paddle over my daughter and saying, 'You will say you're sorry to your sister for wearing her dress without asking.' Any apology would not be a real apology, it would just be avoidance. And people who would 'choose' in a second chance would not really be choosing God, his kingdom, or his ways—nor would they be suited for life in his kingdom. They'd be making a prudent 'choice' to avoid judgment only.

"I'll suggest one more thing. God maintains a delicate balance between keeping his existence sufficiently evident so people will know he's there and yet hiding his presence enough so that people who want to choose to ignore him can do it. This way, their choice of destiny is really free."

Objection 9: Isn't Reincarnation More Rational Than Hell?

Hindus reject the idea of hell. Instead, they believe in reincarnation, where people return to this world in another form after their death and are given another opportunity to work off the bad karma they generated in their past life and move toward enlightenment.

"Wouldn't reincarnation be a rational way for a loving God to give people a fresh start so that they might repent the next time around and he wouldn't have to send them to hell?" I asked. "Wouldn't this be preferable to hell?"

"Remember, we don't decide what's true based on what we like or don't like. We have to consider the evidence. I don't know any other way to decide whether something's true except by looking at the evidence," came Moreland's reply.

"Yes," I said, "but isn't there evidence for reincarnation—specifically, individuals who have memories of prior lives or even speak in languages that they wouldn't otherwise know?"

"I think the evidence for reincarnation is weak for several reasons," he said. "For example, it's incoherent. Let me give you an illustration of why. The number two is essentially even. If you were to tell me you're contemplating the number two but it's an odd number, I would tell you, 'You may be thinking about three or five, but you can't be thinking of two, because I'll tell you one thing that's essential to it—it's got to be an even number.'

"Now, it's not essential to me that I'm five-foot-eight. It's not essential to me that I weigh one hundred and sixty-five pounds. But it *is* essential to me that I'm a human.

"If you were to say, 'J. P. Moreland is in the other room and he has lost five pounds,' most people would say, 'Good for him.' What if you said, 'J. P. Moreland is in the other room and guess what? He's an ice cube.' Most people would say, 'That can't be J. P. Moreland, because if there's one thing I know about him, it's that he's human. He's not an ice cube.'

"Well, reincarnation says that I could come back as a dog, as an amoeba—heck, I don't know why I couldn't come back as an ice cube. If that's true, what's the difference between being J. P. Moreland and anything else? There's nothing *essential* to me. And just like being even is essential to the number two, so being human is essential to me—and reincarnation says that what is essential to me isn't really essential after all."

"Therefore," I interjected, "it's incoherent."

"Exactly," Moreland said. "Another reason I don't believe in reincarnation is because most of these evidences you've suggested—things like supposed memories of past lives—can be explained better by other means.

"There can be psychological explanations—people seem to remember certain details, but they're vague or lucky guesses, or there could be demonic explanations for some of this activity. Actually, when you carefully examine the research, you find it fails to support reincarnation.[15]

"Finally, I don't believe in reincarnation because there's an expert on this question, and he's Jesus of Nazareth. He's the only person in history who died, rose from the dead, and spoke authoritatively on the question. And Jesus says reincarnation is false, and that there's one death and after that comes the judgment. His apostles, whom he instructed carefully, reiterated his teachings on this."

Instead, Jesus taught about the reality of hell. In fact, he discussed the subject more than anyone else in the Bible. "It's ironic," I pointed out, "that many atheists embrace Jesus as having been a great teacher, and yet he's the one who had the most to say about hell."

"Yes," said Moreland, "and remember this: the evidence is that Jesus and his followers were virtuous people. If you want to know how to view the poor, you ask someone who's like Mother Teresa. You don't ask Hugh Hefner, because a person like Mother Teresa has got more character than he does. If you want to know whether hell is ultimately fair, you ask Jesus. And here's the thing: he saw no problem with the doctrine.

"I think we're on thin ice when we compare our moral sentiments and moral intuitions with Jesus'. We're saying we have greater insight into what's fair and what isn't than he does. And I think that's not the kind of arena we want to step into."

THE TRUTH ABOUT HELL

I leaned back on the couch and thought for a moment. Moreland had adroitly responded to the toughest objections to the issue of hell. I had to admit that when I took all of his answers together, they did seem to provide a reasonable rationale for the doctrine.

Yet that didn't remove my discomfort. And I was in good company. C. S. Lewis once said the doctrine of hell is "one of the chief grounds on which Christianity is attacked as barbarous and the goodness of God impugned."[16]

As for Moreland, he had spoken as a philosopher and theologian, but I was curious about his personal reaction to this issue. "What about you, J. P.?" I asked. "You've woven some convincing arguments in favor of the doctrine, but be honest—don't you have times when you feel terribly uncomfortable about the existence of hell?"

Moreland removed his silver-rimmed glasses and rubbed his eyes before speaking. "Absolutely," he said. "No question. But, again, feeling uncomfortable about something is not the same thing as having a rational, considered judgment that it's wrong. I believe that hell is morally justifiable, but I don't feel comfortable about it because it's sad."

He paused, then continued. "Keep in mind that God doesn't feel comfortable about it, either. He doesn't like it. So what's the proper response to feeling uncomfortable? It's not to try to create a view of the afterlife that keeps me from feeling uncomfortable. That's a terrible way to approach truth. The proper thing to do is to admit that hell is real and to allow our feelings of discomfort to motivate us to action.

"For those who don't know Christ, it should motivate them to redouble their efforts to seek him and to find him. For those of us who know him, it should cause us to redouble our efforts to extend his message of mercy and grace to those who need it.

"And we need to keep the right perspective through it all. Remember that hell will forever be a monument to human dignity and the value of human choice. It is a quarantine where God says two important things: 'I respect freedom of choice enough to where I won't coerce people, and I value my image-bearers so much that I will not annihilate them.'"

"Can you see how the doctrine of hell can be a stumbling block for spiritual seekers?"

"Yes, I do, and I'd like to say something about that. Whenever you're trying to start a friendship with any person, you don't understand everything about him and you don't necessarily agree or feel good about every view he holds. But you have to ask, on balance, do you trust this person enough to want to enter a friendship with him?

"The same is true with Jesus. Every single issue isn't going to be resolved before we enter into a relationship with him. But the question is, on balance, can you trust him?

"I'd encourage any seeker to read the gospel of John and then ask, 'Can I trust Jesus?' I think the answer is yes. And I believe that, over time, as we develop our relationship with him, we'll even come to trust him in those areas where right now we lack complete understanding."

"WHAT IS GOD TO DO?"

I let Moreland's words take root for a moment before standing and thanking him for his time and expertise. "This was a tough topic," I said. "I appreciate your willingness to talk about it."

He nodded and smiled. "No problem," he said. "I hope it was helpful."

He walked me outside, where we shook hands and I climbed into the car to head back toward the airport. The heavy traffic didn't bother me; I had plenty of time before my flight. In fact, I appreciated the leisurely drive because it gave me an opportunity to reflect on the interview.

Was hell the only option open to God? Is it just and moral? Is the doctrine logically consistent? Clearly, Jesus thought it was. And I believed that Moreland's analysis, overall, was sufficient to knock down hell as an obstacle.

That didn't mean I was totally comfortable with every single nuance of the points he had made. But it did mean his explanations, when taken as a whole, were strong enough so that I wasn't going to let this issue derail my spiritual journey.

While entangled in the inevitable Los Angeles traffic jam, I reached into my briefcase and rummaged around for the research materials I had compiled in preparation for my talk with Moreland. Finally, I managed to pull out the tape of a previous interview about hell that I had conducted with renowned theologian D. A. Carson.

Popping it into my tape player, I fast-forwarded to some remarks that seemed to be an apt conclusion for the afternoon:

> Hell is not a place where people are consigned because they were pretty good blokes, but they just didn't believe the right stuff. They're consigned there, first and foremost, because they defy their maker and want to be at the center of the universe. Hell is not filled with people who have already repented, only God isn't gentle enough or good enough to let them out. It's filled with people who, for all eternity, *still* want to be the center of the universe and who persist in their God-defying rebellion.
>
> What is God to do? If he says it doesn't matter to him, then God is no longer a God to be admired. He's either amoral or positively creepy. For him to act in any other way in the face of such blatant defiance would be to reduce God himself.[17]

DELIBERATIONS

Questions for Reflection or Group Study

- What was your concept of hell before you read this chapter? How has Moreland's analysis either re-enforced or challenged those beliefs?
- Mark Twain once quipped, "Heaven for the climate; hell for the companionship." In light of Moreland's description of hell, how would you respond to someone who offered that observation?
- Has the doctrine of hell been a stumbling block to you as a spiritual seeker or a believer in Christianity? In what specific ways has Moreland dealt with the concerns that held you back in your spiritual journey?

FOR FURTHER EVIDENCE

More Resources on This Topic

- Gary R. Habermas and J. P. Moreland. *Beyond Death: Exploring the Evidence for Immortality.* Wheaton, Ill.: Crossway, 1998.
- Michael J. Murray. "Heaven and Hell." In *Reason for the Hope Within,* ed. by Michael J. Murray, 287–317. Grand Rapids, Mich.: Eerdmans, 1999.
- William V. Crockett, editor. *Four Views on Hell.* Grand Rapids, Mich.: Zondervan, 1996.

7

OBJECTION #7: CHURCH HISTORY IS LITTERED WITH OPPRESSION AND VIOLENCE

Christianity has (by certain people) been used throughout history as an excuse for some of the most brutal, heartless, and senseless atrocities known to man. The historical examples are not difficult to recall: the Crusades; the Inquisitions; the witch-burnings; the Holocaust. . . . I did not see much in Christianity that I considered to be worth the having.

Ken Schei, atheist[1]

Christianity has been a boon to mankind . . . (and) has had a beneficent effect upon the human race. . . . Most people today who live in an ostensibly Christian environment with Christian ethics do not realize how much we owe Jesus of Nazareth. . . . What goodness and mercy there is in this world has come in large measure from him.

D. James Kennedy, Christian[2]

Wayne W. Olson was always the life of the party. An imposing, avuncular judge, with pale blue eyes and a crown of white hair, Olson would regale everyone with side-splitting stories from his often-bizarre experiences at Cook County Criminal Court. He had a keen wit, a prodigious capacity for booze, and the backslapping friendliness of an old-time Chicago alderman.

Olson was an undistinguished but seemingly conscientious jurist. He especially liked to see his name in the paper, so he would frequently slip me stories when I was the *Chicago Tribune*'s reporter at the Criminal Courts Building on Chicago's West Side.

At the end of the day, sometimes we would lounge around his chambers and swap jokes. Occasionally we'd have some laughs over drinks at Jean's, a popular hangout down the block, where he would entertain everyone with stories about how he worked his way through law school as a drummer in a polka band. An inveterate extrovert, he couldn't stand to be alone.

Once he called the press room and invited me to a wedding. I went up to his chambers and found a jovial Olson presiding over the impromptu marriage of a handcuffed burglar—whom he had just sentenced to three years in prison—and his very pregnant girlfriend. Olson instantly designated me as the best man.

"Sorry," he said with a smile as deputies led away the groom after a two-minute ceremony. "No honeymoon."

As a narcotics judge hearing routine criminal cases, Olson wasn't in a position to pave any new judicial paths. At least, not on purpose. However, on Thanksgiving weekend of 1980, Olson unwittingly became entangled in an incident that was unprecedented in American jurisprudence.

After Olson had driven away from the courthouse, anticipating a restful four-day vacation, a team of FBI agents surreptitiously broke into his darkened chambers and planted a judicially approved listening device. This marked the first time in United States history that federal investigators had bugged the chambers of a sitting judge—an honor that Olson, had he known, would have gladly relinquished to someone else.

Terrence Hake, the prosecutor assigned to work in Olson's courtroom, actually was an undercover agent who was part of a clandestine government investigation called "Operation Greylord." After Olson returned from the holiday, whenever anyone under surveillance would walk into his chambers, Hake would use a hidden transmitter to send a coded message to an FBI agent stationed in a car parked outside. The agent would then signal another investigator to activate the bug so that agents could eavesdrop on what transpired behind the closed doors.[3]

In all, more than two hundred and fifty hours of conversations were secretly recorded—and they confirmed government suspicions that the judge had been leading a double life. The likable, easy-going Olson—Mr. Popularity of the county courthouse—turned out to be a thoroughly corrupt extortionist who was cynically selling justice to the highest bidder.

Preserved forever on tape was Olson taking kickbacks from attorneys and perverting justice at every turn. At one point, he was overheard to say, "I love people that take dough because you know exactly where you stand."[4] In fact, within days after the bug was planted, agents listened in astonishment as Olson brazenly fixed a narcotics case with a crooked lawyer:

> Olson: I'm a coin collector.
>
> Attorney: Is two [hundred dollars] enough—sufficient, judge? I cleared seven hundred and sixty five [dollars] for the day.
>
> Olson: Well, I made a deal with somebody, but I'd rather give it to you; you'd do a better job.
>
> Attorney: I gave you a deuce [two hundred dollars]. If it's not enough, just tell me. Whatever the deal is....
>
> Olson: I like the guy that gives me half of ... what he gets.... It's just that some days I get nothing. It's a shame to have a guy come here and not have anything.[5]

I had already left the *Tribune* to edit another newspaper when the stunning news broke: Olson had been indicted on fifty-five counts of bribery, extortion, and racketeering. I shook my head. He had deceived me, his colleagues, and the public for so many years. I felt betrayed and angered over his cavalier trashing of the very laws he had sworn to uphold. It was an incredible reversal of fortune—the judge who had once presided so regally over the fate of others now found himself sentenced to twelve years in a federal penitentiary.

And he didn't go to prison alone. Dozens of other crooked judges and lawyers also found themselves swept up in the net of Operation Greylord, the most successful undercover probe in the history of the Cook County court system—and an investigation which raised questions that, by analogy, also are relevant to Christianity.

CORRUPT TO THE CORE?

One of the issues that surfaced through Operation Greylord was this: when the history of Chicago is written, will the crimes of Wayne Olson and other corrupt court officials be seen as anomalies in an otherwise honest system of justice? In other words, is the criminal justice apparatus fundamentally untainted and impartial except for those rare blemishes that have occurred when a rogue judge has tried to cash in for himself?

Or are Olson and his cronies symptomatic of widespread and systematic corruption that has corroded the very DNA of justice in Cook County? Is the court system compromised to its core by extortion and favoritism, so that Olson's case was actually a window into "business as usual" among the local judiciary?

Essentially these same questions could be asked about Christianity. Christians tend to see the instances of church abuse and violence through the centuries as anomalies in an otherwise positive institution. Critics, however, are more apt to see travesties like the Crusades, the Inquisition, and the Salem witch trials as illustrative of a deeper problem: that Christianity itself is tainted to its core by a power-hungry desire to impose its will on others—even through violence and exploitation, if necessary. One of modern history's most famous atheists, Bertrand Russell, said this was inevitable:

> As soon as absolute truth is supposed to be contained in the sayings of a certain man, there is a body of experts to interpret his sayings, and these experts infallibly acquire power, since they hold the key to truth. Like any other privileged caste, they use their power for their own advantage.... They become necessarily opponents of all intellectual and moral progress.[6]

Certainly the atrocities committed in the name of Jesus have been lightning rods for opponents to the faith. Said Nobel Prize-winning physicist Steven Weinberg: "With or without religion, you would have good people doing good things and evil people doing evil things. But for good people to do evil things, that takes religion."[7]

Abuses by the church were one factor that promoted Ken Schei to take the oxymoronic step of founding an organization called "Atheists for Jesus," which endorses what it calls Jesus' "message of love and kindness" without embracing him as God or the church as his institution.

Charles Templeton's distaste for much of what has happened through churches was evident in our conversation as well as in his writings. While conceding that organized religion has done "immeasurable good," he charged that it "has seldom been at its best. Too often it has been a negative influence.... Across the centuries and on every continent, Christians—the followers of the Prince of Peace—have been the cause of and involved in strife."[8] For example, he likened the church during the Middle Ages to "a terrorist organization."[9]

Is that assessment warranted by the historical data? Is it possible for Christians to defend themselves against the brutal bloodbath of the Crusades and the cruel torture of the Inquisition? Do these examples of violence and exploitation represent a persistent pattern of behavior that should justifiably prompt spiritual seekers to steer clear of organized religion?

These are troubling questions, but fortunately I didn't have to travel very far to get some answers. One of Christianity's leading historians lived less than an hour from my home when I resided in suburban Chicago.

THE SEVENTH INTERVIEW: JOHN D. WOODBRIDGE, PH.D.

After receiving his master's degree in history from Michigan State University, the bilingual Woodbridge earned his doctorate at the University of Toulouse in France. He has received a Fulbright Fellowship and grants from the National Endowment for the Humanities and the American Council of Learned Societies, and has taught at a number of secular universities, including the division of religion, Hautes Etudes, the Sorbonne, Paris. Currently, he is a research professor of church history at Trinity Evangelical Divinity School in Deerfield, Illinois.

Woodbridge's numerous history-related books include such technical works as *Revolt in Pre-Revolutionary France: The Prince de Conti's Conspiracy against Louis XV, 1755–1757*, published by Johns Hopkins University Press, and more popular-level efforts, including *Great Leaders of the Christian Church*, *More Than Conquerors*, and *Ambassadors for Christ*. He also has written books on theology and biblical studies, such as *Hermeneutics, Authority and Canon* and *Scripture and Truth*, both co-authored with D. A. Carson, and *Biblical Authority*. In addition, he served as senior editor of *Christianity Today* for two years.

Woodbridge is a member of several key historical societies in the United States and France, including the American Catholic Historical Association, American Society of Church History, American Society of Eighteenth Century Studies; the Société française du XVII siècle; and the Société d'histoire moderne et contemporaine.

When I met Woodbridge at his traditionally decorated Dutch colonial home, I experienced a bit of déjà vu. Only later did I realize that he bears an uncanny resemblance to the actor Peter Boyle. The fifty-nine-year-old, balding father of three was wearing a white fisherman's net sweater over a blue button-down shirt. We sat across from each other at his dining room table, which was strewn with papers for a book he was completing while on a sabbatical.

There was no way to ease into our discussion. Not with this topic. Although our interview took place a few months before Pope John Paul II made his historic public confession and asked God's forgiveness for sins committed or condoned by the Roman Catholic church during the last two millennia,[10] I pulled out a newspaper clipping about an earlier admission by the Pope and pointed to it as I posed my first challenge.

CONFESSING THE CHURCH'S SINS

"As far back as 1994," I began, "Pope John Paul II called upon the church to acknowledge 'the dark side of its history' and said: 'How can one remain silent about the many forms of violence perpetrated in the name of the faith—wars of religion, tribunals of the Inquisition and other forms of violations of the rights of persons?'[11] Isn't it true that the church through the centuries has intentionally glossed over these instances of abuse?"

As he listened, Woodbridge sat with his elbows on the table and his hands laced together in front of him. He analyzed my question for a few moments before responding.

"I think the Pope's statement is courageous," he replied, "because he is acknowledging that the Roman Catholic church has glossed over some things that have been done in the name of Christ and which are obviously fodder for criticism of Christianity in general.

"I would quickly add, though, that we should be careful in using the expression 'the church,' because that gives the impression that there has only been one representative institution of Christianity. I would make a clear line of demarcation between people who are part of 'the church'—people who are the sheep who hear the shepherd's voice and would be true Christians—and the institutional churches," he said, emphasizing the plural of that last word.

"Now, obviously," he added, "there are many, many true Christians who are in the visible churches, but just because a person is part of a church doesn't necessarily mean he or she is a follower of Jesus. Some people are *cultural* Christians but not *authentic* Christians."

I squinted with skepticism. "Isn't that a bit of twenty-first century revisionism?" I asked. "That makes it rather easy to look back and say that all of the atrocities committed in the name of Christianity were actually perpetrated by those who said they were Christians but who really weren't. That seems like a convenient escape hatch."

"Oh, no, this distinction isn't new," he insisted. "In fact, it goes back to Jesus himself." He reached for his Bible, which was hidden beneath some stray papers, and read the words of Jesus from the Gospel of Matthew:

> "Not everyone who says to me, 'Lord, Lord,' will enter the kingdom of heaven, but only he who does the will of my Father who is in heaven. Many will say to me on that day, 'Lord, Lord, did we not prophesy in your name, and in your name drive out demons and perform many miracles?' Then I will tell them plainly, 'I never knew you. Away from me, you evildoers!'"[12]

Looking up from the book, Woodbridge said, "So Jesus talked about this distinction two millennia ago. And certainly through the centuries much has been done in the name of Christianity that does not reflect his teachings.

"For example, Adolph Hitler tried to color his movement as being Christian, but obviously he didn't represent what Jesus stood for. When theologian Karl Barth was asked to begin a lecture in Germany by saying, 'Heil Hitler,' he replied, 'It's pretty hard to say, 'Heil Hitler' just before you're exegeting the Sermon on the Mount!' Those two things just don't go together. So if we accept this distinction, then we can more accurately analyze some of the things that have been attributed to the Christian faith."

I remained dubious. "So you're saying that if something bad was done in history, it couldn't have been committed by authentic Christians?"

"No, no, I'm not suggesting that," Woodbridge replied. "The Bible makes it clear that because of our sinful nature, we continue to do things as Christians that we shouldn't. We're not perfect in this world. And unfortunately, some of the evil deeds committed through history may have, indeed, been committed by Christians. When that has happened, they've acted contrary to the teachings of Jesus.

"At the same time, we should recognize that there has often been a minority voice that has spoken out against abuses that some institutional churches have perpetrated. For instance, I was just reading this morning that during Spain's colonization of Latin America, there were Roman Catholics who were appalled at how native peoples were being exploited for economic purposes in the name of Christ. They said, 'No, you can't do that!' These Christians were willing to speak out against abuses by representatives of the state or church."

"Let's get back to the Pope's statement," I said. "Is it appropriate at this point in history to be confessing the past sins of the church?"

"Yes, it's totally appropriate to admit that some things Christians have done are, in fact, sins. The Bible tells us to confess our sins. Confession should be one of the hallmarks of Christians—a willingness to admit fault, seek forgiveness, and endeavor to change our ways in the future. In fact, it's not just the Pope who is doing this. In the Southern Baptist Convention there was a recent initiative to acknowledge that early Southern Baptists had badly erred concerning the issue of slavery, and a few years ago a Canadian Lutheran group apologized to Jews for anti-Semitism in Martin Luther's writings."

"As a historian, can you see why skeptics seize upon the abuses from church history as arguments against Christianity or as a way to attack the faith?"

"Oh, I can understand that," he replied. "Unfortunately, certain incidents in history have created cynicism in some people toward Christianity. At the same time, there are a number of misleading stereotypes about what Christians have and haven't done. Some critics have attacked a cultural Christianity, failing to grasp that it is not an authentic Christianity.

"This has been one of our problems for centuries. Voltaire was a major critic of Christianity, yet when he went to England he ran into some Quakers and Presbyterian Christians and was very impressed by their faith. So there can be an institutional form of Christianity that sometimes repels people, while authentic expressions of faith can be quite attractive when non-Christians encounter them."

With that background, I decided to go back to the dawning of Christianity and then move ahead through history by hitting some of the most disturbing episodes that have been attributed to the faith.

WHY CHRISTIANITY SPREAD

Historians have long marveled at—and theorized about—the amazing speed with which Christianity spread throughout the Roman Empire despite brutal persecution. I asked Woodbridge to assess the comments made by atheist-turned-Christian Patrick Glynn:

> Part of the reason for Christianity's rapid spread, historians have remarked, was simply that the early Christians were such nice people. The very kindness of the Christians and their service to the poor and downtrodden attracted new adherents. "Christians astounded the ancients with their charity," as one historian has put it.[13]

Woodbridge nodded in response. "Yes, I think Glynn's reference to the rapid spread of Christianity is accurate," he said. "Tertullian writes at the end of the second century, 'We are but of yesterday and yet we already fill your cities, island, your palace, senate and forum, we have left to you only your temples.' So in a hundred and fifty years, Christianity spread very, very quickly.

"One explanation of its rapid spread, as Glynn indicated, is that many Christians were not just taking care of their own, but they were caring for neighbors, the poor, and widows, the hurting, and they were basically very loving. They showed compassion toward children, who were often treated very callously by the Romans and Greeks at birth, especially baby girls. The lifestyle of Christians matched their teachings, so that many early Christians were not afraid to say, 'Imitate us as we imitate Christ.'"

Having said that, Woodbridge added a bit sheepishly: "Unfortunately, in contemporary evangelicalism sometimes people say, 'Don't look at us, look at Christ,' because we are worried what people will find if our own lives are scrutinized. That wasn't true of many of these early Christians—there was consistency between their beliefs and behavior."

Woodbridge pulled out a piece of paper. "We can also gain some insights into why Christianity grew so quickly from a few early non-Christians," he said, reading aloud the observations of Lucian, a second-century Greek satirist and critic of Christianity:

> These misguided creatures start with the general conviction that they are immortal for all time, which explains the contempt of death and voluntary self-devotion which are so common among them; and then it was impressed on them by their original lawgiver that they are all brothers, from the moment that they are converted, and deny the gods of Greece, and worship the crucified sage, and live after his laws. All this they take quite on faith, with the result that they despise all worldly goods alike, regarding them merely as common property.[14]

"He's confirming the fact that Christians treated each other as brothers and freely shared their possessions with each other. Add to that another important factor to which he alludes: Christians believed that to die is to be with Christ. Justin Martyr, in the *First Apology*, says: 'You can kill us, but you can't hurt us.'[15] Most of us think killing is a big-time hurt, but from their point of view, being killed doesn't matter too much. As Paul said, 'To live is Christ and to die is gain.'[16]

"So when you take into consideration the early Christians' fearless devotion to the faith; their willingness to testify through their own martyrdom to the truth of Christ; their humble and compassionate lifestyle; their care for each other and the helpless and hurting and disenfranchised in the community; their commitment to prayer; and their empowerment by the Holy Spirit, you can begin to understand why the faith spread so rapidly."

"Ultimately," I asked, "was it a good or bad thing for Christianity that it was adopted as the state religion of the Romans?"

"On one hand, it was very nice to have the persecutions cease, so that was a good thing," Woodbridge said with a smile. "But as the church became closely related to the state, then the church began to use the state as a persecuting agency, and that became a very bad thing. Also, worldliness swept into the church."

"How so?" I asked.

"The rumor was abroad that Constantine promised if you became a Christian, you'd get a beautiful robe and pieces of gold. Well, those aren't very good reasons to become a Christian. So the door was opened wide to persons who may have professed Christianity, but who didn't really embrace Jesus."

"In other words, cultural Christians rather than authentic followers of Jesus?"

"Exactly," he said.

With the groundwork concerning early Christianity having been established, I turned the page in my list of questions and began to focus on the five major blots on Christian history that troubled me the most when I was a skeptic—the Crusades, the Inquisition, the Salem witch trials, exploitation by missionaries, and anti-Semitism. Unquestionably, it was an unsavory and unholy litany.

Sin #1: The Crusades

"Let's skip ahead," I said to Woodbridge. "Christian crusaders tried for two centuries to expel the Muslims from the Holy Land." I opened a history book and paged through it until I found the right entry. "One horrific account described the Crusaders' entry into Jerusalem in the First Crusade this way," I said, reading to Woodbridge the following description from an eyewitness:

> Some of our men ... cut off the heads of their enemies; others shot them with arrows, so that they fell from the towers; others tortured them longer by casting them into the flames.... It was necessary to pick one's way over the bodies of men and horses. But these were small matters compared to what happened at the Temple of Solomon (where)... men rode in blood up to their knees and bridle reins. Indeed it was a just and splendid judgment of God that this place should be filled with the blood of the unbelievers, since it had suffered so long from their blasphemies.[17]

Slamming the book shut with disgust, I looked hard at Woodbridge and asked in a voice laden with sarcasm: "Do you agree that the Crusades were 'just and splendid?'"

Woodbridge pursed his lips. "That kind of bloodshed is repugnant and abhorrent," he said firmly. "Did it happen? Yes, it did. Is it heartbreaking to contemplate? Yes, it is. I'm not going to try to excuse it or rationalize it away. However, your question—were the Crusades just or not—demands an either-or answer, and I think it might be more helpful to provide a little broader context."

I sat back in my chair. "Go ahead," I said.

"Pope Urban II launched the first crusade in 1095, when he gave a very famous sermon and the crowds responded by declaring, 'God wills it!'" Woodbridge began. "The Crusades continued until the loss of the last Christian stronghold in the Holy Land in 1291, when a town called Acre was taken over once again by Muslims. Jerusalem was back in the hands of the Muslims by 1187.

"The Pope called upon barons and others to go to the Holy Land and retrieve it from the Muslims who were occupying it and who were thought to be the foes of Christ. So if we put ourselves back into the shoes of those early crusaders, we can understand that they thought they were doing something magnificent for Christ. But when you study the details of what actually happened, you become deeply troubled. In fact, in one Crusade, the Fourth, the participants didn't even make it to the Holy Land. They got as far as Constantinople, seized it, and set up their own kingdom. Tremendous bloodshed ensued. Western 'Christians' killed Eastern Christians.

"In addition to the violence, another major problem was the motivation of some who went. In 1215, Pope Innocence III actually instructed people that if they went on the Crusades, this could earn their salvation. And if they sent someone to fight in their place, this, too, would earn their salvation. This counsel was an obvious distortion of true Christianity. It makes a mockery of the teachings of the Bible and can't in any way be squared with historic Christian beliefs.

"The motivations of the Crusaders become more difficult to assess after the Muslims took back Jerusalem. Some of the later Crusades involved Christians going to the Holy Land in an attempt to save other Christians who were in desperate straits. All in all, though, it's fair to say that despite anyone's intentions, the general avarice and slaughter associated with the Crusades have created an ugly stain on the reputation of the Christian faith.

"And that's not just a liberal, twenty-first century perspective. In the early part of the thirteenth century, a number of Christians were saying the same thing. One reason why the crusading ideal disintegrated was due to the enormous travesties associated with the Crusades. Popes tried in later centuries to launch crusades, but they couldn't gain political and popular support. The genuine discrepancy between authentic Christianity and the reporting of what the Crusades had been like contributed to this loss of interest or enthusiasm for new crusades.

"This takes us back to the distinction between things done in the name of Christ and those things that really represent Jesus' teachings. When you try to mesh Jesus' teachings with the slaughter of the Crusades—well, there's no way they can be reconciled."

I asked: "What do you say to a non-Christian who says the Crusades just show that Christians want to oppress others and are as violent as anybody else is?"

Woodbridge pondered the question for a moment before answering. "I would say that there is some truth in that statement as it relates to the Crusades," he began. "There have been people who have done things in the name of Christ they never should have done. Then I would point out that not everything done in the name of Christ should, in point of fact, be attributed to Christianity.

"But I would not try to dodge the point that terrible things occurred during the Crusades. They need to be confessed as being totally contrary to the teachings of the one the crusaders were supposedly following. It's important to remember that it's not Jesus' teachings that are at fault here; it's the actions of those who, for whatever reason, greatly strayed from what he clearly taught: we are to love our enemies. A 'just war' theory must interact with this principle.

"Nobody was more outspoken against hypocrisy or cruelty than Jesus. Consequently, if critics believe that aspects of the Crusades should be denounced as hypocritical and violent—well, they'd have an ally in Christ. They'd be agreeing with him."

Sin #2: The Inquisition

The Inquisition began in 1163 when Pope Alexander III instructed bishops to discover evidence of heresy and take action against the heretics. What developed was a campaign of terror, with secret proceedings, supreme authority vested in the inquisitor, and a complete lack of due process, where the accused didn't know the names of their accusers, there was no defense attorney, and torture was used to extract confessions. Those who refused to repent were turned over to the government to be burned at the stake.

"What precipitated the Inquisition?" I asked. "And more important, how could authentic Christians participate in such atrocities?"

"The roots of the Inquisition can be traced back to the papacy's deep concern about the problem of heresy, especially in southern France among the Albigenses," Woodbridge explained. "Actually, there's no question that the Albigeneses were proponents of heretical teachings and practices. Traditional means of persuasion—for instance, sending them missionaries—didn't work. The Inquisition was an alternative approach or tactic to try to prevent this heresy from spreading. And there were political factors at work too—the northern French were looking for any excuse to intervene in southern provinces."

"So that was the first phase of the Inquisition?" I asked.

"Yes, it was," he said. "There were basically three waves of Inquisitions. First, the one I just mentioned. The second one began in 1472 when Isabella and Ferdinand helped establish the Spanish Inquisition, which also had the Pope's authority behind it.[18] The third wave began in 1542 when Pope Paul III determined to hunt down Protestants, especially Calvinists."

"So," I said, "you have Catholics who call themselves Christians persecuting Protestants who call themselves Christians."

"Yes, this shows once again that you can't really talk about the 'one church,'" he replied. "And things get more complicated because contemporaries often identified heresy with political sedition. If a person was deemed to be a heretic, he or she was also thought to be politically seditious. For instance, in the trial of Michael Servetus, the state ultimately put him to death. One accusation was that he was a heretic, but what was possibly the state's great fear? It's that he was also politically seditious. Religion and politics were bound up together."

"Is it possible that some authentic Christians were actually the victims of the Inquisition? We typically think of Christians as perpetrating the terror and wonder how true Christians could torture anyone, but could it be that the true Christians really were the ones being killed?"

"Yes, it's very possible," he said. "We don't know the identities of all those who died, but it's likely many were the ones upholding the true faith. Certainly there's evidence that the Catholic church had lost its way in launching these inquisitions. Protestants sometimes used inappropriate tactics to suppress heresy as well."

"Was the Inquisition an anomaly or part of a broader pattern of abuse and oppression by churches through history?"

"I think that the Inquisition is a tragedy that Christians cannot run away from. But I don't think that it's representative of the history of the Christian churches. It's too much of an extrapolation to say that this kind of hateful activity is part of a pattern.

"For much of their existence, many Christian churches have been in a minority situation and therefore not even in a position to persecute anyone. In fact, talk about persecution—millions of Christians themselves have been victims of brutal persecution through the ages, continuing to the present day in some places. In fact, there have been apparently more Christian martyrs in the twentieth century than in any other. To this very day, Christians are being killed for their faith around the world. So, no, the Inquisition is by far an exception in church history, not the norm."

Woodbridge's remarks reminded me of a magazine column about Christians being on the receiving end of persecution. While most people think of the average Christian today as being a United States resident living far away from any danger for their faith, journalist David Neff set the record straight.

"The typical Christian," he said, "lives in a developing country, speaks a non-European language, and exists under the constant threat of persecution—of murder, imprisonment, torture, or rape."[19]

Sin #3: The Salem Witch Trials

The Salem witch trials at the end of the 1600s are frequently cited as a kind of Christian hysteria. In all, nineteen people were hanged and one pressed to death for refusing to testify.[20]

"Isn't this another example of how Christian beliefs can result in the trampling of the rights of others?" I asked.

"Yes, it's an example—if, in point of fact, true Christianity is involved here. When you unpack the episodes leading to the trials, you see there are many factors that precipitated them. There are issues related to people scheming to get land from other people; there are issues related to hysteria; there are issues of believing in astral appearances, whereby people testify that somebody did something even when they were in another place. When you study the legal context for the trials, there are variables that take you into issues unrelated to Christianity."

"Are you saying the churches were innocent?"

"This may not be a total exculpation of Christianity's influence in the trials, but historians who work with matters of this sort know that you should not be monocausational in sorting out such events. Life is more complex than just saying 'Christianity' was responsible. Although there were witch trials in Europe, this was an aberration, not part of a bigger pattern in the colonies. You have to question the psychological equilibrium of some of the people who were involved in the witch trials and consider their false reporting of things.

"Again, we have to emphasize that the Salem witch trials constituted a terrible episode. I'm not trying to downplay their seriousness. But historians recognize that the story line is considerably more complicated than merely blaming the churches."

"One of the presuppositions at the time was that witches exist," I pointed out. "How about you? Do you believe there are witches?"

"Yes, I believe that they do exist," he replied. "In fact, a number of years ago I was watching French television when Robert Mandrou, a very distinguished historian, was proposing that once people become enlightened, they don't believe in witches anymore. Then a woman called to say, 'Mr. Mandrou, I'm very impressed by all you've said, but I just want to tell you that I'm a witch.' And, indeed, witchcraft is practiced in France, the United States, and elsewhere.

"So part of the problem in dealing with the Salem witch trials is the assumption that all of this was totally hokum, that there's no such thing as witches and witchcraft. The hardcore reality is that there are; even many non-Christians recognize that.

"Does this excuse what happened at Salem? No, of course not. But when you sort through the complexities, this situation can't be simply written off as an example of Christianity having run amok. Life—and history—just aren't that simple."

"What ended the trials?" I asked.

"This isn't commonly known," he said, "but it was a Christian who played the key role. A Puritan leader named Increase Mather spoke out forcefully against what was happening and that was the beginning of the end. Ironically, it was a Christian voice that silenced the madness."

Sin #4: Exploitation by Missionaries

> The missionaries arrive uninvited. Despite noble intentions, they are ignorant of the place where they set up shop and indifferent to the hearts and values of the people they have come to help. They meddle in things which are none of their business. They assume that the natives' traditional spirituality is defective, even devilish. They bribe or coerce the people to abandon their traditional ways until, in the process of trying to 'save' the people, the missionaries wind up destroying them.[21]

I read that accusation to Woodbridge, following it with these questions: "Haven't missionaries through history contributed to the demise of native cultures? Haven't they ended up exploiting the very people they claimed they wanted to help? On balance, haven't missionaries done more harm than good?"

This issue struck close to home for Woodbridge, whose family has a long tradition of serving on the mission field. But he didn't seem to take the challenge personally, responding instead with his characteristic evenhandedness and balance.

"Let me start with the Spanish incursion into Latin America as an example, because it illustrates how complicated this issue can become," he said.

When I nodded my assent, he continued. "Was there exploitation and abuse of native people there? Yes, unfortunately, there was. But was this the result of the missionaries? Well, history tells us that the missionary movement was often associated with an economic policy of the colonial powers known as *mercantilism.*"

"Could you define that?"

"Mercantilism was the belief that the country with the most gold would be the most powerful. The political balance of power in Europe was thought to be in part determined by which country successfully explored Latin America and elsewhere. As a result, mercantilist motivations became, unfortunately, mixed with missionary enterprises. It is, indeed, true that the Spanish did horrible things in Latin America, but much of it was instigated by adventurers and mercantilist types while many missionaries did praiseworthy things."

Woodbridge opened a book that was sitting nearby. "In fact, historian Anthony Grafton of Princeton University talks about the valuable things that the missionaries did," he said, reading from the book *New Worlds, Ancient Text:*

> The Roman church insisted on the humanity of the Indians, and large numbers of missionaries—especially idealistic mendicant friars bent on bringing what they saw as the simple, incorrupt people of the New World to Christ—arrived. They built churches and religious communities.[22]

"Now, Grafton is not an evangelical," Woodbridge continued, "but he has carefully studied the missionary movement and acknowledges the enormous amount of good that the missionaries did. Unfortunately, missionaries as a group get discussed as agents of mercantilism, and so they often get blamed for some of the horrible things the Spanish did in Latin America.

"And as I noted earlier, in the sixteenth century there were debates in Spain about whether what was going on in Latin America was Christian. There were major defenders of the Indians who insisted they shouldn't be exploited. One key figure, Bartolomé de Las Casas, was driven to his reforming attitude after reading a passage in Ecclesiasticus in the Roman Catholic Bible, which says: 'The bread of the needy is their life. He that defraudeth him thereof is a man of blood.'[23] Having read this, he and other Roman Catholics opposed the malevolent things that were taking place in Latin America."

His comments triggered my memory of seeing a statue outside the United Nations building in New York City a number of years earlier. Now I understood the background: Francesco de Vitoria, the founder of international law, had been one of the theologians who had argued for the full dignity of the New World Indians and who had fearlessly opposed their exploitation at the Spanish Court.

"So while it is indeed true that sometimes 'Christian civilization' has done some of the things you pointed out earlier, there have also been thousands of acts of charity that have been God-honoring. The Catholic Church has an impressive record of taking care of the poor during the Middle Ages. In California, their missions all up the coast took care of people. When you read the journals of a number of Protestant missionaries who went to other lands, it's very difficult to come to the conclusion that they were self-consciously determined to oppress or destroy all aspects of native cultures."

While Woodbridge's answer was providing some context, I wanted to press him further for a more personal response. "Your family has included missionaries," I said. "What were their experiences?"

"Well, I've read the diary of my grandfather, who was one of the earliest Protestant missionaries to China. I certainly didn't get the sense that he was doing what you said earlier. Instead, he had a burning desire that the Chinese people come to know Christ, and he was very concerned about the poverty of the Chinese people and about some of their practices that were very detrimental to the humanity of individuals. He respected aspects of their culture and wore a pig-tail on occasion so that he would be accepted by them.

"It has to be pointed out that sometimes the critics of missionaries have almost a Rousseauist idealism that native peoples were always happy and living perfect lives and that there was none of the demonic or negative spiritism going on in their cultures. But when you read the accounts of people going into certain regions, you see that some of these native people were in dire physical and spiritual circumstances and that the missionaries greatly helped them.

"I've also read letters written by my mother, who worked as a missionary in Africa when she was single. She would ride a motorcycle deep into the jungles, going from village to village. She worked in a leper colony taking care of the sick. She desired to show them the love of Christ and to serve them and to see them healed. She served even at great personal risk due to malaria and other dangers associated with living in a jungle.

"So, yes, sometimes there can be a transformation of a culture, but often that transformation brought about some good. When native people became Christians, they experienced the love and joy of Christ. That's a wonderful thing. It's when other motivations creep into the minds of those seeking to change a culture, like a quest for economic gain or a twisted sense of racial superiority, that very bad things result."

"Perhaps," I observed, "some critics of missionaries see no value in the Christian message and therefore no benefit to the people who become followers of Jesus."

"Right!" he declared. "Often that's the underlying presupposition. But if a person has the presupposition that the gospel is the power of God unto salvation, then the gain to the various cultures of the world that hear the gospel is incalculable.

"I have a colleague who is a leading African theologian. He's had to battle the literature that says Christianity is a western imperialist ideology bent on destroying African religions. His perspective is quite different. He sees the wonderful contributions that Christianity has made to African societies. It's brought hope, it's brought redemption, and countless Africans are very grateful for the gospel. At the same time, he does not deny that the bearers of the Christian message sometimes did not live up to the teachings of Christ in their dealings with Africans."

Sin #5: Anti-Semitism

One of the ugliest blights on Christianity's history has been anti-Semitism—certainly an ironic circumstance, since Jesus was Jewish and claimed to be the long-awaited Messiah of Israel and the world. His disciples were Jewish, and Jews also wrote the entire New Testament, with the exception of Acts and the third gospel, which were authored by the physician Luke.

In 1998, the Roman Catholic church apologized for "errors and failures" of some Catholics for not aiding Jews during the Nazi Holocaust, while Cardinal John O'Connor of New York expressed "abject sorrow" for anti-Semitism in churches through the years, saying, "We most sincerely want to start a new era."[24]

Woodbridge readily conceded that, regrettably, anti-Semitism has soiled Christian history. The key question was why it happened in the first place.

"One factor was this: most Jews didn't think Jesus was the Messiah. The Jews' refusal to accept him often transformed Jews in the minds of some Christians into foes of Christ," he said. "Add to this that the Jews were thought to be responsible for Jesus' crucifixion and you have two powerful components of 'Christian' anti-Semitism."

That wasn't sufficient for me. "There has to be more to it than that," I insisted.

"Yes, I believe there is," he replied. "Heiko Oberman, the distinguished historian at the University of Arizona, has tried to identify a number of the other factors. For example, by the time you get to the Middle Ages and the Reformation, there were abundant false rumors about Jews that even added more fuel to the anti-Semitic fires."

"What kind of rumors?"

"That they had been involved with the poisoning of wells at the time of the Black Death of 1348, that they desecrated Christian sacraments when they could, that they privately had sacrificial deaths, that they tampered with Christian Scriptures, and so forth. Now, keep in mind that these accusations weren't true. Nevertheless, they did stoke feelings of anger and resentment."

Yet that didn't seem to satisfy Woodbridge. He gazed off to the side as if he were searching for another explanation, finally turning to me in obvious frustration.

"It seems to me that this doesn't totally handle the issue," he said. "One would have thought—or, should I say, one would have *hoped*—that Christians by the Middle Ages and going up to Martin Luther's day would have realized that the teachings of Jesus absolutely forbade them from doing and saying some of the things that were said and done in his name."

"You mentioned Luther," I said. "His own anti-Semitism is well-documented. Where did that come from?"

"Obviously, he knew some of the rumors about Jews. Early in his life, however, he was apparently philo-Semitic—a lover of Jews—and because of this love he hoped there would be a mass conversion in which they would embrace Jesus as their Messiah. When they didn't, particularly as Luther became more irritable in his later years, he said some very ugly things about them."

His answer puzzled me. "I was under the impression that his anti-Semitism was a lifelong affliction," I said.

"Some scholars contend there's a continuity of his views about Jewish people all through his life, but I would argue that Luther's most virulent statements of hostility come towards the end of his life. Perhaps he was saying them out of deep-seated frustration because they didn't come to Christ.

"All that being said, though, some of his statements are so horrific that it is totally appropriate for Lutherans to repudiate them and for all Christians thoroughly to reject them. Christians simply cannot be anti-Semitic. It should be unthinkable to any follower of Jesus.

"Now, on the other side of the coin, in contemporary times, evangelical Christians have often been some of Israel's greatest friends. And the general attitude I see in many churches toward Jewish people today is one of respect."

"What do you say to a Jewish person who says to you that he or she could never even consider Christianity because of its anti-Semitic history?"

Woodbridge nodded slightly. "I've been hit by that before," he said with sadness in his voice. "I was teaching at a secular university and a young Jewish student said, 'I want to do a paper on Luther. My grandmother told me he hated Jews. Is that true?' I said, 'It probably is, but go ahead and do the paper.' She came back with research that just made me weep. She found things I didn't even know Luther said; it's *that* bad."

"What can you say to someone like her?"

"That I'm very, very sorry for what Luther said; those things are absolutely out of line with the teachings of Christ, and this is one of the problems that we, as Christians, face—we don't always live up to the ideals of Jesus. And I would say, 'I realize how difficult this is, but I hope you would think through what Jesus said and did and examine Christianity on the merits of what it actually teaches.'"

Woodbridge tried to elaborate but apparently could think of nothing else to add that would be very helpful. "I'm afraid that's not very elegant," he conceded. "But that's what I'd say from my heart."

"Some Jewish people believe Hitler was a Christian—," I began, but Woodbridge jumped in and cut me off.

"Oh, yes, that's exactly right," he said. "Again, that's why we have to make the distinction between cultural and authentic Christianity. During the rise of the National Socialists, Hitler tried to wrap himself around Christianity and Martin Luther. It was a clever ideological ploy. But Christian critics, like Karl Barth and others, didn't buy for a moment that Hitler represented orthodox Christianity.

"Let me give you another historical illustration. Many Jewish people in 1665 and 1666 believed that a certain individual was the Messiah. But then he converted to Islam, which dashed the aspirations of a lot of Jewish folks. Now, if I said to a Jewish historian today, 'Do you want to identify that man as the Messiah?' He'd say, 'Of course not. He was a fraud.'

"Well, in a similar fashion, we Christians would say that Hitler was not any sort of Christian Messiah. People often claim things that are false. He was a fraud, an evil individual, who could not have been an authentic Christian, much less a representative of true Christian teachings."

A PORTRAIT OF CHRISTIANITY

We could have gone on to discuss other historical blots on Christianity, including the oppression of women, which has occurred despite Jesus' countercultural attitude toward them, and the way many people in the South once quoted the Bible in a twisted attempt to justify racism and slavery. But I had already spent a long time grilling Woodbridge. Without trying to defend the indefensible, he had sought to provide some context and explanations. In order to establish whether these episodes were exceptions or the norm for Christianity, it was time to explore the other side of Christian history.

"Given all we've talked about," I said, "what's the bottom line? Is the world worse off or better off because of Christianity?"

Woodbridge sat bolt upright in his chair. "Better off," he insisted. "No question about it. These are regrettable historical instances that shouldn't be swept under the rug. We should apologize for them and efforts should be made to make sure they don't recur. At the same time, though, the vast sweep of Christian history has been very beneficial to the world."

"I suppose it's easy in talking about the sins of Christianity to forget the role of atheism in trampling human rights," I observed. I took out a book and read Woodbridge some remarks by prominent Christian Luis Palau:

> The seismic shock of out-and-out atheism sent tidal waves across Europe and beyond, accounting directly for the annihilation and butchering of more than one hundred million people this past century alone. Humanity has paid a steep,

> gruesome price for the awful experiments in deliberate antitheism carried out by Lenin, Hitler, Stalin, Mao Tse-tung and others—each of whom was profoundly influenced by the writings of the apostles of atheism.... After watching atheism proliferate ... it's clearer than ever that ... without God, we're lost.[25]

"I agree that without God, we're lost," Woodbridge responded. "That's not to say an atheist could never govern well, because, from the Christian point of view, the atheist benefits from God's common grace. But given the lack of framework in atheism for making moral decisions, it's easy to see why the world has experienced the horrors of these regimes. Where there's no absolute moral standard, raw power often wins."

"What would you say are the positive ways Christianity has contributed to civilization?"

Woodbridge settled deeper into his chair. He ruminated on my question for a few moments and then answered in a voice whose sincerity and wonder and enthusiasm conveyed his deeply felt love for the church.

"I see Christianity's influence as a resplendent mural with many scenes, each depicted in bright, brilliant, and beautiful colors," he said. "Without Christianity, there would be an awful lot of grays and only a few scattered and disconnected lines here and there giving any sense of meaning. But Christianity adds so much meaning, hope and beauty and richness to the picture."

Intrigued by the imagery, I asked, "What would the painting show?"

"The very center scene would portray the story of Jesus and his redemption for our sins. Finally, once and for all, he dealt with the issues of our guilt, our loneliness, and our alienation from God. Through his atoning death and resurrection, he opened up heaven for everyone who follows him. That's the greatest contribution Christianity ever could have made. It's summarized in John 3:16: 'For God so loved the world that he gave his one and only Son, that whoever believes in him shall not perish but have eternal life.'

"Also, Christianity provides us a revelation as to the meaning of life and the existence of universal morality. Without that revelation, it's very difficult to have any sense of what meaning is. You end up like Albert Camus, who said in the opening paragraph of *The Myth of Sisyphus*, 'Why should I or anyone not commit suicide?' Well, Christianity explains why not. It gives us a frame of reference for living, for following a moral path, for relating to God and others in a healthy and deeply meaningful way.

"Brush strokes in the painting would depict scenes revealing vast humanitarian impulses that have been inspired by Christ's life and teaching. Roman Catholics, Orthodox, Protestants—all have been deeply involved in helping the poor, the disadvantaged, the disenfranchised. They've been willing to work against their own personal interests to serve others. Losing all of that—all the missionary work, all the hospitals, all the homeless shelters, all the rehabilitation programs, all of the orphanages, all of the relief organizations, all the selfless feeding of the hungry and clothing of the poor and encouraging of the sick—would be a devastating blow to the world.

"In addition, the impact of Christian thought adds other scenes and gives shading and nuance and depth to the painting. Christians have given their minds to God, and their literary, musical, architectural, scientific, and artistic contributions, if taken away, would render the world much more dull and shallow. Think of all the great educational institutions that Christians built, including Harvard, Yale, and Princeton, which were originally conceived and constructed to advance the gospel.

"Finally, there's the power of the Holy Spirit that colors everything good. Can you imagine what the world would be like if the Holy Spirit were withdrawn? I mean, talk about your local horror show! It's bad enough the way things are now, but if the restraining power of the Holy Spirit were not here, then the horrible side of life would emerge even more graphically than it already does."

"As you look at this painting of history," I asked, "do you see the positives of Christianity overwhelming the negative instances that we've discussed?"

"Yes, I do," he said without hesitating. "I'm heartsick about the times when we, as Christians, have not lived according to Jesus' teachings and thereby created barriers to the faith. But I'm just so grateful for the nameless men and women who have humbly and courageously upheld the faith through the centuries, who have served in obscurity, who have given their lives to help others, who have left the world a far better place, and who have struggled to do the right thing despite incredible pressure to do otherwise.

"When I think of Christian history," he concluded, "they're the first to come to my mind. They're the heroes who are too often forgotten."

He stopped. Then, with a wistful smile, he gave them his greatest tribute: "They're what Jesus envisioned."

THE GIFTS OF CHRISTIANITY

Woodbridge's impassioned words were still ringing in my mind when I arrived back home, exhausted from a long day. I collapsed into my favorite chair and picked up a magazine to thumb through. There, quite by coincidence, I encountered an article in which several scholars, writing in the waning days of the twentieth century, speculated about where civilization would have been without Christianity. Their observations picked up right where Woodbridge had left off.[26]

Michael Novak extolled Christianity's gift of dignity. "Both Aristotle and Plato held that most humans are by nature slavish and suitable only for slavery," he wrote. "Most do not have natures worthy of freedom. The Greeks used 'dignity' for only the few, rather than for all human beings. By contrast, Christianity insisted that every single human is loved by the Creator, made in the Creator's image, and destined for eternal friendship and communion with him."

He pointed to the civilizing ideas of liberty, conscience, and truth that can be traced to Christianity. "Without the Christian foundations laid for us in the high Middle Ages and again in the sixteenth century our economic and political life together would not only be far poorer," he contended, "but far more brutal as well."

David N. Livingstone, a professor in the School of Geosciences at the Queen's University of Belfast, Northern Ireland, focused on Christianity's gift of science. "The idea that Christianity and science have constantly been at loggerheads is a gross distortion of the historical record," he wrote. "Indeed, Robert Boyle, the great English student of chemistry, believed that scientists more than anyone else glorified God in the pursuit of their tasks because it was given to them to interrogate God's creation."

He pointed out that those in the Reformation "believed that God has revealed himself to humanity in two ways—in Scripture and in nature. This enabled them to engage in the scientific investigation of the natural world." The results have been sweeping contributions by scientists who were spurred on by their Christian faith.

David Lyle Jeffrey, a professor of English literature at the University of Ottawa, described Christianity's gift of literacy. "It would hardly be too much to say that literary culture in Europe, much of Africa and the Americas is inseparable from the culturally transformative power of Christianity," he said. "In most of Europe, as in Africa, South America, and in many other parts of the world, the birth of literacy and literature essentially, not accidentally, coincides with the arrival of Christian missionaries."

Perhaps most captivating, however, was historian Mark Noll's exploration of Christianity's gift of humility, a little-noted contribution that had special relevance in light of my discussions with Woodbridge about the ugly side of Christian history. Wrote Noll:

> Over the long course of Christian history, the most depressing thing—because repeated so often—has been how tragically far short of Christian ideals we ordinary Christians so regularly fall. Over the long course of Christian history, the most remarkable thing—because it is such a miracle of grace—is how often believers have acted against the pride of life to honor Christ. Of all such "signs of contradiction," the most completely Christlike have been those occasions when believers who are strong—because of wealth, education, political power, superior culture, or favored location—have reached out to the despised, the forsaken, the abandoned, the lost, the insignificant, or the powerless.[27]

Power, he said, nurtures the idolatry of self. It corrupts and almost never apologizes. But then Noll went on to recount several episodes through history in which powerful people, in whole or in part because of their Christian faith, willingly humbled themselves in public repentance for their abuse of power—an enduring and countercultural testimony to the power of the gospel.

One story particularly piqued my interest because it concerned an obscure but illuminating incident at the conclusion of an episode that Woodbridge and I had discussed: the Salem witch trials.

One of the judges, a prominent Puritan named Samuel Sewall of Boston, became terribly distressed over the role he had played in that debacle. His Christian conscience was finally moved to action when he heard his son recite a familiar Bible passage: "But if ye had known what this meaneth, I will have mercy and not sacrifice, ye would not have condemned the guiltless."[28] The words broke Sewall's heart.

At church services on January 14, 1697, he gave his pastor a statement to read as a contrite Sewall stood ashamed before the congregation. The statement confessed Sewall's guilt for much of what had happened, saying that he "Desires to take the Blame and shame of it, Asking pardon of men, And especially desiring prayers that God, who has an Unlimited Authority, would pardon that sin and all other sins." His humble act of sorrow and repentance prompted several other jurors to confess their failures, too.

I shut the magazine and tossed it on the coffee table. That, I thought to myself, is perhaps one of Christianity's most amazing legacies—the willingness of the mighty to bend the knee of repentance when wrongs have been committed. It was yet another reminder of the power of faith to change lives—and history—for the good.

DELIBERATIONS

Questions for Reflection or Group Study

- Before reading this chapter, what aspect of Christian history bothered you the most? If it was addressed by Woodbridge, how well did he deal with the issue? Is your opinion about that episode the same or different now?
- Do you think the historical sins discussed by Woodbridge are anomolies in church history or reflective of something that's terribly wrong in the very DNA of the faith? What facts helped you form your opinion?
- Has the world been better off because of Christianity? Why or why not? On balance, have the contributions of atheism been positive or negative for the humankind?

FOR FURTHER EVIDENCE

More Resources on This Topic

- Mark A. Noll. *A History of Christianity in the United States and Canada.* Grand Rapids, Mich.: Eerdmans, 1992.
- Bruce L. Shelley. *Church History in Plain Language.* Dallas: Word, 1982, 1995, updated 2nd edition.
- Rodney Stark. *The Rise of Christianity*. Princeton, N. J.: Princeton University Press, 1996.
- D. James Kennedy and Jerry Newcomb. *What If Jesus Had Never Been Born?* Nashville: Nelson, 1994.

8

OBJECTION #8: I STILL HAVE DOUBTS, SO I CAN'T BE A CHRISTIAN

In their most inner thoughts, even the most devout Christians know that there is something illegitimate about belief. Underneath their profession of faith is a sleeping giant of doubt.... In my experience, the best way to conquer doubt is to yield to it.

Dan Barker, pastor-turned-atheist[1]

Those who believe they believe in God but without passion in the heart, without anguish of mind, without uncertainty, without doubt, and even at times without despair, believe only in the idea of God, and not in God himself.

Madeleine L'Engle, Christian[2]

The lawyer had a tip for me—a human interest story, he said. The tale of a reformed gang member. An inspiring yarn about a former street terrorist who had found religion and gone straight. It will be heartwarming, he promised. A good Sunday read.

I rolled my eyes. The story sounded much too saccharine for me. I was on the prowl for something hard hitting, something gritty, something that would land me on the front page of the weekend *Tribune.* I wasn't interested in a naïve fairy tale about some flaky born-again fugitive.

But the weekend was approaching fast, and the story leads I had been pursuing had taken me down nothing but blind alleys. So I reluctantly wrote down the lawyer's tip. Who knows, I thought, maybe I can expose this con man's phony story and get the kind of article I was after.

I picked up the telephone and started calling my police sources. Had anyone ever heard of this Ron Bronski character? Sure enough, my contacts in the Gang Crimes Unit were well acquainted with him. He was the street-toughened second-in-command of the Belaires, a gang that terrorized parts of Chicago's Northwest Side. He was dangerous and violent, they said. He had a hair-trigger temper, an appetite for illicit drugs, and an encyclopedic arrest record.

"The guy's a sociopath," said one investigator. Another snorted at the mention of his name, then dismissed him with a single word: "Garbage."

They told me there was a warrant out for his arrest on a charge of aggravated battery for shooting a rival gang member in the back. I scrawled the word *coward* in my notebook.

"We haven't seen him around for a long time," one undercover cop told me. "We figure he's fled the city. The truth is, we don't care where he is as long as he's not around here."

Then I called some church leaders in Portland, Oregon, where the lawyer told me Bronski had been living for the last couple of years. While working at a metal shop, he had met some Christians and supposedly abandoned his life of crime, married his live-in girlfriend, and became a devout follower of Jesus.

"Ron is one of the most beautiful, loving people I know," his pastor told me. "He's totally committed to Christ. We pray together several times a week, and he's always doing things like visiting the sick and praying with them, and using his street knowledge to preach to troubled kids. I guess people would call him a 'Jesus freak.'"

He said that Bronski had been reconciled with God but not with society. "He knew there was still a warrant out for his arrest," he said, "so he saved his money and took the train to Chicago to turn himself in."

That piqued my curiosity. A guilty plea to aggravated battery could bring twenty years in the penitentiary. I decided I would go the next step in my research by interviewing Bronski as soon as his lawyer could arrange a meeting.

That night I was sitting at our kitchen table, mulling the conflicting portraits that the police and pastor had painted of Bronski. "On the surface, it sounds like a miraculous change," I commented to Leslie as she stood at the stove, brewing her evening tea.

"On the surface?" she asked.

"Yeah," I said. "When I dig deeper, I'll find out his scam."

She eased into the chair across from me and sipped from a mug. "The police weren't hunting for him, but he gave himself up anyway. What would motivate him to do that?"

"That's what I'm going to find out," I said. "He's probably pretending he's reformed so he'll get a lighter sentence. Or his lawyer is trying to cut some sort of deal with the prosecutor. Or he knows the witnesses are all dead and they can't convict him anyway. Or he's hoping to get some positive publicity to influence the judge. Or he's setting up an insanity defense. . . ."

I went on and on, my hypotheses getting more and more outlandish as I speculated about the real reason he was turning himself in. I considered every far-out possibility—except that his life had legitimately changed and that he had decided to do the right thing by facing the consequences for his crime.

Finally, Leslie put up her hand. "Whoa, whoa," she said. "Those are pretty bizarre theories." She put down her cup and looked me in the eyes. "Tell me something," she said with an edge to her voice. "Are you trying to poke holes in his story because you really think he's a con man? Or are you raising objections because you don't want his story to be true?"

I jumped on the defensive. "Hey," I shot back, "it's my job to be skeptical!"

But she had struck a nerve. To be honest, I didn't want to believe that Christianity could radically transform someone's character and values. It was much easier to raise doubts and manufacture outrageous objections than to consider the possibility that God actually could trigger a revolutionary turn-around in such a depraved and degenerate life.

PIERCING THE SMOKE SCREEN

As it turned out, Ron Bronski survived my cynical attempts to skewer his story. The street-savvy police detectives were absolutely convinced that the changes in his life were authentic. So was the prosecutor. After hearing the evidence, the judge agreed, and instead of sentencing him to the penitentiary, he set him free on probation. "Go home and be with your family," he told a surprised and grateful Bronski.

Today, more than twenty years later, Bronski is still a minister to street kids in the inner city of Portland—and he remains a close friend of mine.[3]

My initial attitude toward Bronski was reminiscent of the doubts that I had raised as a spiritual skeptic. At first I had heartfelt and thoughtful objections to the Christian faith. But over time, after I began finding adequate answers to those issues, I started to bring up new and increasingly marginal challenges.

Then one day I remembered Leslie's comment about Ron Bronski, and I imagined how she might confront me again with similar words: "Lee, are you trying to poke holes in Christianity because you really think it's an illusion—or are you raising objections because you don't *want* it to be true?"

That stung. Admittedly, I had a lot of motivation to find faults with Christianity when I was an atheist. I knew that my hard-drinking, immoral, and self-obsessed lifestyle would have to change if I ever became a follower of Jesus, and I wasn't sure I wanted to let go of that. After all, it was all I knew. Consequently, instead of trying to find the truth, I found myself attempting to fend off the truth with fabricated doubts and contrived objections.

I don't think I'm alone in doing this. Many spiritual seekers have legitimate questions concerning Christianity and need to pursue answers that will satisfy their heart and soul. Yet I think some seekers get to the point where they are subconsciously raising smoke screens to mask their deep-seated motivations for rejecting the faith.

The same is true for Christians who fall prey to doubts about their beliefs. Often, they're having a bout of sincere misgivings about some aspect of their faith; other times, however, their professed doubts may actually be a subtle defense mechanism. They may think they're hung up over an objection to some part of Christianity, when the reality is that they're actually just casting around for some excuse—*any* excuse—not to take Jesus more seriously.

For many Christians, merely having doubts of any kind can be scary. They wonder whether their questions disqualify them being a follower of Christ. They feel insecure because they're not sure whether it's permissible to express uncertainty about God, Jesus, or the Bible. So they keep their questions to themselves—and inside, unanswered, they grow and fester and loom until they eventually succeed in choking out their faith.

"The shame is not that people have doubts," Os Guinness once wrote, "but that they are ashamed of them."[4]

At the same time, many Christians have a completely different perspective. They believe that having doubts isn't evidence of the absence of faith; on the contrary, they consider them to be the very essence of faith itself. "The struggle with God is not lack of faith," said André Resner. "It *is* faith!"[5]

Do spiritual seekers have to resolve each and every one of their questions before they can follow Jesus? Can a person be a Christian and nevertheless have reservations or doubts? What can people do if they want to believe in Christ—much like Charles Templeton professed he did in my interview—but they feel that questions about Christianity are blocking their way? Is there a process for resolving doubts when they arise? And is there hope for those whose melancholy personality seems to draw them inexorably toward uncertainty in matters of faith?

Scholars have wrestled with these issues for years, but I didn't want to talk with some professor whose interest in doubt was merely antiseptic and academic. I wanted to get answers from someone who has personally known the confusion, the guilt, the maddening ambiguity of uncertainty—and that lured me to Dallas to interview a Christian leader whose faith journey has repeatedly taken him on torturous detours through the valley of the shadow of doubt.

THE EIGHTH INTERVIEW: LYNN ANDERSON, D.MIN.

Outside his 1929-vintage house, filled with primitive typewriters, quaint candlestick telephones, and other antiques from that era, Lynn Anderson works in a cozy office above his garage. His working space has a rustic feel, with Indian and western art on the walls, wooden bookcases from floor to ceiling, and a photo of the cabin where he was born in Saskatchewan sixty-three years ago. There was no electricity on the homestead where he grew up, just one beloved battery-powered radio that kept the family connected to the outside world.

Anderson has an easy-going cowboy charm that belies his deep intellect and impressive accomplishments. He has a master's degree from the Harding Graduate School of Religion and a doctor of ministry degree from Abilene Christian University, where he has been an adjunct professor for more than two decades. Anderson was a senior pastor for thirty years at churches in Canada and the United States, leaving the pulpit in 1996 to found Hope Network Ministries, through which he coaches, mentors, and equips church leaders.

He has written a number of books, including *Navigating the Winds of Change, Heaven Came Down, In Search of Wonder, The Shepherd's Song,* and *They Smell Like Sheep.*

The book that especially grabbed my attention, however, was the provocatively titled, *If I Really Believe, Why Do I Have These Doubts?* It was this candid and astute book that disclosed Anderson's recurring personal battles with uncertainty.

After chatting for a while to get to know each other, Anderson and I sat down in straightback chairs at an austere wooden table underneath a ceiling fan that gently washed us with cool air. Anderson has rugged good looks, with rusty-colored hair, a ruddy complexion, and gold-rimmed glasses.

He's demonstrative as he speaks, his arms reaching out at times for understanding and expression. His voice, rich with rough-hewn honesty and sincerity, would occasionally dip to a sandpapery whisper, as if he were confiding some embarrassing secret to me.

My opening questions took Anderson back to his childhood experiences in rural western Canada as I searched for the genesis of his chronic uncertainties. I suspected that many who wrestle with doubts could relate to his story.

THE ROOTS OF DOUBT

Anderson was the son of committed Christians who were part of a small but tight-knit church in an area largely devoid of Christians. He said he derived his identity and sense of value from his family and church community, but even so his doubts about Christianity started early.

"Even as a little kid, I had a melancholy, contemplative personality," he began. "I brooded a lot. I was always looking at the underside of things, not taking anything at face value, always questioning, always probing one level deeper. I've never been able to totally shake that."

I smiled. I've often been accused of asking too many questions myself. "When did you become a Christian?" I said.

"I made a profession of faith at a summer camp when I was eleven, but I felt unclean afterwards. I was supposed to have committed my life to Jesus, but I wasn't even sure there was a Jesus. I felt deceptive."

"Did you mention your feelings to anyone?"

"I talked with a minister, but he didn't seem to understand," he said. "I just kind of swallowed it. But of course I still prayed for things. I remember praying and praying that I'd get a bike and I never got one. That made me feel like God wasn't connected to me. I thought, 'Let's get real. When you pray, there's nothing up there but blue sky.'"

I asked if he only felt doubt or whether there were eras when his faith flourished.

"Sometimes I would really sense God's presence," he told me. "I would ride home from school in a snowstorm at twilight, singing hymns and feeling I was in God's hands. But much of the time, I didn't believe in him—at least, not like my church peers did."

"Were you afraid they might find out?"

"Absolutely, because I had an enormous need to be loved and accepted and have status in that believing community. I was scared that they'd think I was bad, they'd be angry, they'd think my parents were spiritual failures. I was afraid my parents would be disappointed or ashamed."

Obviously, parents can play a significant role in shaping a child's view of God. In fact, one study showed that most of history's most famous atheists—including Bertrand Russell, John Paul Sartre, Friedrich Nietzsche, Albert Camus, Sigmund Freud, Madalyn Murray O'Hair, and Karl Marx—had a strained relationship with their father or their dad died early or abandoned them at a young age, thus creating difficulty in them believing in a heavenly Father.[6] So I decided to probe in this area with Anderson.

"Tell me a little about your parents," I said a bit tentatively, hoping I wasn't getting too personal.

Anderson removed his glasses and laid them on the Bible that sat open in front of him. "In retrospect," he said, "I guess some of my doubts might have stemmed from the parenting style of my mother. She loved me more than life but had no emotional tools to show it. Her way of getting you to improve was to show what you did wrong. She was taught that mothers aren't supposed to show physical affection to sons or it might make them homosexual, and that you don't affirm people because that could give them a big head."

"Did that color your view of God?"

"As you know, people often define God as a parent image. And for good reason—the Bible calls him a father and even a mother sometimes. So part of the distance I felt from God might have been the distance I felt from my mother. On the other hand, my father was an outgoing, affectionate, affirming person, but I think there's something in our fallen nature that hears the bad news come through the good news."

"And so what was the basic Christian message that you perceived in your early years?" I asked.

"It was, 'If you don't meet this standard, you're lost—but nobody can meet this standard, especially you.' As a result, the closer I would get to God—when I'd start believing and get serious about connecting with him—the more hopeless I felt because I couldn't meet his expectations. Then I would think, 'This is sick! Why would I believe in something that's going to condemn me no matter what I do? Surely, if there's a God, he couldn't be like that. Some monster invented this.'"

"Did you think you'd outgrow this?"

"I hoped this was part of being a kid. But at college, the doubts moved from the emotional to the intellectual. I ran into questions about the Bible, and I wondered why there's so much suffering in the world."

He smiled as he recalled a story. "I remember one day a student raised some huge biblical dilemma. The teacher couldn't answer it. Finally, after stumbling around for a while, the teacher said, 'When all the facts are in, we'll see it underscores the credibility of the Bible.'"

Anderson let out a laugh. "I remember thinking, 'Oh, no! This guy's hoping it's true, too! If you scratch under the surface, he's as scared as I am!'"

SPECIES OF DOUBT

Anderson has described himself as being a "congenital doubter," or someone who's always asking, "What if?" Like lawyers and accountants who are trained to identify what could possibly go wrong, congenital doubters are drawn like magnets to uncertainties and questions. They may be filled with angst or have a melancholy personality. For them, faith doesn't come naturally.

But that's just one species of doubt. I asked Anderson for examples of others.

He leaned back in his chair, lifting the front two legs slightly off the floor and then rocking gently back and forth. "Oh, there are lots of different kinds," he said. "Some doubters are rebellious, even though they may not identify themselves that way. They have the attitude, 'I'm not going to let somebody run my life or do my thinking.' This can take the form of an arrogant pride. Sometimes, a young person wants to rebel against his parents, and one way to do that is to rebel against the God they believe in.

"Then there are people whose doubts stem from their disappointment with God. Like the girl I visited with yesterday. God says, 'Seek and ask,' but she's asked and he hasn't given. So she's wrestling with uncertainty. Was God serious? Was he even there?

"Others have personal or family wounds. I talked a few weeks ago with a lady who underwent physical abuse from her mom and dad who were deeply religious—they'd make her kneel by the bed and pray and then beat her. I can see why she's got a problem with God! Others have been personally hurt in the sense of being rejected by a mate or their business has gone south or their health has gone bad. They're wondering, 'If there's a God, why does this stuff happen?'

"Then there are the intellectual doubts. This was where I was at. I was doing my best to intellectually undergird my faith, but there were people a lot smarter than me who didn't believe in God. I started to think, 'Is faith only for the brilliant? How can faith be so important to God, and yet you've got to have an IQ of 197 to hang onto it?'"

I wondered whether there are some factors that can accentuate doubt in people. I asked Anderson, "What things contribute to doubt, even though a person may not be aware of it?"

"Seasons of life can make a big difference," he replied. "Sometimes people are great believers while in college, but when they're young parents with their second baby and they're working sixty or eighty hours a week and their wife's sick all the time and the boss is on their back—they simply don't have time to reflect. And I don't think faith can develop without some contemplative time. If they don't make room for that, their faith is not going to grow and doubts will creep in.

"Another factor can be making comparisons with the faith of others. I met with a young woman who said, 'I hate to go to church because I hear all these claims that I'm not experiencing. I believe, I study the Bible, I pray, I work as hard at ministry as any of them do, but I don't get this joy, I don't get my prayers answered, I don't get a great sense of peace, I don't feel like I'm in the hands of a God who's guiding me down the road and is going to take care of me.' People like this begin to think, 'What's wrong with God that he won't give me those things?'"

I was curious about how he handled her situation. "What did you say to her?" I asked.

"I encouraged her to read the Psalms, because that will alter her perspective on what normal faith looks like. We like to focus on the upbeat Psalms, but sixty percent of them are laments, with people screaming out, 'God, where are you?' Normal faith is allowed to beat on God's chest and complain."

"There's a lot of fear of commitment in our culture," I pointed out. "Does that affect a person's willingness to have faith in God?"

"Yes, it can," he replied. "In this narcissistic country, our definition of freedom is the freedom to get my own way and keep my options open. Some young people are afraid to get married because it's a lifetime commitment. Well, the ultimate commitment is to God. We have a Baskin-Robbins culture where the most-dreaded sentence would be to serve a life with no options. And I do think that contributes to people's fear of committing themselves to Christ."

WHAT FAITH ISN'T

I knew that misconceptions about faith often open the door to doubts because they can create false expectations or misunderstandings about the nature of God. For instance, if people incorrectly think God has promised to heal everyone or make everyone wealthy if they just exhibit sufficient faith, they can fall prey to doubts when illness strikes or bankruptcy looms. In order to arrive at an accurate view of faith, I decided to first clear out the theological underbrush by defining what faith *isn't*.

"What are some common misunderstandings about faith?" I asked.

"People mix up faith and feelings," Anderson replied. "For example, some people equate faith with a perpetual religious high. When that high wears off, as it inevitably does, they start to doubt whether they have any faith at all."

I interrupted. "Are you saying there's no connection between feelings and faith?"

"No," he said. "Feelings are connected with some dimensions of faith, but a lot of that has to do with people's temperaments. Some folks are just not wired to feel very much, even though they may have strong values and convictions."

"How about you?" I asked.

He chuckled. "I tend to be emotionally up and down. It took me years to figure out that this is not a fluctuation of faith. That's why we have to be careful about our feelings—they can be fickle. Let me give you an example.

"A guy once told me, 'I don't like my wife anymore.' My response was to tell him, 'Go home and love her.' But he said, 'You don't understand—I have no feelings for her anymore.' I said, 'I wasn't asking how you felt. I was saying, 'Go home and love her.' Then he said, 'But it would be emotionally dishonest for me to treat my wife that way when I don't feel it.'

"So I asked, 'Does your mother love you?' That seemed to insult him. He said, 'Yeah, of course.' I said, 'About three weeks after she had brought you home from the hospital and you were screaming with dirty diapers and she had to wake up dog tired and put her bare feet on the cold floor, clean up your miserable diapers, and feed you a bottle—did you think she really got a bang out of that?' He said, 'No.' I said, 'Well, then, I think your mother was being emotionally dishonest.'

"Here was the point I was making: the measure of her love wasn't that she felt good about changing the diapers, but that she was willing to do it even when she wasn't feeling particularly happy about it. And I think we need to learn that about faith. Faith is not always about having positive emotional feelings toward God or life."

"Okay, that's one misconception," I said. "What about the idea that faith is the absence of doubt?"

"Yes, some people think that faith means a lack of doubt, but that's not true," he said. "One of my favorite Bible texts is about the man who comes to Jesus with his demon-possessed son, hoping that the boy would get healed. Jesus says all things are possible to those who believe. And the man's response is so powerful. He says, 'I believe, but would you help me with my unbelief?'"[7]

Anderson slapped his knee. "Oh, man!" he exclaimed. "I can really connect with that!"

"So doubt and faith can co-exist?" I asked.

"Yeah, it means you can have doubts even when you believe. That was even true of Abraham. He clearly believed, but at the same time, he had doubts. You can see that by what he did at times and what he said. Now, I don't know where you cross the line into corrosive, eroding, negative doubt, but I do believe that where there's absolutely no doubt, there's probably no healthy faith."

"So doubt can actually play a positive role?"

"I think so. I always get a little nervous at what I call the 'true believer' mentality—people with bright smiles and glassy eyes who never have a doubt in the world, who always think everything's wonderful, everything's great. I don't think they run in the same world I do. I'm afraid of what's going to happen to them when something bad occurs.

"For example, I know a physician whose four-year-old child was stricken with cancer. I remember many nights when forty or fifty people would jam into a house to fervently pray for that child. Some of them thought, 'Of course he's going to be healed because we prayed.' And when he was not, it devastated them.

"Their theology had been misguided and unexamined. It had never been challenged by doubts or thoughtful questions. Doubts could have helped them develop a more substantial and realistic faith—to trust God in the face of death and not just in the face of healing."

Anderson's eyes bored into me as if to emphasize his next words. "You see," he stressed, "a faith that's challenged by adversity or tough questions or contemplation is often a stronger faith in the end."

DELVING BENEATH THE SURFACE

Admittedly, doubts can sometimes serve a positive purpose. I have learned through the years, however, that it can be deceiving to take all doubts at face value. Like my first response to the Ron Bronski story, at times skepticism can be subtly used as a shield to keep people away from deeper motivations. I didn't want to invalidate the legitimacy of people seeking answers to their sincere obstacles to God, but I needed to get to the root of why some individuals raise smokescreen issues.

"In your experience," I said to Anderson, "do some people claim to have intellectual objections, even though their doubts have another underlying source?"

"Yes, that's certainly true," he said as he nodded and planted the front feet of his chair firmly on the floor once again. "In fact, I personally think all unbelief ultimately has some other underlying reason. Sometimes a person may honestly believe their problem is intellectual, but actually they haven't sufficiently gotten in touch with themselves to explore other possibilities."

"Can you give me an example?" I asked.

It only took him a moment to come up with one. "When I was a youngster, a brilliant novelist—an atheist from an atheistic, communist family—came to our little town in Canada to gather local color for a book he was writing. One day he was visiting with our family and he got real serious. He said, 'Can I ask you questions about your religion?' Even though I had been wrestling with doubts from time to time, I said yes.

"He asked, 'Do you really believe there's a God who knows my name?' I said, 'Yeah, that's what I believe.' He said, 'Do you believe the Bible's true? Babies born from virgins, dead people coming out of the cemetery?' I said, 'Yes, that's what I believe.'

"Then he said with great emotion, 'I'd give *anything* to believe that because I've traveled all over the world and I've seen that most people are miserable. The only people who really seem to be getting out of life what they want are the people who say they believe what you believe. But I just can't believe because my head keeps getting in the way!'"

Anderson's eyes got wide. "I was blown away, Lee. I didn't know what to say next because his head was a lot smarter than mine!"

Then Anderson leaned closer to me. "But, in retrospect, I don't think his head was the real problem," he said. "I started thinking about what he would lose if he followed Jesus. He was part of a guild of brilliant writers who all think religion is a total crock. I really believe his professional pride and the rejection of his peers would have been too high of a price for him to pay."

He let the story soak in. "Let me give you another example," he offered.

"Once I was talking with an ex-Marine who said, 'I'm miserable. I've got a wife and kids, and I'm making more money than I can spend with both hands, and I'm sleeping with every woman in town—and I hate myself. You've got to help me, but don't give me any of that God talk because I can't believe that stuff.'

"We talked for hours. Finally, I said, 'Maybe you think you're shooting straight with me, but I'm not sure you are. I don't think your problem is that you *can't* believe; I think it's that you won't believe because you're afraid to give up the things that help get you through the night.'

"He thought for a while and then said, 'Yeah, I guess that's true. I can't imagine sleeping with just one woman. I can't imagine going with less money than I make—which I'd have to do because I lie to get it.' He was finally trying to be honest."

With that, Anderson's voice dropped to an intense whisper. "And here's my point," he said. "That man would argue and argue for hours about his cerebral doubts. He would convince people that he couldn't believe because he had too many intellectual objections. But they were just a smokescreen. They were merely a fog he used to obscure his real hesitations about God."

Anderson leaned back in his chair. "I talked with another girl who had been sexually abused," he continued. "Every way God had been represented to her, as filtered through her parents' religion, was horrible. I don't blame her for having trouble believing. But her arguments were always in the intellectual realm. When you tried to dig deeper into her real obstacles, she didn't want to go through the pain of facing them. She used intellectual doubts to deflect people.

"Then there was the time I had a conversation about God with a guy in the Pacific Northwest. He was raising all kinds of intellectual issues. But when we got beneath that, it turned out he didn't want to believe in God because he didn't want to sell his topless bar. The money was too good and he was having too much fun making it.

"Here's my experience," Anderson said in summary. "When you scratch below the surface, there's either a will to believe or there's a will not to believe. *That's* the core of it."

I stroked my chin in thought. "So you're saying faith is a choice," I said.

Anderson nodded in agreement. "That's exactly right," he replied. "It's a choice."

THE DECISION TO BELIEVE

When I asked Anderson to elaborate on the roles of faith and the will, he immediately brought up the Old Testament character Abraham as an illustration.

"He was called the 'father of the faith,'" said Anderson, "but it wasn't that he never doubted, it wasn't that he always did the right thing, it wasn't that his motives were always pure. He failed on all three counts. But listen—*Abraham never gave up on his will to follow God.* He said, 'I'm going to trust him—will not the king of all the earth do right?' He wouldn't give up on God. And one definition of faith is that it's the will to believe. It's the decision to follow the best light you have about God and not quit.

"The idea of choice runs all the way through Scripture. Look at Joshua. He says to choose this day whom you're going to serve, but as for him and his house, they will serve the Lord. So faith, at its taproot, is a decision of the will."

I lifted my hand to stop him. "But isn't there also a sense in which faith is a gift from God?" I asked.

"Yes," he conceded, "and that raises a big mystery about choice and free will. But I look at it like the power steering on a car. Good luck trying to move the car's tires without it. But with one finger you can supply the impulse of request and the power steering will empower you to turn the wheels. In a similar way, our wills make the decision to put our trust in Christ, and God empowers us."

Anderson reached over to remove his glasses from atop his Bible. He slipped them on and then rustled through the book's wafer-thin pages until he came to the gospel of John.

"Listen to John 7:17," he said, clearing his throat. "Jesus says, 'If a man chooses to do God's will, he will find out whether my teaching comes from God or whether I speak on my own.' So, somehow, if we have the will to believe, God then confirms that Jesus is from God."

He turned a few pages to John 12:37. "The Bible elaborates on this when it says, 'Even after Jesus had done all these miraculous signs in their presence, they still *would not* believe in him.' Then two verses later, it says, 'For this reason they *could not* believe."[8]

"In other words, they made a decision of the will to deny the message of the miracles—the evidence that Jesus is God—because they wouldn't pay the price, which would be their whole religious system being blown out of the water," he explained. "And they had made this decision not to believe for so long that they had dismantled their capacity to believe. Consequently, at its core, faith is a decision of the will that we keep on making, but we're given that option by God's grace. We're empowered to keep making it by his Spirit."

"And," I observed, "it's a choice we must make without having all the complete information we'd like to have."

"That's right. Otherwise, what we would have is knowledge, not faith."

"Talk about the difference."

Anderson laid the Bible back on the table and then scanned the room in a search of an impromptu illustration. Apparently unable to find a suitable prop, he reached into his pocket and withdrew his hand. "Okay," he said, "I'm holding something. Do you know what it is?"

I ventured a guess: "A coin."

"But you don't know for sure," he said. "That's your opinion. Our faith is not our opinion. Let me tell you I've got a quarter in my hand. Do you believe that?"

"Sure," I said.

"I'm telling you it's true, but you haven't seen it. That's faith. Hebrews says faith is the evidence of things not seen."

Anderson smiled. "Watch as I completely destroy your faith." With that, he opened his hand to reveal a quarter. "Now it's no longer faith; it's knowledge."

He tossed the quarter on the table. "Sometimes people think that faith is knowing something is true beyond any doubt whatsoever, and so they try to prove faith through empirical evidence," he said. "But that's the wrong approach."

He gestured toward the coin. "You can see and touch that quarter, so you don't need faith. God, for his own reasons, has not subjected himself to that kind of proof.

"Instead, people should do what you did in *The Case for Christ*—you relied on corroborative evidence. You showed how various strands of evidence point convincingly toward God. And that does something very important—it leaves room for us to make a choice by taking a step of faith in the same direction that the evidence is pointing."

DEALING WITH DOUBT

The afternoon was wearing on, but I didn't want to end our conversation without getting advice from Anderson on how people can deal with the doubts that may be plaguing them. I knew there was no simple formula for overcoming uncertainty; at the same time, there are some steps people can take to help ease their doubts. And everything begins with the will.

"When you teach on this topic, you tell people that initially they need to decide whether or not they really want to believe," I said. "Why do you start there?"

"Because some people say they want to believe when they really don't. As I said earlier, they raise intellectual issues when they're just trying to deflect attention away from why they really don't want to believe. For instance, a college girl told me, 'It looks to me like this whole Christian crock is invented by people who have a psychological need to believe.'

"My answer was, yes, people have a psychological need to believe—just as some people have psychological needs *not* to believe. I said to her, 'What's the reason you don't want to believe? Is it because you don't want the responsibility faith brings with it? Is it because of despair over your own incorrigibility? Or is it because you don't want to give up parties?'

"She was startled. She said, 'Who told you that? It's a little bit of all three.' Okay, she's got emotional reasons for not wanting to believe. Other people have different reasons.

"But people really have to decide why they want to believe. Is it because they've seen some evidence Christianity is true? Or because they're desperate without God? And if they don't want to believe, why not?

"If they have intellectual doubts, that's fine, but don't stop there. They need to go deeper into what really may be driving them to back away from God. For ten years I've been visiting a young girl whose family had been abusive, and she has just finally admitted to me that it's not God she has trouble with, it's not her questions—it's her scars, her emotions. She needs to start there."

"Assuming a person wants to believe," I said, "what do you recommend as a next step?"

"I suggest they go where faith is. If you want to grow roses, you don't buy an acre at the North Pole. You go where roses grow well. If you're going to do faith, you probably don't want to join American Atheists, Inc. Get around people who you respect for their life, their mind, their character, and their faith, and learn from them. Watch their life.

"And I encourage people to put faith-building materials into their mind. By that, I mean books, tapes, and music that build strong motivation for faith, that clarify the nature of God, that examine the evidence pro and con, that deal intelligently with the critic of the faith, that give hope that you can connect with God, that give you tools to develop your spirituality."

These suggestions made sense. But something was missing. "Faith for the sake of faith is meaningless," I said. "Isn't it important to establish exactly where you're putting your faith?"

"Precisely, which is why the next step is to clarify the object of your faith," Anderson replied. "We Canadians know there are two kinds of ice: thick and thin. You can have very little faith in thick ice and it will hold you up just fine; you can have enormous faith in thin ice and you can drown. It's not the amount of faith you can muster that matters up front. It may be tiny, like a mustard seed. But your faith must be invested in something solid.

"So people need to clarify their reasons for believing. Why should they believe in Jesus rather than the Maharishi? Why do they believe in crystals or in Oriental mysticism? Where's the substance?" Anderson gestured toward the leather-bound Bible on the table. "Obviously, I'm prejudiced," he said, "but when it comes right down to it, the only object of faith that is solidly supported by the evidence of history and archaeology and literature and experience is Jesus."

THE FAITH EXPERIMENT

Deciding to believe, going where faith is, consuming faith-building materials, clarifying the object of faith—certainly these were all good recommendations. But something still seemed to be absent. "At some point, the faith journey needs to begin," I said. "How does that happen?"

"Sitting and brooding over faith and doubt will never make a believer out of anybody," came Anderson's response. "Neither will reading all the right books or hanging out with the right people or even making the decision to believe. Ultimately, you must embark on your experiment of faith by doing what faith would do.

"Jesus said that if we continue in his Word—that is, continue doing what Jesus says—then we are truly his disciples.[9] Being a disciple means you're a 'following learner.' And when you're a following learner, you will know the truth and the truth will set you free.

"Knowing the truth doesn't mean filling your head with knowledge; this is the Hebrew 'know,' which isn't gathering information. It's experiential knowledge. Like Adam knew Eve—he didn't just know her name and address; he experienced her.

"To experience the truth and be set free, you have to be a following learner. In other words, do what Jesus says and you'll experience the validity of it. It's kind of like riding a bicycle. You can't watch a video or read a book about it; you've got to get on one and get the feel of it."

"How does a person do that?" I asked.

"You say, 'I've heard some things that Jesus taught. They sound like good ideas to me, but I don't know if they're true. For instance,

I've heard Jesus say it's more blessed to give than to receive. How can I know if that's true?' Well, a thousand debates won't prove it. But when you become generous, you'll realize this is truth. You might say, 'Oh, maybe Jesus accidentally guessed right about that one.' Then just keep going. You'll be amazed at how often he 'guessed' right!"

I reached over to pick up Anderson's Bible, rummaging through it until I came to Psalm 34:8. "King David said, 'Taste and see that the Lord is good,'" I said. "Is that what you're talking about?"

"That's the idea. The more you do this," he said with conviction, "the more you will experientially be woven into a web of faith."

I expected Anderson to elaborate, but he momentarily stopped with that comment. He glanced off to the side as he gathered his thoughts. Then he went on to talk movingly about the experience of faith.

FAITH AS A VERB

"I know, Lee, that you're a former atheist," Anderson said. "You could probably come up with a hundred questions about God that I wouldn't know how to answer. But do you know what? It doesn't matter, because I've discovered that this is true.

"I didn't develop a silly grin and glassy eyes. I've discovered it is more blessed to give than it is to receive. I've walked and walked with this. Every time I discover a new insight, every time Jesus speaks to me personally in ways I can't even articulate, every time I practice his teachings and experience the results—well, after a while I don't care how many intellectual questions you have about why this can't be true. I *know* it's true.

"It's like you say, 'Prove to me that a rainbow is beautiful.' I say, 'Well, it's red and green.' But you say, 'I don't like green and red together.' I'd say, 'But the way they are in the rainbow, it's beautiful!' I've never heard of anyone who thought a rainbow was ugly. When you are able to actually look at it for yourself, then I don't need to say any more. You've seen it, you've experienced it, and you *know* it's beautiful.

"I think faith is like that. Eventually, you have to move out and do it. By the way, in the gospel of John, faith is never a noun, it's always a verb. Faith is action; it's never just mental assent. It's a direction of life. So when we begin to do faith, God begins to validate it. And the further we follow the journey, the more we know it's true."

While his analysis had appeal, nevertheless there was an apparent loophole. "If faith is experiential, then you could get into Buddhism and find that meditation lowers your blood pressure and makes you feel good," I pointed out. "But that doesn't necessarily mean Buddhism is true."

"But remember that experience is just one avenue of evidence," he cautioned. "You also have to clarify the object of your faith, to determine if there are valid reasons for believing it's true. But the ultimate test of the pudding is in the eating. Buddhism does work for some things; atheism works for some things. But if you pursue the whole Jesus journey, you find that his teachings work consistently because they're true. Christianity isn't true because it works; it works because it's true."

I smiled. "It sounds like you're speaking from experience."

"Well, I'll tell you what—my faith is a lot better than it was thirty years ago. Do I have it all together? That would be stretching it. But I am so much more at peace with who God is, I'm so much more confident that I'm in his arms, and I believe that he accepts my feeble attempts to glorify him with my life."

"Do you ever have moments when you still doubt?" I asked.

"Oh, man, yeah!" he exclaimed. "I struggle with why I don't make more progress in overcoming my pet sins. Surely this can't be God's fault—but on the other hand, why is he making it so hard for me? I have those kind of doubts. I struggle with the horrible things happening in Kosovo and Indonesia and parts of Africa, where whole races are being annihilated—some of it in the name of religion. Why doesn't a loving God deal with this? I'm not saying I don't believe in him. I'm saying I don't have the complete and final answer to that question."

"Is there hope for congenital doubters like yourself?"

Anderson was adamant. "Yes, yes," he insisted. "Absolutely. When I say I struggle with my doubts and sins, I don't want to sound like someone who is being defeated or who has no hope. One guy from my church read my book on doubt and said, 'Oh, no! You mean you don't really believe?' I told him, 'No, I really *do* believe—but would you help me with my unbelief?'

"These days, I'm experiencing God more than ever. I can even see God's grace in those times when he feels absent from me, just like the attributes of my wife seem more real when I'm away from her because I long for her. I pray more these days, and I see more of God's response to prayer than I ever have in my life. I feel less need to control other people or outcomes because I know God is in control.

"And ironically, I feel less equipped to answer all the objections that come from brilliant skeptics. But do you know what? That doesn't matter to me like it used to. Because I know this is true. I see it.

"I see it in my life, I see it in my marriage, I see it in my children, I see it in my relationships, I see it in other people's lives when they're changed by the power of God, when they're renewed by him, when they're freed by his truth."

Anderson's voice had an undercurrent of confident authority. Then, with a ring of finality, he declared: "Lee, I've tasted. I'm telling you—I've tasted! And I have seen that the Lord is good."

My mind flashed back to the image of a rural Canadian youngster in anguish over his doubts, desperately searching for solid spiritual ground to build his life upon. And now—*not despite the doubts but because of them*—he's found it. His personal experience with God is confirming to him over and over what no empirical evidence could ever prove.

I reached over and turned off my tape recorder. "Thanks, Lynn," I said, "for being so honest."

HAVING FAITH IN DOUBT

I continued to replay the mental tape of my interview with Anderson as I flew back to Chicago on a half-empty flight that night. I found myself agreeing with his evaluation of the role of doubt. While it can be disconcerting, and although it can eventually become destructive if left untended, doubt clearly can have benefits. I resonated with the view of Gary Parker in his book *The Gift of Doubt:*

> If faith never encounters doubt, if truth never struggles with error, if good never battles with evil, how can faith know its own power? In my own pilgrimage, if I have to choose between a faith that has stared doubt in the eye and made it blink, or a naïve faith that has never known the firing line of doubt, I will choose the former every time.[10]

I would too. I knew that my fundamental trust in Jesus would be stronger, surer, more confident, more steadfast because it had been refined through the purifying fire of doubt. In the end, despite questions, challenges, and obstacles, my faith would not just survive, but it would thrive.

Then my thoughts wandered to Charles Templeton. Were his intellectual objections to God really responsible for dismantling his faith—or was there something lurking beneath those doubts, some unspoken, subterranean motivation that was secretly fueling his challenges to Christianity? There was no way for me to be sure. I had no desire to poke around in his private life to try to find out. At this point, the best I could do would be to continue to take his objections at face value.

There was another important implication of Anderson's interview. If doubt and faith can co-exist, then this means people don't have to fully resolve each and every obstacle between them and God in order to have an authentic faith.

In other words, when the preponderance of all the evidence tilts decisively in God's favor, and a person then makes the rational choice to put their trust in him, they can hold some of their more peripheral objections in tension until the day comes when they're resolved.

In the meantime, they can still make the choice to believe—and ask God to help them with their unbelief.

DELIBERATIONS

Questions for Reflection or Group Study

- What part of Anderson's story could you especially relate to? In what ways is your spiritual journey different or similar to his?
- What kind of doubts do you wrestle with? Is it possible that they're fueled by a motivation not to believe? If so, can you pinpoint why you're reluctant to pursue faith in Christ?
- How has your picture of God been affected by the family in which you grew up or the church you attended as a child? In retrospect, did you grow up with a biblically accurate view of God?
- Anderson offered several suggestions for getting off dead center in your spiritual journey—making the decision to believe, going where faith is, consuming faith-building materials, clarifying the object of your faith, and experimenting with following Jesus' teachings. Which of these steps do you believe would be most helpful to you and why?

FOR FURTHER EVIDENCE

More Resources on This Topic

- Lynn Anderson. *If I Really Believe, Why Do I Have These Doubts?* 2d Edition. West Monroe, La.: Howard, 2000.
- Gary E. Parker. *The Gift of Doubt.* San Francisco: Harper & Row, 1990.
- Os Guinness. *In Two Minds.* Downers Grove, Ill.: InterVarsity Press, 1976.
- Gary R. Habermas. *The Thomas Factor.* Nashville: Broadman & Holman, 1999.

CONCLUSION: THE POWER OF FAITH

Somebody, somewhere, love me!

Written repeatedly in the diary of the late atheist Madalyn Murray O'Hair[1]

A man rejects God neither because of intellectual demands nor because of the scarcity of evidence. A man rejects God because of a moral resistance that refuses to admit his need for God.

Ravi Zacharias, Christian[2]

It had taken me all day to get back from my interview in Texas. My flight was delayed because of stormy weather, then cancelled due to mechanical problems, and I had to reroute myself through two other cities in order to get home. The flights were bumpy and crowded. Physically, I was exhausted—but my mind was working overtime.

I had finally finished retracing and expanding upon my original spiritual journey by interviewing experts about "The Big Eight" objections to Christianity. Once again, Faith had stared Doubt squarely in the eye—and the only question was which one would blink.

I sank into my favorite overstuffed chair, my mind whirring as it sought to assimilate all of the data and opinions and evidence I had been gathering for the previous year. I had filled a stack of legal pads with research. My collection of interview tapes overflowed two shoe boxes. My office was choked with books.

All eight obstacles to faith raised troublesome issues. The experts I interviewed, however, had been masterful in providing satisfying answers. In several matters they were able to offer clear-cut explanations that definitively settled the issue in my mind. For some subjects that didn't lend themselves to that kind of decisive resolution, the scholars managed to dilute the potency of the objections by providing important context and insights. Misconceptions were cleared away, increased clarity was achieved, and in the end the sting of each challenge had been successfully eased.

For me personally, two of the obstacles—the existence of suffering and the doctrine of hell—proved to be the most vexing. The more I would delve into them, the more I found myself in jeopardy of losing my perspective. As I closed my eyes and thought about the investigation, looking for overarching themes that would help me make sense of it all, three distinct scenes came into my mind—starting with a short discussion in which J. P. Moreland had helped me regain my equilibrium.

SCENE #1: FINDING PERSPECTIVE

I was about to leave Moreland's home on the day of our interview about the doctrine of hell. I knew he needed to get over to the seminary, so I thanked him for his time and started packing my recording equipment. But something was still nagging at him. As we stood, he asked if he could make one more point.

"Lee, there's something else I need to mention," he said as he searched his mind for the right way to say it. He sighed, seemingly frustrated on how to sum it up. Then, as I leaned against his doorframe and listened intently, he described an analogy that created an "Aha!" moment for me.

"When you're trying to make a decision about something and weighing the evidence for and against it, it's important to consider all the relevant evidence and not just a little piece of it," he began.

That made sense, but I asked why he felt compelled to say it.

"Because," he explained, "we've been focusing on one common objection to Christianity—namely, the existence of hell. If you just concentrate on one obstacle, though, you're missing the big, overarching picture.

"Let me give you an illustration. Suppose I saw my wife holding hands with another man at the mall. Would it be reasonable to conclude she was cheating on me? Well, it depends on what evidence I consider. If the only evidence I weigh is what I saw at the mall, then I'd say to myself, 'I don't see anything to indicate she's not cheating.' But that leaves something out, doesn't it?

"It ignores a huge chunk of evidence that has nothing to do with the mall situation, but which has everything to do with the last quarter of a century I've spent with her. I've known her well enough, day by day, to be confident she could never cheat on me like that. So if I'm allowed to bring in that lifetime of evidence, I'd say: 'On the surface it looks like something's funny, but it simply can't be true that she's cheating. There's got to be another explanation.'

"Now, suppose that unbeknownst to me she had received a call from a person she had helped become a Christian twenty years earlier. He happened to be in town and she hadn't seen him in two decades, so they got together at the mall and were showing family pictures and reminiscing. He was getting ready to leave for a foreign country and she might never see him again. And so, like a brother and sister, they innocently held hands and talked at the mall.

"Well, this is similar to our examination into the rationality of hell. You may be asking yourself, 'Do I buy hell or not?' If the only evidence you're factoring into your deliberation is the pros and cons of hell by itself, that's like deliberating about my wife's situation and only allowing the evidence for and against what I saw at the mall.

"I want to submit that there's a lot of other evidence that you should consider that has nothing to do with hell *per se*, but it's relevant. What is that? It's all the evidence that there's a God, that he created you, that the New Testament is historically trustworthy, that Jesus performed miracles and rose from the dead, that God wants to spend eternity with you in heaven.

"When you factor all of that in, you might say to yourself, 'Even though I might not have a completely good explanation at this point for why there's a hell, I know there's got to be one because I have too much evidence that Jesus Christ really is the Son of God and he taught about it.

"'And because I can trust him and his deep love for people—as demonstrated by his death for us on the cross—I can have confidence that hell will eventually make sense, that I'll see its fairness, and I will ultimately recognize it as being the best moral alternative.'"

A Litany of Evidence

Moreland's simple illustration was extremely helpful to me. As I delved into the most troublesome obstacles to faith, they tended to loom so large in my mind that they crowded out other relevant information. And maybe as you've focused on an issue that's particularly nettlesome for you, the same phenomenon has occurred.

Debunking Christianity takes more than just trying to poke a hole in it by raising an objection. That's because there's a backdrop of other relevant evidence that creates a strong presumption in favor of faith in Jesus Christ. Simply examining individual challenges isn't enough; this broad sweep of evidence needs to be kept in mind as each individual objection is weighed.

What kind of evidence? My interviews with the experts elicited these persuasive facts that point powerfully toward the existence of God and his unique Son, Jesus Christ:

• *The Big Bang.* William Lane Craig, co-author of Oxford University Press' *Theism, Atheism, and Big Bang Cosmology,* showed that the universe and time itself had a beginning at some point in the finite past. Scientists refer to this as the Big Bang. Craig argued that whatever begins to exist has a cause, the universe began to exist, and therefore the universe has a cause—that is, a Creator who is uncaused, changeless, timeless, and immaterial. Even renowned atheist Kai Nielsen once said: "Suppose you suddenly hear a loud bang . . . and you ask me, 'What made that bang?' and I reply, 'Nothing, it just happened.' You would not accept that." To which Craig said that if there is obviously a cause for a little bang, doesn't it also make sense that there would be a Cause for a Big Bang?

• *The fine-tuned universe.* In the past thirty-five years, scientists have been stunned to discover how life in the universe is astoundingly balanced on a razor's edge. The Big Bang was actually a highly ordered event that required an enormous amount of information, and from the moment of inception the universe was finely tuned to an incomprehensible precision for the existence of life like ourselves. An infinitesimal difference in the rate of the universe's initial expansion, the strength of gravity or the weak force, or dozens of other constants and quantities would have created a life-prohibiting rather than a life-sustaining universe. All of this contributes to the conclusion that there's an Intelligent Designer behind creation.

• *The moral law.* Without God, morality is simply the product of sociobiological evolution and basically a question of taste or personal preference. For instance, rape may become taboo in the course of human development because it's not socially advantageous, but it's also conceivable that rape could have evolved as something that's beneficial for survival of the species. In other words, without God there is no absolute right and wrong that imposes itself on our conscience. But we know deep down that objective moral values *do* exist—some actions like rape and child torture, for example, are universal moral abominations—and, therefore, this means God exists.

• *The origin of life.* Darwinism can offer no credible theory for how life could have emerged naturally from nonliving chemicals. Earth's early atmosphere would have blocked the development of the building blocks of life, and assembling even the most primitive living matter would be so outrageously difficult that it absolutely could not have been the product of unguided or random processes. On the contrary, the vast amount of specific information contained inside every living cell—encoded in the four-letter chemical alphabet of DNA—strongly confirms the existence of an Intelligent Designer who was behind the miraculous creation of life.

• *The Bible's credibility.* Scholar Norman Geisler convincingly argued that there's more evidence that the Bible is a reliable source than there is for any other book from the ancient world. Its essential trustworthiness has been corroborated repeatedly by archaeological discoveries, "and if we can trust the Bible when it's telling us about straightforward earthly things that can be verified, then we can trust it in areas where we can't directly verify it in an empirical way," he said. Further, the Bible's divine origin has been established in two ways. First, in defiance of all mathematical odds, dozens of ancient prophecies about the Messiah—including the precise time frame in which he would appear—were miraculously fulfilled in only one person throughout history: Jesus of Nazareth. Second, biblical prophets performed miracles to confirm their divine authority. Jesus' own miracles were even acknowledged by his enemies. By contrast, in the Koran when unbelievers challenged Muhammad to perform a miracle, he refused and merely told them to read a chapter in the Koran, even though he conceded, "God hath certainly power to send down a sign."

• *The resurrection of Jesus.* Craig built a compelling case that Jesus Christ returned from the dead in the ultimate authentication of his claim to divinity. He presented four facts that are widely accepted by New Testament historians from a broad spectrum. First, after being crucified, Jesus was buried by Joseph of Arimathea in a tomb. This means its location was known to Jew, Christian, and Roman alike. Second, on the Sunday after the crucifixion the tomb was found empty by a group of his women followers. Indeed, nobody claimed the tomb was anything but vacant. Third, on multiple occasions and under various circumstances, different individuals and groups experienced appearances of Jesus alive from the dead. This cannot be dismissed as legendary because of the extremely early date of these accounts. Fourth, the original disciples suddenly and sincerely came to believe Jesus was risen from the dead despite their predisposition to the contrary. They were willing to go to their death proclaiming Jesus was resurrected and thus proved he was the Son of God—and nobody knowingly and willingly dies for a lie.

In addition, the thirteen scholars and experts I interviewed for my previous book, *The Case for Christ*, established that the biographies of Jesus in the New Testament stand up to intellectual scrutiny; that they were reliably passed down to us through history; that there's corroborating evidence for Jesus outside the Bible; that Jesus wasn't psychologically imbalanced when he claimed he was God; and that he fulfilled all the attributes of deity. [Please see the "Appendix: A Summary of *The Case for Christ*" in the back of this book for an overview of these findings.]

Accounting for the Evidence

Every single one of "The Big Eight" objections needs to be weighed in light of this overwhelming positive evidence for the existence of God and the deity of Jesus Christ. For example, as Peter Kreeft conceded in our interview, the suffering in this world does constitute some evidence against the existence of God—but in the end it's buried by an avalanche of *other* evidence that he does exist, that he does love us, and that he can even redeem our suffering and draw good from it. This mountain of evidence can give us confidence that even though we may not fully understand why there's suffering or why hell exists, we can trust that God is just, that he is acting appropriately, and that someday we'll have a deeper explanation.

While each of these eight obstacles is serious, none of them was able to overcome the other data that persuasively point toward Christianity as being true. When I was an atheist, I realized that I would need to do more than merely raise random objections in order to cripple Christianity; I would have to come up with a nontheistic scenario that would better accommodate all of the facts that I've just listed. But atheism cannot credibly account for the Big Bang, the fine-tuning of the universe, the emergence of life, the existence of moral laws, the supernatural confirmation of the Bible, and the Resurrection. The only hypothesis that explains them all is that there's a divine Creator whose unique Son is Jesus of Nazareth.

I had examined each obstacle on its own merits, interviewing experts who were able to provide satisfying explanations and analysis. Then I evaluated each of the objections in the context of the convincing evidence that Christianity is true and that therefore God is ultimately trustworthy and loves us deeply.

My conclusion is that Christianity emerged unscathed. After spending a year investigating "The Big Eight" objections, I remained utterly convinced that the most rational and logical step people can take is to invest their faith in Jesus of Nazareth.

SCENE #2: MAKING A CHOICE

At the University of Southern California, inside a red brick building with the words "Truth Shall Make You Free" etched in its exterior, Leslie and I found ourselves sitting in an office that looked like the aftermath of a tornado in a trailer park. Surrounding us—on the desk and floor and spare chairs—were papers piled high. Shelves were bursting with heavy books, dog-earned journals, and a variety of mementos. And sitting serenely in the midst of it all was philosopher Dallas Willard, one of the most influential Christian thinkers of our day.

It was a rare opportunity to talk with the author of two of the most celebrated Christian books of recent decades: *The Spirit of the Disciplines* and *The Divine Conspiracy.* Our conversation with the gray-haired, bespectacled professor of philosophy was centering on how faith is exercised through prayer.

At one point, as we discussed how people respond to God, Willard made an especially interesting observation: "The issue is, what do we want? The Bible says that if you seek God with all your heart, then you will surely find him. *Surely* find him. It's the person who wants to know God that God reveals himself to. And if a person doesn't want to know God—well, God has created the world and the human mind in such a way that he doesn't have to."

He reached over and dug through a stack of papers on his desk, withdrawing a single sheet. "This is a handout I gave to the students in my class," he said. I took the paper and read the words:

> Next Tuesday morning, just after breakfast, all of us in this one world will be knocked to our knees by a percussive and ear-shattering thunderclap. Snow swirls, leaves drop from trees, the earth heaves and buckles, buildings topple and towers tumble. The sky is ablaze with an eerie silvery light, and just then, as all the people of this world look up, the heavens open, and the clouds pull apart, revealing an unbelievably radiant and immense Zeus-like figure towering over us like a hundred Everests. He frowns darkly as lightning plays over the features of his Michelangeloid face, and then he points down, at me, and explains for every man, woman, and child to hear, "I've had quite enough of your too-clever logic chopping and word-watching in matters of theology. *Be assured, Norwood Russell Hanson, that I most certainly do exist!*"[3]

"So," said Willard, "I asked the class, 'If this really happened, how would Hanson respond?'"

I said, "You think he'd explain it away."

"Absolutely!" Willard replied. "It's very unfortunate, but I think he'd explain it away. We need to be alert to the fact that, in nearly every case imaginable, answered prayer can be explained away if you want to. And that's what people normally do. They say, 'Well, I'm very smart; I can't be fooled by all these things.'"

I could relate to that. I told Willard about the time when my newborn daughter was rushed into intensive care because of a mysterious illness that was threatening her life. The doctors weren't able to diagnose it. Even though I was an atheist, I was so desperate that I actually prayed and implored God—if he existed—to heal her. A short time later, she astounded everyone by suddenly getting completely better. The doctors were left scratching their heads.

"My response," I told Willard, "was to explain it away. I said, 'What a coincidence! She must have had some bacteria or virus that spontaneously disappeared.' I wouldn't even consider the possibility that God had acted. Instead, I stayed in my atheism."

Willard smiled at the story. "I don't mean to diagnose your case in your presence," he said gently, "but might it be that your pride got in the way? You were too smart! You weren't going to be taken in by this. Let all the little old ladies be fooled, but not you. As long as a person has that attitude, that's their response."

Bingo! He was right on target. Even if there had been a proliferation of corroborating evidence that God had intervened, I would have come up with *any* explanation—no matter how bizarre, no matter how nonsensical—other than the possibility that he had answered my prayer. I was too proud to bend the knee to anyone, and too enmeshed in my immoral lifestyle to want to give it up.

"I guarantee you," continued Willard, "that it wouldn't take five minutes to explain away a clear-cut miracle like the fire that came down out of the heavens to consume the altar in the case of Elijah in the Old Testament. And do you know what? People *did* explain it away! If they hadn't, the history of Israel would have been very different from what it was.

"And God has set up prayer in such a way that, if you want to explain it away, you can. That's the human mind. God set it up like that for a reason, which is this: *God ordained that people should be governed in the end by what they want.*"

A Will to Believe

That insight from Willard cut to the heart of my spiritual journey. If I wanted to, I could continue to try to explain away the words of the experts I had interviewed, no matter how outlandish or nitpicking my arguments would eventually become. And, believe me, my mind is quite capable of manufacturing all kinds of elaborate rebuttals, excuses, and counter-arguments—even in the face of obvious truth.

Ultimately, though, faith isn't about having perfect and complete answers to every single one of "The Big Eight" objections. After all, we don't demand that level of conclusive proof in any other area of life. The point is that we certainly do have sufficient evidence about God upon which to act. And in the end, *that's* the issue. Faith is about a choice, a step of the will, a decision to want to know God personally. It's saying, "I believe—please help my unbelief!" As Willard said, "It's the person who wants to know God that God reveals himself to." Or as Lynn Anderson had told me: "When you scratch below the surface, there's either a will to believe or there's a will not to believe. *That's* the core of it."

I was thankful that I didn't have to throw out my intellect to become a Christian. The positive evidence for Jesus being the unique Son of God and the convincing answers to "The Big Eight" objections cleared the way for me to take that step. But I *did* have to overcome my pride. I *did* have to drive a stake through the egoism and arrogance that threatened to hold me back. I *did* have to conquer the self-interest and self-adulation that were keeping my heart shut tight from God.

To apply Willard's words to myself, the biggest issue was: "What did I want?" Did I *want* to know God personally—to experience release from guilt, to live the way I was designed to live, to pursue his purposes for my life, to tap into his power for daily living, to commune with him in this life and for eternity in the next? If so, there was plenty of evidence upon which to base a rational decision to say "yes" to him.

It was up to me—just as it's up to you. As William Lane Craig expressed it:

> If God does not exist, then life is futile. If the God of the Bible does exist, then life is meaningful. Only the second of these two alternatives enables us to live happily and consistently. Therefore, it seems to me that even if the evidence for these two options were absolutely equal, a rational person ought to choose biblical Christianity. It seems to me positively irrational to prefer death, futility, and destruction to life, meaningfulness, and happiness. As [Blaise] Pascal said, we have nothing to lose and infinity to gain.[4]

SCENE #3: CHANGING A LIFE

This third episode occurred after my Atlanta interview with Craig about the issue of miracles. I got into my rental car and took a leisurely drive up Interstate 75 to Rome, Georgia. The next morning was cool but sunny, and I got dressed and headed over to a church for Sunday services.

Outside, politely greeting everyone with a handshake as they arrived, was William Neal Moore, looking handsome in a tan suit with dark stripes, a crisp white shirt and brown tie. His face was deep mahogany, his black hair was close-cropped, but what I remember most was his smile: it was at once shy and warm, gentle and sincere, winsome and loving. It made me feel welcome.

"Praise the Lord, Brother Moore!" declared an elderly woman as she grasped his hand briefly and then shuffled inside.

Moore is an ordained minister at the church, which is sandwiched between two housing projects in the racially mixed community. He is a doting father, a devoted husband, a faithful provider, a hard-working employee, a man of compassion and prayer who spends his spare time helping hurting people who everyone else seems to have forgotten. In short, a model citizen.

But turn back the calendar to May, 1984. At that time, Moore was locked in the death-watch cell at the Georgia State Penitentiary, down the hallway from the electric chair where his life was scheduled to be snuffed out in less than seventy-two hours.

This was not the case of an innocent man being railroaded by the justice system. Unquestionably, Moore was a murderer. He had admitted as much. After a childhood of poverty and occasional petty crimes, he had joined the Army and later became depressed by marital and financial woes. One night he got drunk and broke into the house of seventy-seven-year-old Fredger Stapleton, who was known to keep large amounts of cash in his bedroom.

From behind a door, Stapleton let loose with a shotgun blast, and Moore fired back with a pistol. Stapleton was killed instantly, and within minutes Moore was fleeing with $5,600. An informant tipped police and the next morning he was arrested at his trailer outside of town. Caught with the proceeds from the crime, Moore admitted his guilt and was sentenced to death. He had squandered his life and turned to violence, and now he himself would face a violent end.

But the William Neal Moore who was counting down the hours to his scheduled execution was not the same person who had murdered Fredger Stapleton. Shortly after being imprisoned, two church leaders visited Moore at the behest of his mother. They told him about the mercy and hope that was available through Jesus Christ.

"Nobody had ever told me that Jesus loves me and died for me," Moore explained during my visit to Georgia. "It was a love I could feel. It was a love I wanted. It was a love I *needed.*"

On that day, Moore said yes to Christ's free gift of forgiveness and eternal life, and he was promptly baptized in a small tub that was used by prison trusties. And he would never be the same.

For sixteen years on Death Row, Moore was like a missionary among the other inmates. He led Bible studies and conducted prayer sessions. He counseled prisoners and introduced many of them to faith in Jesus Christ. Some churches actually sent people to Death Row to be counseled by him. He took dozens of Bible courses by correspondence. He won the forgiveness of his victim's family. He became known as "The Peacemaker," because his cellblock, largely populated by inmates who had become Christians through his influence, was always the safest, the quietest, the most orderly.

Meanwhile, Moore inched closer and closer to execution. Legally speaking, his case was a hopeless cause. Since he had pleaded guilty, there were virtually no legal issues that might win his release on appeal. Time after time, the courts reaffirmed his death sentence.

"A Saintly Figure"

So profound was the depth of Moore's transformation, however, that people began to take notice. Mother Teresa and others started campaigning to save his life. "Billy's not what he was then," said a former inmate who had met Moore in prison. "If you kill him today, you're killing a body, but a body with a different mind. It would be like executing the wrong man."[5]

Praising him for not only being rehabilitated but also being "an agent of the rehabilitation of others," an editorial in the *Atlanta Journal and Constitution* declared: "In the eyes of many, he is a saintly figure."[6]

Just hours prior to Moore's being strapped into the electric chair, shortly before Moore's head and right calf would be shaved so that the lethal electrodes could be attached, the courts surprised nearly everyone by issuing a temporary halt to his execution.

Even more amazingly, the Georgia Board of Pardons and Parole later voted unanimously to spare his life by commuting his sentence to life in prison. But what was *really* astounding—in fact, unprecedented in modern Georgia history—was when the Parole and Pardon Board decided that Moore, an admitted and once-condemned armed robber and murderer, should go free. On November 8, 1991, he was released.

As I sat with Moore in his home overlooking a landscape of lush pine trees, I asked him about the source of his amazing metamorphosis.

"It was the prison rehabilitation system that did it, right?" I asked.

Moore laughed. "No, it wasn't that," he replied.

"Then it was a self-help program or having a positive mental attitude," I suggested.

He shook his head emphatically. "No, not that, either."

"Prozac? Transcendental Meditation? Psychological counseling?"

"Come on, Lee," he said. "You know it wasn't any of those."

He was right. I knew the real reason. I just wanted to hear him say it. "Then what was responsible for the transformation of Billy Moore?" I asked.

"Plain and simple, it was Jesus Christ," he declared adamantly. "He changed me in ways I could never have changed on my own. He gave me a reason to live. He helped me do the right thing. He gave me a heart for others. He saved my soul."

That's the power of faith to change a human life. "Therefore," wrote the apostle Paul, "if anyone is in Christ, he is a new creation; the old has gone, the new has come!"[7]

Billy Moore the Christian is not the same as Billy Moore the killer. God had intervened with his forgiveness, with his mercy, with his power, with the abiding presence of his Spirit. That same kind of transforming grace is available to everyone who acts on the ample evidence for Jesus Christ by making the decision to turn away from their sin and embrace him as their forgiver and leader.

It's awaiting all those who say yes to God and his ways.

Reaffirming the Faith

Those three scenes summarized my year-long quest for answers to "The Big Eight." The first scene emphasizes the magnitude of the overall case for Christ and the availability of solid responses to the toughest questions about the Christian faith. In other words, there's ample justification for a thinking person to put his or her trust in Jesus. The second scene highlights our human tendency to explain away that evidence out of pride or self-interest. In the end, faith is a step of the will; God will give us what we want. The third scene uses one radical example to illustrate God's willingness to change the lives of those who respond to the evidence, overcome their pride, and open their hearts to him.

All of this can be boiled down to a three-word process—*investigation . . . decision . . . transformation*—that I experienced in my spiritual journey. It was in 1981 when I originally responded to the evidence by deciding to abandon atheism and cling to Christ. And like Moore, I've never been the same. Opening my life wider and wider to God and his ways, I've found my values, my character, my priorities, my attitudes, my relationships, my desires have been changing over time—for the better.

Today, having now retraced my original investigation, my confidence in that 1981 decision has only been reinforced. Asking uncomfortable questions hasn't diminished my faith; it has strengthened it. Probing the "soft spots" of Christianity has reaffirmed for me once more the fundamental soundness and logical integrity of the faith. Refined by the rigors of intellectual scrutiny, my faith has emerged deeper, richer, more resilient, and more certain than ever.

Yet as I reclined on that chair in my living room and mentally reviewed my investigation, I realized that my task was not quite complete. Preacher-turned-skeptic Charles Templeton, who resolutely denied the existence of a loving God but who wept out of his longing for Jesus, provided much of the impetus for this flurry of interviews about "The Big Eight" obstacles to faith.

The intention of my investigation was to get answers to the issues that had most troubled me in my spiritual journey, not to try to spell out a point-by-point rebuttal of Templeton and his writings. But there was considerable overlap between the issues that blocked his path to faith and the topics that disturbed me when I was a spiritual seeker.

How, I wondered, would Templeton have reacted to my interviews with these eight experts? Would he have been receptive to their evidence and arguments? Or would the inexorable advance of Alzheimer's have already robbed him of the capacity to rethink spiritual issues anew?

A Note of Hope

It was mid-afternoon on a bright spring day in Orange County, California, where Leslie and I had recently moved. I had just printed out the nearly five hundred pages of the manuscript of this book and was in the midst of packing them into a box when Leslie poked her head into my office.

"What are you doing?" she asked.

I gestured toward the manuscript. "There's someone I want to send this to," I replied.

Leslie put down her cup of tea and walked over to put her arm around my shoulder. "Chuck Templeton, right?" she said. "I think about him from time to time. In fact, I've been praying for him."

That didn't surprise me. "Praying what?" I asked.

"That he'd still be healthy enough to reconsider his conclusions about God. That he'd be open to the explanations you've received from the experts. That he'd respond to that tug inside of him that seems to be pulling him toward Jesus."

I nodded. I had been praying too. "I talked to his wife on the phone a few minutes ago," I said. "She told me the Alzheimer's hasn't been very kind to Chuck and that now he has some other health problems. When I got a chance to talk to Chuck and ask him how his Alzheimer's was, he answered with just one word in a very despondent voice—he said, '*Devastating.*'"

"Oh, I'm so sorry," Leslie said quietly.

"Me too," I sighed. "It's very sad." I put some more pages into the box. "She also said Billy Graham came to see Chuck a few months ago."

Leslie's eyes widened. "Really?" she said. "What happened?"

"They hadn't seen each other in quite a while. She said when Chuck recognized him, it was as if a chill went through him and he started crying and threw his arms around Billy and hugged him. She couldn't say enough wonderful things about how kind and loving Billy was. They visited for a while and ate together. Billy prayed before the meal—she said, 'That's the first time grace has ever been said at our table.' Then before he left, Billy prayed for Chuck."

I could see that Leslie's eyes were moist. "I'm so glad they were able to spend some time together," she said. "Maybe something will come out of it."

I nodded and then turned to resume packing the manuscript. "Madeleine said she was anxious to see my book and promised to read it to Chuck," I said. "I just hope he hasn't waited too long and that his mind will be clear enough to understand what these scholars have said. But I feel like I've got to send it—just in case."

With that, I sat down to write him a letter, wishing him well and encouraging him, as best he can, to keep an open mind and take a fresh look at the evidence for Jesus. I signed my name and put down the pen, but I hesitated to fold the letter. I wanted to write something else; I just wasn't sure what was left to say.

I glanced out the window. Saddleback Mountain was majestic against the deep blue sky. For a while I was lost in thought. And then, suddenly, words flooded into my mind. I picked up the pen, and with Leslie peering over my shoulder, quickly added this postscript:

> Chuck, I hope you'll take to heart what Proverbs 2:3–5 says: "If you scream for insight and call loudly for understanding, if

you pursue it like you would money, and search it out as you would hidden treasure, then the Lord will be awesome to you, and you will come into possession of the knowledge of God."

I sealed the note in an envelope and tossed it into the box, then picked up the car keys.

"Let's go mail this," I said.

APPENDIX: A SUMMARY OF *THE CASE FOR CHRIST*

In *The Case for Christ,* I retraced and expanded upon my 1980–81 journey from atheism to Christianity by interviewing thirteen leading experts on the historical evidence for Jesus Christ. Below is a summary of the answers to the issues I investigated.

• CAN THE BIOGRAPHIES OF JESUS BE TRUSTED?

I once thought the gospels were merely religious propaganda, hopelessly tainted by overactive imaginations and evangelistic zeal. But Craig Blomberg of Denver Seminary, one of the country's foremost authorities on the biographies of Jesus, built a convincing case that they reflect eyewitness testimony and bear the unmistakable earmarks of accuracy. So early are these accounts of Jesus' life that they cannot be explained away as legendary invention. "Within the first two years after his death," Blomberg said, "significant numbers of Jesus' followers seem to have formulated a doctrine of the atonement, were convinced that he had been raised from the dead in bodily form, associated Jesus with God, and believed they found support for all these convictions in the Old Testament." A study indicates that there was nowhere near enough time for legend to have developed and wiped out a solid core of historical truth.

• DO JESUS' BIOGRAPHIES STAND UP TO SCRUTINY?

Blomberg argued persuasively that the gospel writers intended to preserve reliable history, were able to do so, were honest and willing to include difficult-to-explain material, and didn't allow bias to unduly color their reporting. The harmony among the gospels on essential facts, coupled with divergence on some incidental details, lends historical credibility to the accounts. What's more, the early church could not have taken root and flourished right there in Jerusalem if it had been teaching facts about Jesus that his own contemporaries could have exposed as exaggerated or false. In short, the gospels were able to pass all eight evidential tests, demonstrating their basic trustworthiness as historical records.

• WERE JESUS' BIOGRAPHIES RELIABLY PRESERVED FOR US?

World-class scholar Bruce Metzger, professor emeritus at Princeton Theological Seminary, said that compared with other ancient documents, there is an unprecedented number of New Testament manuscripts and that they can be dated extremely close to the original writings. The modern New Testament is 99.5 percent free of textual discrepancies, with no major Christian doctrines in doubt. The criteria used by the early church to determine which books should be considered authoritative have ensured that we possess the best records about Jesus.

• IS THERE CREDIBLE EVIDENCE FOR JESUS OUTSIDE HIS BIOGRAPHIES?

"We have better historical documentation for Jesus than for the founder of any other ancient religion," said Edwin Yamauchi of Miami University, a leading expert on ancient history. Sources from outside the Bible corroborate that many people believed Jesus performed healings and was the Messiah, that he was crucified, and that despite this shameful death, his followers, who believed he was still alive, worshiped him as God. One expert documented thirty-nine ancient sources that corroborate more than one hundred facts concerning Jesus' life, teachings, crucifixion, and resurrection. Seven secular sources and several early Christian creeds concern the deity of Jesus, a doctrine "definitely present in the earliest church," according to Dr. Gary Habermas, the scholar who wrote *The Historical Jesus*.

• DOES ARCHAEOLOGY CONFIRM OR CONTRADICT JESUS' BIOGRAPHIES?

John McRay, a professor of archaeology for more than fifteen years and author of *Archaeology and the New Testament*, said there's no question that archaeological findings have enhanced the New Testament's credibility. No discovery has ever disproved a biblical reference. Further, archaeology has established that Luke, who wrote about one-quarter of the New Testament, was an especially careful historian. Concluded one expert: "If Luke was so painstakingly accurate in his historical reporting [of minor details], on what logical basis may we assume he was credulous or inaccurate in his reporting of matters that were far more important, not only to him but to others as well?" Like, for instance, the resurrection of Jesus—the event that authenticated his claim to being the unique Son of God.

• IS THE JESUS OF HISTORY THE SAME AS THE JESUS OF FAITH?

Gregory Boyd, a Yale- and Princeton-educated scholar who wrote the award-winning *Cynic Sage or Son of God,* offered a devastating critique of the Jesus Seminar, a group that questions whether Jesus said or did most of what's attributed to him. He identified the Seminar as "an extremely small number of radical-fringe scholars who are on the far, far left wing of New Testament thinking." The Seminar ruled out the possibility of miracles at the outset, employed questionable criteria, and some participants have touted myth-riddled documents of extremely dubious quality. Further, the idea that stories about Jesus emerged from mythology fails to withstand scrutiny. Said Boyd: "The evidence for Jesus being who the disciples said he was . . . is just light years beyond my reasons for thinking that the left-wing scholarship of the Jesus Seminar is correct." In sum, the Jesus of faith is the same as the Jesus of history.

• WAS JESUS REALLY CONVINCED HE WAS THE SON OF GOD?

By going back to the very earliest traditions, which are unquestionably safe from legendary development, Ben Witherington III, author of *The Christology of Jesus,* was able to show that Jesus had a supreme and transcendent self-understanding. Based on the evidence, Witherington said: "Did Jesus believe he was the Son of God, the anointed one of God? The answer is yes. Did he see himself as the Son of Man? The answer is yes. Did he see himself as the final Messiah? Yes, that's the way he viewed himself. Did he believe that anybody less than God could save the world? No, I don't believe he did." Scholars said that Jesus' repeated reference to himself as the Son of Man was not a claim of humanity, but a reference to Daniel 7:13–14, in which the Son of Man is seen as having universal authority and everlasting dominion and who receives the worship of all nations. Said one scholar: "Thus, the claim to be the Son of Man would be in effect a claim to divinity."

• WAS JESUS CRAZY WHEN HE CLAIMED TO BE THE SON OF GOD?

Gary Collins, a professor of psychology for twenty years and author of forty-five books on psychology-related topics, said Jesus exhibited no inappropriate emotions, was in contact with reality, was brilliant and had amazing insights into human nature, and enjoyed deep and abiding relationships. "I just don't see signs that Jesus was suffering from any known mental illness," he concluded. In addition, Jesus backed up his claim to being God through miraculous feats of healing, astounding demonstrations of power over nature, unrivaled teaching, divine understanding of people, and with his own resurrection, which was the ultimate evidence of his deity.

• DID JESUS FULFILL THE ATTRIBUTES OF GOD?

While the incarnation—God becoming man, the infinite becoming finite—stretches our imaginations, prominent theologian D. A. Carson pointed out that there's lots of evidence that Jesus exhibited the characteristics of deity. Based on Philippians 2, many theologians believe Jesus voluntarily emptied himself of the independent use of his divine attributes as he pursued his mission of human redemption. Even so, the New Testament specifically confirms that Jesus ultimately possessed every qualification of deity, including omniscience, omnipresence, omnipotence, eternality, and immutability.

• DID JESUS—AND JESUS ALONE—MATCH THE IDENTITY OF THE MESSIAH?

Hundreds of years before Jesus was born, prophets foretold the coming of the Messiah, or the Anointed One, who would redeem God's people. In effect, dozens of these Old Testament prophecies created a fingerprint that only the true Messiah could fit. This gave Israel a way to rule out imposters and validate the credentials of the authentic Messiah. Against astronomical odds—one chance in a trillion, trillion, trillion, trillion, trillion, trillion, trillion, trillion, trillion, trillion, trillion, trillion, trillion—Jesus, and only Jesus throughout history, matched this prophetic fingerprint. This confirms Jesus' identity to an incredible degree of certainty. The expert I interviewed on this topic, Louis Lapides, is an example of someone raised in a conservative Jewish home and who came to believe Jesus is the Messiah after a systematic study of the prophecies. Today, he's the pastor of a church in California and former president of a national network of fifteen messianic congregations.

• WAS JESUS' DEATH A SHAM AND HIS RESURRECTION A HOAX?

By analyzing the medical and historical data, Dr. Alexander Metherell, a physician who also holds a doctorate in engineering, concluded Jesus could not have survived the gruesome rigors of crucifixion, much less the gaping wound that pierced his lung and heart. In fact, even before the crucifixion he was in serious to critical condition and suffering from hypovolemic shock as the result of a horrific flogging. The idea that he somehow swooned on the cross and pretended to be dead lacks any evidential basis. Roman executioners were grimly efficient, knowing that they themselves would face death if any of their victims were to come down from the cross alive. Even if Jesus had somehow lived through the torture, his ghastly condition could never have inspired a worldwide movement based on the premise that he had gloriously triumphed over the grave.

• WAS JESUS' BODY REALLY ABSENT FROM HIS TOMB?

William Lane Craig, who has earned two doctorates and written several books on the Resurrection, presented striking evidence that the enduring symbol of Easter—the vacant tomb of Jesus—was a historical reality. The empty grave is reported or implied in extremely early sources—Mark's gospel and a creed in First Corinthians 15—which date so close to the event that they could not possibly have been products of legend. The fact that the gospels report that women discovered the empty tomb bolsters the story's authenticity, because women's testimony lacked credibility in the first century and thus there would have been no motive to report they found the empty tomb if it weren't true. The site of Jesus' tomb was known to Christians, Jews, and Romans, so it could have been checked by skeptics. In fact, nobody—not even the Roman authorities or Jewish leaders—ever claimed that the tomb still contained Jesus' body. Instead, they were forced to invent the absurd story that the disciples, despite having no motive or opportunity, had stolen the body—a theory that not even the most skeptical critic believes today.

• WAS JESUS SEEN ALIVE AFTER HIS DEATH ON THE CROSS?

The evidence for the post-Resurrection appearances of Jesus didn't develop gradually over the years as mythology distorted memories of his life. Rather, said renowned Resurrection expert Gary Habermas, his resurrection was "the central proclamation of the early church from the very beginning." The ancient creed from 1 Corinthians 15 mentions specific individuals who encountered the risen Christ, and Paul even challenged first-century doubters to talk with these individuals personally to determine the truth of the matter for themselves. The Book of Acts is littered with extremely early affirmations of Jesus' resurrection, while the gospels describe numerous encounters in detail. Concluded British theologian Michael Green: "The appearances of Jesus are as well authenticated as anything in antiquity.... There can be no rational doubt that they occurred."

• ARE THERE ANY SUPPORTING FACTS THAT POINT TOWARD THE RESURRECTION?

Professor J. P. Moreland presented circumstantial evidence that provided strong documentation for the Resurrection. First, the disciples were in a unique position to know whether the Resurrection happened, and they went to their deaths proclaiming it was true. Nobody knowingly and willingly dies for a lie. Second, apart from the Resurrection, there's no good reason why such skeptics as Paul and James would have been converted and would have died for their faith. Third, within weeks of the Crucifixion, thousands of Jews became convinced Jesus was the Son of God and began following him, abandoning key social practices that had critical sociological and religious importance for centuries. They believed they risked damnation if they were wrong. Fourth, the early sacraments of Communion and Baptism affirmed Jesus' resurrection and deity. And fifth, the miraculous emergence of the church in the face of brutal Roman persecution "rips a great hole in history, a hole the size and shape of Resurrection," as C. F. D. Moule put it.

Taken together, I concluded that this expert testimony constitutes compelling evidence that Jesus Christ was who he claimed to be—the one and only Son of God. The atheism that I had embraced for so long buckled under the weight of historical truth.

For the details that support this summary, please refer to *The Case for Christ.*

LIST OF CITATIONS

Adams—Candace Adams, "Leading Nanoscientist Builds Big Faith," *Baptist Standard,* March 15, 2000.

Albright—William F. Albright, *Archaeology and the Religion of Israel* (Baltimore: John Hopkins Press, 1953).

Alston—William Alston, "Religious Diversity and Perceptual Knowledge of God," *Faith and Philosophy* 5 (1988).

Anderson—Lynn Anderson, *If I Really Believe, Why Do I Have These Doubts?* (Minneapolis: Bethany House, 1992).

Angeles—ed. Peter A. Angeles, *Critiques of God* (Buffalo: Prometheus Books, 1997).

Atlanta Journal and Constitution—"When Mercy Becomes Mandatory," *The Atlanta Journal and Constitution,* August 21, 1990.

Bacchiocchi—Samuele Bacchiocchi, "Hell: Does it Have an End?" *Sings of the Times,* August 1999.

Barker—Dan Barker, *Losing Faith in Faith* (Madison, Wis.: Freedom from Religion Foundation, 1992).

Behe—Michael Behe, *Darwin's Black Box* (New York: The Fress Press, 1996).

Boyd—Gregory A. Boyd and Edward K. Boyd, *Letters From a Skeptic* (Wheaton, Ill.: Victor, 1994).

Bradley—Walter L. Bradley and Charles B. Thaxton, "Information and the Origin of Life," *The Creation Hypothesis* (Downers Grove, Ill.: InterVarsity Press, 1994).

Boudreaux—Richard Boudreaux, "Pope Apologizes for Catholic Sins Past and Present," *The Los Angeles Times,* March 13, 2000.

Buell—eds. J. Buell and G. Hearn, *Darwinism: Science or Philosophy?* (Dallas: Foundation for Thought and Ethics, 1994).

Bultmann—Rudolf Bultmann, *Jesus* (Berlin: 1926).

Cairns-Smith—A. G. Cairns-Smith, *Genetic Takeover and the Mineral Origins of Life* (New York: Cambridge University Press, 1982).

Campbell—eds. John H. Campbell and J.W. Schoff, *Creative Evolution* (New York: James and Bartlett, 1994).

Chicago Tribune—"Cardinal's Yom Kippur Letter Seeks Atonement for Church Anti-Semitism," *The Chicago Tribune,* September 21, 1999.

Chicago Tribune—"Catholic Clerics Apologize for Past Cruelties," *The Chicago Tribune,* November 14, 1999.

Colson—Charles Colson, *How Now Shall We Live?* (Wheaton, Ill.: Tyndale House, 1999).

Copan—Paul Copan, *True for You, But Not for Me* (Minneapolis: Bethany House, 1998).

Craig—William Lane Craig, *God, Are You There?* (Norcross, Ga.: Ravi Zacharias International Ministries, 1999).

Craig—William Lane Craig, *Reasonable Faith* (Wheaton, Ill.: Crossway, 1994).

Crick—Francis Crick, *Life Itself* (New York: Simon and Schuster, 1981).

Darwin—Charles Darwin, *Origin of Species,* 6th ed., (New York: New York University Press, 1988).

Darwin—Francis Darwin, *The Life and Letters of Charles Darwin* (New York: D. Appleton, 1887).

Dauvillier—A. Dauvillier, *The Photochemical Origin of Life* (New York: Academic Press, 1965).

Davies—P. C. W. Davies, "The Anthropic Principle," *Particle and Nuclear Physics* 10 (1983).

Davies—P. C. W. Davies, *Other Worlds* (London: Dent, 1980).

Dawkins—Richard Dawkins, *The Blind Watch Maker* (New York: Norton, 1987).

Day—William Day, *Genesis on Planet Earth* (East Lansing, Mich.: House of Talos, 1979).

Dembski—William Dembski, *The Design Interference* (Cambridge: Cambridge University Press, 1998).

Dembski—William Dembski and Michael Behe, *Intelligent Design* (Downers Grove, Ill.: InterVarsity Press, 1999).

Denton—Michael Denton, *Evolution: A Theory in Crises* (Chevy Chase, Md.: Adler & Adler, 1986).

Dose—Klaus Dose, "The Origin of Life: More Questions Than Answers," *Interdisciplinary Science Reviews* 13 (1988).

Eddington—Arthur Eddington, *The Expanding Universe* (New York: Macmillan, 1933).

Forsyth—P. T. Forsyth, *Justification of God* (London: Duckworth, 1916).

Fowler—trans. H. W. Fowler and F. G. Fowler, *The Works of Lucian of Samosata* 4 vols. (Oxford: The Clarendon Press, 1949).

Futuyma—Douglas Futuyma, *Evolutionary Biology* (Sunderland, Mass.: Sinauer, 1986).

Geivett—R. Douglas Geivett and Gary Habermas, *In Defense of Miracles* (Downers Grove, Ill.: InterVarsity Press, 1997).

Geisler—Norman L. Geisler, *Baker Encyclopedia of Christian Apologetics* (Grand Rapids, Mich.: Baker Books, 1999).

Geisler—Norman L. Geisler and J. Yutaka Amano, *The Reincarnation Sensation* (Wheaton, Ill.: Tyndale, 1986).

Geisler—Norman L. Geisler and Thomas Howe, *When Critics Ask* (Grand Rapids, Mich.: Baker Books, 1992).

Glynn—Patrick Glynn, *God: The Evidence* (Rocklin, Calif.: Forum, 1997).

Gomes—Alan Gomes, "Evangelicals and the Annihilation of Hell, Part II," *Christian Research Journal* 13 (Summer 1991).

Gould—Stephen Jay Gould, "Will We Figure Out How Life Began?" *Time,* April 10, 2000.

Grafton—Anthony Grafton, with April Shelford and Nancy Siraisi, *New Worlds, Ancient Text* (Cambridge, Mass.: Belknap Press, 1992).

Graham—Billy Graham, *Just As I Am* (Grand Rapids, Mich.: Zondervan, 1997).

Greig—ed. J. Y. T. Greig, *The Letters of David Hume* (Oxford: Clarendon Press, 1932).

Guinness—Os Guinness, *In Two Minds* (Downer's Grove, Ill.: InterVarsity Press, 1976).

Gumble—Nicky Gumble, *Searching Issues* (Eastbourne: Kingsway Publications, 1994).

Habermas—Gary R. Habermas and J. P. Moreland, *Beyond Death: Exploring Evidence for Immortality* (Wheaton, Ill.: Crossway, 1998).

Haeckel—Ernst Haeckel, trans. J. McCabe, *The Wonders of Life* (London: Watts, 1905).

Hanegraaff—Hank Hanegraaff, *The Face that Demonstrates the Farce of Evolution* (Nashville: Word, 1998).

Hawking—Stephen W. Hawking, *A Brief History of Time* (New York: Bantam Books, 1988).

Hawking—Stephen W. Hawking and Roger Penrose, *The Nature of Space and Time* (Princeton, N.J.: Princeton University Press, 1996).

Hemer—Colin J. Hemer, *The Book of Acts in the Setting of Hellenistic History* (Winona Lake, Ind.: Eisenvrauns, 1990).

Herschel—J. F. W. Herschel, *Preliminary Discourse on the Study of Natural Philosophy* (London: Longman, Rees, Orme, Brown and Green, 1831).

Hick—eds. John Hick and Paul F. Knitter, *The Myth of Christian Uniqueness* (London: SCM Press, 1987).

Horgan—J. Horgan, "In the Beginning..." *Scientific American,* February 1991.

Hunter—W. Bingham Hunter, *The God Who Hears* (Downers Grove, Ill.: InterVarsity Press, 1986).

International Herold Tribune—"Why Are We Here: The Great Debate," *International Herold Tribune,* April 26, 1999.

Jastrow—Robert Jastrow, "The Secret of the Stars," *New York Times,* June 25, 1978.

Johnson—B. C. Johnson, *The Atheist Debator's Handbook* (Buffalo: Prometheus, 1979).

Johnson—George Johnson, "Science and Religion: Bridging the Great Divide," *New York Times,* June 30, 1998.

Johnson—Luke Timothy Johnson, *The Real Jesus* (San Francisco, Calif.: HarperSanFrancisco, 1996).

Johnson—Philip E. Johnson, *Darwin on Trial,* 2d. Ed. (Downers Grove, Ill.: InterVarsity Press, 1993).

Jones—Charles T. Jones, "DNA Tests Clear Two Men in Prison," *The Oklahoman,* April 16, 1999.

Kaiser—Walter C. Kaiser Jr., Peter H. Davids, F. F. Vruse, and Manfred T. Brauch, *Hard Sayings of the Bible* (Downers Grove, Ill.: InterVarsity Press, 1996).

Kennedy—D. James Kennedy, *Why I Believe* (Dallas: Word, 1980).

Kenny—Anthony Kenny, *The Five Ways: St. Thomas Aquinas' Proofs of God's Existence* (New York: Schocken Books, 1969).

Kenyon—Dean Kenyon and G. Steinman, *Biological Predestination* (New York: McGraw Hill, 1969).

Knechtle—Cliffe Knechtle, *Give Me an Answer* (Downers Grove, Ill.: InterVarsity Press, 1986).

Kok—Randall A. Kok, John A. Taylor, and Walter L. Bradley, "A Statistical Examination of Self-Ordering of Amino Acids in Proteins," *Origins of Life and Evolution of the Biosphere* 18, 1988.

Kreeft—Peter Kreeft and Ronald Tacelli, *Handbook of Christian Apologetics* (Downers Grove, Ill.: InterVarsity, 1994).

Kreeft—Peter Kreeft, *Making Sense Out of Suffering* (Ann Arbor, Mich.: Servant: 1986).

Kushner—Harold Kushner, *When Bad Things Happen to Good People* (New York: Schocken Books, 1981).

Larsen—Dale and Sandy Larsen, *Seven Myths about Christianity* (Downers Grove, Ill.: InterVarsity Press, 1996).

Leslie—John Leslie, *Universes* (London: Routledge, 1989).

Lewis—C. S. Lewis, *The Problem of Pain* (New York: Macmillan, 1962).

Ludemann—Gerd Ludemann, trans. John Bowden, *What Really Happened to Jesus?* (Louisville: Westminster John Knox Press, 1995).

Maas—Peter Maas, "Top Ten War Crimes Suspects," *George,* June 1999.

Martin—Michael Martin, *The Case Against Christianity* (Philadelphia: Temple University Press, 1991).

Martyr—Justin Martyr, eds. Alexander Roberts and James Donaldson, *First Apology: Ante-Nicene Fathers* (Grand Rapids, Mich.: William B. Eerdmans, 1973).

McCullagh—C. Behan McCullagh, *Justifying Historical Descriptions* (Cambridge: Cambridge Universtiy Press, 1984).

Mills—Gordon C. Mills, Malcolm Lancaster, and Walter L. Bradley, "Origin of Life and Evolution in Biology Textbooks—A Critique," *The American Biology Teacher*, February 1993.

Mills—Steven Mills and Ken Armstrong, "Convicted By a Hair," *The Chicago Tribune*, November 18, 1999.

Montgomery—Bill Montgomery, "U.S. Supreme Court Halts Execution: Even Victim's Family Pleaded For Mercy," *The Atlanta Journal and Constitution*, August 21, 1990.

Neff—David Neff, "Our Extended, Persecuted Family," *Christianity Today*, April 29, 1996.

Nielsen—Kai Nielsen, *Reason and Practice* (New York: Harper & Row, 1971).

Noll—Mark A. Noll, *A History of Christianity in the United States and Canada* (Grand Rapids, Mich.: William B. Eerdmans, 1992).

Novak—Michael Novak, David N. Livingstone, David Lyle Jeffrey, et. al., "Where Would Civilization Be Without Christianity?" *Christianity Today*, December 6, 1999.

O'Neill—ed. Gerard O'Neill, Dick Lehr, and Bruce Butterfield, "A Judgment on Sentences: Some Judges Balk at Present Penalties," *The Boston Globe*, September 27, 1995.

Palau—Luis Palau, *God is Relevant* (New York: Doubleday, 1997).

Parker—Gary E. Parker, *The Gift of Doubt* (San Francisco, Calif.: Harper & Row, 1990).

Polk—Peggy Polk, "Papal State: Despite His Recent Ills, Pope John Paul II is Focused on the Future," *The Chicago Tribune*, June 5, 1995.

Polkinghorne—John Polkinghorne, *Serious Talk: Science and Religion in Dialogue* (London: Trinity Press International, 1995).

Poole—Garry Poole and Judson Poling, *Tough Questions 4* (Grand Rapids, Mich.: Zondervan, 1998).

Possley—Maurice Possley, "Records Charge Deals by Judge: 'We Can Make $1,000 a Week,' Olson Quoted," *The Chicago Tribune*, February 21, 1985.

Possley—Maurice Possley, "Court Hears How FBI Agents Bugged Judge," *The Chicago Tribune*, April 26, 1985.

Possley—Maurice Possley, "Judge Liked 'People Who Take Dough,' Greylord File Shows," *The Chicago Tribune*, April 27, 1985.

Prigogine—Ilya Prigogine and Isabelle Stengers, *The End of Certainty: Time, Chaos, and the New Laws of Nature* (New York: Free Press, 1997).

Radetsky—Peter Radetsky, "How Did Life Start?" *Discover*, November 1992.

Ramsay—William M. Ramsay, *St. Paul the Traveler and the Roman Citizen* (Grand Rapids, Mich.: Baker Books, 1982).

Rana—Fazale R. Rana and Hugh Ross, "Life from the Heavens? Not this Way," *Facts for Faith*, October 2000.

Robertson—Archibald Robertson, *The Origins of Christianity* (New York: International Publishers, 1954).

Ross—Hugh Ross, *Creator and the Cosmos* (Colorado Springs: Navpress, 1993).

Ruse—Michael Ruse, "Evolutionary Theory and Christian Ethics," *Darwinian Paradigm* (London: Routledge, 1989).

Ruse—Michael Ruse, *Darwinism Defended* (London: Addison-Wesley, 1982).

Russell—Bertrand Russell, *Why I Am Not a Christian* (New York: Touchstone, 1957).

Sagan—Carl Sagan, *Broca's Brain* (New York: Random House, 1979).

Shapiro—Robert Shapiro, *Origins* (New York: Summit Books, 1986).

Shelley—Bruce L. Shelley, *Church History in Plain Language* 2d. ed. (Dallas: Word, 1995).

Sherwin-White—A. N. Sherwin-White, *Roman Society and Roman Law in the New Testament* (Oxford: Clarendon Press, 1963).

Smith—George H. Smith, *Atheism: The Case Against God* (Amherst, N.Y.: Prometheus Books, 1989).

Sproul—R. C. Sproul, *Reason to Believe* (Grand Rapids, Mich.: Lamplighter Books, 1991).

Stott—John R. Stott, *The Cross of Christ* (Downers Grove, Ill.: InterVarsity Press, 1986).

Stott—John R. Stott and David L. Edwards, *Essentials: A Liberal-Evangelical Dialogue* (London: 1988).

Strobel—Lee Strobel, "Thanksgiving Near; Only Food Rice," *The Chicago Tribune*, November 25, 1974.

Strobel—Lee Strobel, "Reformed Hood Comes Back to Pay His Dues," *The Chicago Tribune*, October 27, 1977.

Strobel—Lee Strobel, *The Case for Christ* (Grand Rapids, Mich.: Zondervan, 1998).

Strobel—Lee Strobel, *God's Outrageous Claims* (Grand Rapids, Mich.: Zondervan, 1997).

Strobel—Lee Strobel, *Inside the Mind of Unchurched Harry and Mary* (Grand Rapids, Mich.: Zondervan, 1993).

Taylor—Paul S. Taylor, *The Illustrated Origins Answer Book,* 4th ed., (Meda, Ariz.: Eden, 1993).

Tax—ed. S. Tax, *Evolution After Darwin* (Chicago: University of Chicago Press, 1960).

Templeton—Charles Templeton, *Farewell to God* (Toronto: McClelland & Stewart, 1996).

Thaxton—Charles B. Thaxton, Walter L. Bradley, and Roger L. Olsen, *The Mystery of Life's Origin* (Dallas: Lewis and Stanley, 1984).

Time—"Iconoclast of the Century, Charles Darwin (1809–1882)," *Time,* December 31, 1999.

Tolstoy—Leo Tolstoy (David Patterson, translator), *Confession* (New York: W. W. Norton & Co.: 1996).

Vallery-Radot—R. Vallery-Radot, trans. R. L. Devonshire, *The Life of Pasteur,* (New York: Doubleday, 1920).

Vardaman—ed. E. Jerry Vardaman, *Teacher's Yoke* (Waco, Tx.: Baylor University, 1964).

Vitz—Paul C. Vitz, "The Psychology of Atheism," *Truth: An International Interdisciplinary Journal of Christian Thought,* vol. 1 (1958).

Wagman—Robert J. Wagman, *The First Amendment Book* (New York: Pharos Books, 1991).

Wiersbe—Warren Wiersbe, *Classic Sermons on Suffering* (Grand Rapids, Mich.: Kregel Publications, 1984).

Wilford—John Noble Wilford, "Sizing Up the Cosmos: An Astronomer's Quest," *New York Times,* March 12, 1991.

Wilson—Clifford A. Wilson, *Rocks, Relics and Biblical Reliability* (Grand Rapids, Mich.: Zondervan, 1977).

Witherington—Ben Witherington III, *The Christology of Jesus* (Minneapolis: Fortress Press, 1990).

Yancey—Philip Yancey, *Where Is God When It Hurts?* (Grand Rapids, Mich.: Zondervan, 1990).

Yockey—H. P. Yockey, "A Calculation of the Probability of Spontaneous Biogenesis by Information Theory," *Journal of Theoretical Biology* 67.

Zacharias—Ravi Zacharias, *Can Man Live Without God* (Nashville: Word, 1994).

NOTES

INTRODUCTION: THE CHALLENGE OF FAITH

1. George H. Smith, *Atheism: The Case Against God* (Amherst, N.Y.: Prometheus Books, 1989), 51.

2. Charles Colson, *How Now Shall We Live?* (Wheaton, Ill.: Tyndale House, 1999), 31–32.

3. "Billy Graham Indiana Crusade." Available: www.billygraham.org/newsannouncement12.asp [1999, June 4].

4. Billy Graham, *Just As I Am* (Grand Rapids, Mich.: Zondervan, 1997), 137–138.

5. Charles Templeton, *Farewell to God* (Toronto: McClelland & Stewart, 1996), 3.

6. Ibid., 11.

7. Ibid., 9.

8. Ibid., 5–6.

9. Billy Graham, *Just As I Am*, 139.

10. George H. Smith, *Atheism: The Case Against God*, 98.

11. W. Bingham Hunter, *The God Who Hears* (Downers Grove, Ill.: InterVarsity Press, 1986), 153.

12. Charles Templeton, *Farewell to God*, vii.

13. Ibid., 200–202.

ON THE ROAD TO ANSWERS

1. Michael Martin, *The Case Against Christianity* (Philadelphia: Temple University Press, 1991), 3, 5.

2. Patrick Glynn, *God: The Evidence* (Rocklin, Calif.: Forum, 1997), 20.

3. See: Lee Strobel, *The Case for Christ* (Grand Rapids, Mich.: Zondervan, 1998), 131–143; Ben Witherington III, *The Christology of Jesus* (Minneapolis, Minn.: Fortress Press, 1990); and William Lane Craig, *Reasonable Faith* (Wheaton, Ill.: Crossway, 1994), 233–54.

4. See: 1 Corinthians 15:3–8.

5. See: Lee Strobel, *The Case for Christ*, 35, 208–11, 229–33, 264–65.

6. Jeremiah 29:13.

OBJECTION #1: SINCE EVIL AND SUFFERING EXIST, A LOVING GOD CANNOT

1. John R. W. Stott, *The Cross of Christ* (Downers Grove, Ill.: InterVarsity Press, 1986), 311.

2. See: Lee Strobel, "Thanksgiving Near; Only Food Rice," *The Chicago Tribune*, November 25, 1974.

3. Peter Maass, "Top Ten War Crimes Suspects," *George*, June, 1999.

4. Peter Kreeft, *Making Sense Out of Suffering* (Ann Arbor, Mich.: Servant: 1986), viii.

5. Philip Yancey, *Where Is God When It Hurts?* (Grand Rapids, Mich.: Zondervan, 1990), 15.

6. Ibid., 20, quoting novelist Peter De Vries.

7. The OmniPoll, conducted by Barna Research Group, Ltd., January, 1999.

8. Charles Templeton, *Farewell to God*, 201–2.

9. See: Matthew 7:7.

10. See: Peter Kreeft and Ronald K. Tacelli, *Handbook of Christian Apologetics* (Downers Grove, Ill.: InterVarsity, 1994), 48–88.

11. See: Leo Tolstoy (David Patterson, translator), *Confession* (New York: W. W. Norton & Co.: 1996), Reprint edition.

12. Harold Kushner, *When Bad Things Happen to Good People* (New York: Schocken Books, 1981), 43.

13. See: Romans 5:3–4.

14. Hebrews 5:8: "Although he was a son, he learned obedience from what he suffered...."

15. 2 Peter 3:9: "The Lord is not slow in keeping His promise, as some understand slowness. He is patient with you, not wanting anyone to perish, but everyone to come to repentance."

16. C. S. Lewis, *The Problem of Pain* (New York: Macmillan, 1962), 93.

17. See: Matthew 9:12–13.

18. Jeremiah 6:13a.

19. Isaiah 64:6a.

20. Charles Templeton, *Farewell to God*, 201.

21. Philippians 3:8 (KJV): "I count all things but loss for the excellency of the knowledge of Christ Jesus my Lord: for whom I have suffered the loss of all things, and do count them but dung, that I may win Christ."

22. Philip Yancey, *Where Is God When It Hurts?*, 255–56.

23. Warren W. Wiersbe, *Classic Sermons on Suffering* (Grand Rapids, Mich.: Kregel Publications, 1984), 92.

24. Jesus said in John 16:33: "These things I have spoken to you, that in me you may have peace. In the world, you have tribulation, but take courage; I have overcome the world" (NASB).

25. John R.W. Stott, *The Cross of Christ*, 335–36, the last sentence quoting P. T. Forsyth, *Justification of God* (London: Duckworth, 1916), 32.

OBJECTION #2: SINCE MIRACLES CONTRADICT SCIENCE, THEY CANNOT BE TRUE

1. Richard Dawkins, "Snake Oil and Holy Water." Available: www.forbes.com/asap/99/1004/235.htm [1999, Nov. 19].

2. R. Douglas Geivett and Gary R. Habermas, *In Defense of Miracles* (Downers Grove, Ill.: InterVarsity Press, 1997), 280.

3. Charles Templeton, *Farewell to God*, 21.

4. Quoted in: Nicky Gumble, *Searching Issues* (Eastbourne, East Sussex, UK: Kingsway Publications, 1994), 99.

5.———. "Interviews." Available at: www.pbs.org/faithandreason [1999, Nov. 21].

6. Dale and Sandy Larsen, *Seven Myths about Christianity* (Downers Grove, Ill.: InterVarsity Press, 1996), 86.

7. Michael Ruse, *Darwinism Defended* (London: Addison-Wesley, 1982), 322.

8. See: William Dembski, *The Design Inference* (Cambridge: Cambridge University Press, 1998); Michael Behe, *Darwin's Black Box* (New York: The Fress Press, 1996); and William Dembski and Michael Behe, *Intelligent Design* (Downers Grove, Ill.: InterVarsity Press, 1999).

9. Rudolf Bultmann, *Jesus* (Berlin, 1926), 159.

10. George H. Smith, *Atheism: The Case Against God*, 215.

11. Archibald Robertson, *The Origins of Christianity* (New York: International Publishers, 1954), 82, quoted in: George H. Smith, *Atheism: The Case Against God*, 216.

12. Norman L. Geisler writes in *Baker Encyclopedia of Christian Apologetics* (Grand Rapids, Mich.: Baker Books, 1999), 512: "Most miracle claims for Muhammad do not occur in the *Qur'an* [or Koran], the only book in Islam for which divine inspiration is claimed.... The vast majority of alleged miracles are reported in the *Hadith* (Islamic tradition), considered by Muslims to contain many authentic traditions. There are hundreds of miracle stories in the *Hadith*."

13. Richard Robinson, "Religion and Reason," in *Critiques of God*, ed. Peter A. Angeles (Buffalo, N.Y.: Prometheus Books, 1997), 121.

14. Alvin Plantinga, "Two Dozen (or so) Theistic Arguments," Lecture presented at the 33d Annual Philosophy Conference, Wheaton College, Wheaton, Illinois, October 23–25, 1986.

15. For a booklet summarizing Craig's five reasons for believing God exists, see: William Lane Craig, *God, Are You There?* (Norcross, Ga.: Ravi Zacharias International Ministries, 1999).

16. Stephen W. Hawking and Roger Penrose, *The Nature of Space and Time* (Princeton, N.J.: Princeton University Press, 1996), 20.

17. Anthony Kenny, *The Five Ways: St. Thomas Aquinas' Proofs of God's Existence* (New York: Schocken Books, 1969), 66.

18. David Hume to John Stewart, February, 1754, in *The Letters of David Hume*, ed. J. Y. T. Greig (Oxford: Clarendon Press, 1932), vol. I, 187.

19. Kai Nielsen, *Reason and Practice* (New York: Harper & Row, 1971), 48.

20. Arthur Eddington, *The Expanding Universe* (New York: Macmillan, 1933), 124.

21. Stephen W. Hawking, *A Brief History of Time* (New York: Bantam Books, 1988), 123.

22. For a list of examples, see: John Leslie, *Universes* (London: Routledge, 1989).

23. P. C. W. Davies, *Other Worlds* (London: Dent, 1980), 160–61.

24. Ibid., 168–69.

25. For example, see: P. C. W. Davies, "The Anthropic Principle," in *Particle and Nuclear Physics* 10 (1983), 28; and Patrick Glynn, *God: The Evidence*, 29–31.

26. John Polkinghorne, *Serious Talk: Science and Religion in Dialogue* (London: Trinity Press International, 1995), 6.

27. Patrick Glynn, *God: The Evidence*, 53–54, 26.

28. Michael Ruse, "Evolutionary Theory and Christian Ethics," in *The Darwinian Paradigm* (London: Routledge, 1989), 262, 269.

29. John Healey, fund-raising letter, 1991.

30. See: I Corinthians 15:4ff.

31. Gerd Lüdemann, *What Really Happened to Jesus?*, trans. John Bowden (Louisville, Ky.: Westminster John Knox Press, 1995), 8.

32. Luke Timothy Johnson, *The Real Jesus* (San Francisco: Harper San Francisco, 1996), 136.

33. For a list of these historical tests, see: C. Behan McCullagh, *Justifying Historical Descriptions* (Cambridge: Cambridge University Press, 1984), 19. To see how the Resurrection meets these criteria, see: William Lane Craig, *God, Are You There?*, 46–47.

34. John Hick, Introduction, in *The Existence of God*, ed. with an Introduction by John Hick, Problems of Philosophy Series (New York: Macmillan, 1964), 13–14.

35. See: William Alston, "Religious Diversity and Perceptual Knowledge of God," in *Faith and Philosophy* 5 (1988), 433–48.

36. Romans 8:16: "The Spirit himself testifies with our spirit that we are God's children."

OBJECTION #3: EVOLUTION EXPLAINS LIFE, SO GOD ISN'T NEEDED

1. "Iconoclast of the Century, Charles Darwin (1809–1882)," *Time*, December 31, 1999.

2. Michael Denton, *Evolution: A Theory in Crisis* (Chevy Chase, Md.: Adler & Adler, 1986), 77.

3. See: Charles T. Jones, "DNA Tests Clear Two Men in Prison," *The Oklahoman*, April 16, 1999.

4. See: Steven Mills and Ken Armstrong, "Convicted By a Hair," *The Chicago Tribune*, November 18, 1999.

5. Ibid.

6. Patrick Glynn, *God: The Evidence*, 2–3.

7. "Iconoclast of the Century: Charles Darwin (1809–1882)," *Time*, December 31, 1999.

8. Charles Templeton, *Farewell to God*, 232.

9. Francisco Ayala, *Creative Evolution*, John H. Campbell and J. W. Schoff, eds. (New York: James and Bartlett, 1994), 4–5.

10. Michael Denton, *Evolution: A Theory in Crisis*, 67.

11. Ibid., 66.

12. Douglas Futuyma, *Evolutionary Biology* (Sunderland, Mass.: Sinauer, 1986), 3.

13. Richard Dawkins, *The Blind Watchmaker* (New York: Norton, 1987), 6.

14. Phillip E. Johnson, *Darwin on Trial*, 2d ed. (Downers Grove, Ill.: InterVarsity Press, 1993), 126–27.

15. Michael Behe, *Darwin's Black Box* (New York: The Free Press, 1996), 232.

16. Ibid., 193, 251, 243 (emphasis in original).

17. Introduction by Bill Hybels in: Lee Strobel, *Inside the Mind of Unchurched Harry and Mary* (Grand Rapids, Mich.: Zondervan, 1993), 7.

18. David M. Raup, "Conflicts Between Darwin and Paleontology," *Bulletin, Field Museum of Natural History*, January 1979, quoted in Paul S. Taylor, *The Illustrated Origins Answer Book*, 4th ed., (Meda, Ariz.: Eden, 1993), 108; and in Hank Hanegraaff, *The Face that Demonstrates the Farce of Evolution* (Nashville, Tenn.: Word, 1998), 34.

19. Phillip E. Johnson, *Darwin on Trial*, 2d ed., 54.

20. Charles Darwin, *Origin of Species*, 6th ed. (New York: New York University Press, 1988), 154.

21. George Johnson, "Science and Religion: Bridging the Great Divide," *The New York Times*, June 30, 1998.

22. Charles B. Thaxton, Walter L. Bradley, and Roger L. Olsen, *The Mystery of Life's Origin* (Dallas, Tex.: Lewis and Stanley, 1984), back cover.

23. Ibid.

24. Francis Darwin, *The Life and Letters of Charles Darwin* (New York: D. Appleton, 1887), 202.

25. R. Vallery-Radot, *The Life of Pasteur*, trans. by R. L. Devonshire (New York: Doubleday, 1920), 109.

26. Robert Shapiro, *Origins* (New York: Summit Books, 1986), 99.

27. William Day, *Genesis on Planet Earth* (East Lansing, Mich.: House of Talos, 1979), 7.

28. Quoted in: S. Tax, ed., *Evolution After Darwin* (Chicago: University of Chicago Press, 1960), 1:57.

29. See: Gordon C. Mills, Malcolm Lancaster, and Walter L. Bradley, "Origin of Life and Evolution in Biology Textbooks—A Critique," *The American Biology Teacher*, February, 1993.

30. Ernst Haeckel, *The Wonders of Life*, trans. by J. McCabe (London: Watts, 1905), 111, quoted in: Stephen C. Meyer, "The Explanatory Power of Design" in *Mere Creation* (Downers Grove, Ill.: InterVarsity Press, 1998), 114.

31. Klaus Dose, "The Origin of Life: More Questions Than Answers," in *Interdisciplinary Science Reviews* 13 (1988), 348.

32. Francis Crick, *Life Itself* (New York: Simon and Schuster, 1981).

33. "How Did Life Begin?" *Newsweek*, August 6, 1979.

34. J. Buell and G. Hearn, eds., *Darwinism: Science or Philosophy?* (Dallas, Tex.: Foundation for Thought and Ethics, 1994), 68–69; quoted in: Stephen C. Meyer, "The Explanatory Power of Design," *Mere Creation*, 126.

35. See: Dean Kenyon and G. Steinman, *Biological Predestination* (New York: McGraw Hill, 1969).

36. See: Randall A. Kok, John A. Taylor, and Walter L. Bradley, "A Statistical Examination of Self-Ordering of Amino Acids in Proteins," *Origins of Life and Evolution of the Biosphere* 18 (1988).

37. Ilya Prigogine and Isabelle Stengers, *The End of Certainty: Time, Chaos, and the New Laws of Nature* (New York: The Free Press, 1997), 71.

38. H. P. Yockey, "A Calculation of the Probability of Spontaneous Biogenesis by Information Theory," *Journal of Theoretical Biology* 67, 380.

39. See: Charles B. Thaxton, Walter L. Bradley, and Roger L. Olsen, *The Mystery of Life's Origin*, 191–96.

40. Ibid., 194.

41. Phillip E. Johnson, *Darwin on Trial*, 111.

42. A. Dauvillier, *The Photochemical Origin of Life* (New York: Academic Press, 1965), 2.

43. Peter Radetsky, "How Did Life Start?" *Discover*, November 1992.

44. Fazale R. Rana and Hugh Ross, "Life from the Heavens? Not This Way," *Facts for Faith*, October, 2000 (emphasis in original).

45. Ibid. (emphasis in original).

46. Peter Radetsky, "How Did Life Start?" *Discover*, November, 1992.

47. Ibid.

48. Ibid.

49. See: A. G. Cairns-Smith, *Genetic Takeover and the Mineral Origins of Life* (New York: Cambridge University Press, 1982).

50. Quoted in: Walter L. Bradley and Charles B. Thaxton, "Information and the Origin of Life," *The Creation Hypothesis* (Downers Grove, Ill.: InterVarsity Press, 1994), 194.

51. William A. Dembski, ed., *Mere Creation*, 46.

52. Fazale R. Rana and Hugh Ross, "Life from the Heavens? Not This Way," *Facts for Faith*, Quarter 1, 2000.

53. Klaus Dose, "The Origin of Life: More Questions than Answers," *Interdisciplinary Science Review* 13 (1998), 348.

54. Robert Shapiro, *Origins,* 99.

55. Francis Crick, *Life Itself,* 153.

56. J. Horgan, "In the Beginning . . ." *Scientific American,* February 1991.

57. See: Stephen Jay Gould, "Will We Figure Out How Life Began?," *Time,* April 10, 2000.

58. J. F. W. Herschel, *Preliminary Discourse on the Study of Natural Philosophy* (London: Longman, Rees, Orme, Brown and Green, 1831), 149.

59. Carl Sagan, *Broca's Brain* (New York: Random House, 1979), 275.

60. Phillip E. Johnson, *Darwin on Trial,* 103.

61. See: Candace Adams, "Leading Nanoscientist Builds Big Faith," *Baptist Standard,* March 15, 2000.

62. Michael Denton, *Evolution: A Theory in Crisis,* 358.

OBJECTION #4: GOD ISN'T WORTHY OF WORSHIP IF HE KILLS INNOCENT CHILDREN

1. Quoted in: Garry Poole and Judson Poling, *Tough Questions 4* (Grand Rapids, Mich.: Zondervan, 1998), 12.

2. Psalm 86:15.

3. Charles Templeton, *Farewell to God*, 71.

4. George H. Smith, *Atheism: The Case Against God*, 77.

5. Ibid., 76.

6. Thomas Paine, *Age of Reason*, Part I (First printed 1794; reprinted by The Freethought Press Association, New York, 1954), 18–19, quoted in George H. Smith, *Atheism: The Case Against God,* 78.

7. Judges 19:25, 29.

8. 2 Samuel 12:31 (KJV).

9. Malachi 3:6a.

10. 1 Samuel 15:3.

11. Mark 10:14.

12. See: 2 Kings 2:23–25.

13. Walter C. Kaiser Jr., Peter H. Davids, F. F. Bruce, and Manfred T. Brauch, *Hard Sayings of the Bible* (Downers Grove, Ill.: InterVarsity Press, 1996), 233, 234.

14. Ibid. See also: 1 Kings 20:14–15.

15. Charles Templeton, *Farewell to God*, 197 (emphasis removed), 198, 199.

16. Genesis 1:29–30. After the Flood, God told Noah and his sons in Genesis 9:3: "Everything that lives and moves will be food for you. Just as I gave you the green plants, I now give you everything."

17. Isaiah 65:17, 25.

18. Proverbs 12:10.

19. George H. Smith, *Atheism: The Case Against God,* 210–11.

20. Charles Templeton, *Farewell to God,* 38.

21. John 3:12.

22. See: Clifford A. Wilson, *Rocks, Relics and Biblical Reliability* (Grand Rapids, Mich.: Zondervan, 1977), 42.

23. William F. Albright, *Archaeology and the Religion of Israel* (Baltimore, Md.: Johns Hopkins Press, 1953), 176.

24. See: Colin J. Hemer, *The Book of Acts in the Setting of Hellenistic History* (Winona Lake, Ind.: Eisenbrauns, 1990).

25. William M. Ramsay, *St. Paul the Traveler and the Roman Citizen* (Grand Rapids, Mich.: Baker, 1982), 8.

26. A. N. Sherwin-White, *Roman Society and Roman Law in the New Testament* (Oxford: Clarendon Press, 1963), 189.

27. See: William F. Albright, "Retrospect and Prospect in New Testament Archaeology," in *The Teacher's Yoke,* E. Jerry Vardaman, ed. (Waco, Tx.: Baylor University, 1964), 288ff.

28. Norman L. Geisler, *Baker Encyclopedia of Christian Apologetics* (Grand Rapids, Mich.: Baker, 1999), 544.

29. See: Bertrand Russell, "What Is an Agnostic?", *Look* magazine, 1953, quoted in Norman L. Geisler, *Baker Encyclopedia of Christian Apologetics,* 455–56.

30. John 10:37.

31. John 3:2.

32. See Sura 2:118; 3:181–84; 4:153; 6:8, 9, 37 in the Koran.

33. Sura 6:37.

34. Ibid.

35. Luke 7:22.

36. Norman Geisler and Thomas Howe, *When Critics Ask* (Grand Rapids, Mich.: Baker, 1992).

37. Matthew 16:16, Mark 8:29, Luke 9:20.

38. Gregory A. Boyd and Edward K. Boyd, *Letters From a Skeptic* (Wheaton, Ill.: Victor, 1994), 120.

39. Revised Standard Version.

40. John Noble Wilford, "Sizing Up the Cosmos: An Astronomer's Quest," *New York Times*, March 12, 1991, quoted in: Hugh Ross, *Creator and the Cosmos* (Colorado Springs: NavPress, 1993), 116.

41. Hugh Ross, *Creator and the Cosmos,* 17.

42. Robert Jastrow, "The Secret of the Stars," *New York Times Magazine,* June 25, 1978, quoted in: Hugh Ross, *Creator and the Cosmos,* 116.

43. See: Bertrand Russell, "What Is an Agnostic?" *Look* magazine, 1953, quoted in Norman L. Geisler, *Baker Encyclopedia of Christian Apologetics,* 455–56.

44. Gregory A. Boyd and Edward K. Boyd, *Letters From a Skeptic,* 189.

45. John 6:68.

46. John 8:58.

OBJECTION #5: IT'S OFFENSIVE TO CLAIM JESUS IS THE ONLY WAY TO GOD

1. Available at: http://cnn.com/Transcripts/0001/12/lkl.00.html [2000. January 13].

2. R. C. Sproul, *Reason to Believe* (Grand Rapids, Mich.: Lamplighter Books, 1982), 44–45.

3. See: Robert J. Wagman, *The First Amendment Book* (New York: Pharos Books, 1991), 106. Also see: Chapkinsky v. New Hampshire, 315 U.S. 568 (1942).

4. See: Cohen v California, 403 U.S. 15 (1971).

5. John 14:6.

6. See: John Hick and Paul F. Knitter, eds., *The Myth of Christian Uniqueness* (London: SCM Press, 1987), 141, quoted in: Paul Copan, *True for You, But Not for Me* (Minneapolis, Minn.: Bethany House, 1998), 78.

7. Available at: http://cnn.com/Transcripts/0001/12/lkl.00.html [2000. January 13].

8. Quoted in: Paul Copan, *True for You, But Not for Me*, 34.

9. Ravi Zacharias, *Can Man Live Without God* (Nashville, Tenn.: Word, 1994), from introduction by Charles Colson, ix.

10. Charles Templeton, *Farewell to God*, 27.

11. Acts 4:12.

12. Charles Templeton, *Farewell to God*, 27, emphasis added.

13. Quoted in: Ravi Zacharias, *Can Man Live Without God*, back cover.

14. 2 Peter 1:16.

15. See: "The Exclusivism of Religious Pluralism," in: Paul Copan, *True For You, But Not For Me*, 71–77.

16. John 1:1, 14.

17. Genesis 18:25c.

18. See: Psalm 24:3–4.

19. See: Matthew 20:1–16.

20. See: Luke 7:36–50.

21. Acts 17:26–27.

22. Romans 1:20.

23. Romans 2:14–15.

24. Romans 10:14–15.

25. Jeremiah 29:13.

OBJECTION #6: A LOVING GOD WOULD NEVER TORTURE PEOPLE IN HELL

1. Bertrand Russell, *Why I Am Not a Christian* (New York: Simon and Schuster, 1957), 17.

2. Quoted in: Cliffe Knechtle, *Give Me An Answer* (Downers Grove, Ill.: InterVarsity Press, 1986), 42.

3. This story, including the interview with Judge Cortland A. Mathers, originally was reported in an excellent investigation into mandatory sentencing by *The Boston Globe's* Spotlight Team. See: Gerard O'Neill, ed., Dick Lehr and Bruce Butterfield, "A Judgment on Sentences: Some Judges Balk at Preset Penalties," *The Boston Globe*, September 27, 1995.

4. B. C. Johnson, *The Atheist Debater's Handbook* (Buffalo, N.Y.: Prometheus, 1979), 237.

5. Ezekiel 33:11: "Say to them, 'As surely as I live, declares the Sovereign LORD, I take no pleasure in the death of the wicked, but rather that they turn from their ways and live....'"

6. George H. Smith, *Atheism: The Case Against God*, 300.

7. See: Alan Gomes, "Evangelicals and the Annihilation of Hell, Part II," *Christian Research Journal* 13 (Summer 1991), 8–13.

8. Luke 10:27.

9. See: Samuele Bacchiocchi, "Hell: Does it Have an End?", *Signs of the Times*, August 1999, 8–10.

10. Daniel 12:2: "Multitudes who sleep in the dust of the earth will awake: some to everlasting life, others to shame and everlasting contempt."

11. John Stott and David L. Edwards, *Essentials: A Liberal-Evangelical Dialogue* (London: 1988), 316.

12. See: Hebrews 9:27.

13. See: 2 Peter 3:9.

14. See: Hebrews 11:6.

15. For further analysis of evidence concerning reincarnation, see: Gary R. Habermas and J. P. Moreland, *Beyond Death: Exploring the Evidence for Immortality* (Wheaton, Ill.: Crossway, 1998), 237–53; and Norman L. Geisler and J. Yutaka Amano, *The Reincarnation Sensation* (Wheaton, Ill.: Tyndale, 1986).

16. C. S. Lewis, *The Problem of Pain* (Glasgow: William Collins Sons, 1983), 107.

17. See: Lee Strobel, *The Case for Christ*, 164–66.

OBJECTION #7: CHURCH HISTORY IS LITTERED WITH OPPRESSION AND VIOLENCE

1. Ken Schei, "What Is an Atheist for Jesus?" Available: www.atheists-for-Jesus.com/about.htm [2000, January 10].

2. D. James Kennedy, *Why I Believe* (Dallas: Word, 1980), 118, 121.

3. Maurice Possley, "Court Hears How FBI Agents Bugged Judge," *The Chicago Tribune*, April 26, 1985.

4. Maurice Possley, "Judge Liked 'People Who Take Dough,' Greylord File Shows," *The Chicago Tribune*, April 27, 1985.

5. Maurice Possley, "Records Charge Deals By Judge; 'We Can Make $1,000 a Week,' Olson Quoted," *The Chicago Tribune*, February 21, 1985.

6. Bertrand Russell, *Why I am Not a Christian* (New York: Simon and Schuster, 1957), 25–26.

7. "Why Are We Here: The Great Debate," *International Herald Tribune*, April 26, 1999.

8. Charles Templeton, *Farewell to God*, 127, 129.

9. Ibid., 154.

10. See: Richard Boudreaux, "Pope Apologizes for Catholic Sins Past and Present," *The Los Angeles Times*, March 13, 2000.

11. Peggy Polk, "Papal State: Despite His Recent Ills, Pope John Paul II is Focused on the Future," *The Chicago Tribune*, June 5, 1995.

12. Matthew 7:21–23.

13. Patrick Glynn, *God: The Evidence*, 157.

14. See: Lucian, *The Death of Peregrine*, 11–13, in *The Works of Lucian of Samosata*, trans. by H. W. Fowler and F. G. Fowler, 4 vols. (Oxford: The Clarendon Press, 1949), vol. 4.

15. See: Justin Martyr, *First Apology: Ante-Nicene Fathers*, ed. by Alexander Roberts and James Donaldson (Grand Rapids, Mich.: Eerdmans, 1973).

16. Philippians 1:21.

17. Bruce L. Shelley, *Church History in Plain Language* (Dallas, Tex.: Word, 1982, 1995, updated 2d edition), 189.

18. As the Third Millennium approached, Spanish priests and nuns publicly asked forgiveness for "those religious workers who worked closely with the Inquisition and the monks who were soldiers." See: "Catholic Clerics Apologize for Past Cruelties," *The Chicago Tribune*, November 14, 1999.

19. David Neff, "Our Extended, Persecuted Family," *Christianity Today*, April 29, 1996, 14.

20. Mark A. Noll, *A History of Christianity in the United States and Canada* (Grand Rapids: Eerdmans, 1992), 51.

21. Dale and Sandy Larsen, *Seven Myths About Christianity* (Downers Grove, Ill.: InterVarsity Press, 1998), 110.

22. Anthony Grafton, with April Shelford and Nancy Siraisi, *New Worlds, Ancient Text* (Cambridge, Mass.: Belknap Press, 1992), 132.

23. Ibid., 136. Ecclesiasticus, or Sirach, is not considered to be divinely inspired scripture by Protestants, although it is part of the Roman Catholic and Orthodox canons. It is also known as "The Wisdom of Jesus, the son of Sirach," after its author, a scholar who apparently wrote the book between 195 and 171 B.C.

24. "Cardinal's Yom Kippur Letter Seeks Atonement for Church Anti-Semitism," *The Chicago Tribune*, September 21, 1999.

25. Luis Palau, *God Is Relevant* (New York: Doubleday, 1997), 23, 82.

26. See: Michael Novak, David N. Livingstone, David Lyle Jeffrey, et al., "Where Would Civilization Be Without Christianity?", *Christianity Today*, December 6, 1999, 50–59.

27. Ibid., 56.

28. Matthew 12:7 (KJV).

OBJECTION #8: I STILL HAVE DOUBTS, SO I CAN'T BE A CHRISTIAN

1. Dan Barker, *Losing Faith in Faith* (Madison, Wis.: Freedom from Religion Foundation, 1992), 106, 109.

2. Quoted in: Lynn Anderson, *If I Really Believe, Why Do I Have These Doubts?* (Minneapolis, Minn.: Bethany House, 1992), 60 (emphasis added).

3. See: Lee Strobel, "Reformed Hood Comes Back to Pay His Dues," *The Chicago Tribune,* Oct. 27, 1977; and Lee Strobel, *God's Outrageous Claims* (Grand Rapids, Mich.: Zondervan, 1997), 63–67.

4. Os Guinness, *In Two Minds* (Downers Grove, Ill.: InterVarsity Press, 1976), 61.

5. André Resner, *Grief and Faith—Three Profiles of Struggle in the Face of Loss,* Annual Lectures, Pepperdine University, April 19, 1989, quoted in: Lynn Anderson, *If I Really Believe, Why Do I Have These Doubts,* 78 (emphasis in original).

6. See: Paul C. Vitz, "The Psychology of Atheism," *Truth: An International Interdisciplinary Journal of Christian Thought* 1 (1958), 29.

7. See: Mark 9:14–27.

8. Emphasis added.

9. John 8:31–32: "To the Jews who had believed him, Jesus said, 'If you hold to my teaching, you are really my disciples. Then you will know the truth, and the truth will set you free.'"

10. Gary E. Parker, *The Gift of Doubt* (San Francisco: Harper & Row, 1990), 69.

CONCLUSION: THE POWER OF FAITH

1. Quoted in: *Leadership* magazine, Spring 1999, 75.

2. Quoted in: *Servant* magazine, Spring, 1999, 8.

3. From the essay, "What I Do Not Believe," by Russell Hanson, quoted in: William A. Dembski, *Intelligent Design* (Downers Grove, Ill.: InterVarsity Press, 1999), 27, emphasis added.

4. William Lane Craig, *Reasonable Faith* (Wheaton: Crossway, 1984), 72.

5. Bill Montgomery, "U.S. Supreme Court Halts Execution: Even Victim's Family Pleaded for Mercy," *The Atlanta Journal and Constitution,* August 21, 1990.

6. "When Mercy Becomes Mandatory," *The Atlanta Journal and Constitution,* August 16, 1990.

7. 2 Corinthians 5:17.

ACKNOWLEDGMENTS

I am deeply indebted to many people for the roles they played in helping to produce this book. Special thanks goes to Rick Warren, for providing an encouraging and supportive environment in which the creation of Christian resources is valued, and Bill Hybels, whose mentoring has shaped me in more ways than I'll ever know. I admire the two of them beyond words.

Mark Mittelberg, as ever, kept me motivated when the demands of writing and ministry seemed overwhelming. He is simply the best friend I have ever had.

At Zondervan Publishing House, I can never thank John Sloan enough for his guidance that put me on the right trajectory for *The Case for Christ* and this volume. More than anyone else, he is responsible for the way these two books have turned out. Scott Bolinder, Stan Gundry, John Topliff, Greg Stielstra, Bob Hudson, and the rest of the Zondervan team are the best partners I could ever imagine.

Thanks, too, goes to Kay Warren, Jim Mellado, Hank Hanegraaff, Paul Young, Bob Gordon, Garry Poole, and Paul Braoudakis for their encouragement; Bob and Gretchen Passantino for their input; Jodi Walle, Parker VanderPloeg, and Barbara Hoglund for their assistance; and the staffs and congregations of Saddleback Valley Community Church and Willow Creek Community Church, especially Glen Kreun, Doug Slaybaugh, Forrest Reinhardt, Brad Johnson, and John Ortberg.

I am especially grateful for the participation of the experts who agreed to be interviewed for this book. Their wisdom and character influenced me deeply. And, of course, this book would never have become a reality without my wife, Leslie, my daughter, Alison, and my son, Kyle, whose love means the world to me.

ABOUT THE AUTHOR

Lee Strobel, who holds a Master of Studies in Law degree from Yale Law School, as well as a journalism degree from the University of Missouri, is the former legal affairs editor of the *Chicago Tribune*. His awards include Illinois's highest honors for both investigative reporting and public service journalism from United Press International.

His journey from atheism to faith has been documented in the Gold Medallion–winning books *The Case for Christ* and *The Case for Faith*. His other best-sellers include *Inside the Mind of Unchurched Harry and Mary*, which also won a Gold Medallion; *Surviving a Spiritual Mismatch in Marriage*, which he coauthored with his wife, Leslie; *God's Outrageous Claims*; and *What Jesus Would Say*, all published by Zondervan. His book *Reckless Homicide* has been used as a supplementary text at several law schools.

Lee has been a teaching pastor at two of America's largest churches: Willow Creek Community Church in suburban Chicago and Saddleback Valley Community Church in Orange County, California. He is a contributing editor and columnist for *Outreach* magazine and formerly taught First Amendment Law at Roosevelt University.

Lee and Leslie, who have been married for more than thirty years, reside in Southern California. Their daughter, Alison, is a teacher and novelist; their son, Kyle, received his master's degree in philosophy of religion and is pursuing a second master's degree in New Testament studies.

Willow Creek Association

Vision, Training, Resources for Prevailing Churches

This resource was created to serve you and to help you build a local church that prevails. It is just one of many ministry tools that are part of the Willow Creek Resources® line, published by the Willow Creek Association together with Zondervan.

The Willow Creek Association (WCA) was created in 1992 to serve a rapidly growing number of churches from across the denominational spectrum that are committed to helping unchurched people become fully devoted followers of Christ. Membership in the WCA now numbers over 10,500 Member Churches worldwide from more than ninety denominations.

The Willow Creek Association links like-minded Christian leaders with each other and with strategic vision, training, and resources in order to help them build prevailing churches designed to reach their redemptive potential. Here are some of the ways the WCA does that.

- **A2: Building Prevailing Acts 2 Churches—Today**—an annual two-and-a-half day event, held at Willow Creek Community Church in South Barrington, Illinois, to explore strategies for building churches that reach out to seekers and build believers, and to discover new innovations and breakthroughs from Acts 2 churches around the country.
- **The Leadership Summit**—a once a year, two-and-a-half-day conference to envision and equip Christians with leadership gifts and responsibilities. Presented live at Willow Creek as well as via satellite broadcast to over one hundred locations across North America, this event is designed to increase the leadership effectiveness of pastors, ministry staff, volunteer church leaders, and Christians in the marketplace.

- **Ministry-Specific Conferences**—throughout each year the WCA hosts a variety of conferences and training events—both at Willow Creek's main campus and offsite, across the U.S., and around the world—targeting church leaders and volunteers in ministry-specific areas such as: evangelism, small groups, preaching and teaching, the arts, children, students, women, volunteers, stewardship, raising up resources, etc.
- **Willow Creek Resources®**—provides churches with trusted and field-tested ministry resources in such areas as leadership, evangelism, spiritual formation, spiritual gifts, small groups, stewardship, student ministry, children's ministry, the use of the arts-drama, media, contemporary music—and more.
- **WCA Member Benefits**—includes substantial discounts to WCA training events, a 20 percent discount on all Willow Creek Resources®, *Defining Moments* monthly audio journal for leaders, quarterly *Willow* magazine, access to a Members-Only section on WillowNet, monthly communications, and more. Member Churches also receive special discounts and premier services through WCA's growing number of ministry partners—Select Service Providers—and save an average of $500 annually depending on the level of engagement.

For specific information about WCA conferences, resources, membership, and other ministry services contact:

Willow Creek Association
P.O. Box 3188
Barrington, IL 60011-3188
Phone: 847-570-9812
Fax: 847-765-5046
www.willowcreek.com

"My road to atheism was paved by science. . . . But, ironically, so was my later journey to God."—Lee Strobel

The Case for a Creator:
A Journalist Investigates Scientific Evidence That Points Toward God

Lee Strobel, Author of
The Case for Christ *and*
The Case for Faith

During his academic years, Lee Strobel became convinced that God was outmoded, a belief that colored his ensuing career as an award-winning journalist at the *Chicago Tribune.* Science had made the idea of a Creator irrelevant—or so Strobel thought.

But today science is pointing in a different direction. In recent years, a diverse and impressive body of research has increasingly supported the conclusion that the universe was intelligently designed. At the same time, Darwinism has faltered in the face of concrete facts and hard reason.

Has science discovered God? At the very least, it's giving faith an immense boost as new findings emerge about the incredible complexity of our universe. Join Strobel as he reexamines the theories that once led him away from God. Through his compelling and highly readable account, you'll encounter the mind-stretching discoveries from cosmology, cellular biology, DNA research, astronomy, physics, and human consciousness that present astonishing evidence in *The Case for a Creator*.

Hardcover: 0-310-24144-8
Unabridged Audio Pages® CD: 0-310-25439-6

ebooks:
Adobe Acrobat eBook Reader®: 0-310-25977-0
Microsoft Reader®: 0-310-25978-9
Palm™ Edition: 0-310-25979-7
Unabridged ebook Download: 0-310-26142-2

A student-friendly edition of The Case for Christ, *to help teenagers find Christ or deepen their faith.*

The Case for Christ—Student Edition

Lee Strobel with Jane Vogel

There's little question that he actually lived. But miracles? Rising from the dead? Some of the stories you hear about him sound like just that—stories. A reasonable person would never believe them, let alone the claim that he's the only way to God!

But a reasonable person would also make sure that he or she understood the facts before jumping to conclusions. That's why Lee Strobel—an award-winning legal journalist with a knack for asking tough questions—decided to investigate Jesus for himself. An atheist, Strobel felt certain his findings would bring Christianity's claims about Jesus tumbling down like a house of cards.

He was in for the surprise of his life. Join him as he retraces his journey from skepticism to faith. You'll consult expert testimony as you sift through the truths that history, science, psychiatry, literature, and religion reveal. Like Strobel, you'll be amazed at the evidence—how much there is, how strong it is, and what it says.

The facts are in. What will your verdict be in *The Case for Christ*?

Softcover 0-310-23484-0
Padded Hardcover Edition 0-310-24608-3

Pick up a copy today at your favorite bookstore!

ZONDERVAN®
.com

one.